Graph Data Management:
Techniques and Applications

Sherif Sakr
University of New South Wales, Australia

Eric Pardede
LaTrobe University, Australia

A volume in the Advances in Data Mining
and Database Management (ADMDM)
Book Series

Information Science
REFERENCE
An Imprint of IGI Global

Senior Editorial Director:	Kristin Klinger
Director of Book Publications:	Julia Mosemann
Editorial Director:	Lindsay Johnston
Acquisitions Editor:	Erika Carter
Development Editor:	Mike Killian
Production Editor:	Sean Woznicki
Typesetters:	Adrienne Freeland, Jennifer Romanchak
Print Coordinator:	Jamie Snavely
Cover Design:	Nick Newcomer

Published in the United States of America by
Information Science Reference (an imprint of IGI Global)
701 E. Chocolate Avenue
Hershey PA 17033
Tel: 717-533-8845
Fax: 717-533-8661
E-mail: cust@igi-global.com
Web site: http://www.igi-global.com

Library of Congress Cataloging-in-Publication Data

Graph data management: techniques and applications / Sherif Sakr and Eric Pardede, editors.
    p. cm.
  Includes bibliographical references and index.
  Summary: This book is a central reference source for different data management techniques for graph data structures and their applications, discussing graphs for modeling complex structured and schemaless data from the Semantic Web, social networks, protein networks, chemical compounds, and multimedia databases --Provided by publisher.
  ISBN 978-1-61350-053-8 (hardcover) -- ISBN 978-1-61350-054-5 (ebook) -- ISBN 978-1-61350-055-2 (print & perpetual access) 1. Information visualization. 2. Graphic methods. I. Sakr, Sherif, 1979- II. Pardede, Erric, 1975-
  QA276.3.G68 2012
  001.4'226--dc23
                                        2011021482

This book is published in the IGI Global book series Advances in Data Mining and Database Management (ADMDM) (ISSN: 2327-1981; eISSN: 2327-199X)

British Cataloguing in Publication Data
A Cataloguing in Publication record for this book is available from the British Library.

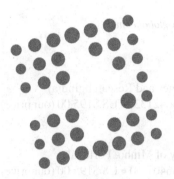

Advances in Data Mining and Database Management (ADMDM) Book Series

David Taniar
Monash University, Australia

ISSN: 2327-1981
EISSN: 2327-199X

MISSION

With the large amounts of information available to businesses in today's digital world, there is a need for methods and research on managing and analyzing the information that is collected and stored. IT professionals, software engineers, and business administrators, along with many other researchers and academics, have made the fields of data mining and database management into ones of increasing importance as the digital world expands. The **Advances in Data Mining & Database Management (ADMDM) Book Series** aims to bring together research in both fields in order to become a resource for those involved in either field.

COVERAGE

- Cluster Analysis
- Customer Analytics
- Data Mining
- Data Quality
- Data Warehousing
- Database Security
- Database Testing
- Decision Support Systems
- Enterprise Systems
- Text Mining

IGI Global is currently accepting manuscripts for publication within this series. To submit a proposal for a volume in this series, please contact our Acquisition Editors at Acquisitions@igi-global.com or visit: http://www.igi-global.com/publish/.

Titles in this Series

For a list of additional titles in this series, please visit: www.igi-global.com

Data Mining in Dynamic Social Networks and Fuzzy Systems
Vishal Bhatnagar (Ambedkar Institute of Advanced Communication Technologies and Research, India)
Information Science Reference • copyright 2013 • 412pp • H/C (ISBN: 9781466642133) • US $195.00 (our price)

Ethical Data Mining Applications for Socio-Economic Development
Hakikur Rahman (University of Minho, Portugal) and Isabel Ramos (University of Minho, Portugal)
Information Science Reference • copyright 2013 • 359pp • H/C (ISBN: 9781466640788) • US $195.00 (our price)

Design, Performance, and Analysis of Innovative Information Retrieval
Zhongyu (Joan) Lu (University of Huddersfield, UK)
Information Science Reference • copyright 2013 • 508pp • H/C (ISBN: 9781466619753) • US $195.00 (our price)

XML Data Mining Models, Methods, and Applications
Andrea Tagarelli (University of Calabria, Italy)
Information Science Reference • copyright 2012 • 538pp • H/C (ISBN: 9781613503560) • US $195.00 (our price)

Graph Data Management Techniques and Applications
Sherif Sakr (University of New South Wales, Australia) and Eric Pardede (LaTrobe University, Australia)
Information Science Reference • copyright 2012 • 502pp • H/C (ISBN: 9781613500538) • US $195.00 (our price)

Advanced Database Query Systems Techniques, Applications and Technologies
Li Yan (Northeastern University, China) and Zongmin Ma (Northeastern University, China)
Information Science Reference • copyright 2011 • 410pp • H/C (ISBN: 9781609604752) • US $180.00 (our price)

Knowledge Discovery Practices and Emerging Applications of Data Mining Trends and New Domains
A.V. Senthil Kumar (CMS College of Science and Commerce, India)
Information Science Reference • copyright 2011 • 414pp • H/C (ISBN: 9781609600679) • US $180.00 (our price)

Data Mining in Public and Private Sectors Organizational and Government Applications
Antti Syvajarvi (University of Lapland, Finland) and Jari Stenvall (Tampere University, Finland)
Information Science Reference • copyright 2010 • 448pp • H/C (ISBN: 9781605669069) • US $180.00 (our price)

Text Mining Techniques for Healthcare Provider Quality Determination Methods for Rank Comparisons
Patricia Cerrito (University of Louisville, USA)
Medical Information Science Reference • copyright 2010 • 410pp • H/C (ISBN: 9781605667522) • US $245.00 (our price)

DISSEMINATOR of KNOWLEDGE

www.igi-global.com

701 E. Chocolate Ave., Hershey, PA 17033
Order online at www.igi-global.com or call 717-533-8845 x100
To place a standing order for titles released in this series, contact: cust@igi-global.com
Mon-Fri 8:00 am - 5:00 pm (est) or fax 24 hours a day 717-533-8661

Table of Contents

Section 1
Basic Challenges of Data Management in Graph Databases

Chapter 1
D. Dominguez-Sal, Universitat Politècnica de Catalunya, Spain
V. Muntés-Mulero, Universitat Politècnica de Catalunya, Spain
N. Martínez-Bazán, Universitat Politècnica de Catalunya, Spain
J. Larriba-Pey, Universitat Politècnica de Catalunya, Spain

Chapter 2
Marko A. Rodriguez, AT&T Interactive, USA
Peter Neubauer, Neo Technology, Sweden

Chapter 3
Srinath Srinivasa, International Institute of Information Technology, India

Chapter 4
Sherif Sakr, University of New South Wales, Australia
Ghazi Al-Naymat, University of Tabuk, Saudi Arabia

Chapter 5
Alfredo Ferro, Università di Catania, Italy
Rosalba Giugno, Università di Catania, Italy
Alfredo Pulvirenti, Università di Catania, Italy
Dennis Shasha, Courant Institute of Mathematical Sciences, USA

Section 2
Advanced Querying and Mining Aspects of Graph Databases

Foreword

In recent years, many database researchers have become fascinated by graphs, of which I am one. Like many others, I have spent years working with the relational model, including its data access methods, optimizing techniques, and query languages. The rise of the graph model has been somewhat disruptive, and our natural tendency is to ask, "Can we address new challenges using the existing relational model?" Unfortunately, many efforts along this direction do not seem to work well.

The advent of the Web, and in particular large social networks on the Web, highlights the urgency of developing a native graph database. The embracing of the graph model is anything but surprising. After all, data management is about modeling the data and the relationships between the data. Can there be a more natural model than the graph itself? The question, however, was not new. About three or four decades ago, network and hierarchical models, which are also graph based, fought and lost the battle against the relational model. Today, however, we are facing many new challenges that the relational model is not designed for. For example, as graphs are becoming increasingly larger, storing a graph in a relational table and using relational self-joins to traverse the graph are simply too costly.

Over the last decade, much research has been conducted on graphs. In particular, the study of large-scale social networks has been made possible, and many interesting and even surprising results have been published. However, the majority of research focuses on graph analytics using specific graph algorithms (for example, graph reachability, sub-graph homomorphism and matching), and not enough effort has been devoted to developing a new data model to better support graph analytics and applications on graphs.

This book is the *first* that approaches the challenges associated with graphs from a data management point of view; it connects the dots. As I am currently involved in building a native graph database engine, I encounter problems that arise from every possible aspect: data representation, indexing, transaction support, parallel query processing, and many others. All of them sound familiar to a database researcher, but the inherent change is fundamental as they originate from a new foundation. I found that this book contains a lot of timely information, aiding my efforts. To be clear, it does not offer the blueprint for building a graph database system, but it contains a bag of diamonds, enlightening the readers as they start exploring a field that may fundamentally change data management in the future.

Haixun Wang
Microsoft Research Asia

Haixun Wang, *who earned a PhD in Computer Science from UCLA in 2000, joined Microsoft Research Asia in 2009. Before then, he spent nine years as a research staff member at IBM Research Center, where he was a technical assistant to Stuart Feldman, then-vice president of Computer Science, and to Mark Wegman, head of Computer Science. Wang's interest lies in data management and mining, and he is working on building a large-scale knowledge base for advanced applications, including search. Wang is on the editorial board of IEEE Transactions on Knowledge and Data Engineering, Knowledge and Information Systems, and the Journal of Computer Science and Technology. He has held key leadership roles in various top conferences in his field*

Preface

The graph is a powerful tool for representing and understanding objects and their relationships in various application domains. Recently, graphs have been widely used to model many complex structured and schemaless data such as semantic web, social networks, biological networks, protein networks, chemical compounds and business process models. The growing popularity of graph databases has generated interesting data management problems. Therefore, the domain of graph databases have attracted a lot of attention from the research community and different challenges have been discussed such as: subgraph search queries, supergraph search queries, approximate subgraph matching, short path queries and graph mining techniques.

This book is designed for studying various fundamental challenges of storing and querying graph databases. In addition, it discusses the applications of graph databases in various domains. In particular, the book is divided into three main sections.

The first section discusses the basic definitions of graph data models, graph representations and graph traversal patterns. It also provides an overview of different graph indexing techniques and evaluation mechanisms for the main types of graph queries. The second section further discusses advanced querying aspects of graph databases and different mining techniques of graph databases. It should be noted that many graph querying algorithms are sensitive to the application scenario in which they are designed and cannot be generalized for all domains. Therefore, the third section focuses on presenting the usage of graph database techniques in different practical domains such as: semantic web, chemoinformatics, bioinformatics, business process model and transportation networks.

In a nutshell, the book provides a comprehensive summary from both of the algorithmic and the applied perspectives. It will provide the reader with a better understanding of how graph databases can be effectively utilized in different scenarios.

Sherif Sakr
University of New South Wales, Australia

Eric Pardede
La Trobe University, Australia

Acknowledgment

We would like to thank the editorial advisory board of the book for their efforts towards the successful completion of this project.

We also would like to thank all contributing authors of the chapters of the book. The efforts of all reviewers in advancing the material of this book are highly appreciated!

Thank you all.

Sherif Sakr
University of New South Wales, Australia

Eric Pardede
La Trobe University, Australia

Section 1
Basic Challenges of Data Management in Graph Databases

Chapter 1
Graph Representation

D. Dominguez-Sal
Universitat Politècnica de Catalunya, Spain

V. Muntés-Mulero
Universitat Politècnica de Catalunya, Spain

N. Martínez-Bazán
Universitat Politècnica de Catalunya, Spain

J. Larriba-Pey
Universitat Politècnica de Catalunya, Spain

ABSTRACT

In this chapter, we review different graph implementation alternatives that have been proposed in the literature. Our objective is to provide the readers with a broad set of alternatives to implement a graph, according to their needs. We pay special attention to the techniques that enable the management of large graphs. We also include a description of the most representative libraries available for representing graphs.

INTRODUCTION

Graphs are a mathematical abstraction to represent a set of entities and their relationships. These entities are represented as the nodes of the graph and the edges correspond to the relationships among these entities.

The use of graphs is very appropriate for many datasets where we want to obtain information about how the entities are related or how the topology of the network evolves. For example, if we want to represent the data associated to a social network we may represent the users as nodes of the graphs and draw friendship relations among those users.

The analysis of this topology can be exploited to find communities of users with similar interests or find influential people (i.e. authorities) in the network.

Another common scenario is travelling routes, where the nodes are the destinations and the edges are the communication routes among them. In this scenario, some important questions are related to obtaining the shortest or cheapest route from a certain spot to a different place. Also, building routes to visit a large set of destinations in the minimum travel time or finding travel routes that may have an important impact in the overall travelling structure in case of malfunction.

DOI: 10.4018/978-1-61350-053-8.ch001

In order to analyze the previous problems and others, it is necessary to efficiently represent graphs in computers. Graph data structures should be able to compute common operations such as finding the neighbors of a node, checking if two nodes are connected by an edge, or updating the graph structure in a short time. However, no data structure is optimal for all graph operations and hence depending on the applications one representation may be preferable than another. Here, we review some of the most relevant graph representation solutions found in the literature.

The chapter is organized as follows. First, we describe simple data structures for representing graphs, which are especially adequate for implementations without big spatial or temporal constraints. Next, we review advanced techniques for improving the in-memory graph representations and compress the graph when performance is important. Then, we describe some distributed graph techniques that aim at providing highly scalable architectures for graph processing. We describe the approach by the Resource Description Framework (RDF) community to describe graph datasets. Finally, we review some of the graph software libraries that are available for representing graphs, showing DEX as an example of the internals of a modern graph database.

CLASSICAL STRUCTURES FOR REPRESENTING GRAPHS

In this section, we introduce some of the most popular data structures for representing graphs. They are important because some of the techniques described later in the chapter are based on these data structures. We summarize the representations described in this section in Figure 1, depicting the four different graph representations for a sample graph.

Adjacency Matrix

A graph $G = (V, E)$ is commonly modeled as the set of nodes (also called vertices, V) plus an associated set of edges E. Edges can be expressed as pairs of the two nodes that are connected. We can represent this neighboring information with the aid of a bidimensional array m of $n \cdot n$ boolean values, in which $n = |V|$. The indexes of the array correspond to the node identifiers of the graph, and the boolean junction of the two indices indicates whether the two nodes are connected through an edge in the graph. If the graph is undirected, then the matrix is symmetric: m_{ij} and λ have the same value, which indicates that there is an edge between nodes i and j. If the graph is directed, $E_{i}, ..., E_{i}$ indicates an edge that is going from the node i to j, *and* m_{ij} indicates an edge going from the node j to i. A variant of the adjacency matrix representation for weighted graphs is to substitute the boolean entries by integers, and these integers can be used to encode the weights of the edges.

Although this implementation is very efficient for adding/removing edges or checking if two nodes are connected because the operation is immediate, it has three important drawbacks. First, it takes a quadratic space with respect to the number of nodes, independently of the number of edges, and hence it is not adequate if the graph is sparse, which tends to be the case. Second, the addition of nodes is expensive because a new matrix is reallocated and the contents copied to the new structure. Finally, third, the operation to retrieve all the neighboring nodes takes linear time with respect to the number of vertices in the graph. Since the most used operation for traversals is obtaining the neighbors of one node, matrix arrays are not adequate for traversing large graphs.

Figure 1. (a) Sample graph represented as (b) adjacency matrix, (c) adjacency lists, (d) incidence matrix, (e) laplacian matrix

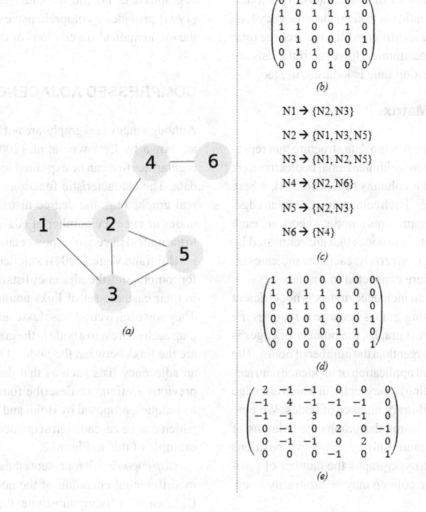

$$\begin{pmatrix} 0 & 1 & 1 & 0 & 0 & 0 \\ 1 & 0 & 1 & 1 & 1 & 0 \\ 1 & 1 & 0 & 0 & 1 & 0 \\ 0 & 1 & 0 & 0 & 0 & 1 \\ 0 & 1 & 1 & 0 & 0 & 0 \\ 0 & 0 & 0 & 1 & 0 & 0 \end{pmatrix}$$

(b)

N1 → {N2, N3}

N2 → {N1, N3, N5}

N3 → {N1, N2, N5}

N4 → {N2, N6}

N5 → {N2, N3}

N6 → {N4}

(c)

$$\begin{pmatrix} 1 & 1 & 0 & 0 & 0 & 0 & 0 & 0 \\ 1 & 0 & 1 & 1 & 1 & 0 & 0 \\ 0 & 1 & 1 & 0 & 0 & 1 & 0 \\ 0 & 0 & 0 & 1 & 0 & 0 & 1 \\ 0 & 0 & 0 & 0 & 1 & 1 & 0 \\ 0 & 0 & 0 & 0 & 0 & 0 & 1 \end{pmatrix}$$

(d)

$$\begin{pmatrix} 2 & -1 & -1 & 0 & 0 & 0 \\ -1 & 4 & -1 & -1 & -1 & 0 \\ -1 & -1 & 3 & 0 & -1 & 0 \\ 0 & -1 & 0 & 2 & 0 & -1 \\ 0 & -1 & -1 & 0 & 2 & 0 \\ 0 & 0 & 0 & -1 & 0 & 1 \end{pmatrix}$$

(e)

(a)

Adjacency List

A graph represented as an adjacency list is implemented using a set of lists where each one accounts for the neighbors of one node. The data structure implements a vector of n pointers to adjacency lists (where $n = |V|$), where each entry indexes one node of the graph. Each adjacency list contains the list of node identifiers that are neighbors to this node. If the graph is undirected and an edge connects nodes i and j, then the list of neighbors of i contains the node j and vice versa. If the graph is directed the adjacency list of i, contains only the outgoing edges of i. Thus, if an edge goes from node i to node j, the adjacency list of i will contain the node identifier of j.

In contrast to matrix representations, adjacency list representations are very adequate for obtaining the neighbors of a node, and allow for a cheaper addition of nodes to the structure. Furthermore, they are a more compact representation of sparse matrices because the nodes that are not connected do not consume space.

On the other hand, adjacency lists are not the most suitable structure for checking if there is an edge between two nodes. If the edge is not present, then the algorithm scans the adjacency list of neighbors, which can be expensive for nodes with a large number of connections. An alternative implementation is to keep the adjacency lists sorted by node identifier, which reduces the time to search to logarithmic. However, if the lists are sorted the insertion time is logarithmic, too.

Incidence Matrix

An incidence matrix is a data structure that represents the graph as a bidimensional boolean matrix of n rows and e columns ($n \cdot e$ positions), where $n=|V|$ and $e=|E|$. Each column represents an edge, and each row represents a node. Therefore, each column indicates the nodes that are connected by a certain edge. Conversely, each row indicates all the edges that are connected to a node.

Generally, an incidence matrix is not efficient for implementing graphs because it requires $n \cdot e$ bits, and for most graphs, the number of edges is significantly larger than the number of nodes. The most significant application of incidence matrices is for representing hypergraphs, in which one edge connects an arbitrary number of nodes. We note that although for regular graphs the columns of the incidence matrix always have two positions set to true, for hypergraphs the number of positions set in one column may be arbitrarily large.

Laplacian Matrix

The laplacian matrix is a variant of the matrix representation. The laplacian matrix is a bidimensional array of $n \cdot n$ integers, where $n=|V|$. The diagonal of the laplacian matrix indicates the degree of the node. The rest of positions are set to -1 if the two vertices are connected and 0 otherwise.

The main advantage of the laplacian representation of a graph is that it allows analyzing the graph structure by means of spectral analysis. The spectral analysis calculates the eigenvalues of the laplacian matrix, which can be interpreted and applied to extract properties of the graph. In this

chapter, we show an example of spectral analysis application for improving the cache locality access of graphs later. For the interested reader, F. Chung (1994) provides a comprehensive description of the mathematical foundations of this topic.

COMPRESSED ADJACENCY LISTS

Although many real graphs are not homogeneous as shown by Leskovec et al. (2008), they have regularities that can be exploited for compressing data. The characteristic functions of these large real graphs (e.g. the degree distributions of the nodes or even the number of edges with respect to the nodes) fit very well power law distributions.

Boldi and Vigna (2004) exploited such features for compressing the adjacency lists of large graphs, in their case the set of links among web pages. They sort each web address lexicographically and map each address to a node in the graph. The edges are the links between the nodes. Departing from an adjacency lists such as that described in the previous section, we describe four compression techniques, proposed by Boldi and Vigna (2004), which can be cascaded in sequence. We show an example of this in Figure 2.

Gap encoding: It represents the adjacency lists by differential encoding of the node identifiers. Differential encoding substitutes the original node identifiers by the difference between two consecutive nodes, which turns into a reduction of the overall size of the lists. The adjacency list for node x: $A(x) = (a_1, a_2, a_3 \ldots, a_n)$ is encoded as $(v(a_1 - x), a_2 - a_1 - 1, a_3 - a_2 - 1, \ldots, a_{n-1} - 1)$ Since the adjacency list A(x) is originally sorted, all the elements but the first are positive numbers. In order to keep all node identifiers positive, the mapping for the first node is the following:

$$v(x) = \begin{cases} 2x, & \text{if } x \geq 0 \\ 2\,|\,x\,|-1, & \text{if } x < 0 \end{cases}$$

Figure 2. Compressed adjacency lists

Node	Outdegree	Successors
21	9	20,23,24,25,26,28,30,31,58
22	7	23,24,25,29,30,31,58
...	...	...

(a) Adjacency list

Node	Outdegree	Successors
21	9	1,2,0,0,0,1,1,0,26
22	7	2,0,0,3,1,0,26
...	...	...

(b) Gap encoding

Node	Outdegree	Reference	Copy List	Successors
21	9	0		20,23,24,25,26, 28,30,31,58
22	7	1	011100111	29
...				...

(c) Reference compression

Node	Outdegree	Reference	Blocks	Copy blocks	Successors
21	9	0			20,23,24,25,26,28,30,31,58
22	7	1	4	0,0,2,1	29
...	...			...	...

(d) Differential compression

Node	Outdegree	Reference	Blocks	Copy blocks	Intervals	Left extreme	Length	Residuals
21	9	0			2	4,2	2,0	1,7,29
22	7	1	4	0,0,2,1	0			14
...	...	...		...				...

(e) Interval representation

- *Reference compression*: Since nodes may share a large set of neighbors, it is more compact to represent a node with respect to the differences in the adjacency lists of previous nodes. The reference compression splits the adjacency lists in three values: the reference, the copy list and the extra nodes. The reference is an offset to the node identifier adjacency list over which the compression is performed. The selected node for reference is the one among the previous nodes where the compression is the largest (it has been tested that selecting the node which compresses the best among the three previous node identifiers yields good compression ratios). The copy list for node x, with reference y is a bitmap of |A(y)| positions where the i-th bit is set if the i-th entry of A(y) is in A(x). The extra nodes are a regular adjacency list that contains the node identifiers in A(x) – A(y).

- *Differential compression*: The copy list, obtained by reference compression, is divided in blocks of consecutive 0's and 1's. This step compresses the copy lists into two values: a block counter and a copy block. The block counter accounts for the number of blocks in the copy block. The copy block is a list of integers that indicate the length of each block of 0's and 1's. By agreement, it is assumed that the first block is a block of 1's, and thus if the first block is a 0's block the first element of the copy block is a 0. Since only the first number may be a 0, each element of the copy block can be decremented by one for all the blocks except for the first one. In order to generate a more compact copy block, the last element can be deduced from the block counter and the outdegree of the node. it is assumed that the first block is a one block, i.e. if the first block is a block with 0's the counter.

- *Interval representation*: This procedure aims at compacting the extra nodes lists. If the list has more than two consecutive integers, then they are encoded as an interval, which is represented as two values: the left extreme and the length of the interval. The left extreme is coded as the difference between the left extreme of the current interval and the right extreme minus two (because at least there are two elements in the interval). For the case of the first interval, the node identifier is subtracted to the left extreme and is represented with the $v(x)$ function. The nodes that do not belong to an interval of more than two nodes are represented using the differential compression. The length of the interval is computed as the number of elements minus the minimum number of elements in the interval. The node sequences that are too short to become an interval, are called residuals and are encoded with gap encoding.

We summarize the previously described compression mechanism in the Table 1.

Example: Figure 2 depicts an example of the compression scheme described previously. In Figure 2(a), we enumerate the neighbors of nodes 21 and 22 with their respective adjacency lists. In the first step, gap encoding reduces the magnitude of the node identifiers enabling less bits per identifier (Figure 2(b)). The reference column in Figure 2(c) indicates the offset from where the copy list is compressed. For node 21, the zero indicates that no compression is performed, and the one for the second node indicates that the reference points to the previous node identifier, which is node 21. The copy list for node 22 is a bitmap that indicates the elements that are shared with node 21, such as identifiers 23 or 24. Differential compression in Figure 2(d) compresses the previously defined copy lists: the copy list of node 22 contained four sections of consecutive bits of length 1, 1, 3 and 2 (given that a section of consecutive bits has at least length one, these numbers can be decreased by one unit to reduce the space). Finally, interval representation compresses the two ranges of consecutive residuals of node 21: from 23 to 26 and 30 to 31. For the former: the left extreme is encoded $v(E_1 - x)_1 = 2° \cdot (23 - 21) = 4$, and its length $L_1 - 2 = 4 - 2 = 2$ Similarly for the latter range, the left extreme is encoded as $E_2 - E_1 - L_1 - 1 = 30 - 23 - 4 - 1 = 2$ and the length $L_2 - 2 = 2 - 2 = 0$ The residuals remaining 20, 28, 58 are encoded as $v(R_1 - x) = 2 \cdot |20 - 21| - 1 = 1, R_2 - R_1 - 1 = 7$ and $R_3 - R_2 - 1 = 58 - 28 - 1 = 29$.

In particular, the previously stated compression techniques are very effective because many graphs, and particularly web graphs, have the following characteristics (Boldi and Vigna (2004)]:

- Some nodes act as a hub with a number of connections significantly over the average degree of the graph.

Table 1. Compressed adjacency lists summary of the representation

Name	Symbol	Calculated as
Node identifier	x	Unique node identifier
Outdegree	d	Number of neighbors
Reference	r	Difference with the node identifier that references
Blocks	b	Number of copy blocks
Copy blocks	$B_1, \ldots, B_b$	$B_1, B_2 - 1, \ldots, B_b - 1$
Intervals	i	Number of intervals
Left extreme	$E_1, \ldots, E_i$	$v(E_1 - x), E_2 - E_1 - L_1 - 1, \ldots, E_i - E_{i-1} - L_{i-1} - 1$
Length	$L_1, \ldots, L_i$	$L_1 - 2, \ldots, L_i - 2$
Residuals	$R_1, \ldots, R_k$	$v(R_1 - x), R_2 - R_1 - 1, \ldots, R_k - R_{k-1} - 1)$

• Many relations are found in a community. In the case of web graphs it is likely that a large portion of websites are linking to other sections of the same website.

• There are many nodes with shared neighbors. In the case of web graphs, two pages have either a very similar set of links, or they are completely disjoint.

IMPROVING THE DATA LOCALITY OF A GRAPH

In addition to the design of the data structures to reach a good performance, it is important to take into account the impact of the computer architecture in the data structures. Computers are prepared to take advantage of both the spatial and temporal localities thanks to the design of the memory hierarchy. Thus, the way data is laid out physically in memory determines the locality to be obtained. In this section, we review techniques that are adequate to improve the L1 and L2 cache levels for graph management. We describe several techniques that relabel the sequence of node

identifiers in order to improve the data locality. In other words, in a graph adjacency matrix representation, these techniques would exchange rows and columns of the graph to improve the cache hit ratio.

We observe that operations on graphs exhibit an important component of spatial locality. Spatial locality is obtained when once a certain data item has been accessed; the nearby data items are likely to be accessed in the following computations. This is particularly evident in graph algorithms, such as traversals, in which once a node is accessed it is likely that its neighbors are explored in the near future. Bearing this in mind, a graph whose data items are mapped taking into account the accesses will be faster than one with the nodes randomly mapped.

Breadth First Search Layout (BFSL)

Al-Furaih and Ranka (1998) proposed a method to augment the space locality of large graphs based on breadth first search traversals. This algorithm takes as input the sequence of vertices of a graph, and generates a permutation of the vertices which obtains better cache performance for graph traversals. The algorithm selects a node at random that is the origin of the traversal. Then, the graph is traversed following a breadth first search algorithm, generating a list of vertex identifiers in the order that they are visited. Finally, BFSL takes the generated list and assigns the node identifiers sequentially.

The rationale of the algorithm is that when a node is explored using a BFS algorithm, the neighboring nodes are queued to be explored together. Thus, BFSL is packing the neighboring vertices of a node together. BFSL is the optimal policy for the BFS traversal starting from the selected origin node, but for traversals starting from a different node it might be far from the optimal. This difference is more severe for traversals that start from nodes distant from the origin node.

Cuthill-Mckee

Since graphs may be seen as matrices we can map the locality problem to a similar one from matrix reorganization that is called minimum bandwidth problem. The bandwidth of a row in a matrix is the maximum distance between non-zero elements, with the condition that one is on the left of the diagonal and the other on the right of the diagonal. The bandwidth of a matrix is the maximum of the bandwidth of its rows. The bandwidth minimization problem is known to be a NP problem, and thus for large matrices (or graphs) the solutions are only approximated. Matrices with low bandwidths are more cache friendly, because the non zero elements (i.e. the edges of the graph) are clustered across the diagonal of the matrix. Therefore, if the graph matrix has a low bandwidth the neighbors of a node are close to the diagonal of the matrix and are all clustered.

Cuthill and Mckee (1969) proposed one of the most popular bandwidth minimization techniques for sparse matrices. This method relabels the vertices of a matrix according to a sequence, with the aid of a heuristically guided traversal. The node

with the first identifier, which is the node from where the traversal starts, is the node with the smallest degree in the whole graph. Then, a BFS traversal starts, applying a heuristic that selects those nodes that have the smallest degree and have not been visited yet. The nodes are labeled sequentially as they are visited by the traversal.

Recursive Spectral Bisection

Recursive Spectral Bisection (RSB) is a graph layout method designed by Barnard and Simon (1993) that takes advantage of the spectral analysis of a graph. Spectral methods are based on the mathematical properties of the eigenvectors of a matrix. If we represent a graph G using its laplacian representation L(G), the eigenvectors of the graph are the vectors $\vec{x}$ that satisfy the following relation:

$$L(G) \cdot \vec{x} = \lambda \cdot \vec{x},$$

where λ is an scalar value. RSB orders the set of eigenvalues of a graph by increasing value, and selects the eigenvector $\vec{x}_2$, which correspond to the second smallest eigenvalue λ_2. The second smallest eigenvalue is known as the Fiedler vector, which is an indicator of how close are two vertices in a graph. Two nodes are close in a graph if the difference between its components in the Fiedler vector is small. RSB applies this to keep nodes that are close in the graph, also close in memory to improve the spatial locality of the graph. Therefore, RSB sorts the nodes by its value in the Fiedler vector, and labels sequentially the vertices.

Although the Fiedler vector may be computed by regular linear equation resolution techniques, such as the Lanczos (1950) algorithm, its direct application to large graphs is unfeasible. RSB provides an approximated procedure to find the eigenvalues of a graph. RSB is divided in a three step recursive process that contracts the graph until it can be computed efficiently with the Lanczos algorithm, and then interpolates the results for the uncontracted graph using the rayleigh quotient iteration:

- *Contraction:* The contraction phase finds a maximal independent set of the original graph. An independent set of vertices is a selection of vertices that none of them are connected by an edge. This set is maximal if no further vertices can be added to the set. Note that the maximal independent may not be unique.
- Then, the new contracted graph has as vertices those that are part of the maximal independent set. Two nodes of the contracted graph are connected if the neighbors of the maximal independent sets share nodes. Therefore, the contracted graph has fewer nodes than the original graph, but it still keeps the original graph structure, and the inference of properties on the contracted graph allows for their extrapolation to the uncontracted graph. Once the size of the graph is small enough to be computed with the Lanczos algorithm, the Fiedler vector is computed finishing the recursivity.
- *Interpolation:* Given a Fiedler vector of the contracted graph, RSB estimates the Fiedler vector of the uncontracted graph. The value of the Fiedler vector is copied from the contracted graph to the uncontracted one, for the nodes that were part of the maximal set (i.e. the nodes that were in both graphs). For the rest of nodes, the value in the Fiedler vector is obtained averaging the components of their neighboring nodes. Since the interpolated nodes must have at least a neighboring node in the contracted graph due to the maximal independent set construction, the value of the Fiedler vector is defined for all components.

- *Refinement:* In order to increase the quality of the approximation, RSB applies a refinement step that uses the rayleigh quotient iteration (RQI) (Parlett (1974)), which is an iterative algorithm that in each iteration estimates an approximation of the eigenvalues of the matrix that converges to the exact solution. Since the Fiedler vector obtained in the interpolation phase is already a good approximation to the exact solution, the RQI process converges fast.

GRAPH PARTITIONING IN DISTRIBUTED REPRESENTATIONS

As we have been discussing in previous sections, an important aspect of network/graph information is its size. Some graphs are too large to be fully loaded into the main memory of a single computer and this implies an intensive usage of secondary storage that degrades the performance of graph applications. A scalable solution consists on distributing the graph on multiple computers in order to add the computing resources.

Most of the initial work in handling graph-like data in parallel or distributed data management has been done in the context of the relational model, where flat tables make it easy for partitioning. In the late 1980s, there have been interesting attempts to deal with complex objects (mostly trees) in the context of object-oriented databases (Khoshafian, Valduriez and Copeland (1988); Valduriez, Khoshafian and Copeland (1986)). This work can be useful to deal with XML documents (trees) in parallel/distributed systems but requires major rethinking to deal with more general graphs.

More recent work has been oriented to the parallel aspects of the algorithms to solve some important algorithms over graphs such as the shortest path problem (Crobak et al. (2007); Madduri et al. (2007)) or finding frequent patterns as the work presented by Reinhardt and Karypis (2007). Other graph algorithms like the shortest path or graph isomorphism have been used to assess their scalability on new parallel architectures (Bader, Cong and Feo (2005) and Underwood et al. (2007)). Parallelism in graph algorithms has also been largely exploited for other typical graph operations such as BFS, graph partitioning, spanning tree search, graph coloring, etc. Some examples may be found in (Bader and Cong (2005); Devine et al. (2006); Yoo et al. (2005)).

One and Two Dimensional Graph Partitioning

Yoo et al. (2005), proposed partitioning the graph at random into parts and distribute them into the nodes of a shared-nothing parallel system in order to solve BFS more efficiently. More precisely, they present two approaches for distributing BFS: BFS with 1D and 2D partitionings, which propose two different ways of partitioning the adjacency matrix of a graph. Although adjacency matrices can grow enormously if the graph has many nodes, as we saw previously, they handled this problem by deploying their system in a huge supercomputer: the BlueGene/L system with over 30000 computing nodes. Following, we compare the two partitioning strategies in relation to the distributed BFS algorithm (DBFS) that Yoo et al. used for their work.

With 1D partitioning (1D), matrix rows are randomly assigned to the p nodes in the system (Figure 3(a)). Therefore, each row contains the complete list of neighbors of the corresponding vertex. With 2D partitioning (2D), the idea is to benefit from the fact that nodes are organized in R x C = p processor meshes in the architecture of the system that they are using, i.e. in a two-dimensional grid such that each node is connected to its four immediate neighbors. The adjacency matrix is divided into R x C blocks of rows and C blocks of columns such that each node is assigned those values in the adjacency matrix corresponding to the intersection between C blocks of rows and a block of columns, as shown in

Figure 3.b. Therefore, the list of adjacencies of a given vertex is divided into R nodes, and the set of vertices in the graph is assigned to C groups of R nodes. Thanks to this, the number of nodes to which a certain node sends data can be reduced drastically, since each node only communicates with at most R + C = 2 instead of p nodes as in the case of 1D partitioning.

However, these previous attempts to partition a graph and parallelize BFS ignore the possible effect that different partitioning techniques of the graph might have on the amount of inter-node communication, which could degrade system performance. This problem becomes critical depending on the query. For instance, the scalability of communications might be a problem for all those types of queries that visit the graph globally and need to traverse the graph using operations such as BFS repeatedly from multiple source vertices.

Other Partitioning Techniques

Comprehensive studies on data partitioning strategies have also been conducted for other database models. For instance, in OODBMSs, the vertices could be viewed as the objects and, the edges could be understood as the relationships between objects. A comprehensive survey of partitioning techniques for OODBMSs was written by Özsu and Valduriez (1999). However, typical graph database queries are completely different from those in OODBMSs. For example, structural queries such as finding the shortest distance between two vertices in a very large graph might be crucial in graph databases but irrelevant in OODBMSs, making previous partitioning strategies unsuitable for these new requirements.

Graph partitioning. In the light of all these analyses, a possible solution might be partitioning the graph guaranteeing that the amount of edges is minimum or as small as possible. Much work has been devoted to the general problem of balanced graph partitioning in the last four decades.

Figure 3. 1D and 2D graph partitioning

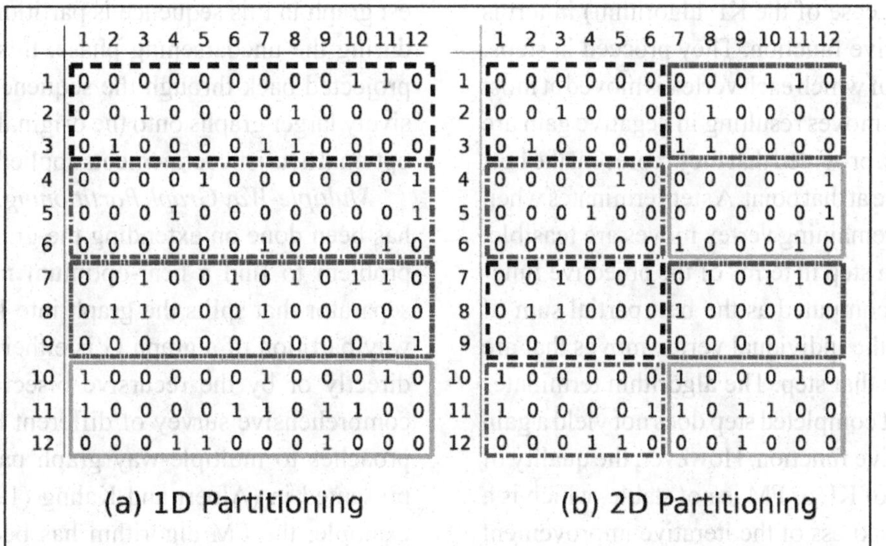

(a) 1D Partitioning

	1	2	3	4	5	6	7	8	9	10	11	12
1	0	0	0	0	0	0	0	0	0	1	1	0
2	0	0	1	0	0	0	0	1	0	0	0	0
3	0	1	0	0	0	0	1	1	0	0	0	0
4	0	0	0	0	1	0	0	0	0	0	0	1
5	0	0	0	1	0	0	0	0	0	0	0	1
6	0	0	0	0	0	0	1	0	0	0	1	0
7	0	0	1	0	0	1	0	1	0	1	1	0
8	0	1	1	0	0	0	1	0	0	0	0	0
9	0	0	0	0	0	0	0	0	0	0	1	1
10	1	0	0	0	0	0	1	0	0	0	1	0
11	1	0	0	0	0	1	1	0	1	1	0	0
12	0	0	0	1	1	0	0	0	1	0	0	0

(b) 2D Partitioning

	1	2	3	4	5	6	7	8	9	10	11	12
1	0	0	0	0	0	0	0	0	0	1	1	0
2	0	0	1	0	0	0	0	1	0	0	0	0
3	0	1	0	0	0	0	1	1	0	0	0	0
4	0	0	0	0	1	0	0	0	0	0	0	1
5	0	0	0	1	0	0	0	0	0	0	0	1
6	0	0	0	0	0	0	1	0	0	0	1	0
7	0	0	1	0	0	1	0	1	0	1	1	0
8	0	1	1	0	0	0	1	0	0	0	0	0
9	0	0	0	0	0	0	0	0	0	0	1	1
10	1	0	0	0	0	0	1	0	0	0	1	0
11	1	0	0	0	0	1	1	0	1	1	0	0
12	0	0	0	1	1	0	0	0	1	0	0	0

Although most of the work has been generalized to hypergraphs, we will focus on the particular case of graphs, where edges only connect two vertices. Given a graph, the objective is to divide it into k partitions such that each partition approximately contains the same number of vertices and the number of edges connecting vertices located in different partitions is minimal. In particular, when k = 2, the problem is called minimum graph bisection. This problem is also known as finding the minimum edge-separator, i.e. the minimal set of edges whose removal from the graph leaves two disconnected subgraphs of equal size (containing the same number of vertices), and has been deeply studied in many different fields, such as VLSI Computer-Aided Design (see the work by Alpert and Kahng (1995), for example) or in communication networks (Arora, Rao and Vazirani (2004)). Finding an optimal graph bisection has been proven to be NP-Hard by Garey and Johnson (1990) and, as a consequence, finding an optimal k-way partition is also at least NP-Hard. Because of this, most of the work presented in the literature has focused on developing polynomial-time heuristic algorithms that give good sub-optimal solutions.

First steps on Balanced Graph Bisection. The proposals on graph partitioning presented in the literature can be classified into two different categories (Ashcraft and Liu (1997)): (i) direct approaches which construct partitions, such as the nested dissection algorithm presented by George and Liu (1978), based on alternating level structures and spectral methods (Pothen, Simon and Liou (1990)), and (ii) iterative approaches which improve these partitions, such as those presented by Kernighan and Lin (1970) (KL) or its faster version presented by Fiduccia and Mattheyses (1982) (FM), which uses an iterative approach by swapping vertices between the existing partitions or moving a vertex from one partition to the other, respectively. Iterative improvement algorithms have been preferred in general to other well-known optimization techniques such as simulated annealing and genetic algorithms because they have the potential to combine good sub-optimal solutions with fast run times. These algorithms rely on a priority queue of vertex moves to greedily select the best vertex move (in the case of the FM algorithm) or the best vertex swap (in the case of the KL algorithm) in terms of the objective function. They proceed in steps, during each of which each vertex is moved at most once. Vertex moves resulting in negative gain are also possible, provided that they represent the best feasible move at that point. A step terminates when none of the remaining vertex moves are feasible. The gain of a step in terms of the objective function is then computed as the best partial sum of the gains of the individual vertex moves that are made during that step. The algorithm terminates when the last completed step does not yield a gain in the objective function. However, the quality of the solution of KL or FM is not stable, which is a common weakness of the iterative improvement approaches based on moves. Because of this, random multi-start approaches are used to alleviate this problem by applying the algorithm repeatedly starting from random initial partitions and return the best solution found (Alpert and Kahng (1995)). A complete overview on stochastic methods is provided by Battiti and Bertossi (1999).

The main disadvantage of the above algorithms is that they make vertex moves based solely on local information (the immediate gain of the vertex move) and this has caused the appearance of several enhancements to the basic algorithms that attempt to capture global properties or that incorporate look-ahead. In addition, flat partitioning algorithms, i.e. algorithms that directly work on the original graph, suffer significant degradation in terms of quality and running time when the size of the graph increases.

Thus, algorithms based on the multilevel paradigm have been proposed as an alternative to mitigate this problem. Some examples are the work presented by Hendrickson and Leland (1995), Karypis, et al. (1997), Karypis and Kumar (1998) or Trifunovic and Knottenbelt (2008). In this type of algorithms, the original graph is successively approximated by smaller graphs during the coarsening phase, where each vertex in the coarse graph is usually a connected subset of vertices in the original one. Next, the smallest graph in this sequence is partitioned. Finally, during the uncoarsening phase, this partition is projected back through the sequence of successively larger graphs onto the original graph, with optional heuristic refinements applied at each step.

Multiple-Way Graph Partitioning. Much effort has been done on extending the graph bisection problem to find a near-optimum multiple-way separator that splits the graph into k parts. A k-way partition of a graph G is either constructed directly or by the recursive bisection of G. A comprehensive survey of different heuristic approaches to multiple-way graph partitioning is presented in (Alpert and Kahng (1995)). As an example, the FM algorithm has been extended in order to compute a k-way partition directly by Sanchis (1989) (a k-way extension to the KL algorithm was first proposed in the original paper by Kernighan and Lin). However, this first k-way formulation of the FM algorithm is dominated by the FM algorithm implemented in a recursive bisection framework. Hence an enhanced k-way algorithm based on a pair-wise application of the FM algorithm is proposed by Cong and Lim (1998). Another randomized greedy refinement algorithm presented by Karypis and Kumar (1999) has been shown to yield partitions of good quality with fast run times.

Although the first papers on multi-way graph partitioning were written two decades ago, research on this topic is still very active, as shown by recent publications such as that by Trifunovic et al. (2008), where authors propose new parallel algorithms for the hypergraph partitioning problem (only scalable when the maximum vertex and hyperedge degrees are small, which may not be the case in real graphs). Although this algorithm allows for easy parallelization and improves the quality of results with respect to previous approaches, this is done at the cost of increasing the execution time, which might make it unsuitable for very large graphs.

Minimum-vertex separators. Most of the work on finding balanced graph partitions has focused on finding the minimum-edge separator. However, some effort is also devoted to the analogous problem of finding minimal size vertex separators. This problem was shown to be NP-Hard by Bui, T. N. and Jones (1992), even in graphs with nodes having a maximum degree of three. In addition, it is generally conjectured that problems on vertex separators are harder than the corresponding problems on edge separators. Much of the previous work on approximating vertex separators piggy-backed on work for approximating edge separators. For general graphs (with no bound on the degree), while there are simple reductions from the problem of approximating edge separators to the problem of approximating vertex separators, there is not any known reduction into the reverse direction. An iterative approach is given by Liu (1989) based on bipartite graph matching. For example, Ashcraft and Liu (1997) extend previous work using a method similar to that presented by Kernighan and Lin (1970) that operates directly on a vertex separator by moving nodes to and from the corresponding partitions. Some years later, Catalyurek and Aykanat (1999) present a proposal that allows minimizing the total number of boundary vertices by hypergraph partitioning. However, it requires optimizing partition shapes which need for using immature additional techniques. A substantial number of publications continue the research on this topic. Feige, Hajiaghayi and Lee (2005) study approximation algorithms that find vertex separators whose size is not much larger than the optimal separator of the input graph. Edge-separator techniques were also used by Evrendilek (2008) on the linear graph of the original graph so that, afterward, the solutions obtained are refined to find a good vertex separator.

Relaxing the balanced restriction. Most of the work on balanced graph partitioning is intended to divide the graph into partitions such that all of them have the same vertex weight (or the same number of vertices in the case of unweighted graphs). In some situations, we are able to relax this restriction by allowing some partitions to be slightly larger than others. Andreev and Räcke (2004) propose an approximation algorithm able to find a (k;v)-partitioning of a graph. That is, a graph must be partitioned in k parts of size at most $v\cdot(n/k)$ where n is the number of vertices in the graph. However, the execution time of their proposal is quadratic in the number of vertices, which makes it unrealistic for very large graphs.

Tools for graph partitioning. Several tools have been designed for graph partitioning. Among these, two of the most frequently used are Metis and Cluto (http://glaros.dtc.umn.edu/gkhome/software).

Graph Partitioning for Graph Distribution. Recent work by Muntés-Mulero et al. (2010) applies a heuristic graph partitioning algorithm in order to distribute a graph and reduce the inter-machine communication in a parallel shared-nothing system during the execution of a BFS traversal. This partitioning is devised to be used when a massive graph is queried by a large number of users concurrently. In general, many of the previously mentioned graph partitioning techniques cannot be applied to massive graphs because of the complexity of the algorithms proposed. Because of this, heuristic algorithms become reasonable candidates to partition such graphs.

Finally, many commercial graph databases such as Neo4J or HyperGraphDB have just started releasing distributed versions of their applications. Even more remarkable, Google Inc. has recently presented Pregel in Malewicz, et al. (2010), a distributed model to compute graph operations on highly scalable distributed systems. Although all these graph tools are currently implementing very simple techniques for distributing data among the machines of the network (for example, using a hash function), in the upcoming years, the distribution of graphs will be a very active research area.

REPRESENTING GRAPHS VIA RESOURCE DESCRIPTION FRAMEWORK (RDF)

Existing database models such as the relational model, lack native support for data structures such as trees and graphs. Many results in storing and querying graph data have been presented. In the last two decades, XML has emerged as the *de facto* data exchange format causing the proliferation of many data models considering tree-like structures (or even graphs). In this scenario looking for exact or approximate patterns represented by trees or graphs efficiently becomes essential.

Many XML indexing techniques have been proposed for pattern matching such as DataGuide, presented by Goldman et al (1997), Index Fabric, presented by Cooper et al. (2001), or APEX, proposed by Chung, Min and Shim (2002), to give some examples. DataGuide, for example, provides a summary of the path structure in a tree-structured database. Index Fabric encodes each label path to each XML element with a string and inserts this encoded information into an index for strings. APEX uses data mining algorithms to find paths that appear frequently. However, the use of the Resource Description Framework (RDF) (http://www.w3.org/RDF) is probably the first widely adopted standard for manipulating graph-like data.

RDF is a W3C standard that was designed as a framework for representing information in the Web. Even though it was not designed for graph representation, this standard has become a popular representation for graphs in the recent years. In addition, large web search enterprises, such as Google, have announced supporting microformats and the RDF format. In this section, we limit our description of RDF to its application to graph datasets.

SPARQL (Prudhommeaux and Seaborne (2005)), for instance, which has been adopted as the *de facto* standard for querying RDF datasets, is based on the use of Basic Graph Pattern (BGP) queries (Gutierrez et al. (2004)) (join queries in the database terminology). A basic graph pattern contains a set of triple patterns. Triple patterns can be regarded as RDF triples except that each subject, predicate, or object entry can either be a variable or a fixed value. The limitation of languages such as SPARQL to support graph-oriented queries such as subgraph extraction in RDF databases has lead to the proposal of extensions of these languages such as SPARQ2L, presented by Anyanwu et al. (2007). In this chapter, we will ignore the discussion related to query language aspects and we will only concentrate on storage aspects.

There exist a direct mapping between BGP queries and SQL queries. Therefore, an RDF graph can be directly mapped to a three-column table in a relational database, containing the subject, the predicate and the object, respectively. Because of this, many methods use this mapping for storing RDF graphs. Some examples of this architecture are Hexastore, presented by Weiss, Karras and Bernstein (2008), or Redland, which are implemented based on extensions of the relational persistent storage systems. Additionally, the use of auxiliary indexes on the RDF data to improve the overall query performance for RDF graphs is common. In general, two proposals are the most typically used in the existing solutions for native RDF indexing: multiple access patterns (MAP) and HexTree.

Multiple Access Patterns (MAP)

In MAP, the three positions of a triple, S, P and O, are indexed using some of their possible permutations (SPO, SOP, OSP, etc). Therefore, MAP may require up to six separate indexes (for example, implemented using B+-trees). Evaluating a BGP join requires accessing to these indexes at least two times, and using sort merge join afterwards.

Some examples of well-known systems which use the MAP technique are Virtuoso, presented by Erling (2008), YARS2, presented by Harth et al. (2007) (which uses exhaustive indexes of triples and all their embedded sub-triples -pairs and single values- in 6 separate B+-tree or hash indexes), and RDF-3X, presented by Neumann and Weikum (2008), which incorporates both index compression and a join index to facilitate BGP query processing. Their structures are built on B+-trees.

HexTree

HexTrees have been also used in well-known systems such as Hexastore. The basic idea of HexTrees is presented by Weiss et al. (2008), where they propose indexing two roles at a time. This requires for six separate data structures which correspond to the six possible ways of ordering the roles (S, P and O) in a RDF triple. In general, this representation is very bulky causing the graph representation to grow beyond the memory limits, for moderately large graphs. Note that Hexastore has only been proposed and evaluated as a main-memory data structure.

It is also relevant to remark that in both MAP and HexTree, information of a specific entity may be scattered and replicated among the database through the different indexes. For instance, in the MAP indexing scheme, looking for triples related to a certain atom A may imply accessing to all the indexes since A may act as a subject, a predicate or an object. Analogously, getting the information from HexTree for that specific atom also requires three separate lookups. A preliminary proposal on solving problems related to data locality and, consequently, to redundant storage and increased query processing cost, is presented by Fletcher and Beck (2009).

Bitmap Based Representations

The use of graph management implementations based on the efficient use compact structures, such as bitmaps, is becoming crucial, specifically for massive graphs where the amount of information to store usually exceeds the memory limits.

In the area of RDF graph management, Oren, Gueret and Schlobach (2008) propose using Bloom filters for rapid evaluation of the solutions generated by the system, although it focuses on imperfect approximate query answering.

A more recent proposal in the same area is BitMat, which is an in-memory RDF graph storage. The basic idea is representing massive graphs through a set of bitmaps that allow for storing them in a very compact way, making it possible to increase the size of data that fit entirely in memory. This compressed representation serves as the primary storage without being necessary to use any additional indexing technique.

BitMat is a 3-dimensional bitmatrix where each dimension corresponds to subject, predicate and object, respectively, which is flattened in 2 dimensions without any loss of information in order to represent RDF triples. *Figure 4* shows an example of a bitmatrix generated from a toy RDF triple set. Firstly, the RDF graph shown is conceptualized as a 3-column (subject, predicate, object) and then it is transformed into a Subject BitMat where we can distinguish three dimensions: the first (horizontal) is the subject, the second (vertical) is the object and the third (the three slices) is the predicate. The fundamental idea is that each bit denotes the presence or absence of the corresponding triple depending on the value of that bit. In order to diminish the size of this structure, which would grow tremendously as the number of different subjects, predicates and objects grow, authors use compressing techniques using a form of *Run Length Encoding*, used for sparse bit-vectors. An important aspect is that BitMats do not need to be uncompressed in order to perform operations on them.

Figure 4. A Subject BitMat for an RDF triple set

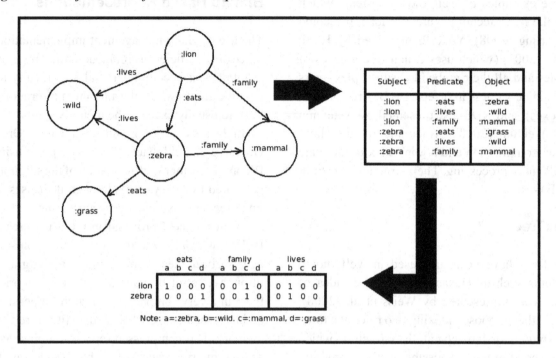

Note: a=:zebra, b=:wild. c=:mammal, d=:grass

This allows a system to represent a very large RDF triple set in a BitMat. This structure is especially interesting to enable efficient join queries expressed as conjunctive triple patterns, by using bitwise AND/OR operations, such as that presented in *Figure 5*. More specifically, it is very suitable in those situations where individual triple patterns in a join query are not selective but the combined join result is selective. On the other side, this structure is suitable for scenarios where it is only necessary to query data but not to modify it.

Other Approaches

Other approaches depend on indexing or partitioning RDF data, such as Jena (running on the TDB backend) or C-Store. In the case of C-Store, a vertical partitioning method is used where triples are partitioned by using distinct predicates, in order to help on the execution of BGP queries constrained by predicates. This approach gets less suitable as the number of predicates grows.

Other techniques have also been proposed in order to improve performance for RDF data management. For instance, Virtuoso uses bitmap indexes to favor performance as explained by Erling (2006). The SwiftOWLIM Semantic Repository uses in-memory hash-tables to load and process large data. Other RDF graph stores, such as BRAHMS, presented by Janik and Kochut (2005), and GRIN, presented by Udrea, Pugliese and Subrahmanian (2007), propose in-memory systems oriented to solve variable-length-path queries over RDF graphs. BRAHMS has evaluated their system for up to 6 million LUBM triples and GRIN was executed with up to 17,000 triples. The RDFCube, presented by Matono, Pahlevi and Kojima (2006), proposes building a 3D cube of subject, predicate, and object dimensions, approximating the mapping of a triple to a cell by treating each cell as a hash bucket containing multiple triples. In this work, the RDFCube proved to store up to 100,000 triples efficiently.

Finally, other approaches such as that presented by Bönström, Hinze and Schweppe (2003), pro-

Figure 5. A Subject BitMat for an RDF triple set

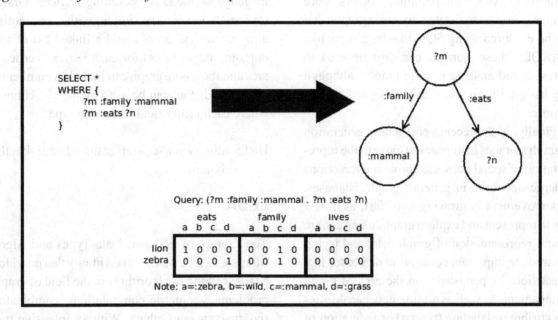

pose storing RDF data as a graph in an Object Oriented DBMS (OODBMS). The basic idea is that the mapping between the RDF graph induced from the conjunction of all the RDF triples and the objects of an object oriented database is more natural.

LIBRARIES IMPLEMENTING GRAPHS

There are many different approaches to store and explore graphs, and the evolution has been closely related to the computational resources and the graph sizes, while the problems are in general the same. The first set of libraries for graph management were designed for single CPU systems with enough memory to load the whole graph, which have evolved to more advanced graph databases (GDB) that can store arbitrarily large graphs using secondary storage.

One of the first attempts was the Stanford GraphBase, a very strict interface to study some classical graph problems, which was followed

by the two most widely used libraries: LEDA, the Library of Efficient Data types, and BGL, the Boost Graph Library. Both are implemented in C++ and make an intensive use of templates, and while the former is for generic data types and algorithms with some packages specialized in graphs, the latter is devoted only to graph storage and analysis. More recently, with the popularization of Java programming, the JDSL appeared as a simple Java interface to graphs.

As computers evolved to multiprocessor systems, parallel and distributed processing demanded for a new representation of graphs. Libraries such as Parallel BGL support the split of the graph in partitions, also named as distributed graphs. Algorithms over distributed graphs are a very active area of research, while the storage or the partitioning of the graph is still in an early stage.

The consolidation of Internet, with billions of web pages connected like in a very large network and, more specifically, the Semantic WEB based on RDF graph and ontologies led to a new generation of graph storage approaches and analytical tools. RDF triple storages, like Jena, OpenLink

Virtuoso, or AllegroGraph, among others, store billions of triples to create very large graphs that can be explored using SQL-like languages like SPARQL. These storages can also be used to represent and analyze generic graphs, although they have not been specifically designed for this purpose.

Finally, in the recent years a new generation of graph storages has appeared close to the representation of social networks, protein interactions or large networks in general: graph databases. This movement is growing very fast, as a new way to represent and explore graphs using a more natural representation of graph data, and trying to introduce important concepts in databases like transactions or persistence in the area of graph management, as well as adding new capabilities like attributes, labeling (typing) or federation of multiple graphs. Some of the proposals are implemented only in Java, like Neo4J, with a proprietary storage; HypergraphDB, using the key-value model in BerkeleyDb; InfoGrid, which allows different open-source storages; or InfiniteGraph, based on Objectivity, an object oriented database. Out of the Java world there is VertexDb, another key-value based on web-services over Tokyo-Cabinet, or Sones, in C# (Mono-compatible) that has also its own storage system. Finally, DEX is a high-performance graph database with a hybrid approach: C++ for an efficient implementation of the core engine, and Java for a public API.

Following there is a short description of some of the most relevant proposals in graph storages and graph databases, with the goal to show different approaches to graph storage and manipulation. Redundant proposals, or those who does not provide enough details of the internals, have been removed for the sake of clarity.

Stanford GraphBase

The Stanford GraphBase is a collection of programs and datasets to manipulate graphs and networks, written with a mix of C programming

language and the TEX typesetting language. Graph representation is very simple, with a sequential array of vertex records, and a linked list of the outgoing edges (arcs) for each vertex. Vertices, arcs and the whole graph can include a number of utility fields that can be used by the algorithms, where each utility field is a union type.

URL: http://www-cs-staff.stanford.edu/~knuth/sgb.html

LEDA

The Library of Efficient Data Types and Algorithms (LEDA), is a C++ class library that provides a large catalog of algorithms in the field of graph problems, geometric computations, combinatorial analysis, and others. With an intensive use of templates, LEDA represents different types of graphs, such as directed, undirected, bidirected, planar or geometric. Most of the graph algorithms do not change the underlying graph and they work on a constant or static graph. LEDA has a cache efficient implementation of these static graphs, a fixed sequence of vertices and edges, as well as standard graph iterators over the edges and the neighbors of a vertex.

URL: http://www.algorithmic-solutions.com/leda/index.htm

BGL and PBGL

The Boost Graph Library (BGL) is one of the most widely used libraries for graph analysis. It provides a generic open interface to the graph structure that hides the details of the implementation. Designed as a C++ library with an intensive use of templates, it provides two graph classes: adjacency list, and adjacency matrix. Adjacency list is a two-dimensional structure, where each element of the first dimension represents a vertex, and each of the vertices contains a one-dimensional structure that is its edge list. Adjacency lists can be parameterized to different kinds of graphs: directed, undirected, with or without parallel edges, optimized for outgoing (or ingoing) edges, fast updates, etc. By contrast, an adjacency matrix implements the traditional representation with a V x V matrix for V vertices, where each element a_{ij} is a boolean flag representing whether there is an edge from vertex i to vertex j. The latter representation is very suitable for very dense graphs.

The Parallel Boost Graph Library (Parallel BGL) is a special version of the BGL library for parallel and distributed computation of graphs. It contains distributed graph structures and distributed graph algorithms. A distributed graph is a graph whose storage is spread across multiple processors. The basic idea is to distribute the vertices among the processors, and each vertex has a distributed adjacency list with all its outgoing edges. There are also distributed property maps which allow the association of properties to vertices and edges, such as weights or ids. The properties and edges are assigned to the same processor as their referencing vertex in order to keep a good performance for multicore systems.

URL: http://osl.iu.edu/research/pbgl/

JDSL

The Data Structures Library in Java (JDSL) is a collection of Java interfaces and classes that implement a simple graph storage in the form of several incidence lists of vertices and edges (the global lists). In addition, each vertex has its own list of incident edges (the local list).

URL: http://www.cs.brown.edu/cgc/jdsl/

Jena (RDF)

Jena is one of the RDF data managers. Jena can be run on two storage backends, which store the RDF triplets: SDB and TDB. TDB is the fastest backend, and the recommended by Jena because it offers specialized RDF data management structures. TDB stores the graph as a set of tables and indexes: (a) the node table and (b) the triple indexes (An additional small table, called prefix table, is also used to export the results to other formats such as XML. This table is not used in a regular query execution). The node table stores a map of the nodes in the graph to the node identifiers (which are a MD5 hash), and vice versa. The storage is a sequential access file for the identifier-to-node mapping, and a B-tree for the node-to-identifier mapping. The triple indexes store the RDF tuples, which describe the structure of the graph. Jena does not implement a table with the three attributes of the RDF tuple, but three separate indexes. Each of these three indexes takes each one of the three attributes of an RDF structure as the sorting key. However, the value stored in the index is the full tuple for all the three indexes. In other words an access to any of the three indexes is able to retrieve a RDF relationship

URL: http://jena.sourceforge.net/.

AllegroGraph (RDF)

AllegroGraph is a triple-store based on the storage of *assertions*, or extended triples with five fields: the subject (s), the predicate (p), the object (o), the graph (g), and the triple-id (i). All of s, p, o and g are strings of arbitrary size that are stored as string identifiers of fixed size, the Unique Part Identifier (UPI). There is a string dictionary manager which maps each unique string with its UPI. The representation model favors also the federation of multiple and disparate triple-stores, to connect and treat them as a single one.

URL: http://www.franz.com/agraph/allegrograph/

Neo4j

Neo4j is a Java-based transactional graph database that stores data structured as graphs. It provides a graph-oriented model for data representation with nodes, relationships and properties; a disk-based storage manager optimized for storing graph structures; a traversal framework for traversals in the node space; and a simple object-oriented Java API. In addition, Neo4j includes the usual database features: ACID transactions, durable persistence, concurrency control and transaction recovery.

URL: http://neo4j.org/

HypergraphDB

Hypergraph is a GDB, which was designed for artificial intelligence and semantic web projects. As a consequence of the requirements from these environments, HypergraphDB stores not only graphs but also hypergraph structures. A hypergraph is a mathematical generalization of the concept of a graph, in which the edges are substituted by hyperdges. The difference between edges and hyperedges is the number of nodes that they connect: a regular edge connects two nodes of a graph, but a hyperedge connects an arbitrary set of nodes. HypergraphDB stores all the graph information in the form of key-value pairs.

Each object of the graph, either nodes or edges, is identified with a single key that is called atom. Each atom is related to a set of atoms, which can contain zero or any number of elements. These relationships create the topological structure of the graph. HypergraphDB also supports node and edge typing. The types are also implemented as atoms that contain all the elements of a particular type. The key-value structures are stored on an external library, BerkeleyDB, which does not support relational queries but provides specialized structures for this type of storage. BerkeleyDB offers three access methods to data: linear hash, which in case of multiple collisions performs multiple

hashes to redistribute the colliding keys; B-trees to store the data in the leaves of a balanced tree; and logical record identifiers to each pair, which are indexed for direct access.

URL: http://www.kobrix.com/hgdb.jsp

OrientDB

OrientDB is an open source GDBMS written in Java. It is a document-based database where the relationships are managed as in a graph databases with direct connections among records. It supports schema-less, schema-full and schema-mixed modes, with SQL support and a security profiling system based on user and roles.

The storage is based on its own RB+Tree algorithm as mix of Red-Black Tree and B+Tree, which consumes about half memory of the Red-Black Tree implementation maintaining the original speed while it balances the tree on insertion/update. There is also an OrientDB Key/Value Server that has been built on top of OrientDB Document Database. It can run in a cluster with multiple running machines where the load is divided among all the nodes.

URL: http://www.orientechnologies.com/

InfiniteGraph

InfiniteGraph is a distributed graph database designed to support applications that generate data models across multiple databases and multiple graphs. It supports a variety of system implementations and deployments from server-based systems, cloud platforms, and embedded appliances.

It provides both a dedicated graph Java API for direct use with a graph data model, along with a scalable distributed persistence layer and indexing capabilities using the Lucene search engine library. There are plug-ins to support the most common graph types, with different graph processing operations such as traversals, item lookups, selection by range, full text and regular expression search, and path finding.

URL: http://www.infinitegraph.com/

Sones

The Sones GraphDB is an object-oriented data management system based on graphs. It enables the storage, management and evaluation of databases with networked data, allowing the linking of unstructured, semi-structured and structured data sources. It is only offered in .NET supported operating systems (compatibility through the mono project).

It includes an object-oriented storage solution (Sones GraphFS) for unstructured and semi-structured data storage as well as the graph-oriented database management system (Sones GraphDB), which links the data to each other. The GraphFS stores the objects in data streams of storage engines, where a storage engine is not limited to a disk-based system; it can support TCP/IP and iSCSI to external systems. The GraphDB layer provides the graph structure, with support for attributes on objects, inheritance, versioning, data safety and data integrity. Finally, the Graph Query Language (Sones GQL) is an extension of SQL with a graph-oriented approach.

URL: http://www.sones.com/

CASE STUDY: DEX

DEX is an efficient GDB implementation based on bitmap representations of the entities. It is devised to directly handle labeled and directed multigraphs containing an undetermined number of attributes in both nodes and edges. In Martínez-Bazan et al. (2007), authors propose a logic bitmap-based organization to store a graph that does not fit in memory and has to be handled out-of-core. In this scenario, several aspects must hold:

- Solving a query should not imply loading the whole graph into memory.
- The graph organization must be as compact as possible in order to fit as many graph structures in memory as possible.
- The most commonly used graph-oriented operations, such as edge navigation, should be executed as efficiently as possible.
- Attributes in the graph should be accessed very fast.

In DEX, all the nodes and edges are encoded as collections of objects, each of which has a unique oid that is a logical identifier. DEX converts a logical adjacency matrix into multiple small indexes to improve the management of out-of-core workloads, with the use of efficient I/O and cache policies. It encodes the adjacency list of each node in a bitmap, which for the adjacent nodes has the corresponding bit set. Given that bitmaps of graphs are typically sparse, the bitmaps are compressed, and hence are more compact than traditional adjacency matrices.

DEX Structures

The basic logical data structure in DEX is a labeled and directed attributed multigraph. A *labeled* graph has a label for each node and edge, that denotes the object type. A *directed* graph allows for edges with a fixed direction, from the *tail* or source node to the *head* or destination node. An *attributed* graph allows a variable list of attributes for each node and edge, where an *attribute* is a value associated to a string which identifies the attribute. A *multigraph* allows multiple edges between two nodes. This means that two nodes can be connected several times by different edges, even if two edges have the same tail, head and label. A directed multigraph helps to represent the richness of the multiple relationships between objects which is a usual situation in complex social networks.

In this system, nodes and edges are uniquely identified by a set of ids separated in two disjoint domains (*oids* and *eids*), and the whole graph is built using a combination of two different types of structures: *bitmaps* and *maps*.

A bitmap or bit-vector is a variable-length sequence of presence bits that denotes which objects are selected or related to other objects. They are essential for speeding-up the query execution and reducing the amount of space required to store and manipulate the graph. In a bitmap, each bit is only set to 1 if the corresponding oid is selected. The first bit in a bitmap is always considered to be in position 1 (the first valid oid) and the last one is the last bit set (the highest oid considered in the bitmap). In order to know the length of the bitmap, the number of actual bits set to 1 in the structure is kept updated. The main advantage of this structure is that it is very easy to manage, operate, compress, iterate, etc.

A map is an inverted index with key values associated to bitmaps, and it is used as an auxiliary structure to complement bitmaps, providing full indexed access to all the data stored in the graph.

These two types of structures are combined to build a more complex one: the *link*. A link is a binary association between unique identifiers and data values. It provides two basic functionalities: given an identifier, it returns the value; and given a value, it returns all the identifiers associated to it.

Graph Representation using Bitmaps

A DEX graph is built using a combination of links, maps and bitmaps to provide a logical view of a labeled and directed attributed multigraph.: each node or edge type has a bitmap which contains the *oids* of all the objects (nodes or edges) that belong to the type; each attribute of a type is a link; and, finally, the edges are decomposed into two different links, one for the tails, where for each node contains all the edges outgoing connected to it, when this node acts as their tail or origin, and in the same way another one for the heads which contains the ingoing edges. Thus, an edge is represented as a double join, one between the tail and the edge, and the other one between the head and the edge. If the edge is undirected, then both nodes of the edge are set as tails and heads for the edge.

More specifically, there are two different kinds of DEX graphs: the DbGraph, a regular graph contains all the persistent data, and the RGraphs, temporal graphs used to retrieve the result of DEX queries. In particular, a RGraph is a collection of inherited nodes from the DbGraph, where each *oid* key is a node that maps to its inherited or referenced *oid* node in the DbGraph.

Thus, DbGraphs and RGraphs or, in general, all DEX graphs are basically built as a collection of bitmaps: one for each type to store the objects in the database, one for each distinct value of each attribute, one for each node that is the tail of one or more edges, and finally one for each node that is the head of one or more edges. With these bitmaps, solving distinct operations such as selecting all the objects of a type, retrieving the objects that have a specific value for an attribute or finding the number of edges or degree of a node, becomes straightforward.

DEX Example

Figure 6 shows an example of a graph extracted from a bibliographic data source (left side), and the mapping of the previous graph into the internal structures as defined above (right side).

The graph contains four object types: *author* (ovals) and *paper* (boxes) nodes, *writes* and *references* edges. These types are represented in the gray boxes at the right, where each type has one bitmap with its collection of objects, represented in the lighter gray frame, and their inner boxes represent the attributes, with one link each. Bitmaps are variable length sequences of 0's and 1's prefixed with the number of bits set. Links have the name, the collection of distinct values and the bitmap for each value. Maps are hidden in this representation because they are only used to index collections, for example the types or the attribute values.

For example, if we look at the node type *paper*, we can see that there are 3 bits set in bitmap $B5$, one for each node. There is also a bitmap for each distinct attribute value ($L1$ to $L5$ in the example) which indicates the oids of the objects containing this value in the attribute. If an object does not have any value then it will not appear in any bitmap of the attribute. Thus, the union of all the bitmaps of all the values of an attribute is equal to or a subset of the bitmap of the objects of the type. For example, $(B6 \cup B7 \cup B8) = B5$ in attribute *title* of *paper*, but $(B11 \cup B12) \subset B5)$ because node 5 has no value for the attribute *year*.

There are two extra links at the rightmost side: one for the tails and the other for the heads. Each one has one value for each node that has edges, with its corresponding bitmap containing the edges where the node is connected. Again, the union of all the bitmaps of each of these links is equal to the union of all the collections of edge types, because all edges have one tail and one head. We can verify that $(B17 \cup B18 \cup B19 \cup B20) = (B21 \cup B22 \cup B23) = (B13 \cup B16)$.

As an example of the meaning of the structures, in the bitmaps we have marked all the occurrences of the *oid* 6, which identifies the node of the PAPER with title 'TITLE-Z'. These are the value '6' in $L6$ and $L7$, and the bit '6' in bitmaps $B5$, $B8$, $B9$ and $B12$. Note that $B5$ tells us it is a node *PAPER;* and $B8$, $B9$ and $B12$ show which are the values for the attributes of this node (*title*, *conference* and *year* respectively). Finally, $L6$ has the edges where this node is the tail, and $L7$ which are the edges where it is the head.

As we can see, with these structures now it is very easy to define graph-based operations just by combining one or more bitmap and map operations. For example:

- Number of authors: $|B1|=3$

- Papers in conference 'CONF-R' of year 2007: $(B9 \cup B11) = \{4\}$
- In-degree of paper 'TITLE-Y': $|B22|=2$

In conclusion, this representation presents some advantages inherent to the structures and others more subtle that appear as a consequence of how the structures are being used. For example, the use of bitmaps directly provides some statistics without extra penalties, like the number of objects for each type, or the number of objects that have the same value for an attribute, the equivalent of a clustering or a GROUP BY / COUNT(*) operation of the relational model. The out-degree and in-degree of nodes are also the count of a bitmap stored into the tails or heads collections respectively. Also, the capability to add or remove attributes becomes easier because they are independent from the object storage. This is crucial for graph mining algorithms that typically require the creation of temporary attributes like weights or distances.

URL: http://www.sparsity-technologies.com/

FUTURE RESEARCH TRENDS AND CONCLUSIONS

In this chapter we have reviewed different techniques for representing graphs. On one hand, we have visited the basic data structures and the state of the art in the distribution of graphs in parallel computers. On the other hand, we have paid attention to issues related to graph representations to improve the performance of applications. In this sense, we have visited approaches such as compression or physical data reorganization. We also reviewed the application of the Resource Description Framework (RDF) standard to represent graphs and the main research publications in this field. We have finalized the chapter with a visit to different graph libraries that allow for the represen-

Figure 6. Example of DEX representing a graph

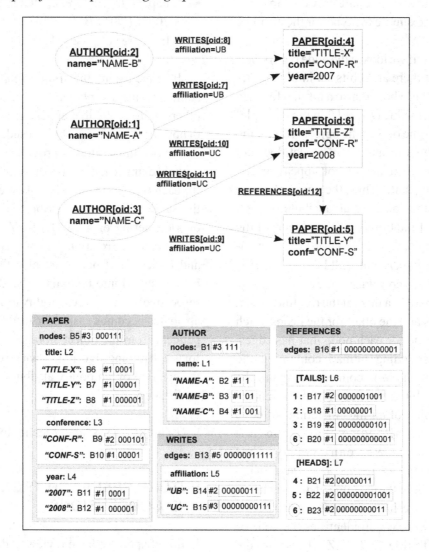

tation and querying of graphs. We have used DEX as a case study of a graph database management system oriented to high performance using bitmap representations of the data represented by graphs.

There are different aspects which will be important for the future research in graph representation:

1. High performance representations and development of more advanced graph databases. The need for data representations that allow for a high performance querying and analysis will be paramount for the different applications arising in the field. We

expect the creation of more advanced graph representations and indexes that will allow for the improvement of the performance, especially for huge graphs where it is necessary to access the secondary storage of the system.

2. Large datasets. One of the issues in the future will be the large graphs that will have to be represented, queried and analyzed. In this sense, the need for compacting the data without damaging the performance of query resolution will become a fundamental research topic. Also, approximate answers to

graph queries will have an important impact in this scenario.

3. Parallel and distributed systems. The newest processors are coming with a large number of cores, and many computing tasks related to the management of large amounts of data are being deployed on clusters. Although these architectural advances have been exploited by relational databases, graph databases are still exploring its implications and most vendors are still in the first steps of this task. Therefore, we expect an increasing interest in how to adapt the graph database engines to these scalable and massively parallel architectures.

4. Languages for high performance graph databases. Graph data management currently lacks a language which allows an easy and efficient definition of graph operations. Given the flexibility of graph operations this definition is an important challenge, which will be attractive not only from a theoretical point of view but will also attract the interest of graph database developers in order to have a common language to write graph related algorithms.

REFERENCES

Al-Furaih, I. (1998). S. Memory hierarchy management for iterative graph structures. In *IPPS/SPDP* (pp. 298–302). Ranka.

Alpert, C. J. & Kahng, (1995). A. B. Recent directions in Net list partitioning: *A Survey. Integr. VLSI J., 19*(1-2), 1–81.

Andreev, K., & Räcke, H. (2004). *Balanced graph partitioning. In ACM symposium on Parallelism in algorithms and architectures*, pages 120—124.

Anyanwu, K., Maduko, A., & Sheth, A. (2007). Q2L: *Towards support for sub graph extraction queries in rdf databases*. In *ACM WWW* (pp. 797–806). SPAR.

Arora, S., Rao, S., & Vazirani, U. (2004). *Expander flows, geometric embeddings and graph partitioning. In ACM symposium on Theory of computing*, pages 222–231.

Ashcraft, C., & Liu, J. W. H. (1997). Using domain decomposition to find graph bisectors. *BIT Numerical Mathematics, 37*(3), 506–534. doi:10.1007/BF02510238

Bader, D. A., & Cong, G. (2005). A Fast (smps). *Parallel Spanning Tree Algorithm for Symmetric Multiprocessors, 65*(9), 994–1006.

Bader, D. A., Cong, G., & Feo, J. (2005). *On the architectural requirements for efficient execution of graph algorithms* (pp. 547–546). ICPP.

Barnard, S., Pothen, A., & Simon, H. (1993). A spectral algorithm for envelope reduction of sparse matrices. In *ACM/IEEE Conference on Supercomputing*, pages 493—502.

Battiti, R., & Bertossi, A. (1999). Greedy, prohibition, and reactive heuristics for graph partitioning. *IEEE Transactions on Computers, 48*(4), 361–385. doi:10.1109/12.762522

Boldi, P., & Vigna, S. (2004). The Web graph framework I: Compression techniques. In *ACM WWW*, pages 595—602.

Bönström, V., Hinze, A., & Schweppe, H. (2003). Storing RDF as a Graph. In *Conference on Latin American Web Congress*, pages 27—36.

Bui, T. N., & Jones, C. (1992). Finding good approximate vertex and edge partitions is np-hard. *Information Processing Letters, 42*(3), 153–159. doi:10.1016/0020-0190(92)90140-Q

Catalyurek, U., & Aykanat, C. (1999). Hypergraph-partitioning-based decomposition for parallel sparse-matrix vector multiplication. *IEEE Transactions on Parallel and Distributed Systems, 10*(7), 673–693. doi:10.1109/71.780863

Chung, C., Min, J., & Shim, K. (2002). APEX: An adaptive path index for XML data. In *SIGMOD Conference*, pages 121—132.

Chung, F. (1994). *Spectral Graph Theory*. Published by the American Mathematical Society.

Cong, J., & Lim, S. K. (1998) Multiway partitioning with pairwise movement. In *IEEE/ACM International Conference on Computer-aided Design*, pages 512–516

Cooper, B. F., Sample, N., & Franklin, M. Hjaltason, & G., Shadmon, M. (2001). A fast index for semistructured data. In *VLDB Conference*, pages 341–350, 2001.

Crobak, J. R., Berry, J., Madduri, K., & Bader, D. A. (2007). *Advanced shortest paths algorithms on a massively-multithreaded architecture* (pp. 1–8). MTAAP.

Cuthill, E., & McKee, J. (1969). Reducing the bandwidth of sparse symmetric matrices. *ACM Annual Conference*, pages 157—172.

Devine, K., Boman, E., & Robert, T. (2006). Parallel hypergraph partitioning for scientific computing. In *IPDPS* (pp. 10–20). Heaphy, Bisseling R., & Çatalyürek U.

Erling, O. *(2006)*. Advances in Virtuoso RDF triple storage (Bitmap Indexing), *from* http://virtuoso.openlinksw.com/ -wiki/ main/ Main/ VOSBitmapIndexing.

Evrendilek, C. (2008). Vertex separators for partitioning a graph. *Sensors (Basel, Switzerland), 8*(2), 635–657. doi:10.3390/s8020635

Feige, U., Hajiaghayi, M., & Lee, J. R. (2005). Improved approximation algorithms for minimum-weight vertex separators. In *ACM Symposium on Theory of Computing*, pages 563—572.

Fiduccia, C. M., & Mattheyses, R. M. (1982). A linear-time heuristic for improving network partitions. In *Design Automation Conference*, pages 175—181.

Fletcher, G. H., & Beck, P. W. (2009). Scalable indexing of RDF graphs for efficient join processing. In *ACM Conference on Information and Knowledge Management*, pages 1513—1516.

Garey, M. R., & Johnson, D. S. (1990). *Computers and Intractability: A Guide to the Theory of NP-Completeness*. W. H. Freeman and Co.

George, A., & Liu, J. W. H. (1978). An automatic nested dissection algorithm for irregular finite element problems. *SIAM Journal on Numerical Analysis, 15*(5), 1053–1069. doi:10.1137/0715069

Goldman, R., & Widom, J. (1997). Enabling query formulation and optimization in semistructured databases. I. In *VLDB* (pp. 436–445). San Francisco, CA, USA: Data Guides.

Gutiérrez, C., Hurtado, C., & Mendelzon, A. (2004). Foundations of Semantic Web databases. In *ACM PODS*, pages 95—106.

Harth, A., Umbrich, J., Hogan, A., & Decker, S. (2007). S2: A federated repository for querying graph structured data from the Web. In *ISWC* (pp. 211–224). YAR.

Hendrickson, B., & Leland, R. (1995). A multilevel algorithm for partitioning graphs. In *ACM/IEEE Conference on Supercomputing*, pages 28—42.

Janik, M., & Kochut, K. (2005). BRAHMS: A WorkBench RDF Store and high performance memory system for semantic association discovery. In *International Semantic Web Conference*, pages 431—445.

Karypis, G., Aggarwal, R., Kumar, V., & Shekhar, S. (1997). Multilevel hypergraph partitioning: Application in VLSI domain. In *Design Automation Conference*, pages 526–529.

Karypis, G., & Kumar, V. (1998). A fast and high quality multilevel scheme for partitioning irregular graphs. *SIAM Journal on Scientific Computing*, *20*(1), 359–392. doi:10.1137/S1064827595287997

Karypis, G., & Kumar, V. (1999). Multi-level k-way hypergraph partitioning. In *Design Automation Conference*, pages 343–348.

Kernighan, B. W., & Lin, S. (1970). An efficient heuristic procedure for partitioning graphs. *The Bell System Technical Journal*, *49*(1), 291–307.

Khoshafian, S., Valduriez, P., & Copeland, G. (1988). Parallel query processing of complex objects. In *IEEE Int. Conf. on Data Engineering (ICDE)*, pages 202—209.

Lanczos, C. (1950). An iteration method for the solution of the eigenvalue problem of linear differential and integral operations. *Journal of Research of the National Bureau of Standards*, *45*(4), 255–282.

Leskovec, J., Backstrom, L., Kumar, R., & Tomkins, A. (2008): Microscopic evolution of social networks. In *Knowledge Discovery and Data Mining Conference KDD*, pages 462—470.

Liu, J. W. H. (1989). A graph partitioning algorithm by node separators. *ACM Transactions on Mathematical Software*, *15*(3), 198–219. doi:10.1145/66888.66890

Madduri, K., Bader, D. A., Berry, J. W., & Crobak, J. R. (2007). An experimental study of a parallel shortest path algorithm for solving large-scale graph instances, In *ALENEX'07*, pages 23—35.

Malewicz, G., Austern, M. H., Bik, A. J., Dehnert, J. C., Horn, I., Leiser, N., & Czajkowski, G. (2010). A system for large-scale graph processing. In *SIGMOD* (pp. 135–146). Pregel.

Martínez-Bazan, N., Muntés-Mulero, V., Gómez-Villamor, S., Nin, J., Sánchez-Martínez, M. A., & Larriba-Pey, J. L. (2007). *Dex: High-performance exploration on large graphs for information retrieval* (pp. 573–582). CIKM.

Matono, A., Pahlevi, S. M., & Kojima, I. (2006). RDFCube: A P2P-based three-dimensional index for structural joins on distributed triple stores. In *DBISP2P*, pages 323—330.

Muntés-Mulero, V., Martínez-Bazán, N., Larriba-Pey, J. L., Pacitti, E., & Valduriez, P. (2010). Graph partitioning strategies for efficient BFS in shared-nothing parallel systems. In *International Workshop on Graph Databases*, pages 13—24.

Neumann, T., & Weikum, G. (2008). 3X: A RISC-style engine for RDF. In *VLDB* (pp. 647–659). RDF.

Oren, E., Gueret, C., & Schlobach, S. (2008). *Anytime query answering in RDF through evolutionary algorithms* (pp. 98–113). ISWC.

Özsu, M. T., & Valduriez, P. (1999). *Principles of distributed database systems* (2nd ed.). Upper Saddle River, NJ, USA: Prentice-Hall, Inc.

Parlett, B. (1974). The Rayleigh Quotient Iteration and some generalizations for non-normal matrices. *Mathematics of Computation*, *28*(127), 679–693. doi:10.1090/S0025-5718-1974-0405823-3

Pothen, A., Simon, H., & Liou, K. (1990). Partitioning sparse matrices with eigenvectors of graphs. *SIAM Journal on Matrix Analysis and Applications*, *11*(3), 430–452. doi:10.1137/0611030

Prudhommeaux, E., & Seaborne, A. (2005). *SPARQL query language for RDF*. http://www.w3.org/ TR/ rdf-sparql-query/

Reinhardt, S., & Karypis, G. (2007). *A multi-level parallel implementation of a program for finding frequent patterns in a large sparse graph.* (pp. 214–222). HIPS.

Sanchis, L. A. (1989). Multiple-way network partitioning. *IEEE Transactions on Computers, 38*(1), 62–81. doi:10.1109/12.8730

Stonebraker, M., Abadi, D. J., Batkin, A., Chen, X., Cherniack, M., & Ferreira, M. ...Zdonik, S. (2005). C-store: A column-oriented DBMS. In *VLDB*, pages 553—556.

(2008). Towards Web scale RDF. In *SSWS* (pp. 52–66). Karlsruhe, Germany: Erling. O.

Trifunovic, A., & Knottenbelt, W. J. (2008). Parallel multilevel algorithms for hypergraph partitioning. *Journal of Parallel and Distributed Computing, 68*(5), 563–581. doi:10.1016/j.jpdc.2007.11.002

Udrea, O., Pugliese, A., & Subrahmanian, V. (2007). A graph based RDF index. In *AAAI* (pp. 1465–1471). GRIN.

Underwood, K., Vance, M., Berry, J., & Hendrickson, B. (2007). *Analyzing the scalability of graph algorithms on Eldorado* (pp. 496–504). MTAAP.

Valduriez, P., Khoshafian, S., & Copeland, G. (1986). *Implementation techniques of complex* (pp. 101–110). VLDB.

Weiss, C., Karras, P., & Bernstein, A. (2008). Sextuple indexing for Semantic Web data management. In *VLDB* (pp. 1008–1019). Hexastore.

Yoo, A., Chow, E., Henderson, K., McLendon, W., Hendrickson, B., & Catalyurek, U. (2005). *A scalable distributed parallel breadth-first search algorithm on BlueGene/L* (pp. 25–49). Supercomputing.

KEY TERMS AND DEFINITIONS

Bitmap: Data structure, typically used to represent a subset of elements in a given domain. It contains an array of bits (which may be compressed), where the state of the i-th bit indicates the presence of the i-th element in the subset.

Breadth First Search: Graph traversal that explores the nodes of a graph following a FIFO policy. The FIFO queue is initialized with the source node of the traversal. At each step, the head of the queue is visited and the neighbors of this node are inserted into the queue.

Differential Encoding: Representation scheme that only represents the changes in a sequence.

Minimum Edge Cut Problem: Finding the minimum set of edges that if removed from a graph, then the graph is disconnected in multiple connected components.

NP Complexity Class: Complexity set of decisional (yes/no) problems. One of its main characteristics is a positive validation of a given answer to the problem can be computed in polynomial time, but it is unknown if there exist a polynomial time algorithm to find if this positive answer exists.

Permutations: Lists of elements that contain a given set, but with a different order.

RDF: specifications used to represent interrelated objects in the form of triplets containing: subject, predicate and object. The semantic of the relation is that "the subject applies the predicate on the object".

Shared Nothing Architecture: Distributed computer architecture where each computing node has its own private address memory space and disks.

Chapter 2
The Graph Traversal Pattern

Marko A. Rodriguez
AT&T Interactive, USA

Peter Neubauer
Neo Technology, Sweden

ABSTRACT

A graph is a structure composed of a set of vertices (i.e. nodes, dots) connected to one another by a set of edges (i.e. links, lines). The concept of a graph has been around since the late 19th century, however, only in recent decades has there been a strong resurgence in both theoretical and applied graph research in mathematics, physics, and computer science. In applied computing, since the late 1960s, the interlinked table structure of the relational database has been the predominant information storage and retrieval model. With the growth of graph/network-based data and the need to efficiently process such data, new data management systems have been developed. In contrast to the index-intensive, set-theoretic operations of relational databases, graph databases make use of index-free, local traversals. This chapter discusses the graph traversal pattern and its use in computing. (Angles & Guiterrez, 2008)

INTRODUCTION

The first paragraph of any publication on graphs usually contains the iconic G = (V,E) definition of a graph. This definition states that a graph is composed of a set of vertices V and a set of edges E. Normally following this definition is the definition of the set E. For directed graphs, $E \subseteq (V \times V)$ and for undirected graphs,

$E \subseteq \{V \times V\}$. That is, E is a subset of all ordered or unordered permutations of V element pairings. From a purely theoretical standpoint, such definitions are usually sufficient for deriving theorems. However, in applied research, where the graph is required to be embedded in reality, this definition says little about a graph's realization. The structure a graph takes in the real-world determines the efficiency of the operations that are applied to it. It is exactly those efficient graph operations that

DOI: 10.4018/978-1-61350-053-8.ch002

yield an unconventional problem-solving style. This style of interaction is dubbed the graph traversal pattern and forms the primary point of discussion for this chapter[1].

THE REALIZATION OF GRAPHS

Relational databases have been around since the late 1960s (Codd, 1970) and are today's most predominate data management tool. Relational databases maintain a collection of tables. Each table can be defined by a set of rows and a set of columns. Semantically, rows denote objects and columns denote properties/attributes. Thus, the datum at a particular row/column-entry is the value of the column property for that row object. Usually, a problem domain is modeled over multiple tables in order to avoid data duplication. This process is known as data normalization. In order to unify data in disparate tables, a "join" is used. A join combines two tables when columns of one table refer to columns of another table.[2] This is the classic relational database design which affords them their flexibility (Mishra & Eich, 1992).

In stark contrast, graph databases do not store data in disparate tables. Instead there is a single data structure – the graph (Angles & Guiterrez, 2008). Moreover, there is no concept of a "join" operation as every vertex and edge has a direct reference to its adjacent vertex or edge. The data structure is already "joined" by the edges that are defined. There are benefits and drawbacks to this model. First, the primary drawback is that it's difficult to shard a graph (a difficulty also encountered with relational databases that maintain referential integrity).

Sharding is the process of partitioning data across multiple machines in order to scale a system horizontally.[3] In a graph, with unconstrained, direct references between vertices and edges, there usually does not exist a clean data partition. Thus, it becomes difficult to scale graph databases beyond the confines of a single machine and at the same time, maintain the speed of a traversal across sharded borders. However, at the expense of this drawback there is a significant advantage: there is a constant time cost for retrieving an adjacent vertex or edge. That is, regardless of the size of the graph as a whole, the cost of a local read operation at a vertex or edge remains constant. This benefit is so important that it creates the primary means by which users interact with graph databases – traversals. Graphs offer a unique vantage point on data, where the solution to a problem is seen as abstractly defined traversals through its vertices and edges.[4]

The Indices of Relational Tables

Imagine that there is a gremlin who is holding a number between 1 and 100 in memory. Moreover, assume that when guessing the number, the gremlin will only reply by saying whether the guessed number is greater than, less than, or equal to the number in memory. What is the best strategy for determining the number in the fewest guesses? On average, the quickest way to determine the number is to partition the space of guesses into equal size chunks. For example, ask if the number is 50. If the gremlin states that its less than 50, then ask, is the number 25? If greater than 25, then ask, is the number 37? Follow this partition scheme until the number is converged upon. The structure that these guesses form over the sequence from 1 to 100 is a binary search tree. On average, this tree structure is more efficient in time than guessing each number starting from 1 and going to 100. This is ultimately the difference between an index-based search and a linear search. If there were no indices for a set, every element of the set would have to be examined to determine if it has a particular property of interest.[5] For n elements, a linear scan of this nature runs in $O(n)$. When elements are indexed, there exists two structures – the original set of elements and an index of those

Figure 1. A table representation of people and their friends

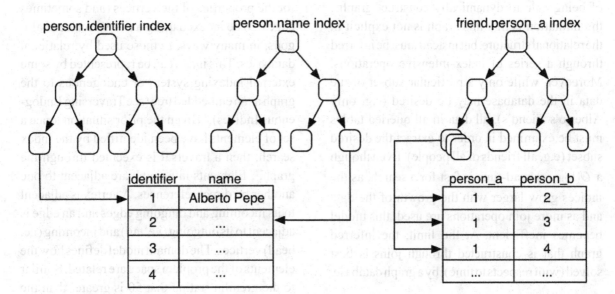

elements. Typical indices have the convenient property that searching them takes $O(\log_2 n)$. For massive sets, the space that indices take is well worth their weight in time.

Relational databases take significant advantage of such indices. It is through indices that rows with a column value are efficiently found. Moreover, the index makes it possible to efficiently join tables together in order to move between tables that are linked by particular columns. Assume a simple example where there are two tables: a person table and a friend table. The person table has the following two columns: unique identifier and name. The friend table has the following two columns: person *a* and person *b*. The semantics of the friend table is that person *a* is friends with person *b*. Suppose the problem of determining the name of all of Alberto Pepe's friends. Figure 1 and the following list breaks down this simple query into all the micro-operations that must occur to yield results.[6]

- Query the person.name index to find the row in person with the name "Alberto Pepe." $[O(\log_2 n)]$
- Given the person row returned by the index, get the identifier for that row. $[O(1)]$
- Query the friend.person a index to find all the rows in friend with the identifier from previous. $[O(\log_2 x) : x << m]$[7]
- Given each of the *k* rows returned, get the person b identifier for those rows. $[O(k)]$
- For each *k* friend identifiers, query the person identifier index for the row with friend identifier. $[O(k \log_2 n)]$
- Given the *k* person rows, get the name value for those rows. $[O(k)]$

The final operation yields the names of Alberto's friends. This example elucidates the classic join operation utilized in relational databases. By being able to join the person and friend table, it's possible to move from a name, to the person, to his or her friends, and then, ultimately, to their names. In effect, the joint operation forms a graph that is dynamically constructed as one table is linked to another table. While having the benefit of being able to dynamically construct graphs, the limitation is that this graph is not explicit in the relational structure, but instead must be inferred through a series of index-intensive operations. Moreover, while only a particular subset of the data in the database may be desired (e.g. only Alberto's friend's), all data in all queried tables must be examined in order to extract the desired subset (e.g. all friends of all people). Even though a $O(\log_2 n)$ read-time is fast for a search, as the indices grow larger with the growth of the data and as more join operations are used, this model becomes inefficient. At the limit, the inferred graph that is constructed through joins is best solved (with respects to time), by a graph database.

The Graph as an Index

Most of graph theory is concerned with the development of theorems for single-relational graphs (Chartrand & Lesniak, 1986). A single-relational graph maintains a set of edges, where all the edges are homogeneous in meaning. For example, all edges denote friendship or kinship, but not both together within the same structure. In application, complex domain models are more conveniently represented by multi-relational, property graphs.[8] The edges in a property graph are typed or labeled and thus, edges are heterogeneous in meaning. For example, a property graph can model friendship, kinship, business, communication, etc. relationships all within the same structure. Moreover, vertices and edges in a property graph maintain a set of key/value pairs. These are known as properties and allow for the representation of non-graphical data—e.g. the name of a vertex, the weight of an edge, etc. Formally, a property graph can be defined as $G = (V, E, \lambda, \mu)$, where edges are directed (i.e. $E \subseteq V \times V$, edges are labeled (i.e. $\lambda : E \to \Sigma$), and properties are a map from elements and keys to values (i.e. $\mu : (V \cup E) \times R \to S)$).

In the property graph model, it is common for the properties of the vertices (and sometimes edges) to be indexed using a tree structure analogous, in many ways, to those used by relational databases. This index can be represented by some external indexing system or endogenous to the graph as an embedded tree (see Traversing Endogenous Indices).[9] Given the prior situation, once a set of elements have been identified by the index search, then a traversal is executed through the graph.[10] Elements in a graph are adjacent to one another by direct references. A vertex is adjacent to its incoming and outgoing edges and an edge is adjacent to its outgoing (i.e. tail) and incoming (i.e. head) vertices. The domain model defines how the elements of the problem space are related. Similar to the gremlin stating that 50 is greater than the number to be guessed, an edge connecting vertex i and j and labeled friend states that vertex i is friend related to vertex j. Indices create "short cuts" in the graph as they partition elements according to specialized, compute-centric semantics (e.g. numbers being less than or greater than another). Likewise, a domain model partitions elements using semantics defined by the domain modeler. Thus, in many ways, a graph can be seen as an indexing structure.

In the relational example previous, a person in the person table has two properties: a unique identifier and a name. The analogue in a property graph would be to have the identifier and name} values represented as vertex properties. Moreover, the friend table would not exist as a table, but as direct friend-labeled edges between vertices. This idea is diagrammed in Figure 2. The micro-operations used to find the name of all of Alberto Pepe's friends are provided in the following enumeration.

1. Query the vertex.name index to find all the vertices in G with the name "Alberto Pepe." $[O(\log_2 n)]$

Figure 2. A graph representation of people and their friends. Given the tree-nature of the vertex.name index, it is possible, and many times useful to model the index endogenous to the graph.

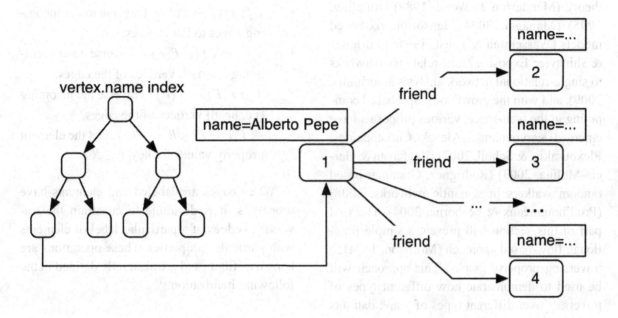

2. Given the vertex returned, get the *k* friend edges emanating from this vertex. [$O(k+x)$] [11]

3. Given the *k* friend edges retrieved, get the *k* vertices on the heads of those edges. [$O(k)$]

4. Given these *k* vertices, get the *k* name properties of these vertices. [$O(ky)$]

The final operation yields the names of Alberto's friends. In a graph database, there is no explicit join operation because vertices maintain direct references to their adjacent edges. In many ways, the edges of the graph serve as explicit, "hard-wired" join structures (i.e. structures that are not computed at query time as in a relational database). The act of traversing over an edge is the act of joining. However, what makes this more efficient in a graph database is that traversing from one vertex to another is a constant time operation. Thus, traversal time is defined solely by the number of elements touched by the traversal. This is irrespective of the size/topology of the graph as a whole. The time it takes to make a single step

in a traversal is determined by the local topology of the subgraph surrounding the particular vertex being traversed from. [12]

The real power of graph databases makes itself apparent when traversing multiple steps in order to unite disparate vertices by a path (i.e. vertices not directly connected). First, there are no $O(\log_2 n)$ operations. Second, the type of path taken, defines the "higher order", inferred relationship that exists between two vertices. [13] Traversals based on abstractly defined paths is the core of the graph traversal pattern. The next section discusses the graph traversal pattern and its application to common problem-solving situations.

GRAPH TRAVERSALS

A traversal refers to visiting elements (i.e. vertices and edges) in a graph in some algorithmic fashion. [14] There are numerous techniques for traversing graphs (Barcelo, Hurtado, Libkin, &

Wood, 2010). In this space there exist algebras based on formal language and finite state automata theory (Mendelzon & Wood, 1989) (Russling, 1995) (Manager, 2004), tensor/matrix-based models (Wasserman & Faust, 1994; Rodriguez & Shinavier, Exposing multi-relational networks to single-relational network analysis algorithms, 2009), and with the growth of graph-based computing in the web-space, various proposals have emerged (Karvounarakis, Alexaki, Christophides, Plexousakis, & Scholl, 2002) (Raghavan & Garcia-Molina, 2003) (Rodriguez, Grammar-based random walkers in semantic networks, 2008) (Prud'hommeaux & Seaborne, 2004). The first part of this section will present a simple functional, flow-based approach (Morrison, 1994) to traversing property graphs. This approach will be used to demonstrate how different types of traversals over different types of graph datasets support different types of problem-solving. This presentation is not intended to be complete and is only provided as a means of creating a simple language for which the examples in the latter half of this section can be explicated.

The most primitive, read-based operation on a graph is a single step traversal from element i to element j, where $i, j \in (V \cup E)$. While it is possible to write and delete elements from a graph, such operations will not be discussed.[15] For example, a single step operation can answer questions such as "which edges are outgoing from this vertex?", "which vertex is at the head of this edge?", etc. Single step operations expose explicit adjacencies in the graph (i.e. adjacencies that are "hard-wired"). The following list itemizes the various types of single step traversals. Note that these operations are defined over power multiset domains and ranges.[16] The reason for this is that it naturally allows for function composition, where a composition is a formal description of a traversal.

- $e_{out} : \hat{P}(v) \to \hat{P}(E)$: Traverse to the outgoing edges of the vertices.
- $e_{in} : \hat{P}(v) \to \hat{P}(E)$: Traverse to the incoming edges to the vertices.
- $v_{out} : \hat{P}(E) \to \hat{P}(V)$: Traverse to the outgoing (i.e. tail) vertices of the edges.
- $v_{in} : \hat{P}(E) \to \hat{P}(V)$: Traverse the incoming (i.e. head) vertices of the edges.
- $\in : \hat{P}(V \cup E) \times R \to \hat{P}(S)$: Get the element property values for key $r \in R$

When edges are labeled and elements have properties, it is desirable to constrain the traversal to edges of a particular label or elements with particular properties. These operations are known as filters and are abstractly defined in the following itemization.[17]

- $e_{lab\pm} : \hat{P}(E) \times \sum \to \hat{P}(E)$: Allow (or filter) all edges with the label $\sigma \in \sum$.
- $e_{p\pm} : \hat{P}(V \cup E) \times R \times S \to \hat{P}(V \cup E)$: Allow (or filter) all elements with the property $s \in S$ for key $r \in R$.
- $\in_{\in\pm} : \hat{P}(V \cup E) \times (P \cup E) \to \hat{P}(V \cup E)$: Allow (or filter) all elements that are the provided element.

Through function composition, we can define graph traversals of arbitrary length. A simple example is traversing to the names of Alberto Pepe's friends. If i is the vertex representing Alberto Pepe and

$$f : \hat{P}(V) \to \hat{P}(S),$$

where

$$f(i) = \in (v_{in}(e_{lab+}(e_{out}(i), friend)), name,$$

*Figure 3. A single path along the **f** traversal*

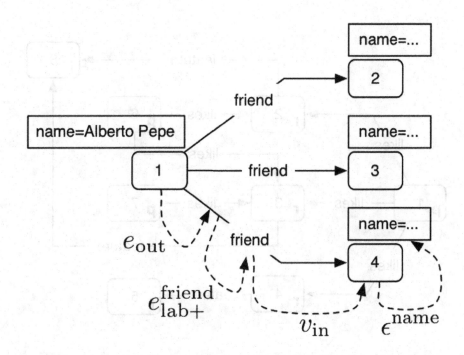

then *f(i)* will return the names of Alberto Pepe's friends. Through function currying and composition, the previous definition can be represented more clearly with the following function rule,

$$f(i) = (\in^{name} \circ v_{in} \circ e_{lab}^{friend} \circ e_{out})(i).$$

The function f says, traverse to the outgoing edges of vertex i, then only allow those edges with the label friend, then traverse to the incoming (i.e. head) vertices on those friend-labeled edges. Finally, of those vertices, return their name property.[18] A single legal path according to this function is diagrammed in Figure 3. Though not diagrammed for the sake of clarity, the traversal would also go from vertex *1* to the name of vertex *2* and vertex *3*. The function *f* is a "higher-order" adjacency defined as the composition of explicit adjacencies and serves as a join of Alberto and his friend's names.[19] The remainder of this section demonstrates graph traversals in real-world problems-solving situations.

Traversing for Recommendation

Recommendation systems are designed to help people deal with the problem of information overload by filtering information in the system that doesn't pertain to the person (Perugini, Goncalves, & Fox, 2004). In a positive sense, recommendation systems focus a person's attention on those resources that are likely to be most relevant to their particular situation. There is a standard dichotomy in recommendation research – that of content- vs. collaborative filtering-based recommendation. The prior deals with recommending resources that share characteristics (i.e. content) with a set of resources. The latter is concerned with determining the similarity of resources based upon the similarity of the taste of the people modeled within the system (Herlocker, Konstan, Terveen, & Riedl, 2004). These two seemingly different

Figure 4. A graph data structure containing people (p), their liked resources (r), and each resource's features (f)

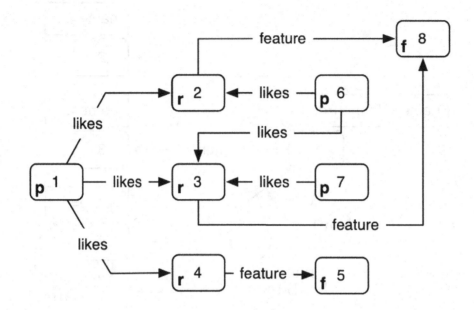

techniques to recommendation are conveniently solved using a graph database and two simple traversal techniques (Mirza, Keller, & Ramakrishnan, 2003) (Griffith, O'Riordan, & Sorensen, 2006).

Figure 4 presents a toy graph data set, where there exist a set of people, resources, and features related to each other by likes}- and feature-labeled edges. This simple data set is used for the remaining examples of this subsection.

Content-Based for Recommendation

In order to identify resources that that are similar in features (i.e. content-based recommendation) to a resource, traverse to all resources that share the same features. This is accomplished with the following function, $f : \hat{P}(V) \rightarrow \hat{P}(V)$, where

$$f(i) = (\in_{\in-}^{i} \circ v_{out} \circ e_{lab+}^{feature} \circ e_{in} \circ v_{in} \circ e_{lab+}^{feature} \circ e_{out})(i)$$

Assuming i = 3, function f states, traverse to the outgoing edges of resource vertex 3, only allow feature-labeled edges, and then traverse to the incoming vertices of those feature-labeled edges. At this point, the traverser is at feature vertex 8. Next, traverse to the incoming edges of feature vertex 8, only allow feature-labeled edges, and then traverse to the outgoing vertices of these feature-labeled edges. At this point, the traverser is at resource vertices 3 and 2. However, since we are trying to identify those resources similar in content to vertex 3, we need to filter out vertex 3. This is accomplished by the last stage of the function composition. Thus, given the toy graph data set, vertex 2 is similar to vertex 3 in content. This traversal is diagrammed in Figure 5.

It's simple to extend content-based recommendation to problems such as: "Given what person *i* likes, what other resources have similar features?" Such a problem is solved using the previous function *f* defined above combined with

Figure 5. A traversal that identifies resources that are similar in content to a set of resources based upon shared features

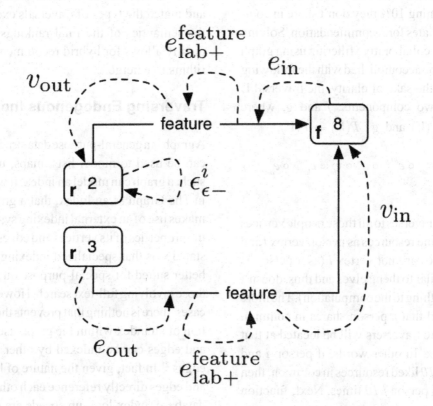

a new composition that finds all the resources that person i likes. Thus, if $g : \hat{P}(V) \to \hat{P}(V)$, where

$$g(i) = (v_{in} \circ e_{lab+}^{likes} \circ e_{out})(i)$$

then to determine those resources similar in features to the resources that person vertex 7 likes, compose function f and g: $(f \circ g)$ (7). Those resources that share more features in common will be returned more by $(f \circ g)$.[20]

What has been presented is an example of the use of traversals to do naive content-based recommendation. It is possible to extend the functions presented to normalize paths (e.g. a resource can have every feature and thus, is related to everything), find novelty (e.g. feature paths that are rare and only shared by a certain subset of re-

sources), etc. In most cases, when creating a graph traversal, a developer will compose different predefined paths into a longer compositions. Along with speed of execution, this is one of the benefits of using a functional, flow-based model for graph traversals (Yoo & Kaplan, 2009). Moreover, each component has a high-level meaning (e.g. the resources that a person likes) and as such, the verbosity of longer compositions can be minimal (e.g. $(f \circ g)$).

Collaborative Filtering-Based for Recommendation

With collaborative filtering, the objective is to identify a set of resources that have a high probability of being liked by a person based upon identifying other people in the system that enjoy similar likes. For example, if person *a* and person *b* share 90% of their liked resources in common, then the remaining 10% they don't share in common are candidates for recommendation. Solving the problem of collaborative filtering using graph traversals can be accomplished with the following traversal. For the sake of clarity, the traversal is broken into two components: *f* and *g*, where $f : \hat{P}(V) \rightarrow \hat{P}(V)$ and $g : \hat{P}(V) \rightarrow \hat{P}(V)$.

$$f(i) = (\in_{\in -}^{i} \circ v_{out} \circ e_{lab+}^{like} \circ e_{in} \circ v_{in} \circ e_{lab+}^{like} \circ e_{out})(i)$$

Function *f* traverses to all those people vertices that like the same resources as person vertex *i* and who themselves are not vertex *i* (as a person is obviously similar to themselves and thus, doesn't contribute anything to the computation). The more resources liked that a person shares in common with *i*, the more traversers will be located at that person's vertex. In other words, if person *i* and person *j* share *10* liked resources in common, then *f(i)* will return person *j 10* times. Next, function *g* is defined as

$$g(j) = (v_{in} \circ e_{lab+}^{like} \circ e_{out})(j)$$

Function *g* traverses to all the resources liked by vertex *j*. In composition, $(g \circ f)(i)$ determines all those resources that are liked by those people that have similar tastes to vertex *i*. If person *j* likes 10 resources in common with person *i*, then the resources that person *j* likes will be returned at least 10 times by $(g \circ f)$ (perhaps more if a path exists to those resources from another person vertex as well).

Figure 6 diagrams a function path starting from vertex 7. Only one legal path is presented for the sake of diagram clarity.

With the graph traversal pattern, there exists a single graph data structure that can be traversed in different ways to expose different types of recommendations – generally, different types of relationships between vertices. Being able to mix and match the types of traversals executed alters the semantics of the final rankings and conveniently allows for hybrid recommendation algorithms to emerge.

Traversing Endogenous Indices

A graph is a general-purpose data structure. A graph can be used to model lists, maps, trees, etc. As such, a graph can model an index. It was assumed, in The Graph as an Index, that a graph database makes use of an external indexing system to index the properties of its vertices and edges. The reason stated was that specialized indexing systems are better suited for special-purpose queries such as those involving full-text search. However, in many cases, there is nothing that prevents the representation of an index within the graph itself – vertices and edges can be indexed by other vertices and edges.[21] In fact, given the nature of how vertices and edges directly reference each other in a graph database, index look-up speeds are comparable. Endogenous indices afford graph databases a great flexibility in modeling a domain. Not only can objects and their relationships be modeled (e.g. people and their friendships), but also the indices that partition the objects into meaningful subsets (e.g. people within a 2D region of space).[22] The remainder of this subsection will discuss the representation and traversal of a spatial, 2D-index that is explicitly modeled within a property graph.

The domain of spatial analysis makes use of advanced indexing structures such as the quadtree (Finkel & Bentley, 1974) (Samet, 2006). Quadtrees partition a two-dimensional plane into rectangular boxes based upon the spatial density of the points being indexed.

Figure 7 diagrams how space is partitioned as the density of points increases within a region of the index.

In order to demonstrate how a quadtree index can be represented and traversed, a toy graph data set is presented. This data set is diagrammed in Figure 8.

The top half of Figure 8 represents a quadtree index (vertices 1-9). This quadtree index is partitioning "points of interest" (vertices a-i) located within the diagrammed plane.[23] All vertices maintain three properties – bottom-left (bl), top-right (tr), and type. For a quadtree vertex, these properties identify the two corner points defining a rectangular bounding box (i.e. the region that the quadtree vertex is indexing) and the vertex type which is equal to "quad". For a point of interest vertex, these properties denote the region of space that the point of interest exists within and the vertex type which is equal to "poi".

Quadtree vertex *1* denotes the entire region of space being indexed. This region is defined by its bottom-left (bl) and top-right (tr) corner points

– namely $[0,0]$ and $[100,100]$, where $bl_x = 0, bl_y = 0, tr_x = 100$, and $tr_y = 100$. Within the region defined by vertex *1*, there are *8* other defined regions that partition that space into smaller spaces (vertices *2-9*). When one vertex subsumes another vertex by a directed edge labeled sub} (i.e. subsumes), the outgoing (i.e. tail) vertex is subsuming the space that is defined by the incoming (i.e. head) vertex. Given these properties and edges, identifying point of interest vertices within a region of space is simply a matter of traversing the quadtree index in a directed/ algorithmic fashion.

In Figure 8, the shaded region represents the spatial query: "Which points of interest are within the rectangular region defined by the corner points $bl = [25,20]$ and $tr = [90,45]$?" In order to locate all the points of interest in this region, iteratively execute the following traversal starting from the root of the quadtree index (i.e. vertex 1).

Figure 6. A traversal that identifies resources that are similar in content to a resource based upon shared features

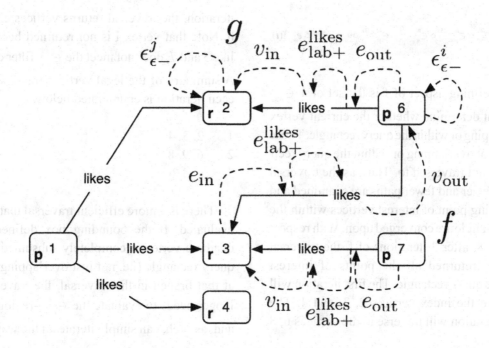

Figure 7. A quadtree partition of a plane. This figure is an adaptation of a public domain image provided courtesy of David Eppstein.

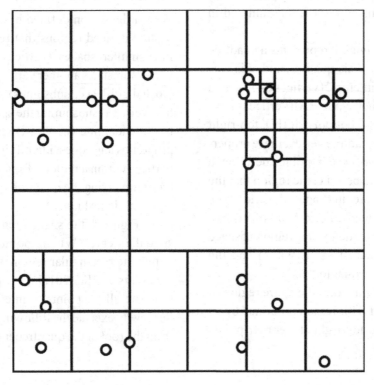

The function is defined as $f : \hat{P}(V) \rightarrow \hat{P}(V)$, where

$$f(i) = (\in_{p+}^{tr_y \geq 20} \circ \in_{p+}^{tr_x \geq 25} \circ \in_{p+}^{bl_y \leq 45} \circ \in_{p+}^{bl_x \leq 90} \circ v_{in} \circ e_{lab+}^{sub} \circ e_{out})(i)$$

The defining aspect of f is the set of 4 $\in_{p+}$ filters that determine whether the current vertex is overlapping or within the query rectangle. Those vertices not overlapping or within the query rectangle are not traversed to. Thus, as the traversal iterates, fewer and fewer paths are examined and the resulting point of interest vertices within the query rectangle are converged upon. With respect to Figure 8, after 3 iterations of f, the traversal will have returned all the points of interest within the query rectangle. The first iteration will traverse to the index vertices 2, 3, and 4. The second iteration will traverse to the vertices 6, 8

and 9. Note that vertices 5 and 7 do not meet the criteria of the $\in_{p+}$ filters. Finally, on the third iteration, the traversal returns vertices c, d, and h. Note that vertex i is not returned because it, like 5 and 7, does not meet the $\in_{p+}$ filter criteria. A summary of the legal vertices traversed to at each iteration is enumerated below.

1. 2, 3, 4
2. 6, 9, 8
3. c, d, h

There is a more efficient traversal that can be evaluated. If the bounding box defined by a quadtree vertex is completely subsumed by the query rectangle (i.e. not just overlapping), then, at that branch in the traversal, the traverser no longer needs to evaluate the $\in_{p+}$ -region filters and, as such, can simply iterate all the way down

Figure 8. A quadtree index of a space that contains points of interest. The index is composed of the vertices 1-9 and the points of interest are the vertices a-i. While not diagrammed for the sake of clarity, all edges are labeled sub (meaning subsumes) and each point of interest vertex has an associated bottom-left (bl) property, top-right (tr) property, and a type property which is equal to "poi".

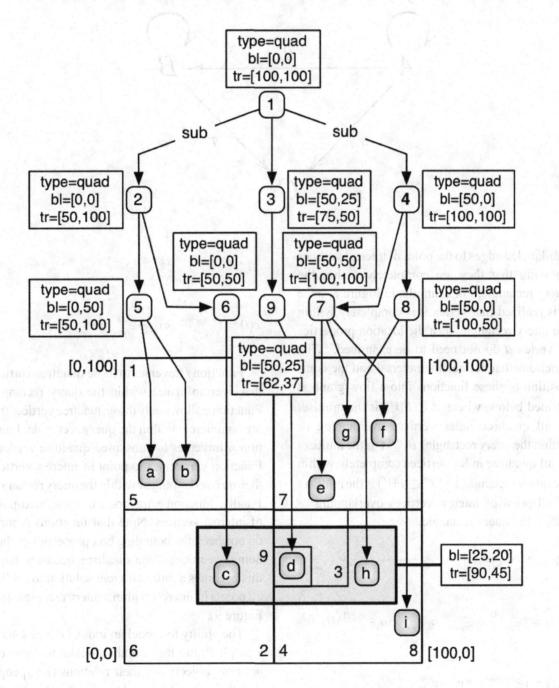

Figure 9. Quadtree vertices and query rectangle

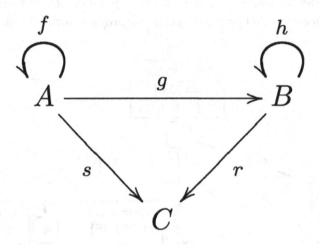

sub-labeled edges to the point of interest vertices knowing that they are completely within the query rectangle. For example, in Figure 8, once it is realized that vertex 9 is completely within the query rectangle, then the location properties of vertex d do not need to be examined.[24] The functions that define this traversal and the composition of these functions into a flow graph is defined below, where $A \subset \hat{P}(V)$ is the multiset of all quadtree index vertices overlapping or within the query rectangle, $B \subseteq A$ is the multiset of all quadtree index vertices completely within the query rectangle, and $C \subset \hat{P}(V)$ is the multiset of all point of interest vertices overlapping or within the query rectangle.

$$f(i) = (\in_{p+}^{tr_y \geq 20} \circ \in_{p+}^{tr_x \geq 25} \circ \in_{p+}^{bl_y \leq 45} \circ \in_{p+}^{bl_x \leq 90} \in_{p+}^{type=quad} \circ v_{in} \circ e_{lab+}^{sub} \circ e_{out})(i)$$

$$g(i) = (\in_{p+}^{tr_y \leq 45} \circ \in_{p+}^{tr_x < 90} \circ \in_{p+}^{bl_y \geq 20} \circ \in_{p+}^{bl_x \geq 25})(i)$$

$$h(i) = (\in_{p+}^{type=quad} \circ v_{in} \circ e_{lab+}^{sub} e_{out})(i)$$

$$s(i) = (\in_{p+}^{tr_y \geq 20} \circ \in_{p+}^{tr_x \geq 25} \circ \in_{p+}^{bl_y \leq 45} \circ \in_{p+}^{bl_x \leq 90} \circ \in_{p+}^{type=poi} \circ v_{in} \circ e_{lab+}^{sub} \circ e_{out})(i)$$

$$r(i) = (\in_{p+}^{type=poi} \circ v_{in} \circ e_{lab+}^{sub} \circ e_{out})(i)$$

Function f traverses to those quadtree vertices that overlap or are within the query rectangle. Function g allows only those quadtree vertices that are completely within the query rectangle. Function h traverses to subsumed quadtree vertices. Function s traverses to point of interest vertices that are overlapping or within the query rectangle. Finally, function r traverses to subsumed point of interest vertices. Note that functions h and r do no check the bounding box properties of their domain vertices. As a quadtree becomes large, this becomes a more efficient solution to finding all points of interest within a query rectangle (see Figure 9).

The ability to model an index endogenous to a graph allows the domain modeler to represent not only objects and their relations (e.g. people and their friendships), but also "meta-objects" and their relationships (e.g. index nodes and their subsumptions). In this way, the domain modeler can organize their model according to partitions that make sense to how the model will be used to solve problems. Moreover, by combining the traversal of an index with the traversal of a domain, there exists a single unified means by which problems are solved within a graph database – the graph traversal pattern.

CONCLUSION

Graphs are a flexible modeling construct that can be used to model a domain and the indices that partition that domain into an efficient, searchable space. When the relations between the objects of the domain are seen as vertex partitions, then a graph is simply an index that relates vertices to vertices by edges. The way in which these vertices relate to each other determines which graph traversals are most efficient to execute and which problems can be solved by the graph data structure. Graph databases and the graph traversal pattern do not require a global analysis of data. For many problems, only local subsets of the graph need to be traversed to yield a solution. By structuring the graph in such a way as to minimize traversal steps, limit the use of external indices, and reduce the number of set-based operations, modelers gain great efficiency that is difficult to accomplish with other data management solutions.

REFERENCES

Angles, R., & Guiterrez, C. (2008). Survey of graph database models. *ACM Computing Surveys*, *40*, 1–39. doi:10.1145/1322432.1322433

Barcelo, P., Hurtado, C., Libkin, L., & Wood, P. (2010). Expressive languages for path queries over graph-structured data. *Proceedings of Symposium on Principles of Database Systems of Data*, 3-14.

Chartrand, G., & Lesniak, L. (1986). *Graphs & digraphs*. Belmont, CA: Wadsworth Publishing Company.

Codd, E. F. (1970). A relational model of data for large shared data banks. *Communications of the ACM*, *13*(6), 377–387. doi:10.1145/362384.362685

DeCandia, G., Hastorun, D., Jampani, M., Kakulapati, G., Lakshman, A., & Pilchin, A. (2007). Dynamo: Amazon's highly available key-value store. *SIGOPS Operating Systems Review*, *41*(6), 205–220. doi:10.1145/1323293.1294281

Finkel, R. A., & Bentley, J. L. (1974). Quad trees a data structure for retrieval on composite keys. *Acta Informatica*, *4*(1), 1–9. doi:10.1007/BF00288933

Griffith, J., O'Riordan, C., & Sorensen, H. (2006). Knowledge-based intelligent information and engineering systems. *Lecture Notes in Artificial Intelligence, chapter A Constrained Spreading Activation Approach to Collaborative Filtering, 4253*, 766-773.

Herlocker, J. L., Konstan, J. A., Terveen, L. G., & Riedl, J. T. (2004). Evaluating collaborative filtering recommender systems. *ACM Transactions on Information Systems*, *22*(1), 5–53. doi:10.1145/963770.963772

Karvounarakis, G., Alexaki, S., Christophides, V., Plexousakis, D., & Scholl, M. (2002). RQL: A declarative query language for RDF. *Proceedings of the 11th International Conference on World Wide Web*, 592-603.

Larsson, P. (2008). Analyzing and adapting graph algorithms for large persistent graphs. *Master's thesis*.

Lennon, J. (2009). *Beginning CouchDB*. New York, NY: Apress. doi:10.1007/978-1-4302-7236-6

Manager, R. (2004). A new path algebra for finding paths in graphs. *Proceedings of the International Conference on Information Technology Interfaces, 1*, 657–662.

Martinez-Bazan, N., Muntes-Mulero, V., Gomez-Villamor, S., Nin, J., Sanchez-Martinez, M.-A., & Larriba-Pey, J.-L. (2007). DEX: Highperformance exploration on large graphs for information retrieval. *Proceedings of the Sixteenth ACM Conference on Information and Knowledge Management*, 573-582.

Mendelzon, A. O., & Wood, P. T. (1989). Finding regular simple paths in graph databases. *Proceedings of the 15th International Conference on Very Large Data Bases*, 185-193.

Mirza, B. J., Keller, B. J., & Ramakrishnan, N. (2003). Studying recommendation algorithms by graph analysis. *Journal of Intelligent Information Systems, 20*(2), 131–160. doi:10.1023/A:1021819901281

Mishra, P., & Eich, M. H. (1992). Join processing in relational databases. *ACM Computing Surveys, 24*(1), 63–111. doi:10.1145/128762.128764

Monro, G. P. (1987). The concept of multiset. *Mathematical Logic Quarterly, 33*(2), 171–178. doi:10.1002/malq.19870330212

Morrison, J. P. (1994). *Flow-based programming: A new approach to application development*. Van Nostrand Reinhold.

Perugini, S., Goncalves, M. A., & Fox, E. A. (2004). Recommender systems research: A connection-centric survey. *Journal of Intelligent Information Systems, 23*(2), 107–143. doi:10.1023/B:JIIS.0000039532.05533.99

Prud'hommeaux, E., & Seaborne, A. (2004, October). SPARQL query language for RDF. *Technical report, World Wide Web Consortium*.

Raghavan, S., & Garcia-Molina, H. (2003). Complex queries over Web repositories. *Proceedings of the International Conference on Very Large Data Bases*, 33-44.

Rodriguez, M. A. (2008). Grammar-based random walkers in semantic networks. *Knowledge-Based Systems, 21*(7), 727–739. doi:10.1016/j.knosys.2008.03.030

Rodriguez, M. A. (2008). Mapping semantic networks to undirected networks. *International Journal of Applied Mathematics and Computer Science, 5*(1), 39–42.

Rodriguez, M. A., & Shinavier, J. (2009). Exposing multi-relational networks to single-relational network analysis algorithms. *Journal of Informatrics, 4*(1), 29–41. doi:10.1016/j.joi.2009.06.004

Russling, M. (1995). A general scheme for breadth-first graph traversal. *Mathematics of Program Construction, 947*, 380–398.

Samet, H. (2006). *Foundations of Multidimensional and Metric Data Structures*. Morgan Kaufmann.

Stonebraker, M. (1986). The case for shared nothing. *IEEE Database Engineering Bulletin, 9*(1), 4–9.

Wasserman, S., & Faust, K. (1994). *Social network analysis: Methods and applications*. Cambridge, UK: Cambridge University Press.

Yoo, A., & Kaplan, I. (2009). Evaluating use of data flow systems for large graph analysis. *Proceedings of the 2nd Workshop on Many-Task Computing on Grids and Supercomputers*, 1-9.

KEY TERMS AND DEFINITIONS

Adjacency: Used to denote that a vertex is directly connected to another vertex.

Edge: A link, relationship, line connecting two vertices.

Index: A data structure that is optimized for looking up elements by a property of the element.

Graph: A data structure composed for vertices and edges.

Graph Database: A database optimized for storing and traversing graph data structures.

Quad Tree Index: A type of index optimized for querying rectangles on a 2D plane.

Recommendation Algorithm: An method for determining if two objects are similar to each other by some semantic quality.

Relational Database: A database optimized for storing and joining table structures.

Traversal: A algorithmic walk over the vertices and edges of a graph. Usually taking into account the adjacency of elements.

Vertex: A node, object, dot that is connected to other vertices by edges.

ENDNOTES

1 The term *pattern* refers to data modeling/processing patterns found in computing such as the relational pattern, the map-reduce pattern, etc. In this sense, a pattern is a way of approaching a data-centric problem that usually has benefits in terms of efficiency and/or expressibility.

2 Maintaining these references in a consistent state is known as a referential integrity.

3 Sharding is easily solved by other database architectures such as key/value stores [5] and document databases [11]. In such systems, there is no explicit linking between data in different "collections" (i.e. documents, key/value pairs). Strict partitions of data make it easier to horizontally scale a database [27].

4 The space of graph databases is relatively new. While it is possible to model and process a graph in most any type of database (e.g. relational databases, key/value stores, document databases), a graph database, in the context of this chapter, is one that makes use of direct references between adjacent vertices and edges. As such, graph databases are those systems that are optimized for graph traversals. The Neo4j graph database is an example of such a database [10].

5 In a relational database, this process is known as a full table scan.

6 Assume that the number of rows in person is n and the number of rows in friend is m. Moreover, for the sake of simplicity, assume that names, like identifiers, in the person table are unique.

7 Given that an individual will have many friends, the number of index nodes in the friend.person_a index will be much less than m.

8 In the parlance of graphs, a property graph is a directed, edge-labeled, attributed multi-graph. For the sake of simplicity, such structures will simply be called property graphs. These types of graph structures are used extensively in computing as they are more expressive than the simplified mathematical objects studied in theory. However, note that expressiveness is defined by ease of use, not by the limits of what can be modeled (Rodriguez & Shinavier, Exposing multi-relational networks to single-relational network analysis algorithms, 2009).

9 The reason for using an external indexing system is that it may be optimized for certain types of lookups such as full-text search.

10 This is ultimately what is accomplished in a relational database when a row of a table is located and a value in a column of that row is fetched (e.g. see the second micro-operation of the relational database enumeration previous). However, when that row doesn't have all the requisite data (usually do to database normalization), it requires the joining with another table to locate that data. It is this situation which is costly in a relational database.

11   If a graph database does not index the edges of a vertex by their labels, then a linear scan of all edges emanating from a vertex must occur to locate the set of friend-labeled edges. Thus, $k+x$ is the total number of edges emanating from the current vertex.

12   The consequence of this is that traversing through a "super node" (i.e. a highdegree vertex) in a graph is slower than traversing through a small-degree vertex.

13   In many ways, this is the graph equivalent of the joint operation used by relational databases – though no global indices are used. When traversing a multi-step path, the source and sink vertices are united by a semantic determined by the path taken. For example, going from a person, to their friends, and then to their friends friends, will unite that person to people two-steps away in the graph. This popular path is known FOAF (friend of a friend).

14   In general, the term "algorithm" is used in a looser sense than the classic definition in that it allows for randomization and sampling when traversing.

15   While it is possible to write and delete elements from a graph, such operations will not be discussed.

16   The power set of set A is denoted P(A) and is the set of all subsets of A (i.e. 2^A). The power multiset of A, denoted $\hat{P}(A)$, is the infinite set of all subsets of multisets of A. This set is infinite because multisets allow for repeated elements (Monro, 1987).

17   Filters can be defined as allowing or disallowing certain elements. For allowing, the symbol + is used. For disallowing, the symbol - is used.

18   Note that the order of a composition is evaluated from right to left.

19   This is known as a virtual edge in the graph system called DEX (Martinez-Bazan, Muntes-Mulero, Gomez-Villamor, Nin, Sanchez-Martinez, & Larriba-Pey, 2007).

20   Again, path traversal functions are defined over power multisets. In this way, its possible for a function to return repeated elements. In some situations, deduplicating this set is desired. In other situations, repeated elements can be used to weight/rank the results.

21   One of the primary motivations behind this chapter is to stress the importance of thinking of a graph as simply an index of itself, where the primary purpose is to traverse the various defined indices in ways that elicit problem solving within the domain being modeled.

22   Those indices that have a graph-like structure are suited for representing as a graph. It is noted that not all indices meet this criteria.

23   The plane depicted does not actually exist as a data structure, but is represented here to denote how the different vertices lying on that plane are spatially located (i.e. spatial information is represented explicitly in the properties of the vertices). Thus, vertices closer to each other on the plane are closer together.

24   In general, disregarding bounding box property checks holds for both quadtree vertices and point of interest vertices that are subsumed by a quadtree vertex that is completely within the query rectangle.

Chapter 3
Data, Storage and Index Models for Graph Databases

Srinath Srinivasa
International Institute of Information Technology, India

ABSTRACT

Management of graph structured data has important applications in several areas. Queries on such data sets are based on structural properties of the graphs, in addition to values of attributes. Answering such queries pose significant challenges, as reasoning about structural properties across graphs are typically intractable problems. This chapter provides an overview of the challenges in designing databases over graph datasets. Different application areas that use graph databases, pose their own unique set of challenges, making the task of designing a generic graph-oriented DBMS still an elusive goal. The purpose of this chapter is to provide a tutorial introduction to some of the major challenges of graph data management, survey some of the piecemeal solutions that have been proposed, and suggest an overall structure in which these different solutions can be meaningfully placed.

INTRODUCTION

Increasingly, management of data representing *relationship structures* across entities is an important issue in several application domains. Often, semantics are hidden in the way different entities are related, which may not be obvious by studying each entity in isolation. Querying on properties

of such relationship structures are sometimes as important, if not more so, as querying for values of specific attributes.

Some application examples follow:

- In proteomics – or the study of proteins, it is well known that the conformation, or the 3D structure, of a protein is strongly correlated to the functioning of the protein (Ex: Graves et. al, 1995; Colinge and Bennett,

DOI: 10.4018/978-1-61350-053-8.ch003

2007). The conformation map of a protein is formed by interactions between the different atoms that make up the protein molecule. Studying these interaction patterns hence, is of immense importance

- In the field of computer-aided design of electrical circuits, some interconnection patterns across electrical devices keep recurring in different problems. Managing data about electrical circuits and comparing similarities between two or more circuits is of significant importance

- In the field of information security, a commonly occurring challenge is to look for anomalous behavior by one or more entities, like people, software, etc. in the system. Anomalies constitute deviations from the norm that are distinct from "noise" or "novel" deviations – both of which also constitute deviations from the norm (Chandola et. al 2009). A central aspect of anomaly detection constitutes studying and reasoning about the *relationship patterns* that an entity has with other entities in the system

- Designers of public infrastructure like airports, hospitals, etc. face a number of conflicting requirements concerning safety, efficiency, reachability, cost, etc. Conflicting requirements like these are often modeled as *network design* and *facility location* problems (cf. Brandes and Erlebach, 2005) over graphs. Since designing a facility from scratch is often a hard problem, architects use design patterns depicting best practices and architectural features that have been recorded over time. Management of such datasets requires the database to support structural queries over graphs.

Management of graph structured data is not a new problem in the field of databases. Most data structures at the application level usually need to deal with some form of graph structure. Early

approaches to data management did not have clear separations between logical and physical views of data. As a result, graph structured data from the application were stored directly as a networked set of records at the physical level. An example of this is the Network data model (Taylor and Frank, 1976).

Later approaches towards data management had clearer separations between the physical layout of records on disk and the logical structuring of the database schema. The most popular among these is of course, the relational data model (Codd 1983), which has become the standard for most commercial DBMS today. The relational data model gave mathematical underpinnings to the logical structuring of data, based on concepts of relations, functional dependencies and normal forms. Relations in a relational schema are captured in two different forms: an n-ary relation across several attributes of a given semantic entity; and relations across entities. The former kind of relation is represented in the form of a table – every column in a table is related to every other, by virtue of being attributed to a single entity. The second form of relation is represented by means of foreign keys across tables.

So, in a sense, every relational database represents a graph structured logical model for the data. However, conventional relational databases are inadequate for the challenges of managing graph data as illustrated in the application examples. They can be summarized as follows:

- A relational database represents several instances of a single graph structure that is captured by the schema. Graph databases on the other hand, may need to contend with several graphs with different structures as part of the same database

- While a graph can be represented as a set of relations (for example, modeling each edge as a relation) and stored as a set of rows in a table, doing so would violate an implicit assumption in relational databases that each row of a table represents an entity instance that is independent of all other instances of that type

- Index structures in relational databases are focused on answering queries over values of attributes. Answering queries concerning relationship structures usually requires a large amount of joins, making it very expensive.

The motivation for developing native database models for graph structures have been varied. Graph based logical data models generated a lot of interest in object-oriented databases in the late 1980s and early 1990s (Kim, 1990). The primary motivation for using graphs in object-oriented databases was to enable representation of complex objects, type systems, associations and inheritances natively in the database.

Some examples are: GOAL (Hidders & Paredaens, 1993), GOOD (Gemis et al., 1993), and GraphDB (Güting, 1994). As mentioned earlier, the main motivations behind using graphs in object databases, centered upon *representation of complex objects* and relationships. However, these are inadequate for the kinds of challenges that require graph data management today. For instance, supporting queries over structural properties across several graphs, has not been one of the main elements of interest in object databases. In addition, in most object databases, graph structured data needed to conform to a predefined schema (Angles & Gutierrez, 2008), thus making their structural properties known a priori.

Graph data management has been addressed in several problems involving knowledge management. Some of the early applications included knowledge representation problems in artificial intelligence, where management of *semantic networks* have been a primary concern. Examples include: Telos (Mylopoulos et al., 1990), Controlled Decomposition Model (CDM) (Topaloglou, 1993), etc. Semantic networks represent relationships across disparate entities, thus forming a large

graph data structure. Such databases also need to provide support for inference, which typically requires indexing *paths* over the semantic networks.

Later, in the fields of digital libraries and the Semantic Web, representing knowledge constructs have become a primary focus. In addition, research efforts on management of semi-structured data address a variety of graph related problems as part of data management, like path constraints, inclusions, extents, inverses etc. Some examples include (Abiteboul, 1997; Abiteboul & Vianu, 1997), (Bertino et al., 2003), (Buneman et al., 1998).

Application areas like bioinformatics, have posed significant problems of graph data management. Many concepts concerning bioinformatics – be they molecular structures, metabolic pathways or protein interaction structures – are naturally represented in the form of graphs. The late 1990s and the early 2000s have seen several research models for representation of biological data in the form of graphs. Some examples include: GRACE (Srinivasa et al., 2002; Kumar & Srinivasa 2003; Srinivasa et al., 2005), (Borgelt & Berthold, 2002), GraphGrep (Guigno & Shasha, 2002), gSpan (Yan & Han, 2002), etc. Management of graph data in bioinformatics applications continues to be an area of active research interest.

In more recent times, the popularity of online social networking and collaborative bookmarking sites have created huge amounts of graph structured data, which cannot be reliably stored and managed using relational databases. As a result, there have been several approaches to create custom storage and query models for managing such large graph data. Several of these disparate efforts have also come together under a banner called NoSQL (which, rather than representing a rejection of SQL, is claimed to stand for "Not Only SQL") databases. To be sure, NoSQL is not just about storing graph structured data – but web scale data. There are several underlying models that are used by databases that call themselves NoSQL. For instance, CouchDB[1] from the Apache Foundation, is a document store that supports ACID (atomicity, consistency, isolation and durability) semantics on a large document repository. It employs the MapReduce[2] model for creating views and interacting with applications. Cassandra[3], also by the Apache Foundation, implements a column store based on Google's BigTable model. Cassandra is used by several sites like FaceBook, Twitter and Digg to manage large graph datasets. The Java based neo4j[4] implements a transactional graph data store that provides native support for describing several graph related properties like nodes, edges, paths, etc.

It is quite clear that graph data management is a pertinent issue in several application areas. However, research efforts towards graph data management have been piece-meal and isolated, with no overarching theory of a graph DBMS emerging. Even more fundamentally, there is no clear consensus on what constitutes a graph database – other than the fact that the data elements of interest lie in the patterns of relationships, in addition to values of attributes.

The objective of this chapter is to introduce some issues of concern pertaining to graph data management, and where relevant, contrast it with similar problems in relational databases. The chapter is not primarily meant to be a survey of existing graph databases; however relevant literature would be cited as part of the process of characterizing this space.

Specifically three kinds of issues are considered: data models, storage models and index structures for graph databases. Data models address the logical model of the graph database. This in turn depends on the type of graph that is to be stored as well as the way in which the graph data is envisaged to be used. Storage models look into physical storage structures for graph data. Specifically, we shall look into the contrasting approaches of mapping graph databases onto relational data stores versus native storage structures for graph databases. The last issue of concern – that of index structures – looks into structural indexes. A

structural index is a augmented data structure for a graph database that extracts and pre-computes certain structural features of the graph data and stores it in a global index structure. This index is then used for quick answering of structure-based queries.

A topic conspicuous by its absence, is query language and query processing for graph databases. This is a vast area of research interest in itself and is omitted from this chapter for reasons of brevity and space constraints. The interested reader is recommended to read (Angles & Gutierrez, 2008; Sakr & Al-Naymat, 2010) for surveys addressing query models in graph databases.

DATA MODELS FOR GRAPH DATABASES

Data models are concerned with the logical structure of the database. Based on constraints posed by the application areas, there are different paradigms of logical models for graph databases. To understand this space, we need to first consider the different kinds of graph data that are typically handled by applications requiring graph databases.

Types of Graph Data

A graph represents a set of relationships among a set of objects or entities of interest. In the most generic form, a graph is represented as a tuple: $G = (V, E)$, where V is a set of *nodes* or *vertices* and $E \subseteq V \times V$ represents pair-wise relationships across the nodes.

Nodes and edges of a graph may contain attributes, whose values may be of interest. However, they can usually be searched by storing them in a relational data store. We will not be concerned with querying for values of attributes of nodes and edges – rather, we will be interested in queries over the graph structure itself.

A graph is said to be *directed* if for any pair of nodes $u, v \in V, (u, v) \neq (v, u)$. The graph is said to be undirected if the direction of the relationship does not matter. In such cases, an edge is also represented as a 2-element subset of vertices, rather than an ordered pair.

A dataset depicting hyperlinks across web pages can be seen as a directed graph, where the nodes are web pages and edges are hyperlinks. On the other hand, a dataset representing friendships on a social networking site like Facebook, can be seen as an undirected graph, where a friendship relation from A to B implies a similar relationship from B to A.

In terms of storage, in undirected graphs, a pair of nodes that are connected by an edge, need to be stored only once in order to represent their relationship, while for a directed graph, a pair of nodes may need to be stored twice depending on the existence of bi-directional relationships. The directed nature of graphs also has a bearing on some indexing structures. Some kinds of structure indexes depend upon reducing a graph structured data into a string by performing a depth-first traversal (DFS) of the graph and then encoding the resultant DFS tree into a string. A DFS traversal on an undirected connected graph always results in a tree, while for directed graphs, a DFS traversal may result in a forest, depending on where the traversal started (Cormen, et al., 2001).

A graph is said to be *labeled* if there exist sets V_L and E_L, representing sets of node and edge labels, and label assignment functions $\delta : V \to V_L$ and $\gamma : E \to E_L$ respectively. Usually the following holds: $|V_L| \ll |V|$ and $|E_L| \ll |E|$. That is, the number of node and edge labels are much less than the number of nodes and edges of the graph.

A label can be seen as a *type* assignment for nodes and edges. All nodes and edges having the same label can be seen as belonging to the same type. Labels are *categorical* values – that is, they cannot be ordered or compared using a relation like less-than-or-equal-to $(\leq)$.

As an example, an organic molecule comprises of a large number of relatively small types of atoms like Carbon, Hydrogen, Oxygen, etc. Each Carbon atom is a different node in the graph, but has the same label as all other Carbon atoms. Similarly, edge types representing covalent bonds in an organic molecule can have one of three labels: single bond, double bond or triple bond.

For graph databases, labels provide a means by which nodes and edges can be bucketed together. Such a bucketing can be used to address problems in both storage and indexing of graphs in the database.

A special form of labeled graph data are *bi-partite* or more generally, k-*partite* graphs. A k-partite graph is a labeled graph where $|V_L| = k$ and $|E_L| = 1 |$ with the following constraint on the edges: an edge can connect two nodes if and only if they do not have the same label.

Bi-partite and k-partite graphs depict data sets showing interaction between two or more *classes* of entities. For instance, an online bookstore like Amazon.com contains data about customers buying books. This entire dataset can be represented as a bi-partite graph where nodes belong to one of two types – customer and book. Edges connecting customers and books depict which customers have bought which book. Similarly, a social bookmarking engine like del.icio.us (now called delicious.com) has a tri-partite dataset made of the following kinds of nodes: users, tags and URLs. Users use tags to annotate URLs. This can be captured in the tri-partite graph as edges across: users and tags, users and URLs and tags and URLs.

Edges in a graph may also be associated with numerical weights. Such graphs are called *weighted graphs*. Here, the edge set E is defined as: $E \subseteq V \times V \times \Re$, where $\Re$ is the set of real numbers. Depending on the application context, these weights may take on different meanings. For instance, a road network can be represented in the form of a graph, where intersections are denoted by nodes and roads by weighted edges. The weight on each edge in this case, would depict the distance across intersections. Unlike labels in a labeled graph, weights represent quantities, rather than types, and can be compared.

Queries over a weighted graph typically require some form of a min/max computation over paths or substructures. Examples include shortest path queries in road network datasets, finding near-cliques with maximum pair-wise energy in molecular structures, etc.

Nodes in a graph can be sometimes associated with *spatial coordinates* in the form of (x,y,z) or latitude, longitude and altitude values. Such forms of graphs are called spatial graphs – graph structures embedded inside S^3 – the 3-dimensional sphere (Kobayashi, 1994). Examples include road networks, where each node – representing an intersection, can be annotated with a latitude, longitude and altitude coordinates. Similarly, the tertiary structure of a protein molecule is represented as a spatial graph. Here, nodes represent atoms and links represent covalent bonds across atoms. In addition to these, a protein is also characterized by its 3D conformance, where the 3D coordinates of each atom is important to determine the structural (and hence functional) characteristics of the protein molecule.

In spatial graphs, the neighborhood of a node can be defined in two ways – the *spatial neighborhood*, comprising of other nodes that are close in terms of their coordinates; and the *logical neighborhood* defined by edge connectivity. The existence of two kinds of neighborhoods can be exploited in problems like facilitating routing and shortest-path queries in spatial graphs.

Some kinds of applications require management of *hypergraph* data. A hypergraph is a generalization over a graph structure, where an edge may connect any number of nodes, rather than just a pair of nodes. Formally, a hypergraph is of the form H = (V,E), where V is the set of nodes and $E \subseteq 2^v - \{\phi\}$, where 2^v is the powerset (set of all subsets) of V and, ϕ is the empty set. Hypergraph data management have been explored in fields like knowledge representation

and object databases. Examples include GROOVY (Levene & Poulovassilis, 1991) and Hy+ (Consens & Mendelzon, 1993). Higher-order relationships – relationships that relate more than a pair of entities – often cannot be reduced to a set of pair-wise relationships without losing semantics.

Another concept related to that of hypergraphs is the notion of a *hypernode*. A hypernode in a graph is a vertex that represents another graph structure (which in turn may contain more hypernodes). Hypernodes represent a way by which graph structures can be aggregated into a conceptual hierarchy, and enable graphs to be used both as a data element and a schema element. Examples of graph databases supporting hypernodes include (Levene & Poulovassilis, 1990), (Jonyer, et al., 2000) and (Srinivasa, et al., 2005).

As is apparent, although management of graph data is required in several application areas, there are different kinds of graph data that needs to be managed – each suitable for a different application area, and having its own specific forms of queries that need to be supported. It is not surprising then that, there is no single data model for a graph database. The next subsection explores some of the different data models of graph databases and their suitability for specific forms of graph data.

Data Models

Different kinds of graph database models have been proposed, each of them being designed in the context of some application area. Broadly however, data models for graph databases can be divided into the following kinds:

1. Database as a collection of graphs
2. Database as a nested graph
3. Database as a graph

Each of these data models are explained in more detail below.

Database as a collection of graphs. In the first model of graph databases, the database can be seen modeled as D = (M,I), where M represents a set of *member* graphs and I represents a set of *auxiliary* graphs that make up the database. Each member graph $G \in M$ represents a data structure distinct from all other member graphs. The set I also comprises of one or more graphs that provides navigational support for the database management system to index into the database.

The graphs in I are strictly meta-data and cannot be part of the result set of a query. The actual data of interest are confined to the graphs in M. Each member graph in M may have a different structure, and there is no overarching schema that describes this collection. While meta-data is managed separately as index structures, this is different from having a schema that is defined a priori, and that describes how the database is organized.

Member graphs are also typically small in comparison with the size of the database. Queries on such databases focus on matching structural properties that are common *across* member graphs in the database and return zero or more member graphs from M as the query result.

Datasets of molecular structures and protein conformance datasets can be seen as examples of such a database. Many such databases exist in the field of bioinformatics, that provide various query services, including queries that search the dataset based on structural properties of the member graphs. The NAR database summary[5] lists several such databases providing online services pertinent to nucleic acid research, many of which manage datasets in the form of a collection of graphs. Other examples of databases as a collection of graphs, include: GraphGrep (Guigno & Shasha, 2002; Shasha et al., 2002) and GRACE (Srinivasa, et al., 2002).

Database as a nested graph. In the second form of graph databases, the database is still a collection of member graphs. But, member graphs are connected together by other graphs describing schematic structures, which in turn can be described by higher level schema graphs; convert-

ing the entire database into a single *nested graph* model. One of the main design objectives behind such graph databases is the *rich expressiveness* that is obtained by treating data and meta-data seamlessly using a common data structure.

Database as a nested graph model has been primarily employed in object database models and database models for knowledge management. In such databases, meta-data elements do not play just an auxiliary role. Data and meta-data are both part of the dataset stored in the database and can be returned in response to a query. Some examples follow.

The hypernode database model (Levene & Poulovassilis, 1990; Levene & Loizou, 1995) models the database as a single data structure called the *hypernode*. A hypernode is a graph structure comprising of nodes and edges, where each node in turn can represent other hypernodes.

Figure 1 shows an example hypernode database showing two "Person" nodes, where each node in turn represents a graph showing relationships between attribute names and values. Formally, a hypernode is defined as a triple (G,V,E), where G is the label of the hypernode, V is a set of nodes and E is a set of directed edges connecting the nodes. Hypernodes can be used to represent a variety of concepts including aggregation, composition, encapsulation and cyclic relationships. The hypernode model also comes with a programming language over hypernodes, supporting a specific operator called INFER, that can infer new hypernodes based on existing hypernodes in the database based on a specified set of rules.

The *Safari* data model described as part of the GRACE graph database (Srinivasa et al., 2005) has a somewhat similar approach. The graph database comprises of several graphs, where a node in a graph can be classified as either a "data" node or a "meta" node. A data node comprises of atomic data objects, while meta nodes refer to other graphs in the database. When a new database is created, it creates a single graph called **_default**, which comprises of a single meta-node pointing

Figure 1. An example hypernode database comprising of a single hypernode with two nodes, each of which represents a graph

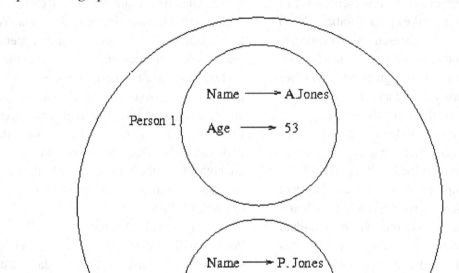

to itself. On insertion of a member graph into the database, a corresponding meta node is automatically created in the **_default** graph, which points to the new member graph. By default, the **_default** graph contains no edges, but edges can always be added to member graphs at any time. Member graphs can in turn, contain a combination of data and meta nodes, and relationships between them.

Figure 2 schematically depicts a graph database in the Safari model. A meta node in any graph can refer to another graph in one of two ways – *statically* using the graph id of the target graph, or *dynamically*, using a standing query. The Safari data model comes with a query language that supports closed operations on graph selections. That is, the input and output to these operators is a *single graph*. There are three such closed operators: select-in, select-on and select-graph. The first two

induces new graph structures by searching "inside" (by unfolding the meta nodes and expanding the search) a graph or "on" a graph (without unfolding the meta nodes). The select-graph operator takes a graph that has one or more meta-nodes and returns one of the target graphs pointed by the meta nodes that match the query. The closed nature of the graph select operators enable them to be composed to form complex queries.

A meta-node with a standing query hence can point to graphs that don't physically exist in the database, and are materialized at query time.

A third example for nested graph database models are RDF[6] databases. RDF, which is a W3C (World Wide Web Consortium) standard is used to provide precise meta-data for web resources. RDF is made of triples of the form (subject, predicate, object). Here, subject and object are resources, where a resource is anything that has

Figure 2. A schematic diagram of a Safari database. Not all member graphs are shown as meta-nodes in the **_default** *graph, however, in the implementation, each member graph contains a representative meta node in* **_default.**

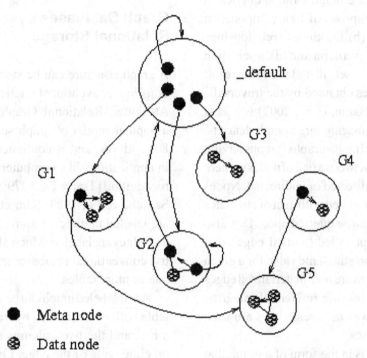

a Universal Resource Identifier (URI) associated with it. A collection of RDF triples that describes a web resource can be seen as a directed graph with edge labels. Since such an RDF description can be made available as a web resource, an RDF description can describe resources that are in turn RDF descriptions themselves, making an RDF store a nested graph.

Database as a graph. The third model for graph databases represents the entire database as one big graph. Unlike the previous approach, the graph comprises of only data elements. There may be other augmented graphs for indexing into the data graph, however, these data structures are not integrated into the data graph. This is a common approach used for handling web-scale graph data like hyperlink networks, social-network data, etc.

In principle, the database as a graph model can be seen as a special case of the "Database as a collection of graphs" model, where the collection size

is 1. However, in practice, the design principles of these two kinds of databases have very different motivations. In web-scale graph data, structural queries *on* the graph is of primary concern, while in a collection of graphs, structural queries *across* the graphs are of interest. Also, web-scale graph data usually need to support several kinds of structural queries like shortest-path queries, community or near-clique detection queries, centrality queries, etc. that are of little interest in a collection of graphs where each member graph is relatively small in size.

Some examples of this model of graph databases follow.

The neo4j graph database represents the entire database as a graph[7]. It supports two kinds of first-class objects – nodes and relations. Both of them can store one or more properties in the form of attributes and their values. The entire database is then modeled as a set of nodes and relations across nodes. For graph related queries, a framework called "Traverser" is provided that can support a variety of traversal and neighborhood queries. A Traverser query comprises of four components: (a). A starting node, (b). the kinds of relationships to traverse, (c). a stop criteria and (d). a selection criteria that selects a set of nodes as the result from the set of nodes obtained by the traversal.

Dex (Martínez-Bazan, et al., 2007) is a Java based library for managing large graph datasets. Dex supports labeled multi-graphs (graphs having more than one edge between a pair of nodes), where edges can be either directed or undirected. Nodes and edges can be associated with a set of attributes and values, which can be queried upon. Dex also introduces a concept called "virtual edge" that connects nodes having the same value for a given attribute. Virtual edges are non-materialized edges and are used for managing referential integrity, in much the same way as foreign keys are used in relational databases.

A Dex database is in the form of a graph that is an instance of the DbGraph class. Dex supports a set of basic graph traversal queries over which other sophisticated algorithms are implemented. The basic support includes operations like "Explode" that gets the set of all edges of a given type from a given node, and "Neighbors" that returns the set of nodes that are adjacent to a given node. Dex also implements a number of graph algorithms in packages. These include shortest-path algorithms, graph traversal algorithms (breadth-first and depth-first traversals), algorithms to find strongly connected components of directed graphs, etc.

STORAGE MODELS FOR GRAPH DATABASES

As with any non-standard database, storage models for graph databases can be seen from two perspectives – graph databases implemented on a relational store, and graph databases implemented over native storage models.

Graph Databases over Relational Storage

A graph structure can be stored as a set of relations in a conventional relational database table. Attributed Relational Graph (ARG) has been a popular model of graph structures in the late 80s and 90s, and is continued to be used today in applications like computer vision and pattern recognition (Tsai & Fu, 1979; Chang & Fu, 1980; Sanfeliu & Fu, 1983; Kim et. al., 2010). ARGs are labeled undirected graphs where both nodes and edges are labeled. Much of the work on ARGs use conventional databases and store an ARG in one or more tables.

An unlabeled graph can be stored in a relational table with two columns, by treating each edge as a row and the two columns representing nodes on either side of the edge. Labels and attributes can be maintained separately in other tables and referred by foreign keys.

Another example for a graph database implemented over relational storage is Periscope/GQ, by the University of Michigan (Tian, 2008). Periscope/GQ implements a graph database as an application over the PostgreSQL relational database engine. The graph database supports labeled graphs that are either directed or undirected. The database uses three relational tables – a "Graphs" table, a "Nodes" table and an "Edges" table to implement the entire database.

While a relational representation of graphs does capture every property of the graph data structure, storing graphs as relational tables is inefficient for large graphs. Even fairly simple traversal algorithms like finding the k-hop neighbors of a given node would require costly self joins on the table making it impractical for managing large graph datasets.

Native Models for Graph Storage

For managing large graphs and/or large collections of graphs, several innovative models of native storage have been proposed. We review some example methods of native graph storage below.

Graph Fingerprinting. GraphGrep (Guigno & Shasha, 2002) is an application independent graph database that manages a collection of undirected, labeled graphs. Here, only nodes are assumed to have labels, while edges are considered unlabeled.

Graph storage in GraphGrep comprises of two elements – label paths and a fingerprint table. A member graph of a GraphGrep database is of the form $G = (V, E, V_L, \delta)$ where V is a set of nodes, E is a set of edges V_L is the set of node labels and $\delta : V \to V_L$ represents label assignment for the nodes. Each node in such a member graph is said to have a unique identifier that distinguishes it from all other nodes.

For such a member graph, two kinds of paths are defined: an *id-path* and a *label-path*. An id-path of length k comprises of a sequence of k node ids such that there exists an edge between any two consecutive node ids. A label-path of length k comprises of a sequence of k node labels, such that there exist at least one id path of length k, where the node ids have the corresponding labels of the label path. A member graph is then represented as a set of label-paths, up to some maximum length (denoted as l_p), where each label-path comprises of a set of id-paths. Label-paths are computed starting from all nodes in the graph up to the maximum length.

Figure 3 shows an example member graph and a computation of label-paths with the corresponding set of id-paths.

Once the label-paths of a member graph are computed, the entire database itself is stored in the form of a table called the fingerprint table. The table lists all label-paths occurring in the database and for each member graph, denotes the number of id-paths that the graph has for the given label-path.

Figure 4 shows an example fingerprint table for a GraphGrep database. This table also serves as an index structure that is used to filter the candidate set of graphs in response to a structural query. A later version of GraphGrep called RelaxGrep (Bonnici et al., 2010) also supports *relaxed graph matching* – that is matching a query graph Q with some of its nodes and edges removed.

Minimum DFS sequence. Another innovative method of storing graphs is to encode them in the form of unique sequences in a way that comparisons related to graph structure can be mostly reduced to string comparisons.

String comparisons are much faster than structure comparisons. As a result, such an encoding can answer structural queries efficiently. The complexity is relegated to the task of reducing a graph to a unique string so that string comparisons are possible. Since this operation is a one-time operation and performed off line, it has no bearing on the query response time. However, such an approach would be suitable primarily for graph databases that are read-only, since any modification to the member graphs will require re-computation of its unique string.

An example of such an approach is gSpan (Yan & Han, 2002), where a member graph is reduced to a unique string that represents a depth-first search (DFS) tree of the graph. The approach is called minimum DFS encoding and is explained below.

Consider a connected, undirected graph as shown in Figure 5. A depth-first search on such a graph starting from a node (v_0 in the example) creates a DFS tree, by traversing the graph in a depth-first manner. The edges that form the DFS tree are called *tree edges* (or *forward edges*) and the rest of the edges of the graph are termed *back edges*.

Figure 3. Label-paths and the corresponding set of id-paths for an example graph

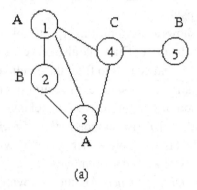

(a)

A = {(1), (3)}
B = {(2), (5)}
C = {(4)}
A–A = {(1,3), (3,1)}
A–B = {(1,2), (3,2)}
A–C = {(1,4), (3,4)}
B–A = {(2,1), (2,3)}
B–C = {(5,4)}
C–A = {(4,1), (4,3)}
C–B = {(4,5)}
A–B–A = {(1,2,3)}

Figure 4. An example fingerprint table for a GraphGrep database

Path	g1	g2	g3	...
A	4	1	3	
B	3	3	5	
-				
AB	2	1	2	
AC	1	0	4	
-				

The classification of edges into tree and back edges are based on the discovery times of the nodes on either side of an edge (Cormen, et al., 2001). For a given node v, let d(v) be the discovery time of node v. Discovery time is a logical time stamp that denotes the time at which the node was first encountered. An edge of the form (u,v) is a tree edge if $d(u) < d(v)$ and is a back edge if $d(u) > d(v)$.

A given graph generates several DFS trees when the process begins from each node separately. Each DFS tree generated is written in the form of a sequence of edges. If $e_1 = (u_1, v_1)$ and $e_2 = (u_2, v_2)$ are both forward edges in the sequence, then e_1 precedes e_2 in the DFS sequence iff $d(v_1) < d(v_2)$. Similarly, if e_1 and e_2 are both

back edges, then e_1 precedes e_2 if either $d(u_1) < d(u_2)$ or $d(u_1) = d(u_2)$ and $d(v_1) < d(v_2)$. If e_1 and e_2 are not the same kind of edge, then e_1 precedes e_2 iff the following holds:

1. e_1 is a back edge, e_2 is a forward edge and $d(u_1) < d(v_2)$
2. e_1 is a forward edge, e_2 is a back edge and $d(v_1) \leq d(u_2)$

The above rules are collectively shown to create a linear ordering over all edges of a DFS tree. Once all DFS trees from a graph are mapped to sequences, the lexicographically smallest DFS sequence is chosen to represent the *canonical labeling* of the graph. It is also shown that isomorphic graphs have the same canonical labeling.

Basis Graph. Storing graphs as path indexes or DFS sequences have several advantages. They can support fast searches based on structural properties of member graphs. However, they are mainly suitable for read-only databases. This is because conversion of graph structures into fingerprints or canonical DFS sequences is a costly operation. This is carried out at graph insertion time, and is a one-time operation. However, if member graphs are modified, then every modification requires re-calculation of the fingerprint or canonical DFS sequence, making such an approach unsuitable for graph databases where member graphs are subject to frequent modifications.

Singh and Srinivasa (Singh & Srinivasa, 2006) propose an alternative approach to graph storage that favors a graph database that is read-write in nature, but which also needs to support structural similarity searches. This model, called "Basis Graph" represents a combined storage and index structure for member graphs in a database supporting labeled, undirected graphs.

In this model, the entire database is represented as a single graph called the Basis Graph. The nodes of the Basis Graph represent all unique node labels that are present in the database. Edges in the Basis Graph represent one or more labeled edges from one or more graphs in the database. The undirected Basis Graph also supports edges from a node to itself. This indicates the presence of edges between two nodes of the same label, somewhere in the database.

Figure 6 schematically shows the basis graph created from two member graphs. Edges of the basis graph are shown in bold and the dashed triangles in the graph depict B+ tree structures that are associated with each node and edge of the basis graph. Every node of the basis graph has an associated B+ tree[8], while every edge connecting distinct labels have two B+ trees associated with them. For edges connecting a node to itself, there is one B+ tree associated with it.

B+ trees are efficient data structures to store, access and delete sorted records. The primary key for the B+ trees associated with node C of the basis graph maintains records of the form (*gid*,

nid, rid). Here, gid is the identifier of a member graph, nid is the identifier of a node in the member graph having label C and rid is the identifier of the record (in a conventional record store) that contains attributes and values associated with the node. The pair gid and nid jointly form the primary key for the records of the B+ tree. Similarly, for a B+ tree associated with an edge of the form C-D of the basis graph, maintains records of the form (*gid, nid1, nid2, rid*), where gid is the graph identifier, and the record represents a C-D edge in the graph between nodes nid1 and nid2. The other B+-tree with this edge stores records of the form (*gid, nid2, nid1, rid*) representing the same edge in the opposite direction. Although this appears redundant, maintaining two B+ trees helps in fast retrieval and structure matching.

Algorithms are proposed over the basis graph for insertion, modification, deletion and query based on gids as well as structural similarity on the member graphs. Even though a B+ tree is an index structure, in this model, it forms part of the database storage system as well, since the member graph structures are not stored elsewhere other than in the basis graph.

Figure 5. A DFS traversal on an undirected graph with tree and back edges

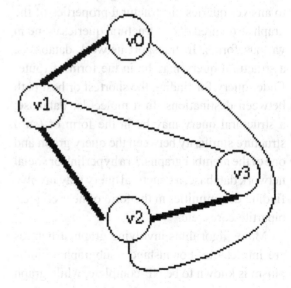

Figure 6. Basis graph for two labeled member graphs

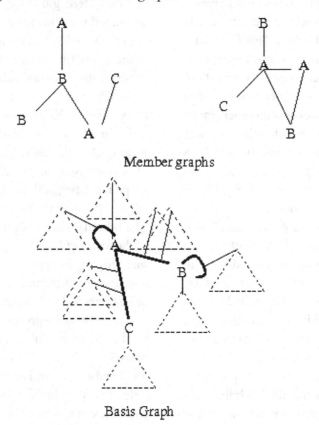

Member graphs

Basis Graph

STRUCTURE INDEXES FOR GRAPH DATABASES

One of the main objectives of graph databases is to answer queries on structural properties of the graph structured data. Structural queries come in various forms. In transport network databases, a structural query may be in the form of route-finder query for finding the shortest or best path between destinations. In a molecular database, a structural query may be in the form of (sub) structure similarity between the query graph and one of the member graphs. In a hyperlink or social network database, a structural query may involve finding communities in the form of near cliques, bipartite cores, etc.

Many algorithms involving graph structures are intractable. For instance, subgraph isomorphism is known to be NP-complete, while graph isomorphism is one of the few problems, which although known to be in NP, it is not known whether it belongs to P or NP-complete[9]. Given that graph databases have to contend with several member graphs, graphs of extremely large sizes and the requirement for an interactive query response time, it is unrealistic to compute exact structural match algorithms at query time.

To address this, a variety of structure indexes have been proposed. The design principle behind a structural index is to extract and index structural properties of member graphs, typically at insertion time, and use this to filter the search space rapidly in response to a query. Optionally, the filtration phase is followed by an exact matching phase in which, precise results are returned. Alternatively, some approaches view graph database queries as *information retrieval* queries, and resort to *ranking* the query results with some confidence measure,

Figure 7. The LWI tree for two labeled member graphs

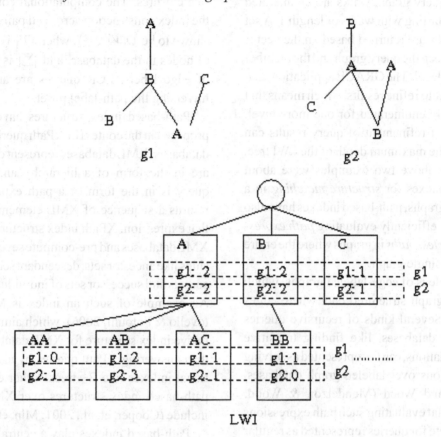

rather than performing exact matches. In any case, the structural index is one of the most important components of a graph database.

Structure indexes can be seen as belonging to one of different indexing paradigms. These are explained in detail below.

Path-Based Index Structures

A path-based structural index extracts paths from member graphs and indexes them in a global data structure. Depending on the nature of the graphs, the extracted paths may be reassembled into a single data structure like a tree, poset or another graph. Path information so extracted, is used to answer queries like shortest-paths and (sub) structure similarity.

The fingerprint table used in GraphGrep (Guigno & Shasha, 2002) can be seen as a path-based

structure index. Here, label paths up to a maximum length are enumerated starting from every node in member graphs and the number of such label paths are recorded in the fingerprint table. This table is used for fast filtering of candidate graphs for structural similarity queries.

The labeled walk index (LWI) of the GRACE graph database (Srinivasa, et. al., 2005) takes a similar approach. All label walks of member graphs are enumerated and organized in the form of a tree. Since GRACE manages only undirected graphs, only the lexicographically smaller label walk is maintained. At each level l in the tree, each member graph is represented as a vector showing the number of label walks of each type of length l.

Figure 7 shows a set of two member graphs and the resultant LWI tree for the graphs. Similar to the fingerprint table of GraphGrep, LWI is used for answering structural similarity queries.

For a given query graph, walks are enumerated in steps of 1 starting with walks of length 1. A set of query results are returned based on the vector distance between the query graph and the member graphs at this level. The GRACE application then allows the user to refine results, which means that label walks are enumerated for one more level. The process of refinement of query results can continue till the maximum depth of the LWI tree.

While the above two examples were about path-based indexes for *structure matching* in a collection of graphs, path-based indexes have also been used for efficiently evaluating *path expressions* and *shortest paths* in graphs where the entire database is a single graph.

An example is of edge-labeled graphs, which are directed-graph structured data where edges have labels. Several kinds of recursive queries on relational databases, like finding transitive closures of relations, can be represented as solving path-expressions over labeled graph databases. Mendelzon and Wood (Mendelzon & Wood, 1995) show that evaluating such path expressions is NP-complete for queries represented as regular expressions over path labels.

Jin, et al (Jin, et. al., 2010) address the issue of answering labeled constraint reachability (LCR) queries in a database represented as a directed, edge-labeled graph. An LCR query takes a set of edge labels A and a pair of nodes u and v, and returns true if there exists a path between u and v whose edge labels are wholly contained in A. In order to answer such queries, a poset is constructed that maintains path-label sets between all pairs of nodes. For any two elements M, N of the path-label poset $M \leq N$, if $M \subseteq N$. The maximal elements of the poset would then contain what are termed "minimal sufficient path-label sets" between the pairs of nodes.

Figure 8 shows a sample graph database and the path-label poset between nodes 0 and 9. The poset is constructed using a dynamic programming approach that is a generalization of the Floyd-Warshall algorithm[10] for shortest paths and transi-

tive closures. The computational complexity of the index construction across all pairs of nodes is shown to be $O(|V|^3 2^{|\Sigma|})$, where $|V|$ is the number of nodes in the database, and $|\Sigma|$ is the number of edge labels. LCR queries are answered by traversing the path-label poset.

Path-based index structures have also been proposed in the context of XPath queries for XML databases. XML databases represent data sets that are in the form of a hierarchy and an XPath query is in the form of a path expression that returns a sequence of XML elements matching that expression. XPath index structures index the XML databases and pre-compute several relationships like ancestor sets, descendant sets, predecessor sets and successor sets of individual elements. An example of such an index is MTree (Pettovello & Fotouhi, 2006), which aims to create a native index structure for XML databases, rather than answering XPath queries by using conventional indexes like B+ trees. Other examples of path-based index structures over XML datasets include (Cooper, et. al., 2001; Min, et. al., 2005).

Path-based indexes play a central role in answering shortest-path and route-finder queries in transportation network datasets. Sanders and Schultes (Sanders & Schultes, 2007) provide a good overview of several indexing approaches to aid in route planning algorithms.

Subgraph-Based Index Structures

The second model of structural index is to extract and index *subgraph structures* from the database. A common strategy here is to use *data mining* techniques to look for frequently occurring subgraphs (sometimes, frequently occurring substructures are also called motifs, in applications like computational proteomics). These motifs are then combined together in a global index structure, which is used to filter candidate graphs in response to a query. Some examples follow.

Figure 8. A sample graph database and path-label poset between nodes 0 and 9

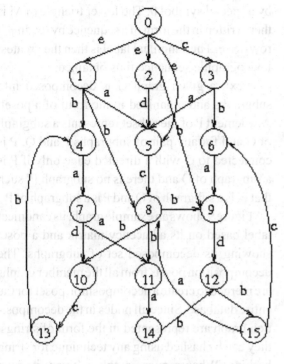

Database graph

{a,b,c,d,e}

[a,b,c,d]   [a,b,c,e]   [b,c,d,e]

[a,b,c]   [b,c,e]

[b,e]

Path–label poset between 0 and 9

Yan et. al., (Yan, et. al., 2004) present a data structure called gIndex for maintaining frequently occurring substructures in a database of labeled, undirected graphs. Member graphs are searched in a breadth-first fashion and all *discriminative fragments* having a minimum support in the database are indexed. A frequently occurring structural fragment x is called "discriminative" if its presence cannot be predicted by the set of all frequently occurring subgraphs of x. In order to facilitate sub-graph isomorphism checks required for extracting frequent subgraphs, the graphs are first encoded into sequences using the canonical DFS encoding developed in their earlier work gSpan (Yan & Han, 2002), and that was introduced in the subsection on storage models for graph databases. Canonical encoding reduces sub-graph isomorphism checks to sequence comparisons. It also facilitates representation of the frequent subgraph index (called gIndex) as a prefix tree

of all canonical sequences of all frequently occurring subgraphs.

He and Singh (He & Singh, 2006) present an index structure called "Closure Tree" for labeled, undirected collection of graphs, that is analogous to R-trees in spatial databases. A closure tree is a structure based index based on the concept of a *graph closure*. A graph closure is defined using a union function over graphs, where the union of two nodes results in a node with attributes and labels as unions of the corresponding sets of attributes and labels. The closure of two graphs is obtained by first establishing a correspondence between the nodes and edges of the two graphs. Where nodes and edges are missing, dummy nodes and edges are created. The best correspondence between graphs is hence a mapping that minimizes the number of dummy nodes and edges. Computing the closure of two graphs gives properties similar to that of the Minimum Bounding Rectangle

(MBR) computation in spatial databases. Closures are then aggregated into a closure tree, forming the structural index. A closure tree is a tree structure whose leaves represent member graphs and internal nodes represent closures. Each internal node is a closure of all its children.

Zhang et. al (Zhang, et. al, 2007), propose an approach based on indexing frequently occurring *tree* structures in a database containing a collection of labeled, undirected graphs. Tree structures are mined from a database with a level-wise edge-increasing graph mining method. The minimum support for frequent trees is a non-decreasing function that increases with the size of the trees being mined. For trees of size 1 (single edges), a minimum support of 1 is used, hence indexing all edges in the graphs. Once tree structures are mined, they are re-written in a canonical form starting from their centers. A node in a graph is said to be its "center" if it has the smallest radius (the longest of the shortest paths from the node to all other nodes). Trees are shown to have either a single center or two centers that are connected by an edge. Using this property, a canonicalization scheme is proposed where each frequent subtree is reduced into a string and stored in a conventional index structure like a trie or a B+ tree. When a query graph Q is provided, it is first partitioned into a set of feature trees that are indexed. A partitioning of a graph Q is a set of subgraphs such that they don't overlap and they collectively cover all nodes of Q. The partitions are then compared against the index structure to retrieve structurally similar member graphs.

Williams et. al (Williams, et al, 2007) present a technique for graph decomposition, where structural features can be extracted from small dense graphs with labeled nodes and edges. First, graphs are represented in a canonical form based on their adjacency matrix. Given a labeled graph G with n nodes, containing node and edge labels, its adjacency matrix M is an n x n matrix where each diagonal element captures the corresponding node label and each off-diagonal element captures

the edge label. The absence of an edge is indicated by a special symbol 0. The lower triangle of M is then written in the form of a sequence by reading it row-wise. The canonical label is then the greatest lexicographic sequence thus obtained.

Next, a given graph G is decomposed into subgraphs and organized in the form of a poset. An element P of the subset represents a subgraph of G and for any pair of subgraphs P and Q, P is connected to Q with a directed edge only if P is a subgraph of Q and there is no subgraph P' such that P' is a subgraph of Q and P is a subgraph of P'.

Figure 9 shows an example graph, its canonical label based on its adjacency matrix and a poset showing its decomposed set of subgraphs. The decomposition posets from all the member graphs are merged to create a decomposition poset for the entire database. Since all nodes in the decomposition graph are represented in the form of strings, they can be hashed using any technique for string hashing. When a query graph is given, its own decomposition matrix is created and the hash of each of the nodes of its decomposition poset are computed. If the top element of this poset matches a maximal element in the decomposition poset of the database, it means that the query graph is isomorphic to a member graph. If it matches an internal element of the database poset, then it means that the query graph is a subgraph of a member graph. Maximal common subgraphs between a given query graph and one or more of the member graphs can also be computed using the decomposition poset.

Spectral Methods for Indexing

Spectral methods for indexing graph databases employ concepts from spectral graph theory, where features of member graph(s) are represented as *vectors in a hypothetical space*. Optionally, multi-dimensional index structures may be used to efficiently search this space for answering structural queries.

Figure 9. An example graph, its canonical label and decomposition poset

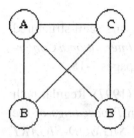

A1B11B111C

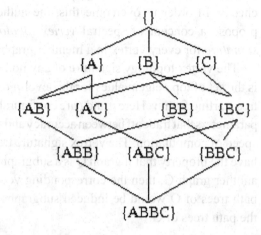

Shokoufandeh et. al (Shokoufandeh et al, 2005) present a spectral indexing method for indexing a database of hierarchical structures represented in the form of directed acyclic graphs (DAGs). The proposed technique is aimed at managing databases of image representations, but could easily be applied to databases of DAGs in other domains as well.

Member DAGs in the database are represented in the form of adjacency matrices whose elements take on values from {-1, 0 1} representing a back edge, no edge and a forward edge respectively. Hence a DAG over *n* nodes becomes an anti-symmetric $n \times n$ matrix. Given a member graph G, its *spectrum* $\Gamma(G)$ is defined as a vector comprising of the magnitudes of all its eigenvalues placed in non-ascending order.

The spectrum hence becomes the feature vector of a member graph. The spectrum of a DAG can also be used to match graphs with distortions, where distortions represent a set of edits (addition, deletion and modification of nodes and edges) from the original graph. If $A^{m \times m}$ represents a DAG, and if it is distorted to another DAG of the form $H^{n \times n}$ by the addition of n-m new nodes, the transformation $\psi : A \rightarrow H$ is called the *lifting operator*. A lifting operator is said to be spectrum preserving, if A and $\psi(A)$ have the same set of non-zero eigenvalues. The authors also show that

any arbitrary lifting operator can be represented as the sum of a spectrum preserving lifting operator and the addition of a noise matrix.

The spectrum of member graphs in the database are thus computed and stored in an index structure representing a multi-dimensional space. Similarity match is computed by performing a k nearest neighbor (kNN) search in the index space.

Zou et. al (Zou, et al, 2008) propose a spectral method for graph indexing based on computing the eigenvalues of member graphs. Given a simple, undirected graph G, a theorem called the Interlacing Theorem in Graph Theory, relates the eigenvalues of G and any *induced subgraph* H of G. An induced subgraph of a graph G is made of a subset of all the vertices of G and any edges among them. Given a graph G with n eigen values $\lambda_1, \ldots, \lambda_n$ sorted in descending order and an induced subgraph H of G with m eigen values $\beta_1, \ldots, \beta_n$ sorted in descending order, the interlacing theorem states that $\lambda_{n-m+i} \leq \beta_i \leq \lambda_i$ for $i = 1 \ldots m$.

However, any arbitrary subgraph of a given graph G, may not correspond to the induced subgraph having the same set of nodes from G. This is because an induced subgraph is expected to have all edges between its nodes that are present in the original graph G. Hence the interlacing theorem cannot be directly used for subgraph isomorphism checks. In order to overcome this, the authors propose a concept of spectral *vertex topology signature* for every vertex in a member graph.

The vertex topology signature of any node *v*, is the set of top *t* eigenvalues for the level-*n* path tree starting from *v*. Here *n* and *t* are configurable parameters that tradeoff between accuracy and the speed of computation. The vertex signature trees have the property that if graph Q is a subgraph of another graph G, then the corresponding vertex path trees of Q would be induced subgraphs of the path trees of G.

CONCLUSION

The objective of this chapter was to provide an overview of the main challenges in designing graph databases. To this end, three specific challenges were chosen – data models, storage models and index structures. Some representative approaches from the literature were also introduced for each of the above challenges.

As is apparent, graph data management has attracted immense research attention, but has still eluded strong foundations or an overarching best practice or design principles. Research and commercial interest in graph databases is still strong as of this writing. One of the first international workshops dedicated to graph databases was held on July 15th 2010[11] in China. Similarly, neo4j which claims to be the first industry-grade, commercial graph database was released in 2009.

As the amount of data grows and the need for identifying patterns and extracting semantics becomes stronger, graph data management becomes an imminent challenge. Much of the research efforts introduced in this chapter go a long way in addressing such challenges.

REFERENCES

Abiteboul, S. (1997). Querying semi-structured data. *Proceedings of the 6th International Conference on Database Theory*, pages 1-18.

Abiteboul, S., & Vianu, V. (1997). Regular path queries with constraints. In *Proceedings of the Sixteenth ACM SIGACT-SIGMOD-SIGART Symposium on Principles of Database Systems, Tucson, Arizona, United States (PODS '97)* (pp. 122-133). New York, NY: ACM Publishing.

Angles, R., & Gutierrez, C. (2008). Survey of graph database models. *ACM Computing Surveys*, *40*(1), 1–39. doi:10.1145/1322432.1322433

Bertino, E., Elmagarmid, A. K., & Hacid, M.-S. (2003). Ordering and path constraints over semistructured data. *Journal of Intelligent Information Systems*, *20*(2), 181–206. doi:10.1023/A:1021880119937

Bonnici, V., Giugno, R., Pulvirenti, A., Ferro, A., & Shasha, D. (2010). RelaxGrep: Approximate graph searching by query relaxation. *Supplementary Proceedings of Pattern Recognition in Bioinformatics. 5th IAPR International Conference, PRIB 2010*, Nijmegen, The Netherlands.

Borgelt, C., & Berthold, M. R. (2002). Mining molecular fragments: Finding relevant substructures of molecules. In *Proceedings of the 2002 IEEE International Conference on Data Mining (December 09-12, 2002), ICDM*. IEEE Computer Society, Washington DC, USA, 51.

Brandes, U., & Erlebach, T. (Eds.). (2005). *Network analysis: Methodological foundations (outcome of a Dagstuhl seminar, April, 2004)* (LNCS 3418). Springer 2005.

Buneman, P., Fan, W., & Weinstein, S. (1998). Path constraints on semi-structured and structured data. In *Proceedings of the Seventeenth ACM SIGACT-SIGMOD-SIGART Symposium on Principles of Database Systems (PODS '98, Seattle, Washington, United States)* (pp. 129 - 138). New York, NY: ACM.

Chang, N. S., & Fu, K. S. (1980). A relational database system for images. *Pictorial Information Systems.* [Springer.]. *Lecture Notes in Computer Science,* 80.

Codd, E., F. (1983). A relational model of data for large shared data banks. *Communications of the ACM, 26*(1), 64–69. doi:10.1145/357980.358007

Colinge J., Bennett K., L. (2007). Introduction to computational proteomics. *PLoS Computational Biolology, 3*(7), e114. doi:10.1371/journal.pcbi.0030114.

Consens, M., & Mendelzon, A. (1993). Hy+: A hygraph-based query and visualization system. *SIGMOD Record, 22*(2), 511–516. doi:10.1145/170036.171537

Cooper, B., Sample, N., Franklin, M. J., Hjaltason, G. R., & Shadmon, M. (2001). A fast index for semistructured data. In *Proceedings of the 27th International Conference on Very Large Data Bases* (September 11 - 14, 2001). In P. M. Apers, P. Atzeni, S. Ceri, S. Paraboschi, K. Ramamohanarao, & R. T. Snodgrass (Eds.). Very large data bases (341-350). San Francisco, CA: Morgan Kaufmann Publishers.

Cormen, T. H., Leiserson, C. E., Rivest, R. L., & Stein, C. (2001). *Introduction to algorithms, 22*(3), pp. 540 – 549, second edition. Depth-first search. Cambridge, MA: MIT Press and New York, NY: McGraw-Hill.

Gemis, M., Paredaens, J., Thyssens, I., & van den Bussche, J. (1993). GOOD: A graph-oriented object database system. *SIGMOD Record, 22,* 505–510. doi:10.1145/170036.171533

Giugno, R., & Shasha, D. (2002). GraphGrep: A fast and universal method for querying graphs. In *Proceedings of the International Conference in Pattern recognition (ICPR)*, Quebec, Canada.

Graves, M., Bergeman, E. R., & Lawrence, C. B. (1995). A graph-theoretic data model for genome mapping databases. In *28th Annual Hawaii International Conference on System Sciences (HICCS'95)*.

Güting, R. H. (1994). GraphDB: Modeling and querying graphs in databases. *Proceedings of the 20th International Conference on Very Large Databases (VLDB '94)*, pages 297—308.

He, H., & Singh, A. (2006). Closure-Tree: An index structure for graph queries. *Proceedings of the 22nd International Conference on Data Engineering, (ICDE '06)*, IEEE Computer Society Press.

Hidders, J., & Paredaens, J. (1993). *GOAL: A graph-based object and association language. Advances in database systems: Implementations and applications* (pp. 247–265). CISM.

Jin, R., Hong, H., Wang, H., Ruan, N., & Xiang, Y. (2010). Computing label-constraint reachability in graph databases. In *Proceedings of the 2010 International Conference on Management of Data (SIGMOD '10)* (pp. 123 - 134). New York, NY: ACM.

Jonyer, I., Holder, L. B., & Cook, D. J. (2000). Graph-based hierarchical conceptual clustering in structural databases'. In the *Proceedings of the Seventeenth National Conference on Artificial Intelligence*.

Kim, D. H., Yun, I. D., & Lee, S. U. (2010). Attributed relational graph matching based on the nested assignment structure. *Pattern Recognition, 43*(3), 914–928. doi:10.1016/j.patcog.2009.09.012

Kim, W. (1990). *Introduction to object-oriented databases*. Cambridge, MA: The MIT Press.

Kobayashi, K. (1994). On the spatial graph. *Kodai Math. Journal, 17*(3), 511–517. doi:10.2996/kmj/1138040046

Kumar, S., & Srinivasa, S. (2003). A database for storage and fast retrieval of structure data: A demonstration. In *Proceedings of the 19th International Conference on Data Engineering (ICDE'03)*.

Kuper, G. M., & Vardi, M. Y. (1984). A new approach to database logic. In *Proceedings of the 3rd ACM SIGACT-SIGMOD Symposium on Principles of Database Systems,* Waterloo, Ontario, Canada *(PODS '84) (pp. 86-96)*. New York, NY: ACM.

Levene, M., & Loizou, G. (1995). A graph-based data model and its ramifications. [TKDE]. *IEEE Transactions on Knowledge and Data Engineering, 7*(5), 809–823. doi:10.1109/69.469818

Levene, M., & Poulovassilis, A. (1990). The hypernode model and its associated query language. In *Proceddings of the 5th Jerusalem Conference on Information Technology* (520 – 530). IEEE Computer Society Press.

Levene, M., & Poulovassilis, A. (1991). An object-oriented data model formalised through hypergraphs. [DKE]. *Data & Knowledge Engineering, 6*(3), 205–224. doi:10.1016/0169-023X(91)90005-I

Martínez-Bazan, N., Muntés-Mulero, V., Gómez-Villamor, S., Nin, J., Sánchez-Martínez, M., & Larriba-Pey, J. (2007). Dex: High-performance exploration on large graphs for information retrieval. In *Proceedings of the Sixteenth ACM Conference on Conference on information and Knowledge Management,* Lisbon, Portugal (CIKM '07) (573-582). New York, NY: ACM.

Mendelzon, A. O., & Wood, P. T. (1995). Finding regular simple paths in graph databases. *SIAM Journal on Computing, 24*(6). doi:10.1137/S009753979122370X

Min, J., Chung, C., & Shim, K. (2005, Sep.). An adaptive path index for XML data using the query workload. *Information Systems, 30*(6), 467–487. doi:10.1016/j.is.2004.04.003

Mylopoulos, J., Borgida, A., Jarke, M., & Koubarakis, M. (1990). Telos: Representing knowledge about Information Systems. [TOIS]. *ACM Transactions on Information Systems, 8*(4), 325–362. doi:10.1145/102675.102676

Pettovello, P. M., & Fotouhi, F. (2006). MTree: An XML XPath graph index. In *Proceedings of the 2006 ACM Symposium on Applied Computing,* Dijon, France, (SAC '06) (pp. 474 – 481). New York, NY: ACM.

Sakr, S., & Al-Naymat, G. (2010). Graph indexing and querying: A review. *International Journal of Web Information Systems, 6*(2), 101–120. doi:10.1108/17440081011053104

Sanders, P., & Schultes, D. (2007). Engineering fast route planning algorithms. In *6th Workshop on Experimental Algorithms (WEA)*, Springer (LNCS 4525, pp. 23-36).

Sanfeliu, A., & Fu, K. S. (1983). A distance measure between attributed relational graphs for pattern recognition. *IEEE Transactions on Systems, Man, and Cybernetics, 13*, 353–363.

Shasha, D., Wang, J. T.-L., & Giugno, R. (2002). Algorithmics and applications of tree and graph searching. In *Proceedings of the ACM Symposium on Principles of Database Systems (PODS)*, Madison, Wisconsin.

Shokoufandeh, A., Macrini, D., Dickinson, S., Siddiqi, K., & Zucker, S. W. (2005). Indexing hierarchical structures using graph spectra. *IEEE Transactions on Pattern Analysis and Machine Intelligence, 27*(7), 1125–1140. doi:10.1109/TPAMI.2005.142

Singh, M. H., & Srinivasa, S. (2006). BasisGraph: Combining storage and structure index for similarity search in graph databases. *Proceedings of the 13th International Conference on Management of Data (COMAD '06)*, New Delhi, India.

Srinivasa, S., Acharya, S., Agrawal, H., & Khare, R. (2002). Vectorization of structure to index graph databases. *Proceedings of IASTED Int'l Conf. on Information Systems and Databases (ISDB '02)*, Tokyo, Japan. Calgary, Canada: Acta Press.

Srinivasa, S., Maier, M., & Mutalikdesai, M. (2005). LWI and Safari: A new index structure and query model for graph databases, *COMAD 2005*, Goa, India.

Srinivasa, S., & Singh, M. H. (2005). GRACE: A graph database system. *COMAD 2005b*, Hyderabad, India.

Chandola, V., Banerjee, A., & Vipin Kumar. 2009. Anomaly detection:Survey, A.. *ACM Computing Surveys*, *41*(3).

Taylor, R. W., & Frank, R. L. (1976). CODASYL Data-base Management Systems. *ACM Computing Surveys*, *8*(1), 67–103. doi:10.1145/356662.356666

Tian, Y. (2008). *Querying graph databases*. PhD Thesis, The University of Michigan.

Topaloglou, T. (1993). Storage management for knowledge bases. In B. Bhargava, T. Finin, & Y. Yesha (Eds.), *Proceedings of the Second international Conference on information and Knowledge Management (CIKM '93)*, Washington D. C., United States (95 - 104). New York, NY: ACM.

Tsai, W. H., & Fu, K. S. (1979). Error-correcting isomorphisms of attributed relational graphs for pattern analysis. *IEEE Transactions on Systems, Man, and Cybernetics*, *9*, 757–768. doi:10.1109/TSMC.1979.4310127

Williams, D., Huan, J., & Wang, W. (2007). Graph database indexing using structured graph decomposition. In *Proceedings of the 23rd IEEE International Conference on Data Engineering (ICDE)*.

Yan, X., & Han, J. (2002). gSpan: Graph-based substructure pattern mining. In *Proceedings of ICDM, 2002*, 721–724.

Yan, X., Yu, P. S., & Han, J. (2004). Graph indexing: A frequent structure-based approach. In *Proceedings of the 2004 ACM SIGMOD International Conference on Management of Data (SIGMOD '04)*, Paris, France (pp. 335 – 346). New York, NY: ACM.

Zhang, S., Hu, M., & Yang, J. (2007). TreePi: A novel graph indexing method. *Proceedings of IEEE International Conference on Data Engineering (ICDE)*, 966-975.

Zou, L., Chen, L., Yu, J. X., & Lu, Y. (2008) A novel spectral coding in a large graph database. In *Proceedings of the 11th international conference on Extending database technology: Advances in database technology (EDBT '08)* (pp. 181 – 192). New York, NY, USA: ACM.

ENDNOTES

[1] CouchDB Technical Overview. http://couchdb.apache.org/docs/overview.html

[2] Wikipedia page for MapReduce. http://en.wikipedia.org/wiki/MapReduce

[3] Cassandra home page. http://cassandra.apache.org/

[4] Neo4j website. http://neo4j.org/

[5] NAR database summary. http://www.oxfordjournals.org/nar/database/a/

[6] Resource Description Framework (RDF). http://www.w3.org/RDF/

[7] Neo4j Technical Introduction. http://dist.neo4j.org/neo-technology-introduction.pdf

[8]   Wikipedia page for B+ tree. http://en.wikipedia.org/wiki/B%2B_tree

[9]   Wikipedia page on Graph Isomorphism Problem. http://en.wikipedia.org/wiki/Graph_isomorphism_problem

[10]   Wikipedia page on the Floyd-Warshall algorithm http://en.wikipedia.org/wiki/Floyd%E2%80%93Warshall_algorithm

[11]   First International Workshop on Graph Databases (WGD 2010) home page http://www.icst.pku.edu.cn/IWGD2010/index.html

Chapter 4
An Overview of Graph Indexing and Querying Techniques

Sherif Sakr
University of New South Wales, Australia

Ghazi Al-Naymat
University of Tabuk, Saudi Arabia

ABSTRACT

Recently, there has been a lot of interest in the application of graphs in different domains. Graphs have been widely used for data modeling in different application domains such as: chemical compounds, protein networks, social networks and Semantic Web. Given a query graph, the task of retrieving related graphs as a result of the query from a large graph database is a key issue in any graph-based application. This has raised a crucial need for efficient graph indexing and querying techniques. In this chapter, we provide an overview of different techniques for indexing and querying graph databases. An overview of several proposals of graph query language is also given. Finally, we provide a set of guidelines for future research directions.

INTRODUCTION

The field of graph databases and graph query processing has received a lot of attention due to the constantly increasing usage of graph data structure for representing data in different domains such as: chemical compounds (Klinger & Austin, 2005), multimedia databases (Lee et al., 2005), social networks (Cai et al., 2005), protein networks (Huan et al., 2004) and semantic web (Manola & Miller, 2004). To effectively understand and utilize any collection of graphs, a graph database that efficiently supports elementary querying mechanisms is crucially required. Hence, determining graph database members which constitute the answer set of a graph query q from a large graph database

DOI: 10.4018/978-1-61350-053-8.ch004

is a key performance issue in all graph-based applications. A primary challenge in computing the answers of graph queries is that pair-wise comparisons of graphs are usually really hard problems. For example, subgraph isomorphism is known to be NP-complete (Garey & Johnson, 1979). A naive approach to compute the answer set of a graph query q is to perform a sequential scan on the graph database and to check whether each graph database member satisfies the conditions of q or not. However, the graph database can be very large which makes the sequential scan over the database impracticable. Thus, finding an efficient search technique is immensely important due to the combined costs of pair-wise comparisons and the increasing size of modern graph databases. It is apparent that the success of any graph database application is directly dependent on the efficiency of the graph indexing and query processing mechanisms. Recently, there are many techniques that have been proposed to tackle these problems. This chapter gives an overview of different techniques of indexing and querying graph databases and classifies them according to their target graph query types and their indexing strategy.

The rest of the chapter is organized as follows. The Preliminary section introduces preliminaries of graph databases and graph query processing. In Section (Subgraph Query Processing), a classification of the approaches of subgraph query processing problem and their index structures is given while the section (Supergraph Query Processing) focuses on the approaches for resolving the supergraph query processing problem. Section (Graph Similarity Queries) discusses the approach of approximate graph matching queries. Section (Graph Query Languages) gives an overview of several proposals of graph query languages. Finally, Section (Discussion and Conclusions) concludes the chapter and provides some suggestions for possible future research directions on the subject.

PRELIMINARIES

In this section, we introduce the basic terminologies used in this chapter and give the formal definition of graph querying problems.

Graph Data Structure

Graphs are very powerful modeling tool. They are used to model complicated structures and schemeless data. In graph data structures, *vertices* and edges represent the *entities* and the relationships between them respectively. The attributes associated with these entities and relationships are called labels. A graph database D is defined as a collection of member graphs $D = \{g_1, g_2, \ldots, g_n\}$ where each member graph database member g_i is denoted as $(V, E, L_v, L_e, F_v, F_e)$ where V is the set of vertices; $E \subseteq V * V$ is the set of edges joining two distinct vertices; L_v is the set of vertex labels; L_e is the set of edge labels; F_v is a function $V \rightarrow L_v$ that assigns labels to vertices and F_e is a function $E \rightarrow L_e$ that assigns labels to edges. In general, graph data structures can be classified according to the direction of their edges into two main classes:

- *Directed-labeled graphs*: such as XML, RDF and traffic networks.
- *Undirected-labeled graphs*: such as social networks and chemical compounds.

In principle, there are two main types of graph databases. The first type consists of few numbers of very large graphs such as the Web graph and social networks (*non-transactional graph databases*). The second type consists of a large set of small graphs such as chemical compounds and biological pathways (*transactional graph databases*). The main focus of this chapter is on giving an overview of the efficient indexing and querying mechanisms on the second type of graph databases.

Graph Queries

In principle, queries in transactional graph databases can be broadly classified into the following main categories:

1. **Subgraph queries:** this category searches for a specific pattern in the graph database. The pattern can be either a small graph or a graph where some parts of it are uncertain, e.g., vertices with wildcard labels. Therefore, given a graph database $D = \{g_1, g_2, ..., g_n\}$ and a subgraph query q, the query answer set $A = \{g_i \mid q \subseteq g_i, g_i \in D\}$. A graph q is described as a subgraph of another graph database member gi if the set of vertices and edges of q form subset of the vertices and edges of g_i. To be more formal, let us assume that we have two graphs $g_1(V_1, E_1, L_{v1}, L_{e1}, F_{v1}, F_{e1})$ and $g_2(V_1, E_2, L_{v2}, L_{e2}, F_{v2}, F_{e2})$, g_1 is defined as subgraph of g_2, if and only if:

    ○   For every distinct vertex $x \in V_1$ with a label $v_l \in L_{v1}$, there is a distinct vertex $y \in V_2$ with a label $v_l \in L_{v2}$.

    ○   For every distinct edge edge $ab \in E_1$ with a label $e_l \in L_{e1}$, there is a distinct edge $ab \in E_2$ with a label $e_l \in L_{e2}$.

    Figure 1(a) illustrates the subgraph search problem. Figure 2(a) shows an example of a graph database. Figure 2(b) illustrates examples of graph queries (q_1 and q_2). Let us assume that these queries are subgraph queries. If we evaluate these queries over the sample graph database (Figure 2(a)) then the answer set of q_1 will consist of the graph database members g_1 and g_2 while the

answer set of q_2 will be empty. The more general type of the subgraph search problem is the *subgraph isomorphism* search problem, which is defined as follows. Let $g_1(V_1, E_1, L_{v1}, L_{e1}, F_{v1}, F_{e1})$ and $g_1(V_2, E_2, L_{v2}, L_{e2}, F_{v2}, F_{e2})$ be two graphs, g_1 is defined as a graph isomorphism to g_2, if and only if there exists at least one bijective function $f : V_1 \rightarrow V_2$ such that: 1) for any edge $uv \in E_1$, 2) there is an edge $f(u)f(v) \in E_2$ 2)$F_{v1}(u) = F_{v2}(f(u))$ and $F_{v1}(v) = F_{v2}(f(v))$. 3) $F_{e1}(uv) = F_{e2}(f(u)f(v))$.

2. **Supergraph queries:** searches for the graph database members of which their whole structures are *contained* in the input query. Therefore, given a graph database $D = \{g_1, g_2, ..., g_n\}$ and a supergraph query q, the query answer set $A = \{g_i \mid q \supseteq g_v, g_i \in D\}$. Figure 1(b) illustrates the subgraph search problem. Let us assume that the graph queries of Figure 2(b) are supergraph queries.

    If we evaluate these queries over the sample graph database (Figure 2(a)) then the answer set of q_1 will be empty while the answer set of q_2 will contain the graph database member g_3.

3. **Similarity (Approximate Matching) queries:** this category finds graphs which are *similar*, but not necessarily isomorphic to a given query graph. Given a graph database $D = \{g_1, g_2, ..., g_n\}$ and a query graph q, similarity search is to discover all graphs that are approximately similar to the graph query q. A key question in graph similarity queries is how to measure the similarity between a target graph member of the database and the query graph. In fact, it is difficult to give a precise definition of graph similarity. Different approaches have proposed

Figure 1. Graph database querying: (a) Subgraph search problem, (b) Supergraph search problem

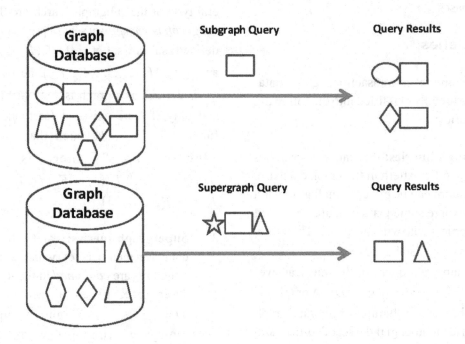

Figure 2. An example graph database and graph queries: (a) Sample graph database, (b) Graph queries

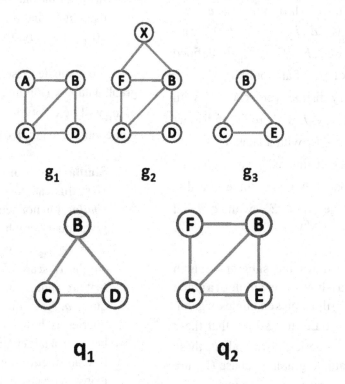

different similarity metrics for graph data structures (Bunke & Shearer, 1998; Fernandez & Valiente, 2001; Raymond et al., 2002). Discussing these different similarity metrics is out of the scope of this chapter. We refer the interested reader to a detailed survey in (Gao et al., 2009).

SUBGRAPH QUERY PROCESSING

There are many graph indexing techniques that have been recently proposed to deal with the problem of subgraph query processing (Sakr, 2009; Yan et al., 2004; Zhang et al., 2007; Zhao et al., 2007). Subgraph query processing techniques can be divided into the following two approaches:

- **Non Mining-Based Graph Indexing Techniques:** The techniques of this approach focus on indexing the whole constructs of the graph database instead of indexing only some selected features (Giugno & Shasha, 2002; He & Singh, 2006; Jiang et al., 2007; Sakr, 2009; Williams et al., 2007). The main criticisms of these approaches are that: 1) they can be less effective in their pruning power; 2) they may need to conduct expensive structure comparisons in the filtering process and thus degrades the filtering efficiency. Therefore, these techniques need to employ efficient filtering and pruning mechanisms to overcome these limitations. However, The techniques of this approach have a clear advantage in that they can handle the graph updates with less cost as they do not rely on the effectiveness of the selected features and they do not need to rebuild their whole indexes.
- **Mining-Based Graph Indexing Techniques:** The techniques of this approach apply graph-mining methods (Kuramochi & Karypis, 2001, 2004; Wang

et al., 2004; Washio & Motoda, 2003; Yan & Han, 2002, 2003) to extract some features (sub-structures) from the graph database members (Cheng et al., 2007; Yan et al., 2004; Zhang et al., 2007; Zhao et al., 2007). An inverted index is created for each feature. Answering a subgraph query q is achieved through two steps:

1. Identifying the set of features of the subgraph query.
2. Using the inverted index to retrieve all graphs that contain the same features of q.

The rationale behind this type of query processing techniques is that if some features of graph q do not exist in a data graph G, then G cannot contain q as its subgraph (inclusion logic). Formally, Clearly, the effectiveness of these filtering methods depends on the quality of mining techniques to effectively identify the set of *features*. Therefore, important decisions need to be made about: the indexing feature, the number and the size of indexing features. These decisions crucially affect the cost of the mining process and the pruning power of the indexing mechanism. A main limitation of these approaches is that the quality of the selected features may degrade over time after lots of insertions and deletions. In this case, the set of features in the whole updated graph database need to be re-identified and the index needs to be re-build from scratch. It should be noted that, achieving these tasks is quite time consuming.

Non Mining-Based Graph Indexing Techniques

GraphGrep. The *GraphGrep* (Giugno & Shasha, 2002) index structure uses enumerated paths as index features to filter unmatched graphs. For each graph database member, it enumerates all paths up to a certain maximum length and records the number of occurrences of each path. Hence, in this index table, each row stands for a path and each column stands for a graph. Each entry in the table is the number of occurrences of the path in the graph. In the query processing, the path indexes is used to find a set of candidate graphs which contains paths in the query structure and to check if the counts of such paths are beyond the threshold specified in the query. In the verification step, each candidate graph is examined by subgraph isomorphism to obtain the final results. The main strength of this approach is that the indexing process of paths with limited lengths is usually fast. However, the size of the indexed paths could drastically increase with the size of graph database. In addition, the filtering power of paths data structure is limited. Therefore, the verification cost can be very high due to the large size of the candidate set.

GDIndex. Williams et al. (2007) have presented an approach for graph database indexing using a structured graph decomposition named GDIndex. In this approach, all connected and induced subgraphs of a given graph are enumerated. Therefore, a graph of size n is decomposed into at most 2^n subgraphs when each of the vertices has a unique label. However, due to isomor-

phism between enumerated graphs, a complete graph with multiple occurrences of the same label may decompose into fewer subgraphs. If all labels are identical, a complete graph of size n is decomposed into just $n + 1$ subgraphs. A directed acyclic graph (DAG) is constructed to model the decomposed graphs and the contained relationships between them. In this DAG, there is always one node that represents the whole graph G, and one node that represents the null graph. The children of a node P are all graphs Q where there is a directed link in the DAG between P and Q. Moreover, the descendants of a node P are all nodes that are reachable from P in the DAG. Figure 3 depicts a sample of graph decomposition using the GDIndex approach.

A hash table is used to index the subgraphs enumerated during the decomposition process. The hash key of each subgraph is determined from the string value given by the canonical code of the subgraph. This canonical code is computed from its adjacency matrix. In this way, all isomorphic graphs produce the same hash key. Since all entries in the hash table are in canonical form, only one entry is made for each unique canonical

Figure 3. Sample graph decomposition

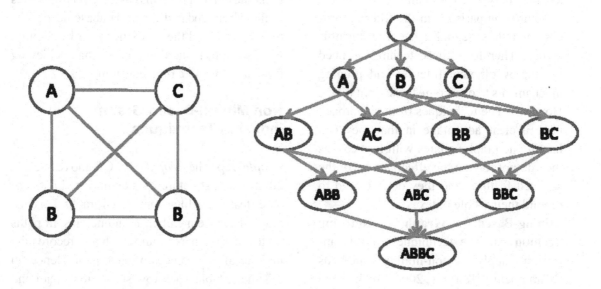

code. This hash table enables the search function to quickly locate any node in the decomposition DAG, which is isomorphic to a query graph, if it exists. Therefore, in the query-processing step, the hash key of the graph query q is computed from the query's canonical code. This computed hash value of the graph query is then used to identify and verify the set of queries that matches the canonical codes of the graph query. A clear advantage of the GDIndex approach is that no candidate verification is required. However, the index is designed for databases that consist of relatively smaller graphs and do not have a large number of distinct graphs.

GString. The *GString* approach (Jiang et al., 2007) considers the semantics of the graph structures in the database. It focuses on modeling graph objects in the context of organic chemistry using basic structures (*Line*, *Star* and *Cycle*) that have semantic meaning and use them as indexing features. *Line* structure denotes a structure consisting of a series of vertices connected end to end, *Cycle* structure denotes a structure consisting of a series of vertices that form a close loop and *Star* structure denotes a structure where a core vertex directly connects to several vertexes. For a graph g, GString first extracts all Cycle structures, then it extracts all Star structures, and finally, it identifies the remaining structures as Line structures. Figure 4

represents a sample graph representation using the GString basic structures. GString represents both graphs and queries on graphs as string sequences and transforms the subgraph search problem to the subsequence string-matching domain.

A suffix tree-based index structure for the string representations is then created to support an efficient string matching process. Given a basic structure, its GString has three components: *type*, *size*, and a set of annotations (*edits*). For Line or Cycle, the size is the number of vertices in the structure. For Star, the size indicates the fanout of the central vertex. For a query graph q, GString derives its summary string representation which is then matched against the suffix-tree of the graph database. An element of a summary string matches a node in the suffix-tree if their types match, sizes are equal or the size in the query is no more than the size in the node and the counts of corresponding types of edits in the query are no larger than those in the node. A key disadvantage of the GString approach is that converting subgraph search queries into a string matching problem could be an inefficient approach especially if the size of the graph database or the subgraph query is large. Additionally, GString focuses on decomposing chemical compounds into basic structures that have semantic meaning in the context of organic chemistry and it is not trivial

Figure 4. Sample graph representation using GString basic structures

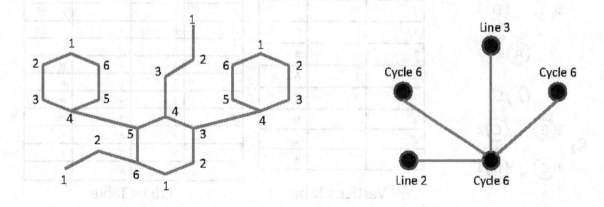

to extend this approach in other domain of applications.

GraphREL. Sakr (2009) has presented a purely relational framework for processing graph queries named GraphREL. In this approach, the graph data set is encoded using an intuitive Vertex-Edge relational mapping scheme ((Figure 5) and the graph query is translated into a sequence of SQL evaluation steps over the defined storage scheme. An obvious problem in the relational-based evaluation approach of graph queries is the huge cost which may result from the large number of join operations which are required to be performed between the encoding relations. Several relational query optimization techniques have been exploited to speed up the search efficiency in the context of graph queries. The main optimization technique of GraphREL is based on the observation that the size of the intermediate results dramatically affects the overall evaluation performance of SQL scripts (Teubner et al., 2008). Therefore, GraphREL keeps statistical information about the less frequently existing nodes and edges in the graph database in the form of simple Markov Tables.

For a graph query q, the maintained statistical information is used to identify the highest pruning point on its structure (nodes or edges with very low frequency) to firstly filter out, as many as possible, of the false positives graphs that are guaranteed to not exist in the final results first before passing the candidate result set to an optional verification process. This statistical information is also used to influence the decision of relational query optimizers by selectivity annotations of the translated query predicates to make the right decision regarding the selection of most efficient join order and the cheapest execution plan (Bruno et al., 2009).

Based on the fact that the number of distinct vertices and edges labels are usually far less than the number of vertices and edges in graph databases, GraphREL utilizes the powerful partitioned B-trees indexing mechanism of the relational databases to reduce the access costs of the secondary storage to a minimum. GraphREL applies an optional verification process only if more than one vertex of the set of query vertices has the same label. For large graph queries, GraphREL

Figure 5. Sample GraphREL encoding of graph databases

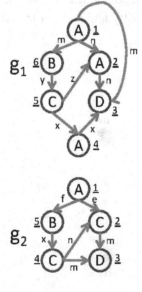

graphID	vertexID	vLabel
1	1	A
1	2	A
1	3	D
1	4	A
1	5	C
1	6	B
2	1	A
2	2	C
2	3	D
2	4	C
2	5	B

Vertices Table

graphID	sVertex	dVertex	eLabel
1	1	2	n
1	1	3	m
1	2	3	n
1	4	3	x
1	5	4	x
1	6	5	y
1	5	2	z
1	1	6	m
2	1	2	e
2	2	3	m
2	4	3	m
2	4	2	n
2	5	4	x
2	1	5	f

Edges Table

applies a decomposition mechanism to divide the large and complex SQL translation query into a sequence of intermediate queries (using temporary tables) before evaluating the final results. This decomposition mechanism reuses the statistical summary information an effective selectivity-aware decomposition process and reduces the size of the intermediate result of each step.

Mining-Based Graph Indexing Techniques

Graph-Based Mining. The *GIndex* technique (Yan et al., 2004) is the first work that used pattern-mining techniques to index graph databases. It makes use of frequent subgraphs as the basic indexing unit. The main observation of this approach is that graph-based index can significantly improve query performance over a path-based one due to the high pruning power of graph data structures. However, the limitation of using subgraphs as the indexing unit is that the number of graph structures is usually much larger than the number of paths in a graph database. To deal with this problem, GIndex considers only frequent subgraphs. Therefore, in order to avoid the exponential growth of the number of frequent subgraphs, the support threshold is progressively increased when the subgraphs grow large. Any subgraph is considered as being frequent if its support is greater than a minimum support threshold. GIndex uses low support for small subgraphs and high support for large subgraphs. Given a query graph q, if q is a frequent subgraph, the exact set of query answers containing q can be retrieved directly without performing any candidate verification since q is indexed. Otherwise, q probably has a frequent subgraph f whose support maybe close to the support threshold. A candidate answer set of query q is then retrieved and verified. If the query graph q is infrequent that means this subgraph is only contained in a small number of graphs in the database. Therefore, the number of subgraph isomorphism tests is going to be small.

Among similar fragments with the same support, GIndex only index the smallest common fragment since more query graphs may contain the smallest fragment. Therefore, the subgraph indexes can be more compact and more effective.

Cheng et al. (2007) have extended the ideas of GIndex (Yan et al., 2004) by using nested inverted-index in a new graph index structure named *FG-Index*. In this index structure, a memory-resident inverted-index is built using the set of frequent subgraphs. A disk-resident inverted-index is built on the closure of the frequent graphs. If the closure is too large, a local set of closure frequent sub-graphs can be computed from the set of frequent graphs and a further nested inverted-index can be constructed. The main advantage of this approach is that it can answer an important subset of queries (frequent graph queries) directly without verification.

Tree-Based Mining. Zhang et al. (2007) have presented an approach for using frequent subtrees as the indexing unit for graph structures named *TreePI*. The main idea of this approach is based on two main observations: 1) Tree data structures are more complex patterns than paths and trees can preserve almost equivalent amount of structural information as arbitrary subgraph patterns. 2) The frequent subtree mining process is relatively easier than general frequent subgraph mining process. Therefore, the TreePI starts by mining the frequent tree on the graph database and then selecting a set of frequent trees as index patterns. In the query processing, for a query graph q, the frequent subtrees in q are identified and then and then matched with the set of indexing features to obtain a candidate set. In the verification phase, the advantage of the location information partially stored with the feature trees is utilized for devising an efficient subgraph isomorphism tests. As the canonical form of any tree can be calculated in polynomial time, the indexing and searching operations can be effectively improved. Moreover, operations on trees, such as isomorphism and normalization are asymptotically simpler than graphs, which are usually NP-complete (Fortin, 1996).

Zhao et al. (2007) have extended the ideas of TreePi (Zhang et al., 2007) to achieve better pruning ability by adding a small number of discriminative graphs (Δ) to the frequent tree-features in the index structure. They propose a new graph indexing mechanism, named (Tree+Δ), which first selects frequent tree-features as the basis of a graph index, and then on-demand selects a small number of discriminative graph-features that can prune graphs more effectively than the selected tree-features, without conducting costly graph mining beforehand.

SUPERGRAPH QUERY PROCESSING

The *supergraph* query-processing problem is important in practice. However, it has not been extensively considered in the research literature. Only two approaches have been presented to deal with this problem. Chen et al. (2007) have presented an approach named *cIndex* as the first work on supergraph query processing. The indexing unit of this approach is the subgraphs which extracted from graph databases based on their rarely occurrence in historical query graphs. Sometimes, the extracted subgraphs are very similar to each other. Therefore, cIndex tries to find a set of contrast subgraphs that collectively perform well. It uses a redundancy-aware selection mechanism to sort out the most significant and distinctive contrast subgraphs. The distinctive subgraph is stored in a hierarchical fashion using bottom-up and top-down proposed approaches. During query processing, cIndex reduces the number of subgraph isomorphism testing by using the filtering and verification methodology. An advantage of the cIndex approach is that the size of the feature index is small. On the other hand, the query logs may frequently change over time

so that the feature index maybe outdated quite often and need to be recomputed to stay effective.

Zhang et al. (2009) have investigated the supergraph query-processing problem from another angle. They proposed an approach for compact organization of graph database members named *GPTree*. In this approach, all of the graph database members are stored into one graph where the common subgraphs are stored only once. An algorithm for extracting the key features from graph databases is used to construct the feature indexes on graph database members. Based on the containment relationship between the support sets of the extracted features, a mathematical approach is used to determine the ordering of the feature set which can reduce the number of subgraph isomorphism tests during query processing.

GRAPH SIMILARITY QUERIES

The problem of similarity (approximate) subgraph queries has been addressed by different research efforts in the literature. Given a query graph and a database of graphs, these approaches try to find subgraphs in the database that are *similar* to the query. Therefore, these approaches can allow for node mismatches, node gaps (Gap node is a node in the query that cannot be mapped to any node in the target graph), as well as graph structural differences. Approximate graph matching techniques are used in some cases when the graph databases are noisy or incomplete. In these cases, using approximate graph matching query-processing techniques can be more useful and effective than exact matching. In this section, we give an overview of the main approaches which address this problem.

Grafil. Yan et al. (2005) have proposed a feature-based structural filtering algorithm, named *Grafil* (*Gra*ph Similarity *Fil*tering) to perform substructure similarity search in graph databases. Grafil models each query graph as a set of features and transforms the edge deletions into the feature misses in the query graph. With an upper bound on the maximum allowed feature misses, Grafil can filter many graphs directly without performing pair-wise similarity computation. It uses two data structures: *feature-graph matrix* and *edge-feature matrix*.

The feature-graph matrix is used to compute the difference in the number of features between a query graph and graphs in the database. In this matrix, each column corresponds to a target graph in the graph database, each row corresponds to a feature being indexed and each entry records the number of the embeddings of a specific feature in a target graph. The edge-feature matrix is used to compute a bound on the maximum allowed feature misses based on a query relaxation ratio. In this matrix, each row represents an edge while each column represents an embedding of a feature. Grafil uses a multi-filter composition strategy, where each filter uses a distinct and complimentary subset of the features. The filters are constructed by a hierarchical, one-dimensional clustering algorithm that groups features with similar selectivity into a feature set.

During the query processing, the feature-graph matrix is used to calculate the difference in the number of features between each graph database member g_i and the query q. If the difference is greater than a user-defined parameter d_{max} then it is discarded while the remaining graphs constitute a candidate answer set. The substructure similarity is then calculated for each candidate to prune the false positives candidates. A loop of query relaxation steps can be applied if the user needs more matches than those returned from the current value of d_{max}.

Closure Tree. He & Singh (2006) have proposed a tree-based index structure named *CTree* (*C*losure-*Tree*). CTree index is very similar to the R-tree indexing mechanism (Guttman, 1984) but extended to support graph-matching queries. In this index structure, each node in the tree contains discriminative information about its descendants

in order to facilitate effective pruning. The closure of a set of vertices is defined as a generalized vertex whose attribute is the union of the attribute values of the vertices. Similarly, the closure of a set of edges is defined as a generalized edge whose attribute is the union of the attribute values of the edges. The closure of two graphs g_1 and g_2 under a mapping M is defined as a generalized graph (V, E) where V is the set of vertex closures of the corresponding vertices and E is the set of edge closures of the corresponding edges (Figure 6). Hence, a graph closure has the same characteristics of a graph. However, the only difference is that the graph database member has singleton labels on vertices and edges while the graph closure can have multiple labels.

In a closure tree, each node is a graph closure of its children where the children of an internal node are nodes and the children of a leaf node are database graphs. A subgraph query is processed in two phases. The first phase traverses the CTree and the nodes are pruned based on a *pseudo subgraph isomorphism*. A candidate answer set is returned. The second phase verifies each candidate answer for exact subgraph isomorphism and returns the answers. In addition to pruning based on pseudo subgraph isomorphism, a lightweight histogram-based pruning is also employed. The histogram of a graph is a vector that counts the number of each distinct attribute of the vertices and edges. For similarity queries, CTree defines graph similarity based on edit distance, and computes it using heuristic graph mapping methods. It conceptually approximates subgraph isomorphism by sub-isomorphism using adjacent subgraphs then it approximates sub-isomorphism by using adjacent subtrees.

SAGA. Tian et al. (2007) have presented an approach of approximate graph query matching named *SAGA* (*S*ubstructure Index-based *A*pproximate *G*raph *A*lignment). SAGA measures graph similarity by a distance value such that graphs

Figure 6. Graph closure

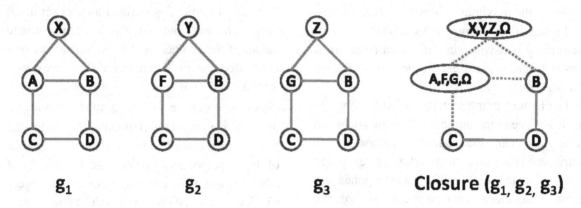

g_1 g_2 g_3 **Closure (g_1, g_2, g_3)**

that are more similar have a smaller distance. The distance model contains three components:

1. The *StructDist* component measures the structural differences for the matching node pairs in the two graphs.
2. The *NodeMismatches* component is the penalty associated with matching two nodes with different labels.
3. The *NodeGaps* component is used to measure the penalty for the gap nodes in the query graph.

SAGA index is built on small substructures of graphs in the database (*Fragment Index*). Each fragment is a set of k nodes from the graphs in the database where K is a user-defined parameter. The index does not enumerate all possible k-node sets. It uses another user-defined parameter $dist_{max}$ to avoid indexing any pair of nodes in a fragment if its distance measure is greater than $dist_{max}$. The fragments in SAGA do not always correspond to connected subgraphs. The reason behind this is to allow node gaps in the matching process. To efficiently evaluate the subgraph distance between a query graph and a database graph, an additional index called *DistanceIndex* is also maintained. This index is used to look up the precomputed distance between any pair of nodes in

a graph. The graph matching process goes through the following three steps:

1. The query is broken into small fragments and the Fragment Index is probed to find database fragments that are similar to the query fragments.
2. The hits from the index probes are combined to produce larger candidate matches. A hit-compatible graph is built for each matching graph. Each node in the hit-compatible graph corresponds to a pair of matching query and database fragments. An edge is drawn between two nodes in the hit-compatible graph if and only if two query fragments share zero or more nodes, and the corresponding database fragments in the hit-compatible graph also share the same corresponding nodes. An edge between two nodes tells us that the corresponding two hits can be merged to form a larger match which is then a candidate match.
3. Each candidate is examined to produce the query results. For each candidate, the percentage of the gap nodes is checked. If it exceeds a user-defined threshold P_g, then the candidate match is ignored otherwise, the *DistanceIndex* is probed to calculate the real subgraph matching distance. If two

Figure 7. Summary of the graph indexing and querying techniques

Indexing Technique	Supported Query Types	Indexing Unit	Indexing Mechanism
CIndex (Chen et al., 2007)	Supergraph queries	Subgraph structure	Rarely occurring features
Closure-Tree (He & Singh, 2006)	Subgraph and similarity	Closure Tree	Enumeration of graph closures
FG-Index (Cheng et al., 2007)	Subgraph queries	Subgraph structure	Frequent features
GDIndex (Williams et al., 2007)	Subgraph queries	Decomposed subgraph	Full enumeration
GIndex (Yan et al., 2004)	Subgraph queries	Subgraph structure	Frequent features
GPTree (Zhang et al., 2009)	Supergraph queries	Subgraph structure	Full enumeration
Grafil (Yan et al., 2005)	Similarity queries	Any	Full enumeration
GraphGrep (Giugno & Shasha, 2002)	Subgraph queries	Path structure	Full enumeration
GraphREL (Sakr, 2009)	Subgraph queries	Nodes and Edges	Full enumeration
GString (Jiang et al., 2007)	Subgraph queries	Subgraph structure	Full enumeration
SAGA (Tian et al., 2007)	Similarity queries	Subgraph structure	Full enumeration
TreeDelta (Zhao et al., 2007)	Subgraph queries	Tree structure	Frequent features
TreePi (Zhang et al., 2007)	Subgraph queries	Tree structure	Frequent features

matches have the same matching distance and one is a submatch of the other, only the supermatch is considered.

Figure 7 provides a comparison between the different graph indexing techniques in terms of their supported query types, indexing unit and indexing strategy.

GRAPH QUERY LANGUAGES

With the prevalence of graph data in a variety of application domains, there is an increasing need for a suitable language to query and manipulate graph data structure (Angles & Gutierrez, 2008). In this section, we give an overview of representative proposals for graph query languages in the literature.

In (Leser, 2005) Leser has proposed a special-purpose graph query language for biological networks called *PQL* (*Pathway Query Language*). PQL is a declarative language whose syntax is similar to SQL. The language targets retrieving specific parts of large, complex networks. It is based on a simple graph data model with extensions reflecting properties of biological objects. PQL queries match arbitrary subgraphs in the database based on node properties and paths between nodes. The general syntax of PQL is as follows:

SELECT subgraph-specification FROM node-variables
WHERE node-condition-set

During query evaluation node variables are bound to nodes of the database graph such that all node-conditions in the WHERE clause evaluate to TRUE. The query result is constructed from these variable bindings according to the subgraph-specification of the SELECT clause. Query evaluation considers each node variable in the FROM clause. For each of these variables, all possible assignments of the variable to nodes of the graph are determined for which the conditions of the WHERE clause mentioning only this variable evaluates to TRUE. Node variables are equally assigned to molecules and interactions. Once all possible bindings are computed for each node variable, the Cartesian product of these sets is computed. From this set, all instances are removed for which the entire WHERE clause evaluates to FALSE and all distinct assignments from the remaining elements of the Cartesian product are combined to form the match graph. In general, SQL query operates on tables and produces a table (a set of rows), in the same manner as a PQL query operates on a graph and produces a graph (a set of nodes) and not a set of graphs. In the result of the SQL query the rows from the Cartesian product are preserved, columns might be removed, added, or changed in their value. In PQL, the concrete combinations of bindings of different node variables that together fulfill the WHERE clause are not preserved in the match graph of a PQL query. The match graph simply consists of all bindings present in the filtered Cartesian product into a flat, duplicate-free list of nodes.

In (He & Singh, 2008) He and Singh have proposed a general graph query and manipulation languages called GraphQL. In this language, graphs are considered as the basic unit of information and each query manipulates one or more collections of graphs. It also targets graph databases that supports arbitrary attributes on nodes, edges, and graphs. The core of GraphQL is its data model and its graph algebra. In the GraphQL data model, a graph pattern is represented as a graph structure and a predicate on attributes of the graph. Each node, edge, or graph can have arbitrary attributes. A tuple with a list of name and value pairs is used to denote these attributes. In GraphQL algebra, graphs are the basic unit of information. Each operator takes one or more collections of graphs as input and generates a collection of graphs as output. For example, the selection operator takes a collection of graphs as input and produces a collection of graphs that match the graph pattern as an output. A graph pattern can match a specific graph database member many times. Therefore, an exhaustive option is used to specify whether it should return one or all possible matches. A Cartesian product operator takes two collections of graphs C and D and produces a collection of graphs as output where each output graph is composed of a graph from C and another from D. The join operator is defined as a Cartesian product operator followed by a selection operator. The composition operator generates new graphs by combining information from matched graphs based on graph templates that specify the output structure of the graphs.

Consens & Mendelzon (1990) have proposed a graphical query language for graph databases called GraphLog. Graphlog queries ask for patterns that must be present or absent in the database graph. In GraphLog, the query graph can define a set of new edges that are added to the graph whenever the search pattern is found. Awad has followed a similar approach in (Awad, 2007) where he presented a visual query language for business process definitions called BPMN-Q. BPMN-Q allows expressing structural queries and specifies proceedings of determining whether a given process model graph is structurally similar to a query graph. BPMN-Q relies on the notations of BPMN languages as its concrete syntax and provides a set of new visual constructs that can be seen as abstractions over the existing modeling constructs. For example a Path construct connecting two nodes in a query represents an abstraction over whatever nodes could be in between in the matching process model while Negative Path used to express that two nodes must have no connection between them.

There are some other proposal for graph query languages that have been proposed in the literature such as: GOQL (Sheng et al., 1999), GOOD (Gyssens et al., 1994) and SPARQL (Prud'hommeaux & Seaborne, 2008). For example, GOQL and GOOD are designed based on an extension of OQL (Object-Oriented Query Language) and rely on an object-oriented graph data model. SPARQL query language is a W3C recommendation for querying RDF graph data. It describes a directed labeled graph by a set of triples, each of which describes a (attribute, value) pair or an interconnection between two nodes. The SPARQL query language works primarily through a primitive triple pattern matching techniques with simple constraints on query nodes and edges.

Figure 8 provides a comparison between the graph query languages in terms of their target domain, query unit and query style.

Figure 8. Summary graph query languages

Query Language	Target Domain	Query Units	Query Style
BPMN-Q (Awad, 2007)	Business Process Models	Subgraphs	Graphical
GOOD (Gyssens et al., 1994)	General	nodes/edges	Declarative (OQL-Like)
GOQL (Sheng et al., 1999)	General	nodes/edges	Declarative (OQL-Like)
GraphLog (Consens & Mendelzon, 1990)	General	nodes/edges	Graphical
GraphQL (He & Singh, 2008)	General	Subgraphs	Declarative (XQuery-Like)
PQL (Leser, 2005)	Biological networks	Subgraphs	Declarative (SQL-Like)
SPARQL (Prud'hommeaux & Seaborne, 2008)	Semantic Web	Subgraphs	Declarative (SQL-Like)

DISCUSSION AND CONCLUSION

In this chapter, we give an overview of the problem of graph indexing and querying techniques. The problem is motivated by the continued emergence and increase of massive and complex structural data. Due to the very expensive cost of pair-wise comparison of graph data structures, recently proposed graph query processing techniques rely on a strategy which consists of two steps: *filtering* and *verification*. For a given graph database D and a graph query q, the main objective of the filtering and verification methodology is to avoid comparing the query graph q with each graph database member g_i that belongs to D to check whether g_i satisfies the conditions of q or not. Therefore, most of the proposed graph indexing strategies shift the high online graph query processing cost to the off-line index construction phase. Index construction is thus, always computationally expensive because it requires the use of high quality indexing features with great pruning power from the graph database. However, the number of indexing features should be as small as possible to keep the whole index structure compact so that it is possible to be held in the main memory for efficient access and retrieval. Hence, a high quality graph indexing mechanism should be time-efficient in index construction and indexing features should be compact and powerful for pruning purposes. Moreover, candidate verification can be still very expensive as the size of the candidate answer set is *at least* equal to

that of the exact answer set in the optimal case but it is usually larger. Hence, reducing the size of the candidate answer set by removing as much as possible of the false positive graphs is the main criteria to evaluate the effectiveness of any filtering technique.

There is a clear imbalance between the number of developed techniques for processing supergraph queries and the other types of graph queries. The reason behind this is that the supergraph query type can be considered to be relatively new. Therefore, there are many technical aspects which still remain unexplored.

A clear gap in the research efforts in the domain of graph database is the absence of a *standard* graph query language which plays the same role as that SQL for the relational data model or XPath and XQuery for the XML hierarchical model. Although there are a number of query languages that have been proposed in the literature (Consens & Mendelzon, 1990; Gyssens et al., 1994; Sheng et al., 1999), none of them has been universally accepted as they are designed to deal with different representations of the graph data model. A *standard* definition of a general purpose graph query language with more powerful and flexible constructs is essentially required. A concrete algebra behind this expected query language is also quite important.

The proposed graph query processing techniques concentrate on the retrieval speed of their indexing structures in addition to their compact size. Further management of these indexes is rarely taken into account. Although efficient query processing is an important objective, efficient update maintenance is also an important concern. In the case of dynamic graph databases, it is quite important that indexing techniques avoid the costly recomputation of the whole index and provide more efficient mechanisms to update the underneath index structures with minimum effort. Therefore, efficient mechanisms to handle dynamic graph databases are necessary.

Finally, query processing usually involves a cost-based optimization phase in which query optimizers rely on cost models to attempt on choosing an optimal query plan from amongst several alternatives. A key issue of any cost model is the cardinality estimation of the intermediate and final query results. Although there is an initial effort has been proposed by Stocker et al. (2008) for estimating the selectivity estimation of basic graph patterns, there is still a clear need for summarization and estimation frameworks for graph databases. These frameworks need to provide accurate selectivity estimations of more complex graph patterns which can be utilized in accelerating the processing of different types of graph queries.

REFERENCES

Angles, R., & Guti¥errez, C. (2008). Survey of graph database models. *ACM Computing Surveys*, *40*(1), 1–39. doi:10.1145/1322432.1322433

Awad, A. (2007). BPMN-Q: A language to query business processes. In *Proceedings of the 2nd International Workshop on Enterprise Modelling and Information Systems Architectures (emisa)* (p. 115-128).

Bruno, N., Chaudhuri, S., & Ramamurthy, R. (2009). Power hints for query optimization. In *Proceedings of the 25th International Conference on Data Engineering (ICDE)* (pp. 469 -480).

Bunke, H., & Shearer, K. (1998). A graph distance metric based on the maximal common subgraph. *Pattern Recognition Letters*, *19*(3-4), 255–259. doi:10.1016/S0167-8655(97)00179-7

Cai, D., Shao, Z., He, X., Yan, X., & Han, J. (2005). Community mining from multi-relational networks. In *Proceedings of the 9th European Conference on Principles and Practice of Knowledge Discovery in Databases (PKDD)* (p. 445-452).

Chen, C., Yan, X., Yu, P. S., Han, J., Zhang, D.-Q., & Gu, X. (2007). Towards graph containment search and indexing. In *Proceedings of the 33rd International Conference on Very Large Data Bases (VLDB)* (p. 926937).

Cheng, J., Ke, Y., Ng, W., & Lu, A. (2007). FG-Index: Towards verification-free query processing on graph databases. In *Proceedings of the ACM Sigmod International Conference on Management of Data* (p. 857872).

Consens, M. P., & Mendelzon, A. O. (1990). GraphLog: A visual formalism for real life recursion. In *Proceedings of the 9th ACM Sigact-Ssigmod-Sigart Symposium on Principles of Database Systems (PODS)* (p. 404-416).

Fern•andez, M.-L., & Valiente, G. (2001). A graph distance metric combining maximum common subgraph and minimum common supergraph. *Pattern Recognition Letters, 22*(6/7), 753-758.

Fortin, S. (1996). *The graph isomorphism problem (Tech. Rep.).* Albetrta, Canada: Department of Computing Science, University of Alberta.

Gao, X., Xiao, B., Tao, D., & Li, X. (2009). A survey of graph edit distance. *Pattern Analysis & Applications*.

Garey, M. R., & Johnson, D. S. (1979). *Computers and intractability: A guide to the theory of NP-completeness*. USA: W. H. Freeman.

Giugno, R., & Shasha, D. (2002). GraphGrep: A fast and universal method for querying graphs. In *Ieee International Conference in Pattern Recognition (ICPR)* (pp. 112-115).

Guttman, A. (1984). R-Trees: A dynamic index structure for spatial searching. In *Proceedings of the ACM Sigmod International Conference on Management of Data* (pp. 47-57).

Gyssens, M., Paredaens, J., den Bussche, J. V., & Gucht, D. V. (1994). A graph-oriented object database model. [TKDE]. *IEEE Transactions on Knowledge and Data Engineering, 6*(4), 572–586. doi:10.1109/69.298174

He, H., & Singh, A. K. (2006). Closure-Tree: An index structure for graph queries. In *Proceedings of the 22nd International Conference on Data Engineering (ICDE)* (pp. 38-52).

He, H., & Singh, A. K. (2008). Graphs-at-a-time: Query language and access methods for graph databases. In *Proceedings of the ACM Sigmod International Conference on Management of Data* (pp. 405-418).

Huan, J., Wang, W., Bandyopadhyay, D., Snoeyink, J., Prins, J., & Tropsha, A. (2004). Mining protein family specific residue packing patterns from protein structure graphs. In *Proceedings of the 8th Annual International Conference on Computational Molecular Biology (RECOMB)* (p. 308-315).

Jiang, H., Wang, H., Yu, P. S., & Zhou, S. (2007). GString: A novel approach for efficient search in graph databases. In *Proceedings of the 23rd International Conference on Data Engineering (ICDE)* (pp. 566-575).

Klinger, S., & Austin, J. (2005). Chemical similarity searching using a neural graph matcher. In *Proceedings of the 13th European Symposium on Artificial Neural Networks (ESANN)* (pp. 479-484).

Kuramochi, M., & Karypis, G. (2001). Frequent subgraph discovery. In *Proceedings of the IEEE International Conference on Data Mining (ICDM)* (p. 313-320).

Kuramochi, M., & Karypis, G. (2004). GREW-A scalable frequent subgraph discovery algorithm. In *Proceedings of the IEEE International Conference on Data Mining (ICDM)* (pp. 439-442).

Lee, J., Oh, J.-H., & Hwang, S. (2005). STRG-Index: Spatio-temporal region graph Indexing for large video databases. In *Proceedings of the ACM Sigmod International Conference on Management of Data* (p. 718-729).

Leser, U. (2005). A query language for biological networks. In *Proceedings of the 4th European Conference on Computational Biology/6th Meeting of the Spanish Bioinformatics Network (ECCB/JBI)* (p. 39).

Manola, F., & Miller, E. (2004, February). *RDF primer: World Wide Web Consortium Proposed Recommendation.* Retrieved from (http://www.w3.org/ TR/ rdf-primer/)

Prud'hommeaux, E., & Seaborne, A. (2008, January). *SPARQL wuery language for RDF. World Wide Web consortium proposed recommendation.* Retrieved from (http://www.w3.org/ TR/ rdf-sparql-query/)

Raymond, J. W., Gardiner, E. J., & Willett, P. (2002). RASCAL: Calculation of graph similarity using maximum common edge subgraphs. *The Computer Journal, 45*(6), 631–644. doi:10.1093/comjnl/45.6.631

Sakr, S. (2009). GraphREL: A decomposition-based and selectivity-aware relational framework for processing sub-graph queries. In *Proceedings of the 14th International Conference on Database Systems for Advanced Applications (DASFAA)* (pp. 123-137).

Sheng, L., Ozsoyoglu, Z. M., & Ozsoyoglu, G. (1999). A graph query language and its query processing. In *Proceedings of the 15th International Conference on Data Engineering (ICDE)* (pp. 572-581).

Stocker, M., Seaborne, A., Bernstein, A., Kiefer, C., & Reynolds, D. (2008). SPARQL basic graph pattern optimization using selectivity estimation. In *Proceedings of the 17th International Conference on World Wide Web (WWW)* (pp. 595-604).

Teubner, J., Grust, T., Maneth, S., & Sakr, S. (2008). Dependable cardinality forecasts for XQuery. [PVLDB]. *Proceedings of the VLDB Endowment, 1*(1), 463–477.

Tian, Y., McEachin, R. C., Santos, C., States, D. J., & Patel, J. M. (2007). SAGA: A subgraph matching tool for biological graphs. *Bioinformatics (Oxford, England), 23*(2), 232–239. doi:10.1093/bioinformatics/btl571

Wang, C., Wang, W., Pei, J., Zhu, Y., & Shi, B. (2004). Scalable mining of large disk-based graph databases. In *Proceedings of the 10th ACM SIGKDD International Conference on Knowledge Discovery and Data Mining (KDD)* (pp. 316-325).

Washio, T., & Motoda, H. (2003). State of the art of graph-based data mining. *SIGKDD Explorations, 5*(1), 59–68. doi:10.1145/959242.959249

Williams, D. W., Huan, J., & Wang, W. (2007). Graph database indexing using structured graph decomposition. In *Proceedings of the 23rd International Conference on Data Engineering (ICDE)* (pp. 976-985).

Yan, X., & Han, J. (2002). gSpan: Graph-based substructure pattern mining. In *Proceedings of the IEEE International Conference on Data Mining (ICDM)* (pp. 721-724).

Yan, X., & Han, J. (2003). CloseGraph: Mining closed frequent graph patterns. In *Proceedings of the 9th ACM SIGKDD International Conference on Knowledge Discovery and Data Mining (KDD)* (pp. 286-295).

Yan, X., Yu, P. S., & Han, J. (2004). Graph indexing: A frequent structure-based approach. In *Proceedings of the ACM SIGMOD International Conference on Management of Data* (pp. 335-346).

Yan, X., Yu, P. S., & Han, J. (2005). Substructure similarity search in graph databases. In *Proceedings of the ACM SIGMOD International Conference on Management of Data* (pp. 766-777).

Zhang, S., Hu, M., & Yang, J. (2007). TreePi: A novel graph indexing method. In *Proceedings of the 23rd International Conference on Data Engineering (ICDE)* (pp. 966-975).

Zhang, S., Li, J., Gao, H., & Zou, Z. (2009). A novel approach for efficient supergraph query processing on graph databases. In *Proceedings of the 12th International Conference on Extending Database Technology (EDBT)* (pp. 204-215).

Zhao, P., Yu, J. X., & Yu, P. S. (2007). Graph indexing: Tree + Delta >= Graph. In *Proceedings of the 33rd International Conference on Very Large Data Bases (VLDB)* (pp. 938-949).

Chapter 5
Efficient Techniques for Graph Searching and Biological Network Mining

Alfredo Ferro
Università di Catania, Italy

Rosalba Giugno
Università di Catania, Italy

Alfredo Pulvirenti
Università di Catania, Italy

Dennis Shasha
Courant Institute of Mathematical Sciences, USA

ABSTRACT

From biochemical applications to social networks, graphs represent data. Comparing graphs or searching for motifs on such data often reveals interesting and useful patterns. Most of the problems on graphs are known to be NP-complete. Because of the computational complexity of subgraph matching, reducing the candidate graphs or restricting the space in which to search for motifs is critical to achieving efficiency. Therefore, to optimize and engineer isomorphism algorithms, design indexing and suitable search methods for large graphs are the main directions investigated in the graph searching area. This chapter focuses on the key concepts underlying the existing algorithms. First it reviews the most known used algorithms to compare two algorithms and then it describes the algorithms to search on large graphs making emphasis on their application on biological area.

DOI: 10.4018/978-1-61350-053-8.ch005

INTRODUCTION

Since the 1970s, many efforts have been spent to solve the subgraph isomorphism problem (Garey & Johnson, 1979). In contrast to other research areas, only a few algorithms have been widely used in applications (Cordella et al., 2004; Ullmann, 1976). They employ backtracking in the search tree (see Figure 1). The search space is reduced by pruning paths in the tree failing the match. Alternative approaches have been designed for special kind of graphs or to match particular typologies of queries (Dessmark et al., 2000; Eppstein, 1999; Matula, 1978; Alon et al, 1995). Another research direction has been focused on the approximate matching problem in which a measure of similarity has to be defined (Nilsson, 1980). Algorithms for subgraph isomorphism are heavily used to discovery frequent patterns which are indexed featured in graphs database (graph database search or graph mining) and/or to search in a selected area of the large graph (Cheng et al., 2007; Giugno et al., 2002; He et al., 2006; Di Natale et al., 2010; Williams et al., 2007; Yan et al., 2005; Zhang et al., 2007). The performance of such techniques strongly depend on the efficiency of the used subgraph isomorphism algorithm.

Because a large number of the real world structures are modeled by large graphs such as web, social and biological networks (Albert et al.,

Figure 1. Exact and Inexact Match. Tree all Possible Mappings represents all the maps between nodes of G_a and G_b. On the right we show a tree search-space to reach the first isomorphism. More precisely, the tree-search space pruned by an exact matching algorithm such as Ullmann's algorithm, and the tree-search space pruned by an inexact matching algorithm such as the Nilsson's algorithm. The leaves in the rectangular frames correspond to subisomorphisms. The writing Delete in the inexact match represents a tree-search node deletion (of course, if the first isomorphism was not reached, such a branch could be investigated). Here we assume that an underlying evaluation function is used to guide the state expansions. Different evaluation functions prune the tree-search differently.

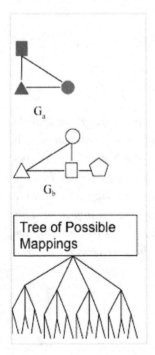
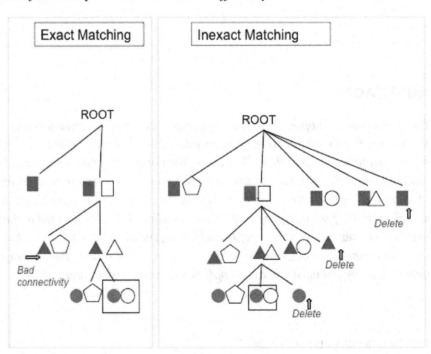

2002; Faloutsos et al., 1999; Pinter et al., 2005), there is increasing research interest in large networks mining and querying. In biological networks analysis, users are usually interested in finding complexes (groups of highly connected nodes) carrying out a specific function (Banks, 2008; Dost, 2007; Ferro et al., 2007). Thus, typical queries rely on the identification of motifs with a specific or approximate topology having unspecified node labels. Other critical problems rely on the comparison of two or more networks (Flannick et al., 2006; Kalaev et al., 2009; Kelley et al., 2004). These problems fall in the area of biological network alignment in which the goal is to efficiently identify subgraphs that are partially shared by several networks. To execute such problems efficiently, researchers use graph preprocessing such as graph partition, pattern and law mining, frequent substructure discovery and sub-graph complex mining.

In this chapter, after reviewing some of most popular exact and inexact graph isomorphism algorithms, we briefly sketch the indexing and mining techniques, which make use of graph isomorphism algorithms. Finally, we describe searching methods for large graphs concentrating on the biological research area.

SEARCHING IN A SINGLE GRAPH

The aim of an *exact* subgraph matching (isomorphism) algorithm is to find the graph G_a in G_b where the isomorphic conditions hold: there exists a subgraph of G_b which has the same number of vertices and the same connections between them presented in G_a. If the graph is labelled[1] then the labels of corresponding nodes must be the same. *Inexact* algorithms employ error correction techniques. These algorithms employ a cost function to measure the similarity of the graphs. For example, a cost function may be defined based on semantic or syntactic transformations to transform one graph into another.

A simple theoretical enumeration algorithm to find the *exact* occurrences of a graph G_a in a graph G_b is to generate all possible maps between the nodes of the two graphs and to check whether each generated map is a match. All the maps can be represented using a *state-space representation* tree: a node represents a pair of matched vertices; a path from the root down to a leaf represents a map between the two graphs. A path from a node at the k_{th} level in the tree up to the root represents a *partial matching* between the graphs; only a subset (k) of vertices have been matched. Only certain leaves correspond to a subisomorphism between G_a and G_b. The complexity of such an algorithm is exponential, but that is to be expected. The problem of subgraph isomorphism is proven to be NP-complete (Garey et al., 1979). On the other hand, there have been many attempts to reduce its combinatorial cost (Shasha et al., 2002; Yannakakis, 1990) by working on particular king of graphs of queries like paths and cycles (Dessmark et al., 2000; Eppstein, 1999; Matula, 1978; Alon et al., 1995).

The fundamental *exact* (and *inexact*) subgraph matching algorithms are described below. They are based on heuristics to improve the state-space representation tree that corresponds to a subisomorphism (see Figure 1).

Ullmann (1976), in seventies, presented an *exact* subgraph matching algorithm based on the *state space search with backtracking* algorithm in (Corneil & Gotlieb, 1970). A depth-first search on the state space tree representation depicts the algorithm's progress. When a node (a pair of matching vertices) is added to the tree, the isomorphism conditions are checked in the partial matching. If the isomorphism condition is not satisfied the algorithm *backtracks* (i.e. the tree-search that would correspond to a full enumeration is pruned). Upon termination only the paths with length equal to the number of nodes in G_a (corresponding to unpruned leaves) represent a subisomorphism. The performance of the above state-space representation algorithm is improved by a refinement procedure called *forward checking*: in order to insert a node in the tree not only must the sub-isomorphism conditions hold, but, in addition, a possible mapping must exist for *all* the unmatched vertices. As a result, the algorithm prunes the tree-search more efficiently at a higher level.

One of the most popular *exact* algorithms is a refinement of the above algorithm (Cordella et al., 2004). This introduces two-look-ahead *semantic* and *syntactic* feasibility rules which result in more selective pruning of the state space. For each intermediate state of the state space tree, the algorithm computes the set of the node pairs that are candidate to be added to the current state. A candidate pair (n, m), $n \in G_a{}^2$ and $m \in G_b$ is valid if: (i) let $(n' \in G_a, m' \in G_b)$ be a pair in the state space tree, if n has an edge with n' then m must have an edge with m', (ii) the number of vertices not already mapped in G_a connecting n such that those vertices have edges with nodes mapped is less than the number vertices in G_b having the same described characteristic for m, (ii) the number of vertices in G_a directed connected to n and not belonging to the two above cases must be less than the number of vertices in G_b connected to m with the same characteristic. Moreover, if the graph is labelled, the semantic rule must apply, that is the label of n must correspond to the one of m.

Related work using alternative heuristics such finding maximum cliques, maximum common subgraphs, enumerations of possible matches, probabilistic functions and so on, can be found in (Akinniyi et al. 1986; Barrow et al., 1976; Cortadella et al., 2000; Henderson, 1990; Horaud et al., 1989; Levi, 1972; Messmer et al. 1995; Myaeng et al., 1992; Nilsson, 1980; Sanfeliu et al., 1983; Wong et al., 1985). In (Akinniyi et al. 1986), a product of graphs is computed and a tree search procedure is applied to detect infeasible subtrees. In (Cortadella et al., 2000; Larrosa et al., 2000), the authors use a representation of graphs by Boolean

functions together with the notion of neighborhood constraints, which allows handling the combinatorial explosion in the case of small subgraph matching. In (Krissinel & Henrick, 2004), authors progressively compute possible mappings of subgraphs of the two graphs, maintaining information about mappings that failed. This speeds up future searches by discarding unpromising recursions of the algorithm on those subgraphs. Some work has been done to treat special cases when graphs have all nodes with different labels or are very poorly labeled (Batz, 2006; Dickinson et al., 2004). Of course their performance, mostly linear, degrades to exponential on growing the number of labels. Recently, Lipets, Vanetik, & Gudes, 2009) describes an algorithm that proceeds by checking first the more dense parts first, in order to rapidly discard infeasible solutions as soon as possible. Authors also work on large graphs by recursively applying their method together with bisection algorithms.

Nilsson (1980) presented an *inexact* subgraph matching algorithm. This time, a breath-first search on the state-space representation tree keeps track of the algorithm's progress. Each node in the tree-search represents a vertex in G_a that has been either matched with a vertex in G_b or deleted. If a vertex in G_a has to be deleted, it is matched to a null vertex in G_b. A cost is assigned to the matching between two vertices (whether null or not). The cost of a partial matching is the sum of the costs of the matched vertices. A function evaluates the partial matching by summing its cost to a lower bound estimation of the cost to match the remaining vertices in G_a. The tree search is expanded to states for which the evaluation function attains the minimum value (among all possible expansion states). The leaves of the tree (that have not been pruned) represent final states, i.e., states where all the vertices of G_a have been matched.

Relevant work and efficient graph edit distances can be found in (Berretti et al., 2004; Bunke, 1999; Bunke et al., 1983; Cordella et al., 1996; Eshera et al., 1984; Fernandez et al., 2001; Lladss et al., 2001; Myers et al., 1998; Tsai, 1979). An interesting direction consists of matching a vertex in one graph with a set of vertices of the other graph; or defining the similarity on the maximal common subgraph computed by maximizing the degree of matching of a single vertex respect to a certain predefined map (Ambauen et al., 2003; Boeres et al., 2004; Champin et al., 2003; Sammoud et al., 2005).

INDEXING AND MINING ON DATABASES OF GRAPHS

Indexing techniques for databases of graphs have the purpose of reducing the number of subgraph isomorphism tests involved in the query process. In a preprocessing phase the database of graphs is analyzed and an index is built. A query is processed in two phases. In the filtering step the index is used to discard the graphs of the database that cannot contain the query, producing a small set of candidate graphs. The set of candidates is then examined by a subgraph isomorphism algorithm (see previous Section) and all the resulting matches are reported. Most graph indexing tools are based on the concept of feature. Depending on the particular system, a feature can be a small graph (Cheng et al., 2007; Williams et al., 2007; Yan et al., 2005), a tree (He & Singh, 2006), or a path (Ferro et al., 2008; Giugno et al., 2002; Di Natale et al., 2010) (see Figure 2).

The filtering property is based on checking whether the features of the query are contained in each target graph. In the preprocessing phase the database of graphs is scanned, the features are extracted from each graph and stored in the index data structure. During the filtering phase, the features are extracted from the query and the index is probed in order to discard all graphs that do not contain some feature of the query.

Unfortunately, the number of graph features grows exponentially with the graph size, leading to a large index that degrades the performance of

Figure 2. Given a database of graphs (G_a, G_b, G_c) and a query Q, the database searching system finds those graphs in the database containing the query. Here, G_a and G_b have an occurrence of Q. Such systems use features (i.e. paths, trees, or circles-small graphs) to index the database.

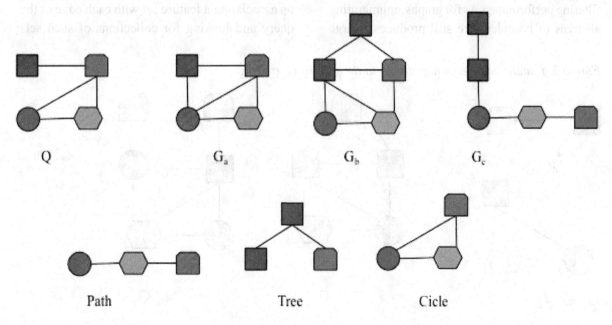

the preprocessing and (to a lesser extent) filtering phases. To solve this problem, (Yan et al., 2005) and GDIndex (Williams et al., 2007) choose as features a set of frequent subgraphs (see Figure 3). gIndex considers also the concept of discriminative subgraphs to further reduce the number of features. All these approaches require the performance of expensive data mining step in the preprocessing phase, leading to a loss of efficiency.

On the other hand, tree features are easier to manage since the tree-isomorphism problem can be solved in polynomial time. TreePi (Zhang et al., 2007) is the first attempt to use trees as features. The authors describe a linear-time algorithm for computing the canonical labeling of a tree. They experimentally show that tree features capture the topological structure well enough. Therefore, using them may result in a good compromise between efficiency and effectiveness of filtering. As shown by the authors, a unique center can be defined for a tree. Consequently the distance (shortest path) between pairs of features in a graph can be computed. TreePi uses an additional pruning rule based on distances between features to improve the quality of the match. Tree $+ \delta$ (Zhao, Yu, & Yu., 2007) uses as features both trees and a restricted class of small graphs to improve the filtering performance. As for graphs, enumerating all trees of bounded size still produces a large

number of features. Consequently, a restricted set of features needs to be selected by an expensive data mining step.

Recently, two non-feature-based graph indexing systems have been proposed (He et al., 2006; Zou et al., 2008). They have been shown to outperform many feature-based indexing systems, probably because they are able to better capture the structure of graphs. CTree organizes the graphs of the database in a R-tree-like data structure. GCoding uses the eigenvalue properties of the adjacency matrix for pruning graphs.

Although a lot of effort has been invested on searching for identical sub-graphs (exact matching problem), solving this problem is still unfeasible for large graphs (see next Section). The situation is even worse when it comes to coping with the more general problem of querying for similar sub-graphs. The latter problem, also known as inexact matching, is fundamental in several research area. Grafil (Yan, Yu, 6 Han, 2005) is the first attempt to propose indexing for inexact searches. It transforms the edge deletions into feature misses in the query graph and uses an upper bound on the maximum number of allowed feature misses for graph filtering. In (Mongiovì et al., 2010), authors present an algorithm based on associating a feature set with each edge of the query and looking for collections of such sets

Figure 3. f_1 and f_2 are frequent patterns in the graphs G_a and G_b

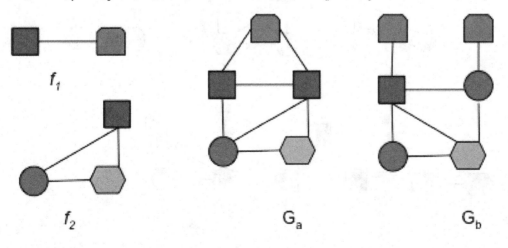

whose removal will allow exact matching of the query with a given graph. This translates into the problem of covering the missing features of the graph with overlapping multi-sets.

LARGE GRAPH ANALYSIS IN BIOLOGY

In computational biology, for a long time, most research attention has been devoted to sequences. They represent a fundamental level of biological description and for this reason they have been considered an evolutionary landmark (Kelley et al. 2003). However, biological networks raise new questions in evolutionary and comparative biology. Thus, biological network analysis has become a central task in bioinformatics and bio-medical analysis.

Several kinds of networks are present in biology, such as Protein-Protein Interaction (PPI) networks, regulatory networks involving protein-DNA interaction and metabolic networks (Alm et al., 2003; Xenarios et al. 2002). For example, PPI networks are important in biological phenomena such as signaling, transcriptional regulation and multi-enzyme complexes. These are deduced by the molecular forces between domains of proteins (Boian et al., 2005; Chen et al., 2008). Interaction networks evolve by losing and gaining nodes (proteins, etc.) and edges (interactions, regulations, etc.) between nodes. Furthermore, network growth is commonly modeled by using specific probability distributions for the gain and loss of nodes and links.

Variations at the protein level often impact how proteins interact with one another, with DNA, and with small molecules to form signaling, regulatory, and metabolic networks. These changes in network organization could have physiological and pathological implications. For example, the mis-regulation of one or more genes could trigger complex diseases such as cancer or neurodegenerative pathologies (Volinia et al., 2010).

Conservation of protein-protein interactions across species follows the same path as sequence conservation (Bork et al, 2004; Matthew et al., 2001; Ramani et al., 2003). By aligning the networks of many species, their ancestral core network can be inferred. Suppose that we have followed the evolution of some proteins and their network up to a common ancestor of human and mouse. After speciation, entities evolve differently in the two lineages of descent yielding two different species. The proteins related by speciation are called orthologous. The inherited interactions and the networks themselves are called orthologous also. The emergence of biological complexity is still poorly understood, and a deeper understanding is of utmost importance. Proteins and their associated interaction networks are commonly represented in a simple graph structure, with vertices representing proteins and edges representing the interactions. Edges can be undirected or directed, depending on the type of interaction. Undirected edges are used to represent a relation between two proteins that interact physically, directed edges represent regulatory mechanisms and include transcription factor binding relationships (i.e. protein-DNA interactions) or where one protein phosphorylates or regulates another (Sharan & Ideker, 2006). Protein interactions can also represent functional associations; two proteins are connected by an edge if they take part in the same biological process. Weights can be assigned to edges to represent the confidence of an interaction.

Recently, several research groups have begun to systematically analyze and compare biological networks. Typical network analysis include (i) network querying (Banks et al., 2008; Dost et al., 2007; Ferro et al., 2007), which is commonly used to establish the presence of structural motifs in a network (even approximated) and if such motifs are functional (over-representation); and (ii) network alignment (Flannick et al., 2006; Kalaev et al., 2009; Kelley et al., 2003) to understand if some functional complexes are conserved among species (by analogy to the multiple sequence alignment approach), to infer the evolutionary relationship among two or more networks. This research area has a further product which is the growth of interaction network datasets (Berglund et al., 2007; O'Brien et al., 2005).

Searching in Biological Networks

In the last few years substantial research effort has been spent on the design of efficient and biologically meaningful tools for network querying (Banks et al., 2008; Dost et al., 2007; Ferro et al., 2007; Flannick et al., 2008; Kalaev et al., 2009; Kelley et al., 2004). Most of the approaches fall into the categories, not strictly separated, of networks alignment, network motif finding, and subgraph queries. Network alignment tools can be used to identify schemas for which the criterion for matching a query protein to a target protein is sequence similarity (see the next subsection). Many tools exist to discover network motifs or over-represented topological patterns in graphs (Kashtan et al., 2004; Schreiber et al., 2005; Wernicke et al., 2006).

In (Kashtan et al., 2004), the authors propose an algorithm based on random sampling to extract all statistically significant subgraphs. Network motifs are detected with a small number of samples in a wide variety of networks. The algorithm samples subgraphs of n nodes by picking random connected edges until a set of n nodes is reached. The sampled subgraph is composed of the set of n nodes together with all the edges that connect these nodes in the original network.

To sample an n-node subgraph, an ordered set of n-1 edges is iteratively randomly picked. Let P_s be the probability of sampling a particular subgraph S. To compute the probability, P_s, all possible ordered sets of n-1 edges that could lead to sampling such a subgraph must be checked. Let S_m be the set of all possible n-1 permutations of the edges from the subgraph edges that could lead to the specific subgraph S, and let E_j be the

j-*th* edge in a specific permutation, say σ. The probability of sampling the subgraph is defined as the sum of the probabilities of all such possible ordered sets of n-1 edges:

$$P_g = \sum_{\sigma \in S_m} \prod_{E_j \in \sigma} P[E_j = e_j \mid (E_1, \cdots, E_{j-1}) = (e_1, \ldots, e_{j-1})]$$

(1)

Each subgraph type, S_i, receives a score. The score is increased by the weight $W=1/P$ after each sample and this is repeated for a total number of samples S_T. Assuming that, after S_T samples, L different subgraphs have been sampled, the concentration of subgraph S_i is computed by:

$$C_i = \frac{S_i}{\sum_{S_j \in L} S_k}$$

(2)

Then, the statistical significance of each sample's subgraph S_i is computed as a z-score.

MAVisto (Schreiber et al., 2005) is a motif search algorithm that discovers all motifs of a particular size. This size is given either by the number of vertices or by the number of edges. All motifs of the given size are analyzed and three kind of frequencies together with z-scores and p-values are computed to establish statistical significance. The p-value and the z-score are obtained by comparing the frequency of all occurrences of a motif in the target network to the frequency values of this motif in an ensemble of randomizations of the target networks (S. Bornholdt, Schuster, & Wiley, 2003). The frequency of a pattern in a target graph is the maximum number of different matches of this pattern. There are different concepts for determining the frequency of a pattern depending on which elements of the graph can be shared by two matches.

Frequency concept F_1 counts every match of this pattern. This concept gives a complete overview of all possible occurrences of a pattern even if elements of the target graph have to be used several times. It does not exclude possible matches (as the other concepts often do) and therefore shows the full potential of the target graph with respect to the pattern. Frequency concepts F_2 and F_3 restrict the reuse of graph elements shared by different matches of a pattern. If different matches share graph elements not allowed by the particular concept, not all matches will be counted for the frequency. In this case the maximum set of non-overlapping matches selected for frequency counting will be computed. This problem is modeled as an instance of the maximum independent set.

In (Wernicke et al., 2006) authors present FANMOD, a tool for network motif detection that implements an algorithm, called RAND-ESU (Wernicke, 2006), which efficiently enumerates and sample subgraphs. As noted in (Kashtan, Itzkovitz, Milo, & Alon, 2004) the probabilities of sampling different specific sub-graphs in the network are biased. For this reason, some subgraphs are sampled more often than others even if they have the same topology. Kashtan et al (Kashtan et al., 2004) corrected this by introducing an unbiased estimator based on normalization over different possible samplings. However, in (Wernicke, 2006), authors observe that many problems are still present. Certain subgraphs are still more likely to be sampled than others. Computing the equation in 1 is expensive since the computation of a single probability could require in the worst case $O(k^k)$ with k the size of the subgraph. Such a computation hides much redundancy in the sampling procedure and there is no estimation of what fraction of subgraphs has been sampled.

The basic idea of FANMOD is to begin with an algorithm able to efficiently enumerate all size-k subgraphs. The algorithm is then adjusted to perform an unbiased sampling by skipping some of the sub-graphs during the execution. A size - k subgraph is a connected subgraph induced by a vertex set of cardinality k. Given an integer k, the set of all size- k subgraphs in G can be partitioned into subsets, $S_i^k(G)$ called subgraph

classes, where two size-k sub-graphs belong to the same subgraph class if and only if they are isomorphic. The concentration of a sub-graph class $S_i^K(G)$ is defined using the Equation (2). The algorithm works as follows. For each vertex v from the input graph, a set $V_{Extenstion}$ is built with nodes having the following two properties: (i) their labels must be larger than the one of v and (ii) they may only be neighbored to the newly added vertex w but not to a vertex already in the constructing subgraph $V_{Subgraph}$. The algorithm proceeds recursively by picking a node w from $V_{Extenstion}$ uniformly and at random and then putting it into $V_{Subgraph}$. The algorithm next upgrades $V_{Extenstion}$ with nodes having the two properties above. Such an algorithm builds a tree, called ESU-tree which completely traverses all the nodes of the graph. The complete traversal could be too time-expensive. For this reason in (Wernicke, 2006) the authors introduced a randomized version of the above algorithm which explores only parts of the ESU-tree.

In (Alon, Dao, Hajirasouliha, Hormozdiari, & Sahinalp, 2008), the authors present a randomized approximation algorithm based on color coding technique (Alon, Yuster, & Zwick, 2005), for biomolecular motif counting, with running time $2^{O(k)} \times n^{O(1)}$ that takes polynomial time providing $k=O(logn)$. Color coding is used to find simple paths and simple cycles of a specified length k within a given graph of size n. The basic idea is to randomly assign k colors to the vertices of the graph and then search for colorful paths in which each color is used exactly once. Thus, rather than having to maintain the list of vertices visited so far (of size $O(n^k)$), one can maintain a list of colors at considerably lower complexity $O(2^k)$.

Given G and a tree T with k vertices, the authors analyze the problem of counting the number of non-induced subtrees of G that are isomorphic to T. A tree T' is said to be a non-induced occurrence of T in G, if T' is a subtree in G that is isomorphic to T. The algorithm counts the number of non-induced occurrences of a tree T with k vertices in G as follows. (i) Color coding. Color each vertex of input graph G independently and uniformly at random with one of the k colors. (ii) Counting. Apply a dynamic programming algorithm to count the number of non-induced occurrences of T in which each vertex has a unique color. (iii) Repeat the two steps above $O(e^k)$ times and add up the number of occurrences of T to get an estimate on the number of its occurrences in G. The authors show that the algorithm is quite efficient in practice and is able to outperform other methods such as (Grochow et al., 2007; Hormozdiari et al., 2009, King et al. 2004). Furthermore, the authors show, for the first time, all possible tree topologies of 8, 9 and 10 vertices in protein-protein interaction networks of various organisms such as S.Cerevisiae (Yeast), E.coli, H.pylori and C.elegans (Worm) protein-protein interaction networks available via the DIP database (Xenarios et al., 2002).

However, in none of these approaches can a user structurally specify a network to be queried. In (Lacroix, Fernandes, & Sagot, 2006) authors propose MOTUS, a tool for non-topology constrained subgraph searches in metabolic networks. The authors introduce a new definition of motif, called *reaction motif*, in the context of metabolic networks. The basic definition based on topological features is enriched with the functional nature of the components that form the motif. Let C be a finite set of labels, referred as colors, drawn from a graph G representing a metabolic network. For each vertex of the graph, a set of colors from C is given. A motif is formally defined as a multiset of elements from the set C of colors. Intuitively, an occurrence is a connected set of vertices labelled by the colors of the motif.

In (Dost et al., 2007) the authors present QNet, an algorithmic framework for handling tree queries under non-exact, homeomorphic, matches. QNet provides an algorithm for querying subnetworks of bounded tree-width and is able to efficiently handle small tree queries in large networks.

Let $G=(V,E,w)$, be a weighted graph with n nodes and m edges representing a protein-protein interaction network, where $w : E \rightarrow R$, measures the interaction reliability. Let $G_Q(V_Q, E_Q)$ be a query graph with k vertices. Let $h(q,v)$ be a similarity score, defined as the sequence similarity, between query node $q \in V_Q$ and vertex $v \in V$. A query node q is homologous to a graph vertex v, if the corresponding similarity score $h(q,v)$ is above a fixed threshold. In order to perform an alignment between the query and the network, the authors introduce the subdivision of an edge (u,v) in a graph $H(U,F)$ by replacing it with two edges (u,w) and (w,v), where $w \notin U$ and creating a new graph $H' = (U \cup w, F \cup \{(u,w),(w,v)\} \setminus \{(u,v)\})$. When the network G can be obtained by a series of subdivisions, H is considered extendible (H is homeomorphic to G). An alignment of the query graph G_Q to G is defined as: (i) a subgraph $G_A = (V_A, E_A)$ of G called alignment subgraph; and (ii) a bijection, $\sigma : V_Q^S \rightarrow V_A^S$, between a subset of query nodes, $V_Q^S \subseteq V_Q$, and the homologous vertices in the alignment subgraph, $V_A^S \in V_A$. The vertices in $V_Q^S \cup V_A^S$ are called skeleton vertices. Pairs of vertices $(q, \sigma(q)) \in V_Q^S \times V_A^S$ are called aligned. An alignment is proper if there exists a pair of skeleton graphs $S_Q = (V_Q^S, E_Q^S)$ and $S_A = (V_A^S, E_A^S)$ such that there is an isomorphism between S_Q and S_A which respects the alignment and G_Q and G_A G_A are homeomorphic (i.e. S_Q is extendable to G_Q and S_A is extendable to G_A). By using this definition, the authors introduce the concept of node deletion (i.e. nodes that are not aligned with network nodes), node insertion, vertices in the alignment subgraph that are not aligned with query nodes. The graph query problem is formally defined as follows: Given a query graph G_Q, a graph G, a similarity score h, and penalty scores for insertions and deletions, find a proper alignment of G_Q in G with maximal weight. By limiting the number of insertions and deletions in the alignment the evolutionary distance between the two subnetworks can be controlled. This can be done by introducing a variation of the problem in which the number of insertions and deletions are limited by N_{ins} and N_{del} respectively.

In the general case, the problem above is equivalent to the subgraph isomorphism problem (Ullmann, 1976). By exploiting the underlying biological constraints and motivated by known pathways in KEGG (Kanehisa, Goto, Kawashima, Okuno, & Hattori, 2004), the authors considered simple and restricted topologies such as tree queries and a graph of bounded tree-width (Pinter, Rokhlenko, Yeger-Lotem, & Ziv-Ukelson, 2005). The authors attack the problem by adapting the color coding method (Alon et al., 1995) to make the problem tractable. The authors build an optimal alignment by extending optimal sub-alignments using dynamic programming (see Dost et al. (2007) for more details). Adding a network vertex to the optimal alignment can be done only if this vertex is not already contained in the sub-optimal alignment. For this reason, each potential sub-optimal alignment should maintain the list of at most k vertices already matched. This yields $O(n^k)$ potential alignments. By using the color coding, each network vertex is randomly colored with one of k colors, looking for a colorful alignment. Thus, a list of used colors of size $O(2^k)$ is enough and reduces the running time significantly. In this way the algorithm become probabilistic and the computation returns a correct answer with probability $\frac{k!}{k^k} = e^{-k}$, if the optimum alignment is colorful. Such a probability can be made small enough (i.e. ε) by repeating the experiment $\ln(1/\varepsilon)e^k$ times. In (Dost et al., 2007), the authors present also the first large scale cross-species comparison of protein complexes, by querying known yeast complexes in the fly protein interaction network.

In (Ferro et al., 2007), authors present Net-Match, a tool that allows users to perform sub-graph queries in biological networks. The tool extends the algorithm presented in (Cordella et al., 2004) allowing it to perform a basic kind of inexact queries. The tool allows also establishing the statistical significance of a found motif. Net-Match is implemented as plug-in to the Cytoscape (Shannon et al., 2003) environment.

SAGA (Tian et al., 2007) is a flexible querying system, which can handle node insertions and deletions. The key point of the algorithm is a distance measure between graphs. Fragments of the query are compared to database fragments using the distance measure. Matching fragments are then assembled into larger matches using clique detection heuristic and, finally, candidate matches are evaluated. SAGA allows inexact matches to a query in multiple networks, and has built-in support for biological networks where proteins are described via orthologous groups.

NetGrep (Banks et al., 2008) is a standalone, multi-platform system supporting flexibility via optional nodes (thereby permitting inexact matches) and proteins and interaction descriptions that may consist of Boolean conjunctions or disjunctions of features. An interaction network is represented as a mixed graph $G=(V_N, E_N, A_N)$ where V_N is the set of nodes (proteins), E_N is the set of undirected edges, and A_N is the set of directed edges. The two kinds of edges allow the representation of different type of interactions. The set of all possible protein labels (i.e. protein IDs) is represented by L, and the set of all possible kinds of edges is represented by T (i.e. regulatory interactions). Each vertex v in the network has an associated set of features $l(v) \subset L$, each edge (u,v) has a set of interaction types $t_e(u,v) \in T$, and each arc (u,v) has an associated a set of types $t_a(u,v) \in T$. A network schema is a mixed graph $H = (V_S, E_S, A_S)$ such that: (i) each vertex $v \in V_S$ has an associated description set D_v such that each $d \in D_v$ is a subset of L; (ii) for every $(u,v) \in E_S \cup A_S$, there is an associated description set $D'_{u,v} \subseteq T$. An instance of a network schema H in an interaction network G (that is, a match in the network for the schema) is a subgraph (V,E,A) where $V_I \subset V_N$, $E_I \subset E_N$, and $A_I \subset A_N$ such that there is a one-to-one mapping $f : V_S \rightarrow V_I$ where: (1) for each $v \in V_S$, there exists $d \in D_v$ such that $d \subseteq l(f(v))$; (2) for each $(u,v) \in E_S \cup A_S$ there exists a $d' \in D'_{u,v}$ such that $d' \subseteq (t_e(f(u), f(v)) \cup t_a(f(u), f(v)))$. In this definition, two distinct instances must differ in at least one protein. Network schemas are used to query the interaction network for sets of proteins that match this description.

NetGrep defines also the interaction reliability following (Mering et al., 2003; Nabieva, et al., 2005) $r(u,v) = 1 - \prod_j (1 - s_{g(j)})$, for a pair of proteins u and v, where j is the number of interactions found between the proteins and $g(j)$ represents the experimental group for the *j-th* interaction. To perform the search, NetGrep preprocesses the interactome and builds look-up tables mapping protein and interaction type labels to proteins associated with the labels. In this way the set of all proteins that match the node's feature set is enumerated. Next, the labeled schema nodes and edges is used to prune the search space. This allows to filter most of the network schema that is useless for the searching process. For the proteins that pass the filter interaction matches along each edge in the schema are determined and stored. These interactions, which are fewer than the original networks, are cached and enumerated for fast lookup. Finally the full list of matches is returned. In this way NetGrep is able to speed up the searching process.

Biological Network Alignment

Network alignment algorithms rely on two components: a scoring function and a search method. The scoring function assigns a numerical value to the network alignment and measures the similar-

ity of aligned subnetworks. High values indicate conservation. The search algorithm searches the set of possible network alignments for the highest scoring network alignment (see Figure 4).

Scoring function research has focused on models of network evolution. Koyuturk et. al. (2004) propose a scoring scheme to model protein evolution together with a duplication-divergence model. Let M be the set of matches among the two subnetworks being compared (that is, two pairs of interacting proteins, one in each subnetwork, with orthology relations between them). Let N be the set of mismatched interactions (that is, two pairs of proteins with orthology relations between them, such that only one pair interacts). Let D be the union of the sets of duplicated protein pairs within each subnetwork. Suppose that scoring functions for a match, mismatch and duplication are provided, the overall score is defined as:

$$\sum_{m \in M} s_m(m) - \sum_{n \in N} s_n(n) - \sum_{d \in D} s_d(d) \qquad (1)$$

In (Kelley et al., 2004) authors propose a scoring function to evaluate the quality of the alignment of two pathways. The two protein interaction networks N_1 and N_2 are combined into a global alignment graph G_{N_1,N_2}. Each vertex in G_{N_1,N_2} represents a protein pair A/a between the two networks. Vertices A/a and B/b in G_{N_1,N_2} are connected by an undirected edge. Three kinds of edges are present: direct, gapped, or mismatched. The type direct is present when the corresponding edges are both present in N_1 and N_2. When one edge is present in N_1 (N_2 respectively) and in N_2 (N_1 respectively), the distance between the two nodes is 2, the type of edge is gapped in N_1 (gap in N_2 respectively). When in both networks the distance between the two nodes is 2, the type of edge in the alignment graph is mismatched. A pathway alignment corresponds to a simple path P through G_{N_1,N_2}. The authors formulated a log probability score as follows:

Figure 4. It shows three networks. In each network are highlited nodes and edges yielding a biologically sound network alignment. Box represents nodes equivalence classes. Each class contains homologous proteins.

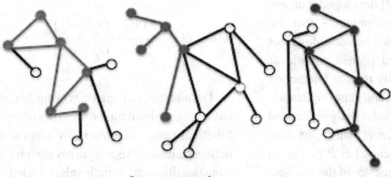

Input networks.

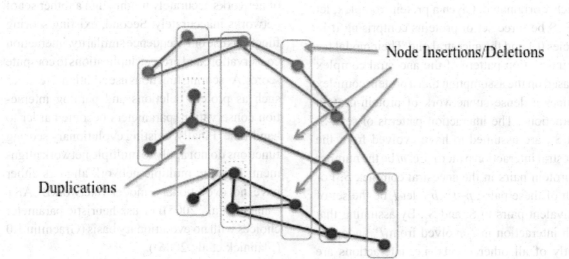

Node Insertions/Deletions

Duplications

Network Alignment.

$$S(P) = \sum_{v \in P} \log_{10} \frac{p(v)}{p_{random}} + \sum_{e \in P} \log_{10} \frac{q(e)}{q_{random}}$$

(2)

$S(P)$ decomposes over the vertices v and edges e of a path P through G_{N_1,N_2}. $p(v)$ represents the probability of true homology, computed using the Bayes rule[3], within the protein pair repre-

sented by v, given its pairwise protein sequence similarity measured by the BLAST E value. $q(e)$ is the probability that the protein-protein interactions represented by e is not false[4]. The background probabilities P_{random} and q_{random} are the expected values of $p(v)$ and $q(e)$ over vertices and edges of G_{N_1,N_2}.

Berg and Lassig (2004) present a stochastic model of network evolution based on observed rates of link and duplication dynamics. The key point of the link dynamics is an asymmetric preferential attachment rule, for which the authors show empirical data support.

Hirsh and Sharan (2007) developed a probabilistic model for protein complexes that are conserved across two species. The model describes the evolution of conserved protein complexes from an ancestral species by protein interaction attachment and detachment and gene duplication events. Let the two species under study be indexed by 0 and 1, respectively. Let P_0 and P_1 be their corresponding sets of proteins. Let P be the set of proteins of a common ancestor of the two species. Let $\varphi(\cdot)$ be a mapping from proteins in $P_0 \cup P_1$ to P. $\varphi(x)$ is the ancestral protein from which x originated. Given a protein complex, let S_0, S_1, S be three set of proteins comprising it in species $0, 1$ and the ancestral one. Their model for the interaction pattern of the ancestral complex is based on the assumption that a protein complex induces a dense subnetwork of protein-protein interactions. The interaction patterns of sets, S_0 and S_1, are assumed to have evolved from the ancestral interaction pattern. Let m be the number of protein pairs in the ancestral complex S. For each of these pairs, $p_i=(a_i b_i)$, let I_i be the set of equivalent pairs in S_0 and S_1. By assuming that each interaction in I_i evolved from P_i, independently of all other events, i.e. interactions are attached with some probability P_A and detached with probability P_D. For two proteins x,y, let T_{xy} be the event that these two proteins interact and let F_{xy} be the event that they do not interact. Let $O_{xy}=\{0,1\}$ denote the observation on whether x and y interact. Let O_S denote the entire set of observations on the members of S. Let D_S be the set of duplicated pairs in S. The likelihood of a set of observations on a conserved complex is defined as follows:

$$P(O_{S_0}, O_{S_1} \mid M_C) = \prod_{i=1}^{m} P(O_{I_i} \mid M_C) \times \prod_{(x,y) \in D_{S_0} \cup D_{S_1}} (O_{xy} \mid M_C)$$

(3)

Given the null model M_N and the corresponding likelihood, the likelihood of a putative conserved complex is defined as:

$$L(O_{S_0}, O_{S_1}) = \frac{P(O_{S_0}, O_{S_1} \mid M_C)}{P(O_{S_0}, O_{S_1} \mid M_N)}$$

(4)

Despite these advances, scoring functions still have several limitations. First, existing scoring functions cannot automatically adapt to multiple network datasets. Because networks have different edge densities and noise levels, which depend on the experiments or integration methods used to obtain the networks, parameters that align one set of networks accurately might align another set of networks inaccurately. Second, existing scoring functions use only sequence similarity, interaction conservation, and protein duplications to compute scores. As scoring functions use additional features such as protein deletions and paralog interaction conservation, parameters become harder to hand-tune. Finally, existing evolutionary scoring functions do not apply to multiple network alignment. Existing multiple network aligners either have no evolutionary model (NetworkBLAST (Sharan et al., 2005)) or use heuristic parameter choices with no evolutionary basis (Graemlin 1.0 (Flannick et al., 2006)).

Given n networks $G_1, ..., G_n$, a multiple network alignment can be defined as an equivalence relation on the nodes $V = V_1 \cup \cdots \cup V_n$. An equivalence relation partitions V into a set of disjoint equivalence classes. The nodes in the same equivalence class are functionally orthologous, the subset of nodes in a local alignment represents a conserved module (i.e. pathway).

The local alignment can be viewed as a relation over a subset of the nodes in V whereas a global alignment is a relation over all nodes in V. Given the scoring function the network alignment problem is to find the maximum score (global or local) network alignment. The local network alignment problem is to find a set of maximal score local network alignments.

The scoring function proposed in (Flannick et al., 2008) computes the features of a network alignment. A vector-valued feature function $f : A \rightarrow R_n$, maps a global alignment to a numerical feature vector. In particular, a node feature function f_N maps equivalence classes to a feature vector and an edge feature function f_E maps pairs of equivalence classes to a feature vector. Given an alignment a the scoring function is defined as:

$$s(a) = \mathbf{w} \times f(a) = \mathbf{w} \times \begin{bmatrix} \sum_{[x] \in a} f_N([x]) \\ \sum_{[x],[y] \in a} f_E([x],[y]) \end{bmatrix}$$

(5)

where $\mathbf{w}$ is a numerical vector. In (Flannick et al., 2008) authors find the best $\mathbf{w}$ through a parameter-learning algorithm.

Most network alignment research has focused on pairwise network alignment search algorithms. PathBLAST uses a randomized dynamic programming algorithm to find conserved pathways (Kelley et al., 2004) and uses a greedy algorithm to find conserved protein complexes. PathBLAST allows the identification of conserved pathways between to two protein interaction networks. It makes use of the alignment graph defined above G_{N_1,N_2}. The computational method has come conceptual similarities with the sequence alignment method BLAST (Altschul et al., 1997). It searches for high-scoring pathway alignments involving two paths, one from each network. Proteins of the first path are paired, allowing gaps and mismatches, with the putative homolog occurring in the same order in the second path. The gap occurs when a protein interaction in one path skips over a protein in the other, whereas a mismatch occurs when aligned proteins do not have sequence similarity (i.e. BLAST *e-value*>E_{cutoff}). The alignment procedure yields the highest-scoring pathway alignment $P *$ of fixed length L (L vertices and L-1 edges). When the alignment graph is directed and acyclic the pathway can be computed in linear time by using dynamic programming. NetworkBLAST (Sharan et al., 2005)) (see (Kalaev, Smoot, Ideker, & Sharan, 2008) for its implementation as web server) extends Path-BLAST to align three species simultaneously.

MaWISh (Tianut & Samatova, 2009) merges pairwise interaction networks into a single alignment graph and formulates network alignment as a maximum weight induced subgraph problem. The aim is to identify conserved multi-protein complexes (clique-like structures). Since, such structures will likely contain hubs (high-degree node), the algorithm starts by aligning a pair of homologous hubs and proceeds greedily.

MetaPathwayHunter (Pinter et al., 2005) uses an efficient tree matching algorithm to find inexact matches to a query pathway in a network database. Given a query pathway and a collection of pathways, the algorithm finds and reports all approximate occurrences of the query in the collection, ranked by similarity and statistical significance. The authors assert that the topology of most metabolic pathways can be easily transformed to multi-source trees without much loss of generality, as cycles are quite rare in these data. A multi-source tree is a directed acyclic graph (DAG), whose underlying undirected graph is a tree, where some of the nodes can have several incoming as well as several outgoing edges. MetaPathwayHunter performs inexact subtree homeomorphism since a single enzyme in one pathway may replace a few consecutively acting enzymes in another pathway due to the fact that the replacing enzyme is multifunctional and can thus catalyze several consecutive reactions, or if the enzyme uses an alternative catalysis that leads directly from the initial substrate to the final product. The authors show similarities and differences in the metabolic networks of the bacterium Escherichia coli and the yeast Saccharomyces cerevisiae, noticing that most subtrees between the species are conserved and thus providing insight into the evolution of metabolic pathways.

In (Kalaev, Bafna, & Sharan, 2009) the authors propose NetworkBAST-M, an algorithm for multiple network alignment based on a novel representation of the network data. The algorithm avoids the explicit representation of every set of potentially orthologous proteins (which form a node in the network alignment graph), thereby achieving a reduction in time and memory requirements. Given k protein-protein interaction networks, the authors represent them through a k-layer graph (layered alignment graph). Each layer corresponds to a species and contains the corresponding network. Additional edges connect proteins from different layers if they have a statistically significant sequence similarity. A set, called k-spine, represents a subgraph of size k that includes a vertex from each of the layers. The basic idea of the algorithm is the assumption that a k-spine corresponding to a set of truly orthologous proteins must be connected and admits a spanning tree. A collection of (connected) k-spines induces a candidate conserved subnetwork. Such networks are scored using a likelihood ratio score as described in equation 5. For fixed m, the algorithm looks for high scoring m-subnets. This problem is computationally hard, so the authors use a greedy heuristic that starts from high weight seeds and expands them using a local search.

Graemlin 2.0 (Flannick et al., 2008) determines the weight vector w in the scoring function of Equation 1 by using a set of known alignments (authors use KEGG Ortholog groups as training sets). Given a set of d training samples in which each sample consists of a set of networks with the corresponding correct alignments, the learning algorithm, based subgradient descent, uses a loss function to establish the distance between a computed alignment and an alignment present in the training set. The parameter vector w will assign higher scores to alignments with smaller loss function values. The authors introduced also a loss function that grows as the alignment diverges from the correct one. Once the optimal parameter vector has been learned, the algorithm finds the highest scoring global alignment.

To compute a global alignment, the authors implemented a local hill-climbing algorithm that, in a greedy way, increases the score of the alignment. At the beginning the alignment contains every node in a separate equivalence class. The algorithm iteratively updates the current alignment. At each iteration, it processes each node and evaluates the following moves: leave the node alone, create a new equivalence class with only the node, move the node to another equivalence class, merge the entire equivalence class with another equivalence class. The algorithm computes the alignment score before and after the move and performs moves that most increases the score. After a complete processing of the nodes it begins another iteration. The algorithm stops when iteration does not increase the alignment score. The algorithm considers as candidates only equivalence classes with a node that has homology (BLAST *e-value* $<10^{-5}$) to the processed node. However, like many greedy algorithms, this algorithm is sensitive the order in which the nodes are processed.

SUMMARY AND THE FUTURE

Exact and inexact subgraph matching are of great practical importance and have given birth to many algorithms, some general and some application-specific. The basic approach is to filter away graphs and parts of graphs first and then to use heuristics to solve the remaining exponential time problems. The heuristics can be domain-independent, but even better ones can be domain-dependent. Filtering involves the construction and traversal of indexing and has advanced thanks to numerous creative insights.

We expect future algorithms to attack (i) web-sized graphs (ii) using new data structures and techniques (iii) for a variety of sociological, scientific, and perhaps even literary applications. We also expect further tight connections between graph matching and machine learning in order to help users gain the most insight possible from the graphs their data reveals.

REFERENCES

Akinniyi, F., Wong, A., & Stacey, D. (1986). A new algorithm for graph monomorphism based on the projections of the product graph. *Trans Systems, Man and Cybernetics* (16), 740-751.

Albert, R., & Barabasi, A. (2002). Statistical mechanics of complex networks. *Reviews of Modern Physics, 74*(1), 47–97. doi:10.1103/RevModPhys.74.47

Alm, E., & Arkin, A. (2003). Biological networks. *Current Opinion in Structural Biology, 13*(2), 193–202. doi:10.1016/S0959-440X(03)00031-9

Alon, N., Dao, P., Hajirasouliha, I., Hormozdiari, F., & Sahinalp, S. (2008). Biomolecular network motif counting and discovery by color coding. *Bioinformatics (Oxford, England), 24*(13), 241. doi:10.1093/bioinformatics/btn163

Alon, N., Yuster, R., & Zwick, U. (1995). Color-coding. [JACM]. *Journal of the ACM, 42*(4), 856. doi:10.1145/210332.210337

Alon, N., Zwick, U., & Yuster, R. (1995). Color-coding. Electronic colloquium on computational complexity. In Nilsson, N. (1980), Principles of artificial intelligence. [Palo Alto, CA: Tioga.]. *Journal of the ACM, 42*(4), 44–856.

Altschul, S., Madden, T., Schaffer, A., Zhang, J., Zhang, Z., & Miller, W. (1997). Gapped blast and psi-blast: A new generation of protein database search programs. *Nucleic Acids Research, 25*(17), 3389. doi:10.1093/nar/25.17.3389

Ambauen, R., Fischer, S., & Bunke, H. (2003). Graph edit distance with node splitting and merging, and its application to diatom identification. *Lecture Notes in Computer Science*, 259–264.

Banks, E., Nabieva, E., Peterson, R., & Singh, M. (2008). Netgrep: Fast network schema searches in interactomes. *Genome Biology, 9*(9), R138. doi:10.1186/gb-2008-9-9-r138

Barrow, H., & Burstall, R. M. (1976). Subgraph isomorphism, matching relational structures and maximal cliques. *Information Processing Letters, 4*, 83–84. doi:10.1016/0020-0190(76)90049-1

Batz, G. (2006). *An optimization technique for subgraph matching strategies (Tech. Rep.)*. Universitat Karlsruhe, Faculty of Informatik.

Berg, J., & Lassig, M. (2004). Local graph alignment and motif search in biological networks. *Proceedings of the National Academy of Sciences of the United States of America, 101*(41), 14689. doi:10.1073/pnas.0305199101

Berglund, A., Sjolund, E., Ostlund, G., & Sonnhammer, E. (2007). Inparanoid 6: Eukaryotic ortholog clusters with inparalogs. *Nucleic acids research*.

Berretti, S., Del Bimbo, A., & Pala, P. (2004). A graph edit distance based on node merging. *CIVR*, 464 - 472.

Boeres, M., Ribeiro, C., & Bloch, I. (2004). A randomized heuristic for scene recognition by graph matching. *WEA*, 100 - 113.

Boiani, M., & Scholer, H. (2005). Regulatory networks in embryo-derived pluripotent stem cells. *Nature Reviews. Molecular Cell Biology, 6*(11), 872–881. doi:10.1038/nrm1744

Bork, P., Jensen, L., Von Mering, C., Ramani, A., Lee, I., & Marcotte, E. (2004). Protein interaction networks from yeast to human. *Current Opinion in Structural Biology, 14*(3), 292–299. doi:10.1016/j.sbi.2004.05.003

Bornholdt, S., Schuster, H., & Wiley, J. (2003). *Handbook of graphs and networks*. Wiley Online Library.

Bunke, H. (1999). Error correcting graph matching: On the influence of the underlying cost function. *IEEE Transactions on Pattern Analysis and Machine Intelligence*, *21*(9), 917–922. doi:10.1109/34.790431

Bunke, H., & Allermann, G. (1983). Inexact graph matching for structural pattern recognition. *Pattern Recognition Letters*, *1*(4), 245–253. doi:10.1016/0167-8655(83)90033-8

Champin, P., & Solnon, C. (2003). Measuring the similarity of labeled graphs. *Conference on case-based reasoning (ICCBR)*, 100 - 113.

Chen, X., Xu, H., Yuan, P., Fang, F., Huss, M., & Vega, V.,…NG, H. (2008). Integration of external signaling pathways with the core transcriptional network in embryonic stem cells. *Cell*, *133*(6), 1106–1117. doi:10.1016/j.cell.2008.04.043

Cheng, J., Ke, Y., Ng, W., & Lu, A. (2007). Fg-index: Towards verification-free query processing on graph databases. *Proceedings of ACM SIGMOD International Conference on Management of Data*.

Cordella, L., Foggia, P., Sansone, C., & Vento, M. (1996). An efficient algorithm for the inexact matching of arg graphs using a contextual transformational model. *Proceedings of the 13th ICPR*, 3, 180 - 184.

Cordella, L., Foggia, P., Sansone, C., & Vento, M. (2004). A (sub)graph isomorphism algorithm for matching large graphs. *IEEE Transactions on Pattern Analysis and Machine Intelligence*, *26*(10), 1367–1372. doi:10.1109/TPAMI.2004.75

Corneil, D., & Gotlieb, C. C. (1970). An efficient algorithm for graph isomorphism. *Journal of the ACM*, *17*(1), 51–64. doi:10.1145/321556.321562

Cortadella, L., & Valiente, G. (2000). A relational view of subgraph isomorphism. *Proceedings of 5th International Seminar on Relational Methods in Computer Science*, 45-54.

Dessmark, A., Lingas, A., & Proskurowski, A. (2000). Faster algorithms for subgraph isomorphism of k-connected partial k-trees. *Algorithmica*, *3*(27), 337–347. doi:10.1007/s004530010023

Di Natale, R., Ferro, A., Giugno, R., Mongiovì, M., Pulvirenti, A., & Shasha, D. (2010). Sing: Subgraph search in non-homogeneous graphs. *BMC Bioinformatics*, 11.

Dickinson, P., Bunke, H., Dadej, A., & Kraetzl, M. (2004). Matching graphs with unique node labels. *Pattern Analysis & Applications*, 7, 243–254.

Dost, B., Shlomi, T., Gupta, N., Ruppin, E., Bafna, V., & Sharan, R. (2007). Qnet: A tool for querying protein interaction networks. *In Research in computational molecular biology* (pp. 1–15).

Eppstein, D. (1999). Subgraph isomorphism in planar graphs and related problems. *Graph Algorithms e Appl*, *3*(3), 1–27.

Eshera, M. A., & Fu, K.-S. (1984). A graph distance measure for image analysis. *IEEE Transactions on Systems, Man, and Cybernetics*, *14*(3), 353–363.

Faloutsos, M., Faloutsos, P., & Faloutsos, C. (1999). On power-law relationships of the Internet topology. In *Proceedings of the Conference on Applications, Technologies, Architectures, and Protocols for Computer Communication*, 251 - 262.

Fernandez, M.-L., & Valiente, G. (2001). A graph distance metric combining maximum common subgraph and minimum common supergraph. *Pattern Recognition Letters*, 753–758. doi:10.1016/S0167-8655(01)00017-4

Ferro, A., Giugno, R., Mongiovì, M., Pulvirenti, A., Skripin, D., & Shasha, D. (2008). Graphfind: Enhancing graph searching by low support data mining techniques. *BMC Bioinformatics*, 9.

Ferro, A., Giugno, R., Pigola, G., Pulvirenti, A., Skripin, D., & Bader, G. (2007). Netmatch: A cytoscape plugin for searching biological networks. *Bioinformatics (Oxford, England)*, *23*(7), 910. doi:10.1093/bioinformatics/btm032

Flannick, J., Novak, A., Do, C., Srinivasan, B., & Batzoglou, S. (2008). Automatic parameter learning for multiple network alignment. *In Proceedings of the 12th Annual International Conference on Research in Computational Molecular Biology*, 214 - 231.

Flannick, J., Novak, A., Srinivasan, B., McAdams, H., & Batzoglou, S. (2006). Graemlin: General and robust alignment of multiple large interaction networks. *Genome Research*, *16*(9), 1169. doi:10.1101/gr.5235706

Garey, M., & Johnson, D. (1979). *Computers and intractability: A guide to the theory of np-completeness*. Freeman and Company.

Giugno, R., & Shasha, D. (2002). Graphgrep: A fast and universal method for querying graphs. *Proceeding of the International Conference in Pattern recognition (ICPR)*.

Grochow, J., & Kellis, M. (2007). Network motif discovery using subgraph enumeration and symmetry-breaking. *In Research in Computational Molecular Biology* (pp. 92 - 106).

He, H., & Singh, A. K. (2006). Closure-tree: An index structure for graph queries. *Proceedings of the 22nd International Conference on Data Engineering (ICDE '06)*.

Henderson, T. C. (1990). *Discrete relaxation techniques*. UK: Oxford University Press.

Hirsh, E., & Sharan, R. (2007). Identification of conserved protein complexes based on a model of protein network evolution. *Bioinformatics (Oxford, England)*, *23*(2), e170. doi:10.1093/bioinformatics/btl295

Horaud, R., & Skordas, T. (1989). Stereo correspondence through feature grouping and maximal cliques. *IEEE Transactions on Pattern Analysis and Machine Intelligence*, *11*(11), 1168–1180. doi:10.1109/34.42855

Hormozdiari, F., Alkan, C., Eichler, E., & Sahinalp, S. (2009). Combinatorial algorithms for structuralvariation detection in high-throughput sequenced genomes. *Genome Research*, *19*(7), 1270. doi:10.1101/gr.088633.108

Kalaev, M., Bafna, V., & Sharan, R. (2009). Fast and accurate alignment of multiple protein networks. *Journal of Computational Biology*, *16*(8), 989–999. doi:10.1089/cmb.2009.0136

Kalaev, M., Smoot, M., Ideker, T., & Sharan, R. (2008). Networkblast: Comparative analysis of protein networks. *Bioinformatics (Oxford, England)*, *24*(4), 594. doi:10.1093/bioinformatics/btm630

Kanehisa, M., Goto, S., Kawashima, S., Okuno, Y., & Hattori, M. (2004). The kegg resource for deciphering the genome. *Nucleic Acids Research*, *32*(Database Issue), D277. doi:10.1093/nar/gkh063

Kashtan, N., Itzkovitz, S., Milo, R., & Alon, U. (2004). Efficient sampling algorithm for estimating subgraph concentrations and detecting network motifs. *Bioinformatics (Oxford, England)*, *20*(11), 1746. doi:10.1093/bioinformatics/bth163

Kelley, B., Sharan, R., Karp, R., Sittler, T., Root, D., & Stockwell, B. (2003). Conserved pathways within bacteria and yeast as revealed by global protein network alignment. *Science's STKE*, *100*(20), 11394.

Kelley, B., Yuan, B., Lewitter, F., Sharan, R., Stockwell, B., & Ideker, T. (2004). Pathblast: A tool for alignment of protein interaction networks. *Nucleic Acids Research, 32*(Web Server Issue), W83.

King, A., Przulj, N., & Jurisica, I. (2004). Protein complex prediction via cost-based clustering. *Bioinformatics*.

Koyuturk, M., Grama, A., & Szpankowski, W. (2004). An efficient algorithm for detecting frequent subgraphs in biological networks. *Bioinformatics (Oxford, England), 20*(Suppl 1), i200. doi:10.1093/bioinformatics/bth919

Krissinel, E., & Henrick, K. (2004). Common subgraph isomorphism detection by backtracking search. *Software, Practice & Experience, 34,* 591–607. doi:10.1002/spe.588

Lacroix, V., Fernandes, C., & Sagot, M. (2006). Motif search in graphs: Application to metabolic networks. *IEEE/ACM Transactions on Computational Biology and Bioinformatics, 3*(4), 360–368. doi:10.1109/TCBB.2006.55

Larrosa, J., & Valiente, G. (2000). Graph pattern matching using constraint satisfaction. *APPLIGRAPH/GETGRATS workshop of graph transformation systems,* 189 - 196.

Levi, G. (1972). A note on the derivation of maximal common subgraphs of two directed or undirected graphs. *Journal of Calcols, 9,* 341–354. doi:10.1007/BF02575586

Lipets, V., Vanetik, N., & Gudes, E. (2009). Subsea: An efficient heuristic algorithm for subgraph isomorphism. *Data Mining and Knowledge Discovery, 19,* 320–350. doi:10.1007/s10618-009-0132-7

Lladss, J., Mart, E., & Villanueva, J. (2001). Symbol recognition by error-tolerant subgraph matching between region adjacency graphs. *IEEE Transactions on Pattern Analysis and Machine Intelligence, 23*(10), 1137–1143. doi:10.1109/34.954603

Matthews, L., Vaglio, P., Reboul, J., Ge, H., Davis, B., & Garrels, J. (2001). Identification of potential interaction networks using sequence-based searches for conserved protein-protein interactions or "interologs". *Genome Research, 11*(12), 2120. doi:10.1101/gr.205301

Matula, D. (1978). Subtree isomorphism in o(n5/2). *Ann Discrete Math*(2), 91 - 106.

Mering, C., Huynen, M., Jaeggi, D., Schmidt, S., Bork, P., & Snel, B. (2003). String: A database of predicted functional associations between proteins. *Nucleic Acids Research, 31*(1), 258. doi:10.1093/nar/gkg034

Messmer, B. T., & Bunke, H. (1995). Subgraph isomorphism detection in polynominal time on preprocessed model graphs. *Proceedings of ACCV.*

Mongiovì, M., Di Natale, R., Giugno, R., Pulvirenti, A., Ferro, A., & Sharan, R. (2010). Sigma: A set-cover-based inexact graph matching algorithm. *Journal of Bioinformatics and Computational Biology, 8*(2). doi:10.1142/S021972001000477X

Myaeng, S. H., & Lopez-Lopez, A. (1992). Conceptual graph matching: A flexible algorithm and experiments. *Journal of Experimental & Theoretical Artificial Intelligence, 4,* 107–126. doi:10.1080/09528139208953741

Myers, R., Wilson, R., & Hancock, E. R. (1998). Bayesian graph edit distance. *Proceedings of the 10th Int. Conf. on Image Analysis and Processing, IEEE.*

Nabieva, E., Jim, K., Agarwal, A., Chazelle, B., & Singh, M. (2005). Whole-proteome prediction of protein function via graph-theoretic analysis of interaction maps. *Bioinformatics (Oxford, England)*, *21*(Suppl 1), i302. doi:10.1093/bioinformatics/bti1054

O'Brien, K., Remm, M., & Sonnhammer, E. (2005). Inparanoid: A comprehensive database of eukaryotic orthologs. *Nucleic Acids Research*, *33*(suppl 1), D476. doi:10.1093/nar/gki107

Pinter, R., Rokhlenko, O., Yeger-Lotem, E., & Ziv-Ukelson, M. (2005). Alignment of metabolic pathways. *Bioinformatics (Oxford, England)*, *21*(16), 3401. doi:10.1093/bioinformatics/bti554

Ramani, A., & Marcotte, E. (2003). Exploiting the co-evolution of interacting proteins to discover interaction specificity. *Journal of Molecular Biology*, *327*(1), 273–284. doi:10.1016/S0022-2836(03)00114-1

Sammoud, O., Solnon, C., & Ghdira, K. (2005). Ant algorithm for the graph matching problem. *EvoCOP*, 213–223.

Sanfeliu, A., & Fu, K. (1983). A distance measure between attributed relational graphs for pattern recognition. *IEEE Transactions on Systems, Man, and Cybernetics*, *13*(3), 353–362.

Schreiber, F., & Schwobbermeyer, H. (2005). Mavisto: A tool for the exploration of network motifs. *Bioinformatics (Oxford, England)*, *21*(17), 3572. doi:10.1093/bioinformatics/bti556

Shannon, P., Markiel, A., Ozier, O., Baliga, N., Wang, J., & Ramage, D. (2003). Cytoscape: A software environment for integrated models of biomolecular interaction networks. *Genome Research*, *13*(11), 2498. doi:10.1101/gr.1239303

Sharan, R., & Ideker, T. (2006). Modeling cellular machinery through biological network comparison. *Nature Biotechnology*, *24*(4), 427–433. doi:10.1038/nbt1196

Sharan, R., Suthram, S., Kelley, R. M., Kuhn, T., McCuine, S., & Uetz, P. (2005). Conserved patterns of protein interaction in multiple species. *Proceedings of the National Academy of Sciences of the United States of America*, *102*(6), 1974–1979. doi:10.1073/pnas.0409522102

Shasha, D., Wang, J.-L., & Giugno, R. (2002). Algorithmics and applications of tree and graph searching. *Proceeding of the ACM Symposium on Principles of Database Systems (PODS)*.

Tatusov, R., Fedorova, N., Jackson, J., Jacobs, A., Kiryutin, B., & Koonin, E. (2003). The cog database: An updated version includes eukaryotes. *BMC Bioinformatics*, *4*(1), 41. doi:10.1186/1471-2105-4-41

Tian, Y., McEachin, R., & Santos, C. (2007). Saga: A subgraph matching tool for biological graphs. *Bioinformatics (Oxford, England)*, *23*(2), 232. doi:10.1093/bioinformatics/btl571

Tianut, W., & Samatova, N. (2009). Pairwise alignment of interaction networks by fast identification of maximal conserved patterns. *In Pacific Symposium on Biocomputing*.

Tsai, W. H., & Fu, K. S. (1979). Error-correcting isomorphism of attributed relational graphs for pattern analysis. *IEEE Transactions on Systems, Man, and Cybernetics*, *9*, 757–768. doi:10.1109/TSMC.1979.4310127

Ullmann, J. (1976). An algorithm for subgraph isomorphism. *Journal of the Association for Computing Machinery*, *23*, 31–42.

Volinia, S., Galasso, M., Costinean, S., Tagliavini, L., Gamberoni, G., & Drusco, A. (2010). Reprogramming of mirna networks in cancer and leukemia. *Genome Research*, *20*(5), 589. doi:10.1101/gr.098046.109

Wernicke, S. (2006). Efficient detection of network motifs. *IEEE/ACM Transactions on Computational Biology and Bioinformatics*, 347–359. doi:10.1109/TCBB.2006.51

Wernicke, S., & Rasche, F. (2006). Fanmod: A tool for fast network motif detection. *Bioinformatics (Oxford, England)*, 22(9), 1152. doi:10.1093/bioinformatics/btl038

Williams, D. W., Huan, J., & Wang, W. (2007). Graph database indexing using structured graph decomposition. *IEEE 23rd International Conference on Data Engineering*.

Wong, A., & You, M. (1985). Entropy and distance of random graphs with application to structural pattern recognition. *IEEE Transactions on Pattern Analysis and Machine Intelligence*, 7(5), 599–609. doi:10.1109/TPAMI.1985.4767707

Xenarios, I., Salwinski, L., Duan, X., Higney, P., Kim, S., & Eisenberg, D. (2002). Dip, the database of interacting proteins: A research tool for studying cellular networks of protein interactions. *Nucleic Acids Research*, 30(1), 303. doi:10.1093/nar/30.1.303

Yan, X., Yu, P. S., & Han, J. (2005a). Graph indexing based on discriminative frequent structure analysis. *ACM Transactions on Database Systems*, 30(4), 960–993. doi:10.1145/1114244.1114248

Yan, X., Yu, P. S., & Han, J. (2005b). Substructure similarity search in graph databases. *Proceedings of ACM SIGMOD International Conference on Management of Data*.

Yannakakis, M. (1990). Graph theoretic methods in database theory. In *Proceedings of the 9th ACM Symp. on Principles of Database Systems*, 230 - 242.

Zhang, S., Hu, M., & Yang, J. (2007). Treepi: A novel graph indexing method. In *Proceedings of IEEE 23rd International Conference on Data Engineering*.

Zhao, P., Yu, J. X., & Yu, P. S. (2007). Graph indexing: Tree + delta ≤ graph. In *Proceedings of the 33rd International Conference on Very large Data Bases (VLDB '07)*, 938 - 949.

Zou, L., Chen, L., Yu, J. X., & Lu, Y. (2008). A novel spectral coding in a large graph database. In *Proceedings of the 11th International Conference on Extending Database Technology (EDBT '08)*, 181 - 192.

KEY TERMS AND DEFINITIONS

Graph Alginment: Given *n* networks (large graphs), a multiple network alignment can be defined as an equivalence relation on the nodes. An equivalence relation partitions into a set of disjoint equivalence classes. The nodes in the same equivalence class are functionally orthologous, the subset of nodes in a local alignment represents a conserved module (i.e. pathway).

Graph Data Mining: Given a database *D* of graphs, the subgraph isomorphism problem is further extended to cover multiple graphs. It finds a set of graphs that are subgraphs of most graphs in *D*.

Isomorphisms or Exact Match: Given a query graph G_Q and a data graph G_A, G_A and G_Q are isomorphic if we can map the vertices of G_A to be vertices of G, maintaining the corresponding edges.

Motif Statistical Significance: Given a query graph G_Q and a biological network *N* finds all the occurrences of the query graph in the network. Execute a permutation test using *m* randomly generated networks to establish if the motif is overrepresented in the original network.

Network Alignment Scoring Function: A numerical value assigned to the network alignment able to measure the similarity (in terms of insertion deletion and duplications) of the aligned subnetworks.

Subgraph Isomorphism or Subgraph Exact Matching: Given a query graph G_Q, and a data graph G_A, G_Q is subgraph isomorphic to G_A if G_Q is isomorphic to a subgraph of G_A. G_Q may be subgraph isomorphic to several subgraphs of G_A.

Subgraph Matching in a Database of Graphs: Given a query graph G_Q and a database of data graphs D, it finds all the occurrences of G_Q in each graph in D.

ENDNOTES

[1]   A labelled graph means that the nodes have names, though two nodes may have the same name.

[2]   Let $G_a(V_a, E_a)$ be a graph, where V_a is the set of vertices, and E_a is the set of edges, $n \in G_a$ is a short way to say n is a vertex, that is $n \in V_a$.

[3] $p(v) = P(Homology \mid E_v)$
$= P(E_v \mid Homology)$
$*P(Homology) / P(E_v), P(E_v \mid Homology)$
is based on E values within the subset of vertices for which both proteins are in the same cluster of orthologous groups (COG) (Tatusov et al., 2003)). The prior probability $P(Homology)$ is computed as the overall frequency of vertices with proteins that are in the same COG.

[4]   Using the guidelines on the accuracy of protein interaction data, the authors estimated the probability of each interaction i using the number of independent experimental studies reporting it and then compute $q(e)$ as the product of these probabilities.

Chapter 6
A Survey of Relational Approaches for Graph Pattern Matching over Large Graphs

Jiefeng Cheng
The University of Hong Kong, China

Jeffrey Xu Yu
The Chinese University of Hong Kong, China

ABSTRACT

Due to rapid growth of the Internet and new scientific/technological advances, there exist many new applications that model data as graphs, because graphs have sufficient expressiveness to model complicated structures. The dominance of graphs in real-world applications demands new graph processing techniques to access and analyze large graph datasets effectively and efficiently. Among those techniques, a graph pattern matching problem receives increasing attention, which is to find all patterns in a large data graph that match a user-given graph pattern. In this survey, we review approaches to process such graph pattern queries with a framework of multi joins, which can be easily implemented in relational databases and requires no specialized native storage for graphs. We also discuss the top-k graph pattern matching problem.

INTRODUCTION

Graph structured data is enjoying an increasing popularity as Web technology and new data management and archiving techniques advance. Due to the sufficient expressive power of graphs

DOI: 10.4018/978-1-61350-053-8.ch006

to model complex relationships among objects, numerous emerging applications need to work with graph data. Instances include navigation behavior analysis for Web usage mining (Berendt & Spiliopoulou, 2000), web site analysis (Fernandez, Florescu, Levy & Suciu, 1997), biological network analysis for life science (Helden et al., 2000) and so on. The dominance of graphs in real-world applications demands new graph processing techniques to access large data graphs effectively and efficiently. In 2002, Shasha, Wang, and Giugno highlighted algorithms and applications for searching trees and graphs.

Among those techniques, a graph pattern matching problem receives increasing attention. Traditionally, graph pattern matching usually stands for problems like the subgraph isomorphism (Ullmann, 1976), which is long investigated. This problem is widely used recently for subgraph containment search (Yan, Yu, & Han, 2004; He & Singh, 2006; Williams, Huan, & Wang, 2007; Cheng, Ke, Ng, & Lu, 2007; Zhao, Yu, & Yu, 2007; Shang, Zhang, Lin, & Yu, 2008). They often work with large number of small candidate graphs with hundreds or thousands of nodes. However, in many cases, the database consists of only one or several very large graphs, such as protein-protein interaction networks, Web information, social networks, etc. Urged by the need to efficient manage and analyze very large graphs, new query semantics for graph pattern matching over very large graphs are developed beyond the subgraph isomorphism semantics: a small graph pattern Q is used to represent structural requirements, in which the connectedness between matched nodes are emphasized. To be more specific, Q implies two kinds of conditions that the matched nodes in G_D should satisfy: (1) The labels conditions specified by Q request that all matched nodes in G_D are labeled identically with Q; (2) the reachability conditions of Q suggest all matched nodes in G_D should have connected paths in G_D, which are required to match all edges in Q.

There are many applications for such graph pattern matching: Taken DBLP[1] as an example (Figure 1(a)). The XML document can be considered as a large graph by categorizing papers into different conferences/journals followed by years. Different papers may link to the same author, which exhibits a graph structure. A simple graph query (Figure 1(b)) finds the authors who have papers published at the major database conferences, namely, EDBT,

ICDE, SIGMOD, and VLDB, in the same year. The answer set includes Christos Faloutsos who did it in 1994, and Hector Garcia-Molina and Surajit Chaudhuri who did it in 1996. In this example, a graph pattern queries the graph-structured XML document, by extending twig queries over the tree-structured XML document (Bruno, Koudas, & Srivastava, 2002). In biological networks such as protein-protein interaction networks (PPI) and metabolic networks, a small graph pattern Q can represent a pattern of some kind of interactions or pathways which is interested by scientists, and can be used to further search similar patterns in exploring different data sets. In software systems, a small graph pattern Q can be used to find interesting dependency patterns in dependency graphs.

One question which may be asked by keen readers is that in connected undirected graphs or strongly connected directed graphs, any node is reachable from (or reaches to) any other node which automatically satisfies the reachability conditions of a given graph pattern query. To explain that our graph pattern matching problem is still useful, we can see that in real applications, many XML graphs and biological networks are still very sparse with the edge/vertex ratio slightly larger than 1 (Wang, He, Yang, Yu, & Yu, 2006); additionally, to handle highly cyclic graphs or even undirected graphs, selection constraints can be deliberately added to prune those reachable nodes which are not needed. For example, in analyzing online social networking systems, such as Facebook, a large graph can be obtained where the "job-title" attribute on each node is regarded as the node label. A small graph pattern Q can be used to discover connections between several people with specified jobs. However, in general, it can return many nodes with obscure connections among them. Therefore, in 2009, Zou, Chen, and Özsu employ a distance threshold to prune all connected nodes whose distances are larger than the threshold. For example, In Figure 2(a), the node-tuple $\langle 3, 5, 6, 8 \rangle$ matches Q in Figure 2(b)

Figure 1. An example: (a) DBLP data, (b) Query

1994
50   George Panagopoulos, Christos Faloutsos: Bit-Sliced Signature Files for Very Large Text Databases an a Parallel Machine Architecture. EDBT 1994: 379-392
49   Manish Arya, William F. Cody, Christos Faloutsos, Joel E. Richardson, Arthur Toya: QBISM: Extending a DBMS to Support 3D Medical Images. ICDE 1994: 314-325
48   Christos Faloutsos, Ibrahim Kamel: Beyond Uniformity and Independence: Analysis of R-trees Using the Concept of Fractal Dimension. PODS 1994: 4-13
47   Christos Faloutsos, M. Ranganathan, Yannis Manolopoulos: Fast Subsequence Matching in Time-Series Databases. SIGMOD Conference 1994: 419-429
46   Rakesh Agrawal, Michael J. Carey, Christos Faloutsos, Sakti P. Ghosh, Maurice A. W. Houtsma, Tomasz Imielinski, Balakrishna R. Iyer, A. Mahboob, H. Miranda, Ramakrishnan Srikant, Arun N. Swami: Quest: A Project on Database Mining. SIGMOD Conference 1994: 514
45   Ibrahim Kamel, Christos Faloutsos: Hilbert R-tree: An Improved R-tree using Fractals. VLDB 1994: 500-509

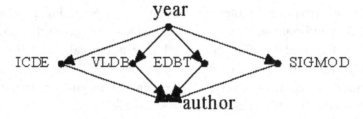

by setting the distance threshold to 2. Notice that $\langle 3,5,6,9\rangle$ cannot be an answer because the distance between 3 and 9 exceeds the distance threshold.

Given a large data graph, we may naturally try to speed up the graph pattern matching with precomputed storage for it, including graph indexes in the database. Here graph encoding schemes are very useful in two ways: the first is to encode the paths in the underlying graph so that the processing of reachability conditions can be supported as potentially very fast primitive operations on the obtained graph codes. Otherwise, to check the required reachability condition for two nodes x, y that appear in a candidate answer,

we have to explore a path from x to y in the underlying graph at querying time, which can be time consuming in a large graph. The other good result includes organizing the storage of underlying graph, usually augmented with graph dencodings, into a number of tables which corresponds to different labels in the underlying graphs. Then, the whole graph pattern query can be processed using join operations over these tables.

In fact, with this framework, different graph encoding schemes and join operations are investigated: Chen, Gupta, and Kurul proposed to use a tree encoding of the underlying graph to find all matches of a given graph pattern query in a directed acyclic graph in 2005; (Cheng, Yu, & Tang, 2006; Cheng, Yu, Yu, & Wang, 2008;

Figure 2. An example for Facebook (Figure 1 in (Zou, Chen, & Özsu, 2009))

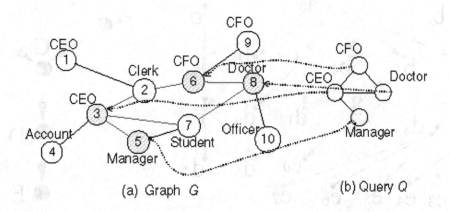

(a) Graph G (b) Query Q

Cheng, Yu, & Yu, 2010) introduce *reachability join* based on the *2-hop code* (Cohen, Halperin, Kaplan, & Zwick, 2002), where semijoins are further considered to improve the performance. In 2008, Wang, Li, Luo and Gao exploited the potentiality of the *multi-interval code* (Agrawal, Borgida, & Jagadish, 1989) and proposed to use hash joins to process a graph pattern query. In 2009, Zou, Chen, and Özsu proposed *distance join* using *graph embedding* (Linial, London, & Rabinovich, 1995; Shahabi, Kolahdouzan, & Sharifzadeh, 2003) for pruning connected nodes which do not satisfy the distance threshold. When the graph pattern Q is limited to be of the tree structure only, Gou and Chirkova also studied efficient algorithm to find top-*k* matches of Q ordered by answer compactness in 2008. It is also based on the join processing with the edge transitive closure of the underlying graph. In this survey, we review these join approaches to process graph pattern. All approaches reviewed in this survey can be easily implemented in relational databases and requires no specialized native storage for graphs. As the next step of this direction, we also discuss the top-*k* graph pattern matching problem.

A JOIN BASED FRAMEWORK FOR GRAPH PATTERN MATCHING

Problem Statement

In this section, we formally give the problem statement for graph pattern matching and outline the overall join processing framework for this problem, where some notations will be used throughout this survey. A data graph is a directed node-labeled graph $G_D = (V, E, \Sigma, \phi)$. Here, V is a set of nodes; E is a set of edges (ordered pairs); Σ is a set of node labels, and ϕ is a mapping function which assigns each node, $v_i \in V$, a label $l_j \in \Sigma$. We use label (v_i) to denote the label of node v_i. Given a label $X \in \Sigma$, the extent of X, denoted as ext(X), is the set of all nodes in G_D whose labels are X. A simple data graph, G_D, is shown in Figure 3(a). There are 5 labels, $\Sigma = \{A, B, C, D, E\}$. In Figure 3(a), a node in an extent ext(X) is represented as x_i where x is a small letter of X with a unique number i to distinguish it from others in ext(X). For example, $ext(C) = \{c_0, c_1, c_2, c_3,\}$. In the following, we use V(G) and E(G) to denote the set of nodes and the set of edges in graph G.

Figure 3. A graph pattern matching example: (a) Data graph, (b) Graph pattern query

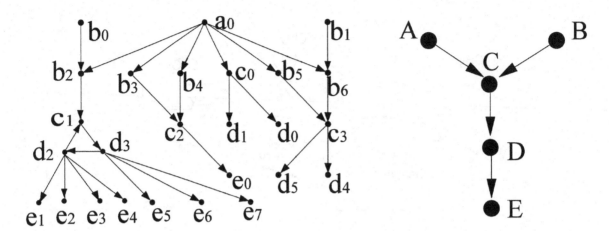

A graph pattern is defined to be a directed node-labeled graph $G_q = (V_q, E_q)$, where V_q is a subset of labels (Σ), and E_q is a set of edges (ordered pairs) between two nodes in V_q. An edge $(X, Y) \in E(G_q)$ represents a reachability condition, denoted X↪Y, for $X, Y \in V_q$. A reachability condition, X↪Y, requests that a graph pattern to be matched in the underlying data graph, G_D, must have two nodes v_i and v_j in G_D, for label (v_i) = X and label(v_j) = Y, v_j is reachable from v_i, denoted $v_i \rightsquigarrow v_j$. A match of graph pattern G_q in G_D satisfies all the reachability conditions conjunctively specified in G_q. A result that matches a n-node graph pattern G_q is a n-ary tuple, $\langle v_1, v_2, \ldots, v_n \rangle$. A graph pattern, G_q, is shown in Figure 3(b). There are five labeled nodes: *A, B, C, D,* and *E*, and there are four edges (reachability conditions), A↪C, B↪C, C↪D, and D↪E, which conjunctively specify a graph pattern query to be matched against the data graph (Figure 3(a)). There is a match $\langle a_0, b_0, c_1, d_2, e_1 \rangle$. In detail, $a_0 \rightsquigarrow c_1$ satisfies A↪C, $b_0 \rightsquigarrow c_1$ satisfies B↪C, $c_2 \rightsquigarrow d_2$ satisfies C↪D, and $d_2 \rightsquigarrow e_1$ satisfies D↪E.

A graph matching problem is to find all matches in a large directed data graph G_D that match all the reachability conditions conjunctively specified in

a graph pattern, G_q. The problem is challenging, because G_D can be a very large directed graph, and a graph pattern, G_q, can be large and complex. Consider a reachability condition A↪D in G_q against a large graph G_D. In G_D, any *A*-labeled nodes can possibly reach any *D*-labeled nodes, and all *A*-labeled nodes and *D*-labeled nodes can appear anywhere in G_D. It is a time consuming process to check all reachability conditions among all *A*-labeled nodes and *D*-labeled nodes over G_D. In addition, it needs to check all such reachability conditions in G_D in a potentially complex graph G_q.

A Join Based Framework

Given a large data graph G_D, we may naturally try to speed up the graph pattern matching with precomputed storage for it in a relational database, denoted G_{DB}. A join based framework is to process graph pattern matching, for a user-given graph pattern $G_q = (V_q, E_q)$, as a sequence of joins, where each reachability condition, X↪Y $\in E(G_q)$ that appears in G_q, can be processed as a join operation in G_{DB}. We illustrate this framework with a baseline approach based on the whole edge transitive closure. It is straightforward to maintain in G_{DB} a single edge relation for G_D, *Edge(Parent, Child, PLabel, CLabel)* where the attributes, *Parent* and

Box 1. With-clause SQL

```
with TC as(
  (select* from Edge)
  union all
  (select TC.Parent, Edge.Child, TC.PLabel, Edge,CLabel
      from TC, Edge where TC.Child=Edge.Parent))
```

Child, record ordered edges from a parent node to a child node, and the attributes, *PLabel* and *CLabel*, record the labels of the two corresponding nodes. To process a graph pattern matching, it requests a transitive closure over the *Edge* relation, as shown in Box 1, using a SQL "with-clause" expression.

Given the transitive closure *TC* computed, a reachability condition X↪Y can be processed as an equijoin using the following SQL expression.

```
select Parent,Child from TC
where TC.PLabel=X and TC.CLabel=Y
```

And the graph pattern matching can be processed using a sequence of equijoins. However, it requests either to compute *TC* on-line or to materialize *TC* with off-line computation. Both are infeasible, because the former requests high computational cost, and the latter requests huge space.

A promising alternative is to maintain a compressed representation of *TC*, called a *graph encoding* of G_D. A graph encoding assigns each node v in G_D a *graph code*. There are different graph codes for a node with different graph encoding. However, with a graph encoding of G_D, the reachability, $v_i \leadsto v_j$, between two nodes, two nodes v_i and v_j in G_D, can be answered using the two corresponding codes, code v_i and code v_j, with a potentially very fast operation. We use a predicate $P(code(v_i), code(v_j))$ to denote the operation over the graph codes. Then, $v_i \leadsto v_j$ is true if and only if $P(code(v_i), code(v_j))$ is true. There are many different graph encoding schemes. We will explain

those schemes applied for graph pattern matching in the context of their detailed applications. Based on the graph encoding of G_D, a relation T_X in the relational database G_{DB} is created for each label $X \in \sum$, which stores all nodes of *ext(X)* and the associated graph codes. T_X has a primary key attribute *X*, which a primary index will be constructed for. With the indexed primary key, we can retrieve the graph code efficiently for a given node identifier. Thus, we can process a reachability condition X↪Y ∈ $E(G_q)$ as a reachability then join (or simply an *R-join*) between two relations T_X and T_Y, dentoed as below:

$$T_R \leftarrow T_X \underset{X \hookrightarrow Y}{\bowtie} T_Y \tag{1}$$

In the following, we call a relation a *base relation* if it is stored in G_{DB}, and a relation a *temporal relation* if it is temporarily generated in query processing. Such an R-join is defined as a subset of Cartesian product of $T_R \subseteq T_X \times T_Y$ such that, for all tuples $\langle x_i, y_j \rangle \in T_R$, $x_i \in T_X$, $y_j \in T_Y$, $x_i \leadsto y_j$ holds, or in other words, $P(code(v_i), code(v_j))$ is true. Consider $T_B \underset{B \hookrightarrow E}{\bowtie} T_E$ in Figure 3(a), $\langle b_0, e_7 \rangle$ appears in its result. Therefore, graph pattern matching for G_q (Figure 3 (b)) can be processed using the SQL in Box 2.

Note that, an R-join over any two (temporal/base) relations, T_R and T_S, can be specified, with a reachability condition, X↪Y, where X and Y indicate the attributes in the corresponding base relations T_X and T_Y. Such R-join attributes appear in a temporal relation because of a previous R-

Box 2. Graph pattern matching for G_q using SQL

select $T_A.A, T_B.B, T_C.C, T_D.D, T_E.E$ from T_A, T_B, T_C, T_D, T_E where $T_A \underset{A \hookrightarrow B}{\bowtie} T_B$ and $T_A \underset{A \hookrightarrow B}{\bowtie} T_B$ and $T_C \underset{D \hookrightarrow D}{\bowtie} T_D$ and $T_D \underset{D \hookrightarrow E}{\bowtie} T_E$

join. Let T_R and T_S be either a base or temporal relation, we have

$$T_{RS} \leftarrow T_R \underset{X \hookrightarrow Y}{\bowtie} T_S \tag{2}$$

In this review, we survey query processing and optimization over multi R-joins. Because it is important to find an optimal left-deep tree query plan, then an R-join is either between two base relations or between a temporal relation and a base relation. As shown in Equation (3) and Equation (4) below, T_X and T_Y represent base relations, and T_R represents either a base or a temporal relation.

$$T_R \underset{X \hookrightarrow Y}{\bowtie} T_Y \tag{3}$$

$$T_X \underset{X \hookrightarrow Y}{\bowtie} T_R \tag{4}$$

As a special case, a self-R-join is a join that can be processed as a selection,

$$T_R \underset{X \hookrightarrow Y}{\bowtie} T_R \tag{5}$$

where T_R can be a base/temporal relation. The following holds for R-joins.

$$T_R \underset{X \hookrightarrow Y}{\bowtie} T_S \equiv T_S \underset{X \hookrightarrow Y}{\bowtie} T_R$$
(**Commutativity**),

$$T_R \underset{X \hookrightarrow Y}{\bowtie} T_S) \underset{W \hookrightarrow Z}{\bowtie} T_T \equiv T_R \underset{X \hookrightarrow Y}{\bowtie} (T_S \underset{W \hookrightarrow Z}{\bowtie} T_T)$$
(**Associativity**).

Given a relation T_R and suppose T_R keeps tuples that satisfy two reachability conditions,

A$\hookrightarrow$B and B$\hookrightarrow$D. Then the tuples in T_R satisfy A$\hookrightarrow$D (**Transitivity**).

It is worth noting that this framework can handle any complex graph pattern, G_q. Consider G_q that consists of A$\hookrightarrow$B and B$\hookrightarrow$C, and C$\hookrightarrow$A, as a cycle. Based on the similar idea of the rename operator used in relational algebra, we can rewrite the above as A$\hookrightarrow$B and B$\hookrightarrow$C, and C$\hookrightarrow$ A' where A' is an alias of A for accessing the same extent ext(A). Then, an additional selection of A= A' over the intermediate join results can remove those that do not contain a required cycle. This strategy can be implemented with self-R-joins. For example, a temporal relation T_{ABC}, where $T_{AB} = T_A \underset{A \hookrightarrow B}{\bowtie} T_B$ and $T_{ABC} = T_{AB} \underset{B \hookrightarrow C}{\bowtie} T_C$, is joined to itself such as $T_{ABC} \underset{C \hookrightarrow A}{\bowtie} T'_{ABC}$ where $T'_{ABC} = T_{ABC}$.

DIFFERENT JOIN APPROACHES

A Holistic Twig Join Approach

Chen, Gupta, and Kurul studied graph pattern matching over a directed acyclic graph (DAG) in 2005. This approach tries to extend the *holistic twig join* of (Bruno, Koudas, & Srivastava, 2002), called *TwigStack* algorithm, which is a fast algorithm to finds tree matches in an XML tree and cannot be used for the graph pattern matching problem directly. In (Bruno, Koudas, & Srivastava, 2002), a node v receives a pair [s,e] where *s* and *e* together specifies an interval. Given two nodes, v_i and v_j in an XML tree, v_i is an ancestor of v_j, $v_i \leadsto v_j$, if and only if $v_i.s < v_j.s$ and $v_i.e > v_j.e$ or simply v_j's interval contains v_i's. Therefore, a table T_A is constructed for each query node of label $A \in V(G_q)$, where T_A contains all nodes and the associated intervals in the underlying graph with the label A. For each $A \in V(G_q)$, a runtime stack S_A is also constructed so that nodes in T_A is scanned sequentially and temporarily buffered in S_A. Figure 4 illustrates the twig-join algorithm with the XML tree data (Figure 4(a)); the tree pattern query in Figure 4(b); the stacks are in Figure 4(c). All nodes v in a table are in the increasing order of $v.s$ and are pushed into stacks according to this order. A node in a stack is popped out if its interval can no longer overlaps with those intervals of newly pushed nodes. Among nodes in stacks, the corresponding ancestor/descendant relationships are maintained by links between them as illustrated by Figure 4(c). Once all nodes correspond to the leaf nodes of the query are found, the tree matches are output based on these links, as shown in Figure 4(d). To further extend this processing towards branching trees instead of the single path here, it can merge all partial solutions corresponding to all paths and matches for tree can thus be obtained.

To process graph pattern query, (Chen, Gupta, & Kurul, 2005) poposes *TwigStackD* algorithm which includes the same *TwigStack* algorithm in (Bruno, Koudas, & Srivastava, 2002) as the first phase. In general, *TwigStackD* has two phases to

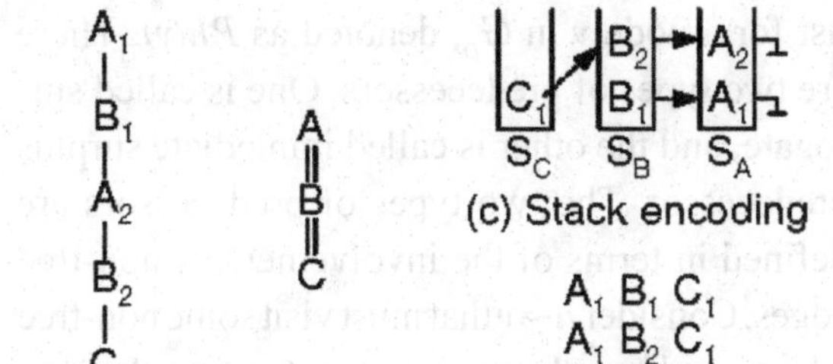

process a tree pattern query, then, it can be straightforwardly extended to handle a given graph pattern query. Therefore, this approach does not explicitly enumerate different join plans because *TwigStack* algorithm performs these joins in a bottom-up batch processing according to the tree query. In the first phase, it finds a spanning tree of the underlying graph and uses the same *TwigStack* algorithm in (Bruno, Koudas, & Srivastava, 2002). Note that all matches contained in the spanning tree are thus found. For example, a DAG is shown in Figure 6(a), where all edges in the identified spanning tree are shown as solid lines while other edges are shown as dashed lines. To process the twig pattern query in Figure 6(b), the *TwigStack* algorithm can successfully find the first two matches in Figure 6(c) in the first phase. It can not find the third match, because $C4$ is not the ancestor of $b1$ and $e2$ in the spanning tree. Then, the second phase is dedicated to find those matches which are missed in the first phase. To achieve this, it further examines each node popped out from stacks by *TwigStack* to further detect reachable nodes in terms of the whole DAG. And the required reachability tests are also based on the interval encoding scheme for trees plus an additional data structure, which is referred as *Tree+SSPI* (Surrogate & Surplus Predecessor Index) and is central to *TwigStackD* (Figure 5). *TwigStackD* needs to buffer all popped nodes (from the stacks) with a number pools, if those nodes are found to satisfy the required reachability tests with any nodes in the DAG. And those reachabilty relationships are also kept as links among nodes in those pools. When *TwigStackD* detects that there are nodes ready in the pool corresponding to the query root, *TwigStackD* enumerates the buffer pool via maintained links and outputs all matched patterns. In the example of Figure 4, $b1$ and $e2$ are kept in the pool when they are popped out from the stacks. Then, when $c4$ is popped out from the stack and inserted into the pool, it is found be the ancestor of $b1$ and $e2$ by

Figure 4. The TwigStack example (Figure 3 in (Bruno, Koudas, & Srivastava, 2002))

(a) Data   (b) Query   (c) Stack encoding

(d) Query results

Figure 5. Tree+SSPI index (Figure 3 in (Chen, Gupta, & Kurul, 2005))

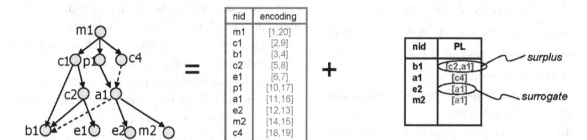

Figure 6. The TwigStackD example (Figure 2 in (Chen, Gupta, & Kurul, 2005))

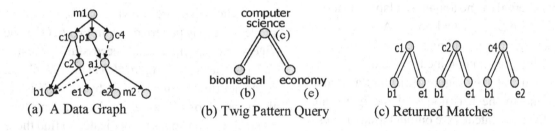

Tree+SSPI. Then, the third match in Figure 6(c) is found and returned.

Tree+SSPI contains two parts. The first one is the tree part, which assigns interval codes to nodes in the spanning tree of the underlying graph, and attempts to reduce the processing time for checking reachability conditions using additional data structures. In particular, Let $T_x(V_S, E_S)$ be a spanning tree of the underlying graph G_D. Here V_S and E_S are sets of nodes and edges of the spanning tree T_S. Note that $V_S = V(G_D)$ and $E_S \subseteq E(G_D)$, where we use E_S to denote the set of tree edges of the graph G_D, and $E_R = E - E_S$ to denote the set of non-tree edges of the graph G_D that do not appear in E_S. The interval enencoding scheme is applied on T_S. For example, the interval code for the sample graph is shown in the middle table in Figure 5. Therefore, to check the corresponding reachability condition for two nodes x, y that appear in a candidate answer, Tree+SSPI first checks whether x's interval contains y's. If

it is true, then $x \rightsquigarrow y$ is true. Otherwise, Tree+SSPI needs to take additional actions to further check the reachability $x \rightsquigarrow y$, because x can reach y through a combination of tree edges and non-tree edges. Below, we discuss the cases that $x \rightsquigarrow y$ cannot be answered simply using the interval enencoding scheme.

The remaining part is the SSPI part: Chen et al. use this "space-economic" index, namely SSPI, to maintain information that needs to be used at run time for reachability tests. For example, the SSPI for the sample graph is shown in the left table in Figure 5. The SSPI keeps a predecessor list for a node v in G_D, denoted as $PL(v)$. There are two types of predecessors. One is called surrogate, and the other is called immediate surplus predecessor. The two types of predecessors are defined in terms of the involvement of non-tree edges. Consider $u \rightsquigarrow v$ that must visit some non-tree edges on the path from u to v. Assume that (v_x, v_y) is the last non-tree edge on the path from u to

Figure 7. The sort-merge join example (Figure 1 in (Cheng, Yu, & Ding, 2007))

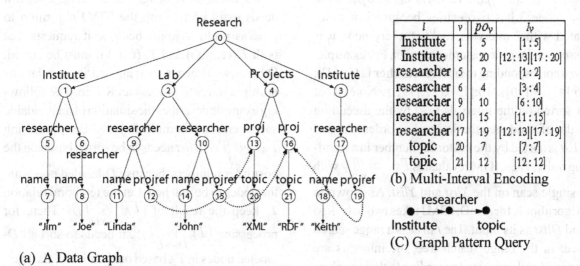

(a) A Data Graph

l	v	po_v	I_v
Institute	1	5	$[1:5]$
Institute	3	20	$[12:13][17:20]$
researcher	5	2	$[1:2]$
researcher	6	4	$[3:4]$
researcher	9	10	$[6:10]$
researcher	10	15	$[11:15]$
researcher	17	19	$[12:13][17:19]$
topic	20	7	$[7:7]$
topic	21	12	$[12:12]$

(b) Multi-Interval Encoding

(C) Graph Pattern Query

v, then v_y is a surrogate predecessor of v if $v_y \neq v$ and v_x is an immediate surplus predecessor of v if $v_x \neq v$. SSPI can be constructed in a traversal of the spanning tree T_S of the graph G_D starting from the tree root. When a node v is visited, all its immediate surplus predecessors are added into $PL(v)$. Also, all nodes in $PL(u)$ are added into $PL(v)$, where u is the parent node of v in the spanning tree. It is sufficient to check any $u \leadsto v$ using both the interval enencoding scheme and the SSPI. For the example in Figure 4, because there is $a1 \in PL(b1)$, it can be decided there are $p1 \leadsto b1$, $c4 \leadsto b1$ and $c4 \leadsto e2$. *TwigStackD* performs well for very sparse DAGs. However, as reported in (Cheng, Yu, & Yu, 2010), its performance degrades noticeably when the DAG becomes dense, due to the high overhead of accessing SSPI recursively.

A Sort-Merge Join Based Approach

A multi-interval code to encode all reachability information in DAGs is given in (Agrawal, Borgida, & Jagadish, 1989). Wang et al. studied processing $T_X \underset{X \hookrightarrow Y}{\bowtie} T_Y$ over any general directed graph (Wang et al., 2005) and proposed a join algorithm, called *IGMJ* (Improved Graph

Merge Join). First, it constructs a DAG G' by condensing a maximal strongly connected component in G_D as a node in G'. Second, it generates a multi-interval code for a node in G' in (Agrawal, Borgida, & Jagadish, 1989). As its name implies, the multi-interval code for enencoding a DAG is to assign a set of intervals and a signle postorder number to each node in the DAG G'. Let $I_v = \{[s_1, e_1], [s_2, e_2], ..., [s_n, e_n]\}$ be a set of intervals assigned to a node v, there is a path from v_i to v_j, $v_i \leadsto v_j$, if the postorder number of v_j is contained in an interval, $[s_k, e_k]$ in I_{vi}. Note: nodes in a strongly connected component in G_D share the same code assigned to the corresponding representative node condensed in the DAG G'. For example, the multi-interval encoding for the graph in Figure 7(a) is given in Figure 7(b). In this example, $17 \leadsto 21$ can be decided because 21's postorder number, 12, is contained in one interval associated with 17, i.e., $[12:13]$.

In the IGMJ algorithm (see Figure 8), given $T_X \underset{X \hookrightarrow Y}{\bowtie} T_Y$, two lists *Xlist* and *Ylist* are formed respectively. Here, in *Xlist*, every node x_i is encoded by the multi-interval I_{vi}, and node x_i has n entries, if it has n intervals in I_{vi}. For example, *Xlist* corresponding to label **institute** in Figure

7(a) is $\{(1:[1,5]),(3:[12,13]),(3:[17,20])\}$. Note that node 3 has two entries because it is associated with 2 intervals. In *Ylist*, every node y_i is associated with a postorder number. For example, *Ylist* corresponding to label **researcher** is $\{(5:[2]),(6:[4]),(9:[10]),(10:[15]),(17:[19])\}$. Note: *Xlist* is sorted on the intervals $[s,e]$ by the ascending order of s and then the descending order of e, and *Ylist* is sorted by the postorder number in ascending order. Then, IGMJ evaluates $T_X \underset{X \hookrightarrow Y}{\bowtie} T_Y$ with a single scan on the *Xlist* and *Ylist*. As shown in Algorithm 1, for A→D, IGMJ takes two lists *Alist* and *Dlist* as its input. The *rstree* is a range search tree. In the range search tree, the intervals are indexed and organized according to their e values of some $[s,e]$. Two operations, *trim(v)* and *insert(n)*, are used such as *trim(v)* is to batch delete the intervals whose e values are smaller than v's and *insert(n)* is to insert a node to the range search tree. For the example in Figure 7, consider the join to process **institute**↝**researcher**, it can be seen that results include $\langle 1:[1,5],5:[2]\rangle, \langle 1:[1,5],6:[4]\rangle$ and $\langle 3:[17,20],17:[19]\rangle$.

As noted in (Cheng, Yu, & Ding, 2007), it needs extra cost to use the IGMJ algorithm to process multi R-joins, because it requests that both T_X (ext(X)) and T_Y (ext(Y)) must be sorted. Otherwise, it needs to scan two input relations multiple times to process an R-join. The following example describes the situation of unavoidable sort operations in multi R-joins. For processing $T_A \underset{A \hookrightarrow D}{\bowtie} T_D$, *Dlist* needs to be sorted based on the postorder numbers, because D-labeled nodes are the nodes to be reached. Let the temporal relation T_R keep the result of $(T_A \underset{A \hookrightarrow D}{\bowtie} T_D)$. Then, for processing $(T_R \underset{D \hookrightarrow E}{\bowtie} T_E)$, it needs to sort all D-labeled nodes in T_R, based on their intervals, $[s,e]$, because D-labeled nodes now become the nodes to reach others. For example, to process the query in Figure 7(c), we obtain the temporal table as

$$\left\{ \langle 1:[1,5],5:[2]\rangle, \langle 1:[1,5],6:[4]\rangle, \langle 3:[17,20],17:[19]\rangle \right\}$$

after we process **institute**↝ researcher. However, this temporal table can not be directly used to further process **researcher**↝ topic, because every

Figure 8. Algorithm 1 IGMJ

Algorithm 1 *IGMJ* ($Alist, Dlist$)

1: $a := Alist.head();$ $d := Dlist.head();$
2: $R := \emptyset;$
3: **while** $a \neq \emptyset \vee d \neq \emptyset$ **do**
4:    **if** $a.s \leq d.PostorderNumber$ **then**
5:      $rstree.trim(a.s);$ $rstree.insert(a);$ $a := a.next();$
6:    **else**
7:      $rstree.trim(d.PostorderNumber);$
8:      **for all** elements $a \in rstree$ **do**
9:        $R.insert(a.NodeID, d.NodeID);$
10:      **end for**
11:      $d := d.next();$
12:    **end if**
13: **end while**
14: **return** $R;$

---

tuple in it has to be attached with the interval for **researcher** labeled nodes and sorted accordingly. Therefore, for this example, we have to obtain the following table on the fly:

$$\{\langle 1:[1,5],5:[1,2]\rangle,\langle 1:[1,5],6:[3,4]\rangle,\langle 3:[17,20],17:[12,13]\rangle,\langle 3:[17,20],17:[17,19]\rangle\}$$

before we can join it with the *Dlist* corresponding to **topic**. The main extra cost is the sorting cost. (Cheng, Yu, & Ding, 2007) uses dynamic programming to select join order for multi R-joins, which requires R-join size estimation. We will discuss it next. The interval-based code was further explored in (Wang et al., 2008).

A Join-Index Based Approach

An R-Join Index Based on 2-Hop: (Cheng, Yu, & Yu, 2010) studies a join index approach for graph pattern matching using a join index built on top of G_D. The join index is built based on the 2-hop cover codes. A 2-hop labeling is a compressed representation of transitive closure (Cohen, Halperin, Kaplan, & Zwick, 2002), which assigns every node v in graph G_D a label $L(v)=(L_{in}(v),L_{out}(v))$, where $L_{in}(v),L_{out}(v)\subseteq V(G_D)$, and $u{\rightsquigarrow}v$ is true if and only if $L_{out}(u)\cap L_{in}(v)\neq 0$. A 2-hop labeling for G_D is derived from a 2-hop cover of G_D, that minimizes a set of $S(U_w,w,V_w)$, as a set cover problem. Here, $w\in V(G_D)$ is called a center, and $U_w,V_w\subseteq V(G_D)$. $S(U_w,w,V_w)$ implies that, for every node, $u\in U_w$ and $v\in V_w$, $u{\rightsquigarrow}w$ and $w{\rightsquigarrow}v$, and hence $u{\rightsquigarrow}v$. We use the same graph in Figure 3(a), an example is $S(U_w,w,V_w)=S(\{b_3,b_4\},c_2,\{e_0\})$. Here, c_2 is the center. It indicates: $b_3{\rightsquigarrow}c_2$, $b_4{\rightsquigarrow}c_2$, $c_2{\rightsquigarrow}e_0$, $b_3{\rightsquigarrow}e_0$, and $b_4{\rightsquigarrow}e_0$. Several algorithms were proposed to fast compute a 2-hop cover for G_D (Cheng, Yu, Lin, Wang, & Yu, 2006, 2008 ; Cheng & Yu, 2009) and to maintain such a computed 2-hop cover (Schenkel, Theobald, & Weikum, 2005; Bramandia, Choi, & Ng, 2008). Let $H=\{S_{w1,}S_{w2},...\}$ be the set of 2-hop cover com-

puted, where $S_{wi}=S(U_w,wi,V_{wi})$ and all w_i are centers. The 2-hop labeling for a node v is $L(v)=(L_{in}(v),L_{out}(v))$. Here, $L_{in}(v)$ is a set of centers w_i where v appears in V_{wi}, and $L_{out}(v)$ is a set of centers w_i where v appears in U_{wi}.

Based on a 2-hop labeling computed for G_D, a relation T_X in the relational database G_{DB}, for a label $X\in\Sigma$, has three attributes, named X, X_{in} and X_{out}. The X attribute records the identifier of a node, x, in the extent of $ext(X)$, and X_{in} and X_{out} attributes are used to maintain the 2-hop labels for x. The X attribute is the primary key attribute in a relation to which a primary index will be constructed. With the indexed primary key, we can retrieve the 2-hop labels of X_{in} and X_{out} efficiently for a given identifier. Note that for a tuple x_i in relation T_X we do not need to maintain x_i in X_{in} and X_{out} attributes and can treat $L_{in}(x_i)=X_{in}\cup\{x_i\}$ and $L_{out}(x_i)=X_{out}\cup\{x_i\}$. $L_{in}(x_i)$ and $L_{out}(x_i)$ are graph codes for x_i, denoted in (x_i) and out (x_i), respectively. The reachability, $x_i{\rightsquigarrow}y_j$, becomes true, if $out(x_i)\cap in(y_j)\neq 0$. For example, the base relations for G_D in Figure 3(a) is shown in Figure 9. There are five base relations: $T_A(A,A_{in},A_{out})$, $T_B(B,B_{in},B_{out})$, $T_C(C,C_{in},C_{out})$, $T_D(D,D_{in},D_{out})$, and $T_E(E,E_{in},E_{out})$. To process a reachability condition $X{\hookrightarrow}Y$, an R-join between two relations T_X and T_Y with the join condition $T_X.X_{out}\cap T_Y.Y_{in}\neq 0$ can be used. Consider $T_B\underset{B{\hookrightarrow}E}{\bowtie}T_E$ in Figure 9, $\langle b_0,e_7\rangle$ appears in the result, because $(b_0)=\{b_0,c_1\},(e_7)=\{c_1,e_7\}$ and $(b_0)\cap(e_7)\neq 0$.

The join index proposed in (Cheng, Yu, & Yu, 2010) is used to index all tuples x_i and y_i that can join between two relations, T_X and T_Y. With such a join-index, an R-join can be efficiently processed as to fetch the corresponding join results. There is a cluster-based R-join index for a data graph G_D based on the 2-hop cover computed, $H=\{S_{w1,}S_{w2},...\}$, using the fast algorithms in (Cheng, Yu, Lin, Wang, & Yu, 2006, 2008 ; Cheng & Yu, 2009), where $S_{wi}=S(U_w,wi,V_{wi})$ and all w_i

Figure 9. Base relations with a 2-hop cover computed for G_D (Figure 3 in (Cheng, Yu, & Yu, 2010))

A	A_{in}	A_{out}
a_0	$\emptyset$	$\{c_1, c_3\}$

(a) T_A Relation

B	B_{in}	B_{out}
b_0	$\emptyset$	$\{c_1\}$
b_1	$\emptyset$	$\{c_3, b_6\}$
b_2	$\{a_0, b_0\}$	$\{c_1\}$
b_3	$\{a_0\}$	$\{c_2\}$
b_4	$\{a_0\}$	$\{c_2\}$
b_5	$\{a_0\}$	$\{c_3\}$
b_6	$\{a_0\}$	$\{c_3\}$

(b) T_B Relation

C	C_{in}	C_{out}
c_0	$\{a_0\}$	$\emptyset$
c_1	$\emptyset$	$\emptyset$
c_2	$\{a_0\}$	$\emptyset$
c_3	$\emptyset$	$\emptyset$

(c) T_C Relation

D	D_{in}	D_{out}
d_0	$\{a_0, c_0\}$	$\emptyset$
d_1	$\{a_0, c_0\}$	$\emptyset$
d_2	$\{c_1\}$	$\{c_1\}$
d_3	$\{c_1\}$	$\{c_1\}$
d_4	$\{c_3\}$	$\emptyset$
d_5	$\{c_3\}$	$\emptyset$

(d) T_D Relation

E	E_{in}	E_{out}
e_0	$\{a_0, c_2\}$	$\emptyset$
e_1	$\{c_1\}$	$\emptyset$
$\vdots$	$\vdots$	$\vdots$
e_7	$\{c_1\}$	$\emptyset$

(e) T_E Relation

are centers. It consists of a B^+-tree and a W-table. In the B^+-tree, non-leaf blocks are used for fast finding a given center w_i. In the leaf nodes, for each center w_i, its U_{wi} and V_{wi}, denoted *F-cluster* and *T-cluster*, are maintained. In addition, w_i's F-cluster and T-cluster are further clustered as labeled *F-subcluster* and *T-subcluster* where every node, x_i, in an X-labeled F-subcluster can reach every node y_i in a Y-labeled T-subcluster, via w_i. B^+-tree is used here because it is a widely used index mechanism supported by almost all DBMSs. It is important to note that in the cluster-based R-join index, node identifiers (tuple identifiers) is kept instead of pointers to tuples in base relations. Together with the B^+-tree, in the cluster-based R-join index, a W-table maintains a set of entries, where an entry $W(X,Y)$ keeps a set of centers. A center w_i will be included in $W(X,Y)$, if w_i has a non-empty X-labeled F-subcluster and a non-empty Y-labeled T-subcluster. The W-table is used to find all the centers, w_i, in the B^+-tree that have an X-labeled F-subcluster and a Y-labeled T-subcluster to be joined. The cluster-based R-join index and W-table for G_D of Figure 3(a) is shown in Figure 10. Figure 10(a) shows its W-table, and Figure 10(b) shows the cluster-based R-join index.

The B^+-tree (Figure 10(b)) maintains six centers, a_0, b_6, c_0, c_1, c_2 and c_3. The W-table (Figure 10(a)) maintains 14 entries. Consider

$T_A \underset{A \hookrightarrow B}{\bowtie} T_B$. The entry $W(A,B)$ in the W-table keeps $\{a_0\}$, which suggests that the answers can only be found in the clusters at the center a_0 in the B^+-tree. As shown in Figure 10(b), the center a_0 has an A-labeled F-subcluster $\{a_0\}$, and a B-labeled T-subcluster $\{b_2, b_3, b_4, b_5, b_6\}$. The answer is the Cartesian product between these two labeled subclusters.

Join Algorithms: We first outline an R-join algorithm between two base relations, and then discuss a two-step R-join algorithm between a temporal relation and a base relation.

The HPSJ algorithm (Algorithm 2) processes an R-join between two base relations, $T_X \underset{X \hookrightarrow Y}{\bowtie} T_Y$. First, it gets all centers, w_k, that have a non-empty X-labeled F-subcluster and a non-empty Y-labeled T-subcluster, using the W-table, and maintains them in C (line 1). Second, for each center $w_k \in C$, it has three actions. (1) It obtains its X-labeled F-subcluster, using getF (w_k, X), and stores them in X_k (line 4). (2) It obtains its Y-labeled T-subcluster, using getT(w_k, Y), and stores them in Y_k (line 5). Both (1) and (2) are done using the cluster-based R-join index. (3) it conducts Cartesian product between X_k and Y_k, and saves them into the answer set R (line 6). The output of an R-join between two base relations contains a set of concatenated tuples $\langle x_i, y_j \rangle$ for $x_i \leadsto y_i$. It is

Figure 10. The cluster-based R-join index and W-table (Figure 3 in (Cheng, Yu, & Yu, 2010))

(A,B)	$\{a_0\}$		(C,D)	$\{c_0, c_1, c_3\}$
(A,E)	$\{a_0, c_1\}$		(A,D)	$\{a_0, c_1, c_3\}$
(A,C)	$\{a_0, c_1, c_3\}$		(C,C)	$\{c_0, c_1, c_2, c_3\}$
(B,C)	$\{c_1, c_2, c_3\}$		(D,E)	$\{c_1\}$
(B,E)	$\{c_1, c_2\}$		(C,E)	$\{c_1, c_2\}$
(B,D)	$\{c_1, c_3\}$		(D,C)	$\{c_1\}$
(B,B)	$\{b_0, b_6\}$		(D,D)	$\{c_1\}$

(a) W-table

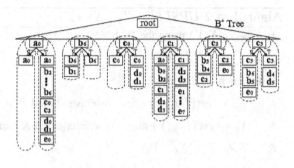

(b) A Cluster-Based R-Join-Index

important to note that there is no need to access base relations because all the nodes are maintained in the cluster-based R-join index to answer the R-join.

In order to process multi R-joins, (Cheng, Yu, & Yu, 2010) proposes a two-step R-join algorithm (Algorithm 3 as shown in Figure 12), called HPSJ+, to process $T_R \underset{X \hookrightarrow Y}{\bowtie} T_Y$, where T_R is a temporal relation that contains R-join attributes related to X, and T_Y is a base relation that has R-join attributes related to Y. The HPSJ+ algorithm takes three inputs, a temporal relation T_R, a base relation T_Y, and an R-join condition $X \hookrightarrow Y$. HPSJ+ first calls a procedure Filter(T_R,$X \hookrightarrow Y$) to filter T_R tuples that cannot possibly be joined with a tuple in T_Y, and stores those that can join into T_W (line 1). Second, it calls a procedure Fetch(T_W,$X \hookrightarrow Y$) to fetch the R-join results. The details of the two procedures are given below.

In Filter(T_R,$X \hookrightarrow Y$), it first initializes T_W to be empty (line 5). Second, in a for-loop, it processes every tuple r_i in T_R iteratively (line 6-9). In every iteration, it obtains a set of centers, for x_i in the X attribute[2] in r_i, where every center w_k in W_i must have some $y_j \in T_Y$ in its T-cluster (line 7). It is done using getCenters (x_i, Y) below.

$$\text{getCenters}(x_i, X, Y) = out((x_i) \cap W(X,Y)$$

(6)

In Equation (6), out (x_i) can be easily retrieved from the base relation given the identifier x_i using the primary index, which contains some centers w_k that an X-labeled node x_i can reach. $W(X,Y)$ is the set of all centers, w_k, such that some X-labeled nodes can reach w_k and some Y-labeled nodes can be reached by w_k. The intersection of the two sets is the set of all centers via which x_i must be able to reach some Y-labeled node y_j. If $W_i \neq 0$, it implies that x_i must be able to reach some y_j (line 6), and therefore the pair of (r_i, W_i) is inserted into T_W (line 8). Otherwise, it will be pruned. Equation (6) needs to access the base relation T_X using the primary index built on the primary key X attribute in T_X. We use a working cache to cache those pairs of $(x_i, out(x_i))$, in our implementation to reduce the access cost for later reuse. In Fetch(T_W,$X \hookrightarrow Y$), it initializes T_{RS} as empty (line 12). For each pair of $(r_i, W_i) \in T_w$, it obtains its Y-labeled T-subcluster maintained in the join-index, using get(w_k, Y), stores them in Y_i (line 15), conducts Cartesian product between $\{r_i\}$ and Y_i and outputs them into T_{RS} (line 16).

As an example, consider $(T_B \underset{B \hookrightarrow C}{\bowtie} T_C) \underset{C \hookrightarrow D}{\bowtie} T_D$ to access G_{DB} (Figure 9) using the R-join index and W-table (Figure 10). First, Algorithm 1 processes $T_A \underset{A \hookrightarrow B}{\bowtie} T_B$ and results in a temporal relation

$$T_{BC} = \{(b_0, c_1), (b_2, c_1), (b_3, c_2), (b_4, c_2), (b_5, c_3), (b_6, c_3)\}$$

Figure 11. Algorithm 2 HPSJ

Algorithm 2 *HPSJ* $(T_X, T_Y, X \hookrightarrow Y)$

1: $\mathcal{C} \leftarrow W(X, Y)$ using the W-table;

2: $\mathcal{R} \leftarrow \emptyset$;

3: **for each** $w_k \in \mathcal{C}$ **do**

4:     $X_k \leftarrow \text{getF}(w_k, X)$ using the cluster-based R-join index;

5:     $Y_k \leftarrow \text{getT}(w_k, Y)$ using the cluster-based R-join index;

6:     $\mathcal{R} \leftarrow \mathcal{R} \cup (X_k \times Y_k)$;

7: **end for**

8: **return** $\mathcal{R}$;

It only uses the clusters maintained in the three centers $W(B,C) = \{c_1, c_2, c_3\}$, (Refer to Figure 10(b)). Next, Algorithm 3 processes $T_{BC} \underset{C \hookrightarrow D}{\bowtie} T_D$. In the Filter(), the two tuples $(b_3,$

Figure 12. Algorithm 3 HPSJ+

Algorithm 3 *HPSJ+* $(T_R, T_Y, X \hookrightarrow Y)$

1: $T_W \leftarrow \text{Filter}(T_R, X \hookrightarrow Y)$;

2: $T_{RS} \leftarrow \text{Fetch}(T_W, X \hookrightarrow Y)$;

3: **return** T_{RS};

4: **Procedure** $\text{Filter}(T_R, X \hookrightarrow Y)$

5: $T_W \leftarrow \emptyset$;

6: **for each** tuple, r_i, in T_R **do**

7:     $W_i \leftarrow \text{getCenters}(x_i, X, Y)$;

8:     insert (r_i, W_i) into T_W if $W_i \neq \emptyset$;

9: **end for**

10: **return** T_W;

11: **Procedure** $\text{Fetch}(T_W, X \hookrightarrow Y)$

12: $T_{RS} \leftarrow \emptyset$;

13: **for each** $(r_i, W_i) \in T_W$ **do**

14:     **for each** $w_k \in W_i$ **do**

15:         $Y_i \leftarrow \text{getT}(w_k, Y)$ using the cluster-based R-join index;

16:         $T_{RS} \leftarrow T_{RS} \cup (\{r_i\} \times Y_i)$;

17:     **end for**

18: **end for**

---

c_2) and (b_4, c_2), in T_{BC} are pruned, because $\text{out}(c_2) = \{c_2\}$, $W(C,D) = \{c_0, c_1, c_3\}$, and the intersection of the two is empty (Equation (6)). Fetch() returns the final results, which are $\{(b_0, c_1, d_2), (b_0, c_1, d_8),$ $(b_2, c_1, d_2), (b_2, c_1, d_8), (b_5, c_8, d_4), (b_5, c_8, d_5), (b_6, c_8, d_4),$ $(b_6, c_8, d_5)\}$.

R-Semijoins: Reconsider HPSJ+$(T_R, T_Y, X \hookrightarrow Y)$ for an R-join between a temporal relation T_R and a base relation T_Y. It can be simply rewritten as Fetch(Filter($T_R, X \hookrightarrow Y$), $X \hookrightarrow Y$) as given in Algorithm 3. Filter() prunes those T_R tuples that cannot join any T_Y using the W-table. The cost of pruning T_R tuples is small for the following reasons. First, W-table can be stored on disk with a B^+-tree, and accessed by a pair of labels, B^+, as a key. Second, the frequently used labels are small in size and the centers maintained in $W(X,Y)$ can be maintained in memory. Third, the number of centers in a $W(X,Y)$ on average is small. Fourth, the cost of getCenters (Equation (6)) is small with caching and sharing. We consider Filter as an R-semijoin Equation (7).

$$T_R \underset{X \hookrightarrow Y}{\ltimes} T_Y = \pi_{T_R} \left(T_R \underset{X \hookrightarrow Y}{\bowtie} T_Y \right)$$

$$(7)$$

Here, the X attribute appears in the temporal relation X and Y attribute appears in the base relation T_Y, as the primary key.

$$T_R \underset{X \hookrightarrow Y}{\ltimes} T_X = \pi_{T_R}(T_R \underset{X \hookrightarrow Y}{\bowtie} T_X) \tag{8}$$

Equation (8) shows a similar case where the attribute Y appears in the temporal relation T_R and the attribute X appears in the base relation T_X.

The R-semijoin discussed in this work is different from the semijoin discussed in distributed database systems which is used to reduce the dominant data transmission cost over the network at the expense of the disk I/O access cost. Here, there is no such network cost involved. A unique feature of our R-semijoin is that it is the first of the two steps in an R-join algorithm. In other words, it must process R-semijoin to complete R-join. Below, we use $\in$ denote Filter() as an R-semijoin and $\bowtie$ denote Fetch(). Then, we have

$$T_R \underset{X \hookrightarrow Y}{\bowtie} T_S \equiv (T_R \underset{X \hookrightarrow Y}{\ltimes} T_S) \underset{X \hookrightarrow Y}{\widetilde{\bowtie}} T_S \tag{9}$$

It is worth noting that the cost for both sides of Equation (9) are almost the same.

Consider $((T_B \underset{B \hookrightarrow C}{\bowtie} T_C) \underset{C \hookrightarrow D}{\bowtie} T_D) \underset{C \hookrightarrow E}{\bowtie} T_E$. Suppose we process $T_A \underset{A \hookrightarrow B}{\bowtie} T_B$ first, and maintain the result in T_{BC}. It becomes $(T_{BC} \underset{C \hookrightarrow D}{\bowtie} T_D) \underset{C \hookrightarrow E}{\bowtie} T_E$. Then,

$$
\begin{aligned}
(T_{BC} \underset{C \hookrightarrow D}{\bowtie} T_D) \underset{C \hookrightarrow E}{\bowtie} T_E &= ((T_{BC} \underset{C \hookrightarrow D}{\ltimes} T_D) \underset{C \hookrightarrow D}{\widetilde{\bowtie}} T_D) \underset{C \hookrightarrow E}{\bowtie} T_E \\
&= (((T_{BC} \underset{C \hookrightarrow D}{\ltimes} T_D) \underset{C \hookrightarrow D}{\widetilde{\bowtie}} T_D) \underset{C \hookrightarrow E}{\ltimes} T_E) \underset{C \hookrightarrow E}{\widetilde{\bowtie}} T_E \\
&= (((T_{BC} \underset{C \hookrightarrow D}{\ltimes} T_D) \underset{C \hookrightarrow E}{\ltimes} T_E) \underset{C \hookrightarrow D}{\widetilde{\bowtie}} T_D) \underset{C \hookrightarrow E}{\widetilde{\bowtie}} T_E
\end{aligned}
$$

In the above equation, the conditions used in the two R-semijoins are C↪D and C↪E. Both access C in relation T_{BC}. If we process the two R-semijoins one followed by another, we need to scan the relation T_{BC}, get another temporal relation T'_{BC}, and then process the second R-semijoin against T'_{BC}. Instead, we can process the two

R-semijoins together, which only requests to scan T_{BC} once. The cost of Filter() can also be shared. It can be done by straightforward modification on Filter(). In general, a sequence of R-semijoins, $(((T_R \underset{C_1}{\ltimes} T_{X_1}) \cdots) \underset{C_k}{\ltimes} T_{X_k}$, can be processed together by one-scan of the temporal relation T_R under the following conditions. First, it is a sequence of R-semijoins, and there is no R-join in the sequence. Second, let C_i be a reachability condition, $X_i \hookrightarrow Y_i$. Either all X_i or all Y_i are the same for a label appearing in T_R. Due to the reusability of cached $(x_i, out(x_i))$ used in all R-semijoins in such a sequence, the cost of all R-semijoins succeeding the first R-semijoin is small, and therefore the ordering of the succeeding R-semijoins will not change the cost significantly.

R-Join/R-Semijoin Order Selection: In order to use multi R-joins to process a graph pattern query, it is important to find an efficient query plan as a sequence of R-joins/R-semijoins, because different costs are associated with different R-join/R-semijoin orders. (Cheng, Yu, & Yu, 2010) uses dynamic programming, as one of the main techniques for join order selection. It investigates two styles of R-join/R-semijoin order selection: The first is a two-step approach, which finds the optimal R-join order first and then consider if R-semijoins can be further used to reduce the cost. The second consider interleaving R-joins with R-semijoins, which can further find better plans that the two-step approach (the first style of order seleciton) cannot find.

The two basic components considered in dynamic programming are *statuses* and *moves*, where statuses maintains the R-joins/R-semijoins already considered while moves is the candidate operation to be considered next. To do R-join order selection, all statues and moves only consider R-joins (the first style of order selection), however, during interleaving R-joins with R-semijoins (the second style of order selection), both R-joins/R-semijoins are considered in statues and moves. The goal is to find the sequence of moves from the initial status toward the final status with the minimum cost among all the possible sequences of moves. For example, consider the graph pattern query in Figure 3(b). The detailed moves for finding the minimum-cost plan are given in Figure 13 using dynamic programming. Figure 13(a) lists all statuses, depicted as subgraphs of G_q, which includes reachability conditions of considered R-joins that far, and moves, which implies a newly included reachability conditions and connects two successive statuses. Each move is labeled with a cost, which is the total cost for that move. A dashed edge indicates a possible move, and a solid edge indicates a move with the minimum total cost. The optimal plan is the path with all solid edges from initial status to the final status. And the corresponding optimal left-deep tree plan to evaluate G_q is shown in Figure 13(b).

The cost is used to reflect the I/O cost of a query plan which can be estimated based on R-join/R-semijoin size estimation. Similar techniques to estimate joins/semijoins sizes and I/O

costs used in relational database systems can be adopted to estimate R-joins/ R-semijoins sizes. (Cheng, Yu, & Yu, 2010) maintains the join sizes and the processing costs for all R-joins between two base relations in a graph database. It maintains the join sizes and the processing costs for all R-joins between two base relations in a graph database. Using this statistical information, a simple method can be developed to estimate R-joins/ R-semijoins sizes. We briefly explain it as below.

$$|T_{RS}| = |T_R| \cdot \frac{|T_X \underset{X \hookrightarrow Y}{\bowtie} T_Y|}{|T_X|} \quad \text{or} \quad |T_R| \cdot \frac{|T_X \underset{X \hookrightarrow Y}{\bowtie} T_Y|}{|T_Y|} \tag{10}$$

$$|T'_{RS}| = |T_{RS}| \cdot \frac{|T_X \underset{X \hookrightarrow Y}{\bowtie} T_Y|}{|T_X| \cdot |T_Y|} \tag{11}$$

$$|T'_R| = |T_R| \cdot \frac{|T_X \underset{X \hookrightarrow Y}{\ltimes} T_Y|}{|X|} \quad \text{or} \quad |T_R| \cdot \frac{|T_Y \underset{X \hookrightarrow Y}{\ltimes} T_X|}{|Y|} \tag{12}$$

Figure 13. R-Join order selection (Figure 4 in (Cheng, Yu, & Yu, 2010))

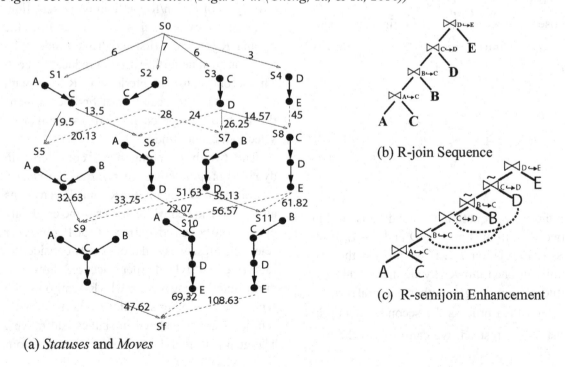

(a) *Statuses* and *Moves*

(b) R-join Sequence

(c) R-semijoin Enhancement

First, Equation (10) estimates the join size for R-joins between a temporal relation and a base relation, where the two cases are for whether T_y is the base table or whether T_x is the base table, respectively. On the right-hand side of Equation (10), the second term after $|T_R|$ estimates how many tuples in a based relation for a tuple in T_R can possibly join. Second, Equation (11) estimates the size of a self-R-join, with condition $X \hookrightarrow Y$, using the join selectivity for the R-join $T_X \underset{X \hookrightarrow Y}{\bowtie} T_Y$ between two base relations T_x and T_y. Here, $|T_{RS}|$ is the size of the relation on which the self-R-join is performed, and $|T_X \underset{X \hookrightarrow Y}{\bowtie} T_Y| / |T_X| \cdot |T_Y|$ is a value between 0 and 1 indicating the selectivity how many tuples will be selected in the self-R-join. Finally, the size estimation of R-semijoins is given by Equation (12), where the two cases are for whether T_y is the base table or whether T_x is the base table, respectively. The second term on the right-hand side of Equation (12) is a semi-join selectivity factor for the ratio of tuples in T_R that satisfy the join condition.

To enhance the R-join plan with R-semijoins, it is intuitive to view every R-join $(X \overset{\bowtie}{\hookrightarrow} Y)$ as a corresponding R-semijoin $(X \overset{\bowtie}{\hookrightarrow} Y)$ and R-join $(X \overset{\widetilde{\bowtie}}{\hookrightarrow} Y)$ and then move those R-semijoin $(X \overset{\bowtie}{\hookrightarrow} Y)$ to an earlier position, so that (i) it prunes the irrelevant intermediate results more progressively, i.e. the input to every R-join in the new plan consists of fewer intermediate tuples than that of the same R-join in the original plan, and (ii) it is still a left-deep tree plan and no extra cost will be introduced. For example, as depicted in Figure 13(c), it moves two R-semijoins to earlier postions for the R-join plan (Figure 13(b)). This strategy assumes that the R-join order, as a left-deep tree, reflects the optimal order of executing R-joins that R-semijoins must also follow. Second, it conducts R-semijoin reordering under a principle such that it does not add additional overhead into

the optimal R-join order identified. In other words, it must not introduce I/O cost that is not planned in the optimal R-join order selection.

For the the second R-join/R-semijoin order selection which considers interleaving R-joins with R-semijoins, a move in the dynamic programming optimization can be either an R-semijoin or an R-join. Note that according to Equation (9), each R-join can be divided and considered in two parts: $\in$ part and $\widetilde{\bowtie}$ part, where the output of the first part becomes the input of the second part. However, the search space can be as as high as $O(3 | E(G_q) |)^{|V(G_q)|-1}$ in (Chen & Yu, 1993), where the constant comes from the important fact that for each join predicate there are 3 candidate operations (the join plus the two semi-joins on the two relations respectively). (Cheng, Yu, & Yu, 2010) proposes a strategy to interleave R-joins with R-semijoins with the overhead being manageable. Particularly, one there is a move for an R-semijoin on X such as $X \overset{\bowtie}{\hookrightarrow} Y$ (or $Y \overset{\bowtie}{\hookrightarrow} X$), where X belongs to the temporal table, all other possible $\in$ on X are also included in this move. This is because all other possible $\in$ on X can be processed while processing the first R-semijoin $X \overset{\bowtie}{\hookrightarrow} Y$ (or $Y \overset{\bowtie}{\hookrightarrow} X$) for they all access the same temporal relation and the same graph code in the base relation. Therefore, we can always consider all possible $\in$ on X together. A corresponding search space is $O(| E(G_q | \cdot | V(G_q) |)5^{|V(G_q)|}$ which is much better than the one in (Chen & Yu, 1993). The details can be found in (Cheng, Yu, & Yu, 2010). The experiment study in (Cheng, Yu, & Yu, 2010) suggests that for a given graph pattern query, the processing with the optimal R-join order using join index is usually 2 or 3 orders of magnitude faster than the holistic twig join approach (Twig-StackD), and 1 order of magnitude faster than the sort-merge join based approach (IGMJ). On the other hand, for all approaches based on the join index, the performance with the optimal R-join order is very close to the performance with the first style of R-join/R-semijoin order selection, namely the optimal R-join order with R-semijoin enhancement. However, for the second style of R-join/R-semijoin order selection, namely, interleaving R-joins with R-semijoins, it significantly outperforms the other two alternatives, even with more time on searching an optimal interleaved R-join/R-semijoin plan.

A Hash Join Based Approach

Wang, Li, Luo and Gao propose a hash join based approach in 2008 to process a graph pattern query. This approach further exploits the potentiality of multi-interval code in (Agrawal, Borgida, & Jagadish, 1989) and extends their IGMJ algorithm to a hash based join algorithm. In particular, it also operates on *Alist* and *Dlist* to process a corresponding reachability condition A↪D. Here, *Alist* is a list of pairs (*val(u),post(u)*) for all $u \in ext(A)$, where *post(u)* is the unique postorder number of u, and *val(u)* is either a start value s or an end value e of the intervals $[s,e]$ assigned to u by the multi-interval encoding scheme. For example, *Alist* corresponding to label institute in Figure 7(a) becomes {(1,1),(1,5),(3,12),(3,13),(3,17),(3,20)}, because node 1 is assigned with the interval [1,5] and node 3 is assigned with the intervals [12,13] and [17,20]. Like the IGMJ algorithm, *Dlist* keeps a list of postorder numbers *post(v)* for all $v \in ext(D)$. *Alist* is sorted in ascending order of *val(u)* values, and *Dlist* is sorted in ascending order of *post(v)* values. The hash based join algorithm, called HGJoin, is outline in Algorithm 4 as seen in Figure 14.

(Wang, Li, Luo & Gao, 2008) investigates how to share the processing cost for the hash join when it needs to process several *Alist* and *Dlist* simultaneously. They propose three basic join operators, namely, IT-HGJoin, T-HGJoin, and Bi-HGJoin. The IT-HGJoin processes a subgraph of a query with one descendant and multiple ancestors such

as, for example, a query graph consists of A↪D∧B↪D∧C↪D∧.... The T-HGJoin process a subgraph of a query with one ancestor and multiple descendants such as, for example, a query graph consists of A↪B∧A↪C∧A↪D∧.... The Bi-HGJoin processes a complete bipartite subgraph for a query with multiple ancestors and multiple descendants such as, for example, a query graph consists of A↪C∧A↪D∧B↪C∧B↪D∧.... A general query graph G_q will be processed by a set of subgraph queries using IT-HGJoin, T-HGJoin, and Bi-HGJoin. (Wang et al., 2008) also proposes cost-based query optimization strategy to study how to decompose a general query graph G_q to a number of IT-HGJoin, T-HGJoin, and Bi-HGJoin operations.

A Brief Summary

We briefly summarize the graph pattern matching based on reachability joins (r-joins). Figure 11 outlines the time/space complexity of the underlying code, the join method and the supported queries for the four representatives, denoted as Baseline, CGK05, WLL08 and CYY10. In particular, the first row is for the baseline approach based on *TC*, which is used to introduce this relational processing framework; (Chen, Gupta, & Kurul, 2005) is described in the second row; the third row is for (Wang, Li, Luo & Gao, 2008) and the last row for (Cheng, Yu, & Yu, 2010). In Figure 11, n and m is the number of nodes and edges in the underlying data graph, respectively. Some approaches are not mentioned here because they are preliminary versions of these representatives, such as (Wang et al., 2005; Cheng, Yu, & Tang, 2006; Cheng, Yu, Yu, & Wang, 2008), or have different query semantics, such as (Zou, Chen, & Özsu, 2009) and (Fan et al., 2010), which we will briefly explain in the next section.

The baseline approach based on the edge transitive closure is not practical due to its prohibitive $O(n^2)$ space consumption. The approach

Figure 14. Algorithm 4 HGJoin

Algorithm 4 HGJoin(*Alist*, *Dlist*)

1: $H \leftarrow \emptyset$;
2: $Output \leftarrow \emptyset$;
3: $a \leftarrow Alist.first$;
4: $d \leftarrow Dlist.first$;
5: **while** $a \neq Alist.last \land d \neq Dlist.last$ **do**
6:     **if** $val(a) \leq post(d)$ **then**
7:         **if** $post(a) \notin H$ **then**
8:             hash $post(a)$ into H;
9:             $a \leftarrow a.next$;
10:        **else if** $val(a) < post(d)$ **then**
11:            delete $post(a)$ from H;
12:            $a \leftarrow a.next$;
13:        **else**
14:            **for all** $post(a)$ in H **do**
15:                append $(post(a), post(d))$ to $Output$;
16:            **end for**
17:            $d \leftarrow d.next$;
18:        **end if**
19:     **else**
20:         **for all** $post(a)$ in H **do**
21:            append $(post(a), post(d))$ to $Output$;
22:         **end for**
23:         $d \leftarrow d.next$;
24:     **end if**
25: **end while**
26: **return** $Output$;

Figure 15. An Overview of different approaches

	Underlying code	Reachabilty test time	Encoding time	Code size	Join method	Query
Baseline	transitive closure	$O(1)$	$O(nm)$	$O(n^2)$	nested loop join	general graph
CGK05	tree+SSPI	$O(m-n)$	$O(n+m)$	$O(n+m)$	holistic twig join	DAG
WLL08	multi-interval code	$O(\log(n))$	$O(nm)$	$O(n^2)$	hash join	DAG
CYY10	2-hop cover	$O(m^{1/2})$	$O(n^3|TC|)$	$O(nm^{1/2})$	join index	general graph

of (Chen, Gupta, & Kurul, 2005) has a much better space consumption, but the overhead of the reachability test time at querying time can be high. Although the multi-interval code used by (Wang, Li, Luo & Gao, 2008) has a high space complexity, but it is usually much smaller than the theoretical value in practice. (Cheng, Yu, Lin, Wang, & Yu, 2006) contains some empirical study for its size. (Cheng, Yu, & Yu, 2010) uses the 2-hop cover which only require $O(nm^{\frac{1}{2}})$ space. The time complexity for constructing an 2-hop cover remains open. In (Cohen, Halperin, Kaplan, & Zwick, 2002), the conjecture is $O(n^3 \cdot |TC|)$ where $|TC|$ is the size of the edge transitive closure of the underlying data graph. Several efficient algorithms are proposed to compute 2-hop cover (Cheng, Yu, Lin, Wang, & Yu, 2006, 2008;

Cheng & Yu, 2009) and to maintain such a computed 2-hop cover (Schenkel, Theobald, & Weikum, 2005; Bramandia, Choi, & Ng, 2008). For the four compared relational approaches, the overall performance for processing a graph pattern is indicated by the underlying code size and the join method. The empirical study to compare different approaches can be found in (Cheng, Yu, & Yu, 2010).

TOP-K GRAPH PATTERN MATCHING

A Top-*k* Join Approach

As we know that in connected undirected graphs or strongly connected directed graphs, any node is reachable from (and can reach to) any other node which automatically satisfies the reachability condition of any graph patterns. Then, any node combinations which have the required labels of Q will be returned as answers. Therefore, Zou, Chen, and Özsu proposed a multi D-join approach to process a graph pattern in 2009, which explicitly requires that for every edge $X \hookrightarrow Y \in E(G_q)$,

the distance between the two corresponding nodes $x, y, \in M_Q$ must be no larger than a user-given threshold. This implies there are $|T_X| \times |T_Y|$ distance computations between all pairs (x,y), where $x \in ext(X)$ and $y \in ext(Y)$, to process $X \hookrightarrow Y \in E(G_q)$. Then, (Zou, Chen, and Özsu, 2009) focus on reducing the number of distance computations. Recently, (Fan et al., 2010) further renovates this problem by assigning each query edge $X \hookrightarrow Y \in E(G_q)$ either a constant k or a *, denoting the corresponding pair of nodes in a data graph are reachable within k hops or any hops, respectively. They use a much different graph simulation approach instead of join algorithms.

We are motivated by the difficulty that too many matches may be found in G_D and returned to users, which are hard to be all digested by users. To remedy the problem, we propose a direct extension on the semantics of the graph pattern matching discussed previously in this chapter, and it becomes a problem of *top-k graph pattern matching*. It only returns the k matches with the smallest total sum of all distances between two corresponding nodes $x, y, \in M_Q$ for $X \hookrightarrow Y \in E(G_q)$. This semantics is different to (Zou, Chen, and Özsu, 2009; Fan et al., 2010) and we will not discuss further details of them for the different semantics and processing paradigm. We continue to explain the preliminary solution for this top-*k* graph pattern matching problem.

The top-*k* graph pattern matching problem is defined in terms of node distances. Formally, let the distance from a node u to a node v be denoted as $\delta(u,v)$; the score of a match M_Q is defined as $score(M_Q) = \sum_{X \hookrightarrow Y \in E(G_a)} \delta(x,y)$, for $x, y, \in M_Q$. Intuitively, the smaller distance between two nodes in G_D indicates a closer relationship between them. Therefore, a match with a smaller score is regarded to be better. In other words, a match M_Q tends to be ranked higher if score(M_Q) is smaller. For example, a top-*k* graph pattern query is shown in Figure 17(a), which request the top-2 matches. When evaluating it against the data graph G_D (Figure 16), the two returned matches are with scores as 3 and 5, as shown in Figure 17(b) and (c), which are the smallest two scores for any matches in G_D. Here, the directed path either from x to y or from y to x in a directed graph G_D can satisfy an edge $X \hookrightarrow Y \in E(G_q)$, which is undirected.

Note that the graph pattern query $E(G_q)$ (Figure 17(a)) contains a circle. And the existing work of finding top-k twig matches (Gou & Chirkova, 2008; Qi, Candan, & Sapino, 2007) cannot be effectively applied here, because their query executions rely on the tree structure of given queries which are required to be cycle-free. On the other hand, as a naive solution, it is possible to find all matches using an existing approach (Wang, Li, Luo & Gao, 2008; Cheng, Yu, & Yu, 2010) and then rank all returned matches by the match scores, and report the top-k matches with the smallest scores. However, this can be very inefficient because there can still be an enormous number of matches in the underlying graph. We first show that a top-k join approach can be used for the top-k graph pattern matching problem based on the materialized transitive closure. As a compact supporting data structure, we also discuss the

R-join index (Cheng, Yu, & Yu, 2010) can be extended with distance-aware 2-hop.

We materialize the edge transitive closure of a data graph G_D, and store it in tables. A table $R_{(A,D)}$ stores information for all paths from A-labeled nodes to D-labeled nodes as a database relation: AD_CONN_TBL(A,D, δ). Here, columns A and D are for A-labeled nodes and D-labeled nodes, respectively. The attribute δ is dedicated for the corresponding $\delta(a,d)$ where a and d are A-labeled and D-labeled nodes respectively. Below, we use $R_{(A,D)}$ to refer to this table. There can be $|\sum|^2$ tables, each corresponding to a different pair of labels in Σ. Later, we use t to signify a tuple in $R_{(A,D)}$, while attribute δ denotes $\delta(a,d)$ for a, b, $\in$ t. It is possible to compute all matches M_Q of a top-k graph pattern query by processing top-k joins over a number of tables $R_{(A,D)}$, where the top-k algorithm (Ilyas, Aref, & Elmagarmid, 2004) can progressively compute top-k joins of several tables without computing all joins of those tables. Therefore, there is a solution as the adaption of a top-k join algorithm to find top-k matches.

Figure 17. Top-k query/answers

Figure 16. Data graph

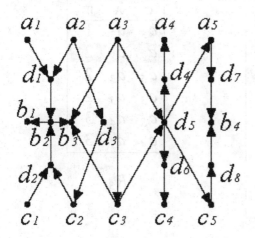

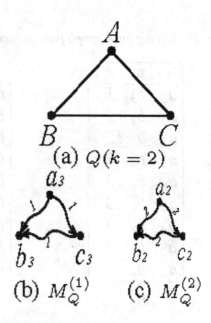

Suppose there are $|E(G_q)| = l$ edges and each edge is identified by a number. Let the i-th edge in $E(G_q)$ be X↪Y, and we use R_i to denote $R_{(A,D)}$. A multi-way join on $R_1, R_2, \ldots,$ and R_i can be used to compute all matches M_Q. Here, R_i and R_j are joined together, if a common query node X appears as an end node in both the i-th and the j-th edges of $E(G_q)$. And the join is based on the equality condition on the corresponding common X columns in table $E(G_q)$ and table R_i and R_j. The whole join condition for this multi-way join can be expressed as below:

$$\bigwedge R_i.X = R_i.X \qquad (13)$$

We briefly describe the adaption of the popular top-k join algorithm (Ilyas, Aref, & Elmagarmid, 2004), called the *hash ripple join*, or simply HRJN. In detail, $R_1, .R_2., \ldots,$ and R_i are required to be sorted in the ascending order of δ. HRJN sequentially scans those tables on disk. The tuples already scanned into memory are referred as *seen tuples*, while those not scanned yet are un*seen tuples*. For each table R_i, a hash index is built for those seen tuples of R_i. In detail, during the sequential scan, when an unseen tuple t from R_i is accessed, HRJN probes all hash indexes to compute all valid join combinations of t between all seen tuples of t, $i \neq j$. In this way, HRJN incrementally joins $R_1, R_2, \ldots,$ and using Equation (13) and a buffer is used to maintain temporary top-k matches that have been found. For example, Figure 18 illustrate the identification of the two returned matches in $R_{(A, B)}$, $R_{(B,C)}$ and $R_{(C,A)}$ for the graph in Figure 16.

To see how HRJN can stop early to avoid totally scanning and joining $R_1, R_2, \ldots,$ and R_l. It is based on the comparison of two bounds of *score* (M_Q), namely, the upper bound of top-k seen matches, denoted as $\overline{score}$, and the lower bound of unseen matches, denoted as $\underline{score}$. In particular, $\overline{score}$ is the largest score of the temporary top-k matches, i.e., the score of the current k-th matches in the buffer, while $\underline{score}$ is the possible smallest score of an match, that is not seen but can be produced with those tuples not scanned yet. $\overline{score}$ and $\underline{score}$ are calculated and updated every time after a tuple has been scanned and consumed. HRJN can stop immediately when $\overline{score} \leq \underline{score}$. Detailed bouding schemes to obtain $\overline{score} \leq \underline{score}$ can be found in (Ilyas, Aref, & Elmagarmid, 2004). We next show how to

Figure 18. Solving top-k graph pattern matching with Top-k joins

A	B	W_p
a_3	b_3	1
a_1	b_2	2
a_2	b_2	2
a_5	b_4	2
a_1	b_1	3
a_2	b_1	3
a_1	b_3	3
a_2	b_3	3
a_3	b_4	4

R_1

B	C	W_p
b_3	c_3	1
b_2	c_1	2
b_2	c_2	2
b_4	c_5	2
b_1	c_1	3
b_1	c_2	3
b_3	c_1	3
b_3	c_2	3
b_4	c_3	4

R_2

C	A	W_p
c_3	a_3	1
c_2	a_2	2
c_5	a_3	2
c_3	a_5	2
c_3	a_4	3
c_4	a_3	3

R_3

replace $R_1, R_2, ..., $ and R_l with a compact supporting data structure with distance-aware 2-hop, because the storage cost of $R_1, R_2, .., $ and R_l based on transitive closure can be prohibitively large.

An Indexing Scheme Based on Distance-Aware 2-Hop

The compact storage which supports retrieving tuples $\langle (a,d) : \delta(a,d) \rangle$ in $R_{(A,D)}$ in the increasing order of $\delta(a,d)$ is studied in (Cheng, Yu, & Cheng, 2010), based on distance-aware 2-hop labeling (Cohen, Halperin, Kaplan, & Zwick, 2002; Schenkel, Theobald, & Weikum, 2005; Cheng & Yu, 2009). The distance-aware 2-hop labeling is further enhanced with distance information: Let $H = \{S_{w1}, S_{w2i}, ...\}$ be the seft of 2-hop cover computed, where $S_{wi} = S(U_w, w_i, V_{wi})$ and all w_i are centers. Now, U_{wi} or V_{wi} is a set $\{\langle (u, w_i) : \delta(u, w_i) \rangle\}$ or $\{\langle (w_i, v) : (w_1, v) \rangle\}$. And $S_{wi} = S(U_w, w_i, V_{wi})$ compactly represents a set of $\{\langle (u,v) : \delta(u,v) \rangle\}$, where there is $\delta(u, w_i) + \delta(w_i, v) = \delta(u, v)$. This suggests that the shortest path from u to v is the concatenation of the shortest path from u to w_i and the shortest path from w_i to v. For example, in the graph of Figure 19, we have 6 centers. Specifically, Figure 19(a) shows the center 7, with a circle on it, marking a number of shortest paths from different u to v going through 7. The set U_7

for all u, U_7, and the set V_7 for all v, are marked by two shadowed areas with two background colors. Similarly, Figure 19(b) and Figure 19(c) show the other centers and clusters.

It is straightforward to use the same B+-tree and W-table of (Cheng, Yu, & Yu, 2010) to design a storage scheme for $H = \{S_{w1}, S_{w2i}, ...\}$. To be different from the B+-tree index used in (Cheng, Yu, & Yu, 2010), all reachable pairs (a,d) indexed by a center should also reflect the increasing order of $\delta(a,d)$, such as illustrated in Figure 20. It shows 6 sorted lists on the 6 clusters in Figure 19, which are indexed by corresponding centers. With these sorted lists, it is straightforward to retrieving tuples $\langle (a,d) : \delta(a,d) \rangle$ in $R_{(A,D)}$ in the increasing order of $\delta(a,d)$, for the W-table gives all centers for those $\langle (a,d) : \delta(a,d) \rangle$. Therefore, the nodes in F-clusters and T-clusters of centers in this B+-tree index has to be further organized to support retrieving those sorted lists in Figure 20 and Figure 22 sequentially.

(Cheng, Yu, & Yu, 2010) organizes these F-clusters and T-clusters based on information in $S_{wi} = S(U_w, w_i, V_{wi})$ for a center w_i. It further groups nodes in U_{wi}/V_{wi} by their distances to/from w_i into a number of *F-buckets/T-buckets*. Those F-buckets/T-buckets are arranged in the increasing order of the node distance. It collects all node labels for all nodes and forms a signature (Zobel, Moffat, & Ramamohanarao, 1998) to indicate all

Figure 19. Distance-aware 2-hop

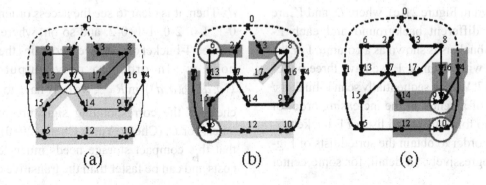

(a) (b) (c)

Figure 20. Reachable pairs indexed by the B⁺-Tree index

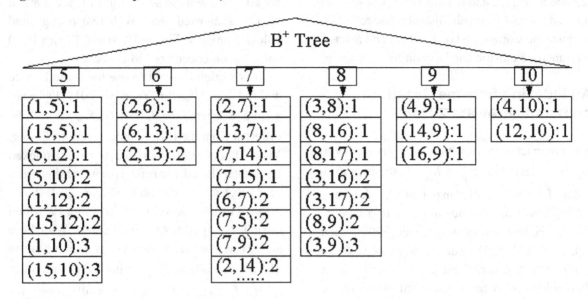

Figure 21. Organize the B⁺-Tree index based on distances

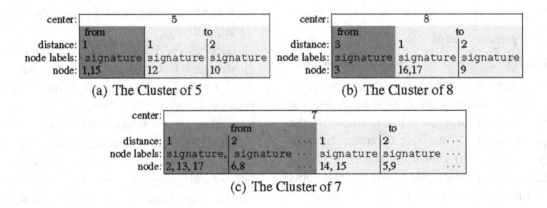

(a) The Cluster of 5   (b) The Cluster of 8

(c) The Cluster of 7

labels included by that bucket. This structure is illustrated in Figure 21. For example, $S(U_7, 7, V_7)$ is illustrated in Figure 21(c), where U_7 and V_7 are shown in different background and each F-buckets/T-buckets is shown as a column. For the F-buckets with distance 1, we have three nodes 2, 13 and 17. We can sequentially scan F-buckets/T-buckets of a center in the increasing order of distances to form the sorted lists of F-buckets/T-buckets in order to obtain the sorted lists of Figure 20 progressively. In detail, for some center

w_i, we use a pair $d_1 - d_2$ to signify the access for the F-bucket of distance d_1 and T-bucket of distance d_2. Then, it is clear to see the access order is 0-0, 0-1, 1-0, 2-0, 1-1, 0-2, and so on, where the F-bucket/ T-bucket of distance 0 contains the single node w_i. In order to only output those $\langle (a, d) : \delta(a, d) \rangle$ in $R_{(A,D)}$, we only have to further check if the corresponding signature matches label A or D. (Cheng, Yu, & Cheng, 2010) shows that this compact storage needs much less I/O costs and can be faster than the transitive closure

Figure 22. Reachable pairs indexed by the B^+-Tree index

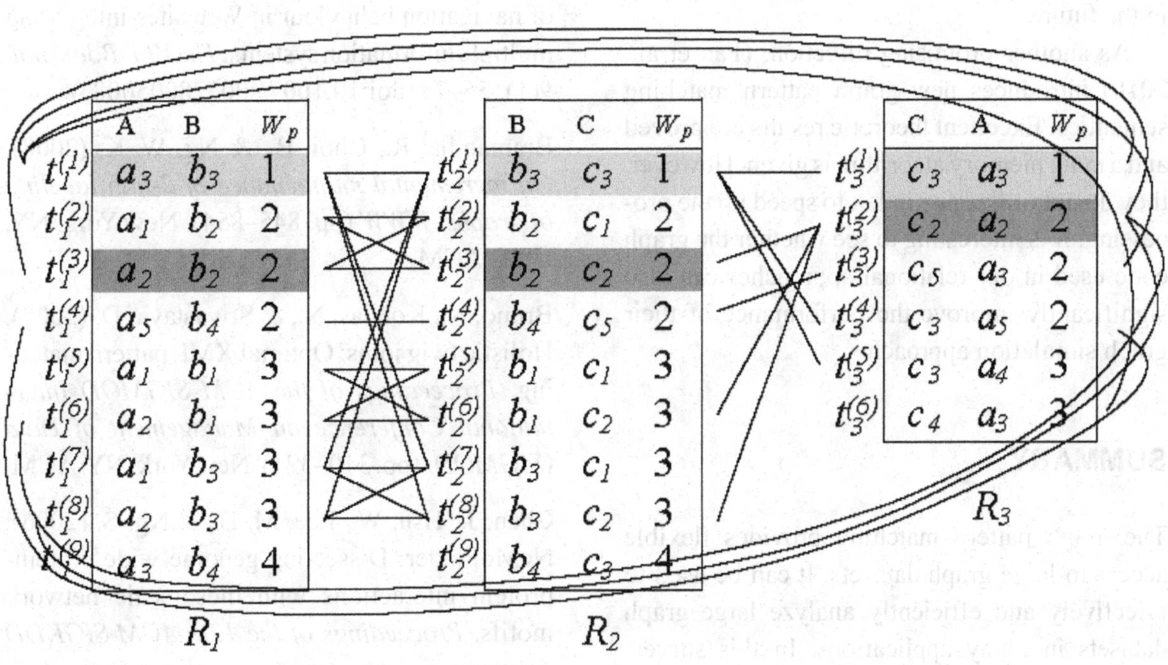

based storage up to an order of magnitude in processing top-k queries for primitive graph patterns .

Limitation of the Top-k Join Solution

Here are some important observations regarding the performance of the solution adapted from top-k joins: it is based on the nested loop style processing, which is costly itself. Moreover, during the top-k join processing, the stop condition $\underline{score} \leq \overline{score}$ may not be easily satisfied, because $\overline{score}$ grows slowly according to its calculation in (Ilyas, Aref, & Elmagarmid, 2004). Figure 18 illustrates computing top-2 matches using this solution. After the top-2 match $\langle a_2, b_2, c_2 \rangle$ is found, it can be easily verified that $\overline{score}$ remains to be less than 6 till both $t_1^{(9)}$ and $t_2^{(9)}$ are accessed. Hence the top-k join solution can not stop early because that $\overline{score}$ is too small. As a result, there is a considerable overhead of repeatedly computing joins between every tuple accessed from disk

and all accessed tuples in memory. In Figure 18, there are many lines between tuples to represent successful joins between two tuples, which also indicates that there exist a large number of partial matches.

FUTURE RESEARCH DIRECTIONS

An acute reader may consider applying the threshold top-k selection algorithm (TA) of (Fagin, Lotem, & Naor, 2001). It is important to note when the object attributes are known, TA algorithm is used to find top-k objects according to a monotonic scoring function combining those object attributes. These objects are respectively sorted by each attribute and formed into different sorted object lists. And TA algorithm requires that one object on a list corresponds (can join to) the same object in another list. However, such conditions are not immediate in our setting. It is interesting to see how to achieve a proper scenario that TA algorithm can successfully renovate this problem in the future.

As another promising direction, (Fan et al., 2010) introduces new graph pattern matching semantics. Excellent theoretic results are proved and a main memory algorithm is given. However, they do not utilize any index to speed up the processing. It is interesting to see whether the graph code used in our relational approaches can also significantly improve the performance of their graph simulation approach.

SUMMARY

The graph pattern matching provides flexible access to large graph datasets. It can be used to effectively and efficiently analyze large graph datasets in many applications. In this survey, we have reviewed different join approaches to process graph pattern queries that can be easily implemented in relational databases. We can see that the graph pattern matching problem involves various primitive join operators based on different graph encoding schemes, and different optimization schemes to combine these joins. As the next step of this direction, it is interesting to further study a successful solution for the top-k graph pattern matching problem.

REFERENCES

Agrawal, R., Borgida, A., & Jagadish, H. V. (1989). Efficient management of transitive relationships in large data and knowledge bases. *Proceedings of the ACM SIGMOD International Conference on Management of Data (SIGMOD)* (pp. 253 – 262). San Francisco, CA: Morgan Kaufmann Publishers Inc.

Berendt, B., & Spiliopoulou, M. (2000). Analysis of navigation behaviour in Web sites integrating multiple information systems. *The VLDB Journal*, *9*(1), 56–75. doi:10.1007/s007780050083

Bramandia, R., Choi, B., & Ng, W. K. (2008). *On incremental maintenance of 2-hop labeling of graphs. WWW* (pp. 845–854). New York, NY, USA: ACM.

Bruno, N., Koudas, N., & Srivastava, D. (2002). Holistic twig joins: Optimal XML pattern matching. *Proceedings of the ACM SIGMOD International Conference on Management of Data (SIGMOD)* (pp. 310–321). New York, NY: ACM.

Chen, J., Hsu, W., Lee, M. L., & Ng, S. (2006). NeMoFinder: Dissecting genome-wide protein-protein interactions with meso-scale network motifs. *Proceedings of the 12th ACM SIGKDD International Conference on Knowledge Discovery and Data Mining (KDD)* (pp. 106–115). Philadelphia, PA: ACM.

Chen, L., Gupta, A., & Kurul, M. E. (2005). Stack-based algorithms for pattern matching on DAGs. *Proceedings of the International Conference on Very Large Data Bases (VLDB)* (pp. 493–504). Vienna, Austria: VLDB Endowment.

Chen, M. S., & Yu, P. S. (1993). Combining joint and semi-join operations for distributed query processing. *TKDE*, *5*(3), 534–542.

Cheng, J., Ke, Y., Ng, W., & Lu, A. (2007). Fg-index: Towards verification-free query processing on graph databases. *Proceedings of the ACM SIGMOD International Conference on Management of Data (SIGMOD)* (pp. 857–872). New York, NY: ACM.

Cheng, J., & Yu, J. X. (2009). On-line exact shortest distance query processing. *Proceedings of the International Conference on Extending Database Technology (EDBT)* (pp.481–492). New York, NY: ACM.

Cheng, J., Yu, J. X., & Cheng, R. C. (2010). On-line preferential nearest neighbor browsing in large attribute graphs. *Proceedings of the 1st International Workshop on Graph Data Management Techniques and Applications (GDM '10)* (invited). Berlin–Heidelberg, Germany: Springer.

Cheng, J., Yu, J. X., & Yu, P. S. (2010). (to appear). Graph pattern matching: A join/semijoin approach. *TKDE*.

Cheng, J., Yu, J. X., Yu, P. S., & Wang, H. (2008). Fast graph pattern matching. *Proceedings of the International Conference on Data Engineering (ICDE)* (pp. 913–922). Los Alamitos, CA: IEEE Computer Society.

Cohen, E., Halperin, E., Kaplan, H., & Zwick, U. (2002). Reachability and distance queries via 2-hop labels. *Proceedings of the ACM-SIAM Symposium on Discrete Algorithms (SODA)* (pp. 937–946). Philadelphia, PA: SIAM.

Fagin, R., Lotem, A., & Naor, M. (2001). Optimal aggregation algorithms for Middleware. *Proceedings of the ACM SIGACT-SIGMOD-SIGART Symposium on Principles of Database Systems (PODS)* (pp. 102–113). New York, NY: ACM.

Fan, W., Li, J., Ma, S., Tang, N., Wu, Y., & Wu, Y. (2010). Graph pattern matching: From intractable to polynomial time. *PVLDB*, *3*(1), 264–275.

Fernandez, M., Florescu, D., Levy, A., & Suciu, D. (1997). A query language for a Web-site management system. *SIGMOD Record*, *26*(3), 4–11. doi:10.1145/262762.262763

Gallagher, B. (2006). Matching structure and semantics: A survey on graph-based pattern matching. *Proceedings of the 2006 AAAI Fall Symposium on Capturing and Using Patterns for Evidence Detection* (AAAI FS.), (pp. 45–53). Menlo Park, CA: AAAI Press.

Gou, G., & Chirkova, R. (2008). Efficient algorithms for exact ranked twig-pattern matching over graphs. *Proceedings of the ACM SIGMOD International Conference on Management of Data (SIGMOD)* (pp. 581–594). New York, NY: ACM.

He, H., & Singh, A. K. (2006). Closure-Tree: An index structure for graph queries. *Proceedings of the International Conference on Data Engineering (ICDE)* (p. 38). Washington D. C., USA: IEEE Computer Society.

Helden, J., Van, , Naim, A., Mancuso, R., Eldridge, M., Wernisch, L., & Gilbert, D.,…Wodak, S. J. (2000). Representing and analysing molecular and cellular function using the computer. *The Journal of Biological Chemistry*, *381*(9-10), 921–935. doi:10.1515/BC.2000.113

Ilyas, F., Aref, G., & Elmagarmid, K. (2004). Supporting top-k join queries in relational databases. *The VLDB Journal*, *13*(3), 207–221. doi:10.1007/s00778-004-0128-2

Linial, N., London, E., & Rabinovich, Y. (1995). The geometry of graphs and some of its algorithmic applications. *COMBINATORICA*, *15*(2), 31–42. doi:10.1007/BF01200757

Qi, Y., Candan, K. S., & Sapino, M. L. (2007). Sum-max monotonic ranked joins for evaluating top-k twig queries on weighted data graphs. *Proceedings of the International Conference on Very Large Data Bases (VLDB)* (pp. 507-518). Vienna, Austria: VLDB Endowment.

Schenkel, R., Theobald, A., & Weikum, G. (2005). Efficient creation and incremental maintenance of the HOPI index for complex XML document collections. *Proceedings of the International Conference on Data Engineering (ICDE)* (pp. 360-371). Washington D. C., USA: IEEE Computer Society.

Shahabi, C., Kolahdouzan, M. R., & Sharifzadeh, M. (2003). A road network embedding technique for k-nearest neighbor search in moving object databases. *GeoInformatica*, *7*(3), 31–42. doi:10.1023/A:1025153016110

Shang, H., Zhang, Y., Lin, X., & Yu, J. X. (2008). Taming verification hardness: An efficient algorithm for testing subgraph isomorphism. *PVLDB*, *1*(1), 364–375.

Shasha, D., Wang, J. T. L., & Giugno, R. (2002). Algorithmics and applications of tree and graph searching. *Proceedings of the ACM SIGACT-SIGMOD-SIGART Symposium on Principles of Database Systems (PODS)* (pp. 39–52). New York, NY: ACM.

Tian, Y., & Patel, J. (2008). TALE: A tool for approximate large graph matching. *Proceedings of the International Conference on Data Engineering (ICDE)* (pp. 963–972). Washington D. C., USA: IEEE Computer Society.

Tong, H., Faloutsos, C., Gallagher, B., & Eliassi-Rad, T. (2007). Fast best-effort pattern matching in large attributed graphs. *Proceedings of the International Conference on Knowledge Discovery and Data Mining (KDD)* (pp. 737–746). New York, NY: ACM.

Ullmann, J. R. (1976). An algorithm for subgraph isomorphism. *Journal of the ACM, 23*(1), 31–42. doi:10.1145/321921.321925

Wang, H., Li, J., Luo, J., & Gao, H. (2008). Hash-base subgraph query processing method for graph-structured xml documents. *PVLDB*, *1*(1), 478–489.

Wang, H., Wang, W., Lin, X., & Li, J. (2005). Labeling scheme and structural joins for graph-structured XML data. *Proceedings of the Asia-Pacific Web Conference (APWeb)* (pp. 277–289). Berlin – Heidelberg, Germany: Springer.

Williams, D., Huan, J., & Wang, W. (2007). Graph database indexing using structured graph decomposition. *Proceedings of the International Conference on Data Engineering (ICDE)* (pp. 976–985). Washington D. C., USA: IEEE Computer Society.

Yan, X., Yu, P. S., & Han, J. (2004). Graph indexing: A frequent structure-based approach. *Proceedings of the ACM SIGMOD International Conference on Management of Data (SIGMOD)* (pp. 335–346). New York, NY: ACM.

Zhao, P., Yu, J. X., & Yu, P. S. (2007). Graph indexing: Tree + delta <= graph. *Proceedings of the International Conference on Very Large Data Bases (VLDB)* (pp. 938–949). Vienna, Austria: VLDB Endowment.

Zobel, J., Moffat, A., & Ramamohanarao, K. (1998). Inverted files versus signature files for text indexing. *ACM Transactions on Database Systems*, *23*(4), 453–490. doi:10.1145/296854.277632

Zou, L., Chen, L., & Özsu, M. T. (2009). Distancejoin: Pattern match query in a large graph database. *PVLDB, 2*(1), 886–897.

ADDITIONAL READING

Besides the techniques surveyed in this paper, different algorithms also exist in other domains: In 2002, Shasha, Wang, and Giugno highlighted algorithms and applications for searching trees and graphs, while (Gallagher, B., 2006) contains a survey of graph pattern matching in a variety of areas. Traditionally, graph pattern matching usually stands for problems like the subgraph isomorphism (Ullmann, 1976), which is long investigated. This problem is widely used recently for subgraph containment search (Yan, Yu, & Han, 2004; He & Singh, 2006; Williams, Huan, & Wang, 2007; Cheng, Ke, Ng, & Lu, 2007; Zhao, Yu, & Yu, 2007; Shang, Zhang, Lin, & Yu, 2008).

The work of XML query processing, especially on processing twig queries against large tree-structured data (Bruno, Koudas, & Srivastava, 2002), renewed the interests of graph matching problem. Approximate graph matching has been studied in (Tian, & Patel, 2008; Tong, Faloutsos, Gallagher, & Eliassi-Rad, 2007) to allow node mismatches/gaps. In biological networks, it is interesting to find network motifs which are patterns (sub-graphs) that recur within a network much more often than expected at random (Chen, Hsu, Lee, & Ng, 2006). Recently, (Fan et al., 2010)

further introduces new graph pattern matching semantics based on graph simulation and proves theoretic performance bounds for this problem.

ENDNOTES

[1] http://www.informatik.uni-trier.de/~ley/db
[2] The X attribute is the same named attribute in the base relation T_X. X appears in T_R because T_X is involved in at least a previous R-join.

Chapter 7
Labelling–Scheme–Based Subgraph Query Processing on Graph Data

Hongzhi Wang
Harbin Institute of Technology, China

Jianzhong Li
Harbin Institute of Technology, China

Hong Gao
Harbin Institute of Technology, China

ABSTRACT

When data are modeled as graphs, many research issues arise. In particular, there are many new challenges in query processing on graph data. This chapter studies the problem of structural queries on graph data. A hash-based structural join algorithm, HGJoin, is first proposed to handle reachability queries on graph data. Then, it is extended to the algorithms to process structural queries in form of bipartite graphs. Finally, based on these algorithms, a strategy to process subgraph queries in form of general DAGs is proposed. It is notable that all the algorithms above can be slightly modified to process structural queries in form of general graphs.

INTRODUCTION

In many applications, data is naturally modeled as a labeled directed graph. For example, the XML document of the relationship of publications and authors adapts to graph structure since one paper may have more than one author and one author may have more than one paper. A fragment of

DOI: 10.4018/978-1-61350-053-8.ch007

such information is shown in Figure 1. Obviously, a graph can be represented in tree structure by duplicating the nodes with more than one incoming paths. But it will result in redundancy. If the information in Figure 1 is represented with a tree, the element "author" will be duplicated.

Among the queries on a graph, the subgraph queries are widely used. A subgraph query on a graph (*subgraph query* for short) is to retrieve the subgraphs matching the graph pattern in the

Figure 1. An example of a graph

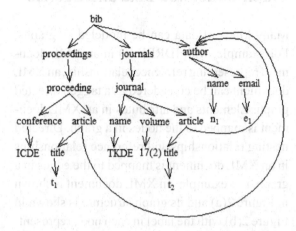

query. For instance, a subgraph query on the graph in Figure 1 is to retrieve the names of authors with publications both in proceedings and journals. Another subgraph query on the graph in Figure 1 is to retrieve the name of the journal with an author who published papers in the conference ICDE.

It is a big challenge to process subgraph queries efficiently. All the four kinds of traditional methods of processing structural queries on tree-structured data, structural join based methods (S. Al-Khalifa&H. V. Jagadish, et. al.(2002)), holistic Twigjoin based methods (Bruno, N. & Koudas, N. et.al. (2002)), structural index based methods (Milo, T. & Suciu, D.(1999)) and subsequence matching based methods (Wang, H. & Park, S. et. al. (2003)), cannot be used to process subgraph queries.

The structural join based methods and the holistic Twigjoin based methods both depend on the labelling scheme especially for tree-structured data. The encoding scheme of graphs is totally different from that of trees. As a result, they cannot be used to process subgraph queries.

Tree-structured index is enough for the structural query processing for tree-structured data. However, structural queries on graphs require graph-structured indices. Thus, the structural index-based methods for tree-structured data

cannot be used to process the subgraph queries efficiently.

The subsequence matching based methods require that the tree-structured data and the queries on the documents must be converted into sequences before query processing. It is difficult to covert a graph into a sequence because the traversal of a graph can only cover a small share of edges while the traversal on a tree can cover all the edges. Therefore, it is not easy to process subgraph queries using the subsequence matching based methods.

To process subgraph queries effectively and efficiently, a natural way is to use interval-based labeling scheme (Agrawal, R. & Borgida, A. (1989)). The reasons for choosing the interval-based labeling scheme (Agrawal, R. & Borgida, A. (1989)) are as following.

• It contains only intervals and identifications (ids). All intervals and ids are numerical values so that there is an order on them, which makes query processing easier.

• Interval-based reachability and adjacent labeling scheme are compatible so that they can be used to process subgraph queries with both reachability and adjacent edges.

• The interval-based labeling scheme can be used to process subgraph queries in various forms, e.g. graphs with circles, non-planar graphs, on general graphs.

Our proposed method is designed step by step. Firstly, a hash-based join algorithm, HGJoin, is proposed for processing reachability queries on a graph to retrieve pairs of nodes in the graph with reachability relationship between nodes in each pair. Second, the HGJoin algorithm is extended to the IT-HGJoin and T-HGJoin algorithms to process the extensive reachability queries with multiple ancestors or multiple descendants. Then, Bi-HGJoin, the combination of IT-HGJoin and T-HGJoin, is designed to process queries in form of complete bipartite graphs with only reachability relationships. Finally, based on all the above algorithms, the method for processing subgraph queries in form of DAGs is proposed.

Without losing generality, the major part of this chapter focus on subgraph queries in form of DAG with only reachability relationships on edges for the convenience of discussion. With a slight modification, the method can be used to process any general subgraph queries.

In some applications, all nodes in the subgraph matching the query are not required to be retrieved. To efficiently process such queries, we extend the algorithm to process such partial subgraph queries.

The content of this chapter are as follows:

- Based on the reachability scheme by Agrawal, R. & Borgida, A. (1989), a family of hash-based join algorithms is presented as basic operators of subgraph query processing.
- For structural queries in form of general graphs, an efficient method is presented. The basic idea is to split a query into bipartite subqueries each of which can be processed by some HGJoin algorithm. In order to find effective splitting strategy, a cost-based query optimization strategy is presented with some acceleration strategies.
- Efficient methods are presented to process partial subgraph queries. With merging intervals, such methods avoid large intermediate results and accelerate the query processing.

BACKGROUND

In this section, the background and notations used in this chapter are presented.

Graph-Structured Data and Queries

Many kinds of data can be modeled as graphs. For example, with IDREF-ID in an XML document representing reference relationship, an XML document can be considered as a tagged directed graph. Elements and attributes in an XML document is mapped to the nodes in a graph. Directed nesting relationships and reference relationships in an XML document is mapped to the edges in a graph. For example, an XML document is shown in Figure 2(a) and its graph structure is shown in Figure 2(b) with the label in each node representing the id of this node in the XML documents.

In the graph-structured data, structural queries are defined based on the structural relationship between nodes. In a graph G, two nodes a and b satisfy *adjacent relationship* if and only if an edge from a to b exists in G; two nodes a and b satisfy *reachability relationship* if and only if a path from a to b exists in G. A *reachability query* $a \rightarrow d$ is to retrieve all pairs of nodes (n_a, n_d), in G where n_a has tag a, n_d has tag d and n_a and n_d satisfy reachabilty relationship in G. For example, the result of reachability $a \rightarrow e$ in the graph in Figure 2(b) includes $(a, e_1), (a, e_2), (a, e_3)$. *Adjacent queries* can be defined similarly. The combination of multiple reachability or adjacent relationships forms subgraph queries.

A subgraph query is a tagged directed graph $Q = (V, E, tag, rel)$, where V is the node set of Q; E is the edge set of Q; the function $tag: V \rightarrow TAG$ is the tag function (TAG is the set of tags); the function $rel: E \rightarrow AXIS$ shows the structural relationships between the nodes in the query ($AXIS$ is the set of relationships between nodes; $PC \in AXIS$ represents adjacent relationship; $AD \in AXIS$ represents reachability relationship). The directed graph (V, E) is called the *query graph*. If $ab \in E$ and $rel(ab) = PC$, then ab is called an *adjacent edge*. If $ab \in E$ and $rel(ab) = AD$, then

Figure 2. An example of graph-structured data

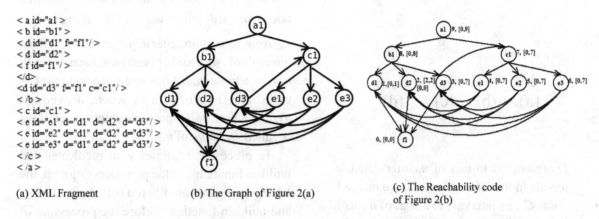

```
< a id="a1" >
< b id="b1" >
< d id="d1" f="f1"/ >
< d id="d2" >
< f id="f1"/ >
</d>
<d id="d3" f="f1" c="c1"/ >
< /b >
< c id="c1" >
< e id="e1" d="d1" d="d2" d="d3"/ >
< e id="e2" d="d1" d="d2" d="d3"/ >
< e id="e3" d="d1" d="d2" d="d3"/ >
< /c >
< /a >
```

(a) XML Fragment   (b) The Graph of Figure 2(a)   (c) The Reachability code of Figure 2(b)

ab is called a *reachability edge*. In V, the nodes without incoming edges are called *sources* and the nodes without outgoing edges are called *sinks*. For simplicity, a subgraph query is represented as $Q=(V, E)$.

The result of a subgraph query $Q = (V_q, E_q, tag, rel)$ on a graph $G=(V_G, E_G)$ is $R_{G,Q} = \{g = (V_g, E_g) \mid V_g \subset V_G$ and $\exists$ bijective mapping $fg : Vg \to VQ$ and $\exists$ injective mapping $g : V_g \to V_G$ satisfying $\forall n \in V_g, tag(n) = tag(f_g(n)) = tag(p_g(n))$; $\forall e = (n_1, n_2) \in E_g, p_g(n_1), p_g(n_2)$ satisfy the relationship $rel(f(n_1), f(n_2))\}$.

For example, Figure 3(b) shows a subgraph query, in which a single line represents an adjacent edge and a double line represents a reachability edge. The result of such a query on the graph shown in Figure 3(c) is the graph in Figure 2(b), where a1 has two children b1 and c1 sharing the same descendent f1.

For a subgraph query $Q=(V, E, tag, rel)$, if $V=V_s \cup \{d\}, d \notin V_s$, and $E=\{(a,d) \mid a \in V_s\}$, then Q is an IT-query. If $V=\{a\} \cup V_s, a \notin V_s$, and $E=\{(a,d) \mid d \in V_s\}$, then Q is a T-query.

Reachability Labelling Scheme

The labelling scheme for a graph is to judge the structural relationship between any two nodes in the graph without retrieving other information, such that subgraph queries can be processed efficiently. The labelling scheme used in this chapter is an extension (Wang, H. & Wang, W. et. al. (2005)) of that in Agrawal, R. & Borgida, A. (1989).

The reachability labelling scheme can be generated in the following steps:

- Each strongly connected component in G is contracted to one node to convert G to a DAG D.
- An optimum tree covering T of the DAG D is found. A depth-first traversal from the root of T accesses all nodes to generate the post-order of each node. Note that during the traversal, when a node n_c generated from a strongly connected component $C \subset G$ is accessed, if the post order of last accessed node is pc, then $pc+1$, $pc+2$,..., $pc+|V_c|$ are assigned to n_c (where V_c is the set of nodes in C). Then, each node $n \in T$ is assigned a number id and an interval $[x, id]$, where id is the post order of n; x is the smallest post order of descendants of n in T.
- All the nodes in D are traversed in the reversed topological order. When a node n is reached, the interval sets of n's children in

Figure 3. Example queries and results

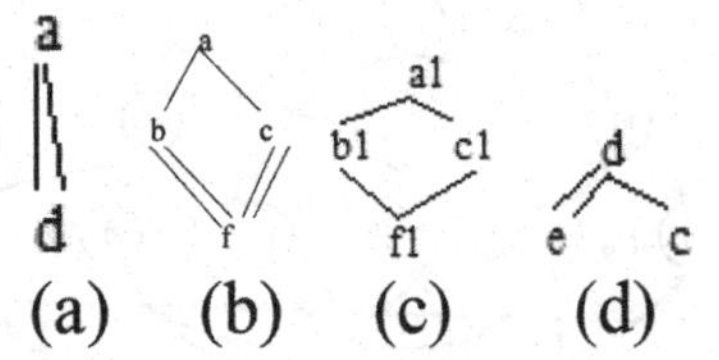

(a)   (b)   (c)   (d)

D are copied to that of *n*. Intersected intervals in the interval set of *n* are merged.

- $\forall n \in C$, its interval set is that of n_c; its *id* is one of the *id*s of n_c. Each node in *C* has a different *id*.

When such steps are finished, each node *n* in *G* is assigned a number *n.id* and a set of intervals I_n. In the labeling scheme by Wang, H. & Wang, W. et. al. (2005), it is proved that a node *a* reaches a node *b* if and only if *b.id* belongs to some interval of I_a. For example, the labelling scheme of the graph in Figure 2(b) is shown in Figure 2(c). Since the *id* of *f1* is in the interval [0,0] of *d2*, it can be judged that *d2* and *f1* satisfy reachability relationship.

In order to retrieve pairs of nodes satisfying a reachability query based on reachability labelling scheme, the following storage strategy is applied. For each tag $t \in TAG$ of a graph, two lists, *t.Alist* and *tDlist*, are stored. N_t is the set of nodes with tag *t*. *tDlist* is the list of the elements in set $\{n.id \mid n \in N_t\}$ sorted incrementally. *t.Alist* contained the elements in set $\{<va\ l, n.id> \mid n \in N_t, [x,y] \in I_n, val=x \text{ or } val=y\}$ sorted by the first item.

From the third step of encoding, for each node *n*, I_n has no overlapping intervals. Therefore, *tag(n).Alist* has the following property which is the base of the algorithms in the following sections.

Proposition 1. For a node *n*, all the elements in *tag(n).Alist* with the second item equalling to *n.id* form an ordered list $(val_{i_1}, n.id)$, $(val_{i_2}, n.id)$, ..., $(val_{i_k}, n.id)$. In such an ordered list,

$l \leq s \leq u \leq r \leq v \leq k$ do not exist such that both $[val_{i_s}, val_{i_r}]$ and $[val_{i_u}, val_{i_v}]$ belong to I_n.

Additionally, in order to judge whether all the intervals of one node has been processed, for each node *n*, a tuple (*null,id*) is inserted next to the last tuple of *tag(n).Alist* with the second item equals to *n.id*, where *null* represents empty. Such tuple is called *endtuple* of *n*.

To process the queries with predicates and build-in functions, as the preprocessing step, the labelling schemes are filtered with the predicates and build-in functions before the processing of subgraph query.

In order to analyze the complexity of algorithms in this chapter, it is defined that $N = max_{t \in TAG} |\{n \in V_g \mid tag(n) = t\}|$. The set of the second items of all elements in *Alist* is ID_{Alist}. Obviously, for each *Alist* and *Dlist*, $|ID_{Alist}| \leq N$.

LABELLING-BASED SUBGRAPH QUERY PROCESSING[1]

In this section, we will discuss the query processing of subgraph queries based on the labeling schemes. The basic idea of subgraph query processing is to split the query graph into some subgraph queries in special forms including one ancestor with one descendent (reachability query), multiple ancestors sharing the same descendent (IT-query), one ancestor with multiple descendents (T-query) as well as multiple ancestors sharing the same set of descendents (CBi-query), process them respectively and combine the results.

HGJoin Algorithms for Subgraph Queries in Special Forms

In this subsection, the algorithms for processing subgraph queries in special forms are presented.

Basic HGJoin Algorithm

Based on the storage strategy, suppose $Alist$=tag(a). $Alist$ and $Dlist$=tag(d).$Dlist$. Intuitively, for any $id_j \in Dlist$, if two tuples in $Alist$, (x, id_i) and (y, id_i), satisfy $x \leq id_i \leq y$ and $[x,y]$ is an interval of the labelling scheme of some node, then (id_i, id_j) belongs to the result set. Proposition 1 assures that the query can be processed with scanning Alist and Dlist alternately only once. During the scan, a hash table H is used to store ids of nodes satisfying the condition that for each node n, the start point x of some interval in I_n has been scanned while corresponding end point y is not met. Proportion 1 shows that before such y is met, none of the start points of other intervals in I_n will be met. When a corresponding y is met, $n.id$ will be removed from H. The step is shown as following. At first, cursors a and d are assigned to Alist and Dlist, respectively. During the scan of Alist, if the current tuple (val_a, id_a) satisfies $val_a \leq id_d$ and $id_a \in H$, it means that the end position of some interval is met and such an interval is impossible to contain id_d. Since the elements in Dlist is in incremental order, and such an interval is impossible to contain other unscanned elements in Dlist. So id_a is removed from H and a is updated. If $val_a = id_d$ and $id_a \in H$ or $val_a > id_d$, it means that id_d is contained in some interval with val_a as the end point. In such an instance, partial results are outputted and the scan is switched to Dlist. During the scan of Dlist, if $id_d < val_a$, or $val_a = id_d$ and $id_a \in H$, then based on the properties of elements in H, for $\forall id \in H$, (id, id_d) is outputted and d is updated; if $id_d > val_a$, or $val_a = id_d$ but $id_a \notin H$, it means that val_a is possibly the start position of an interval containing id_d and the scan is switched to Alist. The pseudo-code of HGJoin is shown in Algorithm 1 (see Box 1).

Example 1. In Figure 4, we give the intuition of Alist and Dlist, where a, b, c, d and e are tags. The elements with tag a are a_1, a_2, a_3 and a_4. Each interval of a_i is represented by a line segment and

denoted by a_{ij}. The start point of the line segment is the start position of the interval and the end point of the line segment is the end position of the interval. The position of element id in the interval is represented by a circle. For example, $a_1.id$ is in the end position of interval a_{12} and $a_2.id$ is in the middle of the interval a_{21}; other symbols have the same meanings. For a reachablity query $a \rightarrow b$, corresponding Alist has an ordered list with first items sorted in form of (the end point) of a_{ij}, $a_i.id$ and Dlist=$\{b_1.id, b_3.id, b_2.id\}$. After Alist and Dlist scanned with HGJoin algorithm, the outputted result is $(a_1.id, b_1.id), (a_1.id, b_3.id), (a_2.id, b_3.id)$, $(a_1.id, b_2.id)$ in order.

Complexity Analysis. The time cost of HGJoin algorithm has three parts, the cost of operations of H, the cost of disk I/O and the cost of result outputting. The time cost is:

Box 1. Algorithm 1 HGJoin(Alist, Dlist)

```
a=Alist.begin
d=Dlist.begin
while a≠ Alist.end AND d≠Dlist.end do
    if val_a≤id_d then
        if id_a ∉ H then
            H.insert(id_a)
            a = a.nextNode
        else if val_a<id_d then
            H.delete(id_a);
            a = a.nextNode;
        else
        for ∀id ∈H do
            append (id, id_d) to OutputList;
        d=d.nextNode;
    else /*id_d < val_a */
        for ∀id ∈H do
            append (id, id_d) to OutputList;
        d=d.nextNode;
```

Figure 4. Labeling schemes for examples

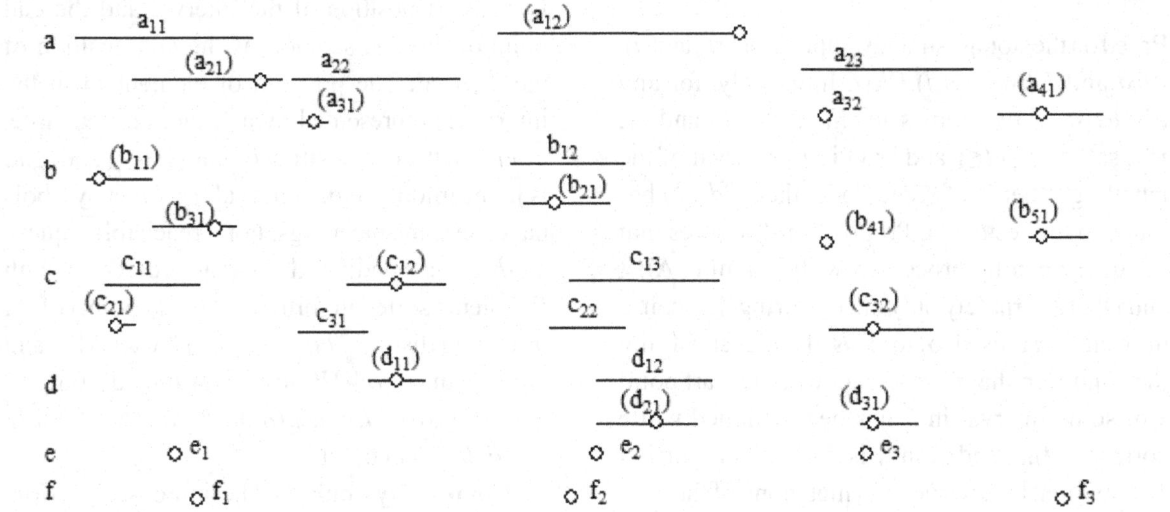

$$\frac{|\,Alist\,|}{2} \cdot (cost_I + cost_D)$$
$$+\,|\,result\,| \cdot cost_{out}$$
$$+(\frac{|\,Alist\,|\,|\,entry_A\,|}{|\,B\,|}$$
$$+\frac{|\,Dlist\,|\,|\,entry_D\,|}{|\,B\,|}) \cdot cost_{I/O}$$

with each item corresponding to each part, where the cost of insertion and deletion of H once are $cost_I$ and $cost_D$, respectively, $|entry_A|$ and $|entry_D|$ are the sizes of each tuple in Alist and Dlist, respectively, B is the size of a disk block, $cost_{I/O}$ is the cost of accessing each disk block and $cost_{out}$ is the cost of outputting one tuple.

The space cost of HGJoin algorithm is the space cost of the hash table H. Therefore, the space complexity is the largest size of H during the algorithm. In the worst case, all the elements in ID_{Alist} are in H. Therefore, the space cost of HGJoin is no more than N.

Algorithm for IT-Queries

In this section, HGJoin is extended to process IT-queries.

For an IT-query Q, suppose its sources are a_1, a_2, ..., a_k and its sink is d. Let $Alist_i$=tag(a_i).Alist, $Dlist$=tag(d).Dlist, $i\in 1,2,...,k$. Similar as HGJoin algorithm, IT-HGJoin algorithm scans $Alist_1$, $Alist_2$, ..., $Alist_k$ and $Dlist$ alternatively once and obtains the results of an IT-query. During the scan, a hash table H_i is assigned to each $Alist_i$, the function of which is the same as H in HGJoin algorithm. In the algorithm, cursors l_1, l_2, ..., l_k point to the current scanned position of $Alist_1$, $Alist_2$, ..., $Alist_k$, respectively. A cursor l points to the current scanned position of $Dlist$. The algorithm scans $Alist_1$, $Alist_2$, ..., $Alist_k$, in turn. id_{l_i} in pairs (val_{l_i}, id_{l_i}) satisfying $val_{l_i} \le id_{l_i}$ and $id_{l_i} \notin H_i$ are inserted to H_i and id_{l_i} s in pairs (val_{l_i}, id_{l_i}) satisfying $val_{l_i} \le id_{l_i}$ and $id_{l_i} \in H_i$ are removed from H_i. After $Alist_k$ is processed, the scan is switched to $Dlist$. Such processing is similar as the Dlist scan in HGJoin algorithm. At that time, the node corresponding to each id in any H_i is an ancestor of the node corresponding to id_l. If any of H_i is not empty, it means that with its ancestors, the node with id_l matches the descendent in the query. Such subgraphs are outputted as partial results. Since each tuple in $H_1 \times H_2 \times ... \times H_k$ corresponds to each group of different ancestors of

id_l, all the tuples in $H_1 \times H_2 \times \ldots \times H_k \times \{id_l\}$ should be outputted. In the step of result output, function OutputTuples($H_1, H_2, \ldots, H_k, id_d$) is invoked. After such partial results are outputted, the scan is switched to $Alist_1$, $Alist_2$, ..., $Alist_k$. IT-HGJoin algorithm is shown in Algorithm 2 (see Box 2).

In the implementation of IT-HGJoin algorithm, the size of $H_1 \times H_2 \times \ldots \times H_k$ may be very large. In order to store partial results efficiently, latency processing strategy is applied. That is, H_1, H_2, ..., H_k and corresponding id_l are stored respectively. The Cartesian production is not performed until such partial result will be used.

Example 2. The case of processing IT-query in Figure 5(a) on the data in Figure 4 is considered. H_b, H_c and H_d are hash tables corresponds to b,

Figure 5. Examples for IT-query and T-query

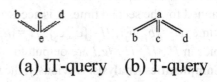

(a) IT-query   (b) T-query

c and d. At first, ids corresponding to intervals b_{1l}, c_{1l} and c_{2l} are inserted to hash tables. Then, when the end point of interval c_{2l} is scanned, c_2 is deleted from H_c. Then the scan is switched to *Dlist*. When e_l is processed, since H_d is empty, no result is outputted. All Alists are scanned in

Box 2. Algorithm 2 IT-HGJoin(Alist_1, Alist_2, ..., Alist_k, Dlist)

```
for i=1 to k do /*initial all the pointers*/
        a_i = Alist_i.begin
d = Dlist.begin
while a_i≠Alist_i.end do

        for i=1 to k do

            while val_{a_i} < id_d do

                if id_{a_i} in H_i then

                    H_i.insert(id_{a_i})
        else

                    H_i.delete(id_{a_i})
                    a_i=a_i.next
            while val_{a_i} = val_d AND id_{a_i}∉H_i do
                    H_i.insert(id_{a_i})
                    a_i=a_i.next
        if none of the hash tables are not empty then /*the id satisfies
the ancestor constraint*/
                OutputList∪=OutputTuples(H_1,…, H_k, id_d)
            for each a_i do /*delete useless ids*/
                while val_{a_i} = val_d AND id_{a_i}∈ H_i do
                        H_i.delete(id_{a_i})
        a_i=a_i.next
        d = d.next
```

turn. The ordered operations are the deletion of b_1, b_3 and c_1 from H_b and H_c in turn, insertion and deletion of c_1 and d_1 to H_c and H_d.... When Dlist is scanned for the second time, e_2 is accessed. At that time, $H_b = \{b_1, b_2\}$, $H_c = \{c_1, c_2\}$, $H_d = \{d_1, d_2\}$, 8 tuples in $H_b \times H_c \times H_d \times \{e_2\}$ are outputted.

Complexities Analysis. Obviously, the worst space complexity is kN. Similar as the analysis of HGJoin, the time complexity is:

$$
\begin{aligned}
Cost &= \sum \frac{|Alist_i|}{2} \cdot (\cos t_I + \cos t_O) \\
&+ |result| \cdot \cos t_{out} \\
&+ \left(\frac{\sum |Alist_i| \cdot |entry_A|}{|B|} \right. \\
&+ \left. \frac{|Dlist| \cdot |entry_D|}{|B|} \right) \cdot \cos t_{I/O}
\end{aligned}
$$

Algorithm for T-Queries

In this section, an algorithm for processing T-queries is presented. In a T-query Q, the source is a and sinks are $d_1, d_2, ..., d_k$. Let $Alist = tag(a)$. Alist, $Dlist_i = tag(d_i)$.Dlist, $i \in \{1, 2, ..., k\}$. Since in Q, the source a has multiples descendants d_1, $d_2, ..., d_k$ and in the reachability labelling scheme, all the nodes with tags $tag(d_1)$, $tag(d_2)$, ..., $tag(d_k)$ do not belong to the same interval of a node with $tag(a)$, in order to obtain the result of Q, all results of reachability query $a \rightarrow d_i$ where $i \in \{1, 2, ..., k\}$ should be obtained and the join operation is performed on such intermediate results.

HGJoin can be applied to process reachability queries $a \rightarrow d_i$. For the interest of efficiency, the k way scans of HGJoin algorithm are combined. That is, during the scans on Alist, $Dlist_1$, $Dlist_2$, ..., $Dlist_k$, are processed together. Such that all intermediate results can be obtained by scanning all lists only once. In order to make a join operation efficient, a hash table IHT_i is assigned to each $Dlist_i$. When a bucket in some IHT_i is full, the intermediate results in such a bucket are sorted based on the first items (the id value of the node matching a) and written out to the disk.

When the intermediate results are obtained, all tuples in form of $(id, id_1) \in IHT_1$, $(id, id_2) \in IHT_2$, ..., $(id, id_k) \in IHT_k$ are joined to generate a tuple, $(id, id_1, ..., id_k)$, the partial result of IT-query. Obviously, the cost of join operation increases fast with $|IHT|$. In order to reduce the cost of join, the size of IHT_i should be decreased during join.

The strategy in T-Join algorithm is that during the scan of Alist, when the end sign $(null, id)$ is met, it means that the following steps of the scan will not generate intermediate result in form of $(id, *)$. Therefore, the join operation can be performed on current IHT_1, IHT_2, ..., IHT_k to generate all results in form of $(id, id_1, ..., id_k)$. Then the tuples with form $(id, *)$ are deleted from IHT_1, IHT_2, ..., IHT_k and corresponding disk blocks are merged.

Even though the above strategy can minimize the size of $|IHT_i|$ during join operation, frequent join operations will make an algorithm inefficient. Additionally, after each join operation, the number of disk blocks to be merged is very limited. In order to make it more efficient, the "join latency" strategy is applied in T-HGJoin algorithm. That is, during T-HGJoin algorithm, an *ancestor table* A with fixed size is maintained. During the scan of Alist, when end sign $(null, id)$ is met, id is inserted to A. When A is full or the scan of Alist is finished, the join operation is performed on current IHT_1, IHT_2, ..., IHT_k to generate partial query results with form $(id, *, ..., *)$ where id is the id of any element in A. Then intermediate results with form $(id, *)$ are deleted and for each bucket in any IHT_i, mergable disk blocks are merged.

In order to reduce the space cost of partial results storage, the latency processing strategy similar as IT-HGJoin can also be applied.

Example 3. The processing of the T-query in Figure 5(b) on the data in Figure 4 is considered. For easy discussion, suppose that each bucket can only contain two tuples and each IHT uses hash function $hash(x) = x \bmod 2$. It means that each IHT has only two buckets. The size of ancestor table A is 2. When T-HGJoin algorithm accesses tuple $(null, a_1.id)$, generated intermediate results

Figure 6. Intermediate results for the example of T-query processing

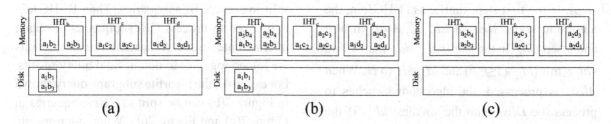

(a)   (b)   (c)

are shown in Figure 6(a). $a_1.id$ is inserted to A. At that time, A is not full, so the join operation is not performed. When the tuple $(null, a_3.id)$ is scanned, the intermediate results are shown in Figure 6(b). $a_3.id$ is inserted to A and A is full, so the join operation is performed on the intermediate results with only a_1 and a_3 and results (a_1, b_1, c_2, d_2), (a_1, b_2, c_2, d_2) and (a_1, b_3, c_2, d_2) are generated. After join, all intermediate results in IHTs related to a_1 and a_3 are deleted. Current intermediate result is shown as Figure 6(c).

Complexities Analysis. The time cost of T-HGJoin includes 4 parts, the cost of operations on H, the disk I/O cost of accessing Alist and all *Dlist*s, the cost of processing intermediate results and the cost of outputting final results. In the worst case, since each element in Alist is the ancestor of any element in each $Dlist_i$, $|IHT_i| \le N^2$. Therefore, the worst time cost of T-HGJoin is

$$
\begin{aligned}
Cost = &\frac{|Alist|}{2}(\cos t_I + \cos t_O) \\
&+ (\frac{|Alist||entry_A|}{|B|} \\
&+ \frac{\sum |Dlist_i||entry_D|}{|B|}) \cos t_{I/O} \\
&+ (kN^2 \cos t_I \\
&+ 2k(\frac{|entry_{IHT}|N^2}{|B|} - n_b) \cos t_{I/O} \\
&+ [(\frac{|entry_{IHT}|N^2}{|B|n_b} - 1) \\
&+ (\frac{N^2}{n_b})^k \cos t_{join}]N) \\
&+ |result_F| \cos t_{out}
\end{aligned}
$$

each item of which corresponds the cost of each part. The cost analysis of the former two and last parts is similar as that of HGJoin. In the third item, $cost_{Join}$ is the cost of generating one output tuple.

The main memory cost of T-HGJoin algorithm includes the space for the hash table H during the scan of Alist and main memory used to store intermediate results in IHT_i. With the symbols discussed above, the main memory space cost of T-HGJoin is $N + kn_b|B|$ in the worst case.

Algorithm for Bipartite Queries

In this section, the processing algorithm for bipartite subgraph queries is presented. At first, the algorithm for the bipartite subgraph queries in a special case that all descendants share the same ancestor (CBi for brief) is presented and then that of bipartite subgraph queries is presented. Suppose that the sources of a CBi query are a_1, a_2, ..., a_m and the sources are d_1, d_2, ..., d_n. Let $Alist_i = tag(a_i).Alist$, $Dlist_j = tag(d_j).Dlist$, $i \in \{1, 2, ..., m\}, j \in \{1, 2, ..., n\}$. In the algorithm, cursors $l_1, l_2, ..., l_m$ points to the current scanned position of $Alist_1, Alist_2, ..., Alist_m$, respectively. $t_1, t_2, ..., t_n$ points to the current scanned positions of $Dlist_1$, $Dlist_2, ..., Dlist_n$, respectively.

Similar as IT-HGJoin, the algorithm assigns a hash table H_i for each source a_i. Similar as T-HGJoin, the algorithm assigns a hash table IHT_j for the intermediate results corresponding to each sink d_j.

Bi-HGJoin algorithm includes two alternative steps. In the first step, similar as IT-HGJoin, the algorithm scans $Alist_1$, $Alist_2$, ..., $Alist_m$ in turn and inserts id_{l_i} in the pair (val_{l_i}, id_{l_i}) satisfying $val_{l_i} \leq \mathbf{min}(id_{t_i})(1 \leq j \leq n)$ and $id_{l_i} \notin H_i$ to H_i. When $Alist_m$ is processed, the algorithm switches to process the $Dlist_j$ with the smallest id_{t_j}. If the hash tables H_1, H_2,..., H_k are not empty, each tuple $(h_1,h_2,...,h_m,id_{t_j}) \in H_1 \times H_2 \times ... \times H_m \times \{id_{t_j}\}$ is inserted to the bucket with hash value $hash(h_1,h_2,...,h_m)$ of IHT_j. The second step is similar as the join of intermediate results in T-HGJoin. When in each $Alist_i$, the end sign $(null, h_i)$ of h_i is met, where $1 \leq i \leq m$, the combination of ancestor $(h_1,h_2,...,h_m)$ is inserted into the ancestor table A. When A is full or all scans on Alists have been finished, for each combination $(h_1,h_2,...,h_m)$ in A, the buckets with hash value $hash(h_1,h_2,...,h_m)$ in IHT_1, IHT_2,..., IHT_n are joined to generate partial query result with form $(h_1,h_2,...,h_m,id_1,id_2,...,id_n)$. Then corresponding intermediate results are deleted and disk blocks in such buckets are merged. When the join operation is finished, the first step resumes. The above steps are repeated until all elements in any $Alist_i$ have been scanned.

Such algorithm cannot process general bipartite subgraph queries. Since sinks may have different sources, it is difficult to find a hash function to assure effective execution of a join operation. Intuitively, such a problem can be processed with following steps. Based on the cost model presented in the above section, a query is split to some CBi subqueries. Then Bi-HGJoin is invoked to process CBi subqueries to obtain intermediate results. At last, intermediate results are joined together to obtain final query results. For example, the bipartite subgraph query shown in Figure 7(b) can be split to CBi subqueries in Figure 7(c) and Figure 7(d). When intermediate results are obtained, the equal join is performed on f elements to obtain final results.

DAG Subgraph Query Evaluation

In this section, we present a hash-based evaluation strategy for subgraph queries in form of DAGs.

The direct processing of a general DAG subgraph query requires not only large main memory space but also large disk space. The efficiency is affected. Hence the strategy presented in this section does not process general subgraph queries directly but also splits a DAG subgraph query to some CBi-queries. Each CBi-subquery is processed to obtain intermediate results. Then, join operations are executed to obtain final results. Such join is performed with sort-merge algorithms. For example, to process the query in Figure 8(a), it is split to the subquerires: q_{11} in Figure 8(b), q_{12} in Figure 8(c) and reachability query $c \rightarrow e$. Then labelling schemes with tags tag(b) and tag(c) are filtered with intermediate results of q_{11}. Then subquery q_{12} is processed on filtered labelling schemes to obtain intermediate results. The reach-

Figure 7. An example for Complex Bipartite query

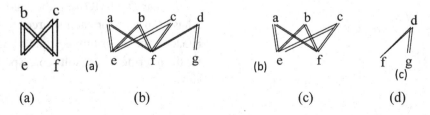

(a)   (b)   (c)   (d)

ability query is processed on filtered data to obtain intermediate results. At last, the join operation is performed on such three groups of intermediate results to obtain final results.

Obviously, the key of the above strategy is how to split the query and construct the query plan. A query plan can be modelled as a DAG $D=(V, E)$, where each node in V represents an operation (possible operations includes HGJoin, IT-HGJoin, T-HGJoin and Bi-HGJoin, Filter and sort-merge operations). The results of the operation in arrow tail is the input of operation in arrow head. For example, in Figure 8(d), T-HGJoin$_{\{(a,b),(a,c)\}}$ represents that T-HGJoin algorithm is performed on the labelling schemes with tag tag(a), tag(b) and tag(c). *Filter$_c$* represents that the labelling schemes with tag tag(c) are filtered to eliminate the labelling schemes which are not in the intermediate results of T-HGJoin$_{\{(a,b), (a,c)\}}$. Other operations have the same meanings.

At first, we design the cost model. Then query plan generation algorithm and query optimization accelerate strategy are presented.

The Cost Model

The query plan of a subgraph query has multiple choices. In order to generate an efficient query plan, a query optimizer is required. As the base of the query optimization, the cost model is presented in this section. For each operation in the query plan, its cost has two parts, execution time and required main memory. The former represents the execution efficiency of query plan and the latter is the main memory space which is required during query plan execution. The estimation of the cost of sort-merge join operation has been studied extensively and the time cost of HGJoin and IT-HGJoin can be estimated as the time complexity of them, respectively. This section focuses on the cost model of T-HGJoin and Bi-HGJoin.

The cost model of T-HGJoin is similar as time analysis in above sections. With intermediate size estimation techniques by Polyzotis, N. & Garofalakis. M. N. (2002) and Polyzotis, N. & Garofalakis. M. N. et. al. (2004), for $\forall a \in ID_{Alist}$ and $\forall i \in \{1, 2, ..., k\}$, $P_{a,i}$, the number of tuples related to a in the intermediate results of join operation of *Alist* and *Dlist$_i$*, can be estimated. Additionally, such technique can be used to estimate $S_{a,i}$, the number of disk blocks of the intermediate results related to a in *IHT$_i$* at the time when (null,a) is met in *Alist*. Therefore, intermediate results related to a can be estimated as selectivity(A,D$_i$)= $\Sigma_{a \in ID_{Alist}} P_{a,i}$. When intermediate results related to a are joined, $S_{a,1}, S_{a,2}, ..., S_{a,k}$ times of disk blocks distributed in *IHT$_1$*, *IHT$_2$*, ..., *IHT$_k$* are required to be accessed in a nest loop join[], respectively. In such step, the number of disk blocks to be accessed is estimated as NL$_a=\prod_{i \in \{1,..k\}} S_{a,i}$. Based on such estimations, the time cost of T-HGJoin is estimated as

Figure 8. An example of query plan generation

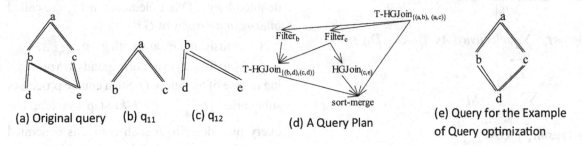

(a) Original query   (b) q_{11} (c) q_{12} (d) A Query Plan   (e) Query for the Example of Query optimization

$$Cost_{T\text{-}HGJoin} = \frac{|Alist|}{2} \cdot (cos\, t_I + cos\, t_O)$$

$$+ \left(\frac{|Alist| \cdot |entry_{Alist}|}{|B|} \right.$$

$$\left. + \frac{\sum |Dlist_i| \cdot |entry_{Dlist}|}{|B|} \right) \cdot cos\, t_{I/O} +$$

$$+ cos\, t_I \cdot \sum_{i=1}^{k} selectivity(A, D_i)$$

$$+ 2 \cdot \sum_{a \in ID_{Alist}} S_a \cdot cos\, t_{I/O}$$

$$+ \sum_{a \in A} NL_a$$

$$+ |result_F| \cdot cos\, t_{output}$$

where selectivity(A, D_i) is the result number of join on A and D_i.

The estimation of Bi-HGJoin is similar as T-HGJoin. The number of intermediate result generation with the join on $Alist_1$, $Alist_2$, ..., $Alist_m$ and $Dlist$ is denoted by sel(A1, A2, ..., Am, Di). The number of intermediate results related to the combination of nodes a_1, a_2,..., a_m ($a_i \in ID_{Alist\,i}$) is denoted by $S_{a1,a2,...am}$. The number of disk blocks for joining intermediate results with a_1, a_2,..., a_m is denoted by $NL_{a1,a2,...am}$. The estimation of these parameters is similar as those of T-HGJoin. The time of Bi-HGJoin operation can be estimated as

$$Cost_{Bi\text{-}HGJoin} = \frac{\sum |Alist_i|}{2} \cdot (cos\, t_I + cos\, t_O)$$

$$+ \left(\frac{\sum |Alist| \cdot |entry_{Alist}|}{|B|} \right.$$

$$\left. + \frac{\sum |Dlist_i| \cdot |entry_{Dlist}|}{|B|} \right) \cdot cos\, t_{I/O}$$

$$+ cos\, t_I \cdot \sum_{i=1}^{n} selectivity(A_1, A_2,...A_m, D_i) +$$

$$+ 2 \cdot \sum_{a_1 \in A_1, a_2 \in A_2,...,a_m \in A_m} S_{a_1,a_2,...a_m} \cdot cos\, t_{I/O}$$

$$+ \sum_{a_1 \in A_{j_1}, a_2 \in A_{j_2},...,a_m \in A_{j_m}} NL_{a_1,a_2,...,a_m}$$

$$+ |result_F| \cdot cos\, t_{output}$$

where selectivity($A_1, A_2, ..., A_m, D_i$) is the results number of join on A_1, A_2, ..., A_m and D_i.

The main memory required by an operation includes fixed main memory and alterable main memory. The fixed main memory is the buffer for the intermediate result. The size of such part equals to a fixed value $fixed_{mm}$. The alterable part is the main memory of the hash tables corresponding to Alists during query processing. The size of such part is linear with the maximum number of ancestors of descendants during query processing. $ancestor_d$ represents the number of ancestors in Alist(s) of d∈$Dlist$. |$entry_H$| is the size of data element in hash table H. The space cost of the operation is $cost_{mm} = fixed_{mm} + max_{d \in Dlist}(|ancestor_d|) \cdot |entry_H|$.

Algorithms for Query Plan Generation

In this section, the process of query execution is represented by state graph and then optimal query plan is generated as the shortest path generation algorithm on the state graph.

Suppose (V_Q, E_Q) is the query graph of a subgraph query Q ($m = E_Q$). The directed graph $G^* = (V_{G^*}, E_{G^*})$ is the *state graph* of the subgraph query Q, where $V_{G^*} = \{g | g = (v_g, e_g)$ and $e_g \subset E_Q\}$. There is a directed edge from $g \in V_{G^*}$ to $g' \in V_{G^*}$ if and only if a subquery $Q_{gg'} = (V_{gg'}, E_{gg'})$ belonging to one of reachability query, T-query, IT-query and CBi-query exists with $E_g - E_{gg'} = E_{g'}$. The node in G^* representing the query graph (V_Q, E_Q) is called the *start state* of G^*, denoted by g_0. The node ($V_Q, \varnothing$) in G^* is called the *end state* of G^*, denoted by g_m. Other elements in V_{G^*} are called *intermediate states* of G^*.

Obviously, in G^*, any path $g_0 = g_{i1}, g_{i2}, ..., g_{ik} = g_m$, ($k \leq m$) from g_0 to g_m corresponds to a processing course of the query Q. Such course processes subqueries $Q_{g_{i_j} g_{i_{j+1}}}$ ($1 \leq j \leq k$) step by step. The query plan describing such course is generated with following steps. For the first edge in the path $g_{i1} g_{i2}$, an operation O_E (where $E = E_{g_{i_1} g_{i_2}}$) is constructed based on the operation type $O \in$ {HGJoin, T-HGJoin, IT-HGJoin, CBi-HG-Join} of $Q_{g_{i_1} g_{i_2}}$.

It is supposed that the query plan for $g_0 = g_{i_1}$ $,g_{i_2},...,g_{i_k} = g_m$ has been generated and the collection of sets of intermediate results is denoted by B_j. The edge $g_{i_j} g_{i_{j+1}}$ in the path is considered. At first, based on the operation type $O \in$ {HGJoin, T-HGJoin, IT-HGJoin, CBi-HGJoin} of $Q_{g_{i_j} g_{i_{j+1}}}$, an operation O_E is added to the query plan (where $E = E_{g_{i_1} g_{i_2}}$). Then each node $a \in V_{g_{i_1} g_{i_2}}$ is considered. If some set of intermediate results exists in B_j, then an operation $Filter_a$ is added to the query plan. An edge from corresponding intermediate result set is added to $Filter_a$ and another edge from $Filter_a$ is added to O_E. Then intermediate results

set of O_E is added to B_j. At that time, if there is mergable intermediate results set in B_j, then an operation sort-merge is added to the query plan and an edge from corresponding intermediate is added result set to new added sort-merge operation. At the same time, the unmerged intermediate results set is deleted from B_j and the merged intermediate result set is inserted. The above steps are repeated until no intermediate result sets can be merged. Let $B_{j+1} = B_j$. The query plan of other edges is generated until all the edges in the path are considered.

For example, the state graph for the query in Figure 8(e) is shown in Figure 9.

During the generation of a query plan for the path $g_0 = g_{i_1}, g_{i_2},...,g_{i_k} = g_m$, a group of operations are added to the query plan for $g_{i_j} g_{i_{j+1}}$.

Figure 9. Example of state graph

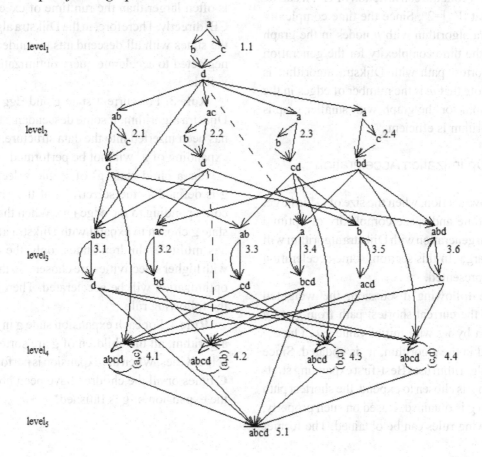

$w_{g_{i_j} g_{i_{j+1}}}$, the sum of time cost of such operation group, and the maximum space cost w are considered. If w is not larger than available main memory space, then let the weight of edge $g_{i_j} g_{i_{j+1}}$ equal to $w_{g_{i_j} g_{i_{j+1}}}$. Otherwise, such group of operations is infeasible and the weight of edge $g_{i_j} g_{i_{j+1}}$ equals to $+\infty$. In such a way, any edge gg' in G^* is unique, since whatever the path to g is, the collection of sets of intermediate results sets are the same. Therefore, the operation added to gg' is the same.

From the above discussion, it can be seen that a path from g_0 to $\boldsymbol{g_m}$ in the weighted query graph $G^*=(V_{G^*}, E_{G^*})$ corresponds to a query plan with the weighted length as the cost of the query plan. Therefore, the generation of the optimal query plan is to find the shortest path from g_0 to g_m in G^*. Such problem can be solved with Dijkstra algorithm. From the construction of $\mathbf{G^*}$, it can be known that $|V_{G^*}|=2^m$. Since the time complexity of Dijkstra algorithm with n nodes in the graph is $O(n^2)$, the time complexity for the generation of the shortest path with Dijkstra algorithm is $O(2^{2m})$. Note that m is the number of edges in the query graph, for the graph with smaller graphs such algorithm is efficient.

Query Optimization Acceleration

In the above section, when the size of G^* is large, both the time and space complexity of optimal query plan generation with Dijkstra algorithm will be very large. In this section, some acceleration rules are presented.

In the following discussion, the weighted length of the current shortest path from $\boldsymbol{g_0}$ to $\boldsymbol{g}$ is denoted by w_0 with initial value $+\infty$. Once g is reached in the algorithm, w_g is updated. Since Dijkstra algorithm uses Best-first expanding strategy, when g is chosen to expend, the shortest path from g_0 to g is obtained. Based on such property, the following rules can be obtained. The former

can halt the algorithm to reduce the run time. The latter will delete the states impossibly belonging to the shortest path to reduce the space cost.

Rule 1. In the Dijkstra algorithm, if the selected state g equals to g_m or $w_g \geq w_{g_m}$, then the current shortest path from g_0 to g_m is outputted and the algorithm halts.

Rule 2. In the Dijkstra algorithm, if the selected state is g and each outgoing edge gg' of g satisfies $w_g + w_{gg'} > w_{g'}$ ($w_{gg'}$ is the weight of the edge gg'), then g is deleted from the data structure of the Dijkstra algorithm.

Proposition 2. Rule 1 and Rule 2 will not affect the result of query optimization.

Intuitively, the time cost of executing a complex operation directly is often smaller than the sum of the time cost of the series of simple operation split from such operation. For example, a CBi-subquery can be split to some T-subqueries or IT-subqueries, but the sum of the run time of these subqueries is often larger than the run time of execution of CBi directly. Therefore, in the Dijkstra algorithm, the states with all descendants expanded can be neglected to accelerate query optimization. This is Rule 3.

Rule 3. For current state g and $\exists gg' \in E_{G^*}$ in Dijkstra algorithm, if some descendant state of g' has been inserted into the data structure, then the expanding of g' will not be performed.

For a child state g' of $\mathbf{g}$, the selectivity of $\mathbf{g}$ is defined as the selectivity of the operations corresponding to the edge $\mathbf{gg'}$. When the current state $\mathbf{g}$ chosen to expand with Dijkstra algorithm has multiple children states, only the children with higher selectivities are chosen. So that query optimization will be accelerated. Then we have the following rule.

Rule 4. For each expansion state $\mathbf{g}$ in Dijkstra algorithm, all the children of $\mathbf{g}$ are sorted by the selectivities. When the expansion is performed for $\mathbf{C}$ times or all the children have been processed, the expansion of $\mathbf{g}$ is finished.

Even though Rule 3 and Rule 4 will result in non-optimal query plan, these two rules can reduce the time complexity of query optimization effectively.

Proposition 3. With Rule 3 and Rule 4, the complexity of Dijkstra algorithm is $O(C \cdot 2^m)$ in the worst case.

General Subgraph Query Processing

In this section, we present the discussions about two variations to make our query processing method to support subgraph queries in form of general graphs. One is how to make the method to support subgraph query in form of graphs with circles. The other is how to make the method to support subgraph queries with adjacent relationships.

Evaluate Queries with Circles

In this section, we present a strategy to adapt the family of HGJoin to support subgraph queries with circles. Such strategy is based on the feature that all reachability labelling scheme of the nodes in the same strongly connected component (SCC for brief) share the same interval sets.

The basic idea is to identify all the SCCs in the nodes in the graph related to the query with labelling schemes. An id is assigned to each SCC and such id is also assigned to the nodes belong to such SCC. All edges in the SCC in the query are deleted. Each separate part of the query is processed individually. Then the results of these parts are joined together with the id of SCC based on the nodes corresponding to the query nodes in the same SCC.

Since We illustrate such strategy with an example.

Example 4. To process the structural query shown in Figure 10(a), in order to eliminate interpretations, we use arrow to represent the reachability relationship in the query. The codes of the elements are shown in Table 1. In the first step, since **c1**, **d1**, and **e1** share same intervals, they are assigned to the same id of SCC. For the same reason, **c2**, **d2** and **e2** are assigned to the same id of SCC. Since there are no **d** node and **e** node with the same intervals as **c3**, **c3** is not considered in the following query processing steps. Then the edges of SCC in the query are deleted and two generated queries are shown in Figure 10(b) and Figure 10(c). The results of these two sub-queries are {(**a1**, **b1**, **c1**, **d1**), (**a2**, **b2**, **c2**, **d2**),(**a1**, **b1**, **c1**, **d2**), (**a2**, **b2**, **c2**, **d1**)} and (**e1**, **f1**), respectively. In the last step, the join is performed based on the ids of SCC. In this step, (**a1**, **b1**, **c1**, **d1**) is joined with (**e1**, **f1**) since **c1**, **d1** and **e1** have same SCC *id*. Tuples (**a1**, **b1**, **c1**, **d2**, **e1**) and (**a2**, **b2**, **c2**, **d1**, **e2**) are neglected because their **c** and **d** nodes have different *id*s of SCC. (**a2**, **b2**, **c2**, **d2**, **e2**) is neglected because there is no corresponding (**e**, **f**) tuple to join with it.

Proposition 4 shows the correctness of this method. Since the proof is intuitive, for the interest of space, its detail is eliminated.

Proposition 4. The strategy above of processing subgraph queries with circles obtains correct results.

Evaluate Queries with Adjacent Edges

Subgraph queries with adjacent edges can be processed in the algorithms similar to the family of HGJoin.

Figure 10. Example for the processing of queries with circles

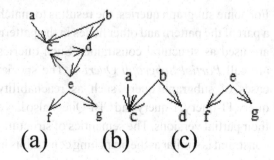

Table 1. The codings of nodes

a1	7, [0,7]	b1	8, [0,6], [8,8]	c1	1, [0,3]
c2	4, [4,6]	c3	9, [9,9]	d1	2, [0,3]
d2	5, [4,6]	e1	3, [0,3]	e2	6, [4,6]
f1	0, [0,0]				

An adjacent labelling schema is assigned to each node. The generation of adjacent labelling scheme is that for each node with postid i, interval $[i,i]$ is assigned to each of its parents. The benefit of such scheme is that the judgment of adjacent relationship is same as that of reachability labelling scheme so that the processing techniques for subgraphs with only reachability relationships can be applied to evaluate structural queries with adjacent edges.

If a query node n as an ancestor has both reachability and adjacent outgoing edges, n should be split to two query nodes with only reachability and adjacent outgoing edges, respectively. It is because different intervals are used to judge reachability and adjacent relationships. Considering only outgoing edges is because the judgements of reachability and adjacent relationship use the same *postid*s. When the query processing method is applied, for the query node with reachability outgoing edges, intervals in reachability scheme are used, while for query node with adjacent outgoing edges, intervals in adjacent scheme are used. The algorithm is same as the corresponding one in the family of HGJoin.

Partial Subgraph Query Processing

For some subgraph queries, the result is to match a part of the pattern and other nodes in the pattern are used as structural constraints. Such queries are call *Partial Subgraph Queries*. The special cases of subgraph query such as reachability query, IT-query, T-query and CBi-Query also have their partial versions. The semantics of structural constraint is similar as the branching constraints in

XPath. For example, a subgraph query shown in Figure 11, where the node in circle represents the constraint. This query is to retrieve the subgraph with a, b, c nodes connected to the same t node and they share the same r node as the ancestor. The r node is not required to be contained in the result. The nodes matching the node in the constraints of the query are called *constraint nodes* and the nodes matching other node in the query are called *materialized nodes*.

Of course, the queries with structural nodes can be processed with the processing strategy of the queries without structural nodes. The constraint nodes are not required to be contained in the final results. It gives us the chances to accelerate the processing partial subgraph queries. In this section, the processing algorithms of partial subgraph queries are presented. We use the same framework of subgraph queries to process partial subgraph queries. At first, the algorithms for basic operators are presented. Corresponding to basic operators for subgraph queries, HGJoin, IT-HGJoin, T-HGJoin, CBi-HGJoin, the basic operators for partial subgraph queries are Semi-HGJoin, Semi-IT-HGJoin, Semi-T-HGJoin and Semi-CBi-HG-Join with the similar style in join operator in relational database.

Semi-HGJoin Algorithms

Partial reachability query is a special case for partial subgraph query with only two nodes. In this subsection, two improved versions of HGJoin are presented to process the partial reachability queries with the nodes matching the ancestor and descendent in the query to be returned, re-

Figure 11. An example of partial subgraph query

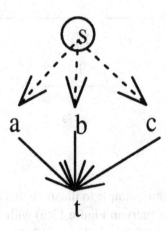

Box 3. Algorithm 3 D-Semi-HGJoin(Alist, Dlist)

```
a=Alist.begin
d=Dlist.begin
b = true;
while a ≠ Alist.end AND d ≠ Dlist.end do
    if val_a ≤id_d then
if val_a=id_d and b=true then
    add id_d to OutputList
    d=d.nextNode
b=¬ba = a.nextNode
    else
if b=true then
    add id_d to OutputList
d=d.nextNode
```

spectively, which are called A-Semi-HGJoin and D-Semi-HGJoin. In the Semi-HGJoin algorithms, only materialized nodes are to be returned as results. With this feature, the id of constraint nodes (as ancestors or descendent) are not required to be stored and only the feature for the judgement of structural relationship.

If in a partial reachabilty query $a \rightarrow d$, a is the constraint, the judgement constraint of whether a d node n_d is the result is that $n_d.id$ is in any interval in the labelling schemes of any a node. That is, $n_d.id$ is in the union of intervals in the labelling schemes of all a nodes. Based on above analysis, we have the D-Semi-HGJoin algorithm, which is shown in Algorithm 3 (see Box 3). In this algorithm, *Alist'* = $\{val | [x,y] \in I_a, val=x$ or $val=y\}$, where I_a is the union of all intervals in each labelling scheme of nodes with tag a. *Alist'* is sorted with the value of val. In this algorithm, a boolean variable b is used to represent whether the hash table contains some element. b is initialized to *false*. Since the intervals in I_a do not overlap, when a value in *Alist'* is met, it means that the status of "in an interval" or "out of all intervals" is changed and b is changed. When an element n_d in *Dlist* is met and b is *true*, n_d is one of the result. An example of the algorithm is shown in Example 5.

Example 5. With union intervals, parts of the labelling schemes in Figure 4 are shown in Figure 12. For the query a→e, the merged intervals of labelling schemes of a nodes are used. b is initialized to 0. At first, the start point of I_{a1} is met and b turns to 1. Then e_1 is to be processed. With $b=1$, e_1 is returned as a result. When the end point of I_{a2} is met, b turns to 0.

The optimization opportunity of A-Semi-HGJoin algorithm is to skip some useless d nodes and remove the ids of a nodes which have been judged as the result from the hash set. In this algorithm, a hash set H_u is used to store the id of the results. In order to reduce the space of H_u, when the end tuple of a result n in the Alist is met, $n.id$ is removed from H_u. The algorithm is shown in Algorithm 4 (see Box 4).

Semi-IT-HGJoin Algorithms

Similar as Semi-HGJoin, Semi-IT-HGJoin also has two types for ancestor and descendent, A-Semi-IT-HGJoin and D-Semi-IT=HGJoin, respectively.

As discussed in the above section, for an partial IT-query $(a_1, a_2, ..., a_n, d)$ with d nodes in the results, a d node n_d is a result if for each a_i, there is a node n_a with tag a_i satisfying $\exists inter \in I_{n_a}, n_d.id$

Figure 12. The labeling schemes with merged intervals

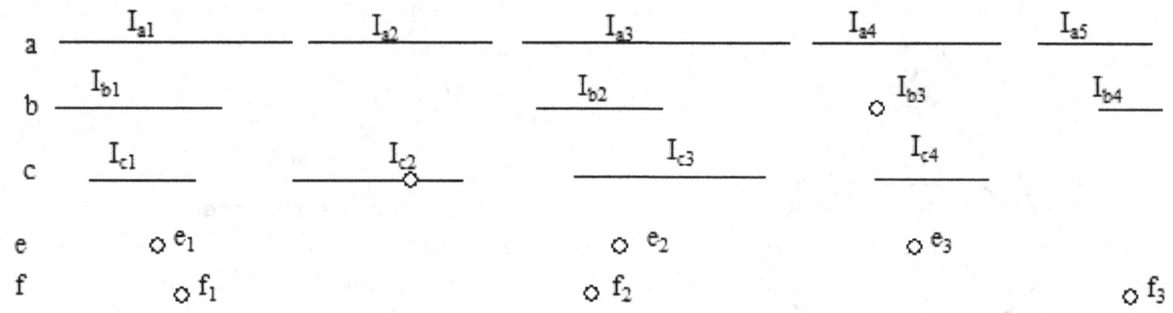

Box 4. Algorithm 4 A-Semi-HGJoin(Alist, Dlist)

```
a=Alist.begin
d=Dlist.begin
while a ≠ Alist.end AND d ≠ Dlist.end do
    if val_a=NULL then
        remove val_id from H_u
    else if val_a · id_d and id_a ∉ H_u then
        if id_a ∉ H then
            H.insert(id_a)
        a = a.nextNode
    else if val_a < id_d then
        H.delete(id_a)
        a = a.nextNode
    elsefor ∀id∈ H do
            append id to OutputList
            insert id to H_u
            d=d.nextNode;
    else
            for ∀id∈ H do
                append id to OutputList
                insert id to H_u
d=d.nextNode;
```

is contained in *inter*. That is, $\forall a_i, \exists inter_i \in I_{na}$, $n_d.id$ is contained in $\bigcap_{i=1}^{n} inter_i$. Therefore, the judgement condition of a d node n_d is that $n_d.id$ is contained in any interval of $\bigcap_{i=1}^{n} \bigcup_{n\in Node(a_i)} I_n$, where symbols ∩ and ∪ represents the intersection and union of the intervals in the interval sets.

We use an example to illustrate this claim. To process the query in Figure 13(a) with the labelling schemes shown in Figure 12, the id of e_i is contained in all of I_{a1}, I_{b1} and I_{c1}. That is e_i is contained in the intersection of these three intervals.

With this property, the D-Semi-IT-HGJoin algorithm is in Algorithm 4. In this algorithm, as the combinations of boolean variables in D-Semi-HGJoin algorithm, a bitmap m is used with each bit $m[i]$ corresponds to whether current status is in some interval of $I_{A i}$ (see Box 5).

Similar as A-Semi-HGJoin, A-Semi-IT-HG-Join can skip some useless d nodes. However, the id of judged a node cannot be removed from corresponding hash set. It is because the result of A-Semi-IT-HGJoin is the combinations of ancestors with different tags. Removing an *id* after it is judged as ancestor will lose the result as the combination of *id* and some unprocessed nodes in other Alists. For example, to process the query in Figure 13(a) on the labelling schemes in Figure 4, when the processing of interval of b_{11} is finished, if all intervals related to b_1 are deleted, the result b1, c1, d1 will be lost.

Semi-T-HGJoin Algorithms

The implementation of D-Semi-T-HJoin is the same as T-HGJoin. The strategy in Section "Semi-HGJoin Algorithms" cannot be applied. It is because the join of partial results requires the id of the node.

Figure 13. Example queries for partial queries

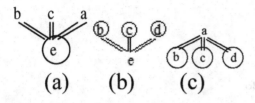

Since the descendent are not required to be included in final results, for each candidate n_a of the ancestor, a bitmap b_{n_a} is used with the ith bit representing that n_a has a descendent with tag d_i. With such bitmap, the join of partial results in T-HGJoin algorithm can be bypassed. The framework of the processing is the same as T-HGJoin algorithm. A hash table H_t is used to store all met a nodes. When some descendent of any node n_a in H_t with tag a_i is met, the ith bit of b_{n_a} is converted to 1. When all bits of b_n is converted to 1, n is outputted as a result and n is inserted to a hash table H_r. With such table, the remaining tuples of n in Alist can be ignored. When the end tuple of n is met, it is removed from H_r. The algorithm is shown in Algorithm 6 (see Box 6).

Example 6 illustrates the process of this algorithm.

Example 6. To process the query in Figure 13(c) on the labelling schemes in Figure 4. Initially, $b_{a_2}[b]=0$. When b_3 is met, $b_{a_2}[b]$ is set to 1. When c_1 is met, $b_{a_2}[c]$ is set to 1 and $b_{a_2}=110$. When d_1 is met, $b_{a_2}[d]$ is set to 1 and $b_{a_2}=111$. a_2 is returned as a result. It is inserted to H_r. When the tuples $(a_{23}.x, a_2)$ and $(a_{23}.y, a_2)$ are met, since a_2 in H_r, no action is performed. When the tuple $(null, a_2)$ is met, a_2 is removed from H_r.

Box 5. Algorithm 5 D-Semi-IT-HGJoin

```
for i = 1 to k do
    aᵢ = Alistᵢ.begin
    d = Dlist.begin
    m=0
    m_f=1...1 (k bits of 1)
    while ai ≠ Alistᵢ.end do
        for i=1 to kdo
            while val_{aᵢ} < id_d do
                m[i]=¬m[i]
            while val_{aᵢ} = val_d AND id_{aᵢ} ∉ Hᵢ do
                Hᵢ.insert(id_{aᵢ})
                aᵢ = aᵢ.next
    if m=m_f then
            append id_d to OutputList
    OutputList∪ =OutputTuples(H₁,...,H_k, id_d)
for each aᵢ do
            while val_{aᵢ} = val_d AND m[i]=1 do
                m[i] = 0
                aᵢ =aᵢ.next
            d = d.next
```

Box 6. Algorithm 6 A-Semi-T-HGJoin

```
a = Alist.begin
for i = 1 to k do
    d_i =Dlist_i.begin
b_f=1...1(k bits of 1)
while a≠Alist.end AND ∀1≤i≤k; d_i≠Dlist_i.end do
        if val_a=NULL then
            remove id_a from H_r
        for i = 1 to kdo
            if id_{di} < val_a and H is not empty then
                for ∀n∈H do
                    b_n[i]=1
                if b_n=b_f then
                    append n to outputList
                    insert n to H_r
                    remove n from H
            while id_{di} < val_a do
                d=d.nextNode
                if id_a ∉ H then
                    insert id_a into H
            else
                for i=1 to k do
                    if id_{di} =val_a then
                        for ∀n∈H do
                            b_n[i]=1
                        if b_n=b_f then
                            append n to outputList
                            insert n to H_r
                            remove n from H
                remove id_a from H
return outputList
```

A-Semi-CBi-HGJoin can be processed in the similar way as A-Semi-T-HGJoin with the bitmap attached to the combinations of nodes instead of a single node.

The Processing Strategy for Partial Subgraph Queries

For a partial subgraph query with complex structure, its processing can be performed with the same framework discussed in Section "DAG

Subgraph Query Evaluation". Since in most of cases semi-HGJoin algorithms can gain better efficiency than corresponding HGJoin algorithm, for the processing of constraint part of the query, Semi-HGJoin operators can be applied.

The framework of subgraph processing presented in Section "DAG Subgraph Query Evaluation" is to split the query graph into bipartite subgraphs and join the result of these subgraph queries. For partial subgraph queries, some subgraphs as split results are to be processed with Semi-HGJoin Operators. The application and selection rule of Semi-HGJoin Operator is that for a bipartite subquery $(a_1, a_2, ..., a_n; d_1, d_2, ..., d_m)$, if $a_1, a_2, ..., a_n$ are in the constraint and none of them are contained in the subqueries in following steps (Property D), corresponding Semi-HGJoin algorithm may be D algorithm; if $d_1, d_2, ..., d_m$ are in the constraint and none of them contained in the subquereis in following steps (Property A), corresponding Semi-HGJoin algorithm may be A algorithm.

During the query optimization for partial subgraph queries, when an edge in the state graph corresponding to the graph satisfying Property D or Property A, the operator assigned on it should be the corresponding Semi-HGjoin operator. It is because some Semi-HGJoin operators have more efficient implementation algorithm than corresponding HGJoin operator and all Semi-HGJoin operator will have the results with smaller size than corresponding HGJoin operator.

The judgment of whether the a node n in the query attached to an edge $e=(g, g')$ in the state graph is to judge whether in g', there is no edge with n as a vertex.

We use an example to illustrate the generation of the state graph of a partial subgraph query. For the partial subgraph query in Figure 13(d), its state graph is the same as that of the subgraph query in Figure 8(e). In the state graph, the operator corresponds to the edge (3.1, 5.1) is A-Semi-IT-Join(b,c,d). It is because d node is used as the

constraint and the nodes matching d node will not be used in further steps.

In the state graph, the query optimization can be performed with the same method and accelerate strategy as in Section "DAG Subgraph Query Evaluation".

Experimental Study

In this section, we perform experimental study on the techniques in this chapter.

Experimental Setup

Experiments were run on Pentium 3GHz with 512M memory. We implemented all our algorithms in this chapter.

The dataset we tested is the XMark benchmark (Schmidt, A. & Waas, W. et. al. (2002)). It can be modeled as a graph with complicated schema and circles. Documents are generated with factors 0.1 to 2.5. Their parameters are shown in Table 2, where Num is the number of numbers in the labelling scheme in the storage.

To test the algorithms on real data, we performs the experiments on DBLP. By connecting "cross-ref" element to corresponding element, the DBLP can be represented as a graph with 3,795,138 nodes and 3,935,751 edges. We use run time as the measure of algorithms (*RT* for brief). In order to evaluate the algorithms on graphs in various forms, we also use synthetic data generated with 2 parameters: the number of nodes with each tag (*node number* for brief) n and the probability between nodes with two different tags(*edge probability* for brief) p. The data set generated in this way is called the random dataset. All the graphs in the random dataset have 8 tags in order { A,B, C, D, E, F, G, H}. The graphs in the random dataset may be DAGs or general graph (*GG* for brief). For a GG, the probability between each pair of nodes with any tag is p. For a DAG, only the probability of an existing edge from a node with smaller tag to a node with larger tag is 0 but

Table 2. Statistics of the XMark datasets

factor	0.1	0.5	1.0	1.5	2	2.5
Size(M)	11	56	113	170	226	284
#Nodes(K)	175	871	1681	2524	3367	4213
#Edges(K)	206	1024	1988	2985	3982	4981
Num(M)	0.98	4.9	9.71	14.7	19.6	24.7

the probability of the edges in inverted direction is 0.

For queries on XMark, we choose two queries for each algorithm, one contains all the nodes not in the circle with smaller selectivity, the other one contains some nodes in the circle with larger selectivity. The queries for HGJoin are XMQS1: text→emph and XMQS2: person→bold. Queries for IT-HGJoin and T-HGJoin are in Figure 14(a), Figure 14(b) and Figure 14(c), Figure 14(d), respectively. For the comparison with the algorithm StackD (Chen, L. & Gupta, A. et. al.(2005)), we also design complex twig queries XMQW1 and XMQW2 shown in Figure 14(g) and Figure 14(h). In order to study the performance of query optimization deeply, we design two complex structured queries XMQC1 and XMQC2 in Figure 14 (i) and Figure 14(j), respectively. Since Bi-HGJoin algorithm is the combination of IT-HGJoin and T-HGJoin and its features are represented by the experiments of these two algorithms, due to space limitation, the experimental results specially for Bi-HGJoin are not shown. In order to make query graphs clear, without confusion, in the query graphs we use arrows to represent AD relationships. Some of these queries are from real instances while some of them are synthetic. For example, XMQS1 represents the query for retrieving the text and the emph part belonging to it and XMQT1 is to retrieve the text with all emph, bold and keywords in it.

For queries on the random dataset, since the selectivity is mainly determined by edge probabil-

ity, we choose one query for each algorithm. The query for HGJoin is RQS: A→E. Queries for IT-HGJoin and T-HGJoin are in Figure 14(e) and Figure 14(f). Twig query and complex query are RQW and RQC, shown in Figure 14 (k) and Figure 14(l).

For queries on DBLP, we choose three queries for comparison. The reachability query for HG-Join is DQS: inproceedings→series. Queries for T-HGJoin and Twig query are shown in Figure 14 (m) and Figure 14 (n), respectively.

Since the query processing methods for the queries in form of circle or with adjacent relationships are the extensions of that for DAG queries, the features of these algorithms are similar. Due to space limitation, the experimental results of such queries are not shown in this chapter.

Comparisons

For comparison, we implemented stackD algorithm by Chen, L. & Gupta, A. et. al.(2005). The comparison is performed on 10M XMark data, DBLP, random graph in form of DAG and general graph with 4096 nodes and edge probability of 0.1, 0.8, 0.4, representing sparse edges, dense edges and the density of edge between those two instances. Note that in such case, the edge probabilities 0.1, 0.4 and 0.8 correspond to the ratio of the numbers of edges and the numbers of nodes of 250, 922 and 1794. The results are shown in Figure 15. From the results, it can be seen that the efficiency of our algorithm outperforms StackD

Figure 14. Query set

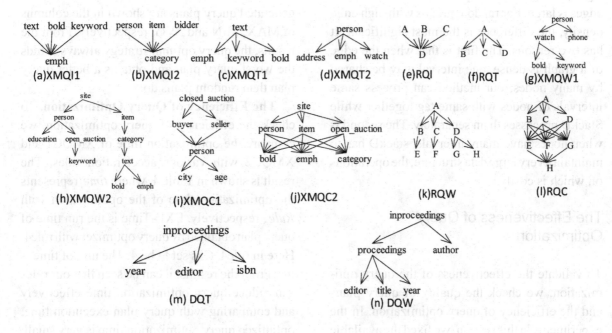

Figure 15. Experimental results of comparisons

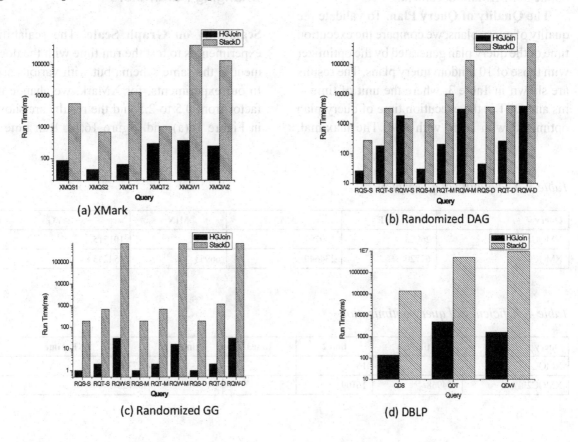

(a) XMark

(b) Randomized DAG

(c) Randomized GG

(d) DBLP

significantly, especially when the density of edges is large. For random graphs with high edge density, the difference is the most significant. It has two reasons. The first is that when the edge of a graph is dense, one interval may be shared by many nodes; our method can process same intervals of nodes with same tag together while StackD processes them separately. The second is when nodes have many intervals, stackD has to maintain a very large data structure, the operations on which is costly.

The Effectiveness of Query Optimization

To validate the effectiveness of the query optimization, we check the quality of query plans and the efficiency of query optimization. In the experiments in this section, we fixed the available memory to 1M and performed query optimization on the 50M XMark document.

The Quality of Query Plan. To validate the quality of query plans, we compare the execution time of the query plan generated by the optimizer with those of 10 random query plans. The results are shown in Table 3, where the unit of time is ms and OPT is the execution time of query plan optimized with rule4 with $k=4$. The maximal,

minimal and average run time of 10 randomly generated query plans are shown in the columns of MAX, MIN and AVG, respectively. From the results, the query optimal strategy always avoids the worst query plan and obtains a better query plan than random plans do.

The Efficiency of Query Optimization. To check the efficiency of query optimization, we compare the optimization time of XMQC1 and XMQC2 with various acceleration rules. The result is shown in Table 4, where $time_i$ represents the optimization time of the optimization with $Rule_i$, respectively. EXE-Time is the run time of query plan obtained by query optimizer with rule4. Here in rule4, C is set to be 4. The unit of time is ms. From the results, it can be seen that our rules can reduce query optimization time effectively and comparing with query plan execution time, optimized query optimization time is very small.

Changing Parameters

Scalability on Graph Scale. The scalability experiment is to test the run time with the document in the same schema but with various size. In our experiments, for XMark, we change the factor from 0.5 to 2.5 and the results are shown in Figure 16(a) and Figure 16(b). Run time of

Table 3. The quality of query plan

Query	OPT	MAX	MIN	AVG
XMQC1	26923	169797	55641	101715
XMQC2	62720	234640	66953	154243.8

Table 4. Efficiency of query optimization

Query	time1	time2	time3	time4	EXE-Time
XMQC1	47	16	2	1	17328
XMQC2	104968	16109	35	34	62720

Figure 16(a) is in log scale. From the results, the run time of XMQS1, XMQS2, XMQI1, XMQI2 and XMQW2 changes almost linearly with the data size. When data size gets larger, the process times of XMQT1, XMQT2, XMQW1, XMWC1 and XMWC2 increase fast. It is because major parts of these queries are related to some circle or bipartite subgraph in data. The results of such part are as the Cartesian production of related nodes and the number of results and intermediate results increase in the power of the number of query nodes. Therefore, the processing time increases faster than linearly. Since the time complexity is related to the size of results, it is inherent. For the random dataset, experiments on DAG were performed. Node number factors are changed with fixed edge probabilities 0.1. The results are shown in Figure 16(c). Note that run time and node number axes of Figure 16(c) are

in log scale. For the same reason discussed in the last paragraph, the query processing time of RQS, RQI, RQT and RQW increases faster than linearly with node number. The run time of RQC does not increase significantly with node number because with query optimizer, RQC is performed bottom-up and the selectivity of subquery ({E, F, G}, H) is very small. As a result, the query processing time increases faster than linearly only when the size of final results increases faster.

Scalability on Edge Density. For the random dataset, we performed experiments on DAGs and changed edge probabilities from 0.1 to 1.0 with fixed node number 4096. The results are shown in Figure 16(d), it shows that the run time of RQS, RQI, RQT and RQW does not change significantly with the number of edges. It is because when the edges become dense, more intervals are copied to ancestors and the intervals of all nodes

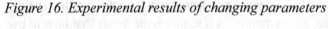

Figure 16. Experimental results of changing parameters

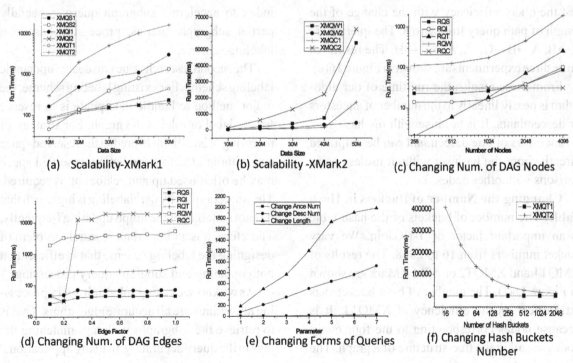

(a)   Scalability-XMark1

(b)   Scalability -XMark2

(c) Changing Num. of DAG Nodes

(d) Changing Num. of DAG Edges

(e) Changing Forms of Queries

(f) Changing Hash Buckets Number

trend to be the same. Based on our data preprocessing strategy, same intervals are merged. Therefore, the query processing time of these queries does not change a lot. RQC is an exception. When the edge probability changes from 0.2 to 0.3, the run time changes significantly. It is because RQC is complex and only when the density of edges reaches a threshold, the number of results becomes large.

Changing the Form of Queries. In this section, we test the efficiency change of our method with the forms of queries. All experiments were performed on a random dataset with node number 4096 and edge probability 0.1. We test the query efficiency with the change of the number of ancestors and descendants in the queries of T-HGJoin and IT-HGJoin from 1 to 7, respectively. The queries for IT-HGJoin algorithm use *H* as the descendant and {A}, {A, B}, ..., {A, ..., G} are the ancestor sets, respectively. The queries for T-HGJoin use *A* as the ancestor and {B}, {B, C}, ..., {B, ..., H} are the ancestor sets, respectively. The run time axes are both in log scale. We also test the query efficiency with the change of the length of path query from 2 to 8. The queries are A→B, A→B→C, ..., A→...→H. The results of these three experiments are shown in Figure 16(e).

From these results, the run time of our algorithm is nearly linearly to the number of ancestors or descendants. It is because with the hash sets, all ancestors of one descendant can be outputted directly from the hash set without useless comparisons with other nodes.

Changing the Number of Buckets in Hash Table. The number of buckets of the hash table is an important factor of T-HGJoin. We vary bucket numbers from 16 to 2048. The results of XMQT1 and XMQT2 on 50M XMark are shown in Figure 16(f). The number of hash buckets has little effect on the efficiency of XMQT1. It is because nodes corresponding to the four query nodes are all in the tree-structure of a graph. The

coding of each node has only one interval. So there are only three intervals to process at the same time. But for XMQT2, the run time is nearly logarithmic related to the number of bucket. It is because during the processing of XMQT2, there are many intermediate results in the hash table. More buckets will reduce not only disk I/O but also the cost of sort and join.

FUTURE RESEARCH DIRECTIONS

With its importance, efficient subgraph query processing algorithms are in great demand. There are three aspects of issues for future research.

The first is more efficient algorithms. To scale the subgraph query to very large graph, it is an interesting problem to design effective storage structure or data distribution for very large graph in parallel computer and to process subgraph queries parallel computation systems. In our method, no index is applied on the labeling schemes. A research issue arises that how to use index to accelerate subgraph query, especially partial subgraph queries, processing based on labeling scheme.

The second research issue is to design updatable labeling scheme. For existing labeling scheme, the major method to handle the update is to reserve for the label or relabel the graph. For strategy of reserving, it is difficult to predict the reserved space and without effective prediction, reserved space may be often used up and relabeling is required. The time complexity of relabeling is high such that it is not suitable for the graph updating frequently. Therefore, it is an important research problem of designing the labeling scheme that is efficient on both updating and subgraph query processing.

As we know, existing subgraph query processing algorithms are all accurate algorithms. That is to retrieve the subgraphs with tags matching the tags in the query accurately. In many applications, because of the quality of data and the typos in the input query, the tags in the data or the query may be error. To retrieve result on dirty data or for dirty subgraph query, the third research issue is to define and process approximate subgraph queries efficiently.

CONCLUSION

When data are modeled as graphs, many challenging research issues arise. In this chapter, we consider the problem of efficient structural query evaluation which is to match a subgraph in a graph. Based on a reachability labelling scheme, we present a hash-based structural join algorithm, HGJoin, to handle reachability queries for a graph. As the extensions of HGJoin, two algorithms are presented to process reachability queries with multiple ancestors and single descendants or single ancestors and multiple descendants, respectively. As the combination of these two algorithms, the query processing algorithm for subgraph queries in form of bipartite graphs is presented. With these algorithms as basic operators, we present a query processing method for subgraph queries in form of DAGs. In this chapter, we also discuss how to extend the method to support subgraph queries in the form of general graphs. For the queries that is to retrieve only part of the nodes in the pattern, we design partial subgraph query processing algorithms. Analysis and experiments show that our algorithms outperform the existing algorithm in efficiency and applicability.

ACKNOWLEDGMENT

This research is partially supported by National Science Foundation of China (No. 61003046,No.), the NSFC-RGC of China (No. 60831160525), National Grant of High Technology 863 Program of China (No. 2009AA01Z149), Key Program of the National Natural Science Foundation of China (No. 60933001), National Postdoctoral Foundation of China (No. 20090450126, No. 201003447), Doctoral Fund of Ministry of Education of China (No.20102302120054), Postdoctoral Foundation of Heilongjiang Province (No. LBH-Z09109), Development Program for Outstanding Young Teachers in Harbin Institute of Technology (No. HITQNJS.2009.052).

REFERENCES

Agrawal, R., & Borgida, A. (1989). Efficient management of transitive relationships in large data and knowledge bases. In J. Clifford, B. G. Lindsay, & D. Maier (Eds.), *Proceedings of the 1989 ACM SIGMOD International Conference on Management of Data,* Portland, Oregon (pp. 253 – 262). New York, NY: ACM Press.

Al-Khalifa, S., Jagadish, H. V., Patel, J., Wu, Y., Koudas, N., & Srivastava, D. (2002). Structural joins: A primitive for efficient XML query pattern matching. *Proceedings of the 18th International Conference on Data Engineering* (pp. 141–152). San Jose, CA: IEEE Computer Society.

Amagasa, T., Yoshikawa, M., & Uemura, S. (2003). A robust numbering scheme for XML documents. In U. Dayal, K. Ramamritham, T. M. Vijayaraman (Eds.), *Proceedings of the 19th International Conference on Data Engineering* (pp. 705 – 707). Bangalore, India: IEEE Computer Society.

Bruno, N., Koudas, N., & Srivastava, D. (2002). Holistic twig joins: Optimal XML pattern matching. In M. J. Franklin, B. Moon, A. Ailamaki (Eds.). *Proceedings of the 2002 ACM SIGMOD International Conference on Management of Data,* Madison, Wisconsin (pp. 310 -321), New York, NY: ACM.

Chen, L., Gupta, A., & Kurul, M. (2005). Stack-based algorithms for pattern matching on DAGs. In K. Böhm, C. S. Jensen, L. M. Haas, M. L. Kersten, P. Larson, & B. C. Ooi (Eds.), *Proceedings of the 31st International Conference on Very Large Data Bases,* Trondheim, Norway (pp. 493 – 504). New York, NY: ACM.

Cheng, J., Yu, J. F., & Ding, B. (2007). Cost-Based Query Optimization for Multi Reachability Joins (*DASFAA '07*) (pp. 18 - 30).

Cheng, J., Yu, J. F., Ding, B., Yu, P., & Wang, H. (2008). Fast graph pattern matching (*ICDE '08) (pp.* 913 - 922).

Cheng, J., Yu, J. F., & Tang, N. (2006). Fast Reachability Query Processing *(DASFAA '06)* (pp. 674 - 688).

Cheng, J., & Yu, J. X. (2006). Fast computation of reachability labeling for large graphs. In Ioannidis, Y. E., Scholl, M. H., Schmidt, J. W., Matthes, F., Hatzopoulos, M., Böhm, K., & Böhm, C. (Eds.), *EDBT, Lecture Notes in Computer Science, 3896, 961 – 979.* Springer.

Cohen, E., Halperin, E., Kaplan, H., & Zwick, U. (2003). Reachability and distance queries via 2-hop labels. *SIAM Journal on Computing, 32*(5), 1338–1355. doi:10.1137/S0097539702403098

Cohen, E., Kaplan, H., & Milo, T. (2002). Labeling dynamic XML trees. In L. Popa (Ed.), *Proceedings of the Twenty-first ACM SIGMOD-SIGACT-SIGART Symposium on Principles of Database Systems*, Madison, Wisconsin (pp. 271 – 281). New York, NY: ACM.

Cordella, L. P., Foggia, P., Sansone, C., & Vento, M. (2004). A (sub)graph isomorphism algorithm for matching large graphs. *IEEE Transactions on Pattern Analysis and Machine Intelligence, 26*(10), 1367–1372. doi:10.1109/TPAMI.2004.75

Cortadella, J., & Valiente, G. (2000). *A relational wiew of subgraph isomorphism (RelMiCS)* (pp. 45 - 54)

DePiero, F. W., & Krout, D. K. (2003). An algorithm using length-r paths to approximate subgraph isomorphism. *Pattern Recognition Letters, 24*(1-3), 33–46. doi:10.1016/S0167-8655(02)00186-1

Garey, M. R., & Johnson, D. S. (1979). *Computers and intractability: A guide to the theory of NP-completeness.* New York, NY, USA: W. H. Freeman & Co.

Giugno, D., & Shasha, D. (2002). GraphGrep: A fast and universal method for querying graphs. *ICPR,* (2), 112-115.

Güting R. H. (1994). GraphDB: Modeling and querying graphs in databases. *VLDB,* 297-308.

He, H., Wang, H., Yang, J., & Yu, P. (2005). Compact reachability labeling for graph-structured data. In O. Herzog, H.-J. Schek, N. Fuhr, et al. (Eds.), *Proceedings of the 2005 ACM CIKM International Conference on Information and Knowledge Management*, Bremen, Germany (pp. 594 – 601). New York, NY: ACM.

Jin, R., Xiang, Y., Ruan, N., & Furhy, D. (2009). 3-HOP: A high-compression indexing scheme for reachability query. *SIGMOD Conference,* (813-826).

Jin, R., Xiang, Y., Ruan, N., & Wang, H. (2008). Efficiently answering reachability queries on very large directed graphs. *SIGMOD Conference* (pp. 595 – 608).

Kameda, T. (1975). On the vector representation of the reachability in planar directed graphs. *Information Processing Letters, 3*(3), 78–80. doi:10.1016/0020-0190(75)90019-8

Li, C., Ling, T. W., & Hu, M. (2006). Efficient processing of updates in dynamic XML data. In Ling Liu, Andreas Reuter, Kyu-Young Whang, et al. (Eds.), *Proceedings of the 22nd International Conference on Data Engineering*. Atlanta, GA, USA: IEEE Computer Society 13.

Li, Q., & Moon, B. (2001). Indexing and querying XML data for regular path expressions. In P. M. G. Apers, P.Atzeni, S. Ceri, et al. (Eds.), *Proceedings of 27th International Conference on Very Large Data Bases* (pp. 361 – 370). Roma, Italy: Morgan Kaufmann.

Messmer, B. T., & Bunke, H. (2000). Efficient subgraph isomorphism detection: A decomposition approach. *IEEE Transactions on Knowledge and Data Engineering, 12*(2), 307–323. doi:10.1109/69.842269

Milo, T., & Suciu, D. (1999). Index structures for path expressions. In C. Beeri, & P. Buneman (Eds.), *Proceedings of the 7th International Conference of Database Theory* (pp. 277 – 295). Jerusalem, Israel: Springer.

O'Neil, P., O'Neil, E. J., Pal, S., Cseri, I., Schaller, G., & Westbury, N. (2004). OrdPaths: Insert-friendly XML node labels. In *Proceedings of the ACM SIGMOD International Conference on Management of Data*, Paris, France (pp. 903–908). New York, NY: ACM.

Polyzotis, N., & Garofalakis, M. N. (2002). Statistical synopses for graph-structured XML databases. In M. J. Franklin, B. Moon, & A. Ailamaki (Eds.), *Proceedings of the 2002 ACM SIGMOD International Conference on Management of Data*, Madison, WI, USA (pp. 358 – 369). New York, NY: ACM, 2002.

Polyzotis, N., & Garofalakis, M. N. (2004). Selectivity estimation for XML twigs. *Proceedings of the 20th International Conference on Data Engineering* (pp. 264 – 275). Boston, MA, USA: IEEE Computer Society.

Schenkel, G. W. R., & Theobald, A. (2004) Hopi: An efficient connection index for complex XML document collections. In E. Bertino, S. Christodoulakis, D. Plexousakis, et al. (Eds.), *Proceedings of 9th International Conference on Extending Database Technology*, Heraklion, Crete, Greece (pp. 237 – 255). LNCS Springer 2004.

Schmidt, A., Waas, W., Kersten, M., Carey, M., Manolescu, I., & Busse, R. (2002). XMark: A Benchmark for XML Data Management. VLDB:974-985

Tatarinov, I., Viglas, S., Beyer, K., Shanmugasundaram, J., Shekita, E., & Zhang, C. (2002). Storing and querying ordered XML using a relational database system. In M. J. Franklin, B. Moon, A. Ailamaki (Eds.), *Proceedings of the 2002 ACM SIGMOD International Conference on Management of Data*, Madison, Wisconsin (pp. 204–215). New York, NY: ACM Press.

TriBl. S., & Leser, U. (2007. Fast and practical indexing and querying of very large graphs. In *Proceedings of the 2007 ACM SIGMOD International Conference on Management of Data* (pp. 845 – 856).

Ullmann, J. R. (1976). An algorithm for subgraph isomorphism. *Journal of the ACM, 23*(1), 31–42. doi:10.1145/321921.321925

Vagena, V. J. T. Z., & Moro, M. M. (2004). Twig query processing over graph-structured XML data. In Sihem Amer-Yahia, Luis Gravano (Eds.), *Proceedings of the Seventh International Workshop on the Web and Databases.Maison de la Chimie*, Paris, France (pp. 43 – 48). New York, NY: ACM.

Wang, H., He, H., Yang, J., Yu, P., & Yu, J. (2006). Dual labeling: Answering graph reachability queries in constant time. In L. Liu, A. Reuter, K. Whang, et Al. (Eds.), *Proceedings of the 22nd International Conference on Data Engineering*, Atlanta, GA, 75. IEEE Computer Society.

Wang, H., Li, J., Luo, J., & Gao, H. (2008). Hash-base subgraph query processing method for graph-structured XML documents. *PVLDB*, *1*(1), 478–489.

Wang, H., Li, J., & Wei, W. 0011, Lin, X. (2008B). Coding-based join algorithms for structural queries on graph-structured XML document. *World Wide Web (Bussum)*, *11*(4), 485–510. doi:10.1007/s11280-008-0050-4

Wang, H., Park, S., Fan, W., & Yu, P. (2003). Vist: A dynamic index method for querying XML data by tree structures. In A. Y. Halevy, Z. G. Ives, & A. Doan (Eds.), *Proceedings of the 2003 ACM SIGMOD International Conference on Management of Data,* San Diego, CA, USA (pp. 110 – 121). New York, NY: ACM.

Wang, H., Wang, W., Lin, X., & Li, J. (2005). Labeling scheme and structural joins for graph-structured XML data. In *APWeb* (pp.277-289).

Wang, W., Jiang, H., Lu, H., & Yu, J. (2003). PBiTree coding and efficient processing of containment joins. In U. Dayal, K. Ramamritham, T. M. Vijayaraman (Eds.), *Proceedings of the 19th International Conference on Data Engineering,* Bangalore, India (pp. 391 – 402). IEEE Computer Society.

Wu, X., Lee, M.-L., & Hsu, W. (2004). A prime number labeling scheme for dynamic ordered XML trees. In *Proceedings of the 20th International Conference on Data Engineering,* IEEE Computer Society, Washington D. C., USA (pp. 66 – 78).

Zhang, C., Naughton, J. F., DeWitt, D., & Luo, Q. (2001). On supporting containment queries in relational database management systems. In Walid G. Aref. (Ed.), *Proceedings of the 2001 ACM SIGMOD ('01) International Conference on Management of Data*, Santa Barbara, CA, USA (pp. 425 – 436). New York, NY: ACM.

Zibin, J. G. Y. (2001). Efficient subtyping tests with pq-encoding. In *Proceedings of the 2001 ACM SIGPLAN Conference on Object-Oriented Programming Systems, Languages and Applications*, San Francisco, CA, USA (pp. 96 – 107). New York, NY: ACM.

KEY TERMS AND DEFINITIONS

Adjacent Relationship: In a graph G, two nodes a and b satisfy adjacent relationship if and only if an edge from a to b exists in G.

Adjacent Query: An adjacent query a/d is to retrieve all pairs of nodes (n_a, n_d) in G where n_a has tag a, n_d has tag d and n_a and n_d satisfy adjacent relationship in G

Labeling Scheme: The labelling scheme for a graph is to judge the structural relationship between any two nodes in the graph without retrieving other information.

Reachability Relationship: Two nodes a and b satisfy reachability relationship if and only if a path from a to b exists in G

Reachability Query: A reachability query $a{\rightarrow}d$ is to retrieve all pairs of nodes (n_a, n_d) in G where n_a has tag a, n_d has tag d and n_a and n_d satisfy reachability relationship in G.

Query Optimization: Query optimization is to find a query plan with minimal execution cost.

Subgraph Query: A subgraph query is a tagged directed graph $Q=\{V,E,tag,rel\}$, where V is the node set of Q; E is the edge set of Q; the function $tag{:}V{\rightarrow}TAG$ is the tag function (TAG is the set of tags); the function $rel{:}E{\rightarrow}AXIS$ shows the structural relationships between the nodes in the query ($AXIS$ is the set of relationships between nodes; $PC \in AXIS$ represents adjacent relationship; $AD \in AXIS$ represents reachability relationship).

Subgraph Query Processing: For a subgraph query $Q=\{V_Q, E_Q, tag, rel\}$ and a graph $G=\{V_G, E_G\}$, the processing of subgraph query Q is to retrieve the set

$$R_{G,Q} = \{g = (V_g, E_g) \mid V_g \subset V_G$$

and $\exists$ bijective mapping $f_g : V_g \rightarrow V_Q$ and $\exists$ injective mapping $g : V_g \rightarrow V_G$ satisfying

$$\forall n \in V_g, tag(n) = tag(f_g(n)) = tag(p_g(n));$$

$$\forall e = (n_1, n_2) \in E_g, p_g(n_1), p_g(n_2)$$

satisfy the relationship $rel(f(n_1), f(n_2))\}$.

APPENDIX

For its importance, subgraph queries have been studied in various fields. The subgraph isomorphism problem which is proven to be an NP-Complete problem (Garey, M. R. & Johnson D. S. (1979)) is related to subgraph query processing but it only requires the judgment of whether some subgraph in a graph is isomorphic to the givn graph. Ullmann, J. R. (1976), Messmer, B. T. & Bunke, H. (2000), DePiero, F. W. & Krout, D. K. (2003), Cordella, L. P.& Foggia, P. et. al. (2004) present various algorithms for this problem. Some research work focus on retrieve all the subgraphs in a graph isomorphic to a given graph such as Cortadella, J.& Valiente, G. (2000). Such work can be considered as the technique of processing subgraph queries with only PC relationship.

From the perspectives of data management, many works have been done about query processing on graphs. For example, GraphDB (Güting R. H. (1994)) manages tagged graphs in object-orient database and retrieves subgraphs with some properties from the database. GraphGrep (Giugno, D& Shasha, D (2002)) retrieves subgraph from a graph database with a regular expression graph query language.

To judge the structural relationship between the nodes in a graph efficiently, labeling scheme is a common-used method such as 2-Hop labeling scheme for reachability and distance queries (Cohen, H & Halperin, E. el. al. (2003)). Data management community focuses on reachability labeling scheme and some reachablity labeling scheme have been presented. For tree-structure data, several reachability labeling schemes are presented including interval-based labeling schemes (Zhang, C. & Naughton, J. F. et. al.(2001), Li, Q. & Moon, B. (2001) and Amagasa, T. & Yoshikawa, M. et. al.(2003)), prefix-based labeling scheme (Cohen, E. & Kaplan, H. et. al. (2002), Tatarinov, I. & Viglas, S. et. al. (2002), O'Neil, P. E. & O'Neil, E. J. et. al. (2004), Li, C. & Ling, T. W. (2006)) and arithmetic labeling schemes(Wang, W. & Jiang, H. et. al. (2003), Wu, X. & Lee, M.-L. et. al. (2004)). The reachability labeling scheme on graph include interval-based labeling scheme (Kameda. T. (1975), Agrawal, R. Borgida, A. (1989), Zibin, J. G. Y.(2001), Wang, H. & Wang, W. et. al. (2005)), set-based labeling scheme (Schenkel, G. W. R. & Theobald, A. (2004), Cheng, J. & Yu, J. X.(2006A), Jin, R. &Xiang, Y. et. al.(2008) and Jin, R. & Xiang, Y. et. al. (2009)) and hybrid labeling scheme (He, H. & Wang, H. et. al.(2005), Wang, H. & He, H. et. al.(2006) and TriBl, S. & Leser, U. (2007)).

Based on 2-hop labeling schemes, the processing algorithms for reachability queries and subgraph queries have been presented by Cheng, J.&Yu, J. F. et. al. (2006B, 2007, 2008). Vagena, V. J. T. Z. & Moro, M. M.(2004), Chen, L. & Gupta, A. et. al.(2005) and Wang, H. & Li, J. et.al.(2008A, 2008B) propose algorithms for subgraph query processing based on interval-based labeling schemes. The major content in this chapter is from Wang, H. & Li, J. et. al. (2008A).

Section 2
Advanced Querying and Mining Aspects of Graph Databases

Chapter 8

G–Hash:
Towards Fast Kernel–Based Similarity Search in Large Graph Databases

Xiaohong Wang
University of Kansas, USA

Jun Huan
University of Kansas, USA

Aaron Smalter
University of Kansas, USA

Gerald H. Lushington
University of Kansas, USA

ABSTRACT

Structured data such as graphs and networks have posed significant challenges to fundamental aspects of data management including efficient storage, indexing, and similarity search. With the fast accumulation of graph databases, similarity search in graph databases has emerged as an important research topic. Graph similarity search has applications in a wide range of domains including chemoinformatics, bioinformatics, sensor network management, social network management, and XML documents, among others.

Our objective in this chapter is to enable fast similarity search in large graph databases with graph kernel functions. In particular, we propose (i) a novel kernel-based similarity measurement and (ii) an efficient indexing structure for graph data management. In our method, we use a hash table to support efficient storage and fast search of the extracted local features from graph data. Using the hash table, we have developed a graph kernel function to capture the intrinsic similarity of graphs and for fast similarity query processing. We have demonstrated the utility of the proposed methods using large chemical structure graph databases.

DOI: 10.4018/978-1-61350-053-8.ch008

INTRODUCTION

Structured data including sets, sequences, trees and graphs, pose significant challenges to fundamental aspects of data management such as efficient storage, indexing, component search (e.g. subgraph/ supergraph search) and similarity search. Among these structured data, the use of graph representations has gained popularity in pattern recognition and machine learning. The main advantage of graphs is that they offer a powerful way to represent structured data. Querying and mining of the graphs can contribute to our understanding in numerous ways: understanding of new connectivity patterns, evolutionary changes and discovery of topological features. Queries in graph databases can be broadly classified into two categories: (i) subgraph query and (ii) similarity query. The aim of subgraph query is to identify a set of graphs that contain a query graph. The aim of similarity query is to identify similar graphs in a graph database to a query, according to a distance metric. There are two types of similarity query, i.e. *k*-NNs query and range query. In *k*-NNs query, the *k* most similar graphs are reported. In range query, all graphs within a predefined distance to the query graph are reported. In this chapter, we address the problem of *k*-NNs similarity search in large database of graphs.

Motivation

Recent scientific and technological advances have resulted in an abundance of data modeled as graphs. Graph has been used extensively in modeling complicated structures and schemaless data, such as proteins (Berman *et al.*, 2000), image (Berretti *et al.*, 2001), visions (Fu, 1986), program flows (Liu *et al.*, 2005), XML documents (McHugh *et al.*, 1997), the Web (Faloutsos *et al.*, 1999), etc. For example, a metabolic pathway is modeled as a set of reactions, enzymes and metabolites, and an edge is placed between a reaction and a metabolite (or enzyme) if it participates in the reaction and

schema of heterogeneous web-based data sources and e-commerce sites can also be modeled as graphs (He and Singh, 2006). With the fast growth of graph databases, *similarity search* in graph databases has emerged as an important research topic. Graph similarity search has applications in a wide range of domains including chemoinformatics, bioinformatics, sensor network management, social network management, and XML documents, among others. For example, in chemistry and pharmacy, there is a fast accumulation of chemical molecule data. Once a new chemical is synthesized, the properties of the chemical may be revealed through querying existing chemicals with known properties. Fast similarity search in large graph databases enables scientists and data engineers to build accurate models for graphs, identify the intrinsic connections between graph data, and reduce the computational cost of processing large databases.

Many researchers have been working on the graph similarity search. The most straightforward approach for similarity measurement is to embed a graph in a high dimensional Euclidian space, known as the feature space, uses spatial indexing techniques for similarity search. Much of this work has naturally tended toward methods that balance the expressivity of substructures with their efficiency of enumeration. General subgraphs are the most expressive, as they are graphs themselves, but that also makes them the most expensive enumeration. The application of frequent subgraph mining has seen much success in this area, as a way to retain high expressivity while allowing fast enumeration. At the other end of the spectrum, sets or bags of vertices and edges are the least expressive and ignore all of the rich information of graph connectivity; hence set representations for graphs are not widely used. Falling between these two extremes are intermediate structures such as paths, cycles, and trees. Substructure enumerations are then the basis for many useful operations such as hashing, indexing, similarity search, etc. In all, current feature extraction methods operate in two different ways: (i) enumeration of substructures in each graph separately (e.g. generating a set of random walks from a graph) (Kashima *et al.*, 2003), and (ii) enumeration of substructures from a set of graphs (e.g. mining frequent patterns) (Cheng *et al.*, 2007; Williams *et al.*, 2007; Yan *et al.*, 2004; Zhao *et al.*, 2007). Though widely used, there are several limitations of adapting the feature extraction and feature indexing strategy for similarity search. First, the feature extraction process is computational intensive, especially for mining large graph databases. Second, feature extraction may produce many features that occupy a large amount of memory. Different feature selection methods have been devised to identify "discriminative" features (Yan *et al.*, 2004). However features that are efficient for database search may not be equally good for similarity search and a trade-off is needed.

Challenges

Similarity search on graphs is challenging. We argue that an ideal design of fast similarity search should solve the following three related (sometimes contradicting) problems:

- how to define similarity measurement between graphs? (accuracy),
- how to store graph databases efficiently? (space efficient),
- how to build efficient index structure to accelerate pattern matching and graph similarity search? (running-time efficient)

By accurate, we emphasize that the similarity measurement should capture the intrinsic similarity of objects. But the application of graphs to a wide variety fields implies that graph themselves have a wide variety of interpretations. This poses a challenge on defining useful similarity measurements, even when the definition is restricted to a single domain, such as chemical structures (Willett *et al.*, 1998). Currently, figure edit distance (Mess-

mer and Bunke, 1998; Sabfeiliu and Fu, 1983) is commonly used and maximum common subgraph distance (Fermandez and Valiente, 2001; Wallis *et al.*, 2001) may be more meaningful. Recently, graph kernel functions also provide similarity measurements (Frohlich *et al.* 2005; Vert, 2008). Rather than extracting features explicitly, a kernel function maps data objects to a high-dimensional functional space and measures the similarity of objects by computing the inner product of the objects in the functional space. The advantage of kernel function based similarity measurement is that kernel functions usually have high statistical power, i.e. affording high classification accuracy. The major difficulty of applying kernel function for database search is that (i) kernel functions for graphs are expensive to compute and (ii) there is no clear way to index the kernel function computation over a large graph database. By running-time efficient, it is well-known that operations on graphs, such as subgraph isomorphism, are NP-complete problems (Cook, 1971). As a result, most meaningful definitions of similarity will result in NP-hard problems. Even a simple comparison, graph isomorphism, defies a polynomial bound for the general case (Fortin, 1996). These costly pair-wise comparisons, when combined with the increasing size of modern graph databases, make finding efficient search techniques difficult. Therefore it is needed to design efficient algorithms to avoid exhaustive search as much as possible. By space efficient, the index structure should not add a significant storage overhead to graph databases. When the databases are very large, it is hard for main memory to hold the whole index structure. That is the reason why some of current methods, such as C-tree, can not handle queries in databases larger than 70K.

Summary

Here we explore a new way of graph similarity search where similarity is defined using graph kernel functions. Our approach, called G-hash, aims to devise a kernel function that can be efficiently computed over a large graph database. In our model, graphs are reduced to point sets that are compared directly via a kernel function. Typically such an approach would lose a great deal of information in the rich graph structure, but we avoid this by compressing much of the topological information into feature vectors describing each graph vertex. This approach provides a compact graph representation that is information rich, yet easy to compare. We then hash graph objects using the compressed set representation. The hash keys are based on these sets and hence similar objects in the hash table are positioned in the same cells. Once we have hashed graphs in a database into the table, we can find all similar nodes and then calculate the distances between the query graph and the graphs in the database based on both those similar nodes and kernel function to obtain the k-NNs of the query graph.

We have implemented our method, and have demonstrated its utility on large chemical graph databases. It has been a challenge in bioinformatics to develop computational techniques to elucidate the roles of small molecules in biological systems. Similarity search in chemical databases is such one of problems. With the rapid growth of public chemical databases, fast similarity search in large chemical databases has started to attract intensive research attention. Although there are many methods addressing this problem, such as Daylight fingerprints (Daylight Fingerprints, 2008), Maximum common subgraph (Cao *et al.*, 2008) and C -tree (He and Singh, 2006), none of them has achieved the goal of fast and effective similarity search in chemical databases, i.e. having computational efficiency in scaling to large chemical databases and computational efficiency in capturing the intrinsic similarity of chemicals. Our method, G-hash, provides a good solution to reach the above goal. Our results show that the G- hash method achieves state-of-the-art performance for k-NNs classification. Most importantly, the new similarity measurement and the index structure is

scalable to large databases with smaller indexing size, faster indexing construction time, and faster query processing time as compared favorably with the state-of-the-art indexing methods such as Daylight fingerprints, C-tree and GraphGrep.

The rest of the text is organized as follows. Firstly, we formally defined graphs and graph similarity search. Secondly, we reviewed related work in the areas of graph indexing and kernels for graphs. Thirdly, we discussed the details of our methodology and presented a comprehensive experimental study using our methods and competing methods. Then, we applied our methods into large chemical databases. Finally, we concluded with a few remarks on the study and future work.

BACKGROUND

Before we proceed to discuss the algorithmic details, we present some general background materials which include graph database mining, graph kernel functions, graph wavelet analysis and chemical structures as graphs.

Graph Database Mining

In this section, we will introduce a few important concepts and definitions for graphs: labeled graph, walk, subgraph, subgraph isomorphism, maximum common subgraph (MCS), MCS distance and graph edit distance. A labeled graph G is described by a finite set of nodes V and a finite set of edges $E \subset V \times V$. In most applications, a graph is labeled, where labels draw from a label set λ. A labeling function $\lambda : V \cup E \rightarrow \Sigma$ assigns labels to nodes and edges. In node-labeled graphs, labels are assigned to nodes only and in edge-labeled graphs, labels are assigned to edges only. In fully-labeled graphs, labels are assigned to nodes and edges. We may use a special symbol to represent missing labels. If we do that, node-labeled graphs, edge-labeled graphs, and graphs without labels are special cases of fully labeled graphs. Without loss of generality, we deal with fully-labeled graphs only in this text. For the label set Σ, we do not assume any structure of Σ now; it may be a field, a vector space, or simply a set. Following convention, we denote a graph as a quadruple G = (V, E, Σ, λ) where V, E, Σ, λ are explained before. A graph database is a set of labeled graphs. A walk of a graph is a list of node $v_1, v_2, \cdots, v_n$ such that v_i and v_{i+1} is connected for all $i \in [1, n-1]$. A path is a walk which contains no repeated nodes, i.e. for all $i \neq j$ we have $v_i \neq v_j$.

Definition 1. *Subgraph Isomorphism*: A graph $G' = (V', E', \Sigma', \lambda')$ is *subgraph isomorphic* to G = (V, E, Σ, λ), denoted by $G' \subseteq G$, if there exists a 1-1 mapping $f : V' \rightarrow V$ such that

$$\forall v \in V', \lambda'(v) = \lambda(f(v))$$
$$\forall (u, v) \in E', (f(u), f(v)) \in E, \text{ and}$$
$$\forall (u, v) \in E', \lambda'(u, v) = \lambda(f(u), f(v)).$$

In other words, a graph is a subgraph of another graph if it preserves the node labels, edge relations, and edge labels. The function f is a *subgraph isomorphism* from graph G' to graph G. It is said G' *occurs* in G if $G' \subseteq G$. Given a subgraph isomorphism f, the image of the domain $V'(f(V'))$ is an embedding of G' in G.

Example 1. *Figure 1 shows a graph database of three labeled graphs. The mapping (isomorphism) $p_1 \rightarrow q_2$, $p_2 \rightarrow q_3$ and $p_3 \rightarrow q_4$ demonstrates that graph P is subgraph isomorphic to Q and P occurs in Q. Similarly, graph G occurs in graph Q but not P.*

Problem statement: Given a graph database G* containing a set of n graphs and a query graph *Q, the graph similarity search problem* is to retrieve all graphs in G* similar to the graph Q according to the similarity measurement. There are different similarity measurements among which *Graph Edit distance* (Messmer and Bunke, 1998; Sanfeliu and Fu, 1983) and *Maximum Common Graph (MCS)* distance (He and Singh, 2006; Fermandz and Valiente, 2001; Wallis *et al.*, 2001) are widely used. The edit distance between two graphs is the minimum cost of transforming one graph into the other. Here the transformations refer to the insertion and removal of vertices and edges, and the changing of attributes on vertices and edges. The MCS distance between two graphs, G_1 and G_2, is defined by

$$d_{MCS}(G_1, G_2) = 1 - \frac{|V_{MCS}|}{\max(|V_1|, |V_2|)}. \qquad (1)$$

Figure 1. A database of three labeled graphs

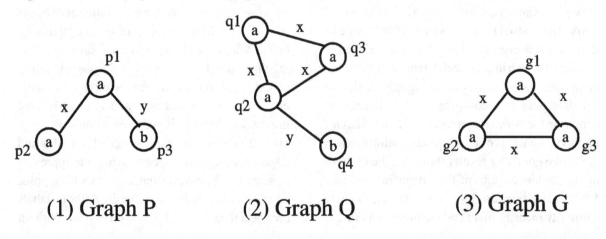

(1) Graph P (2) Graph Q (3) Graph G

where V_{MCS}, V_1, V_2 are the number of vertices of *MCS*, G_1 and G_2 respectively.

Take the three graphs in Figure 1 for example. If we use uniform distance measures for graph edit distance, then the graph edit distance between graph P and Q is d(P,Q)=3 since in order to transform the graph *P* to *Q*, we need to insert the node q1, the edge of q1-q2 and the edge of q1-q3. Similarly, *d(P,G)*=3, *d(Q,G)*=2..

The MCS distance between P and Q is

$$d_{MCS} = 1 - \frac{|V_P|}{\max(|V_P|, |V_Q|)} = 1 - \frac{3}{\max(3,4)} = 0.25.$$

Similarly, the MCS distance between P and G is

$d_{MCS} = 1 - \frac{2}{3} = 0.33$, and the MCS distance

between Q and G is $d_{MCS} = 1 - \frac{3}{4} = 0.25$.

Reproducing Kernel Hilbert Space

Kernel functions are powerful computational tools to analyze large volumes of graph data (Haussler, 1999). The advantage of kernel functions is due to their capability to map a set of data to a high dimensional Hilbert space without explicitly computing the coordinates of the data. This is done through a special function called a *kernel* function.

A binary function $K : X \times X \to \mathbb{R}$ is a *positive semi-definite* function if

$$\sum_{i,j=1}^{m} c_i c_j K(x_i, x_j) \geq 0 \qquad (2)$$

for any $m \in \mathbb{N}$, any selection of samples $x_i \in X (i = [1, n])$, and any set of coefficients $c_i \in \mathbb{R} (i = [1, n])$. In addition, a binary function is *symmetric* if $K(x, y) = K(y, x)$ for all $x, y \in X$. A symmetric, positive semi-definite function ensures the existence of a Hilbert space H and a map $\Phi: X \to H$ such that

$$k(x, x') = \langle \Phi(x), \Phi(x') \rangle \qquad (3)$$

For all $x, x' \in X$, $\langle x, y \rangle$ denotes an inner product between two objects x and y. The result is known as the Mercer's theorem and a symmetric, positive semi-definite function is also known as a Mercer kernel function (Scholkopf and Smola, 2002), or *kernel* function for simplicity.

By projecting the data space to a Hilbert space, kernel functions provide a uniformed analytical environment for various data types including graphs, regardless of the fact that the original data space may not look like a vector space at all. This strategy is known as the "kernel trick" and it has been applied to various data analysis tasks including classification (Vapnik, 1998), regression (Collobert and Bengio, 2001) and feature extraction through principle component analysis (Scholkopf *et al.*, 1999), among others.

Graph Wavelets Analysis

Wavelet functions are commonly used as a means for decomposing and representing a function or signal as its constituent parts, across various resolutions or scales. Wavelets are usually applied to numerically valued data such as communication signals or mathematical functions, as well as to some regularly structured numeric data such as matrices and images. Graphs, however, are arbitrarily structured and may represent innumerable relationships and topologies between data elements. Recent work has established the successful application of wavelet functions to graphs for multi-resolution analysis. Two examples of wavelet functions are the *Haar* and the *Mexican hat*. Crovella et al. (Crovella and Kolaczyk, 2003) have developed a multi-scale method for network traffic data analysis. For this application, they are attempting to determine the scale at which certain traffic phenomena occur. They represent traffic networks as graphs labeled with some measurements such as bytes carried per unit time. Maggioni et al. (Maggioni, 2005) demonstrates a general-purpose biorthogonal wavelet for graph analysis. In their method, they use the

Figure 2. An example chemical structure

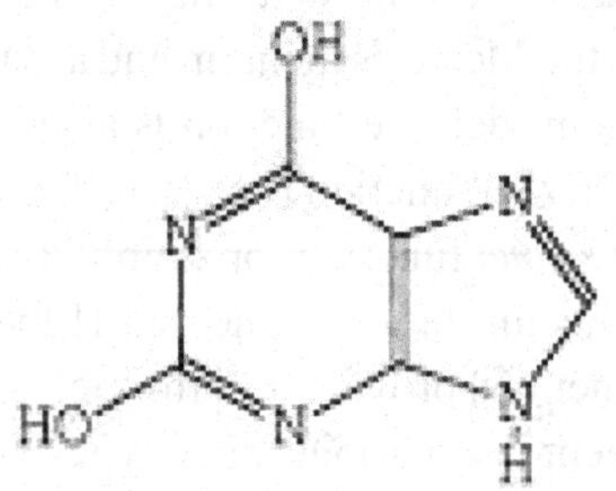

dyadic powers of a diffusion operator to induce a multi-resolution analysis. While their method applies to a large class of spaces, such as manifolds and graphs, the applicability of their method to attributed chemical structures is not clear. The major technical difficulty is how to incorporate node labels in a multi-resolution analysis.

Graph Modeling of Chemical Structures

Chemical compounds are organic molecules that are commonly modeled by graphs. In our study, we adopt the 2D connectivity map where we use *nodes* in a graph to model *atoms* in a chemical structure and *edges* to model chemical *bonds* in the chemical structure. In the representation, nodes are labeled with the atom element type, and edges are labeled with the bond type (single, double, and aromatic bond). The edges in the graph

are undirected, since there is no directionality associated with chemical bonds. Figure 2 shows an example chemical structure, where unlabeled vertices are assumed to be carbon (C). Figure 3 shows one sample chemical structure and its graph representation.

For chemical similarity search, the Tanimoto similarity score (Girke *et al.*, 2005) is a method of calculating the similarity between two ligands' (small molecule) fingerprints. If we describe our molecules by the presence or absence of features, molecules are encoded as binary strings. The Tanimoto score is determined as shown in the equation below:

$$T = \frac{N_c}{(N_a + N_b + N_c)} \tag{4}$$

where T is the Tanimoto score, N_a and N_b are the number of bits set to 1 in fingerprints of ligand a and b respectively and N_c is the total number of bits set to 1 found in fingerprints of both ligand a and b. The result is a value between 0 and 1 with 0 indicating no similarity and 1 indicating 100% similarity. A high Tanimoto score of 0.7 or above is representative of two molecules having high structural similarity which is a good indication of similar biological activity. Tanimoto similarity measurement used by daylight fingerprints (Daylight fingerprints, 2008), a commercial product for compound registration, has already been used

Figure 3. Left: the sample chemical structure. Right: graph representation of the sample chemical structure.

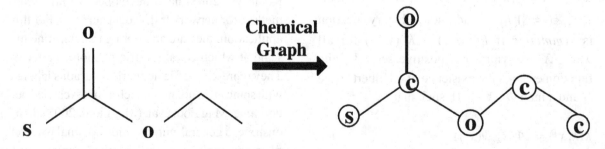

in chemical informatics. Details will be shown later.

RELATED WORK

Given that graphs are such powerful and interesting structures, graph similarity search has been extensively studied with the rapid growth of graph databases. In this section, we will overview related work, starting from indexing in graph databases in general, including graph similarity search, subgraph containment search and approximate subgraph search, and move to graph kernel functions.

Graph Similarity Search

Graph similarity search methods provide quantitative similarity measurements which are used to rank the search results in a meaningful manner. Most of similarity search methods are general methods such C-tree (He and Singh, 2006), Gstring (Jiang et al., 2007) and maximal common subgraph (Cao et al., 2008). Although those methods can be used for chemical similarity search, extending these strategies to similarity search in large compound databases is non-trivial. There are still specific methods for chemical similarity search such as Daylight fingerprints (Daylight fingerprints, 2008).

General Graph Similarity Search

There are several ways used to measure graph similarity. The first one is edit distance. That is, given a set of operations on graph vertices and edges (such as insertion, deletion, relabeling), how many such operations are required to transform graph G into another graph G'. We can parameterize the method by assigning different costs to different operations and summing over the total cost of all operations. Edit distance is an intuitively attractive approach to graph similarity,

but unfortunately in practice it is costly to compute (NP-hard). *C*-tree (He and Singh, 2006) is a widely used graph indexing scheme that also does not use graph pieces as features. Instead, it organizes database graphs in tree based structure, where interior nodes are *graph closures*, and leaf nodes are database graphs. Importantly, *C*-tree also supports similarity queries where the previous two methods, *GraphGrep* and *gIndex*, do not. The second one is maximal common subgraph (Cao *et al.*, 2008; Fermandez and Valiente, 2001; Wallis, 2001). Several heuristic strategies (Raymond and Willet, 2002), based on specific properties of chemical structures, were proposed to improve the efficiency of MCS-based similarity search algorithm. Recently, a new backtracking algorithm was presented to compute MCS in (Cao *et al.*, 2008). Although this method shows better accuracy, the MCS computation is still time-consuming. The third one is graph alignment (Frohlich *et al.*, 2005; Vert, 2008). Unfortunately, for such methods there is no easy way to index both measurements for large graph databases.

There are also other measurements. One method, GString (Jiang et al, 2007) is a subgraph similarity query method and uses graph fragments as features as well. The approach is somewhat different from the previous two feature-based subgraph search methods. Complex graphs are first reduced into connected graphs of fewer nodes, each of which represents a specific fragment. Canonical node numbering is used to create a string representation for each graph in a database. An index that supports similarity search is then constructed in the form of a suffix tree. This method combines the expressive power of subgraphs and simplified graphs with the speed of string querying and matching.

Chemical Similarity Search

Daylight fingerprints (Daylight fingerprints, 2008) is a well-known algorithm for chemical similarity search and is adopted as the default choice in databases such as PubChem (http://pubchem.ncbi.nlmnih.gov). Benefiting from such a system, researchers are able to do screening, designing and knowledge discovery from compound or molecule databases. In Daylight fingerprints, all paths up to a fixed length (e.g. 7) are retrieved as descriptors. A molecule is represented as a bit-string, indexed by the descriptors. Various similarity metric for bit-strings, such as the Taminoto index (Jacob et al., 2008), are used to measure the similarity of chemicals. Though fast, Daylight fingerprints provides only a coarse measurement of the true similarity of chemicals since majority of the features (i.e. paths) may not contribute to the chemical activity of the compounds and there is no feature selection step in the Daylight system. As evaluated in our own experimental study with 12 data sets, using all paths up to length 7 as features (the default parameter in Daylight system), Daylight fingerprints deliver the worst classification results among the five similarity measurements that we use, and provide results scarcely better than random guesses.

Subgraph Search

Many of the recent methods for subgraph search adopt a similar framework, decomposing graphs into a set of smaller pieces, treating each piece as a feature, and building a feature-based index structure for subgraph query. Methods that belong to this category include GraphGrep (Shasha *et al.*, 2002), *gIndex* (Yan *et al.*, 2004), *FG-Index* (Cheng *et al.*, 2007), *Tree+Delta* (Zhao *et al.*, 2007) and *GDIndex* (Williams *et al.*, 2007).

The simplest type of feature in use for graph indexing is walk (including path as special cases) as pioneered in *GraphGrep* (Shasha *et al.*, 2002). Paths are easy to retrieve and easy to work with. The simplicity of paths limits their expressiveness. For example, using paths, we could not distinguish the topology of a ring and a chain (where all paths from the two graphs are paths with different sizes).

Recognizing the limitation of paths, *gIndex* (Yan *et al.*, 2004) and *FG-Index* (Cheng *et al.*, 2007) build indices using general subgraphs, which can easily distinguish between paths and cycles in graphs and hence are more powerful. The limitation of subgraph features is that subgraph enumeration and matching are computational intensive procedures. In order to manage these obstacles, these methods extract only frequent subgraph features. Similar methods, *Tree+Delta* (Zhao *et al.*, 2007) and *TreePI* (Zhang *et al.*, 2007) use frequent tree patterns (as well as some discriminative graph features) instead of frequent subgraph patterns.

The method GDIndex (Williams *et al.*, 2007) also uses subgraphs as the basic index feature, but does not restrict itself to frequent subgraph features. In addition to a subgraph-based index, this method incorporates a hash table of subgraphs for fast isomorphism lookup. While this method's focus is subgraph search, it supports similarity search as well.

Approximate Subgraph Search

Besides strict subgraph search, some methods relax the isomorphism matching constraint and allow partial or approximate matches since in some applications where graphs, i.e. biological graphs, are often noisy and incomplete. This is a relatively new direction, and hence not many methods currently address the problem. One such method, *SAGA* (Tian *et al.*, 2007), was designed for biological pathway analysis. First, it builds an index based on graph fragments. Then it uses a graph distance measure to allow for vertex mismatches and gaps when candidate graphs are matched with a query.

Another method *gApprox* (Chen *et al.*, 2007) is similar to the *gIndex* (Yan *et al.*, 2004) method, in spirit and name, as well as authors. This approach seeks to mine frequent *approximate patterns* from a graph database and use these patterns for indexing. They also explore the notion of *approximately frequent*. The method *TALE* (Tian *et al.*, 2008) is also designed for approximate graph matching. It focuses, however, on handling large graphs with thousands of vertices and edges instead of large graph databases.

Graph Kernel Functions

Several graph kernel functions have been studied. The pioneering work was done by Haussler in his work on *R-convolution* kernel, providing a framework for many current graph kernel functions to follow (Haussler, 1999). The R-convolution kernel is based on the notion of decomposing a discrete structure (e.g. a graph) into a set of component objects (e.g. subgraphs). We can define much such decomposition, as well as kernels between pairs of component objects. The R-convolution framework ensures that no matter the choice of decompositions or component kernels, the result is always a symmetric, positive semi-definite function, or a kernel function between compound objects. This key insight allows the problem of finding kernel functions for discrete structures to be reduced to those of finding decompositions and kernel functions between component objects. The R-convolution kernel can be extended to allow weighting of the kernel between various components, via the Weighted Decomposition Kernel (Menchetti *et al.*, 2005).

Recent progresses of graph kernel functions could be roughly divided into two categories. The first group of kernel functions considers all possible components in a graph (e.g. all possible paths) and hence measures the global similarity of two graphs. These include product graph kernels (Gartner *et al.*, 2003), random walk based kernels (Kashima *et al.*, 2003), and kernels based on shortest paths between pair of nodes (Borgwardt and Kriegel, 2005). The second group of kernel functions tries to capture the local similarity of two graphs by specifying a (finite) subset of components and counting the shared components

only according to the finite subset of components. These include a large class of graph kernels called spectrum kernels [18] and recently frequent subgraph kernels (Smalter et al., 2008). The most efficient kernel function that we notice is proposed by Vishwanathan (Vishwanathan *et al.*, 2006) for global similarity measurement with complexity $O(n^3)$ where n is the maximal number of nodes in graphs. Different from global similarity measure, local similarity capturing is known to be expensive since subcomponent matching (e.g. subgraph isomorphism) is an NP-hard operation.

Graph kernel functions can provide a more accurate similarity measurement but until now they just can handle small databases(less than 10k) since the calculation of kernel matrix is very expensive. In this text, we adopt a recently develop graph wavelet matching kernel and make it scalable for large databases.

FAST GRAPH SIMILARITY SEARCH WITH HASH FUNCTIONS

As discussed above, current methods usually focus on either accuracy or speed. For example, graph query methods provide fast query time but not good similarity measurements. Kernel functions can provide better similarity measurement but the kernel matrix calculation is time-consuming so it is hard to build index structure by using them directly. To address this problem, we propose a new method, *G*-hash. Our proposed method defines similarity based on Wavelet Graph matching kernels (WA) and uses hash table as index structure to speed up graph similarity query.

Methodology

We first give an overview of *G*-hash shown in Figure 4. For graphs in database, firstly node vectors are calculated through extracting node features and using wavelet analysis shown later to exact local node features, and then a hash table is built. For query graphs, firstly node vectors are calculated, and then the nodes of query graphs are hashed into the hash table. Next, distances between query graph and library graphs are calculated and sorted. Finally, top k nearest neighbors are reported.

Node Feature and Local Feature Extraction

In this section, we show how to decompose graphs to node vectors through node feature and local feature extraction. Node features are extracted according to the need. They can be label of the node, histogram of immediate neighbor node labels and histogram of edge labels. For local feature extraction, we use wavelet analysis which will be discussed below in details.

Wavelet analysis method for local feature extraction contains two important concepts: *h-hop neighborhood* and *discrete wavelet functions*. The *h-hop neighborhood* of one node v, denoted by

$N_h(v)$, refers to a set of nodes which are h hops away from the node v according to the shortest path. *Discrete wavelet functions* refer to the defined wavelet functions, shown in Equation (5), applying to h-hop neighborhood.

$$\psi_{j,h} = \frac{1}{h+1} \int_{j/(h+1)}^{(j+1)/(h+1)} \varphi(x)dx \qquad (5)$$

where $\varphi(x)$ is *Haar* or *Mexican Hat* wavelet function and h is the hth partition after $\varphi(x)$ is partitioned into $h+1$ intervals on the domain $[0,1)$ and j is between 0 and h.

Based on the above two definitions, we can now apply wavelet analysis to graphs. Wavelet functions are used to create a measurement summarizing the local topology of a node. Equation (6) shows such a wavelet measurement, denoted by $\Gamma_h(v)$, for a node v in a graph G.

Figure 4. Flowchart of G-hash algorithm

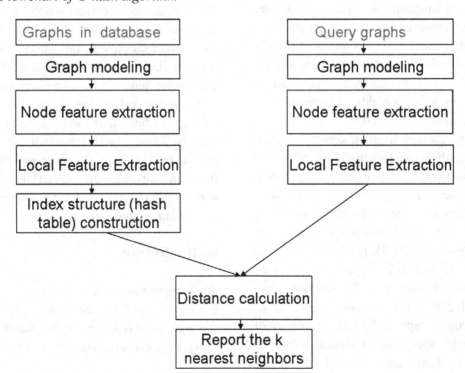

$$\Gamma_h(v) = C_{h,v} \times \sum_{j=0}^{h} \psi_{j,h} \times \bar{f}_j(v) \qquad (6)$$

where $C_{h,v}$ is a normalization factor with

$$C_{h,v} = \left(\sum_{j=0}^{h} \frac{\psi_{j,h}^2}{|N_h(v)|}\right)^{-1/2}, \qquad (7)$$

and $\bar{f}_j(v)$ is the average feature vector value of atoms that are at most j-hop away from v with

$$\bar{f}_j(v) = \frac{1}{|N_j(v)|} \sum_{u \in N_j(v)} f_u, \qquad (8)$$

where f_u denotes the feature vector value of the node v. Such feature vector value can be one of the following four types: nominal, ordinal, internal and ratio. For ratio and internal node features, we directly apply the above wavelet analysis to get local features. For nominal and ordinal node features, we could first build a histogram and then use wavelet analysis to extract local features. After the node v is analyzed, a list of vectors $\Gamma^h(v) = \{\Gamma_1(v), \Gamma_2(v), \cdots, \Gamma_h(v)\}$, called wavelet measurement matrix, can be obtained. The key idea is illustrated by an example shown in Figure 5 below. The output of the wavelet analysis is a set of local averages, indexed by the parameter diameter d. In other words, if each node has a n-element feature vector at the beginning of the wavelet analysis, each node will have a set of d feature vectors, each of which contains n elements after the wavelet analysis. In this way, a graph can be decomposed into a set of node vectors. Since the wavelet has strongly positive and strongly negative regions, these wavelet-compressed properties represent a comparison between the local and distant vertex neighborhood. Structural information of a graph has therefore been compressed into the vertex properties through

wavelets. Further details can be found in (Smalter *et al.*, 2008).

Hash-Based Approximating of Structure Matching Kernel

After graphs are composed into a set of node vectors, we can now ignore the topology and focus on matching vertices. A graph kernel is

Figure 5. Upper: chemical graph centered on vertex v, with adjacent vertices t and u. Vertices more than one hop away are labeled with the hop number, up to hop distance three. Lower: Super-position of a wavelet function on the chemical graph. Note that we can see the intensity of the wavelet function (per the color map) corresponds to the hop distance from the central vertex. In this figure, unlabeled vertices correspond to carbon (C); hydrogens are shown without explicit bonds (edges).

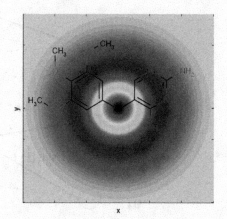

defined on these sets. Given two graphs G and G' for example, the graph matching kernel is

$$k_m(G, G') = \sum_{(u,v)\in V(G)\times V(G')} K(\Gamma^h(u), \Gamma^h(v)),$$
(9)

where K can be any kernel function defined in the co-domain of Γ. We call this function K_m a *structure matching kernel*. The following theorem indicates that K_m is symmetric and positive semi-definite and hence a kernel function.

Theorem 1. *The structure matching kernel is symmetric and positive semi-definite if the function K is symmetric and positive semi-definite.*

Proof sketch: The structure matching kernel is clearly symmetric if K is symmetric. The structure matching kernel is a special case of the *R-convolution* kernel and is hence positive semi-definite as proved in (Haussler, 1999).

We visualize the kernel function by constructing a weighted complete bipartite graph: connecting every node pair $(u,v) \in V[G] \times V[G']$ with an edge weighted by $K(\Gamma(u), \Gamma(v))$. In Figure 6, we show a weighted complete bipartite graph for $V[G] = \{v_1, v_2, v_3, v_4\}$ and $V[G'] = \{u_1, u_2, u_3\}$. From the figure we notice that if two nodes are quite dissimilar, the weight of the related edge is small. Since dissimilar node pairs usually outnumber similar node pairs, in our design, we use the RBF kernel function, as specified below, to penalize dissimilar node pairs.

$$K(X, Y) = e^{\frac{-\|X-Y\|_2^2}{2}}$$
(10)

where $\|X\|_2$ is the L_2 norm of the vector X.

The structure matching kernel shows a good definition of similarity between graphs, as validated in the experimental part (Smalter et al., 2008). One issue, however, is that the overall time complexity of the wavelet-matching kernel is $O(m^2)$, and that of the kernel matrix is $O(n^2 \times m^2)$, where n is the size of the database and m is the average node number of all graphs.

Figure 6. A schematic representation of the structure matching kernel. Highlighted edges (v1,u1),(v2,u1), (v3,u3),(v4,u2) have larger weights than the rest of the edges (dashed).

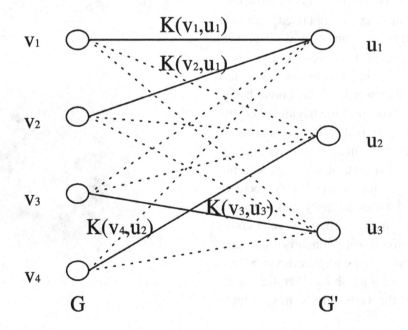

When the size of the database increases, the kernel matrix calculation time grows very quickly. Fortunately, we have the following two observations:

- When the node vector of node u in graph G is dramatically different from that of node v in the graph G', the RBF kernel value between node u and node v is small and has little contribution to the graph kernel. So if we just count those pairs of nodes which have similar node vectors, the kernel matrix will reflect almost the same similarity measurement between two graphs as that of WA method but the time will be saved.

- Similar objects in the hash table are positioned in the same cells if the hash keys are based on the node vectors. So the hash table can help us to find similar node pairs rapidly. Here similar node pair refers to the nodes with the same node vector. In addition, if all graphs in the database are hashed into the table, one cell may contain many similar nodes which belong to different graphs. Since these nodes are all similar, only one time RBF kernel calculation using two nodes of them is enough. Node overlay provides another chance to save time.

Based on the above two observations, we revise the structure matching kernel using an approximation as described below.

$$k_m(G, G') = \sum_{v \in G', u \in simi(v)} K(\Gamma^h(u), \Gamma^h(v)) \quad (11)$$

where $simi(v)$ is the node set containing nodes from graph G that are hashed to the same cell. Clearly, the similarity of two graphs is determined only by similar node pairs instead of all node pairs, which will save computational time. To further save time, since only similar nodes are

involved into the kernel calculation and we have $K(\Gamma^h(u), \Gamma^h(v)) \approx 1$ if the RBF kernel is used, the Equation (11) can be written into

$$k_m(G, G') \approx \sum_{v \in G', u \in simi(v)} 1 = \sum_{v \in G'} |simi(v)|, \quad (12)$$

where $|simi(v)|$ is the number of nodes contained in $simi(v)$. In other words, we only count the number of common nodes belonging to the graph G and G' in this version. We implemented both Equation (11) and (12), and the classification accuracy difference between them is minimal. We hence use Equation (12) for its simplicity.

Index Construction

As we mentioned before, hashing can help us to speed up the query processing. In this section, we will talk bout the construction of the index structure (hash table). After node vectors are obtained, the hash table will be built using graphs in the database. At this time, a hash function needs to be constructed to make sure that similar nodes can be hashed into the same cell. That means the hash keys should be associated with node vectors. Before we construct the hash key, we round the value of all numeric features to the nearest integer. The hash key is a string which concatenates all these features together delimited by underscores. Take the graph P shown in Figure 7 for example.

Example 2. *For simplicity, we apply the hash process to a single graph shown in Figure 7. We assume that we pick d = 0 and use the following features for each node in this example: the node label (a single feature) and the histogram of immediate neighbor label types (with three feature), with a total of 4 features. For example, the feature vector for node P_3 is [b, 2, 0, 1] since its label type is 'b', and it has two neighbors with node label 'a', zero neighbors with node label 'b', and one neighbor with node label 'c'. The feature vectors*

Figure 7. Example graph

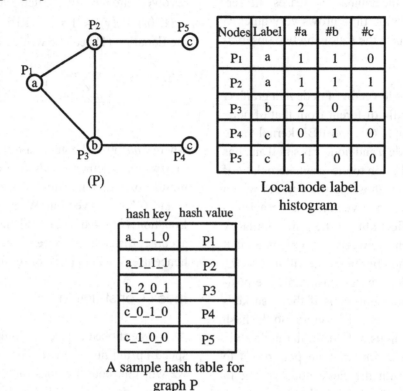

(P)

Nodes	Label	#a	#b	#c
P1	a	1	1	0
P2	a	1	1	1
P3	b	2	0	1
P4	c	0	1	0
P5	c	1	0	0

Local node label histogram

hash key	hash value
a_1_1_0	P1
a_1_1_1	P2
b_2_0_1	P3
c_0_1_0	P4
c_1_0_0	P5

A sample hash table for graph P

for all nodes are shown in the same Figure 7 and the sample hash table is shown in the bottom panel of Figure 7. Notice: In this framework, we assume no information for query graphs when we build the hash table for indexing.

k-NNs Query Processing

During the query processing, we first do the node feature exaction and local feature exaction on the query graph, then hash the nodes of the query graph into the hash table, and calculate the graph kernel according to the Equation (12). In the following, we show the connection between kernel functions and similarity search. The idea is to compute Euclidian distance of two objects between their embeddings in related Hilbert space according to the kernel function. According to Mercer's theorem (Scholopf and Smola, 2002), any symmetric and positive semi-definite function ensures

the existence of a Hilbert space H and a map $\phi : X \rightarrow H$ such that $k(x, x') = \langle \phi(x), \phi(x') \rangle$ for all $x, x' \in X$ where $\langle x, y \rangle$ denotes an inner product between two objects x and y.

Based on the Mercer's theorem, the distance of two objects, as measured in the related Hilbert space, is

$$
\begin{aligned}
d(G, G') &= \sqrt{\left\| \phi(G) - \phi(G') \right\|_2^2} \\
&= \sqrt{\langle \phi(G) - \phi(G'), \phi(G) - \phi(G') \rangle} \\
&= \sqrt{\langle \phi(G), \phi(G) \rangle + \langle \phi(G'), \phi(G') \rangle - 2 \langle \phi(G), \phi(G') \rangle} \\
&= \sqrt{k_m(G, G) + k_m(G', G') - 2 k_m(G, G')}.
\end{aligned}
$$

(13)

where $k_m(X, Y)$ is the structure matching kernel function between graph X and Y. With Equations (12) and (13), we compute distances between the query graph and graphs in a graph database. Finally, we obtain k nearest neighbors of the query graph. To illustrate the whole process of *G*-hash, we take graph G_1, G_2 and Q for example shown in figure 8.

Example 3. *We apply G-hash algorithm to three simple graphs shown in Figure 8. We assume that we pick d = 0 and use the same features as example 2. G_1 and G_2 are graphs in the graph database and Q is the query graph. The feature vectors for all nodes are shown on the right side of the same Figure 8 and the sample hash table is shown in the middle panel of Figure 8. After hashing the query graph into the hash table, we can calculate the distance as follows:* $k_m(G_1, Q) = 1$ since the graph Q just has one node (p5) is hashed to the same cell with the nodes in the graph

G. $k_m(G_1, G_1) = 3$, $k_m(Q, Q) = 5$

$$d(G_1, Q) = \sqrt{1 + 1 - 2\frac{1}{\sqrt{3} \times \sqrt{5}}} = 1.22.$$

Similarly,

$$d(G_2, Q) = \sqrt{1 + 1 - 2\frac{3}{\sqrt{4} \times \sqrt{5}}} = 0.81$$

$$d(G_2, Q) < d(G_1, Q),$$

so G_2 is more similar to Q compared with G_1.

Dynamic Insertion and Deletion

To insert a new graph into the database, we hash all nodes of the new graph into the hash table. After insertion, only those cells associated with these nodes contain more nodes and all other cells have no changes. In addition, since the new graph has a limited number of nodes, insertion operations involve less time and have little effect on the size of index structure. Deletion operations are similar to insertion. To delete a graph from the database, we calculate the key corresponding to each node in this graph and then delete each node from the cell containing them.

Experimental Study

We have performed a comprehensive evaluation of our method by evaluating its effectiveness (in classification), efficiency, and scalability. We will validate our method, *G*-hash, on chemical databases. For chemical compounds, node features include numeric features and boolean atom features. Numeric features include element type, atom partial charge, atom electron affinity, atom free electrons count and atom heavy valence, etc. Boolean atom features include atom in acceptor, atom in terminal carbon, atom in ring, atom is negative, atom is axial, etc. Here, we just use a single of atomic feature: element type for simplicity.

We have compared our methods with the Wavelet Alignment Kernel, *C* -tree, GraphGrep and gIndex as performance benchmarks. Our method, WA method, GrapGrep and gIndex are developed in C++ and compiled using g++. *C* -tree was developed in Java and compiled using Sun JDK1.5.0. All experiments were done on an Intel Xeon EM64T 3.2GHz, 4G memory cluster running Linux.

The parameters for WA, *G*-hash, *C*-tree, Graph-Grep and gIndex are set in the following way. We set *h*=1 and use *haar* wavelet function for WA and *G*-hash. For *C*-tree, we choose the default values, namely, setting the minimum number of child node *m*=20, the maximum number M=2m-1 and the NBM method (He and Singh, 2006) is used for graph mapping. For GraphGrep and gIndex, we use default parameters.

Data Sets

We chose a number of data sets for our experiments. The first five data sets are established data taken from Jorisson/Gilson Data Sets (Jorissen and Gilson, 2005). The next seven data sets are manually extracted from BindingDB data sets (Liu *et. al.*, 2007). The last one is NCI/NIH AIDS Antiviral Screen data set (http://dtp.nci.nih.gov/.). Table 1 shows these data sets and their statistical informa-

Figure 8. Example for G-hash algorithm

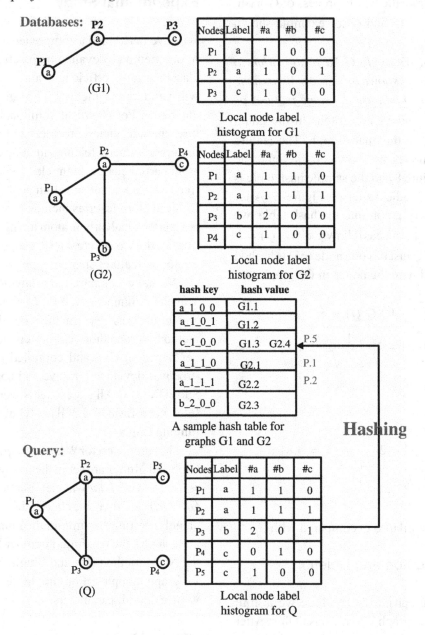

Databases:

(G1)

Nodes	Label	#a	#b	#c
P_1	a	1	0	0
P_2	a	1	0	1
P_3	c	1	0	0

Local node label
histogram for G1

(G2)

Nodes	Label	#a	#b	#c
P_1	a	1	1	0
P_2	a	1	1	1
P_3	b	2	0	0
P_4	c	1	0	0

Local node label
histogram for G2

hash key	hash value	
a_1_0_0	G1.1	
a_1_0_1	G1.2	
c_1_0_0	G1.3 G2.4	P.5
a_1_1_0	G2.1	P.1
a_1_1_1	G2.2	P.2
b_2_0_0	G2.3	

A sample hash table for
graphs G1 and G2

Hashing

Query:

(Q)

Nodes	Label	#a	#b	#c
P_1	a	1	1	0
P_2	a	1	1	1
P_3	b	2	0	1
P_4	c	0	1	0
P_5	c	1	0	0

Local node label
histogram for Q

tion. In the same table, positive compounds refer to those with higher activity values or binding to the target protein and negative compounds refer to those with lower activity values or not binding to the target protein.

The Jorissen data sets contain information about chemical-protein binding activity. The target values are drug's binding affinity to a par-ticular protein. There are five proteins for which 100 chemical structures are selected with 50 chemical structures clearly bind to the protein (called "active" ones) and the other 50 ones similar to the active ones but clearly not bind to the target protein. See the text (Jorissen and Gilson, 2005) for the further details.

Table 1. Data sets statistics. #S: total number of compounds, #P: number of positive compounds, #N: number of negative com- pounds, #Node: average number of nodes, #Edge: average number of edges.

Date Set	#S	#P	#N	#Node	#Edge
PDE5	100	50	50	44.7	47.2
CDK2	100	50	50	38.4	40.6
COX2	100	50	50	37.7	39.6
FXa	100	50	50	45.75	48.03
AIA	100	50	50	48.33	50.61
AChE	183	94	89	29.1	32.0
ALF	151	61	60	23.8	25.2
EGF-R	497	250	247	24.6	27.1
HIV-P	267	135	132	43.0	46.2
HSP90	109	55	54	29.84	32.44
MAPK	336	168	168	28.0	31.1
HIV-RT	482	241	241	22.18	24.39

The BindingDB database contains data for proteins and chemicals that bind to the proteins. We manually selected 6 proteins with a wide range of known interacting chemicals (ranging from tens to several hundreds). For the purpose of classification, we convert the real-valued binding activity measurements to binary class labels. This is accomplished by dividing the data set into two equal parts according to the median activity reading (we also deleted compounds whose activity value is equal to zero).

NCI/NIH AIDS Antiviral Screen data set contains 42,390 chemical compounds retrieved from DTP's Drug Information System. There is a total 63 types of atoms in this data set; the most frequent ones are C, O, N, and S. The data set contains three types of bonds: single-bond, double-bond and aromatic-bond. We selected all chemicals to build our graph database and randomly sampled 1000 chemicals as the query data set.

Similarity Measurement
Evaluation with Classification

We compared classification accuracy using k-NNs classifier on Jorissen sets and BindingDB

sets with different similarity measurement. For the WA method, we use wavelet matching kernel function to obtain kernel matrix, and then calculate distance matrix to obtain k nearest neighbors. For G-hash, we compute graph kernel according to our algorithmic study section and then calculate the k nearest neighbors. For C-tree, we directly retrieve the nearest neighbor. We used standard 5-fold cross validation to obtain classification accuracy, which is defined as $(TP+TN)/S$ where TP stands for true positive, TN stands for true negative and S is the total number of testing samples. We reported the average accuracy. In our experiments, we set $k = 5$.

The accuracy results are shown in Figure 9. The precision and recall results are shown in Table 2 and Table 3 respectively. The accuracy statistical information is shown in Table 4. From Figure 9, we know that C-tree has the worst performance and its performance is just a little better than random algorithm. G-hash outperforms C-tree on all twelve data sets, with at least 8% improvement on all of them. The average accuracy difference between G-hash and C-tree is about 13%. WA method outperforms G-hash, the average difference between them is about 2% because, most

Figure 9. Comparison of averaged classification accuracy over cross validation trials among G-hash, WA and C-tree methods

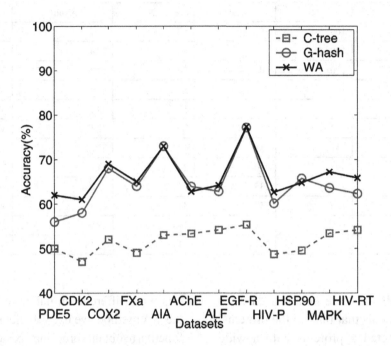

Table 2. Average Precision for different data sets. Asterisk (*) denotes the best precision for the data sets among WA, G-hash and C-tree methods.

Data Set	WA	*G*-hash	*C*-tree
PDE5	83.16*	75.78	31.20
CDK2	73.81*	67.42	51.82
COX2	75.88*	66.98	54.85
FXa	95.78*	91.19	29.36
AIA	98.93*	98.33	36.00
AChE	66.46	73.59*	62.63
ALF	72.14*	69.82	32.59
EGF-R	72.75	80*	55.41
HIV-P	56.90	64.64*	40.81
HSP90	58.19	73.63*	48.72
MAPK	66.31*	66.21	53.25
HIV-RT	69.38*	61.87	54.11

likely because, we adopt some simplifications on distance matrix calculation. From Table 2 and Table 3, we know that *C*-tree provides relatively low precision and recall which are less than 50% on half of these datasets. *G*-hash and WA are comparable on precision and recall. From what is discussed above, it is clear that kernel based similarity measurement is better than edit distance

194

Table 3. Average recall for different data sets. Asterisk (*) denotes the best recall for the data sets among WA, G-hash and C-tree methods.

Data Set	WA	*G*-hash	*C*-tree
PDE5	58.06*	56.20	46.93
CDK2	55.87*	53.54	46.70
COX2	63.57	68.06*	51.46
FXa	58.23	62.41*	42.06
AIA	64.81	66.27*	55.33
AChE	63.63*	62.82	44.15
ALF	61.25	66.16*	53.83
EGF-R	79.64*	77.51	55.81
HIV-P	63.40*	61.96	47.62
HSP90	65.30*	64.32	49.44
MAPK	70.52	73.61*	72.16
HIV-RT	67.78*	66.83	56.78

Table 4. Accuracy results statistical information for G-hash, C-tree and WA on all data sets.

Method	*G*-hash	*C*-tree	WA
average	64.55	51.64	66.23
deviation	2.68	5.95	4.83

based similarity measurement. Since the accuracy of k-NNs classifier is associated with the value of k, we also study the accuracy with respect to the value of k on these data sets to test whether the parameter k has any effect on accuracy performance comparison. We test the accuracy on the HIV-RT data set when the value of k is changed from 1 to 19. Figure 10 shows that accuracy performance comparison is insensitive to the parameter k.

Scalability

In this section, we apply *G*-hash, *C*-tree [28], GraphGrep [44] and gIndex [56] on NCI/NIH AIDS Antiviral Screen data set. Since WA method has no index structure, here we don't compare with it. We compare index size and average index construction time of different methods. Towards that end, we sampled different number of graphs ranging from 10,000 to 40,000. Figure 11 shows the index construction time in milliseconds with respect to the size of database for G-hash, *C*-tree, GraphGrep and gIndex.

gIndex method needs the longest time to build the index structure, then GraphGrep, *C*-tree and *G*-hash. The construction time of *G*-hash is much lower than that of other three methods because of the adoption of a hash table. In addition, when the data set size increases, the construction time of *C*-tree, GraphGrep and gIndex grows faster than that of *G*-hash since the construction of *C*-tree, GraphGrep and gIndex involve relatively complicated index structure. When the dataset size is 40,000, the construction time of gIndex, GraphGrep and *C*-tree are nearly 10,000 times, 1000 times and 100 times as that of *G*-hash respectively. So *G*-hash outperforms *C*-tree, Graph-Grep and gIndex on index construction time.

Figure 10. The average accuracy of EGF-R data set with different k value

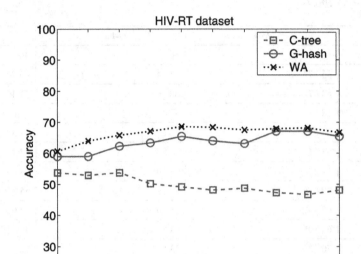

Figure 11. Index construction time for NCI/NIH AIDS data set

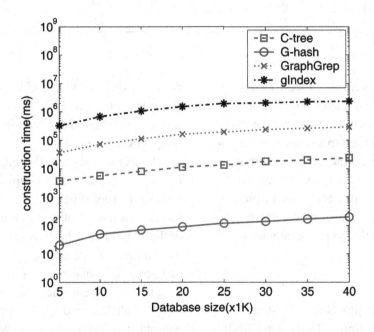

Figure 12 shows index size with respect to database size. C-tree needs the most space for the index structure, then GraphGrep, G-hash needs the smallest space. The index size of G-hash shows a steady growth with increasing database size while that of C-tree increases sharply since C-tree need to save the whole tree structure while G-hash just needs to save the hash table.

Figure 12. Index size for NCI/NIH AIDS data set

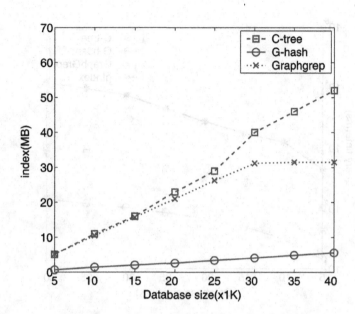

Figure 13 shows the query time in milliseconds with respect to the size of database. There is no direct way that we could compare *G*-hash and subgraph indexing methods such as gIndex and Graphgrep since *G*-hash search for similar graph and gIndex (and Graphgrep) searches for the occurrences of a subgraph in a database. In the following, we sketch one way to use subgraph indexing methods for similarity search. This method contains three steps: (i) randomly sample subgraphs from a query, (ii) use those subgraphs as features and compute the occurrences of the subgraphs in graph databases, and (iii) search for nearest neighbors in the obtained feature space. Clearly the overall query processing time depends on (i) how many subgraphs we use and (ii) how fast we can identify the occurrences of the subgraphs in a graph database. We estimate the lower bound of the overall query processing time by randomly sampling a SINGLE (one) subgraph from each of the 1000 querying graph and use subgraph indexing method to search for the occurrence of the subgraph. We record the average query processing time for each query. This query

processing time is clearly the lower bound since we use only one subgraph from the query graph.

Figure 13 shows gIndex needs the longest time to do the query. The query processing time for *C*-tree and GraphGrep are similar. *G*-hash is the most fast one. When the size of database is 40,000, the query time for *C*-tree, Graphgrep and gIndex are nearly 8 times, 10 times and 100 times as that for *G*-hash respectively. In addition, when the size of database increases, the query time for *G*-hash grows slowly while that for *C*-tree, GraphGrep and gIndex increases a lot. Finally, we compared *C*-tree and *G*-hash with varying *k* values for *k*-NNs search. The results are shown in Figure 14. The query time of *C*-tree increases with the increasing *k* and the running time of *G*-hash is insensitive to the number of *k*.

APPLICATION OF SIMILARITY SEARCH IN CHEMICAL DATABASES

G-hash shows the feasibility in the application of similarity search in chemical databases in

Figure 13. Query time for NCI/NIH AIDS data set

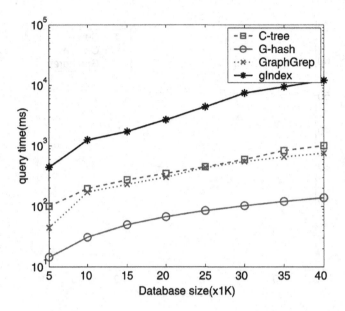

Figure 14. Query time with respect to different k for k-NN query

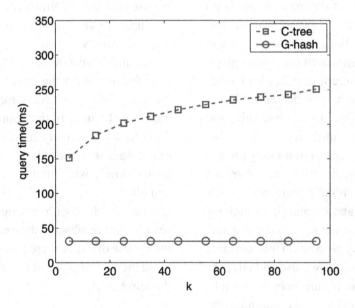

last section. But we just took the chemicals as general graphs and ignored the rich information contained in the structure of chemicals. In this chapter, we focus on application of *G*-hash in chemical databases.

It has been a challenge in bioinformatics to develop computational techniques to elucidate the roles of small organic molecules in biological systems. Traditionally the computational analysis of chemicals was done mainly within pharmaceutical companies for therapeutics discovery, and it was estimated that only 1% of chemical information is in the public domain (Dobson, 2004). This situation, however, has been changed dramatically in the last few years. With the Chemical Genetics Initiative and the Molecular Library Initiative started by NIH in 2002(Tolliday *et al.*, 2006), and 2004(Austin *et al.*, 2004), respectively, publicly-available, digitalized data grow exponentially fast. The PubChem database, just to name an example, contains structures of more than 18 million chemical compounds.

With the rapid growth of public chemical databases, fast similarity search in large chemical databases has started to attract intensive research attentions. There are two approaches for similarity search whether 2D or 3D. Most 3D methods compare three-dimensional shapes using a range of molecular descriptors which are in one way or another related to the geometry of the molecule, such as (Ballester and Richards, 2007; Rush *et al.*,2005). Such methods provide fast query processing in large chemical databases but relatively poor accuracy since they may lose more information during compressing the three-dimensional shapes. Here we focus on the second approach since many researches has shown that structure based methods provide an efficient way to do the query. Current similarity measurement of chemicals used in such type of approach may be roughly divided into four categories. The first and by far the most widely used method is to embed chemical structures in a high dimensional feature space, e.g. through daylight fingerprints (Daylight fingerprints, 2008) with the Tanimoto distance (Girke *et al.*, 2005). This strategy is adopted as the default choice in databases such as PubChem. The second method utilizes the largest common subgraph approach to measure the similarity of two chemical structures. Two graph represented chemicals are "similar" if the graph representations share a large common subgraph and "dissimilar" otherwise (Cao *et al.*, 2008). Third, graph editing distance is utilized to measure the similarity of chemical structures (he and Singh, 2006).

Finally graph alignment algorithms have been recently utilized to measure similarity of chemicals (Frohlich et al., 2005; Vert, 2008). Though these methods have been successfully applied in chemoinformatics research, as evaluated in our experimental study, none of them has achieved the goal of fast and effective similarity search in chemical databases, i.e. having computational efficiency in scaling to large chemical databases and computational efficiency in capturing the intrinsic similarity of graphs. With the fast growing of chemical databases, fast, effective, and indexable approaches are needed.

As mentioned above, our method, *G*-hash, can meet this need since it can quickly provide more accurate results for similarity search in graph databases and chemical databases can also regarded as graph databases. To apply *G*-hash to similarity search in chemical databases, we need to extract some specific chemical features which will be shown below.

Chemical Query Processing Overview

Application of G-hash to chemical databases follows the below steps. In index construction, we utilize the following steps:

1. For each chemical in the chemical database, extract node features for each atom in the chemical
2. Using graph wavelet analysis, extract local features for each atom in the chemical
3. Discretize the combined features and hash the atoms in a hash table.

In the query processing phase, we utilize the following steps:

1. For the query chemical, extract node and local features for each atom in the chemical

2. Discretize the combined features and hash the atoms in a hash table using the same procedure in index construction

3. Compute distances of the query chemical to the rest of chemicals use Equations (13).

4. Report the k nearest neighbors.

Chemical Node Feature Extraction

In the experimental part, we use the same chemical datasets as before to test G-hash method. But at that time, we just use atom type for the node feature and although the results of G-hash are better than C -tree and WA, the accuracy, precision and recall are still not high. To effectively apply G-hash to chemical databases, we need to dive into specific properties of compounds to extract more features. In the following table, we summarize a few features that we may compute for each node in a graph represented chemical compound. We divide these features to three groups: numeric node features, boolean node features, and boolean edge features (see Table 5). All these features can be computed using various chemoinformatics tools including the software package JOELib ((Frohlich et al., 2005). The meaning of the features should be clear from their names. For further details of these features see the literature (Frohlich et al., 2005).

In our experimental study, to simplify kernel function computation we sampled several features from the list. The node features that we use are the atom type, the histogram of atom types of immediate neighbor of the node, the local functional group information, and the histogram of the (immediate) chemical bond information. The atom type of the node is a single number. For histogram of neighboring atom types, we collect information for C, N, O, S, and group the rest to "others" to save spaces and hence we have a total of five numbers. For local functional group information, we collect whether the node is in a 5-node ring, a 6-node ring, a high-order ring, a branch, or a path, as did in (Cheng *et al.*, 2008) and hence have a single number. For the histogram of the (immediate) chemical bond information, we have three numbers corresponding to single, double, and aromatic bonds. Figure 15 shows an example for a chemical graph.

Example 4. *Here we apply the hash process to the single graph shown inFigure 3whose nodes are numbered with p1, p2, p3, p4, p5, p6 shown inFigure 15. We assume d=0 and each node has 10 features. For example, the feature vector for the node with a label of 'S' is [016,1,0,0,0,0,4,1,0,0] since its atomic number is '16'; it has only one neighbor with node label 'C', zero neighbor with node label 'N', zero neighbor with node label of 'O', zero neighbor with node label of 'S', and zero neighbor with node label of other atom symbol; it is in a path; and it connects with the neighbor through only one single bond. The feature vectors for all nodes are also shown in the Figure 15 and the sample hash table is shown in the bottom panel of Figure 15.*

In the previously mentioned node extraction method, we (almost) ignore the topology of the chemical compound completely by focusing on atom physical and chemical properties. To add

Table 5. We divide node and edge features into three groups: numeric node features (N Numeric), boolean node features (N Boolean), and boolean edge features (E Boolean).

N Numeric	N Boolean	E Boolean
Van D. Waals Volume	In Acceptor	In Aromatic
Partial Charge	In Donor	In Ring
#Free Electrons	In Aromatic	Is Carbonyl
Electron Affinity	In Ring	Is Amide
Hybridization	Is Chiral	Is Ester
Mass	Is Terminal Carbon	Is Rotomer

topology information, we utilize a technique called the graph wavelet analysis (Smalter *et al.*, 2008). The output of the wavelet analysis is a set of local averages, indexed by the parameter diameter d.

Finally we compute distances between the query chemical and chemicals in a chemical database to obtain the k nearest neighbors of the query chemical. The idea is to compute the Euclidian distance of two objects between their embeddings in the related Hilbert space according to a kernel function.

Experimental Study

We have performed a comprehensive evaluation of our method by evaluating the classification effectiveness and scalability for large chemical databases. We have compared our method with other related methods including the Daylight fingerprints, Wavelet Alignment Kernel, *C*-tree, GraphGrep, gIndex. For *G*-hash, we extract 30 features for each node. We used the OpenBabel software package to compute Daylight Fingerprints and *k*-nearest neighbors (http://openbabel. org/wiki/Fingerprint). For WA, we set the diameter

Figure 15. An example graph, related feature vectors, and the hash table contents

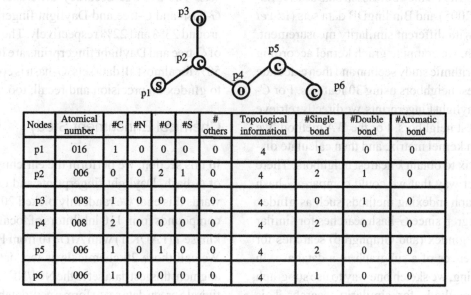

Nodes	Atomical number	#C	#N	#O	#S	# others	Topological information	#Single bond	#Double bond	#Aromatic bond
p1	016	1	0	0	0	0	4	1	0	0
p2	006	0	0	2	1	0	4	2	1	0
p3	008	1	0	0	0	0	4	0	1	0
p4	008	2	0	0	0	0	4	2	0	0
p5	006	1	0	1	0	0	4	2	0	0
p6	006	1	0	0	0	0	4	1	0	0

hash key	hash value
016_1_0_0_0_0_4_1_0_0	p1
006_0_0_2_1_0_4_2_1_0	p2
008_1_0_0_0_0_4_0_1_0	p3
008_2_0_0_0_0_4_2_0_0	p4
006_1_0_1_0_0_4_2_0_0	p5
006_1_0_0_0_0_4_1_0_0	p6

$d = 2$ and use *haar* wavelet function. For *C*-tree, GraphGrep and gIndex, we use default parameters. All methods, except *C*-tree, were implemented using the C++ programming language and compiled using g++ with -O3 optimization. *C*-tree was developed in Java and compiled using SUN JDK1.5.0. We performed our experiments on a Linux cluster where each node has a dual-core Intel Xeon EM64T 3.2GHz processor and 4G memory running CentOS 4.

Similarity Measurement Evaluation with Classification

We have compared classification accuracy using *k*-NN classifier on the 12 Jorissen data sets (Jorissen *et al.*, 2005) and BindingDB data sets (Liu *et al.* 2007) with different similarity measurement. For *G*-hash, we compute graph kernel according to our algorithmic study section and then calculate the *k* nearest neighbors using 30 features. For *C*-tree and Daylight Fingerprints, we directly retrieve the *k* nearest neighbors. For the WA method, we first obtain kernel matrix, and then calculate distance matrix to obtain *k* nearest neighbors. There is no direct way that we could compare *G*-hash and subgraph indexing methods such as gIndex and Graphgrep since *G*-hash searches for similar graph and gindex (and Graphgrep) searches for the occurrences of a subgraph in a database. In the following, we sketch one way to use subgraph indexing methods for similarity search. This method contains three steps: (i) randomly sample subgraphs from a query, (ii) use those subgraphs as features and compute occurrences of the subgraphs in graph databases, and (iii) search for nearest neighbors in the obtained feature space. Clearly, the accuracy depends on the number of features. Here we pick 20 features for gIndex.

We used standard 5-fold cross validation to obtain classification accuracy, and reported the average accuracy, precision and recall in the cross validation experiments. We have tested different *k* values ranging from 3 to 11 in classifications. The

quality of the results are similar and hence we only report results with $k = 5$. The accuracy is shown in Figure 16. The precision and recall results are shown in Table 6 and Table 7 respectively. The accuracy results statistical information is shown in Table 8. *C*-tree and Daylight fingerprints show the worst performance. They just are a little better than the random guess. WA method is better than them since its similarity measurement is based on kernel function. gIndex based similarity measurement and *G*-hash has similar classification performance with about 78% of average accuracy and outperform others. *G*-hash outperforms *C*-tree and Daylight fingerprints on all twelve data sets, with at least 18% improvement on most of data sets. The average accuracy difference between *G*-hash and *C*-tree and Daylight fingerprints are around 23% and 22% respectively. The precision of *C*-tree and Daylight fingerprints are lower than 50% for almost all data sets. *G*-hash is comparable to gIndex on precision and recall, too.

Chemical Enrichment Study

In this section, we perform the enrichment study of *G*-hash, Daylight fingerprints and *C*-tree. Towards this end, we randomly picked 20 chemical compounds from 110 inhibitors of focal adhesion kinase 1 (FADK 1) with AID810 from PubChem. We call those 20 chemicals as test data set. We augment this test data set to the NCI/NIH AIDS Antiviral Screen data set to form a new database. Then we pick one chemical from these 20 chemicals as the query chemical to search the new database and retrieve 100 nearest neighbors. According to these 100 results, we calculate the "precision" curve. Specifically, for the top *k* similarity compound, we compute precision as the percentage of chemicals in the top *k* compounds belonging to the true 19 hits and plot the change of precision along with the number of retrieved chemicals.

Obviously, the high precision shows good performance. After repeating the above steps for 20 times, we calculate the average precision

Figure 16. Comparison of averaged classification accuracy over cross validation trials among G-hash, WA, C-tree, Daylight fingerprint and gIndex methods

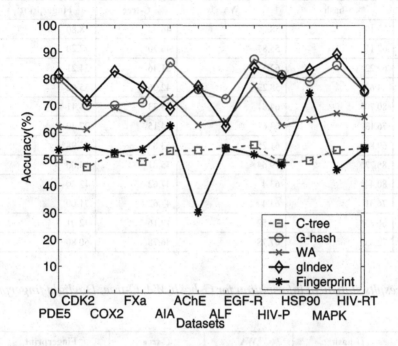

Table 6. Average Precision for different data sets. Asterisk (*) denotes the best precision for the data sets among G-hash, WA, C-tree, Daylight fingerprint and gIndex methods.

Data Set	*G*-hash	WA	*C*-tree	Fingerprint	gIndex
PDE5	95.48	83.16	31.2	53.02	96.0*
CDK2	78.87	73.81	51.82	57.23	87.81*
COX2	92.40*	75.88	54.85	51.62	82.00
FXa	96.93*	95.78	29.36	52.80	93.23
AIA	96	98.93	36	64.61	99.00*
AChE	77	66.46	62.63	27.80	79.62*
ALF	77.38	72.14	32.59	55.61	82.88*
EGF-R	88.62	72.75	55.41	52.42	96.40*
HIV-P	83.64	56.9	40.81	46.99	95.22*
HSP90	85.66	58.19	48.72	76.57	93.00*
MAPK	84.01	66.31	53.25	44.40	95.79*
HIV-RT	80.93	69.38	54.11	54.20	84.61*

curve shown in Figure 17. Although Daylight fingerprints performs better than *C*-tree, both of them show the low precision. *G*-hash performs much better than Daylight fingerprints and *C*-tree.

From Figure 17, we see that the precision is about 0.85 when the total number of retrieved chemicals is equal to 19 for *G*-hash which means that 16 chemicals in the test data are contained in the

Table 7. Average recall for different data sets. Asterisk (*) denotes the best precision for the data sets among G-hash, WA, C-tree, Daylight fingerprint and gIndex methods.

Data Set	*G*-hash	WA	*C*-tree	Fingerprint	gIndex
PDE5	73.19	58.06	46.93	58.80	73.60*
CDK2	67.17	55.87	46.70	47.20	67.82*
COX2	64.22	63.57	51.46	54.21	87.01*
FXa	64.63	58.23	42.06	55.62	71.19*
AIA	80.70*	64.81	55.33	54.41	60.20
AChE	76.13	63.63	44.15	27.40	85.20*
ALF	69.84	61.25	53.83	75.98*	65.00
EGF-R	86.22*	79.64	55.81	54.00	81.61
HIV-P	80.44*	63.4	47.62	42.20	75.40
HSP90	76.31	63.4	47.62	71.00	91.38*
MAPK	86.83*	70.52	72.16	42.01	85.79
HIV-RT	72.83	67.78	56.78	60.80	73.40*

Table 8. Average results statistical information for G-hash, WA, C-tree, Daylight fingerprint and gIndex methods

Method	*G*-hash	WA	*C*-tree	Fingerprint	gIndex
Average	77.81	66.23	51.64	52.92	77.83
Derivation	6.29	4.83	2.68	10.03	7.51

top 19 nearest neighbors of the query chemical. The result is as same as what we expected. Edit distance based similarity measurement used by *C*-tree prefers large graphs. For Daylight fingerprints, two graphs sharing more small substructures or patterns are considered to be similar. But as we all know, the connection or position of these substructures also determines the similarity of graphs. Our method, *G*-hash, not only consider the number of common small substructures but also consider the connection between them through using features reflecting local topological information and chemical information.

Robustness

In this section, we evaluate the robustness of *G*-hash by using four different feature sets for the enrichment study mentioned above. In the first set of features, we use 10 features as discussed before. For other three data sets, we use wavelet analysis to extract features from the local region centered at the particular node. We use $d = 1$ with 10 additional features, $d = 2$ with 20 additional features and $d = 3$ with 30 additional features. So we have 4 feature sets with sizes 10, 20, 30 and 40. The average precision curves over 20 queries and the optimal precision curve are shown in Figure 18. We draw the optimal precision curve in this way: if the number is retrieved chemicals is less than 19, the precision is equal to 1; otherwise, the precision is equal to 19 over the number of retrieved chemicals. *G*-hash with 10 features shows the worst performance which is similar to that of *C*-tree and Daylight fingerprints shown in Figure 17. *G*-hash with 20 features has a large

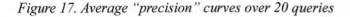

Figure 17. Average "precision" curves over 20 queries

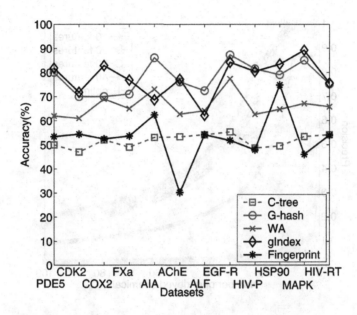

improvement. *G*-hash with 30 features gives the best performance which is near to the optimal performance. *G*-hash with 40 features has a little worse performance than *G*-hash with 30 features. With less features, more nodes pairs are hashed into the same cell. This case prefers those graphs sharing too many small subcomponents. With more features, just a few nodes pairs are hashed into the same cell. This case prefers those small graphs. Therefore the distance between graphs can not accurately represent their similarity with too large or small feature sets.

Scalability

We compare index size and average index construction time for different methods. Towards that end, we have sampled different number of graphs ranging from 5,000 to 40,000. Figure 19 shows the index construction time in milliseconds with respect to the size of database for *G*-hash, *C*-tree, GraphGrep, gIndex and Daylight fingerprints. The construction time for *G*-hash is much less than

those for other four methods with a speed-up up to three orders of magnitudes.

Figure 20 shows the sizes of constructed indexes with respect to different database sizes. The index size of *G*-hash grows slowly with increasing database size while that of *C*-tree increases sharply. Daylight fingerprints method shows a very similar scalability to that of *G*-hash. A sharp index size increase also is observed for GraphGrep. We did not show the index size of gindex since the size is much larger than the rest of the methods. For example, gIndex takes 7.2 MB index spaces for 5,000 chemicals and 20.9MB for 10,000 chemicals.

There is no direct way that we could compare *G*-hash and subgraph indexing methods such as gIndex and Graphgrep and we use the way that we outlined before (random sample a few subgraphs from the query graph and then perform subgraph query search). Clearly the overall query processing time depends on the many subgraphs we sample. To estimate the lower bound of the overall query processing time, we randomly sample a SINGLE (one) subgraph from

Figure 18. Average precision curves over 20 queries for G-hash with different feature sets

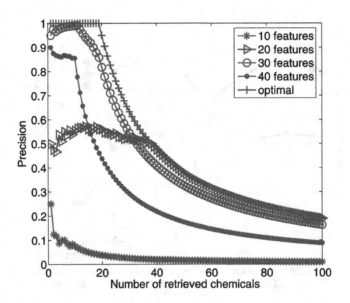

Figure 19. Index construction time for NCI/NIH AIDS data set

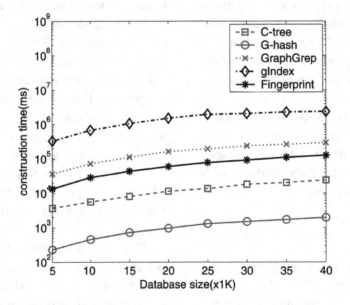

each of the 1000 querying graph and use subgraph indexing method to search for occurrences of subgraphs. We record the average query processing time for each query. This query processing time is clearly the lower bound since we use only one subgraph from the query graph. Figure 21 shows the average query time (over 1000 randomly samples query chemicals) of different index methods in milliseconds with respect to the size of database. gIndex is the worst one. Daylight

Figure 20. Index size for NCI/NIH AIDS data set

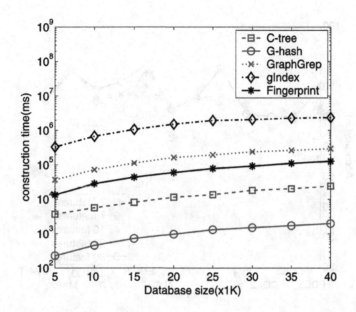

Figure 21. Query time for NCI/NIH AIDS data set

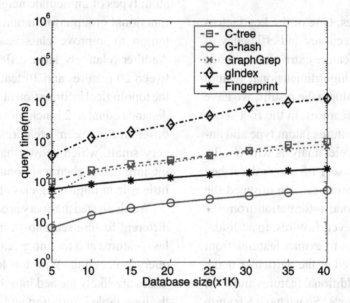

fingerprints performs the query faster than *C*-tree and GraphGrep which are comparable. *G*-hash is the fastest one. When the size of database increases, *G*-hash scales better than Daylight Fingerprints, with around an order of magnitude speedup. *G*-hash performs better than *C*-tree, with two orders of magnitude speedup.

Figure 22. Average accuracy for different feature sets

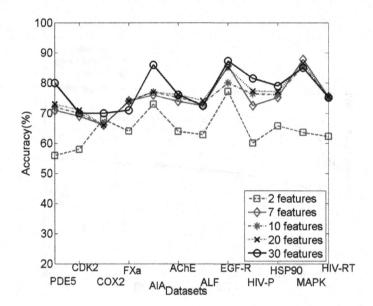

Discussion

Feature Set Influences. One of the key factors for determining both accuracy and efficiency of *G*-Hash method is the feature extraction methods that maps nodes to a high-dimensional feature space Γ. In order to evaluate the results, we have compared five sets of features. In the first set of features, we use two features (atom type and another feature from wavelet analysis with $d = 1$). In the second set, we use 10 features described before. In the third feature set, we dropped the immediate chemical bond information from the first set and obtained seven features. In addition, we use wavelet analysis to extract features from the local region centered at the particular node. We use $d = 1$ with 10 additional features and $d = 2$ with 20 additional features. So we have 5 feature sets with sizes 2, 7, 10, 20, and 30.

We have tested the classification accuracy with different feature sets. The average accuracy on 12 datasets is shown in Figure 22. When more features are used, we can obtain better results. The largest difference happens between 2 features

and 7 features, which means that the histogram of atom types of immediate neighbors and the local functional group information make a big contribution to improve classification performance. Another relatively large difference happens between 20 features and 30 features, which means the topological information of neighbors with hop distance equal to 2 much more makes sense. The difference between 7 features and 10 features is very small, which shows that the histogram of the immediate chemical bond information plays little role in improving classification accuracy.

We also tested the query processing time among different feature sets shown in Table 9. Both too less features and too more features will speed up query processing. With too less features, many nodes are likely hashed into the same cell so that the hash table is too short and less query processing time is needed. With more features, nodes are more likely to be hashed to different cells. If too more features are used so that nodes of the query graph just are hashed into a few cells and hence we could speed up query processing time. So to obtain both good classification performance and

Table 9. Average query running time for different number of features with different database sizes

#of features	Average Running Time(ms)			
	10k	**20k**	**30k**	**40k**
2	30.97	67.71	102.9	139.39
7	109.12	219.2	333.86	451.96
10	107.01	233.13	355.69	471.22
20	23.3	56.6	80.76	113.74
30	14.67	29.94	44.71	61.16

fast query processing, relatively more features should be used. In our case, the feature set with 30 features is the best choice.

CONCLUSION AND FUTURE WORK

Graphs are a kind of general structural data that have been widely applied in many fields such as chemoinformatics and bioinformatics, among others. A lot of significant researchers have been attracted to current data management and mining techniques. Proposing an efficient similarity graph query method is a significant challenge since most existing methods focus on speed and provide poor accuracy. In order to address this problem, we have presented a new graph query method, *G*-hash. In our method, graphs are represented by node vectors describing each graph vertex and the similarity measurement is defined via a kernel function based on a hash table index structure. To avoid losing a great deal of information in the rich graph structure, we compressed much of the topological information into feature vectors. The usage of hash table makes sure that it is fast to locate similar nodes if the hash keys are based on these node vectors and hence similar objects in the hash table are positioned in the same cells. Through our experimental study, we have shown that *G*-hash method achieves the state-of-the-art performance for *k*-NNs classification. Most importantly, the new similarity measurement and the index structure are scalable to large databases with

smaller indexing size, faster indexing construction time, and faster query processing time.

G-hash provides a new way to do similarity search in large chemical databases since chemicals can be represented by graphs. The experimental study validates *G*-hash has the advantages over other methods such as Daylight fingerprints, *C*- tree, GraphGrep and gIndex, i.e. having computational efficiency in scaling to large chemical databases and computational efficiency in capturing the intrinsic similarity of chemicals. In all, the experimental study shows the effectiveness and feasibilities of *G*-hash in the application of querying in chemical databases. In addition, to make our method open to other researchers and easy to use, we also developed an online server for similarity search in chemical databases.

Although *G*-hash showed good performance as discussed above, it still can't handle very large databases containing millions of graphs. Therefore, in the next step, we will work on the index structure improvement to extend our method to effectively perform similarity query in those very graph databases

REFERENCES

Austin, C., Brady, L., Insel, T., & Collins, F. (2004). NIH molecular libraries initiative. *Science, 306*(5699), 1138–1139. doi:10.1126/science.1105511

Ballester, P. J., & Richards, W. G. (2007). Ul-trafast shape recognition for similarity search in molecular databases. *In Proceedings of the ROYAL SOCIETY A.*

Berman, H. M., Westbrook, J., Feng, Z., Gilliland, G., Bhat, T. N., & Weissig, H. (2000). The protein data bank. *Nucleic Acids Research, 28.*

Berretti, S., Bimbo, A. D., & Vicario, E. (2001). Efficient matching and indexing of graph models in content-based retrieval. *IEEE Transactions on Pattern Analysis and Machine Intelligence, 23*(10), 1089–1105. doi:10.1109/34.954600

Borgwardt, K., & Kriegel, H. (2005). Shortest-path kernels on graphs. *Proceedings of the 5th International Conference on Data Mining*, Washington, DC, USA (pp. 74-81).

Cao, Y., Jiang, T., & Girke, T. (2008). A maximum common substructure-based algorithm for searching and predicting drug-like compounds. *Bioinformatics (Oxford, England), 24*(13), i366–i374. doi:10.1093/bioinformatics/btn186

Chen, C., Yan, X. F., Zhu, F. D., & Han, J. W. (2007). Gapprox: Mining frequent approximate patterns from a massive network. *Proceedings of 7th IEEE International Conference on Data Mining*, Omaha, Nebraska, USA (pp. 445-450).

Cheng, H., Yan, X. F., Han, J. W., & Hsu, C. W. (2007). Discriminative frequent pattern analysis for effective classification. *Proceedings of the 23rd IEEE International Conference on Data Engineering* (pp. 716-725).

Cheng, J., Yu, J. X., Ding, B., Yu, P. S., & Wang, H. (2008). Fast graph pattern matching. *Proceedings of the 24th IEEE International Conference on Data Engineering*, Cancun, Mexico (pp. 913-922).

Collobert, R., & Bengio, S. (2001). SVMTorch: Support vector machines for large-scale regression problems. *Journal of Machine Learning Research, 1*, 143–160. doi:10.1162/15324430152733142

Cook, S. A. (1971). The complexity of theorem-proving procedures. *Proceedings of the 3rd Annual ACM Symposium on Theory of Computing (pp. 151-158)*. New York, USA: ACM.

Crovella, M., & Kolaczyk, E. (2003). Graph wavelets for spatial traffic analysis. *Proceedings of the 22nd Annual Joint Conference of the IEEE. Computer Communications, 3*, 1848–1857.

Daylight fingerprints (2008). Software available at http://www.daylight.com.

Deshpande, M., Kuramochi, M., & Karypis, G. (2005). Frequent sub-structure-based approaches for classifying chemical compounds. *IEEE Transactions on Knowledge and Data Engineering, 17*(8), 1036–1050. doi:10.1109/TKDE.2005.127

Dobson, C. (2004). Chemical space and biology. *Nature, 432*(7019), 824–828. doi:10.1038/nature03192

Faloutsos, M., Faloutsos, P., & Faloutsos, C. (1999). On power-law relationships of the Internet topology. *Proceedings of the Conference on Applications, Technologies. Architectures. And Protocols for Computer Communication, New York, USA* (251-262).

Fermandez, M. L., & Valiente, G. (2001). A graph distance metric combining maximum common subgraph and minimum common supergraph. *Pattern Recognition Letters, 22*(6-7), 753–758. doi:10.1016/S0167-8655(01)00017-4

Fortin, S. (1996). *The graph isomorphism problem*. Technical Report. The University of Alberta.

Frohlich, H., Wegner, J. K., Sieker, F., & Zell, A. (2005). Optimal assignment kernels for attributed molecular graphs. *Proceedings of the 22nd International Conference on Machine Learning*, New York, USA (vol. 119, pp. 225-232).

Fu, K. S. (1986). A step towards unification of syntactic and statistical pattern recognition. *IEEE Transactions on Pattern Analysis and Machine Intelligence, 8*(3), 398–404. doi:10.1109/TPAMI.1986.4767800

Gartner, T., Flach, P., & Wrobel, S. (2003). On graph kernels: Hardness results and efficient alternatives. *Proceedings of the 16th Annual Conference on Computational Learning Theory and 7th Kernel Workshop* (pp. 129-143).

Girke, T., Cheng, L., & Raikhel, N. (2005). Chemmine: A compound mining database for chemical genomics. *Plant Physiology, 138*, 573–577. doi:10.1104/pp.105.062687

Haussler, D. (1999). *Convolution kernels on discrete structures. Technical Report (UCSC-CRL099-10), Computer Science Department.* UC Santa Cruz.

He, H., & Singh, A. K. (2006). Closure-tree: An index structure for graph queries. *Proceedings of International Conference on Data Engineering,* Atlanta, Georgia, USA (p. 38).

Jacob, L., Hoffmann, B., Stoven, V., & Vert, J. P. (2008). *Virtual screening of GPCRs: An in silico chemogenomics approach* (Technical Report HAL-00220396). French Center for Computational Biology.

Jiang, H., Wang, H., Yu, P. S., & Zhou, S. (2007). Gstring: A novel approach for efficient search in graph databases. *Proceedings of International Conference on Data Engineering* (pp. 566-575).

Jorissen, R., & Gilson, M. (2005). Virtual screening of molecular databases using a support vector machine. *Journal of Chemical Information and Modeling, 45*(3), 549–561. doi:10.1021/ci049641u

Kashima, H., Tsuda, K., & Inokuchi, A. (2003). Marginalized kernels between labeled graphs. *Proceedings of the International Conference on Machine Learning,* 321-328.

Liu, C., Yan, X., Fei, L., Han, J., & Midkiff, S. P. (2005). Sober: Tatistical odel-based bug localization. *Proceedings of the 10th European Software Engineering Conference* (vol. 30, pp. 286-295).

Liu, T., Lin, Y., Wen, X., Jorrisen, R. N., & Gilson, M. (2007). Bindingdb: A Web-accessible database of experimentally determined protein-ligand binding affinities. *Nucleic Acids Research, 35,* D198–D201. doi:10.1093/nar/gkl999

Maggioni, M., Bremer, J. C. Jr, Coifman, R., & Szlam, A. (2005). Biorthogonal diffusion wavelets for multiscale representations on manifolds and graphs. *Proceedings of the Society of Photographic Instrumentation Engineers, 5914,* 543–555.

McHugh, J., Abiteboul, S., Goldman, R., Quass, D., & Widon, J. (1997). Lore: A database management system for semistructured data. *SIGMOD Record, 26*(3), 54–66. doi:10.1145/262762.262770

Menchetti, S., Costa, F., & Frasconi, P. (2005). Weighted decomposition kernels. *Proceedings of the 22nd International Conference on Machine Learning (pp. 585–592).*

Messmer, B. T., & Bunke, H. (1998). A new algorithm for error-tolerant subgraph isomorphism detection. *IEEE Transactions on Pattern Analysis and Machine Intelligence, 20*(5), 493–504. doi:10.1109/34.682179

Raymond, J. W., & Willet, P. (2002). Maximum common subgraph isomorphism algorithms for the matching of chemical structures. *Journal of Computer-Aided Molecular Design, 16,* 521–533. doi:10.1023/A:1021271615909

Rush, T. S. III, Grant, J. A., Mosyak, L., & Nicholls, A. (2005). A shape-based 3-D scaffold hopping method and its application to a bacterial protein-protein interaction. *Journal of Medicinal Chemistry, 48*, 1489–1495. doi:10.1021/jm040163o

Sanfeliu, A., & Fu, K. S. (1983). A distance measure between attributed relational graphs for pattern recognition. [Part B]. *IEEE Transactions on Systems, Man, and Cybernetics, 13*(3), 353–362.

Scholkopf, B., & Smola, A. J. (2002). *Learning with Kernels*. Cambridge, MA: MIT Press.

Scholkopf, B., Smola, A. J., & Muller, K. R. (1999). Kernel principal component analysis. *Advances in kernel methods: Support vector learning, 327–352.*

Shasha, D., Wang, J. T. L., & Giugno, R. (2002). Algorithmics and applications of tree and graph searching. *Proceeding of the ACM Symposium on Principles of Database Systems*, Madison, Wisconsin (pp. 39-52).

Smalter, A., Huan, J., & Lushington, G. (2008). Graph wavelet alignment kernels for drug virtual screening. *Proceedings of the 7th Annual International Conference on Computational Systems Bioinformatics*, Standford, CA.

Smalter, A., Huan, J., & Lushington, G. (2008). Structure-based pattern mining for chemical compound classification. *Proceedings of the 6th Asia Pacific Bioinformatics Conference*, Kyoto, Japan.

Tian, Y., McEachin, R. C., States, D. J., & Patel, J. M. (2007). SAGA: A subgraph matching tool for biological graphs. *Bioinformatics (Oxford, England), 23*(20), 232–239. doi:10.1093/bioinformatics/btl571

Tian, Y., & Patel, J. (2008). TALE: A tool for approximate large graph matching. *Proceedings of the IEEE International Conference on Data Engineering*, Cancun, Mexico (pp. 963-972).

Tolliday, N., Clemons, P. A., Ferraiolo, P., Koehler, A. N., Lewis, T. A., & Li, X. (2006). Small molecules, big players: The national cancer institute's initiative for chemical genetics. *Cancer Research, 66*, 8935–8942. doi:10.1158/0008-5472.CAN-06-2552

Vapnik, V. (1998). *Statistical Learning Theory*. John Wiley & Sons.

Vert, J. (2008). *The optimal assignment kernel is not positive definite*. (Technical Report HAL-00218278), French Center for Computational Biology.

Vishwanathan, S. V. N., Borgwardt, K. M., & Schraudolph, N. N. (2006). *Fast computation of graph kernels. Advances in Neural Information Processing Systems* (pp. 1449–1456). Cambridge, MA: MIT Press.

Wallis, W. D., Shoubridge, P., Kraetzl, M., & Ray, D. (2001). Graph distances using graph union. *Pattern Recognition Letters, 22*, 701–704. doi:10.1016/S0167-8655(01)00022-8

Willett, P., Barnard, J., & Downs, G. (1998). Chemical similarity searching. *Journal of Chemical Information and Computer Sciences, 38*(6), 983–996. doi:10.1021/ci9800211

Williams, D., Huan, J., & Wang, W. (2007). Graph database indexing using structured graph decomposition. *Proceedings of the 23rd IEEE International Conference on Data Engineering*, Istanbul, Turkey (pp. 976-985).

Yan, X. F., Yu, P. S., & Han, J. W. (2004). Graph indexing: A frequent structure-based approach. *Proceedings of the 2004 ACM SIGMOD International Conference on Management of Data*, Paris, France (pp. 335-346).

Yan, X. F., Yu, P. S., & Han, J. W. (2005). Graph indexing based on discriminative frequent structure analysis. *ACM Transactions on Database Systems*, *30*(4), 960–993. doi:10.1145/1114244.1114248

Zhang, S., Hu, M., & Yang, J. (2007). Treepi: A new graph indexing method. *Proceedings of the 23rd IEEE International Conference on Data Engineering*, Istanbul, Turkey (pp. 966-975).

Zhao, P., Yu, J. X., & Yu, P. S. (2007). Graph indexing: Tree + delta ≥ graph. *Proceedings of the 33rd International Conference on Very Large Data Bases,* Vienna, Austria (pp. 938-949).

Chapter 9

TEDI:
Efficient Shortest Path Query Answering on Graphs

Fang Wei
University of Freiburg, Germany

ABSTRACT

Efficient shortest path query answering in large graphs is enjoying a growing number of applications, such as ranked keyword search in databases, social networks, ontology reasoning and bioinformatics. A shortest path query on a graph finds the shortest path for the given source and target vertices in the graph.

Current techniques for efficient evaluation of such queries are based on the pre-computation of compressed Breadth First Search trees of the graph. However, they suffer from drawbacks of scalability. To address these problems, we propose TEDI, an indexing and query processing scheme for the shortest path query answering. TEDI is based on the tree decomposition methodology. The graph is first decomposed into a tree in which the node (a.k.a. bag) contains more than one vertex from the graph. The shortest paths are stored in such bags and these local paths together with the tree are the components of the index of the graph. Based on this index, a bottom-up operation can be executed to find the shortest path for any given source and target vertices.

Our experimental results show that TEDI offers orders-of-magnitude performance improvement over existing approaches on the index construction time, the index size and the query answering.

DOI: 10.4018/978-1-61350-053-8.ch009

INTRODUCTION

Querying and manipulating large scale graph-like data have attracted much attention in the database community, due to the wide application areas of graph data, such as ranked keyword search, XML databases, bioinformatics, social network, and ontologies. The shortest path query answering in a graph is among the fundamental operations on the graph data.

In a ranked keyword search scenario over structured data, people usually give scores by measuring the link distance between two connected elements. If more than one path exists, it is desirable to retrieve the shortest distance between them, because shorter distance normally means higher rank of the connected elements (Tran, T., Wang, H., Rudolph, S. & Cimiano, P. (2009), He, H., Wang, H., Yang, J. & Yu, P. S. (2007)). In a social network application such like Facebook, registered users can be considered as vertices and edges represent the friend relationship between them. Normally two users are connected through different paths with various lengths. The problem of retrieving the shortest path among the users efficiently is of great importance.

Let $G = (V, E)$ be an undirected graph where $n = |V|$ and $m = |E|$. Given $u, v \in V$, the shortest path problem finds a shortest path from u to v with respect to the length of paths from u to v. One obvious solution for the shortest path problem is to execute the Breadth First Search (BFS) on the graph. The time complexity of the BFS method is $O(n)$. If the graph is of large size, the efficiency of query answering is expected to be improved.

The query answering can be performed in constant time, if the BFS tree for each vertex of the graph is pre-computed. However, the space overhead is n^2. This is obviously not affordable if n is of large value. Therefore, appropriate indexing and query scheme for answering shortest path queries must find the best trade-off between these two extreme methods.

Xiao et al. (Xiao, Y., Wu, W., Pei, J., Wang, W. & He, Z. (2009)) proposed the concept of compact BFS-trees where the BFS-trees are compressed by exploiting the symmetry property of the graphs. It is shown that the space cost for the compact BFS trees is reduced in comparison to the normal BFS trees. Moreover, shortest path query answering is more efficient than the classic BFS-based algorithm. However, this approach suffers from scalability. Although the index size of the compact BFS-trees can be reduced by 40% or more (depending on the symmetric property of the graph), the space requirement is still prohibitively high. For instance, for a graph with 20 K vertices, the compact BFS-tree has the size of 744 MB, and the index construction takes more than 30 minutes. Therefore, this approach cannot be applied for graphs with larger size that contain hundreds of thousands of vertices.

OUR CONTRIBUTIONS

To overcome these difficulties, we propose TEDI (Tree Decomposition based Indexing) (Wei, F. (2010)), an indexing and query processing scheme for the shortest path query answering. Briefly stated, we first decompose the graph G into a tree in which each node contains a set of vertices in G. These tree nodes are called bags. Different from other partitioning based methods, there are overlapping among the bags, i.e., for any vertex v in G, there can be more than one bag in the tree which contains v. However, it is required that all these related bags constitute a connected subtree (see Definition 1 for the formal definition).

Based on the decomposed tree, we can execute the shortest path search in a bottom-up manner and the query time is decided by the height and the bag cardinality of the tree, instead of the size of the graph. If both of these two parameters are small enough, the query time can be substantially improved. Of course, in order to compute the shortest paths along the tree, we have to pre-compute the local shortest paths among the vertices in every bag of the tree. This constitutes the major part of the index structure of the TEDI scheme. Our main contributions are the following:

- Solid theoretical background. TEDI is based on the well-known concept of the tree decomposition, which is proved being of great importance in computational complexity theory. The abundant theoretical results provide a solid background for designing and correctness proofs of the TEDI algorithms.
- Linear time tree decomposition algorithm.

In spite of the theoretical importance of the tree decomposition concept, many results are practically useless due to the fact that finding a tree decomposition with optimal treewidth is an NP-hard problem, with respect to the size of the graph. To overcome this difficulty, we propose in TEDI the simple heuristics to achieve a linear time tree decomposition algorithm. To the best of our knowledge, TEDI is the first scheme that applies the tree decomposition heuristics dealing with graphs of large size, and based on that, enables efficient query answering algorithms to be developed.

- Flexibility of balancing the time and space efficiency. From the proposed tree decomposition algorithm, we discover an important correlation between the query time and the index size. If less space for the index is available, we can reduce the index size by increasing some parameter k during the tree decomposition process, while the price to pay is longer query time. On the other hand, if the space is less critical, and the query time is more important, we can decrease k to achieve higher efficiency of the query answering. This flexibility offered by TEDI enables the users to choose the best time/space trade-off according to the system requirements.

Finally we conduct experiments on real and synthetic datasets, and compare the results with the compact BFS-tree approach. The experimental results confirm our theoretical analysis by demonstrating that TEDI offers orders-of-magnitude performance improvement over existing algorithms. Moreover, we conduct the experiments over large graphs such as DBLP and road networks. The encouraging results show that TEDI scales well on large datasets.

BACKGROUND

The classic shortest path algorithm deploys Breadth First Search, which can be implemented with a queue (Knuth, D. E. (1997)). In recent years, efficient algorithms with preprocessing have been proposed for finding the shortest paths. The graphs under consideration have some special constraints such as edge weights. The labeling method for finding shortest paths from the source to all vertices in the graph is a classical implementation of the greedy algorithm, and can be found in any algorithm design textbook.

For point-to-point shortest path problem, the so-called Bidirectional Dijkstra algorithm (Nicholson T. A. J. (1966)) works as follows. It alternates between running the two algorithms, each maintaining its own set of distance labels: one is for the vertices which are reached from u, and the other is for those vertices which reach v. Let $d_u(x)$ and $d_v(x)$ be the distance labels of x maintained by the forward and the reverse algorithms, respectively. During the initialization, the forward search scans u and the reverse search scans v. The algorithm also maintains the length of the shortest path seen so far, μ, and the corresponding path. Initially, $\mu = \infty$. When an edge (v_1, v_2) is scanned by the forward search and v_2 has already been scanned by the reverse search, we know the shortest $u \rightarrow v_1$ and $v_2 \rightarrow v$ paths have lengths $d_u(v_1)$ and $d_v(v_2)$ respectively. If $\mu > d_u(v_1) + (v_1, v_2) + d_v(v_2)$, we have found a path shorter than μ, so we update μ and its path accordingly. We perform similar updates during the reverse search. When the search in one direction selects a vertex x already scanned in the other direction, the algorithm terminates. Heuristics such as A* search has been investigated to speed up the search procedure (Goldberg A. V. & Harrelson, C. (2005)).

In recent years, many algorithms with preprocessing have been proposed for finding the shortest paths. Theses preprocessing-based algorithms contain two parts: *preprocessing algorithm* and *query algorithm*. The former can also be called index construction using the database jargon. This procedure may take longer, but runs only once for all. The latter need to be fast and may run on a small device.

The ALT family of algorithms (Goldberg A. V. & Harrelson, C. (2005)) uses *landmarks* and triangle inequality to compute feasible lower bounds. A small subset of vertices is selected as landmarks. For each vertex in the graph, distances to and from every landmark are pre-computed. This information can be used to compute lower bounds. Note that the landmarks are of very small sizes (typically 16). With the lower bounds, the search can be considerably accelerated. Of course, the price to be paid is the large overhead of storing the pre-computed distances.

Reach-based approach, proposed by Gutman (Gutman, R. (2004)), is also a preprocessing-based method. The method pre-computes for each vertex x, the *reach* value, represented as $r(x)$. It is defined as follows. Given a path P from u to v and a vertex x on P, the reach of x with respect to P is the minimum of the length of the sub-path from u to x and the length of the sub-path from x to v. The reach of x, $r(x)$, is the maximum, over all shortest paths P through x, of the reach of x with respect to P. With the reach values of all the vertices in the graph, effective pruning can be applied in the Dijkstra's algorithm.

Various versions of the algorithms are presented in (Goldberg, A. V. (2007)). All of these

methods are based on heuristics designed specifically on the underlying datasets (like GIS data). It is unknown, whether the algorithms can be extended to dealing the other graph datasets. Moreover, one assumption common to all those algorithms is that the whole graph can be stored in main memory.

Another related graph query problem – which is more intensively studied in the database community – is the reachability query answering. Many approaches have been proposed to first pre-compute the transitive closure, so that the reachability queries can be more efficiently answered comparing to BFS or DFS. Generally speaking, the existing research on reachability query answering can be categorized into the two main groups. The first group of algorithms is based on the 2-Hop approach first proposed by Cohen et al. (Cohen, E., Halperin, E., Kaplan, H. & Zwick, U. (2003)). The second is based on the *interval labeling* approach by Agrawal et al. (Agrawal R., Borgida A., & Jagadish H. V. (1989)).

2 Hop based algorithms. The basic idea of the 2-Hop approach is to assign for each vertex v a list of vertices which are reachable from v, denoted as $L_{in}(v)$, and a list of vertices which v can reach, denoted as $L_{out}(v)$, so that for any two vertices u and v, $u \rightarrow v$ if and only if $L_{out}(u) \cap L_{in}(v) \neq \varnothing$. The ultimate goal of the algorithm is to minimize the index size of the form $\sum_{v \in V} L_{in}(v) + L_{out}(v)$. Clearly if the index is available, the reachability query answering requires only two lookups. However, this optimization problem is NP-hard. Cohen et al. proposed an approximate algorithm based on set-covering which can produce a 2-Hop cover with size no larger than the minimum possible 2-Hop cover by a logarithmic factor. However, their original algorithm requires the pre-computing of the transitive closure and has the time complexity of $O(n^4)$. Schenkel et al. (Schenkel, R., Theobald, A. & Weikum, G. (2005)) proposed the HOPI algorithm, which deployed the graph partitioning method to reduce the storage requirements for the index construction process. With HOPI the index construction time is reduced to $O(n^3)$. Cheng et al. (Cheng, J., Yu, J. X., Lin, X., Wang H., Yu P. S. (2008)) proposed heuristics to improve the performance of the 2-Hop algorithm by reducing the index construction time and the index size. But no approximation bound was given.

Interval labeling based algorithms. Interval labeling based approaches utilize the efficient method of indexing and querying trees which was applied to XML query processing in recent years. It is well known that given a tree, we can label each node v by an interval (*start(v), end(v)*). Thus the reachability query can be answered by comparing the start and the end labels of u and v in constant time. The labeling process takes linear time and space. Most of the research work along this line considered extending the interval labeling approach to apply it to graphs. The most common method is to first extract a spanning tree from the graph, then process the rest of the edges which are not covered in the tree. The various approaches differ from each other mainly on how to process the non-tree edges.

The Dual Labeling algorithm proposed by Wang et al. (Wang, H., He, H., Yang, J., Yu, P. S. & Yu, J. X. (2006)) achieved to answer reachability queries in constant time. They first identify a spanning tree from the graph and label the vertices in the tree with pre- and post-order values. Then the transitive closure for the rest of the edges is stored. Clearly, the price for the constant query time is paid by the storage cost of t^2 where t is number of the non-tree edges in the graph. Therefore the Dual Labeling approach achieves good performance only if the graph is extremely sparse where $t \ll n$. The Label+SSPI algorithm proposed by Chen et al. (Chen, L., Gupta, A. & Kurul, M. E. (2005)) used an additional data structure, called

SSPI, for storing non-tree edges. Thus the index size is reduced to $O(n+m)$. However, the query time is $O(m-n)$ in the worst case. The GRIPP algorithm proposed by Trißl et al. (Trissl, S. & Leser, U. (2007)) was implemented in an RDBMS and followed the idea of Label+SSPI. Although the worst case complexity of GRIPP is the same as Label+SSPI, the experiments showed that the actual time to answer a reachability query is almost constant over different graphs.

Jin et al. (Jin, R., Xiang, Y., Ruan, N. & Wang, H. (2008)) proposed a different index structure called Path Tree. Like other interval labeling based methods, they extract a tree from the original graph. But every node in the tree contains a path, instead of a single vertex. This index structure is superior to the previous ones since it can encode some non-tree structures such as grid in an elegant way. Furthermore, it is theoretically proved that the Path Tree cover can always perform the compression of transitive closure better than or equal to the optimal tree cover approaches (Agrawal R., Borgida A., & Jagadish H. V. (1989)) and chain decomposition approaches (Jagadish, H. V. (1990)). Recently, Jin et al. have proposed the 3-HOP algorithm for reachability query answering on dense graphs (Jin, R., Xiang, Y., Ruan, N. & Fuhry, D. (2009)).

None of these methods can be extended to cope with the shortest path query answering. Given u, v in a graph, reachability queries require only a boolean answer (yes or no). Therefore, the transitive closure stored in the index can be drastically compressed, as long as the boolean query is correctly answered. On the other hand, shortest path queries require that the paths to be returned. Therefore, the compression methods with the information loss cannot be adapted for answering shortest path queries.

GRAPH INDEXING USING TREE DECOMPOSITION

Tree Decomposition

An undirected graph is defined as $G = (V, E)$, where $V = \{0, 1, ..., n-1\}$ is the vertex set and $E \subseteq V \times V$ is the edge set. Let $n = |V|$ be the number of vertices and $m = |E|$ be the number of edges. In this paper, we consider only undirected graphs, where $\forall u, v \in V: (u,v) \in E \Leftrightarrow (v,u) \in E$ holds. There is an non-negative length function, denoted as l, on each edge $(u,v) \in E$, representing the distance from u to v. The shortest path problem finds a shortest path from u to v with respect to l. To simplify the presentation, we assume that all the edges are labeled with 1. We will point out in the later part of the chapter how our algorithm can be generalized to deal with graphs with labels greater than 1. In the rest of the chapter, we will use the term graph to denote undirected graph.

Definition 1 (Tree Decomposition). A tree decomposition of $G = (V, E)$, denoted as T_G, is a pair $(\{X_i \mid i \in I\}, T)$, where $\{X_i \mid i \in I\}$ is a collection of subsets of V and $T = (I, F)$ is a tree such that:

1. $\cup_{i \in I} X_i = V$.
2. For every $(u,v) \in E$, there is $i \in I$, s.t. $u, v \in X_i$.
3. For all $v \in V$, the set $\{i \mid v \in X_i\}$ induces a subtree of T.

A tree decomposition consists of a set of tree nodes, where each node contains a set of vertices in V. We call the sets X_i bags. It is required that every vertex in V should occur in at least one bag (condition 1), and for every edge in E, both vertices of the edge should occur together in at least one bag (condition 2). The third condition is usually referred to as the connectedness condition, which requires that given a vertex v in the graph, all the bags that contain v should be connected.

Note that from now on, the node in the graph G is referred to as vertex, and the node in the

tree decomposition is referred to as tree node or simply node. For each tree node i, there is a bag X_i consisting of vertices. To simplify the presentation, we will sometimes use the term node and its corresponding bag interchangeably. Given a tree decomposition T_G, we denote its root as R.

Given any graph G, there may exist many tree decompositions that fulfill all the conditions in Definition 1. However, we are interested in those tree decompositions with smaller bag sizes. We call the cardinality of a bag the width of the bag.

Definition 2 (Width, Treewidth). Let $G = (V, E)$ be a graph.

- The width of a tree decomposition $(\{X_i \mid i \in I\}, T)$ is defined as $max\{|X_i| \mid i \in I\}$.
- The treewidth of G is the minimal width of all tree decompositions of G. It is denoted as $tw(G)$ or simply tw.

Example 1. Consider the graph illustrated in Figure 1(a). One of the tree decompositions is shown in Figure 1(b). The width of this tree decomposition is 3. It is not hard to check that this tree decomposition is optimal, thus the treewidth of the graph is 3.

Let $G = (V, E)$ be a graph and $T_G = (\{X_i \mid i \in I\}, T)$ a tree decomposition of G. Due to the third condition in Definition 1, for any vertex v in V there exists an induced subtree of T_G in which every bag contains v. We call it the induced subtree of v and denote it as T_v. Moreover, we denote the root of T_v as r_v and its corresponding bag as Xrv. For instance, X_0, X_1 and X_2 constitute the bags of the induced subtree of vertex 3 in Figure 1(b) because vertex 3 occurs precisely in these three bags. Since X_0 is the root of the induced subtree, we have $r_3 = 0$.

Tree Path

Let $G = (V, E)$ be a graph, and $u, v \in V$. v is reachable from vertex u, denoted as $u \rightarrow v$, if there is a path starting from u and ending at v with the form

Figure 1. The graph G (a) and one tree decomposition T_G(b) with tw = 3

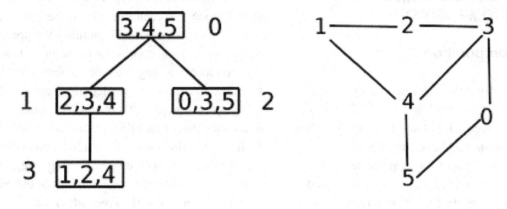

(a)   (b)

$\{u, v_1, ..., v_n, v\}$, where $(u, v_1), (v_i, v_{i+1})_{(1 \leq i \leq n-1)}, (v_n, v) \in E$. The shortest distance from vertex u to vertex v is denoted as *sdist*(u, v). Note that in this chapter, we consider only simple paths. Obviously for undirected graphs, $u \rightarrow v \Leftrightarrow v \rightarrow u$ holds.

Let us consider the graph vertices in the tree nodes. Since a vertex in G may occur in more than one bag of T_G, it is identified with $\{v, i\}$, where v is the vertex and i the node in the tree, meaning that vertex v is located in the bag X_i. We denote it as tree vertex.

Now we define the so-called internal edge in the tree decomposition. Recall that the second condition in Definition 1 requires that for every edge $(u, v) \in E$, both u and v should occur in some bag of T_G. We call these edges inner edges in the tree decomposition.

Definition 3 (Inner Edge). Let $G = (V, E)$ be a graph and $T_G = (\{X_i \mid i \in I\}, T)$ a tree decomposition of G. The inner edges of T_G are precisely the pairs of tree vertices defined as: $\{((\{u, i\}, \{v, i\}) \mid (u, v) \in E, u, v \in X_i (i \in I)\}$.

Intuitively, the set of inner edges consists of precisely those edges in E, with the extra information of the bags in which the edges are located. For instance, the inner edges of the tree decomposition of the graph in Example 1 are: $(\{0, 2\}, \{5, 2\})$,

$(\{1, 3\}, \{2, 3\})$, $(\{2, 1\}, \{3, 1\})$, $(\{3, 2\}, \{0, 2\})$, $(\{4, 1\}, \{3, 1\})$, $(\{4, 0\}, \{3, 0\})$, $(\{4, 3\}, \{1, 3\})$, $(\{4, 0\}, \{5, 0\})$, ... Note that it is possible that the same pair of vertices occurs in more than one bag. For instance, the edge $(4, 3)$ occurs in both bags X_0 and X_1. Thus there are two inner edges: $(\{4, 1\}, \{3, 1\})$ and $(\{4, 0\}, \{3, 0\})$.

In order to traverse from one bag to another in the tree decomposition, we need to define the second kind of edge, the inter edge. Note that two neighboring bags in the tree are in fact connected by the common vertices they share, according to the connectedness condition in Definition 1.

Definition 4 (Inter Edge). Let $G = (V, E)$ be a graph and $T_G = (\{X_i \mid i \in I\}, T)$ a tree decomposition of G. Let $v \in X_i$ and $v \in X_j$, where either $(i, j) \in F$ or $(j, i) \in F$ holds. We call the edge from vertex $\{v, i\}$ to $\{v, j\}$ the inter edge and denote it as $(\{v, i\}, \{v, j\})$.

For instance, in Example 1, $(\{5, 0\}, \{5, 2\})$ is an inter edge, as well as $(\{5, 2\}, \{5, 0\})$, because vertex 5 occurs in bags X_0 and X_2, where 0 is the parent node of 2. Now we are ready to define the tree path on the tree decomposition with inner and inter edges.

Definition 5 (Tree Path). Let $G = (V, E)$ be a graph and $T_G = (\{X_i \mid i \in I\}, T)$ a tree decomposition of G. Let $u, v \in V$. Let further $\{u,i\}$ and $\{v,j\}$ be tree vertices in T_G. A tree path from $\{u,i\}$ to $\{v,j\}$ is a sequence of tree vertices connected with either inter or inner edges.

Lemma 1. Let $G = (V, E)$ be a graph and $T_G = (\{X_i \mid i \in I\}, T)$ a tree decomposition of G. Let $u, v \in V$. Let further $\{u,i\}$ and $\{v,j\}$ be tree vertices in T_G. There is a path from u to v in G if and only if there is a tree path from $\{u,i\}$ to $\{v,j\}$.

Proof. The "if" direction is trivial: given a tree path from $\{u,i\}$ to $\{v,j\}$, we only need to consider the inner edges. Since for each inner edge $\{u,i\},\{v,i\}$, there is an edge $(u,v) \in E$, the path from u to v can be easily constructed.

Now we prove the "only if" direction: assume that there is a path from u to v in G. We prove it by induction on the length of the path.

- Basis: if u reaches v with a path of length 1, that is, $(u,v) \in E$. Then there exists a node k in the tree decomposition, s.t. $u \in X_k$ and $v \in X_k$. We start from $\{u,i\}$, traverse along the induced subtree of u, till we reach $\{u,k\}$. Since the induced subtree is connected, the path from $\{u,i\}$ to $\{u,k\}$ can be constructed with inter edges. Then we reach from $\{u,k\}$ to $\{v,k\}$ with an inner edge. Now we traverse from $\{v,k\}$ to $\{v,j\}$ along the induced subtree of v, which can again be constructed with inter edges. The tree path from $\{u,i\}$ to $\{v,j\}$ is thus completed.

- Induction: assume that the lemma holds with paths whose length is less than or equal to $n - 1$, we prove that it holds for paths with length of n. Assume that there is a path from u to v with length n, where u reaches w with length $n - 1$ and $(w,v) \in E$. From induction hypothesis, we know that there is a tree path form $\{u,i\}$ to $\{w,l\}$ in the tree decomposition, where l is a node in the induced subtree of w. Since $(w,v) \in E$, there is a node n such that $w \in X_n$ and $v \in X_n$. Thus $\{w,n\}$ can be reached from $\{w,l\}$

with inter edges. Then $\{w,n\}$ can reach $\{v,n\}$ with an inner edge. Finally $\{v,n\}$ can reach $\{v,j\}$ with a sequence of inter edges. This completes the proof.

Example 2. Consider the graph in Figure 1(a). Vertex 4 reaches vertex 0 with the path $(4, 1, 2, 3, 0)$. In the tree decomposition in Figure 1(b), there is a tree path from $\{4, 1\}$ to $\{0, 2\}$ as follows: $(\{4, 1\}, \{4, 3\}, \{1, 3\}, \{2, 3\}, \{2, 1\}, \{3, 1\}, \{3, 0\}, \{3, 2\}, \{0, 2\})$.

Shortest Path Query Answering on Tree Decomposition

With the definition of the tree path, we are able to map every path from u to v in the graph G into a tree path in the corresponding tree decomposition T_G. Since all the paths can be traced in the tree decomposition, after inspecting all the corresponding tree nodes, we are able to compute the shortest path from u to v. Our goal is now to restrict the attention of the tree nodes to those that every tree path would pass through.

There is a well-known property of trees that for any two nodes i and j in a tree, there exists a unique simple path, denoted as $SP_{i,j}$, such that every path from i to j contains all the nodes in $SP_{i,j}$. In the following we show that this property can also be applied to tree paths.

Given a tree path P in the tree decomposition, we say P visits a node i, if there is a tree vertex $\{v,i\}$ in P.

Lemma 2. Let $\{u,i\}$ and $\{v,j\}$ be two tree vertices, and $SP_{i,j}$ be the simple path between tree nodes i and j. Let P be a tree path from $\{u,i\}$ to $\{v,j\}$. Then P visits every node in $SP_{i,j}$.

Example 3. The tree path from $\{4, 1\}$ to $\{0, 2\}$ shown in Example 2 visits the nodes in a sequence of $(1, 3, 1, 0, 2)$. It contains not only all the nodes in the simple path, but also node 3, which is not in the simple path.

Theorem 1. Let $G = (V, E)$ be a graph and $T_G = (\{X_i \mid i \in I\}, T)$ a tree decomposition of G. Let

$u, v \in V$, and r_u (resp. r_v) be the root node of the induced subtree of u (resp. v). Then for every node w in $SPr_u r_v$, there is one vertex $t \in X_w$, such that $sdist(u,v) = sdist(u,t) + sdist(t,v)$.

Proof. Let p be the shortest path from u to v in G that generates $sdist(u,v)$. From Lemma 1, we know that there is a corresponding tree path P of p from $\{u, r_u\}$ to $\{v, r_v\}$ in T_G. According to Lemma 2, P visits all the nodes in $SPr_u r_v$. Then for every node n in $SPr_u r_v$, there is a vertex $\{t, n\}$ in P. Therefore, t is in p. Then we have $sdist(u,v) = sdist(u,t) + sdist(t,v)$.

Theorem 1 shows that for every path from u to v in G, although the tree path from $\{u, r_u\}$ to $\{v, r_v\}$ may possibly visit any node in the tree, we only need to concentrate on those vertices which occur in the simple path $SPr_u r_v$. More precisely, we can simply take any node w from $SPr_u r_v$, and for each $t \in X_w$, compute $sdist(u,t)$ and $sdist(t,v)$ respectively. Then, the minimal value of $sdist(u,t) + sdist(t,v)$ is the shortest distance from u to v. However, this is obviously not a solution, since we have to compute the shortest path for $2c$ times, where c is the cardinality of the bag X_w.

The following question thus arises: Can we compute the shortest path from u to the vertices (respectively from the vertices to v) in the simple path more efficiently? The answer is yes. Intuitively, we can compute the shortest distance from u to the vertices occur in the simple path bag after bag, in a bottom-up manner. Let us assume that the current bag be X_c and its parent bag be X_p. Assume further that for all the vertices $t \in X_c$, we have obtained $sdist(u,t)$. Now we start processing X_p. For any vertex $s \in X_p \setminus X_c$, the following property holds:

$$sdist(u,s) = \{\min(sdist(u,t) + sdist(t,s)) \mid t \in X_c \cap X_p\}$$

This is because every path from u to s has to pass through one vertex in $X_c \cap X_p$ (formal proof given in Theorem 2). Therefore, the shortest path must be among them.

Clearly, in order to enable the bottom-up operation, we need to store the shortest distances for each bag in the tree decomposition. That is, in every bag X, for every pair of vertices $x, y \in X$, we pre-compute $sdist(x,y)$ and store them locally. In addition to the local shortest distance, we need to store the vertices in $sdist(x,y)$, denoted as $path(x,y)$, to trace back the vertices along the shortest path later on.

Given the tree decomposition of G and the local shortest distance, as well as u and v, the shortest path query answering is sketched in Theorem 2. See Figure 2 for a graphical illustration.

Theorem 2. Let $G = (V,E)$ be a graph and $u, v \in V$. Let tw be the treewidth of G and $T_G = (\{X_i \mid i \in I\}, T)$ be the corresponding tree decomposition. The shortest distance from u to v can be computed in $O(tw^2 h)$, where h is the height of T_G.

Proof. We show that the bottom-up operation can be executed on T_G, so that the shortest distance (as well as the corresponding shortest path) from u to v can be computed.

Let us make the following assumptions of T_G: T_u (resp. T_v) is the induced subtree of u (resp. v) where r_u (resp. r_v) is the root. a is the youngest common ancestor of r_u and r_v. Assume further that the shortest distance ($sdist$) and shortest path ($path$) for the pairs of vertices in every bag in T_G are pre-computed. We explain the process only for the side of u, the bottom-up process from the v side is identical.

The process starts with the node r_u. From the information of shortest distance in the tree node X_{r_u}, we can simply obtain $sdist(u,t)$ for each $t \in X_{r_u}$.

Next, we consider r_u as the child node and process its parent node, with the available $sdist$ information. This process is executed till a is reached.

We show that at each step of the processing, the shortest distance from u to all the vertices in the current bag can be computed in w^2 time, where w is the width of the current bag. Assume p

Figure 2. Bottom-up processing on the simple tree path

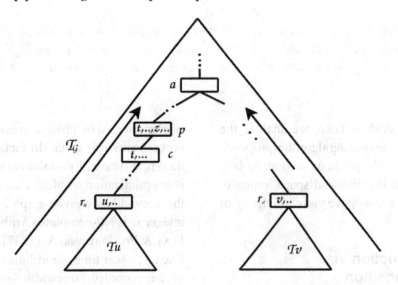

is the current node, c its child node, and we have obtained $sdist(u,t)$ for each $t \in X_c$.

Now we have to compute the shortest distance from u to every vertex in X_p. Let z be a vertex in X_p. We want to compute $sdist(u,z)$. We consider the following two cases:

1. $z \in X_p$ and $z \in X_c$. Since at the child node $sdist(u,z)$ is already obtained, the value $sdist(u,z)$ remains unchanged.

2. $z \in X_p$ and $z \notin X_c$. This is a more complex case. We show that there is a vertex t, where $t \in X_p$ and $t \in X_c$, such that $sdist(u,z) = sdist(u,t)+sdist(t,z)$. In other words, the shortest path from u to z has to pass through some vertex t that occurs in both X_c and X_p. Since z does not occur in X_c, according to the connectedness condition, z does not occur in any bag in the subtree rooted with c. Thus the induced subtrees of u and z do not share any common node in T_G. Since $u \rightarrow z$, there is a tree path from $\{u,r_u\}$ to $\{z,r_z\}$, and $c,p \in SPr_ur_z$. The tree path from $\{u,r_u\}$ to $\{z,r_z\}$ must contain an inter edge of the form $(\{t,c\},\{t,p\})$, where $t \in X_pX_c$, because this is the only possible edge to traverse from c

to p. Therefore, the shortest path from u to z must pass through one vertex $t \in X_pX_c$.

Given the shortest distance from u to every vertex in X_c, we compute the shortest distance from u to the vertices in X_p as follows: First for each vertex $t \in X_c \cap X_p$, set $sdist(u,t)$ the same value as in X_c. Then for each vertex $t \in X_p \setminus X_c$, set $sdist(u,t) = min(sdist(u,s) + sdist(s,t))$ where $s \in X_c \cap X_p$. Clearly the time consumption is in the worst case $O(w^2)$ where w is the width of X_p.

To sum up, at each step, the time cost of updating the shortest distance is $O(tw^2)$, where tw is the treewidth of G. and there are maximally $2h$ steps where h is the height of the tree decomposition. Hence the overall time cost is $O(tw^2h)$.

ALGORITHMS AND COMPLEXITY RESULTS

In this section, we present the detailed algorithms for both the index construction and the shortest path query answering. We begin with the introduction of algorithmic issues on the tree decomposition from a complexity theory perspective, and then justify our choice of an efficient but suboptimal

Algorithm 1. index_construction(G)

```
1:   graph_reduction(k,G); {output the vertex stack S and reduced graph G'}
2:   tree_decomposition(S,G,G'); {output the tree decomposition T_G}
3:   local_shortest_paths(G,T_G); {compute local shortest paths in T_G}
```

decomposing algorithm. Then, we analyze the shortest path query answering algorithm proposed in Theorem 2 from the previous section. At last, we point out that the time and space improvement can be made to achieve more efficiency of our algorithm.

Index Construction via Tree Decomposition

The index construction algorithm consists of three steps (see Algorithm 1). Step 1 and 2 constitute the major part of the index construction task: decomposing the graph G.

Introduced by Robertson and Seymour (Robertson, P. D. & Seymour, N. (1984)), the concept of tree decomposition has been proved to be of great importance in computational complexity theory. The interested readers may refer to an introductory survey by Bodlaender (Bodlaender H. L. (1993)). The theoretical significance of the tree decomposition based approach lies in the fact that many intractable problems can be solved in polynomial time (or even in linear time) for graphs with treewidth bounded by a constant. Problems which can be dealt with in this way include many well known NP-complete problems, such as the Independent Set, the Hamiltonian Circuits, etc. Recent applications of tree decomposition based approaches can be found in Constraint Satisfaction (Kask, K., Dechter, R., Larrosa, J. & Dechter, A. (2005)) and database design (Gottlob, G., Pichler, R. & Wei, F. (2006)).

However, the practical usefulness of tree decomposition based approaches has been limited due to the following two problems: (1) Computing the treewidth of a graph is hard. In the last section, we have always assumed that a tree decomposition is given. In fact, to obtain a tree decomposition with the minimal width (treewidth) is an optimization problem. Determining whether the treewidth of a given graph is at most a given integer w is NP-complete (Arnborg, S., Corneil, D. G. & Proskurowski A. (1987)). Although for a fixed w, linear time algorithms exist to solve the decision problem "treewidth $\leq w$", there is a huge hidden constant factor, which prevents it from being useful in practice. There exist many heuristics and approximation algorithms for determining the treewidth, unfortunately few of them can deal with graphs containing more than 1000 vertices (Koster, A., Bodlaender, H. L. & Hoesel, S. P. M. V. (2001)). (2) The second problem lies in the fact that even if the treewidth can be determined, good performance for solving intractable problems by using the tree decomposition based approaches can only be achieved if the underlying structure has bounded treewidth (i.e. less than 10). Because the time complexity of most of the algorithms is exponential to the treewidth.

As far as the efficiency is concerned, we can only search for an approximate solution, which yields a suboptimal treewidth. On the other hand, we can tolerate a treewidth that is not bounded. As we have seen from Theorem 2, the time complexity is in the worst case quadratic of the treewidth (width). We will show later in this section that our query answering algorithm does not depend on the treewidth, but with some parameter which can be enforced to be bounded, due to the nice property of our dedicated decomposing algorithm.

Inspired by the so-called pre-processing methods from Bodlaender et al. (Bodlaender, H. L., Koster, A. M. C. A. & van den Eijkhof, F.

Figure 3. A graph containing a vertex v with degree 1(a), 2(b) and 3(c)

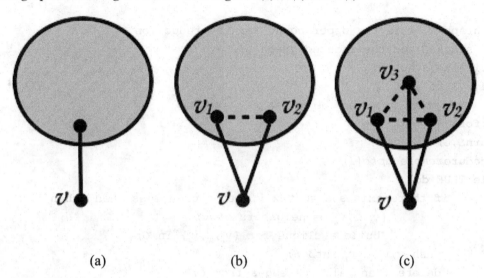

(a)   (b)   (c)

(2005)), we apply the reduction rules on the graph by reducing stepwise a graph to another one with fewer vertices, due to the following simple fact.

Definition 6 (Simplicial). A vertex v is simplicial in a graph G if the neighbors of v form a clique in G.

Proposition 1. If v is a simplicial vertex in a graph G, computing the treewidth of G is equivalent to computing the treewidth of G - v.

Proof. Let T_{G-v} be the tree decomposition of G - v. Let further $\{v_1, ..., v_l\}$ be the neighbors of v. We construct a bag $X_c = \{v, v_1, ..., v_l\}$. Since $\{v_1, ..., v_l\}$ form a clique, there exists a bag in T_{G-v} consisting of all the vertices in $\{v_1, ..., v_l\}$. We denote it as X_p. We can then construct T_G by adding X_c as a child of X_p. It is easy to verify that all the conditions of the tree decomposition are fulfilled. Thus this new tree is also a tree decomposition.

Figure 3 shows some special cases. If a vertex v has degree of one (Figure 3(a)), then we can remove v without increasing the treewidth. Figure 3(b), 3(c) illustrates the cases of degree 2 and 3 respectively.

The main idea of our decomposition algorithm is to reduce the graph by removing the vertices one by one from the graph, and at the same time push the removed vertices into a stack, so that

later on the tree can be constructed with the information from the stack. Each time a vertex v with a specific degree is identified. We first check whether all its neighbors form a clique, if not, we add the missing edges to construct a clique. Then v together with its neighbors are pushed into the stack, which is followed by the deletion of v and the corresponding edges in the graph (see Algorithm 2).

The program begins with removing isolated vertices and vertices with degree 1. Then the reduction process proceeds by increasing the degree of the vertex. We denote such procedure of removing all the vertices with degree l as degree-l reduction.

Example 4. Consider the graph in Example 1. Figure 4 illustrates the reduction process. The process starts with a degree-2 reduction by removing vertex 0 and its edges, after adding the edge between 3 and 5. Vertex 0 and its neighbors are then pushed in the stack. Then vertex 1 is removed, following the same principle as of 0. After vertex 2 is removed, a single triangle is then left.

Algorithm 2 will terminate if one of the following conditions is fulfilled. (1) The graph is reduced to an empty set. For instance, if the graph contains only simple cycles, it will be reduced to

Algorithm 2. graph_reduction(k,G)

```
Input:  graph G, k is the upper bound for the reduction.
Output: stack S and the reduced graph G'
1:  initialize stack S;
2:  for i = 1 to k do
3:          remove_upto(i);
4:  end for
5:  return S,G;
6:  procedure remove_upto(l)
7:  while TRUE do
8:          if there exists a vertex v with degree less than l then
9:                  {v₁,…,v_l} = neighbors of v;
10:                 build a clique for {v₁,…,v_l} in G;
11:             push v,v₁,…,v_l into S;
12:             delete v and all its edges from G;
13:             else
14:                     break;
15:         end if
16: end while
```

an empty set after degree-2 reductions. This is usually the case for extremely sparse graphs. (2) For graphs that are not sparse, one has to define a upper bound k for the reduction, so that the program stops after the degree-k reduction. Note that as the degree increases, the effectiveness of the reduction will decrease, because in the worst case, we need to add $l(l-1)/2$ edges in order to remove l edges.

After the reduction process, the tree decomposition can be constructed as follows: (1) At first we collect all the vertices which were not removed by the reduction process and assign this set as the bag of the tree root R. The size of R depends on

Figure 4. The reduction process on the graph of Example 1

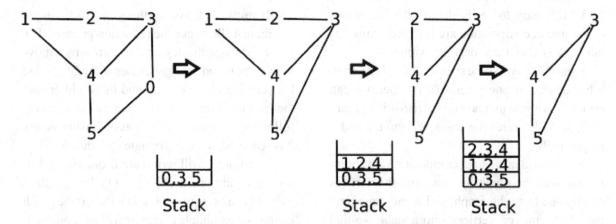

Algorithm 3. tree_decomposition(S,G,G')

```
Input:  S is the stack storing the removed vertices and their neighbors, G is
the graph, G' is the reduced graph of G.
Output:  return tree decomposition T_G
1:  construct the root of T_G containing all the vertices of G';
2:  whileS is not empty do
3:          pop up a bag X_c = {v,v_1,...,v_l} from S;
4:          find the bag X_p containing {v_1,...,v_l};
5:          add X_c into T as the child node of X_p;
6:  end while
```

the structure of the graph (i.e. how many vertices are left after the reduction). For graphs which are not sparse, the bag size of the root is the greatest among all bags in the tree decomposition. (2) The rest of the tree is generated from the information stored in stack S. Let X_c be the set of vertices $\{v,v_1,...,v_l\}$ which is popped up from the top of S. Here v is the removed vertex and $\{v_1,...,v_l\}$ are the neighbors of v which form a clique. After the parent bag X_p which contains $\{v_1,...,v_l\}$ is located in the tree, X_c is added as a child bag of X_p. This process proceeds until S is empty. Algorithm 3 (see Algorithm 3) illustrates the process.

The last step of the index construction is to compute and store the shortest distances and paths for every pair of vertices in the bags of the tree decomposition (see Algorithm 4). We apply the standard BFS algorithms. Due to the property of the tree decomposition, there exist redundancies. For instance, both node 1 and 3 in Figure 1(b) contain the vertex pair (2, 4). Therefore, the same shortest distance is stored in two bags. This re-dundancy can be avoided by storing the shortest distances in a hash table.

Shortest Path Query Answering

Recall from Theorem 2 that the time complexity of the bottom-up query answering is $O(tw^2h)$. This upper bound is optimal, only if the following two conditions are fulfilled: (1) the treewidth of the underlying graph is bounded (that is, $tw^2 \ll n$), and (2) there is an efficient tree decomposition algorithm for it. The first condition has to be fulfilled, since otherwise the linear time BFS algorithm would be more efficient. Unfortunately, as we have seen in above, given an arbitrary graph, neither of them can be guaranteed. Therefore, we have to inspect the tree decomposition heuristics applied in last Section for improvements.

Algorithm 4. local_shortest_paths(G,T_G)

```
Input:  G,T_GOutput:  local shortest paths in T_G
1:  for all bag X in the tree decomposition do
2:          for every vertex pair x,y ∈ Xdo
3:                  compute sdist(x,y) and path(x,y)
4:          end for
5:  end for
```

From Treewidth to |R| and k

According to Algorithm 2, a graph G can be decomposed by the degree-1 reductions by increasing l from 1 to k. As soon as the degree-k reduction is done, all the vertices that are not yet removed are the elements in R of the tree decomposition. Usually if the graph is not extremely sparse, the relationship $k << |R|$ holds. In fact, we could even enforce such a relationship by setting k to be small enough in the tree decomposition algorithm. Hence, the resulting tree decomposition has the following properties: (1) the root is of big size ($|R|$), and (2) the rest of the bags have smaller size (the upper bound is k).

If we inspect the bottom-up query processing more carefully, we could observe that the quadratic time computation over the root can be always be avoided. To see this, let us consider the vertices u and v and the youngest common ancestor of r_u and r_v is the root R. Assume that X_1 (resp. X_2) is the child node of R which locates in the simple path from r_u (resp. r_v) to R. Consider now that for all $x \in X_1$, $sdist(u,x)$ (resp. all $y \in X_2$, $sdist(y,v)$) have been computed. Clearly, any path from u to v has to pass through a vertex in X_1 and X_2 respectively. Therefore, at the root node R, the interface from X_1 to R has to be $X_1 \cap R$, and accordingly, the interface from X_2 to R has to be $X_2 \cap R$. Now, we only need to execute a nested loop on $X_1 \cap R$ and $X_2 \cap R$, to decide

The algorithm for the shortest path query answering is presented in Algorithm 5 (see Algorithm 5). Comparing with the bottom-up query processing shown in Theorem 2, Algorithm 5 is customized with respect to our dedicated tree decomposition algorithm, in the sense that the query time complexity is adapted to be related to k, instead of the treewidth.

Given the graph G, its tree decomposition T_G and the pre-computed local shortest paths in the bags on T_G, as well as the vertices u,v, we first locate the root of the induced subtree of u (v), denoted as r_u (r_v). The algorithm considers special cases, according to the relationship between r_u and r_v. (1) if r_u and r_v are located in one bag, then the shortest path can be immediately returned (line 3). (2) Otherwise, we have to locate the youngest common ancestor of r_u and r_v, denoted as *root*. Here a special case is either r_u or r_v is *root*. If this occurs, the bottom-up operation should be only executed from one side. Note that we stop the processing at the child node of the *root* node. At each step of the bottom-up processing, we update the shortest distance value, as well as the *parent* value, for the later back-trace for the shortest paths(line 12 and 23). As soon as both the child nodes X_1 and X_2 are reached, we obtain the common values with the *root* node by executing the set intersection operation with it (line 26). At last, a nested loop over the bag X_1 and X_2 is executed, to stitch the threads from both sides. Finally, the shortest path can be traced back using the p set we have stored during the bottom-up processing.

Complexity

Index construction time. For the index construction, we have to (1) generate the tree decomposition, and (2) at each tree node, generate the required shortest paths. For (1), both of the reduction step and the tree construction procedure take time $O(n)$. For (2), we deploy the classic BFS algorithm, which costs in worst case $O(n)$. In fact, we need to run for each vertex in G exactly one BFS procedure. Therefore, the overall index construction time is $O(n^2)$.

Index size. In each bag X, for each pair of vertices u,v in X, we need to store the vertices along the shortest path between u and v. Thus the index size is $l|X|^2$, where l is the average length of all the local shortest paths. Since the relationship $k << |R|$ holds, the root size ($|R|$) is dominant among all the bags. Therefore, the index size is $l|R|^2$. The index size consists of the tree structure, constructed by using the tree decomposition al-

Algorithm 5. reach_dist(T_G,u,v)

Input: T_G is the tree decomposition of G and u,v vertices in G. In every bag X of T_G, and any pair of $x,y \in X$, $sdist(x,y)$ stores the shortest distance, and $path(x,y)$ stores the vertices along the path.

Output: the shortest path from u to v.

1: r_u = root of induced subtree of u;

2: r_v = root of induced subtree of v;

3: **if** ($r_u == r_v$) **then** return $path(u,v)$;

4: $root$ = youngest common ancestor of r_u and r_v;

5: **if** ($r_u == root$) **then** switch u and v; switch r_u and r_v;

6: **for** all $x \in X_{ru}$ **do** label x with $d_u(x) = sdist(u,x)$; $p(x) = u$;

7: $X_1 = X_{ru}$;

8: **while** $X_1.parent \neq root$ **do**

9:      $X_p = X_1.parent$

10:        **for** all $t \in X_p \setminus X_1$ **do**

11:           **for** all $s \in X_p \cap X_1$ **do**

12:              **if** $d_u(t) > d_u(s) + sdist(s,t)$ **then** $d_u(t) = d_u(s) + sdist(s,t)$; $p(t) = s$;

13: $X_1 = X_p$;

14: $X_1 = X_1 \cap root$;

15: **if** r_v is the ancestor of r_u **then** $X_2 = \{v\}$; $d_v(v) = 0$;

16:      **else**

17:        **for** all $x \in X_{rv}$ **do** label x with $d_v(x) = sdist(v,x)$; $p(x) = v$;

18:        $X_2 = X_{rv}$;

19:        **while** $X_2.parent \neq root$ **do**

20:           $X_p = X_2.parent$

21:           **for** all $t \in X_p \setminus X_2$ **do**

22:              **for** all $s \in X_p \cap X_2$ **do**

23:                 **if** $d_v(t) > d_v(s) + sdist(s,t)$ **then** $d_v(t) = d_v(s) + sdist(s,t)$; $p(t) = s$;

24:           $X_2 = X_p$;

25:           $X_2 = X_2 \cap root$;

26: $mdist = \{min(d_u(x) + d_v(y) + sdist(x,y)) \mid (x \in X_1, y \in X_2\}$;

27: let $x \in X_1, y \in X_2$ be the vertices along the shortest path;

28: **while** $x \neq u$ **do** output $path(x,p(x))$; $x = p(x)$; the final shortest path. Since both $|X_1|$ and $|X_2|$ have the upper bound of k, the overall time consumption is of $O(k^2h)$, thus independent of $|R|$.

29: output $path(x,y)$;

30: **while** $y \neq v$ **do** output $path(y,p(y))$; $y = p(y)$;

Figure 5. k and |R| relationships for real data

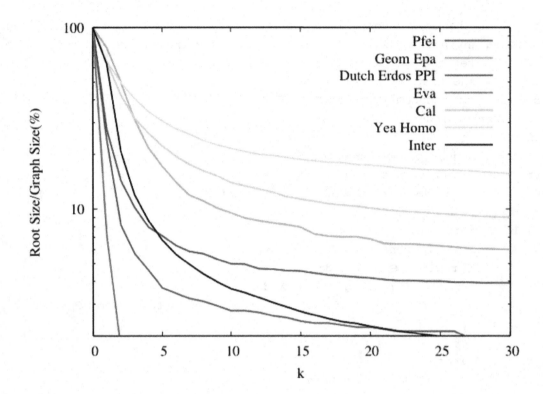

gorithm. However, this space overhead is linear to *n*, thus can be ignored.

Query. The bottom-up query processing for shortest path computation takes time $O(k^2h)$, where *k* is the number of the reductions and *h* is the height of the tree decomposition.

The Trade-Off between Time and Space

The number of the reductions for the tree decomposition algorithm, *k*, and the root size |*R*|, represent the trade-off between the time and space consumptions of the TEDI approach. As analyzed above, the time complexity for the query answering depends on *k*, whereas the index size is decided by |*R*|. Clearly, regarding to the tree decomposition algorithm, |*R*| is a monotonically decreasing function of *k*. Usually |*R*| decreases drastically as

k is small, e.g. from 1 to 5. Then, the decreasing of |*R*| follows diverse trends, which is decided by the characteristics of the underlying graphs. One obvious instance is that for extremely sparse graphs, |*R*| can be decreased rapidly into zero after 3 or 4 steps of reductions. For instance, the graph "Eva" in Figure 5 belongs to this category. However, this correlation cannot be solely reflected by the density of the underlying graph. An exact investigation of such a relationship is left as the future work. Figure 5 depicts the *k*-|*R*| relationship for the real datasets we have tested. In this illustration, the Y-axis depicts the value of |*R*|/*n* in percentage, namely the proportion of the root size with respect to the graph size. Note that due to the wide range of the value on Y-axis, we plot the vertical axis logarithmically. More details of the dataset are given in the experimental section.

Extension to Weighted Graphs

The proposed algorithms can be extended to deal with weighted graphs in a straight-forward manner. The query algorithm presented in Algorithm 5 can be applied to solving shortest distance queries over weighted graphs without any modification. The index size remains to be the same as well. The index construction time is $O(n^2 \log n)$. This increase of the time consumption stems from the higher time complexity of the classic algorithms for finding shortest distances over weighted graphs, which is $O(n \log n)$.

EXPERIMENTAL RESULTS

In this section we evaluate the TEDI approach on real, synthetic, and large datasets respectively, for the shortest path query answering. All tests are run on an Intel(R) Core 2 Duo 2.4 GHz CPU, and 2 GB of main memory. All algorithms are implemented in C++ with the Standard Template Library (STL).

We are interested in the following parameters:

- Index size,
- Index construction time, and
- Query time.

The index size consists of two parts: (1) the size of the tree decomposition. This includes the tree structure and the vertices stored in the bags of the tree decomposition. (2) the local shortest paths stored in the hash table, which is dominant comparing to part (1).

The index construction time consists of two parts as well: (1) time cost for the tree decomposition. (2) the time for the local shortest path generation. Here part (2) is dominant.

Besides the standard measurements, we are also interested in the structure of the tree decomposition, which may influence the performance of the algorithm. These are:

- The number of tree nodes (#TreeN),
- The number of all the vertices stored in the bags (#SumV),
- The height of the tree (h),
- The number of vertex reductions (k), and
- The root size of the tree. ($|R|$).

In our experiments, we compare our approach with the compact BFS trees proposed by Xiao et al. (Xiao, Y., Wu, W., Pei, J., Wang, W. & He, Z. (2009)), which we denote as SYMM. To the best of our knowledge, SYMM is the state-of-the-art implementation for efficient shortest path query answering with pre-computed index structures.

Real Datasets

We test a variety of real graph data including biological networks (PPI, Yea and Homo), social networks (Pfei, Geom, Erdos, Dutch, and Eva), information networks (Cal and Epa) and technological networks (Inter). All the graph data are provided by the authors of (Xiao, Y., Wu, W., Pei, J., Wang, W. & He, Z. (2009)).

Some statistics of the graphs with respect to the tree decomposition algorithm are shown in Table 1. Note that we have chosen the optimal k, in order to achieve the best query time performance.

We measure the time and space cost of the index construction on the real datasets, and compare our results with SYMM (Xiao, Y., Wu, W., Pei, J., Wang, W. & He, Z. (2009)). See Table 2 for details. The index size generated with TEDI has been dramatically reduced comparing with SYMM. In fact, most of the index sizes of TEDI are two orders of magnitude smaller than those generated with SYMM. For the index construction time, improvement can be shown similarly. The index construction time of TEDI on every graph is at least one order of magnitude faster than that with SYMM.

The measurement on the index construction time and the index size confirms the complexity analysis in the previous section. The index con-

Table 1. Statistics of real graphs and the properties of the index

Graph	n	#TreeN	#SumV	h	k	$|R|$
Pfei	1738	1680	3916	16	6	60
Gemo	3621	3000	9985	10	5	623
Epa	4253	3637	11137	7	7	618
Dutsch	3621	3442	8700	9	5	258
Eva	4475	4457	9303	9	2	75
Cal	5925	5095	18591	14	10	832
Erdos	6927	6690	18979	9	7	405
PPI	1458	1359	3638	11	7	101
Yeast	2284	1770	6708	6	9	516
Homo	7020	5778	24359	10	15	1244
Inter	22442	21757	67519	10	13	687

struction time is only dependent on the graph size, whereas the index size is decided by the root size $|R|$. For instance, the graph size of Homo is 3 times small than Inter, while the root size is two times greater than Inter. This is exactly reflected by the index size and index construction time in Table 2 respectively.

We execute the query answering algorithm given in Algorithm 5. For each dataset we randomly generate 10000 pairs of vertices and query the shortest paths between each pair of vertices.

To make a fair comparison, we have implemented the naive BFS algorithm. This way, we could compare the speedup of our method with respect to the BFS algorithm to the speedup of the SYMM algorithm with respect to BFS. The results are shown in Table 3. Surprisingly, the speedup for all the datasets, except for one graph, is higher than that of SYMM.

In summary, TEDI algorithm is superior to SYMM in all aspects.

Table 2. Comparison between TEDI and SYMM on index construction of real dataset

	Index Size (MB)				Index Time (s)			
Graph	paths	tree	TEDI	SYMM	t_{tree}	t_{paths}	TEDI	SYMM
Pfei	0.025	0.008	0.033	7.9243	0.003	0.099	0.102	2.688
Gemo	1.81	0.020	1.830	44.9907	0.068	0.878	0.946	14.859
Epa	1.63	0.022	1.652	28.1992	0.056	0.97	1.026	37.14
Dutsch	0.404	0.016	0.420	20.8559	0.011	0.311	0.322	13.687
Eva	0.026	0.018	0.044	5.5447	0.006	0.239	0.245	289.532
Cal	3.04	0.038	3.078	92.026	0.145	2.535	2.680	34.094
Erdos	0.516	0.018	0.534	32.2695	0.038	0.849	0.887	90.453
PPI	0.052	0.008	0.060	5.954	0.004	0.130	0.134	1.547
Yeast	1.08	0.014	1.094	19.4457	0.019	0.566	0.585	7.578
Homo	6.88	0.048	6.928	21.574	0.198	7.745	7.943	53.985
Inter	1.66	0.136	1.796	744.074	0.796	15.858	16.654	1709.64

Table 3. Comparison between TEDI and SYMM on query time over real dataset

	TEDI			SYMM
Graph	TEDI (ms)	BFS	Speedup	Speedup
Pfei	0.003420	0.052	15.2	13.04
Gemo	0.002933	0.123	42.4	41.10
Epa	0.002096	0.105	50.0	39.62
Dutsch	0.002655	0.097	37.3	28.21
Eva	0.002299	0.089	38.7	20.20
Cal	0.003325	0.187	56.7	59.31
Erdos	0.002037	0.146	71.9	57.72
PPI	0.002629	0.050	19.2	13.30
Yeast	0.002463	0.071	28.4	25.63
Homo	0.007666	0.226	29.7	N.a.
Inter	0.004178	0.693	169.0	N.a.

Synthetic Datasets

We have generated synthetic graphs according to the BA model (Barabasi A. L. and Albert R. (1999)), a widely used model to simulate real graphs. To make a fair comparison, we set $d = 1.1$, so that the average degree of the graph generated is $2d$, which is identical to the synthetic datasets in (Xiao, Y., Wu, W., Pei, J., Wang, W. & He, Z. (2009)). We vary the graph size from 1000 to 10000 vertices by the step of 1000.

Some statistics of those graphs with respect to the tree decomposition algorithm are shown in Table 4. Again, we have chosen the optimal k, in order to achieve the best query time performance. The measurement of the index construction time and index size is similar to those of real dataset.

The index size and the index construction time are shown in Table 5. Figure 6(a) and 6(b) illustrate the comparison of index construction time and the index size on the synthetic datasets with SYMM. Note that due to the wide range of time and space cost, we plot the vertical axis logarith-

Table 4. Statistics of the synthetic graphs and the properties of the index

Graph	n	#TreeN	#SumV	h	k	$|R|$
1k	1000	808	2131	9	3	194
2k	2000	1730	4786	11	5	272
3k	3000	2641	7362	10	6	361
4k	4000	3559	10131	10	7	443
5k	5000	4460	12758	10	8	542
6k	6000	5355	15371	10	9	612
7k	7000	6292	18626	12	9	710
8k	8000	7201	20790	11	9	801
9k	9000	8089	23497	12	9	913
10k	10000	8983	26224	11	9	1019

Table 5. Index Construction of synthetic dataset

	Index Size (MB)			Index Time (s)		
Graph	paths	tree	TEDI	t_{tree}	t_{paths}	TEDI
1k	0.27	0.004	0.274	0.003	0.088	0.091
2k	0.61	0.010	0.620	0.010	0.217	0.227
3k	1.16	0.014	1.174	0.024	0.385	0.409
4k	1.76	0.020	1.780	0.038	0.625	0.663
5k	2.68	0.025	2.705	0.040	0.953	0.993
6k	4.0	0.030	4.030	0.081	1.340	1.456
7k	4.6	0.036	4.636	0.092	1.942	2.134
8k	6.2	0.042	6.242	0.091	2.400	2.491
9k	8.2	0.047	8.247	0.124	3.128	3.252
10k	10.2	0.052	10.052	0.167	4.274	4.441

mically. The results in Figure 6(a) and 6(b) show clearly that on both the index size and the index construction time, TEDI outperforms the approach SYMM with the improvement of more than an order of magnitude.

Since SYMM does not present the query time for the synthetic data, we cannot make a comparison on that. Instead, we report the query time on synthetic graphs with TEDI and compare the results with the BFS algorithms. The results are given in Table 6. Interestingly, the speedup to the naive BFS method increases, as the size of the graph grows. This observation will be confirmed in the next section, namely on very large datasets, the speedup of the query time to BFS can be increased substantially.

Scalability over Large Datasets

To test the scalability of our approach, we conduct the experiments on much larger datasets. We have chosen two datasets. The first one is DBLP dataset. We first generate an undirected graph from the DBLP N-triple dump[1]. The dataset contains

Figure 6. Comparison of index construction time and size on synthetic data

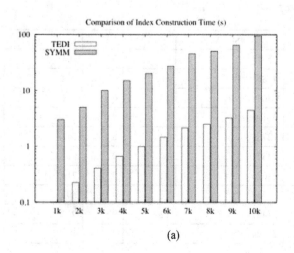
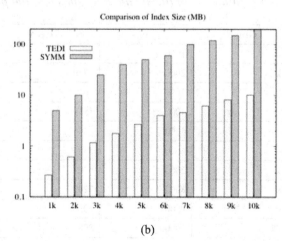

(a)   (b)

Table 6. TEDI query time on synthetic datasets

Graph	Query Time		
	TEDI (ms)	BFS	Speedup
1k	0.001545	0.027	17.5
2k	0.002073	0.050	25.0
3k	0.002645	0.078	29.5
4k	0.003286	0.104	31.6
5k	0.003674	0.145	39.5
6k	0.004155	0.168	40.4
7k	0.004450	0.193	43.4
8k	0.004754	0.226	47.5
9k	0.005135	0.257	50.0
10k	0.005722	0.299	52.3

all the inproceeding records and all proceedings records, with all their persons, publishers, series and relations between persons and inproceedings. To highlight the purpose of shortest path query answering, we removed elements in each paper that are not interesting to keyword search, such as url, ee, etc. Finally, we get a graph containing 593K vertices.

The second large dataset is the road network of the San Francisco Bay area[2] denoted as BAY. The graph contains 321K vertices.

Figure 7 illustrates the relationship of k and $|R|$ with respect to the reduction step of the tree decomposition process. Table 7 shows some characteristics of the graphs. The curves in Figure 7 exposes distinct features of the k-$|R|$ relationship on DBLP and BAY. For DBLP, the root size $|R|$ can hardly be reduced after 4000 (approximately 0.67% of the graph size). On the other hand, the root size of BAY remains decreasing continuously. The results of the tree decomposition reflect these differences. The decomposed tree of BAY has a much smaller root size than that of DBLP (245 vs. 3821). However, the height of BAY is correspondingly greater than DBLP (30 vs. 351). This implies that the BAY dataset requires less space for index structure, but the query time is longer. For DBLP, the query time is much shorter because

of the smaller height of the tree, but the price to pay is greater index size. All of these observations are reflected in the Table 8 and 9.

The experimental results on large graphs demonstrate clearly that the TEDI approach scales well on large dataset. Moreover, the query time speedup is more substantial, in comparison to the relatively smaller graphs.

As far as the index time is concerned, the experimental results are against the complexity analysis of $O(n^2)$. The reason for this is that the average shortest path length of BAY graph is much longer than that of DBLP. Therefore, the time cost of the BFS algorithm for BAY is greater than DBLP.

FUTURE RESEARCH DIRECTIONS

In the future we plan to investigate the following problems: (1) Development more heuristics for the tree decomposition algorithms. (2) The integration of A* heuristics for a more efficient query answering. (3) Maintenance of the index structure. Furthermore, we will consider on-disk algorithms for both index construction and query answering.

Figure 7. k and |R| relationships for large data

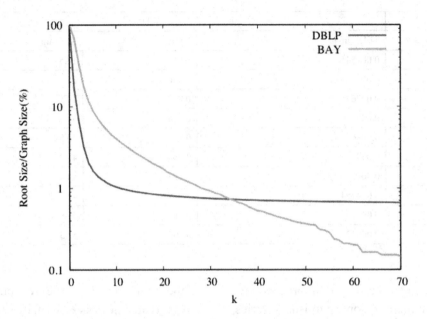

Table 7. Statistics of large graphs and the properties of the index

Graph	n	#TreeN	#SumV	h	k	|R|
DBLP	592 983	589 164	1 309 710	30	100	3821
BAY	321 272	321 028	1 298 993	351	80	245

Table 8. Index construction of large dataset

Graph	Index Size (MB)			Index Time (s)		
	paths	tree	TEDI	t_{tree}	t_{paths}	TEDI
DBLP	117.2	2.6	119.8	102.4	2124.0	2226.4
BAY	24.7	2.6	27.3	182.2	2859.7	3041.9

Table 9. Comparison of TEDI query time on large datasets to BFS

Graph	Query Time		
	TEDI (ms)	BFS (ms)	Speedup
DBLP	0.055	32.47	590.0
BAY	0.258	20.54	80.0

Discuss solutions and recommendations in dealing with the issues, controversies, or problems presented in the preceding section.

CONCLUSION

In this chapter, we introduced an indexing and query answering scheme based on the tree decomposition concept for the shortest path query answering. The careful theoretical analysis has shown that our approach is intuitive and efficient. Through extensive experiments over various datasets, we demonstrate that TEDI achieves the improvement of performance by more than an order of magnitude in all aspects including query time, index construction time and index size. Moreover, the algorithm scales well over large datasets.

REFERENCES

Agrawal, R., Borgida, A., & Jagadish, H. V. (1989). Efficient management of transitive relationships in large data and knowledge bases. In *Proceedings of the ACM SIGMOD International Conference on Management of Data, SIGMOD 1989.*

Arnborg, S., Corneil, D. G., & Proskurowski, A. (1987). Complexity of finding embeddings in a k-tree. *SIAM Journal of Algebraic Discrete Methods, 8*(2), 277–284. doi:10.1137/0608024

Barabasi A. L., & Albert R. (1999). Emergence of scaling in random networks. *Science, 286*(5439), October 1999.

Bodlaender, H. L. (1993). A tourist guide through treewidth. *Acta Cybernetica, 11*, 1–23.

Bodlaender, H. L., Koster, A. M. C. A., & van den Eijkhof, F. (2005). Pre-processing rules for triangulation of probabilistic networks. *Computational Intelligence, 21*(3), 286–305. doi:10.1111/j.1467-8640.2005.00274.x

Chen, L., Gupta, A., & Kurul, M. E. (2005). Stack-based algorithms for pattern matching on dags. In *Proceedings of the 31st International Conference on Very Large Data Bases, VLDB 2005.*

Cheng, J., Yu, J. X., Lin, X., Wang, H., & Yu, P. S. (2008). Fast computing reachability labelings for large graphs with high compression rate. In *11th International Conference on Extending Database Technology, EDBT 2008.*

Cohen, E., Halperin, E., Kaplan, H., & Zwick, U. (2003). Reachability and distance queries via 2-hop labels. *SIAM Journal on Computing, 32*(5), 1338–1355. doi:10.1137/S0097539702403098

Goldberg, A. V. (2007). Point-to-point shortest path algorithms with preprocessing. In *Proceedings of the 33rd Conference on Current Trends in Theory and Practice of Computer Science (Invited Paper) 2007.*

Goldberg, A. V., & Harrelson, C. (2005). Computing the shortest path: A* search meets graph theory. In *Proceedings of the 16th Annual ACM-SIAM Symposium on Discrete Algorithms.*

Gottlob, G., Pichler, R., & Wei, F. (2006). Tractable database design through bounded treewidth. In *Proceedings of the 25th ACM SIGACT-SIGMOD-SIGART Symposium on Principles of Database Systems, PODS 2006.*

Gutman, R. (2004). Reach-based routing: A new approach to shortest path algorithms optimized for road networks. In *Proceedings 6th Workshop on Algorithm Engineering and Experiments (ALENEX) (SIAM, 2004) (pp. 100-111).*

He, H., Wang, H., Yang, J., & Yu, P. S. (2007). Blinks: Ranked keyword searches on graphs. In *Proceedings of the ACM SIGMOD International Conference on Management of Data, SIGMOD 2007.*

Jagadish, H. V. (1990). A compression technique to materialize transitive closure. *ACM Transactions on Database Systems, 15*(4), 558–598. doi:10.1145/99935.99944

Jin, R., Xiang, Y., Ruan, N., & Fuhry, D. (2009). 3-hop: A high-compression indexing scheme for reachability query. In *Proceedings of the ACM SIGMOD International Conference on Management of Data, SIGMOD 2009.*

Jin, R., Xiang, Y., Ruan, N., & Wang, H. (2008). Efficiently answering reachability queries on very large directed graphs. In *Proceedings of the ACM SIGMOD International Conference on Management of Data, SIGMOD 2008.*

Kask, K., Dechter, R., Larrosa, J., & Dechter, A. (2005). Unifying tree decompositions for reasoning in graphical models. *Artificial Intelligence, 166*(1-2), 165–193. doi:10.1016/j.artint.2005.04.004

Knuth, D. E. (1997). Art of Computer Programming: *Vol. 1. Fundamental Algorithms* (3rd ed.). Boston, MA: Addison-Wesley Professional.

Koster, A., Bodlaender, H. L., & Hoesel, S. P. M. V. (2001). Treewidth: Computational experiments. *Electronic Notes in Discrete Mathematics*, 2001.

Nicholson, T. A. J. (1966). Finding the shortest route between two points in a network. *The Computer Journal, 9*(3), 275–280.

Robertson, P. D., & Seymour, N. (1984). Graph minors 3: Planar tree-width. *Journal of Combinatorial Theory Series B*, (36): 49–64. doi:10.1016/0095-8956(84)90013-3

Schenkel, R., Theobald, A., & Weikum, G. (2005). Efficient creation and incremental maintenance of the hopi index for complex XML document collections. In *Proceedings of the 21st International Conference on Data Engineering, ICDE 2005.*

Tran, T., Wang, H., Rudolph, S., & Cimiano, P. (2009). Top-k exploration of query candidates for efficient keyword search on graph-shaped (rdf) data. In *Proceedings of the 25th International Conference on Data Engineering, ICDE 2009.*

Trissl, S., & Leser, U. (2007). Fast and practical indexing and querying of very large graphs. In *Proceedings of the ACM SIGMOD International Conference on Management of Data, SIGMOD 2007.*

Wang, H., He, H., Yang, J., Yu, P. S., & Yu, J. X. (2006). Dual labeling: Answering graph reachability queries in constant time. In *Proceedings of the 22nd International Conference on Data Engineering, ICDE 2006.*

Wei, F. (2010). TEDI: Efficient shortest path answering on graphs. In *Proceedings of the ACM SIGMOD International Conference on Management of Data, SIGMOD 2010.*

Xiao, Y., Wu, W., Pei, J., Wang, W., & He, Z. (2009). Efficiently indexing shortest paths by exploiting symmetry in graphs. In *Proceedings of the 12th International Conference on Extending Database Technology, EDBT 2009.*

ENDNOTES

[1] http://www4.wiwiss.fu-berlin.de/bizer/d2rq/benchmarks

[2] http://www.dis.uniroma1.it/~challenge9/download.shtml

Chapter 10
Graph Mining Techniques:
Focusing on Discriminating between Real and Synthetic Graphs

Ana Paula Appel
Federal University of Espirito Santo at São Mateus, Brazil

Christos Faloutsos
Carnegie Mellon University, USA

Caetano Traina Junior
University of São Paulo at São Carlos, Brazil

ABSTRACT

Graphs appear in several settings, like social networks, recommendation systems, computer communication networks, gene/protein biological networks, among others. A large amount of graph patterns, as well as graph generator models that mimic such patterns have been proposed over the last years. However, a deep and recurring question still remains: "What is a good pattern?" The answer is related to finding a pattern or a tool able to help distinguishing between actual real-world and fake graphs. Here we explore the ability of ShatterPlots, a simple and powerful algorithm to tease out patterns of real graphs, helping us to spot fake/masked graphs. The idea is to force a graph to reach a critical ("Shattering") point, randomly deleting edges, and study its properties at that point.

INTRODUCTION

Traditional data mining algorithms, such as association rule mining, market basket analysis, and cluster analysis, commonly attempt to find patterns in a single relation that stores a collection of independent instances. An emerging challenge for data mining is to tackle the problem of mining collections of inter-related instances, represented as graphs, usually spanning several relations.

Graphs are convenient representations of numerous settings, such as social networks, scientific publication networks, authors vs. conference participation, and others. Over the last decade, the number of data that should be represented as graphs (e.g. social networks in LinkedIn, Facebook

DOI: 10.4018/978-1-61350-053-8.ch010

and Flickr) has increased exponentially (Newman, 2003). Therefore, graph mining has become an essential technique to extract knowledge from networks. Many fascinating non-intuitive network properties, such as small and shrinking diameter, degree distribution, triangles, eigenvalues, and community structures (Faloutsos et al., 1999, Leskovec et al., 2007b, Tsourakakis, 2008, Fortunato, 2010) have been discovered.

Network properties are important to understand the network behavior and formation. For example, if most of the nodes follow a specific pattern, the deviating ones can be outliers and should be more carefully studied. To develop graph analysis techniques, or to test new hypotheses and algorithms for graphs, it is often necessary to drill over synthetic graphs, where the target properties are known to occur within known parameters. Therefore, the generation of synthetic graphs is an important asset. Data generation to evaluate traditional data mining algorithms is a fairly well-understood technique, and several statistical methods have been long available. However, the development of synthetic graphs that resemble real ones requires great efforts and synthetic graph generation is still an open research issue (Chakrabarti et al., 2004). To improve graph generators, especially to generate well-suited graphs to help evaluate social network analysis tools, it is important to identify and describe properties that can distinguish real from synthetic networks.

Spotting synthetic data is another important research topic, since synthetic networks can be generated or mixed with real networks to hide or fake information. For instance, in a network for product recommendation or reliability, unethical participants might try to insert few, well-designed synthetic fake nodes, skewing the scores reliability.

In this context, this chapter presents techniques and properties, such as node degree distribution, number of triangles, adjacency matrix eigenvalues and others (Faloutsos et al., 1999, Tsourakakis, 2008, Leskovec et al., 2007b) developed to mine graphs. However, these traditional properties used alone do not allow distinguishing synthetic network from real ones. For example, if one compares the degree distribution of a real network and a synthetic network generated by preferential attachment, both will have a power law degree distribution.

ShatterPlots (Appel et al., 2009) is a technique that allows distinguishing between real and synthetic graphs. Its process is based on network resilience and randomly removes edges from a network until it reaches a state, known as Shattering point, where the network reaches its largest effective diameter, that is, the node reachability is at its worst point. At this point, it is possible to extract interesting patterns for the number of nodes and edges and the triangles distributions, as well as properties of connected components and adjacency matrix eigenvalues. We will show that the combination of all these properties helps us separate real networks from synthetic ones.

Traditionally, only the node degree, the distributions of the number of triangles and diameter properties have been used to distinguish between synthetic and real networks. Those measurements are generally enough to compare real and random graphs (Erdos and Renyi, 1960), since those characteristics can tell random graphs apart. However, more elaborate network generators, such as the Small World (Watts and Strogatz, 1998) and the Preferential Attachment (Barabasi and Albert, 1999) techniques can closely mimic these properties following a power law (Clauset et al., 2009), enforcing a large number of triangles and a small diameter and better resembling the real networks. Spotting real graphs from synthetic ones created by those newer generators is therefore a tough enterprise. Forcing a graph to a critical state, as the ShatterPlots technique does, and measuring its properties at that state reveals the inner nature of the graph, helping to identify its inherent constitution.

BACKGROUND

Graphs

A complex network, or just network for short, is a discrete mathematical object composed of nodes, also called vertices, interconnected by edges. A complex network is modeled as a graph defined as $G(V,E)$ where V represents the set of nodes, with cardinality $|V| = N$, and E represents the set of edges, with cardinality $|E|=M$ such that $e_k \in E$ and $e_k = \{(v_i, v_j)|v_i, v_j \in V\}$. Following this definition, the complex network study can take into account all the mathematical graph theories developed (Bondy and Murty, 1979).

One of the most traditional ways to computationally process a graph is by representing it in an adjacency matrix. It is the $N*N$ order matrix A, where $A_{i,j} = 1$ if $(v_i, v_j) \in E$ and 0 otherwise. In this chapter, some graph properties will be defined over the corresponding adjacency matrix of a complex network.

Networks have been used in a wide range of applications to model systems and processes, such as World Wide Web, Internet, social network, academic collaboration networks, among others (Newman, 2003).

Power-Laws

Power-law distributions have attracted especial attention over recent years due to their mathematical properties and have several interesting consequences to the understanding of both natural and man-made phenomena. Examples are the evaluation of how a city population grows, earthquake intensity distribution, and variations of power outage ranges. All of these examples have been recognized to follow power-law distributions.

A distribution is a power-law if its probability density function (PDF) follows the equation: $p(x) \propto x^y$, where $p(x)$ is the probability of x to occur and y is the power law exponent (Newman, 2005, Clauset et al., 2009).

Power-laws also occur in many types of graphs properties, such as node degree distribution (Chakrabarti and Faloutsos, 2006), number of triangles distribution over node degree (Tsourakakis, 2008), eigenvalue distribution (Faloutsos et al., 1999) and others.

Power-law distribution is also called scale-free distribution, which means that a distribution looks like itself, no matter the scale where the data is being observed. The notion of self-similarity is implicit in the name "scale-free". Self-similarity means that an element has the same properties of one or more of its constituent parts (Schroeder, 1991). Several researches have argumented that the Web and most biologic networks are self-similar (Dorogovtsev et al., 2002, Dill et al., 2002, Crovella and Bestavros, 1997).

Graph Mining

The research on graph patterns has focused primarily on static patterns that can be extracted from one snapshot of a graph at a given instant.

Most of the interesting features of real-world networks which have attracted the researchers' attention over the last few years are related to why networks are not like Erdős–Rényi graphs. Real networks do not follow a random distribution, and it is hard to describe what distribution they follow. There exist revealing ways that suggest both possible mechanisms that could be employed to guide the network formation and possible ways to exploit the network structure to achieve certain objectives. The speculation about a real network not following a random distribution has created the basis for a new research area called "Graph Mining".

The development of models for graph generation requires a way to compare real graphs to synthetic ones; the better the match, the better the model. A way to compare real and synthetic graphs is usually based on constituent properties, like node degree distribution, cluster coefficient, graph diameter and others. These properties are detailed as follows.

Degree Distribution

The degree of a node in a network is the number of incident edges to that node. A plot of N_φ, where N_φ is the fraction of nodes that have degree φ for the given network, is constructed evaluating the histogram of the node degree distribution of the network. While in graphs similar to the Erdős–Rényi the node degree distribution follows a Poisson distribution, real networks follow distinct distributions.

In real networks, the degree distribution presents a large number of one-degree nodes and few nodes whose degree is far above the average degree, creating a long tail in the plot. This type of distribution indicates that the network follows a power law. The most common way to measure this tail and reduce the evaluation noise is by plotting the cumulative distribution function of the probability that the node degree is higher than or equal to φ. As most networks have their node degree distribution following a power law, they are called scale-free networks. Thus, it is possible to state that $N_\varphi = \varphi^{-y}$, where $V_\varphi = \{v_i \in V \mid d(v_i) = \varphi\}$, $|V_\varphi| = N_\varphi$ and $y>1$ is called degree distribution exponent. For most real networks, the node degree distribution follows a power law with $2<y<3$.

Node degree distributions following power laws (Figure 1) have been described in the literature for many networks, such as phone calls (Abello et al., 1998), Internet (Faloutsos et al., 1999), Web (Kleinberg et al., 1999, Broder et al., 2000, Flaxman et al., 2005, Huberman and Adamic, 1999, Kumar et al., 1999), citation (Redner, 1998), click-stream (Bi et al., 2001), online social network (Chakrabarti et al., 2004) among others.

Small Diameter

Another important characteristic of complex networks is the small-world phenomenon, also called six degrees of separation (Milgram, 1967). In the 1960s Stanley Milgram conducted a famous experiment, in which participants were asked to reach a randomly assigned target individual by sending a chain of letter. He found that, for all the chains that reached the goal the average length was six, which is a very small number considering the large population the participants and targets were chosen from.

Usually the diameter, also called completed diameter, is defined as the longest path among all shortest paths between pairs of nodes in a graph. This type of calculation makes the diameter susceptive to outliers. For example, if the graph has more than one connected component, the diameter is infinity or if the graph has a long chain of nodes, the diameter is dominate by this chain. Also, calculating the diameter is a very expensive computational process ($O(N3)$).

One efficient way to obtain the graph diameter is sampling nodes or using the effective diameter, which is the most preferable way to be more accurate. The main algorithm to calculate effective diameter is ANF (Palmer et al., 2002).

The diameter of a graph is the least integer number D that enables every pair of nodes to be connected by a path of length at most D. Diameter D is susceptible to outliers, therefore, a more robust measurement of the pair wise distances between nodes of a graph is the Effective Diameter (D_e) (Tauro et al., 2001). It is defined as the minimum number of edges (also called 'hops' in this context) in which some fraction (or quartile q, typically q = 90%) of all connected pairs of nodes can reach each other. The effective diameter is usually calculated based on a hop-plot computed as follows:

Starting from a node u in the graph, find the number of nodes $N_h(u)$ reached in a neighborhood of at most h hops. Repeat this process starting from

Figure 1. Node degree distribution from the Oregon network following a power law

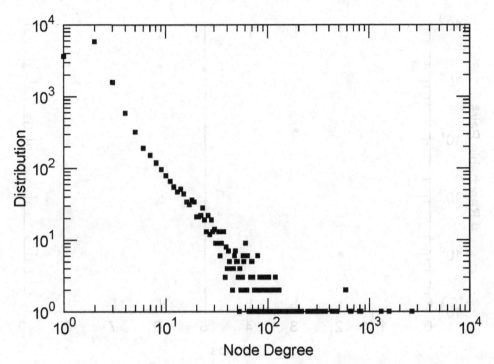

every node in the graph, and add up the results to find the total neighborhood size N_h for h hops $(N_h = \sum_u N_h(u))$. For $h=0$ the value of $N_h=N$, given that for distance zero nodes reach only themselves. For $h=1$ the value of $Nh=M$, that is, total number of edges in the network in question.

The hop-plot is the plot of N_h versus h. An example of a hop-plot from the Oregon network is presented in Figure 2, where the effective diameter is 5.

The effective diameter has been found to be small and decreasing over time for large real-world graphs, like the Internet, the Web, and many social networks (Leskovec et al., 2007b). Another characteristic of real networks is that they present higher transitivity than the synthetic ones.

Transitivity

The network transitivity is measured by its cluster coefficient (Watts and Strogatz, 1998). It has been found that, in several networks, if node v

is connected to a node u and node u to another node w, there is a high probability that node v is also connected to node w. In social networks, this type of connection means that a friend of my friends is also likely to be my friend. In terms of network topology, the transitivity property leads to the presence of many triangles in the network. A triangle is a triad of three inter-connected nodes. Apart from the cluster coefficient, the number of triangles versus node degree distribution follows a power-law that helps detect nodes with a suspicious behavior, like e-mail spammers on the internet.

The cluster coefficient tends to be considerably higher for real networks than for a random graph with similar numbers of nodes and edges. It is also known to be dependent on the node degree (Dorogovtsev et al., 2002, Ravasz and Barabási, 2003), that is, a node vi with degree d(vi) and cluster coefficient C(vi) decreases as the degree d(vi) increases, following a power law for models like scale-free networks. This behavior means that

Figure 2. Hop-plot of the Oregon network, where the effective diameter $D_e=5$

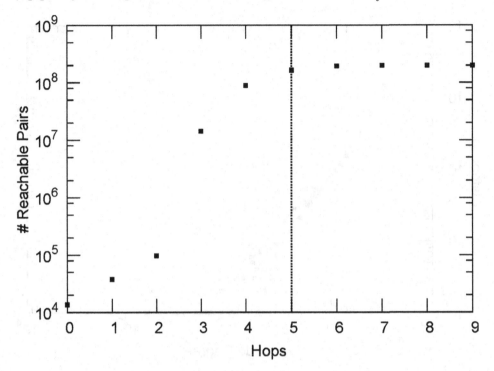

low-degree nodes tend to form highly connected groups, which are connected to each other forming even larger groups. The presence of these larger groups explains the small-world phenomenon (Watts and Strogatz, 1998). In a social network, these groups are seen as communities, in which the nodes represent people and the edges between nodes represent friendship relationships. This property corresponds to the fact that people are more related to people inside their own communities and less related to people outside them.

Other Properties

Besides power laws, small diameters, and community effects, some other patterns have been observed in large real-world graphs. These include the resilience of such graphs to random failures and eigenvalue-based properties.

The resilience of a graph is an indication of its robustness to node or edge failures. This is the classic example of a process often occurring in a network. This process is also called percolation process, that is, a process in which the nodes or the edges of a complex network are randomly designated to be either occupied or unoccupied. The occupied state can be mapped as a node or an edge deletion. Thus, the unoccupied state implies that a node or an edge remains in the network.

The resilience of a network is usually measured evaluating the paths available for a node to reach other nodes in the network. If nodes or edges are removed, the path connecting two given nodes may increase and some nodes can even be disconnected from each other. An example corresponds to disconnecting a computer (nodes) from a communication network, or removing its interconnecting cables (edges). The more computers turned off or cables removed, the more unfeasible the communication in this network.

There is a large variety of techniques to remove a node or an edge in a network. Also, each network has a different behavior with a specific node or edge removal. Many real-world graphs are resilient to random failure, which is a random removal of a node, but vulnerable to targeted attacks, i.e., high-degree nodes removal (Albert et al., 2000).

Network resilience is important not only for communication networks, but also for epidemiology, in which an occupied node can be associated with a node vaccination against a particular disease, for example the flu.

One of the most interesting works in the epidemiology area is presented in (Chakrabarti et al., 2008). The authors have proven that the first (highest) eigenvalue ($\lambda1$) is the epidemic threshold, which is very important to the prevention of a contagious disease spread among a population, in SIS model. Such a model considers individuals as either susceptible (S) or infective (I). However even after being cured, there is some probability that the same individual will become susceptible again.

The epidemic threshold condition links the characteristics of the virus and the network topology such that, if the condition is satisfied, then a viral infection dies out over time.. In that same paper the authors also state that the node that mostly affects the first eigenvalue should be the node to be vaccinated.

In spectral graph theory, an eigenvalue (λ) of a graph is defined as an eigenvalue of the graph's adjacency matrix A presented by $Ax = \lambda x$, where A is the adjacency matrix of graph G, x is a vector and λ is an eigenvalue (Mihail and Papadimitriou, 2002). The set of eigenvalues of graph G is called graph spectrum. Recent developments in spectral graph theory have concerned the effectiveness of eigenvalues in studying general graphs. An example is Google's PageRank algorithm based on a graph's eigenvector (Page et al., 1999).

Moreover spectral graph theory has stated several theorems that help graph mining. An example is the one that states that if a graph does not have cycles and $M=N-1$ thus, the first eigenvalue is dominated by the square root of the highest node degree $(\sqrt{d_{max}} = \lambda_1)$ (Mihail and Papadimitriou, 2002).

GRAPH GENERATORS

Besides the empirical study of large complex networks, there exists a wide range of works on graph generators. Graph generator models are useful tools to innumerous tasks, such as simulation studies to observe the algorithms performance with a graph with different structural properties, sampling or growing to create a larger or smaller graph, and graph evolution to observe how some graph properties emerge.

Also, synthetic networks are important to build better and more efficient graph algorithms, as they enable the generation of large complex networks. For instance, in order to test the next-generation Internet protocol, we could create a graph similar to what the Internet will look like in a few years.

Among the probabilistic complex network models the oldest and simplest model is Erdős–Rényi, also called random graph (Erdos and Renyi, 1960), in which each pair of nodes has an independent and identical probability p of being connected. Erdős–Rényi model originated from a rich mathematical theory about graph generators. However, it does not follow real complex network properties, as node degree distribution and cluster coefficient.

In an Erdős–Rényi network, the node degree distribution follows a Poisson distribution, while a real network follows a power law (Durrett, 2007). Also, the cluster coefficient in real networks is higher than that in Erdős–Rényi network with same number of nodes, edges and node degree average (Dorogovtsev et al., 2002, Ravasz and Barabási, 2003).

An important characteristic analyzed in Erdős–Rényi graph is the "Phase Transition", which is the phase in which a connected graph becomes disconnected. In detail, in this phase the Erdős–Rényi network has few nodes connected that still form a giant connected component, which is a large fraction of nodes connected among themselves. Also, in the phase transition, the presence of cycles among nodes is rare in the giant connected component of an Erdős–Rényi network. If even a small fraction of nodes is removed, the giant connected component will become disconnected and several small connected components of similar size will appear in the network. Thus, it is possible to summarize that below the phase transition there is no giant connected component and above it the giant connected component fills a large fraction of nodes.

Phase Transition is also known in the literature as "Percolation" or "Critical Point" (Kong et al., 2006). This phase is observed in a large number of natural phenomena, like avalanches, forests (with forest fires), mechanical tension causing earthquakes, and others (Chen et al., 1991, Bailey, 1975, Bak, 1996) which can be mapped into a graph problem.

The increasing interest in the study of complex networks has made the development of more realistic graph generators a fruitful research area. Among the models developed we can highlight *Small World* (Watts and Strogatz, 1998) and *Preferential Attachment* (Barabasi and Albert, 1999) as the first and most traditional graph models. Each of them will be detailed below (Figure 3).

The basis of the Small World model is the fulfillment of the small world phenomenon and the high cluster coefficient value in the synthetic graph generation. To achieve its goal the small-world model combines a regular lattice, which is a graph where each node is linked to its four immediate neighbors, and a random graph as

follows: starting with the lattice, it goes through each edge in turn, and with some probability p it "rewires" that edge, meaning it takes one of its ends and moves it to a new location chosen uniformly at random.

However, as previously detailed, neither the small-world model nor Erdős–Rényi model has a power law degree distribution, since they are democratic models, meaning that there is no difference among nodes. Moreover, both models assume that a network has a fixed number of nodes, which are wired together in some clever way and remain unchanged during the network's lifespan. Due to these facts, the research into network model has been driven to a new direction.

In this context, one of the first papers published is the one by Barabási and Albert (1999), who proposed the Preferential Attachment model. In this model the network grows by the addition of a simple new node at each time-step, with m edges connected to it. The other end of each edge is connected to one of the nodes already placed in the network, randomly chosen with probability proportional to node degree. High-degree nodes have higher probability than low-degree ones. Therefore, the Preferential Attachment model is also called "rich get richer" and leads to power law effects on degree distribution. Some of today's most popular models belong to this class.

As observed, most graph generators focus on static and unweighted graph that mimics only in one or two patterns. Even being poor, these

Figure 3. Node degree distribution of Erdös-Rényi, small-world and preferential attachment models

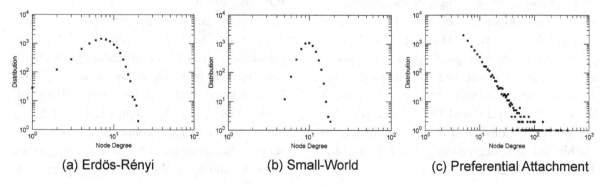

(a) Erdös-Rényi   (b) Small-World   (c) Preferential Attachment

generators provide a good intuitive mechanism for modeling complex networks.

Recently, dynamic and weighted graphs, such as RTM (Recursive Tensor Multiplication) model (Akoglu et al., 2008) and RTG (Random Typing Generator) model (Akoglu and Faloutsos, 2009) have attracted some attention. These models mimic not only more than one graph pattern, as weight, but also the graph evolution over time.

The RTM model is based on tensor multiplication extending the kronecker product of two matrices by adding a third mode. Although RTM model and Kronecker graphs (Leskovec et al., 2005) have been successful in mimicking several real graphs' properties, they have disadvantages, such as generation of multinomial/lognormal degree and eigenvalue distributions instead of a power-law, and have a fixed predetermined number of nodes, in which the addition of more edges than expected does not create additional nodes.

On the other hand, the RTG model is based on a random typing process to generate source and destination nodes identifiers. So far, the RTG has been the most flexible, capable of generating weighted/unweighted, directed/undirected, and bipartite/unipartite graphs, and any combination of these. It is also a simple and intuitive model that generates the emergent macroscopic patterns seen in real graphs.

GRAPH MINING: THE PROBLEM OF DISTINGUISHING REAL NETWORKS FROM SYNTHETIC ONES

The study of complex networks is still in its beginning. Triangles are counted in networks and degree distribution is measured, but it is not clear if these are the only important quantities to be measured or even if there are other more important ones.

Also, due to the evolution in the development of graph generators over the last years, the quantities measured are not enough to separate real networks from synthetic ones. For example, one can mask a

network, and by "masked" we mean a graph that is a non-random sample of a real one, or one can insert a fake user in a recommendation network to obtain a better score in his/her profile.

Thus, how can we separate real networks from synthetic ones? An important tool proposed to tease out the characteristics of large graphs and, based on these characteristic, classify a network into real or synthetic is ShatterPlots (Appel et al., 2009).

SHATTERPLOTS

Our goal is to find patterns to help us spot fake and masked graphs. Thus, we propose to tease out the characteristics of large graphs with the novel tool called ShatterPlots. Moreover, we expect our method to be scalable to handle graphs that span MegaBytes, GigaBytes or more.

The main idea behind ShatterPlots resembles high-energy physics, in which particles are smashed and experts study the results of the collisions to draw conclusions. ShatterPlots randomly removes edges from a network. After each deletion a large number of structural properties of the graph, such as effective diameter, number of reachable pairs of nodes, number of triangles, first eigenvalue of the graph adjacency matrix and size of the largest connected component are measured and their behavior is observed.

During this process there will be a Shattering point, where the connectivity of the graph will be seriously disrupted. A surprising observation is that all criteria shatter at the same point, with the diameter being the only one with a clear sharp spike. Thus at the Shattering point the graph becomes disconnected, the size of the largest component drops, the diameter spikes, and the number of reachable pairs of nodes drops.

As presented in Figure 4, among the several measures we can use to detect critical point/Shattering point, the best is the effective diameter D_e. The reason is that giant component and number of reachable pairs do show a critical point, that is, a sudden increase, as we insert more and more edges, but it is not clear how to define the exact Shattering point. In contrast, the diameter always has a sharp peak, reminding us of the percolation threshold (Schroeder, 1991). Indeed the diameter is widely used to evaluate the network breakdown during the random node deletion or highest degree node deletion (Albert et al., 2000).

ShatterPlots uses an effective diameter and an adaptive number of edges deletion each time-step to be scalable ($O(E)$, in which $|E|$ is the total number of edges of a graph). Another aspect to optimize ShatterPlots is that, instead of the algorithm starting with the full graph and deleting edges at random, it starts with an empty graph and inserts edges at random. The idea is to shuffle the edges file of a graph G and build the temporary graph H adding some number of edges at random. Both of them have the same nodes (N), and will be exactly the same at the end of the algorithm. After each insertion we measure the structural properties of the graph, like, e.g., the diameter, number of reachable pairs of nodes,

number of triangles, first eigenvalue of the graph adjacency matrix or size of the largest connected component. We keep repeating the process until the graph is full, i.e., contains all edges from the edges file.

Ideally, the network properties used would be computed after each edge insertion. However, this approach would be slow requiring that a set of edges be inserted each time-step. The problem is, what should the right number of edges be? Due to this question, ShatterPlots uses an adaptive method, which means the number of edges to be inserted is based on how close the graph is to the Shattering Point. This is evaluated through the analyses of the graph effective diameter.

In detail, we start with a small batch size, and if there is no major difference in the graph structure (the diameter), and then we increase the batch size. Conversely, we decrease it if it seems to be reaching a spike. The same process could be applied the other way round, that is, instead of inserting edges, we could start with a full graph and delete edges at random on it. However, empirically, we have notice that the algorithm is very fast, and

Figure 4. ShatterPlots of Gnutella's network (Ripeanu et al., 2002). The diameter is the only measurement that has a clear and nice spike at the shattering point.

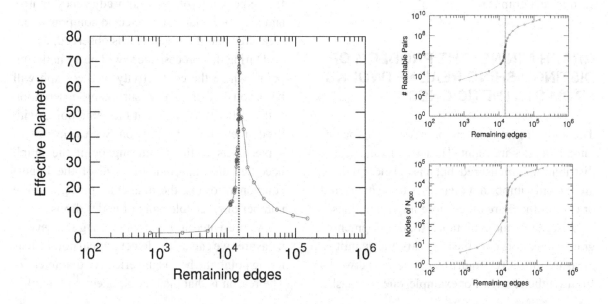

usually needs approximately 250 steps to locate the Shattering point.

OBSERVATIONS

One might expect real graphs, like avalanches, finances of interrelated companies and tectonic plaques, to be barely connected. Therefore they would be just above the Shattering point. However, all real graphs are way above the Shattering point. One might argue that a communication network that is way above Shattering point would be wasting resources. At the Shattering point, a list of surprising observations for several real graphs that allows separating real networks from synthetic ones is given.

The first is the nodes-edges ratio: at the Shattering point the number of nodes (N_{sp}) versus number of edges (E_{sp}) remaining in the graph of all graphs follows a line whose slope is 1.30, meaning at the Shattering Point the number of nodes N_{sp} is approximately 30% higher than E_{sp}, that is, $N_{sp} = 1.30 * E_{sp}$. Figure 5 presents the nodes-edges ratio for several networks. A surprising observation about the nodes-edges ratio pattern is that it is

very close to the phase transition of Erdős–Rényi stated in the literature, i.e., $N_{sp} = 1.26 * E_{sp}$ (Appel et al., 2009).

The real networks are Oregon (cyan square) (Leskovec et al., 2007a), As-Caida (cyan square) (asc, 2007), Gnutella (cyan square) (Ripeanu et al., 2002), WebGoogle (orange circle) (Google, 2002), Amazon (pink box) (Clauset et al., 2004), Epinions (gray diamond) (Richardson et al., 2003), Enron (gray diamond) (Klimt and Yang, 2004), Power Grid (red diamond) (Watts and Strogatz, 1998) and Arxiv (author-to-paper – red +, citation – green x, co-autor – blue *) (Leskovec et al., 2007b, Leskovec et al., 2007c, Gehrke et al., 2003), blog green x) (Leskovec et al., 2007c).

The synthetic ones, represented by triangles in the plot, are Erdős–Rényi (black triangle), Preferential Attachment (cyan triangle), Small World (blue triangle), 2D grid (red triangle) and Hierarchical (pink triangle).

The strictest pattern discovered by ShatterPlots is the Node Shattering Ratio, which presents the relation of nodes at the Shattering point N_{sp} versus total number of nodes N of a graph. This pattern shows that by plotting N_{sp} versus N, we can easily draw a line at $N_{sp} = 0.37 * N$. All real graphs are

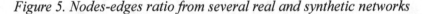

Figure 5. Nodes-edges ratio from several real and synthetic networks

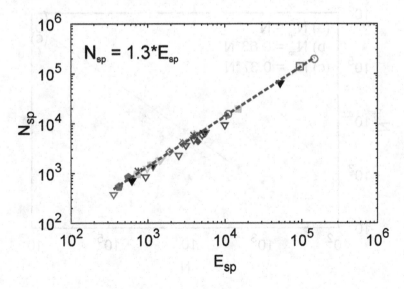

below this line, as shown in Figure 6. The green line (a) is a sanity check (total number of nodes N is equal to N_{sp}, which is the number of nodes at the Shattering Point). The red line (b) is the theoretical line of Erdős–Rényi (black triangles) (Erdos and Renyi, 1960) and the blue line (c) is the line below which all real networks are and above which the synthetic ones are.

Most real graphs have many nodes with degree $d(v_i)=1$, which is a power law degree distribution, and these nodes have a high probability of being isolated at the Shattering point. On the other hand, most of the nodes of graphs 2D-grids and Power Grid have degree four, and Erdős–Rényi graphs have a little variation, with most of their nodes having a degree close to the average degree.

All synthetic graphs have very few isolated nodes when they shatter – 2D-grids are the ones that have the fewest. This is the reason why the red triangles (2D-grids) are above the line of the black triangles (Erdős–Rényi networks), meaning that at the Shattering point they have many more non-isolated nodes than real ones.

However some graphs, like Amazon (pink square) and Gnutella (cyan square close to line (c)

in Figure 6) are masked, meaning that they do not have a nice power law distribution, as shown in Figures 7 (a) and (b), respectively. These graphs (Figure 6) shatter faster than the other real graphs.

The network at the Shattering point is extremely disrupted and still has a large connected component, as shown by TreeGCC pattern. At the Shattering point the number of nodes and edges of the large connected component are almost equal, $N_{spgcc} \approx E_{spgcc}$. As shown in Figure 8, all networks follow a straight line, where $N_{spgcc} = E_{spgcc}$, meaning that the giant connected component looks like a barely connected graph without cycle. Some networks, such as 2D grids (red triangle) and Power grid (red diamond), are a little bit below the line, as they "shatter" fast, that is, the Shattering Point occurs with the deletion of few edges.

Another interesting pattern discovered by ShatterPlots is the Edge Shattering Ratio, where E_{sp}/E is plotted against the epidemic threshold, $1/\lambda_1$. E_{sp}/E is the percentage of edges that still create a giant connected component.

This pattern shows that the percentage of edges remaining in the graph at the Shattering Point has

Figure 6. Node shattering ratio of several networks. The blue line separates all real networks from synthetic ones.

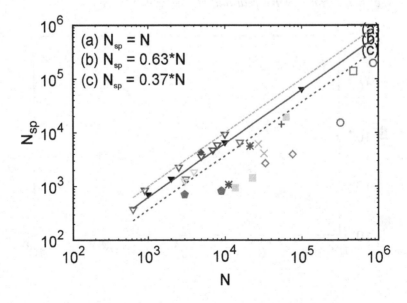

a correlation with the epidemic threshold. Thus, the Edge Shattering Ratio does not depend on the size of the graph, but on the epidemic threshold instead.

Some networks, especially hierarchical (pink triangle), 2D grid (red triangle) and power grid (red diamond), behave as outlier in this pattern, as shown in Figure 9. The percolation threshold of the 2D grid networks is well defined as 0.5 (Kes-

ten, 1980). As the structure of power grid is very close to 2D grids, it displays the same behavior.

As presented in the Background section, if a graph does not have cycles and the number of edges is equal to the number of nodes minus one, then the first eigenvalue is dominated by the square root of the highest node degree. The Root-degree pattern plots the first eigenvalue at the Shattering Point versus the square root of the highest degree node at the Shattering Point. As seen in Figure

Figure 7. Degree distribution of Amazon and Gnutella networks

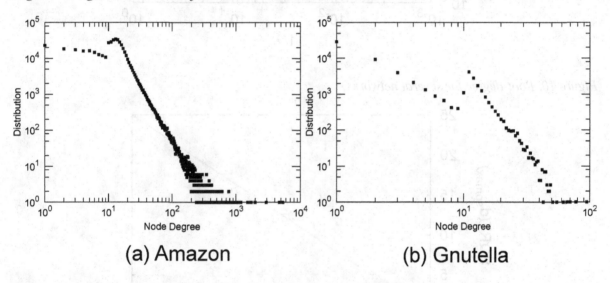

(a) Amazon   (b) Gnutella

Figure 8. Nodes versus edges of a giant connected component at the shattering point

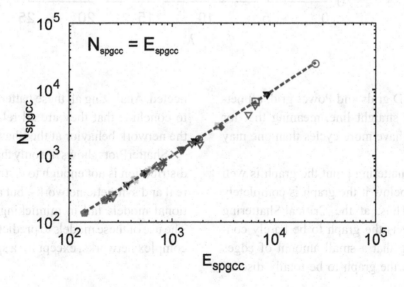

Figure 9. Edge shattering ratio for several networks

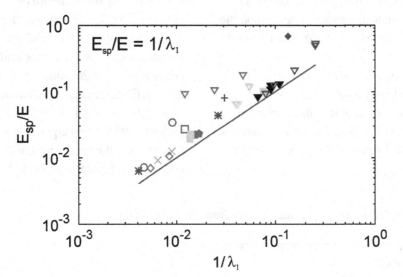

Figure 10. Root-degree for several networks

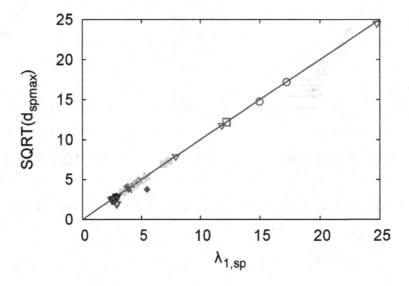

10, except for 2D grids and Power grid, all networks follow a straight line, meaning that for Power Grid we have more cycles than one may expect.

Above the Shattering point the graph is well connected and below it the graph is completely disconnected. Thus, at the Critical/Shattering Point, one expects the graph to be barely connected, meaning that a small amount of edges removed causes the graph to be totally discon-

nected. Analyzing all these patterns, it is possible to conclude that they are all related and reflect the network behavior at the Shattering Point.

ShatterPlots shows not only that a node degree distribution is not enough to distinguish between real and synthetic networks, but also those traditional models fail in mimicking real networks. The use of these models to predict the structure of complex networks, except for a specific propose,

Figure 11. ShatterPlots' scalability

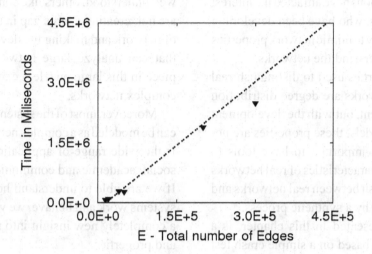

could lead to erroneous conclusions since they have a completely different behavior.

Another interesting observation is that networks that "shatter" fast, as Amazon and Gnutella, might be masked, indicating a possible failure during the network crawled process or some human interference in the network, like the insertion of nodes or edges. Therefore, the node degree distribution might not be enough since there are some real networks, as Power Grid, that do not follow a power law distribution. For these networks, ShatterPlots reveals that they have a completely different behavior, not only regarding the node degree distribution, but also the intrinsic characteristics hidden in a network at the Shattering Point. In the network research area it is important to bear this fact in mind, as some processes or algorithms can be worthy only for some sets of networks, as, for instance, a sampling algorithm (Krishnamurthy et al., 2007).

SCALABILITY

ShatterPlots is a fast tool that just needs to read the edges file once an iteration. The number of

iterations depends on how quickly one can zoom to the shattering point E_{sp}.

Figure 11 shows the scalability of ShatterPlots, plotting the wall-clock time versus the dataset size. The input graphs are synthetic Erdős–Rényi graphs, where we controlled the number of edges E = 14k, 40k, 50k, 200k, 300k, 500k, 600k and number of nodes N=2k, 10K, 10k, 40K, 60k, 80k, 100k, respectively. The experiments ran on a Quad Xeon (2.66 GHz), with 8 GB of RAM, under Linux (Ubuntu). The fit line shows that the method seems to scale up linearly with the graph size.

CONCLUSION

This chapter has reviewed the most traditional properties studied in complex network as well as the models to generate synthetic networks. The aim of the study of the networks structure is to understand and explain what a network looks like, how it becomes a network, how it evolves and so on.

Based on these questions a large number of quantitative measurements were found over the last decade. The main ones are high cluster coefficient, small diameter and skewed degree distribution. These observations have attracted the interest of many researchers, who have been developing network models to try to mimic network properties and thus better understand the networks.

The usual properties used to distinguish real from synthetic networks are degree distribution and cluster coefficient, but with the development of sophisticated models, these properties are not enough. Thus, it is important to have tools to discover intrinsic characteristics of real networks in order to distinguish between real networks and networks generated by a synthetic process.

ShatterPlots, presented in this chapter, is a scalable useful tool based on a simple crash test approach that helps find hidden network patterns by deleting edges and analyzing their behavior in a stage called Shattering Point, which is the highest value reached by the effective diameter during this process.

ShatterPlots is the first initiative to find hidden patterns in order to separate real networks from synthetic ones. There may be other properties that are more important than those presented here to help spot real from synthetic networks.

Moreover, as one can see, the development of more sophisticated models has increased daily, making it impossible to analyze all existent models.

FUTURE RESEARCH DIRECTIONS

The motivation to the study of large complex networks is the wide range of their applications. The observation of new network properties has inspired researchers to the development of new network models that fulfill these properties. This fruitful cycle has made the complex network research area grow over the last years.

However, there is much to be done for the development of more sophisticated models of networks to help us answer questions, such as what does a network look like? While some prop-

erties, as the ones presented in this chapter, are well understood, others like community structure are not, creating a large gap in the understanding of network and making the development of tools that can analyze large networks an important piece in this large puzzle, i.e., the study of large complex networks.

Moreover, most of the systems that surround us can be modeled as a complex network. An example is the wide range of applications of biological, social, academic and communications networks. If we are able to understand how these network systems work and behave, we will probably have a completely new insight into network structure and properties.

REFERENCES

Abello, J., Buchsbaum, A., & Westbrook, J. (1998). A functional approach to external graph algorithms. In *Algorithmica* (pp. 332–343). Springer-Verlag.

Akoglu, L., & Faloutsos, C. (2009). RTG: A recursive realistic graph generator using random typing. *Data Mining and Knowledge Discovery, 19*(2), 194–209. doi:10.1007/s10618-009-0140-7

Akoglu, L., McGlohon, M., & Faloutsos, C. (2008). RTM: Laws and a recursive generator for weighted time-evolving graphs. In *International Conference on Data Mining (ICDM '08)* (pp. 701–706).

Albert, R., Jeong, H., & Barabási, A.-L. (2000). Error and attack tolerance of complex networks. *Nature, 406*, 378–381. doi:10.1038/35019019

Appel, A. P., Chakrabarti, D., Faloutsos, C., Kumar, R., Leskove, J., & Tomkins, A. (2009). Shatterplots: A fast tool for mining large graphs. In *Proceedings of the SIAM International Conference on Data Mining (SDM 2009)*, 802–813.

ASC. (2007). The caida as relationships dataset. Retrieved December 11, 2007, from http://www. caida.org/ data/ active/ as-relationships/.

Bailey, N. T. J. (1975). *The Mathematical Theory of Infectious Diseases and its Applications* (2nd ed.). New York, NY: Hafner Press.

Bak, P. (1996). *How nature works: The science of self-organized criticality*. New York, NY: Copernicus Press.

Barabasi, A. L., & Albert, R. (1999). Emergence of scaling in random networks. *Science, 286*(5439), 509–512. doi:10.1126/science.286.5439.509

Bi, Z., Faloutsos, C., & Korn, F. (2001). The DGX distribution for mining massive, skewed data. In *ACM SIGKDD International Conference on Knowledge Discovery and Data Mining (KDD 2001)* (pp. 17–26).

Bondy, J. A., & Murty, U. S. R. (1979). *Graph Theory with applications*. Amsterdam, Netherlands: Elsevier Science Publishing Co., Inc.

Broder, A., Kumar, R., Maghoul, F., Raghavan, P., Rajagopalan, S., & Stata, R. …Wiener, J. (2000). Graph structure in the Web: Experiments and models. In *Proceedings of the Ninth International World-Wide Web Conference (WWW9) (pp. 309 – 320).*

Chakrabarti, D., & Faloutsos, C. (2006). Graph mining: Laws, generators, and algorithms. *ACM Computing Surveys, 38*(1), 2. doi:10.1145/1132952.1132954

Chakrabarti, D., Wang, Y., Wang, C., Leskovec, J., & Faloutsos, C. (2008). Epidemic thresholds in real networks. *ACM Transactions on Information and System Security, 10*(4), 1–26. doi:10.1145/1284680.1284681

Chakrabarti, D., Zhan, Y., & Faloutsos, C. (2004). R-mat: A recursive model for graph mining. In *Proceedings of the SIAM International Conference on Data Mining (SDM 2004)* (pp. 442 – 446).

Chen, K., Bak, P., & Obukhov, S. P. (1991). Self-organized criticality in a crack-propagation model of earthquakes. *Physical Review A., 43*(2), 625–630. doi:10.1103/PhysRevA.43.625

Clauset, A., Newman, M. E. J., & Moore, C. (2004). Finding community structure in very large networks. *Physical Review E: Statistical, Nonlinear, and Soft Matter Physics, 70*, 066111. doi:10.1103/PhysRevE.70.066111

Clauset, A., Shalizi, C. R., & Newman, M. E. J. (2009). Power-law distributions in empirical data. *SIAM Review, 51*(4), 661–704. doi:10.1137/070710111

Crovella, M. E., & Bestavros, A. (1997). Self-similarity in World Wide Web traffic: Evidence and possible causes. *IEEE/ACM Transactions on Networking, 5*(6), 835–846. doi:10.1109/90.650143

Dill, S., Kumar, R., Mccurley, K. S., Rajagopalan, S., Sivakumar, D., & Tomkins, A. (2002). Self-similarity in the Web. *ACM Transactions on Internet Technology, 2*(3), 205–223. doi:10.1145/572326.572328

Dorogovtsev, S. N., Goltsev, A. V., & Mendes, J. F. F. (2002). Pseudofractal scale-free Web. *Physical Review E: Statistical, Nonlinear, and Soft Matter Physics, 65*, 066122. doi:10.1103/PhysRevE.65.066122

Durrett, R. (2007). *Random Graph Dynamics*. Cambridge, UK: Cambridge University Press.

Erdos, P., & Renyi, A. (1960). On the evolution of random graphs. *Publication of the Mathematical Institute of the Hungarian Acadamy of Science, 5*, 17–67.

Faloutsos, M., Faloutsos, P., & Faloutsos, C. (1999). On power-law relationships of the Internet topology. In *ACM Special Interest Group on Data Communication (SIGCOMM 1999)* (1, pp. 251-262. Cambridge, Massachusetts: ACM Press.

Flaxman, A., Frieze, A., & Fenner, T. (2005). High degree vertices and eigenvalues in the preferential attachment graph. *Internet Math.*, *2*(1), 1–19. doi:10.1080/15427951.2005.10129097

Fortunato, S. (2010). Community detection in graphs. *Physics Reports*, *486*(3-5), 75–174. doi:10.1016/j.physrep.2009.11.002

Gehrke, J., Ginsparg, P., & Kleinberg, J. (2003). Overview of the 2003 KDD Cup. *ACM Special Interest Group on Knowledge Discovery and Data Mining - SIGKDD Explorations*, *5*(2), 149–151. doi:10.1145/980972.980992

Google. (2002). *Google programming contest*. Retrieved on May, 2002 from http://www.google.com/ programming-contest/.

Huberman, B. A., & Adamic, L. A. (1999). Internet: Growth dynamics of the World-Wide Web. *Nature*, *401*(6749), 131.

Kesten, H. (1980). The critical probability of bond percolation on the square lattice equals 1/2. *Communications in Mathematical Physics*, *74*, 41–59. doi:10.1007/BF01197577

Kleinberg, J. M., Kumar, R., Raghavan, P., Rajagopalan, S., & Tomkins, A. S. (1999). The Web as a graph: Measurements, models, and methods. In *Computing and Combinatorics: 5th Annual International Conference (COCOON '99)* (pp. 1–17).

Klimt, B., & Yang, Y. (2004). Introducing the ENRON corpus. In *Collaboration, Electronic messaging, Anti-Abuse and Spam Conference CEAS* (1–2).

Kong, J. S., Rezaei, B. A., Sarshar, N., Roychowdhury, V. P., & Boykin, P. O. (2006). Collaborative spam filtering using e-mail networks. *Computer*, *39*(8), 67–73. doi:10.1109/MC.2006.257

Krishnamurthy, V., Faloutsos, M., Chrobak, M., Cui, J.-H., Lao, L., & Percus, A. G. (2007). Sampling large Internet topologies for simulation purposes. *Computer Networks*, *51*(15), 4284–4302. doi:10.1016/j.comnet.2007.06.004

Kumar, R., Raghavan, P., Rajagopalan, S., & Tomkins, A. (1999). Trawling the Web for emerging cyber-communities. *Computer Networks, 31*(11-16), 1481–1493.

Leskovec, J., Adamic, L. A., & Huberman, B. A. (2007a). The dynamics of viral marketing. (TWEB). *ACM Transactions on the Web*, *1*(1), 2. doi:10.1145/1232722.1232727

Leskovec, J., Chakrabarti, D., Kleinberg, J. M., & Faloutsos, C. (2005). Realistic, mathematically tractable graph generation and evolution, using kronecker multiplication. In *Principles and Practice of Knowledge Discovery in Databases* (pp. 133–145). PKDD.

Leskovec, J., Kleinberg, J. M., & Faloutsos, C. (2007b). Graph evolution: Densification and shrinking diameters. *ACM Transactions on Knowledge Discovery from Data - TKDD*, *1*(1), 1 – 40.

Leskovec, J., McGlohon, M., Faloutsos, C., Glance, N. S., & Hurst, M. (2007c). Patterns of cascading behavior in large blog graphs. In *Proceedings of the SIAM International Conference on Data Mining (SDM 2007)*.

Mihail, M., & Papadimitriou, C. H. (2002). On the eigenvalue power law. In *Proceedings of the 6th International Workshop on Randomization and Approximation Techniques (RANDOM '02)*, (pp. 254–262). London, UK: Springer-Verlag.

Milgram, S. (1967). The small world problem. *Psychology Today*, *2*, 60–67.

Newman, M. E. J. (2003). The structure and function of complex networks. *SIAM Review*, *45*, 167–256. doi:10.1137/S003614450342480

Newman, M. E. J. (2005). Power laws, pareto distributions and zipf's law. *Contemporary Physics, 46,* 323. doi:10.1080/00107510500052444

Page, L., Brin, S., Motwani, R., & Winograd, T. (1999). *The Pagerank citation ranking: Bringing order to the Web. Technical report.* Stanford Digital Library Technologies Project.

Palmer, C. R., Gibbons, P. B., & Faloutsos, C. (2002). Anf: A fast and scalable tool for data mining in massive graphs. In *ACM SIGKDD International Conference on Knowledge Discovery and Data Mining,* Edmonton, Alberta, Canada *(KDD 2002)* (1, pp. 81–90). New York, NY: ACM Press.

Ravasz, E., & Barabási, A.-L. (2003). Hierarchical organization in complex networks. *Physical Review E: Statistical, Nonlinear, and Soft Matter Physics, 67*(2), 026112. doi:10.1103/PhysRevE.67.026112

Redner, S. (1998). How popular is your paper? An empirical study of the citation distribution. *The European Physical Journal B - Condensed Matter and Complex Systems, 2,*131-134.

Richardson, M., Agrawal, R., & Domingos, P. (2003). Trust management for the Semantic Web. In *Second International Semantic Web Conference,* Florida, USA.

Ripeanu, M., Foster, I., & Iamnitchi, A. (2002). Mapping the Gnutella network: Properties of large-scale peer-to-peer systems and implications for system design. *IEEE Internet Computing Journal, 6*(1).

Schroeder, M. (1991). *Fractals, Chaos, Power Laws: Minutes from an Infinite Paradise.* W. H. Freeman.

Tauro, S. L., Palmer, C., Siganos, G., & Faloutsos, M. (2001). A simple conceptual model for the Internet topology. In *Global Internet,* San Antonio, Texas.

Tsourakakis, C. E. (2008). Fast counting of triangles in large real networks without counting: Algorithms and laws. In *International Conference on Data Mining,* Washington, DC, USA (*ICDM '08)* (pp. 608–617). IEEE Computer Society.

Watts, D. J., & Strogatz, S. H. (1998). Collective dynamics of 'small-world' networks. *Nature, 393*(6684), 440–442. doi:10.1038/30918

ADDITIONAL READING

Aggarwal, C. C., Zhao, Y., & Yu, P. S. (2010). On Clustering Graph Streams. *Proceedings of the SIAM International Conference on Data Mining (SDM 2010)* (pp. 478-489).

Amer-Yahia, S., Doan, A., Kleinberg, J. M., Koudas, N., & Franklin, M. J. (2010). Crowds, clouds, and algorithms: Exploring the human side of "big data" applications. *Proceedings of the ACM SIGMOD International Conference on Management of Data (SIGMOD '10)* (pp. 1259-1260).

Barabasi, A.-L. (2002). *Linked: The New Science of Networks.* Perseus Publishing.

Chakrabarti, D., Papadimitriou, S., Modha, D. S., & Faloutsos, C. Fully automatic cross-associations. (2004). *Proceedings of the 2004 ACM SIGKDD International Conference on Knowledge Discovery and Data Mining (KDD04)* (pp. 79-88).

Chen, J., Zaane, O. R., & Goebel, R. (2009). A visual data mining approach to find overlapping communities in networks. *The International Conference on Advances in Social Network Analysis and Mining (ASONAM* 2009) (pp. 338-343).

Getoor, L., & Diehl, C. P. (2005). Link mining: A survey. *ACM SIGKDD Explorations, 7,* 3–12. doi:10.1145/1117454.1117456

Han, J., Sun, Y., Yan, X., & Yu, P. S. (2010). Mining knowledge from databases: An information network analysis approach. *Proceedings of the ACM SIGMOD International Conference on Management of Data (SIGMOD 2010)* (pp. 1251-1252).

Kang, U., Tsourakakis, C. E., Appel, A. P., Faloutsos, C., & Leskovec, J. (2010). Radius plots for mining tera-byte scale graphs: Algorithms, patterns, and observations. *Proceedings of the SIAM International Conference on Data Mining (SDM 2010)* (pp. 548-558).

Kossinets, G., Kleinberg, J. M., & Watts, D. J. (2008). The structure of information pathways in a social communication network. *Proceedings of the 14th ACM SIGKDD International Conference on Knowledge Discovery and Data Mining (KDD 2008)* (pp. 435-443).

Lamberti, F., Sanna, A., & Demartini, C. (2009). A relation-based page rank algorithm for Semantic Web search engines. *IEEE Transactions on Knowledge and Data Engineering, 21*, 123–136. doi:10.1109/TKDE.2008.113

Leskovec, J., Chakrabarti, D., Kleinberg, J. M., Faloutsos, C., & Ghahramani, Z. (2010). Kronecker graphs: An approach to modeling networks. *Journal of Machine Learning Research, 11*, 985–1042.

Leskovec, J., Lang, K. J., & Mahoney, M. W. (2010). Empirical comparison of algorithms for network community detection. *Proceedings of the 19th International Conference on World Wide Web (WWW 2010)* (pp. 631-640).

Liu, L., Zhu, F., Chen, C., Yan, X., Han, J., Yu, P. S., & Yang, S. (2010). Mining diversity on networks. *International Conference on Database Systems for Advanced Applications (DASFAA 2010)* (pp. 384-398).

Newman, M. E. J. (2010). *Networks: An Introduction*. Oxford, UK: Oxford University Press.

Pavlo, A., Paulson, E., Rasin, A., Abadi, D. J., DeWitt, D. J., & Madden, S. …Tatbul, N. (2009). A comparison of approaches to large-scale data analysis. *Proceedings of the ACM SIGMOD International Conference on Management of Data (SIGMOD 2009)* (pp. 165-178).

Prakash, B. A., Sridharan, A., Seshadri, M., Machiraju, S., & Faloutsos, C. (2010). EigenSpokes: Surprising patterns and scalable community chipping in large graphs. *Advances in Knowledge Discovery and Data Mining, 14th Pacific-Asia Conference (PAKDD 2010)* (6119, pp. 435-448).

Tsourakakis, C. E., Kang, U., Miller, G. L., & Faloutsos, C. (2009). DOULION: Counting triangles in massive graphs with a coin *Proceedings of ACM SIGKDD International Conference on Knowledge Discovery and Data Mining (KDD 2009)* (pp. 837-846).

KEY TERMS AND DEFINITIONS

Complex Network: A non-trivial graph whose formation is not based on a random process.

Epidemic Threshold: Level at which a disease becomes an epidemic.

Masked Networks: Networks in which some parts are clipped by a non-random process.

Phase Transition: A stage in which a graph changes from disconnected to connect or vice-versa.

Power Law: A type of data distribution that is very common to occur in natural phenomena; it looks like a line on log-log scale.

Shatter a Graph: Remove edges at random until all nodes have been completely isolated and observe the diameter of the graph during this process.

Shattering Point: A high spike in the graph diameter led by the random edge deletion process.

Small World Phenomenon: Phenomenon in which everybody is connected by few contacts.

Synthetic Networks: Networks created by graph model generators.

Chapter 11
Matrix Decomposition– Based Dimensionality Reduction on Graph Data

Hiroto Saigo
Kyushu Institute of Technology, Japan

Koji Tsuda
National Institute of Advanced Industrial Science and Technology (AIST), Japan

ABSTRACT

Graph is a mathematical framework that allows us to represent and manage many real-world data such as relational data, multimedia data and biomedical data. When each data point is represented as a graph and we are given a number of graphs, a task is to extract a few common patterns that capture the property of each population. A frequent graph mining algorithm such as AGM, gSpan and Gaston can enumerate all the frequent patterns in graph data, however, the number of patterns grows exponentially, therefore it is essential to output only discriminative patterns. There are many existing researches on this topic, but this chapter focus on the use of matrix decomposition techniques, and explains the two general cases where either i) no target label is available, or ii) target label is available for each data point. The reuslting method is a branch and bound pattern mining algorithm with efficient pruning condition, and we evaluate its effectiveness on cheminformatics data.

INTRODUCTION

Graph is a powerful mathematical framework which enables us to represent and manage various real-world objects in a natural way. The examples include XML, social networks and biological net-works. In this chapter, we focus on applications in chemoinformatics where a chemical compound is represented as a labeled graph in which atoms and edges have corresponding labels such as H, C, N and single, double, aromatic bond, respectively. Given a large number of such graphs, a recent

DOI: 10.4018/978-1-61350-053-8.ch011

approach to extract common features is through the use of frequently appearing subgraphs. Even though it involves *subgraph isomorphism* problem, which is NP-hard, after the pioneering work AGM (Inokuchi, 2005), several fast frequent graph miners such as Gaston (Nijssen & Kok, 2004), gSpan gSpan (Yan & Han, 2002a) are proposed. A frequent subgraph mining algorithm enumerates all the subgraph patterns that appear more than m times in a graph database. The threshold m is called *minimum support*. As a next step after mining frequent patterns, we consider learning rules to classify graphs into positive class and negative class according to given labels. In order to achieve the best classification accuracy when classifying graph data, the minimum support threshold (the number of times a subgraph appears in graph data) has to be set to a small value (Wale & Karypis, 2006; Kazius, Nijssen, Kok, Baeck, & Ijzerman, 2006; Helma, Cramer, Kramer, & Raedt, 2004). However, such a setting creates millions of patterns, leading to difficulty when storing patterns and using them in the subsequent learning step. To avoid creating large number of uninformative patterns, we make use of a tree-shaped search space for enumerating frequent patterns (Figure 4). As we go down the tree from the root node, we encounter many child nodes corresponding to supergraphs of the parent node. For an efficiency reason, we desire to traverse only nodes that are necessary for the subsequent learning step.

In this chapter, we assume that the occurrence of subgraphs mined so far are recorded in a design matrix **X**. Since the number of subgraphs can be very large, the size of the design matrix can be too large to store in memory. Thereby we employ a so called *matrix-free* method, which constructs only a part of the whole matrix in an iterative fashion. More precisely, we make advantage of Lanczos method for unsupervised learning, and partial least squares (PLS) regression for supervised learning. The connection between the two appears later in this chapter.

Although we only deal with an application to chemical informatics data in this chapter, the proposed approach is applicable to other data such as protein (Jin, Young, & Wang, 2009), RNA (Tsuda & Kudo, 2006), text (Kudo, Maeda, & Matsumoto, 2005), image (Nowozin, Tsuda, Uno, Kudo, & Bakir, 2007), video (Nowozin, Bakir, & Tsuda, 2007) and so forth.

RELATED RESEARCH

As a next step after mining frequent patterns, many researchers have worked on integrating frequent pattern mining and rule learning algorithm. They are roughly categorized into filter approach and wrapper approach (Kohavi & John, 1997).

A filter approach first enumerates all the frequent patterns, then perform learning step afterwards (PatClass (Cheng, Yan, Han, & Hsu, 2007)). A pro of this approach is that one can employ recent learning algorithms without further change. Fei and Huan considered the spatial distribution of patterns for classifying graph data (Pattern SFS (Fei & Huan, 2009), LPGB (Fei & Huan, 2010)). A major con of filter approach is that the number of frequent pattern can become too large to perform the subsequent learning step because of a memory and storage issue.

A wrapper approach select features while mining patterns. Information gain criterion is often employed to suppress the number of output patterns ($M^\phi T$ (Fan et al., 2008), DDPMine (Cheng, Yan, Han, & Yu, 2008)). In stead of information gain, HARMONY (Wang & Karypis, 2005) and COM (Jin et al., 2009) employ another criterion, which is a relative frequency of a pattern appearing in positive class against that in negative class. CORK (Thoma et al., 2009) uses a submodular quality criterion that can guarantee the quality of selected patterns to some degree. gBoost (Saigo, Nowozin, Kadowaki, Kudo, & Tsuda, 2009) is designed to solve classification problem by selecting patterns that minimize hinge loss function (Schoelkopf &

Smola, 2002). Similarly, gLARS (Tsuda, 2007) is designed to solve regression problem by selecting patterns that minimize squared loss function (Schoelkopf & Smola, 2002). Moreover, it traverses and shows all the solution set along the varying regularization parameter (Efron, Hastie, Johnstone, & Tibshirani, 2004). gSSC (Kong & Yu, 2010) is developed for a case when both labeled and unlabeled data are available. This approach employs standard Laplacian regularizer for semi-supervised learning, and discriminative patterns are searched by branch and bound algorithm. Leap Search (Yan, Cheng, Han, & Yu, 2008) aims at mining patterns that show significant frequency difference between positive and negative class.

Table 1 shows a categorization of existing approaches that integrates mining step and learning step. They are further categorized into either itemset or graph depending on the type frequent pattern miner. However, they are exchangeable, that is, methods developed for itemset data can be ported to graph data, and vice versa.

This chapter is organized as follows: first we introduce terminology and definition of our pattern; subgraphs. Subsequently, supervised learning and unsupervised learning with dimensionality reduction on graph data are presented with computational experiments on chemoinformatics data. We conclude this chapter with discussion and future research direction.

Representation of Graph Data

Throughout the chapter, we deal with undirected, labeled and connected graphs. To be more precise, we define the graph, subgraph and *subgraph isomorphism* as follows:

Definition 1 (Labeled connected graph). *A labeled graph is represented in a 4-tuple G=(V,E,L,l), where V is a set of vertices, $E \subseteq V \times V$ is a set of edges, L is a set of labels, and $l : V \bigcup E \rightarrow L$ is a mapping that assigns labels to the vertices and edges. A labeled connected graph is a labeled graph such that there is a path between any pair of vertices.*

Definition 2 (Isomorphism). *Let $G'=(V',E',L',l')$ and $G=(V,E,L,l)$ be labeled connected graphs. These two graphs are isomorphic if there exists a bijective function $\phi : V' \rightarrow V$ such that: (1) $\forall v' \in V', l'(v') = l(\phi(v'))$, (2) $E = \{\{\phi(v_1'), \phi(v_2')\} \mid \{v_1', v_2'\} \in E'\}$ and (3) $\forall \{v_1', v_2'\} \in E', l'(\{v_1', v_2'\}) = l(\{\phi(v_1'), \phi(v_2')\})$.*

Definition 3 (Subgraph). *Given two graphs $G'=(V',E',L',l')$ and $G=(V,E,L,l)$, G' is a subgraph of G if the following conditions are satisfied: (1) $V' \subseteq V$, (2) $E' \subseteq E$, (3) $L' \subseteq L$, (4) $\forall v' \in V', l(v') = l'(v')$ and (5) $\forall e' \in E', l(e') = l'(e')$. If G' is a subgraph of G, then G is a supergraph of G'.*

Definition 4 (Subgraph Isomorphism). *A graph G' is subgraph-isomorphic to a graph G*

Table 1. Recent mining based structure learning methods

	Filter	Wrapper
Itemset data	PatClass (Cheng et al., 2007)	HARMONY (Wang & Karypis, 2005), CPAR (Thoma et al., 2009), DDPMine (Cheng, Yan, Han, & Yu, 2008), M^bT (Fan et al., 2008)
Graph data	LPBG (Fei & Huan, 2010), Pattern SFS (Fei & Huan, 2009)	COM (Jin et al., 2009), Leap Search (Yan, Cheng, Han, & Yu, 2008), CORK (Thoma et al., 2009), gSSC (Kong & Yu, 2010), gBoost (Saigo, Nowozin, Kadowaki, Kudo, & Tsuda, 2009), gLARS (Tsuda, 2007)

$G' \subseteq G$ () iff it has a subgraph S that is isomorphic to G'.

Supervised Dimensionality Reduction on Graph Data

We begin with defining the supervised learning problem on graph data. The task is to learn a prediction rule from the training examples $\{(G_i, y_i)\}_{i=1}^n$, where G_i is a training graph and $y_i \in \mathbb{R}$ is the associated class label. Let P be the set of all patterns, i.e., the set of all subgraphs included in at least one training graph. Then, each graph G_i is encoded as a $|P|$-dimensional row vector

$$x_{i,p} = \begin{cases} 1 & if \ p \subseteq G_i, \\ -1 & otherwise, \end{cases}$$

and $n \times P$-matrix $X = [x_1, x_2, \ldots, x_n]^\mathrm{T}$. This feature space is illustrated in Figure 1.

Our prediction rule is a convex combination of binary indicators $x_{i,j}$, and has the form

$$f(x_i) = x_i^\mathrm{T} \beta \tag{1}$$

where β is a $|P|$-dimensional column vector such that $\sum_{p \in P_i}^n \beta_p = 1$ and $\beta_p \geq 0$. A simple formulation for minimizing prediction error leads to that of ordinary least squares (OLS):

$$\min_\beta \| X\beta - y \|_2^2, \tag{2}$$

where $\| x \|_2 = \left(\sum_{i=1}^n {}^n_i x_i \mid^2 \right)^{1/2}$ denotes the ℓ_2 norm of $\mathbf{x}$, and response variable $y \in \mathbb{R}^n$ are assumed centered. The solution to this OLS problem is obtained in a closed form as:

$$\beta = (X^\mathrm{T} X)^{-1} X^\mathrm{T} y. \tag{3}$$

However, this requires the whole design matrix $\mathbf{X}$, which is intractable in our setting, since it amounts to enumerating all the frequent subgraphs in advance. Even in the case where we have all the frequent subgraph patterns at hand, the number of subgraphs P easily exceeds the number of graphs n, therefore overfitting problem arises.

In chemometrics, however, it is often the case that many measured variables exists on each of a few observations. Partial Least Squares (PLS) was originally introduced by Wold (H. Wold, 1966) for such a situation, and heavily used in the community as an alternative to OLS. Its statistical property was unclear for a long time, but later recognized as equivalent to conjugate gradient (S. Wold, Ruhe, Wold, & DunnIII, 1984) and shrink coefficients like ridge regression (Frank & Friedman, 1993).

PLS performs dimensionality reduction similar to PCA, and fits regression function in the low-dimensional space. Let $\mathbf{X}$ be our design matrix and $\mathbf{W}$ be the m-dimensional projection matrix, the problem PLS solves can be written as a constrained least squares problem:

$$\min_\beta \| y - X\beta \|_2^2 \tag{4}$$

$$s.t. \beta \in span(W_m), \tag{5}$$

where $span(\mathbf{W_m})$ indicates that the projection matrix $\mathbf{W}$ lies in the m-dimensional *Krylov subspace*

$$K_m(X^\mathrm{T} X, X^\mathrm{T} y) = \{X^\mathrm{T} y, X^\mathrm{T} X X^\mathrm{T} y, \ldots, (X^\mathrm{T} X)^{m-1} X^\mathrm{T} y\}.$$

Therefore one can consider PLS as a two step method; i) it first projects $\mathbf{X}$ onto $\mathbf{W}$, ii) then fits regression coefficients β in a low-dimensional projected space $\mathbf{XW}$. The column vectors of the matrix $W = [w_1, w_2, \ldots, w_m]$ is called as weight vectors in PLS literature. The column vectors of the matrix $XW = [Xw_1, Xw_2, \ldots, Xw_m]$ is called

Figure 1. Feature space based on subgraph patterns. The feature vector consists of binary pattern indicators.

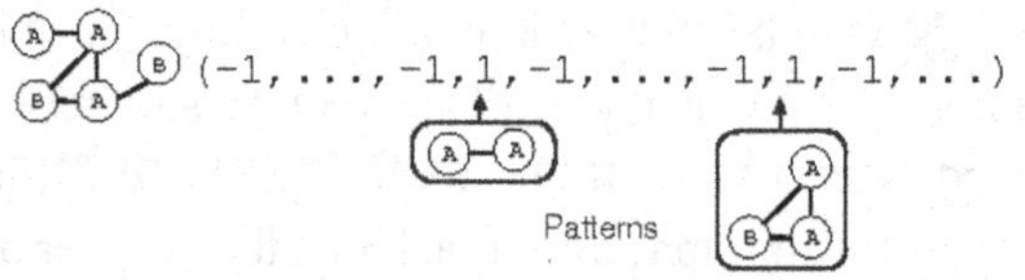

as latent components, and often denoted as $T = [t_1, t_2, \ldots, t_m]$. Typically, each latent component **t** is kept orthogonal to each other. Regression problem in the projected space can be written as

$$\min_{\beta} \| y - XW\hat{\beta} \|_2^2, \qquad (6)$$

where $\hat{\beta} \in \mathbb{R}^m$ is a m-dimensional regression coefficient vector in the projected space. m controls the number of components in PLS, and can be seen as a regularization parameter. If we set $m = P$, then the OLS solution (3) is recovered. As long as m is chosen such that $m < n$, overfitting problem is naturally avoided. Equation (6) can be interpreted as a covariance maximization procedure (Frank & Friedman, 1993). We give a simple proof that the first weight vector $\mathbf{w} = \mathbf{w}_1$ in PLS maximizes the covariance: **cov**$(Xw, y) = y^T Xw$.

Theorem 1. *PLS maximizes squared covariance*

$$\max_{w} \ \mathrm{cov}^2(Xw, y) \qquad (7)$$

Proof. By taking the derivative of Equation (6) with respect to $\hat{\beta}$ and setting it to zero, regression coefficients in the projected space are obtained as

$$\hat{\beta} = \left(W^T X^T X W\right)^{-1} W^T X^T y.$$

Corresponding regression coefficients in the original space are

$$\beta = W\hat{\beta} = W \left(W^T X^T X W\right)^{-1} W^T X^T y. \qquad (8)$$

Replacing this into Equation (6) and solving it with respect to the first weight vector **w** obtains

$$\min_{\beta} \| y - X\beta \|_2^2 = \min_{w} \| y - Xw\left(w^T X^T Xw\right)^{-1} w^T X^T y \|_2^2$$

$$= \min_{w} \| y - Xww^T X^T y \|_2^2,$$

where orthogonal condition $w^T X^T Xw = 1$ is used in the last equality. By extracting the last equation,

$$\min_{w} \| y - Xww^T X^T y \|_2^2$$

$$= \min_{w} \left(y - Xww^T X^T y\right)^T \left(y - Xww^T X^T y\right)$$

$$= \min_{w} y^T y - 2y^T Xww^T X^T y + y^T Xww^T X^T Xww^T X^T y.$$

Removing $y^T y$ and using the orthogonal condition obtains

$$\min_{w} - y^T Xww^T X^T y$$

$$= \max_{w} \ (y^T Xw)(y^T Xw)^T$$

$$= \max_{w} \ \mathrm{cov}^2(Xw, y).$$

Note, however, that each column of **Xw** is not centered in our case. A standard NIPALS algorithm (Algorithm 1) can efficiently compute weight vectors in such a way that they successively maximize covariance. Then after m iterations, the regression coefficients β are recovered from weight vectors using Equation (8).

In each iteration of NIPALS, rank-one deflation of design matrix $\mathbf{X}$ is performed to ensure the orthogonality between latent components $\mathbf{t}$. However, this deflation step completely destroys the structure of $\mathbf{X}$, therefore cannot be used in combination with graph mining. (Since we cannot modify the structure of the design matrix.) To avoid deflation, we make use of the connection between PLS and the Lanczos method (Lanczos, 1950). The Lanczos method is a *matrix free* method, which does not change the structure of design matrix, therefore can be coupled with graph mining (Saigo & Tsuda, 2008). Moreover, this method is proven to be mathematically equivalent to PLS (Lanczos, 1950; Eld_en, 2004). Based on this connection, we give a non-deflation PLS algorithm which does not require deflation at all. Remember that in NIPALS, the first weight vector is obtained as

$$w_1 = X^{(1)\mathrm{T}}y = X^{\mathrm{T}}y.$$

The second weight vector is obtained as

$$w_2 = X^{(2)\mathrm{T}}y = \left(X^{(1)} - t_1 t_1^{\mathrm{T}} X^{(1)}\right)^{\mathrm{T}} y = X^{(1)\mathrm{T}}\left(I - t_1 t_1^{\mathrm{T}}\right)y$$

$$= X^{\mathrm{T}}\left(r_1 - \left(y^{\mathrm{T}}t_1\right)t_1\right),$$

where we used *residual* $r_{k+1} = \left(r_k - \left(y^{\mathrm{T}}t_{k-1}\right)t_{k-1}\right)$ and initialized it as $r_1 = y$. The third weight vector is obtained similarly as

$$w_3 = X^{(3)\mathrm{T}}y = \left(X^{(2)} - t_2 t_2^{\mathrm{T}} X^{(2)}\right)^{\mathrm{T}} y = X^{(2)\mathrm{T}}\left(I - t_2 t_2^{\mathrm{T}}\right)y$$

$$= X^{(1)\mathrm{T}}\left(I - t_1 t_1^{\mathrm{T}}\right)\left(I - t_2 t_2^{\mathrm{T}}\right)y$$

$$= X^{\mathrm{T}}\left(I - t_1 t_1^{\mathrm{T}} - t_2 t_2^{\mathrm{T}}\right)y$$

$$= X^{\mathrm{T}}\left(r_2 - \left(y^{\mathrm{T}}t_2\right)t_2\right).$$

Algorithm 1. NIPALS

Initial: $\tilde{\mathbf{X}}^{(1)} = \mathbf{X}$
For $k = 1, \ldots, m$, do

$$\mathbf{w}_k = \tilde{\mathbf{X}}^{(k)\mathrm{T}}\mathbf{y}. \text{ (Weight vector)}$$

$$\mathbf{t}_k = \tilde{\mathbf{X}}^{(k)}\mathbf{w}_k \text{ (Latent components)}$$

$$\tilde{\mathbf{X}}^{(k+1)} = \tilde{\mathbf{X}}^{(k)} - \mathbf{t}_k \mathbf{t}_k^{\mathrm{T}} \tilde{\mathbf{X}}^{(k)} \text{ (Deflation)}$$

EndFor
Convert $\mathbf{w}$ into regression coefficients using Equation (8)

In the same line, we can represent the k-the weight vector as

$$w_k = X^{\mathrm{T}}\left(r_{k-1} - \left(y^{\mathrm{T}}t_{k-1}\right)t_{k-1}\right).$$

Now it is clear that we do not need to update $\mathbf{X}$, but can update $\mathbf{r}$ instead. This non-deflation PLS algorithm is stated in Algorithm 2.

Below, we discuss how to apply the non-deflation PLS algorithm to graph data. The feature space has already been illustrated in Figure 1. Since $|P|$ is a large number, we cannot keep the whole design matrix. So we need to set $\mathbf{X}$ as the empty matrix first, and grow the matrix as the iterations proceed. In each iteration, we obtain the set of patterns p whose weight $w_{ip} = X_p^{\mathrm{T}}r$ is above the threshold, which can be written as

$$P_i = \{p \mid \left|X_p^{\mathrm{T}}r\right| \geq \varepsilon\}, \tag{9}$$

which corresponds to selecting patterns with largest current *covariance*. Then, the design matrix is expanded to include newly introduced patterns. There are two alternative ways to determine the threshold ε: 1) Sort $|w_{ij}|$ in the descending order, take the top-k elements, and set all the other elements to zero. 2) Set ε to a fixed threshold. In the latter case, the number of non-zero elements in $\mathbf{w}_i$

may vary. In the experiments, we took the former top-k approach to avoid unbalanced weight vectors and to make efficiency comparisons easier. The pseudocode of gPLS is described in Algorithm 3. Most numerical computations are carried over from Algorithm 2.

Our search strategy is a branch-and-bound algorithm that requires a canonical search space in which a whole set of patterns are enumerated without duplication. As to the search space, we adopt the DFS (depth first search) code tree (Yan & Han, 2002a). The basic idea of the DFS code tree is to organize patterns as a tree, where a child node has a supergraph of the parent's pattern (Figure 2). A pattern is represented as a text string called the DFS code. The patterns are enumerated by generating the tree from the root to leaves using a recursive algorithm. To avoid duplications, node generation is systematically done by rightmost extensions. See Appendix for details about the DFS code and the rightmost extension.

All embeddings of a pattern in the graphs $\{G_i\}_{i=1}^{n}$ are maintained in each node. If a pattern matches a graph in different ways, all such embeddings are stored. When a new pattern is created by adding an edge, it is not necessary to perform full isomorphism checks with respect to all graphs in the database. A new list of embeddings are made by extending the embeddings of the parent (Yan & Han, 2002a). Technically, it is necessary to devise a data structure such that the embeddings are stored incrementally, because it takes a prohibitive amount of memory to keep all embeddings independently in each node.

Our aim is to find the optimal hypothesis that maximizes the gain $g(p) = \left| X_p^T r \right|$. Suppose the search tree is generated up to the subgraph pattern p. If it is guaranteed that the gain of any supergraph pattern p' is not larger than ε, we can avoid the generation of downstream nodes without losing the optimal pattern. Our pruning condition is described as follows.

Theorem 2. *Define* $y_i = \mathrm{sgn}(r_i)$. *For any pattern* p' *such that* $p \subseteq p'$, $g(p') < \varepsilon$, *if*

$$\max\{g^+(p), g^-(p)\} < \varepsilon, \tag{10}$$

Figure 2. Schematic figure of the tree-shaped search space of graph patterns (i.e., the DFS code tree). To find the optimal pattern efficiently, the tree is systematically expanded by rightmost extensions.

Algorithm 2. Non-deflation PLS

```
Initial: r₁ = y
For k = 1,...,m do
wₖ = Xᵀrₖ  (Weight vector)
If k = 1 then
t₁ = Xw₁
Else
tₖ = (I − tₖ₋₁tₖ₋₁ᵀ)Xwₖ  (Orthogonaliza-
tion)
EndIf
tₖ = tₖ / ‖ tₖ ‖₂  (Latent component)
rₖ₊₁ = rₖ − (yᵀtₖ)tₖ  (Update residual)
EndFor
Convert W into regression coeffi-
cients using equation (8)
```

Tree of Substructures

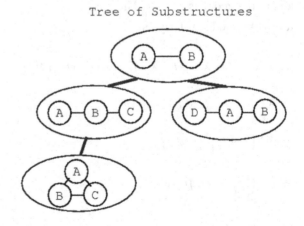

where

$$g^+(p) = 2 \sum_{\substack{i \\ \{i|y_i=+1, x_{i,j}=1\}}}^n |r_i| - \sum_{i=1}^n r_i$$

$$g^-(p) = 2 \sum_{\substack{i \\ \{i|y_i=-1, x_{i,j}=1\}}}^n |r_i| + \sum_{i=1}^n r_i.$$

Other conditions such as the maximum size of pattern (*maxpat*) and the minimum support (*minsup*) can be used in combination with the pruning condition (10). The whole gPLS algorithm is stated in Algorithms 3 and 4.

COMPUTATIONAL EXPERIMENTS

In this subsection, we evaluate the efficiency of gPLS on publicly available chemical datasets. We

Algorithm 3. gPLS

```
Initial: r₁ = y,  X̂ = ∅
For k = 1,...,m do
Pₖ = {p | |Xₚᵀrₖ| ≥ ε}. (Pattern search)
Xₚₖ: design matrix restricted to Pₖ
X̂ ← X̂ ∪ Xₚₖ
wₖ = Xₚₖᵀrₖ (Weight vector)
If k = 1 then
t₁ = X̂w₁
Else
tₖ = (I - tₖ₋₁tₖ₋₁ᵀ)X̂wₖ (Orthogonalization)
tₖ = tₖ/ ‖tₖ‖₂ (Latent component)
rₖ₊₁ = rₖ - (yᵀtₖ)tₖ (Update residual)
        EndIf
EndFor
Convert W and X̂ into regression
coefficients using Equation (8).
```

use four publicly available chemical datasets for evaluation: EDKB[1], CPDB[2], CAS[3] and the AIDS antiviral screen dataset[4]. EDKB is a regression dataset, but the others are classification datasets. The statistics of used datasets are summarized in Table 2. Among them, the AIDS dataset (Kramer, Raedt, & Helma, 2001; Deshpande, Kuramochi, Wale, & Karypis, 2005) is by far the largest both in the number of examples and the graph size. For solving classification problems, we regress examples to a target values that take either +1 or −1.

We did not use minimum support parameter (*minsup*) for relatively small datasets (EDKB, CPDB and AIDS1), but set it to 10% of the number of positives for large datasets (CAS, AIDS2 and AIDS3). Throughout the experiments maximum pattern size (*maxpat*) is set to 10. We used AMD Opteron 2.2GHz system with at most 8GB memory for all experiments.

We evaluate the performance of gPLS for classification and regression in five fold cross validation settings. There are two parameters to tune, namely the number of iterations m and the number of obtained patterns per search k. For each dataset, we exhaustively tried all combinations from $m = \{10, 20, 30, 40, 50\}$, and $k = \{10, 20, 30, 40, 50\}$,. In the following, we always report the best test accuracy among all settings.

The accuracy is measured by Q^2 for regression and by the area under the ROC curve (AUC) for classification. The Q^2 score is defined as

$$Q^2 = 1 - \frac{\sum_{i=1}^n (y_i - f(x_i))^2}{\sum_{i=1}^n \left(y_i - \frac{1}{n}\sum_{i=1}^n y_i\right)^2}$$

which is close to 1 when the regression function fits good, and is close to 0 when it does not. The interpretation is similar to that for the Pearson correlation coefficient.

First we observed the behavior of accuracy and running time in regression (EDKB) and

Algorithm 4. Finding the optimal pattern

```
Procedure Optimal Pattern
Global variables: g*,p*

g* = −∞ p ∈ DFS codes with single nodes do
project p
    ()endfor
return p*
EndProcedure
Function project p
() If p is not a minimum DFS code then
        return
EndIf
If pruning condition (10) holds then
        return
EndIf
If  g(p) > g* then

g* = g(p),  p* = p

EndIf
For p' ∈ rightmost extensions of p do

project p'

() EndFor
EndFunction
```

classification (CPDB) datasets while changing maximum pattern size (Figure 3 and 4). In Figure 4, it is observed that classification accuracy in AUC is almost saturated when *maxpat* is 4, while in Figure 3, regression accuracy in Q^2 kept increasing slightly when *maxpat* is more than 7. This behavior reflects the fact that EDKB consists of graphs with more bonds and edges than that of CPDB dataset (Table 2).

Figure 5 shows the patterns selected by gPLS from the EDKB dataset. It is often observed that similar patterns are extracted together in the same component. This property makes PLS stable, because the regression function is less affected by small changes in graph data.

Results in other datasets are summarized in Table 3. In order to capture the property of large

AIDS datasets, we chose the number of iterations from $m = \{10, 20, 30, 40, 50\}$., and the number of latent components from $k = \{10, 20, 30, 40, 50\}$. In the table, we distinguish the computational time for pattern search (mining time, MT) and the numerical computations (numerical time, NT). Notice that in large AIDS datasets, computation time is dominated by mining time (MT), and time for numerical computation (NT) is negligibly small.

Efficiency Gain by Iterative Mining

The main idea of iterative mining is to gain efficiency by means of adaptive example weights. We evaluated how large the efficiency gain is by comparing gPLS with a naïve method that enumerates

Table 2. Datasets Summary. The number of positive data (POS) and negative data (NEG) are only provided for classification datasets. Average number of atoms (ATOM) and bonds (BOND) are shown for each dataset.

	LABEL	ALL	POS	NEG	ATOM	BOND
CPDB	binary	684	341	343	14.1	14.6
CAS	binary	4337	2401	1936	29.9	30.9
AIDS1 (CAvsCM)	binary	1503	422	1081	58.9	61.4
AIDS2 (CACMvs-CI)	binary	40939	1324	39615	42.7	44.6
AIDS3 (CAvsCI)	binary	39965	350	39615	42.7	44.5
EDKB	real	59	-	-	18.2	19.7

Figure 3. Regression accuracy (left) and computational time (right) against maximum pattern size (max-pat) in the EDKB dataset. In the table on the right, "Mining Time"' stands for computational time for pattern search, and "Numerical Time" stands for computational time for matrix and vector operations.

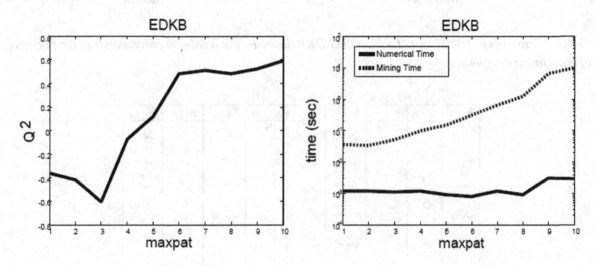

all patterns first and apply PLS afterwards. Table 4 summarizes the results for different maximum pattern sizes (maxpat). In the naïve method, the number of patterns grow exponentially, hence the computational time for PLS grows rapidly as well. gPLS successfully keeps computational time small in all occasions.

Unsupervised Dimensionality Reduction on Graph Data

In this section we present how to perform dimensionality reduction on graph data when no label information associated with each graph is available. We begin with defining the unsupervised dimensionality reduction problem on graph data. Let our training examples be $\{G_i\}_{i=1}^{n}$, and let P be the set of all subgraphs included in at least one training graph. Then each graph G_i is encoded as a $|P|$-dimensional row vector

Figure 4. Classification accuracy (left) and computational time (right) against maximum pattern size (maxpat) in the CPDB dataset. In the table on the right, "Mining Time" stands for computational time for pattern search, and "Numerical Time" stands for computational time for matrix and vector operations.

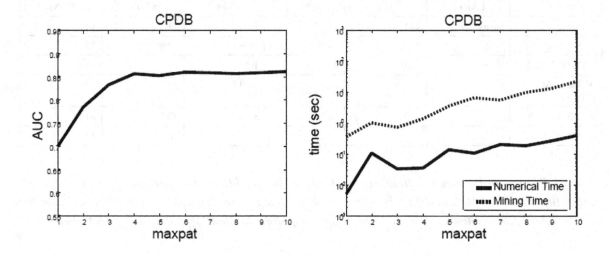

Figure 5. Patterns obtained by gPLS from the EDKB datasets. Each column corresponds to the patterns of each latent component.

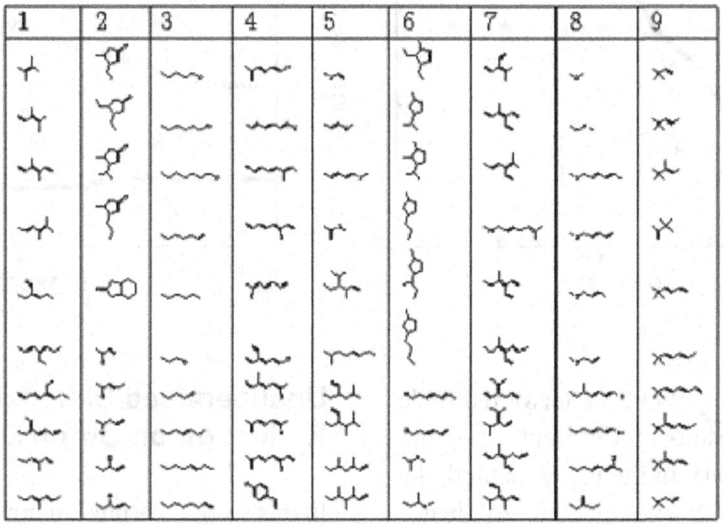

$$x_{i,p} = \begin{cases} 1 & \text{if } p \subseteq G_i, \\ -1 & \text{otherwise,} \end{cases}$$

and $n \times P$-matrix $X = \left[x_1, x_2, \ldots, x_n \right]^{\mathrm{T}}$. This feature space is already illustrated in Figure 1.

Let $\mathbf{z}$ be the $|P| \times 1$ column vector of projection weights such that *variance* in the data covariance matrix $\mathbf{X}^T\mathbf{X}$ is maximized:

Table 3. Results of gPLS in various datasets. Values in the parentheses are optimal parameters achieving the best test accuracy. P: the average number of obtained patterns, MT: mining time, NT: numerical time, ITR: the number of iterations required until convergence.

		gPLS			
	$(m,k)*$	P	MT	NT	AUC/Q ^{2†}
EDKB	(10, 30)	296	16.0	0.0025	$0.647^{\dagger} \pm 0.129$
CPDB	(20, 15)	258	26.8	0.474	0.862 ± 0.0214
CAS	(30, 10)	294	3570	14.1	0.870 ± 0.0098
AIDS1	(10, 10)	99	290	0.0652	0.773 ± 0.0538
AIDS2	(40, 10)	396	50300	167	0.747 ± 0.0266
AIDS3	(50, 20)	946	57100	509	0.883 ± 0.0541

Table 4. Frequent mining + PLS vs gPLS in the CPDB dataset

frequent mining + PLS					gPLS			
P	MT	NT	AUC	maxpat	P	MT	NT	AUC
17	0.0927	0.038	0.696	1	15.2	0.308	0.038	0.700
61	0.148	0.0164	0.770	2	45.8	1.20	0.117	0.782
182	0.212	0.0335	0.812	3	73.8	1.09	0.0573	0.833
515	0.282	0.0923	0.842	4	82.6	2.06	0.0488	0.857
1387	0.602	0.221	0.846	5	93.4	1.97	0.0296	0.844
3500	2.55	0.525	0.852	6	85.6	2.67	0.0222	0.833
8215	4.38	1.60	0.848	7	65.4	3.19	0.0146	0.837
18107	7.6	5.32	0.840	8	172	13.1	0.247	0.857
37719	17.9	7.42	0.840	9	209	12.7	0.282	0.859
74857	40.3	51.2	0.842	10	244	26.8	0.474	0.862
143006	70.3	92.8	0.835	11	244	35.4	0.375	0.862
out of memory				12	244	46.3	0.367	0.862
out of memory				13	244	52.4	0.549	0.861
out of memory				∞	244	66.3	0.586	0.861

$$\max_z \mathrm{var}(Xz) = \max_z (Xz)^\mathrm{T}(Xz) = \max_z (z^\mathrm{T} X^\mathrm{T} Xz).$$

Since this quantity is not normalized, it can take arbitrary large value. Therefore we intro-

duce regularization on **z** such that it lies on a $\|z\|$-dimensional euclidean ball:

$$\max_z z^\mathrm{T} X^\mathrm{T} Xz \qquad (11)$$

$$s.t. \parallel z \parallel = 1. \tag{12}$$

We can rewrite the optimization problem as:

$$\max_{z} z^{\mathrm{T}} X^{\mathrm{T}} X z - \lambda(\parallel z \parallel - 1), \tag{13}$$

where λ is a Lagrangian multiplier. Let us call the above quantity as L, then we can find the global maximum by taking the difference with respect to **z**, then setting it to zero;

$$\frac{\partial L}{\partial z} = 2X^{\mathrm{T}} X z - 2\lambda z = 0.$$

Eventually, this boils down to a familiar eigenvalue form,

$$(X^{\mathrm{T}} X - \lambda I)z = 0,$$

so it is clear that λ is the first eigenvalue and z is the corresponding eigenvector that represents the largest variance in the data.

Below, we aim for principal components $z_1, \ldots, z_m \in \Re^d$ that correspond to m major eigenvalues of the covariance matrix $\mathbf{X}^T\mathbf{X}$. Here, we do not centralize the design matrix **X** as in latent semantic indexing (Deerwester, Dumais, Furnas, Landauer, & Harshman, 1990). Principal components can also be computed from the Gram matrix $\mathbf{A} = \mathbf{X}\mathbf{X}^T$ (Schoelkopf, Smola, & Mueller, 1999). The eigenvalues of **A** are equal to those of $\mathbf{X}^T\mathbf{X}$. If the major eigenvectors of **A** are denoted as $\mathbf{X}^T\mathbf{X}$ $v_1, \ldots, v_m$, then the principal components are recovered as

$$\mathbf{z}_i = \mathbf{X}^T\mathbf{v}_i \tag{14}$$

Our algorithm follows the latter path, namely, computing the eigenvectors of the Gram matrix. However, the exact computation of the Gram matrix and the recovery of principal components (14) requires the whole feature space. In our case,

it is intractable, because all the patterns have to be enumerated a priori.

Therefore, we need to create a restricted design matrix $\overline{X}$ where a tractable number of patterns are used. The selection of patterns is of utmost importance in obtaining accurate approximations z_i. One obvious way to reduce the number of patterns is to use the minimum support threshold, and create a feature space with frequent patterns only. However, as shown in experiments later, it does not lead to accurate approximation due to high correlation among features. We propose an iterative mining method based on the Lanczos method for calculating major eigenvectors. The weighted subgraph mining is embedded to the Lanczos iteration. A handful of patterns are mined with different criteria in each iteration, thereby avoiding the correlation problem effectively.

The Lanczos Algorithm

In this section, we review the Lanczos algorithm briefly. Algorithm 5 shows how to compute the all eigenvalues and eigenvectors of a $n \times n$ symmetric matrix **A**. Let us denote the eigenvalues of **A** as $(\lambda_1, \ldots, \lambda_n)$, and denote by **V** the matrix whose i-th column corresponds to the i-th eigenvector. Let $Q = (q_1, \ldots, q_n)$ denote an orthogonal matrix. Then, the following transformation does not alter the eigenvalues

$$\mathbf{T} = \mathbf{Q}^T\mathbf{A}\mathbf{Q} \tag{15}$$

The Lanczos algorithm finds a matrix **Q** such that **T** is tridiagonal. Here, **T** is parametrized as follows,

$$T = \begin{bmatrix} \alpha_1 & \beta_1 & \cdots & 0 \\ \beta_1 & \alpha_2 & \ddots & \vdots \\ \vdots & \ddots & \ddots & \beta_{n-1} \\ 0 & \cdots & \beta_{n-1} & \alpha_n \end{bmatrix}.$$

The Lanczos algorithm computes the entries of **T** and **Q** progressively using elementary matrix computations. The columns of **Q** are called ``Lanczos vectors''. Since **T** is tridiagonal, the eigendecomposition can be efficiently done via Schur decomposition. Denote by **R** the eigenvectors of **T**. Then, the eigenvectors of **A** are obtained as

V=QR   (16)

This algorithm is employed in many numerical computation software including MATLAB. The orthogonal matrix leading to tridiagonal **T** is not unique. One can start from an arbitrary initial vector q_1, and always obtain a tridiagonal matrix as **T**.

In principal component analysis, we need only top m eigenpairs. In that case, we can stop the Lanczos algorithm after $K(<n)$ steps. Denote by $T_k, Q_k, R_k, V_k, \lambda_k$ the early versions of **T**, **Q**, **R**, **V**, λ after k iterations, respectively. The eigenpairs (λ_k, V_k) are only approximation of top k eigenpairs of **A**. However, there is an important property that the eigenvectors corresponding to larger eigenvalues are approximated more accurately. Thus, if k is sufficiently larger than m, the top-m eigenvectors in V_k are accurate estimates of the top-m eigenvectors of A. For rigorous error analysis, see

Algorithm 5. The Lanczos Algorithm

```
Input: A ∈ ℝ^{n×n}, q_1 ∈ ℝ^n, ‖ q_1 ‖= 1.
Output: All eigenpairs [λ, V]
Initial: r_0 = q_1; β_0 = 1; k = 0
While β_k ≠ 0 do
    q_k = r_k / β_k
    k = k + 1
    α_k = q_k^T A q_k
    r_k = A q_k − β_{k−1} q_{k−1} − α_k q_k
    β_k = ‖ r_k ‖_2
EndWhile
[λ, R] = EigenDecomposition(T)
V = QR
```

(Saad, 1980). An interesting point is that the accuracy depends on the initial vector q_1. If q_1 is set to the first eigenvector of **A**, V_k gives exactly the top-k eigenvectors (Ipsen & Meyer, 1998). However, since we do not know a priori the first eigenvector, q_1 is usually set to an arbitrary vector. In our experiments, we always used $q_1 = /\sqrt{n}$.

Now the question is how to determine when to stop the iteration. Here, the iteration is terminated, if all the m eigenvalues have converged (Sjoestroem, 1996; Golub & Loan, 1996):

$$\frac{\| A V_i - \lambda_i V_i \|_2}{\lambda_i} = \frac{|\beta_k| |R_{ki}|}{\lambda_i} < \sigma, \quad \forall i = 1,\dots,m,$$

(17)

where σ is the parameter controlling error tolerance. We set σ=0.01 in our experiments.

It is known that the Lanczos algorithm is prone to rounding errors and the orthogonality between the Lanczos vectors is quickly lost. Several methods have been proposed for this problem, such as implicitly/explicitly restarted Lanczos and selective/partial orthogonalization(Sjoestroem, 1996). In this paper, we apply the Gram-Schmidt procedure to ensure the orthogonality between the Lanczos vectors. Algorithm 6 summarizes the Lanczos algorithm with early stopping and reorthogonalization.

Application to Graph Data

In this section, we explain how to apply the Lanczos algorithm to graph data. Normal PCA creates principal components depending on all features, assuming that all features can be accessed in memory. For graph data, it is not possible to access all features at the same time. However, due to the structure of the feature space, namely, subgraph-supergraph relationships among patterns, we can solve the following weighted substructure mining problem (Nowozin, Tsuda, et al., 2007). Denote by $\mathbf{w} \in \mathfrak{R}^n$ example weights. The

Algorithm 6. The Lanczos Algorithm with early stopping and reorthogonalization

Input: $\mathbf{A} \in \mathbb{R}^{n \times n}, \mathbf{q}_1 \in \mathbb{R}^n, \parallel \mathbf{q}_1 \parallel = 1, m$
Output: Top eigenpairs $\{(\lambda_i, \mathbf{v}_i)\}_{i=1}^m$
Initial: $\mathbf{r}_0 = \mathbf{q}_1; \ \beta_0 = 1; \ k = 0$
While (17) is not true do
 $\mathbf{q}_k = \mathbf{r}_k / \beta_k$
 $k = k + 1$
 $\alpha_k = \mathbf{q}_k^T \mathbf{A} \mathbf{q}_k$
 $\mathbf{r}_k = \mathbf{A}\mathbf{q}_k - \beta_{k-1}\mathbf{q}_{k-1} - \alpha_k \mathbf{q}_k$
 For $j = 1 : k - 1$ do
  $\mathbf{r}_k = \mathbf{r}_k - \mathbf{q}_j(\mathbf{q}_j^T \mathbf{r}_k)$ (Reorthogonal-ization)
 EndFor
 $\beta_k = \parallel \mathbf{r}_k \parallel$
 $[\lambda_k, \mathbf{R}_k] = EigenDecomposition(\mathbf{T}_k)$
 $V_k = \mathbf{Q}_k \mathbf{R}_k$
EndWhile
Truncate $[\lambda_k, \mathbf{V}_k]$ to top m eigenpairs

Algorithm 7. PCA based on the Lanczos mentod

Input: Design matrix $\mathbf{X} \in \mathbb{R}^{n \times d}$
Output: Principal components
$\mathbf{Z} \in \mathfrak{R}^{d \times m}$
Initial: $\mathbf{r}_0 = \mathbf{q}_1; \ \beta_0 = 1; \ k = 0$
While (17) is not true do
 $\mathbf{q}_k = \mathbf{r}_k / \beta_k$
 $k = k + 1$
 $\mathbf{g}_k = \mathbf{X}^T \mathbf{q}_k$ (Intermediate variable)
 $\alpha_k = \mathbf{g}_k^T \mathbf{g}_k$
 $\mathbf{r}_k = \mathbf{X}\mathbf{g}_k - \beta_{k-1}\mathbf{q}_{k-1} - \alpha_k \mathbf{q}_k$
 For $j = 1 : k - 1$ do
  $\mathbf{r}_k = \mathbf{r}_k - \mathbf{q}_j(\mathbf{q}_j^T \mathbf{r}_k)$
 Endfor
 $\beta_k = \parallel \mathbf{r}_k \parallel$
 $[\lambda_k, \mathbf{R}_k] = EigenDecomposition(\mathbf{T}_k)$
 $V_k = \mathbf{Q}_k \mathbf{R}_k$
EndWhile
Truncate $[\lambda_k, \mathbf{V}_k]$ to top m eigenpairs
$\mathbf{Z} = \mathbf{X}^T \mathbf{V}_m$

weighted mining enumerates the following pattern set,

$$P_w = \{p \ | \ \left| \sum_{j=1}^n \sum_i^n w_j x_{jp} \right| \geq \varepsilon\}, \tag{18}$$

where ε is a predetermined constant. Therefore, we can quickly collect features highly correlated with a given vector **w**. See next section for the mining algorithm. Our question here is how we can use this tool to compute principal components approximately without accessing all features.

To understand the problem better, let us first consider the PCA of d-dimensional vectorial data, i.e., $\mathbf{X} \in \mathbb{R}^{n \times d}$. PCA is done by the eigendecomposition of the Gram matrix $\mathbf{A} = \mathbf{X}\mathbf{X}^T$. Let us consider the following intermediate variable

$$\mathbf{g}_k = \mathbf{X}^T \mathbf{q}_k.$$

where the i-th entry is described as

$$g_{ki} = \sum_{i=1}^n \sum_i^n x_{ip} q_{kj}.$$

Substituting $\mathbf{A} = \mathbf{X}\mathbf{X}^T$ to the equations in Algorithm 6, it turns out that the Lanczos algorithm accesses the design matrix $\mathbf{X}$ through $\mathbf{g}_k$ and $\mathbf{X}\mathbf{g}_k$. The reformulated pseudo code is summarized in Algorithm 7.

What it implies is that the features corresponding to zero entries $\{i \ | \ g_{ki} = 0\}$ need not to be accessed in the k-th iteration. More aggressively, we can reduce the number of accessed features by introducing the tolerance threshold ε as

$$\{i \ | \ | g_{ki} | \geq \varepsilon\}. \tag{19}$$

Alternatively, one can take the best ℓ features with largest $|g_{ki}|$. It provides a reasonable method to trade the number of accessed features and the accuracy of principal components.

For graph data, the features satisfying the criterion (19) can be enumerated by mining (18) with $\mathbf{w}=\mathbf{q}_k$. By incorporating the mining step to Algorithm 10, we finally arrive at our graph PCA algorithm (Algorithm 8). For indexing purposes, we collect mined patterns to the pattern pool P. Each principal components is indexed by the patterns correspond to its major elements. In analogy to text mining, each principal component corresponds to a "topic" and the associated patterns describe that topic.

Optimal Pattern Search

In this section, we briefly describe the way to search optimal patterns. The basic strategy is the similar to that for gPLS, therefore the pseudocode is omitted, but the pruning condition is different. Remember that our task is to enumerate all the patterns whose gain function

$$s(p) = \left| \sum_{i=1}^{n} \overset{n}{\underset{i}{w_i}} x_{ip} \right|$$

is larger than ε. Suppose the search tree is generated up to the pattern p. If it is guaranteed that the score of any supergraph p' is not larger than ε,

Algorithm 8. Graph PCA

```
Input: Graphs G₁....,Gₙ , Tolerance ε
Output: Patterns P , Principal components Z ∈ ℜ^|P|×m
Initial: q₁ = /√n;  r₀ = q₁;  β₀ = 1;  k = 0;  P = ∅
While (17) is not true do
    qₖ = rₖ / βₖ
    k = k + 1
```
$$P_k = \left\{ p \ \middle| \ \left| \sum_{j=1}^{n} \overset{n}{\underset{i}{q_{kj}}} x_{jp} \right| \ge \varepsilon \right\} \quad \text{(Pattern Search)}$$
```
    P ← P∪Pₖ
    Xₚ: design matrix restricted to P
```
$\alpha_k = \mathbf{q}_k^{\mathrm{T}} \mathbf{X}_P \mathbf{X}_P^{\mathrm{T}} \mathbf{q}_k$

$\mathbf{r}_k = \mathbf{X}_P \mathbf{X}_P^{\mathrm{T}} \mathbf{q}_k - \beta_{k-1}\mathbf{q}_{k-1} - \alpha_k \mathbf{q}_k$
```
    For j = 1 : k - 1 do
```
$\quad \mathbf{r}_k = \mathbf{r}_k - \mathbf{q}_j(\mathbf{q}_j^{\mathrm{T}}\mathbf{r}_k)$
```
    EndFor
```
$\beta_k = \| \mathbf{r}_k \|$

$[\lambda_k, \mathbf{R}_k] = EigenDecomposition(\mathbf{T}_k)$

$\mathbf{V}_k = \mathbf{Q}_k \mathbf{R}_k$
```
Endwhile
Truncate [λₖ, Vₖ] to top m eigenpairst
```
$\mathbf{Z} = \mathbf{X}_P^{\mathrm{T}} \mathbf{V}_m$

we can avoid the generation of downstream nodes without losing the optimal pattern. Our pruning condition is described as follows.

Theorem 3. *Define*

$$s^+(p) = 2 \sum_{\{i|w_i \geq 0, p \subseteq G_i\}} |w_i| - \sum_{i=1}^{n} w_i$$

$$s^-(p) = 2 \sum_{\{i|w_i < 0, p \subseteq G_i\}} |w_i| + \sum_{i=1}^{n} w_i.$$

For any supergraph p' of p, the following bound holds.

$$s(p') \leq \max\{s^+(p), s^-(p)\} \qquad (20)$$

Therefore, the search tree is pruned at p, if $\varepsilon > max\{s^+(p), s^-(p)\}$.

Computational Experiments

In this section, we evaluate gPCA in terms of approximation error and computation time. Due to the truncation of the intermediate variables, the principal components obtained by gPCA are not equal to the true principal components which can only be obtained by total enumeration of patterns. Our goal is to build an approximated principal components to the true ones. We test our algorithm in chemical datasets presented in Table 2. We employed relatively small datasets such that total enumeration is possible.

In this experiment, the number of principal components is set to three. In visualization and machine learning applications, it is desirable that the the similarity of graphs are appropriately represented by projected points. We first create ``true'' three-dimensional projections of graphs by total enumeration and PCA. Here, the minimum support is set to 2, and the pattern size is restricted up to 15 nodes. Denote by G_{true} the true Gram matrix, representing the dot product of three

dimensional projections. It is compared with G, the Gram matrix of gPCA projections. Since they differ in scale, the Gram matrix is normalized as

$$\hat{G}_{ij} = \frac{G_{ij}}{\sqrt{G_{ii} G_{jj}}}.$$

Then, the approximation error is measured using the Frobenius norm as $\| \hat{G} - \hat{G}_{true} \|$. The smaller the approximation error means the reconstruction of the subspace closer to the true Gram matrix. In approximating the intermediate variable (19), we employed the top-L approximation rather than fixing the threshold ε.

Figure 7 shows the approximation error of gPCA in the EDKB dataset. As L increases, the Gram matrix is more accurately approximated. The projected points are illustrated in Figure 6. Also, the patterns associated with principal components are shown in Figure 8. It is observed that similar subgraph patterns are clustered together in the same column, but the patterns in different columns are distinctly different. Frequent patterns are often small and boring. When the patterns are listed according to frequency, one has to go down the list up to the bottom to find meaningful features. Our patterns are not immediately interpretable like words in text mining. Nevertheless our PCA-based patterns look much more meaningful because they are relatively large and capture complex features.

The computational time for larger datasets are measured and shown in Table 5. For such medium-sized datasets, the computational time stays within the tractable level (e.g., several hours) in an ordinary PC.

A Connection between PCA and PLS

In this chapter, we have demonstrated the integration of graph mining algorithm with PCA or PLS. An obvious question would be ``why the

Figure 6. A three-dimensional plot of projected points in the EDKB dataset

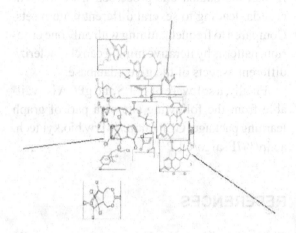

Figure 7. Approximation error using top 3 principal components in the EDKB dataset

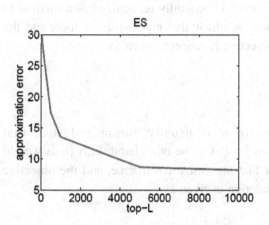

Figure 8. Patterns associated with the top 10 principal components in the EDKB dataset.

1	2	3	4	5	6	7	8	9	10

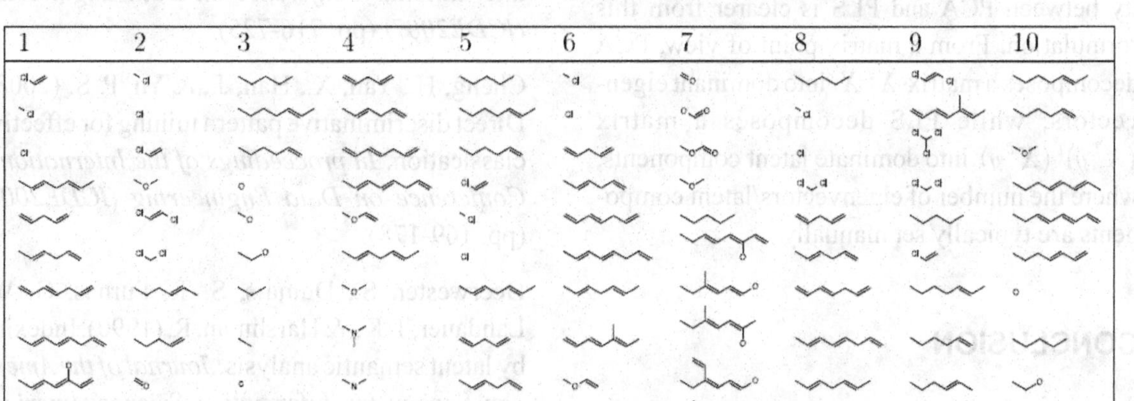

Table 5. Time for finding top 3 principal components in the CAS and CPDB dataset

	CAS		CPDB	
L	time (sec)	# iter	time (sec)	# iter
10	9.038	11	1.611	4
50	46.55	6	6.472	4
100	110.9	6	12.21	4
500	702.8	6	62.57	4
1000	2227	4	90.79	4

resulting gPLS algorithm and gPCA algorithm are so similar to each other".

PCA is generally recognized as a method to find weight **w** that maximize variance, and the objective function is given as

$$\max_{w} w^{\mathrm{T}}(X^{\mathrm{T}}X)w,$$

where **w** is usually normalized such that $\| \mathbf{w} \| = 1$. On the other hand, PLS finds weight **w** that maximize covariance, and the objective function is given as

$$\max_{w} w^{\mathrm{T}}(X^{T}y)^{\mathrm{T}}(X^{T}y)w,$$

where **w** is usually not normalized. The similarity between PCA and PLS is clearer from this formulation. From a matrix point of view, PCA decomposes a matrix $X^{T}X$ into dominant eigenvectors, while PLS decomposes a matrix $(X^{T}y)^{T}(X^{T}y)$ into dominate latent components, where the number of eigenvectors/latent components are typically set manually.

CONCLUSION

We have presented matrix decomposition based dimensionality reduction approaches for graph data. Our methods automatically creates features optimal for a given graph dataset, and save generating redundant and useless subgraph features. On the other hand, we face a problem of selecting subgraph features from a large number of candidates. In our gPLS and gPCA approach, highly-correlated subgraph features are successfully treated by building new orthogonal basis. Our approach is general, since mining part can be replaced by different kind of frequent substructure mining algorithms such as itemset mining, sequence mining and tree mining while reducing the number of patterns to present.

An advantage of iterative mining methods is that; the database is processed with different criteria, leading to several different pattern sets. Compared to frequent mining with only one criterion, patterns by iterative mining can characterize different aspects of the given database.

Finally, a software of gPLS and gPCA is available from the following site as a part of graph learning package (GLP). http://www.bio.kyutech.ac.jp/%7Esaigo/GLP/

REFERENCES

Cheng, H., Yan, X., Han, J., & Hsu, C.-W. (2007). Discriminative frequent pattern analysis for effective classiscation. *In proceedings of the International Conference on Data Engineering (ICDE2007)* (pp. 716-725).

Cheng, H., Yan, X., Han, J., & Yu, P. S. (2008). Direct discriminative pattern mining for effective classication. *In proceedings of the International Conference on Data Engineering (ICDE2008)* (pp. 169-178).

Deerwester, S., Dumais, S. T., Furnas, G. W., Landauer, T. K., & Harshman, R. (1990). Indexing by latent semantic analysis. *Journal of the American Society for Information Science American Society for Information Science*, 41.

Deshpande, M., Kuramochi, M., Wale, N., & Karypis, G. (2005). Frequent sub-structurebased approaches for classifying chemical compounds. *IEEE Transactions on Knowledge and Data Engineering*, *17*(8), 1036–1050. doi:10.1109/TKDE.2005.127

Efron, B., Hastie, T., Johnstone, I., & Tibshirani, R. (2004). Least angle regression. *Annals of Statistics*, *32*(2), 407–499. doi:10.1214/009053604000000067

Elden, L. (2004). Partial least squares vs. lanczos bidiagonalization i: Analysis of a projection method for multiple regression. *Computational Statistics & Data Analysis*, *46*(1), 11–31. doi:10.1016/S0167-9473(03)00138-5

Fan, W., Zhang, K., Cheng, H., Gao, J., Yan, X., & Han, J..... Verscheure, O. (2008). Direct mining of discriminative and essential frequent patterns via model-based search tree. In *Proceedings of the ACM SIGKDD International Conference on Knowledge Discovery and Data Mining (KDD2008)* (pp. 230-238).

Fei, H., & Huan, J. (2009). L2 norm regularized feature kernel regression for graph data. In *Proceedings of the ACM Conference on Information and Knowledge Management (CIKM2009)* (pp. 593-600).

Fei, H., & Huan, J. (2010). Boosting with structure information in the functional space: An application to graph classification. In *Proceedings of the ACM SIGKDD International Conference on Knowledge Discovery and Data Mining (KDD2010)* (pp. 643-652).

Frank, E., & Friedman, J. H. (1993). A statistical view of some chemometrics regression tools. *Technometrics*, *35*(2), 109–135. doi:10.2307/1269656

Golub, G. H., & Loan, C. F. V. (1996). *Matrix computations*. MD, USA: Johns Hopkins University Press.

Helma, C., Cramer, T., Kramer, S., & Raedt, L. (2004). Data mining and machine learning techniques for the identification of mutagenicity inducing substructures and structure activity relationships of noncongeneric compounds. *Journal of Chemical Information and Computer Sciences*, *44*, 1402–1411. doi:10.1021/ci034254q

Inokuchi, A. (2005). Mining generalized substructures from a set of labeled graphs. In Proceedings of the IEEE Internatinal Conference on Data Mining (ICDM2005) *(pp. 415-418).*

Ipsen, I. C. F., & Meyer, C. D. (1998). The idea behind Krylov methods. *The American Mathematical Monthly*, *105*(10), 889–899. doi:10.2307/2589281

Jin, N., Young, C., & Wang, W. (2009). Graph classification based on pattern co-occurrence. In Proceedings of the ACM Conference on Information and Knowledge Management (CIKM2009) (pp. 573-582).

Kazius, J., Nijssen, S., & Kok, J., Back, T., & Ijzerman, A. (2006). Substructure mining using elaborate chemical representation. *Journal of Chemical Information and Modeling*, *46*, 597–605. doi:10.1021/ci0503715

Kohavi, R., & John, G. H. (1997). Wrappers for feature subset selection. *Artificial Intelligence*, *97*(1-2), 273–324. doi:10.1016/S0004-3702(97)00043-X

Kong, X., & Yu, P. S. (2010). Semi-supervised feature selection for graph classification. In *Proceedings of the ACM SIGKDD International Conference on Knowledge Discovery and Data Mining (KDD2010)* (pp. 793-802).

Kramer, S., Raedt, L., & Helma, C. (2001). Molecular feature mining in HIV data. In Proceedings of the ACM SIGKDD International Conference on Knowledge Discovery and Data Mining (KDD2001) *(pp. 136-143).*

Kudo, T., Maeda, E., & Matsumoto, Y. (2005). An application of boosting to graph classification. In *Advances in Neural Information Processing Systems (NIPS2005)* (p. 729-736).

Lanczos, C. (1950). An iteration method for the solution of the eigenvalue problem of linear differential and integral operators. *Journal of Research of the National Bureau of Standards*, *45*, 255–282.

Nijssen, S., & Kok, J. (2004). A quick start in frequent structure mining can make a difference. In *Proceedings of the ACM SIGKDD International Conference on Knowledge Discovery and Data Mining (KDD 2004)* (pp. 647-652).

Nowozin, S., Bakir, G., & Tsuda, K. (2007). Discriminative subsequence mining for action classification. In *Proceedings of the 11th IEEE International Conference on Computer Vision (ICCV 2007)* (pp. 1919-1923).

Nowozin, S., Tsuda, K., Uno, T., Kudo, T., & Bakir, G. (2007). Weighted substructure mining for image analysis. *In IEEE Computer Society Conference on Computer Vision and Pattern Recognition (CVPR 2007)*.

Saad, Y. (1980). On the rates of convergence of the Lanczos and the block Lanczos methods. *SIAM Journal on Numerical Analysis, 17,* 687–706. doi:10.1137/0717059

Saigo, H., Kraemer, N., & Tsuda, K. (2008). Partial least squares regression for graph mining. In *Proceedings of the ACM SIGKDD International Conference on Knowledge Discovery and Data Mining (KDD2008)* (pp. 578-586).

Saigo, H., Nowozin, S., Kadowaki, T., Kudo, T., & Tsuda, K. (2009). gBoost: A mathematical programming approach to graph classiscation and regression. *Machine Learning, 75*(1), 69–89. doi:10.1007/s10994-008-5089-z

Saigo, H., & Tsuda, K. (2008). Iterative subgraph mining for principal component analysis. In *Proceedings of the IEEE International Conference on Data Mining (ICDM 2008)* (pp. 1007-1012).

Schoelkopf, B., & Smola, A. J. (2002). *Learning with kernels: Support vector machines, regularization, optimization, and beyond*. Cambridge, MA: MIT Press.

Schoelkopf, B., Smola, A. J., & Mueller, K.-R. (1999). Kernel principal component analysis . In Schoelkopf, B., Burges, C., & Smola, A. (Eds.), *Advances in kernel methods - support vector learning* (pp. 327–352). Cambridge, MA: MIT Press.

Sjoestroem, E. (1996). *Singular value computations for Toeplitz matrices*. Unpublished doctoral dissertation, Linkoping University, Sweden.

Thoma, M., Cheng, H., Gretton, A., Han, J., Kriegel, H.-P., & Smola, A. ...Borgwardt, K. (2009). Near-optimal supervised feature selection among frequent subgraphs. In *Proceedings of the SIAM International Data Mining Conference (SDM2009)*.

Tsuda, K. (2007). Entire regularization paths for graph data. In *Proceedings of the International Conference on Machine Learning (ICML2007)* (pp. 919-926).

Tsuda, K., & Kudo, T. (2006). Clustering graphs by weighted substructure mining. In Proceedings of the International Conference on Machine Learning (ICML2006) *(p. 953-960)*.

Wale, N., & Karypis, G. (2006). Comparison of descriptor spaces for chemical compound retrieval and classification. In *Proceedings of the IEEE International Conference on Data Mining (ICDM2006)* (pp. 678-689).

Wang, J., & Karypis, G. (2005). HARMONY: Efficiently mining the best rules for classification. In *Proceedings of the SIAM International Data Mining Conference (SDM2005)*.

Wold, H. (1966). Estimation of principal components and related models by iterative least squares. In P. R. Krishnaiaah (Ed.), *Multivariate analysis* (pp. 391-420). Academic Press.

Wold, S., Ruhe, A., Wold, H., & Dunn, W. J. III. (1984). The collinearity problem in linear regression. The partial least squares (PLS) approach to generalized inverses. *SIAM J. Sci. Stat. Comput.*, *5*(3), 735–743. doi:10.1137/0905052

Yan, X., Cheng, H., Han, J., & Yu, P. S. (2008). Mining significant graph patterns by leap search. In *Proceedings of the ACM SIGKDD International Conference on Management of Data (KDD2008)* (p. 433-444).

Yan, X., & Han, J. (2002a). gSpan: Graph-based Substructure Pattern Mining. In *Proceedings of the 2002 IEEE International Conference on Data Mining (ICDM2002)* (p. 721-724).

Yan, X., & Han, J. (2002b). gSpan: *Graph-based substructure pattern mining* (Tech. Rep.). Department of Computer Science, University of Illinois at Urbana-Champaign.

Yin, X., & Han, J. (2003). CPAR: Classification based on predictive association rules. In

KEY TERMS AND DEFINITIONS

Classification: Learning a rule that separates one class from the other classes.

Conjugate Gradient: A method in numerical optimization which solves a system Ax = b.

Graph Mining: Enumeration of subgraphs appearing more than a given frequency in graph data.

Lanczos Method: A numerical method for decomposing a matrix into eigenvalues and eigenvectors.

Regression: Learning a rule so that a predicted value fits close to a true response value.

Principal Component Analysis: A statistical tool which is mainly used for visualizing data.

Partial Least Squares: A regression method frequently used in cheminformatics.

ENDNOTES

[1]   http://edkb.fda.gov/databasedoor.html
[2]   Available from the supplementary information of [?]
[3]   http://www.cheminformatics.org/datasets/bursi/
[4]   http://dtp.nci.nih.gov/docs/aids/aids_screen.html

APPENDIX

DFS Code Tree

Algorithm 6 finds the optimal pattern which optimizes a gain function. To this end, we need an intelligent way of enumerating all subgraphs of a graph set. This problem is highly nontrivial due to loops: One has to avoid enumerating the same pattern again and again. In this section, we present a canonical search space of graph patterns called *DFS code tree* (Yan & Han, 2002b),, that allows to enumerate all subgraphs without duplication. In the following, we assume undirected graphs, but it is straightforward to extend the algorithm for directed graphs.

DFS Code

The *DFS code* is a string representation of a graph G based on a depth first search (DFS). According to different starting points and growing edges, there are many ways to perform the search. Therefore, the DFS code of a graph is not unique. To derive a DFS code, each node is indexed from 0 to n-1 according to the discovery time in the DFS. Denote by E^f the *forward edge* set containing all the edges traversed in the DFS, and by E^b the *backward edge* set containing the remaining edges. Figure 14 shows two different indexing of the same graph.

After the indexing, an edge is represented as a pair of indices (i, j) together with vertex and edge labels, $e = (i, j, l_i, l_{ij}, l_j) \in V \times V \times L_V \times L_E \times L_V$, where $V = \{0, \ldots, n-1\}$, L_V and L_E are the set of vertex and edge labels, respectively. The index pair is set as $i < j$, if it is an forward edge, and $i > j$ if backward. It is assumed that there are no self-loop edges. To define the DFS code, a linear order $\prec_T$ is defined among edges. For the two edges $e_1 = (i_1, j_1)$ and $e_2 = (i_2, j_2)$, $e_1 \prec_T e_2$ if and only if one of the following statements is true:

1. $e_1, e_2 \in E^f$, and $(j_1 < j_2$ or $i_1 > i_2 \wedge j_1 = j_2)$
2. $e_1, e_2 \in E^b$, and $(i_1 < i_2$ or $i_1 = i_2 \wedge j_1 < j_2)$.

Figure 9. Depth first search and DFS code of graph. (a) A graph example. (b), (c) Two different depth-first-searches of the same graph. Red numbers represent the DFS indices. Bold edges and dashed edges represent the forward edges and the backward edges respectively.

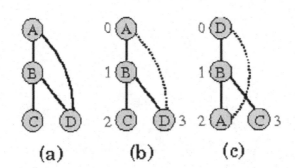

(a)   (b)   (c)

3. $e_1 \in E^b, e_2 \in E^f$, and $i_1 < j_2$.
4. $e_1 \in E^f, e_2 \in E^b$, and $j_1 \leq i_2$.

The DFS code is a sequence of edges sorted according to the above order.

Minimum DFS Code

Since there are many possible DFS codes, it is necessary to determine the minimum DFS code as a canonical representation of the graph. Let us define a linear order for two DFS codes $D_1 = (a_0, \ldots, a_m)$ and $D_2 = (b_0, \ldots, b_n)$. By comparing the vertex and edge labels, we can easily build a lexicographical order of individual edges a_i and b_j. Then, the *DFS lexicographic order* for the two codes is defined as follows: $D_1 < D_2$ if and only if either of the following is true,

1. $\exists t, 0 \leq t \leq \min(m, n), a_k = b_k \quad for \quad k < t, a_t < b_t$.
2. $a_k = b_k$ for $0 \leq k \leq m$ and $m \leq n$.

Given a set of DFS codes, the minimum code is defined as the smallest one according to the above order.

Right Most Extension

As in most mining algorithms, we form a tree where each node has a DFS code, and the children of a node have the DFS codes corresponding to the supergraphs. The tree is generated in a depth-first manner and the generation of child nodes of a node is done according to the right most extension (Yan & Han, 2002b). Suppose a node has the DFS code $D_1 = (a_0, a_1, \cdots, a_n)$ where $a_k = (i_k, j_k)$. The next edge a_{n+1} is chosen such that the following conditions are satisfied:

1. If a_n is a forward edge and a_{n+1} is a forward edge, then $i_{n+1} \leq j_n$ and $j_{n+1} = j_n + 1$.
2. If a_n is a forward edge and a_{n+1} is a backward edge, then $i_{n+1} = j_n$ and $j_{n+1} < i_n$.
3. If a_n is a backward edge and a_{n+1} is a forward edge, then $i_{n+1} \leq i_n$ and $j_{n+1} = i_n + 1$.
4. If a_n is a backward edge and a_{n+1} is a backward edge, then $i_{n+1} = i_n$ and $j_n < j_{n+1}$.

For every possible a_{n+1}, a child node is generated and the extended DFS code $(a_0, \ldots, a_{n+1})$ is stored. The extension is done such that the extended graph is included in at least one graph in the database.

For each pattern, its embeddings to all graphs in the database are maintained. Whenever a new pattern is created by adding an edge, the list of embeddings is updated. Therefore, it is not necessary to perform isomorphism tests whenever a pattern is extended.

DFS Code Tree

The *DFS code tree*, denoted by $\mathbb{T}$, is a tree-structure whose node represents a DFS code, the relation between a node and its child nodes is given by the right most extension, and the child nodes of the same parent is sorted in the DFS lexicographic order.

It has the following completeness property. Let us remove from $\mathbb{T}$ the subtrees whose root nodes have non-minimum DFS codes, and denote by $\mathbb{T}_{min}$ the reduced tree. It is proven that all subgraphs of graphs in the database are still included in $\mathbb{T}_{min}$ (Yan & Han, 2002b). This property allows us to prune the tree as soon as a non-minimum DFS code is found. In Algorithm 6, the minimality of the DFS code is checked in each node generation, and the tree is pruned if it is not minimum (line 9). This minimality check is basically done by exhaustively enumerating all DFS codes of the corresponding graph. Therefore, the computational time for the check is exponential to the pattern size. Techniques to avoid the total enumeration are described in Section 5.1 of (Yan & Han, 2002b), but still it is the most time consuming part of the algorithm.

Chapter 12
Clustering Vertices in Weighted Graphs

Derry Tanti Wijaya
Carnegie Mellon University, USA

Stephane Bressan
National University of Singapore, Singapore

ABSTRACT

Clustering is the unsupervised process of discovering natural clusters so that objects within the same cluster are similar and objects from different clusters are dissimilar. In clustering, if similarity relations between objects are represented as a simple, weighted graph where objects are vertices and similarities between objects are weights of edges; clustering reduces to the problem of graph clustering. A natural notion of graph clustering is the separation of sparsely connected dense sub graphs from each other based on the notion of intra-cluster density vs. inter-cluster sparseness. In this chapter, we overview existing graph algorithms for clustering vertices in weighted graphs: Minimum Spanning Tree (MST) clustering, Markov clustering, and Star clustering. This includes the variants of Star clustering, MST clustering and Ricochet.

INTRODUCTION

Graphs are mathematical structures used to represent pairwise relations between objects from a certain collection. Graphs contain vertices (that represent objects) and edges connecting the vertices (that represent pairwise relations between the objects). A graph G is therefore an ordered

pair $G = (V, E)$ where V is a set of vertices and E is a multiset of edges: unordered pairs of vertices. A simple, weighted graph is an undirected graph that has no self-loops and no more than one edge between any two vertices: i.e. edges form a set rather than a multiset and each edge is an unordered pair of distinct vertices. A number or weight is assigned to each edge, representing the weight of relation between the two vertices connected by the edge.

DOI: 10.4018/978-1-61350-053-8.ch012

Clustering is the unsupervised process of discovering natural clusters so that objects within the same cluster are similar and objects from different clusters are dissimilar according to some similarity measurements. In a vector space, for instance, where objects are represented by feature vectors, similarity is generally defined as the cosine of the angle between vectors. In clustering, if similarity relations between objects are represented as a simple, weighted graph where objects are vertices and similarities between objects are weights of edges; clustering reduces to the problem of clustering vertices in a weighted graph. A natural notion of graph clustering is the separation of sparsely connected dense sub graphs from each other based on the notion of intra-cluster density vs. inter-cluster sparseness. Clustering is the separation of dense from sparse regions of space or components of graphs. Clusters are the dense regions or components.

In this chapter, we first identify graph algorithms related to clustering problem: random walk and minimum spanning tree algorithms. Intuitively, random walk algorithm can produce ranking of vertices in the graph thus identify potentially significant vertices. Minimum spanning tree algorithm can identify potentially significant edges or path in the graph. These issues are closely related to the problem of clustering: identification of significant vertices as candidate centroids (seeds) and the identification of significant edges to merge or split clusters. We present an overview of existing graph algorithms for clustering vertices in weighted graphs: Minimum Spanning Tree (MST) clustering, Markov clustering, and Star clustering. We also present novel family of Star clustering variants, MST clustering variants we call MST-Sim, and Ricochet.

Our variants of Star clustering explore various techniques, including random walk algorithm, to identify centroids (Star centers). MST-Sim explores minimum spanning tree algorithm for clustering, adding to it intra and inter-cluster similarity metrics that have basis in graph theory.

Ricochet uses results of our study on Star clustering to identify centroids and our study of minimum spanning tree algorithm to identify edges to merge clusters. Ricochet also uses the idea of vertices reassignment from K-means to reach terminating condition. Combining these ideas results in Ricochet being unconstrained – it does not require any parameter to be defined a priori – and able to maximize intra-cluster similarities

BACKGROUND

RANDOM WALK ALGORITHM

Suppose we are given a connected, weighted graph $G = (V, E)$. Suppose that the graph is bi-directed, i.e. $(x, y) \in E$ if and only if $(y, x) \in E$. Suppose also that the graph has no self-loops, so that $(x, x) \notin E$ for any $x \in V$. Let $N(x) = \{y \in V: (x, y) \in E\}$ be the set of neighbors of a vertex x. Since G is a weighted graph, there is a weight $c(x, y) > 0$ associated with each edge $(x, y) \in E$. The weight is symmetric such that $c(x, y) = c(y, x)$ for $(x, y) \in E$. Extend the weight c to a function on all $V \times V$ by defining $c(x, y) = 0$ for $(x, y) \notin E$. If, as an analogy, we imagine a fluid flows through the edges of the graph; the weight measures the capacity of the edge. Let $C(x) = \sum_{y \in V} c(x, y)$ and suppose that $C(x) < \infty$ for each $x \in V$. The Markov chain with state space V and transition probability matrix P given by:

$$P(x,y) = \frac{c(x,y)}{C(x)} \qquad (x,y) \in E \qquad (1)$$

is called a random walk on the graph G. This chain governs the movement of a random walker moving along the vertices of G. If the walker is at vertex x at a given time, the walker will be at a neighbor of x at the next time; the neighbor is chosen randomly, in proportion to the weight of the edges connecting *x* to its neighbors.

Random walk has been applied to computer science, economics and various other fields to represent random processes in time. Random walks on graphs have been applied to rank the vertices in the graph (Brin & Page, 1998) or to identify clusters in a graph (Van Dongen, 2000).

To rank vertices in a graph, given a graph where edges are weighted by the probability of traversing from one vertex to another, rank of vertices can be computed according to the structure of the edges by simulating random walks on the graph. As a walker proceeds in his random walk from vertex to vertex, he visits some vertices more often than the others. The vertices can thus be ranked according to the probabilities that a walker will arrive at the vertices after such random walk. To simulate such random walk and compute the scores of the vertices, we can represent the graph by its adjacency matrix and compute the fix point of the product of the matrix with itself (Gondran & Minoux, 1984) or approximate the computation of the fix point with PageRank (Brin & Page, 1998) which introduces 'fatigue' to the random walker.

Random walk on graphs has been used in clustering. Markov clustering (MCL) (Van Dongen, 2000) simulates stochastic flow (or random walks) in the graph. The graph is first represented as stochastic (Markov) matrices where edges between vertices are weighted by the amount of flow between the vertices. MCL algorithm simulates flow using two alternating algebraic operations on the matrices. The flow is eventually separated into different regions, yielding a cluster interpretation of the initial graph.

MINIMUM SPANNING TREE ALGORITHM

Given a connected, weighted, bi-directed graph $G = (V, E)$, a spanning tree of G is a subgraph which is a tree that connects all the vertices in G.

The weight of a spanning tree is the sum of the weights of edges in that spanning tree. A minimum spanning tree (MST) of G is a spanning tree whose weight is less than or equal to weight of every other spanning tree of G. More generally, any weighted, bi-directed graph (not necessarily connected) has a minimum spanning forest, which is a union of MSTs of its connected components. Well known algorithms for finding MST are Kruskal's algorithm (Kruskal, 1956), Borůvka's algorithm (Borůvka, 1926), and Prim's algorithm (Skiena, 1998), which are all greedy algorithms. Faster randomized MST algorithm has also been developed by Karger, Klein, & Tarjan (1995). Randomized MST algorithm uses two important properties of graph, namely the cut and the cycle property. The cut property states that for any proper, non empty subset X of the vertices in the graph, the lightest edge with exactly one end point in X will be in the MST of the graph. The cycle property states that for any cycle C in a graph, the heaviest edge in C will not be in the MST of the graph. This randomized MST runs in expected time linear to the number of edges in the graph.

GRAPH ALGORITHMS FOR CLUSTERING

Graph algorithms for clustering create clusters by cutting or removing edges that are deemed unimportant according to some measurement. We present several existing graph algorithms for clustering vertices in a weighted graph: Minimum Spanning Tree (MST) clustering, Markov clustering, and Star clustering.

MST Clustering

Zahn's MST clustering algorithm (Zahn, 1971) is a well known graph algorithm for clustering (Jain, Murty, & Flynn, 1999). The implementation of Zahn's algorithm starts by finding a minimum spanning tree in the graph and then removes inconsistent edges from the MST to create clusters. Inconsistent edges are defined as edges whose distances are significantly larger (e.g. c times larger) than the average distance of the nearby edges in the MST; where c is a measure of significance and is a user-defined constant. The objective function of Zahn's algorithm is inter-cluster sparseness; i.e. maximum distances in-between clusters. Zahn's algorithm requires constructing the complete MST to determine inconsistent edges.

Grygorash, Zhou, & Jorgensen (2006) propose two variants of MST clustering: HEMST and MSDR. HEMST assumes that the desired number of clusters is given in advance while MSDR does not. MSDR starts by constructing MST in the graph. Next, it computes the standard deviation of the edges in the MST, and removes an edge to obtain a set of disjoint sub-trees such that the overall standard deviation reduction is maximized. This edge removing step is done repeatedly to create more disjoint sub-trees until overall standard deviation reduction is within a threshold. Similar to Zahn's, MSDR requires constructing the complete MST in the graph to compute the standard deviation.

He & Chen (2005) propose an automatic detection of threshold for MST clustering. The method is analogous to finding the cut in hierarchical clustering where the gap between two successive combination similarities is largest. Similar to Zahn's and single-link, this algorithm constructs the complete MST before cutting.

Markov Clustering

Markov Clustering (MCL) algorithm is a form of graph clustering algorithm that is based on simulation of stochastic flow (or random walks) in graphs (Van Dongen, 2000). The aim of MCL is to separate the graph into regions with many edges inside and with only a few edges between regions. Once inside such a region, the flow (or a random walker) has little chance to flow out (Nieland, 2000). To do this, the graph is first rep-

resented as stochastic (Markov) matrices where edges between vertices indicate the amount of flow between the vertices: i.e. similarity measures or the chance of walking from one vertex to another in the graph. MCL algorithm simulates flow using two alternating simple algebraic operations on the matrices: expansion, which coincides with normal matrix multiplication, and inflation, which is a Hadamard power followed by a diagonal scaling. The expansion process causes flow to spread out and the inflation process represents the contraction of flow: it becoming thicker in regions of higher current and thinner in regions of lower current. The flow is eventually separated into different regions, yielding a cluster interpretation of the initial graph. The objective function of MCL is intra-cluster similarity and inter-cluster sparseness.

MCL does not require an a priori number of expected clusters nor a threshold on the similarity values. However, it requires a fine tuning inflation parameter that influences the coarseness and the quality of the resulting clusters.

Star Clustering

Star clustering algorithm, proposed by Aslam, Pelekhov, & Rus (2004), replaces the NP-complete computation of a vertex-cover by cliques by the greedy, simple and inexpensive computation of star shaped dense sub graphs. Star clustering starts by removing edges whose weight is heavier than certain threshold. It then assigns each vertex to its adjacent star center, which is a vertex with equal or higher degree. Each star center and its adjacent vertices is a cluster.

Unlike K-means, Star clustering does not require the indication of an a priori number of clusters. It also allows the clusters produced to overlap. This is a generally desirable feature in information retrieval applications. For document clustering application, Star clustering analytically guarantees a lower bound on the topic similarity between the documents in each cluster and computes more accurate clusters than either the older single-link (Croft, 1977) or average-link (Voorhees, 1985) hierarchical clustering methods. The objective function of Star is both intra-cluster similarity (by selecting star centers with high degree to potentially maximize intra-cluster similarity) and inter-cluster sparseness (by removing edges whose weights are above certain threshold). However, Star clustering requires the value of threshold to be determined a priori.

PROPOSED GRAPH CLUSTERING ALGORITHMS

In this section, we present an overview of our proposed variants of Star and MST clustering algorithms. Combining ideas from Star clustering, MST, and K-means, we also present an overview of our novel family of graph clustering algorithms called Ricochet that does not require any parameters to be defined a priori.

Proposed Variants of Star Clustering

For the task of document clustering, to produce reliable document clusters of similarity σ (i.e. clusters where documents have pair-wise similarities of at least σ, where σ is a user-defined threshold); Star algorithm starts by representing the document collection by its σ-similarity graph. A σ-similarity graph is an undirected, weighted graph where vertices correspond to documents and there is an edge from vertex v_i to vertex v_j if their cosine similarity in a vector space is greater than or equal to σ. Star clustering formalizes clustering by performing a minimum clique cover with maximal cliques on this σ-similarity graph (where the cover is a vertex cover). Since covering by cliques is an NP-complete problem, Star clustering approximates a clique cover greedily by dense sub-graphs that are star shaped.

A star shaped sub-graph of $m + 1$ vertices consists of a single Star center and m satellite vertices,

where there exist edges between the Star center and each satellite vertex. Star clustering guarantees pair-wise similarity of at least σ between the Star and each of the satellite vertices. However, it does not guarantee such similarity between satellite vertices. By investigating the geometry of the vector space model, Aslam, Pelekhov, & Rus (2004) derive a lower bound on the similarity between satellite vertices and predict that the pair-wise similarity between satellite vertices in a Star-shaped sub-graph is high. In their derivation of expected similarity between satellite vertices in a Star cluster, Aslam, Pelekhov, & Rus (2004) show that the lower bound of similarity $cos(\gamma_{i,j})$ between two satellite vertices v_i and v_j in a Star cluster is such that:

$$cos\left(\gamma_{i,j}\right) \geq cos\left(\alpha_i\right)cos\left(\alpha_j\right) + (\frac{\sigma}{\sigma+1})sin(\alpha_i)sin(\alpha_j)$$

(2)

where $cos(\alpha_i)$ is the similarity between the Star center v and satellite v_i and $cos(\alpha_j)$ is the similarity between the Star center v and satellite v_j. They also show empirically that the right hand side of inequality (2) above is a good estimate of its left hand side.

The off-line Star clustering algorithm (for static data) starts by sorting the vertices by degree. Then, it scans the sorted vertices from highest to lowest degree as a greedy search for Star centers. Only vertices that do not yet belong to a Star can become Star centers. Once a new Star center v is selected, its marked bits are set, and for all vertices w adjacent to v, w.marked bit is set. Only one scan of the sorted vertices is needed to determine all Star centers. Upon termination (i.e. when all vertices have their marked bits set) these conditions must be met: (1) the set of Star centers are the Star cover of the graph, (2) a Star center is not adjacent to any other Star center, and (3) every satellite vertex is adjacent to at least one center vertex of equal or higher degree. The algorithm has a running time of $\Theta\left(|V| + |E_\sigma|\right)$ where V is the set of vertices and E_σ edges in the σ-similarity graph G_σ.

Our work on Star clustering (Wijaya & Bressan, 2007) is motivated by the hypothesis that degree is not the best similarity metrics for the selection of Star centers because it does not make use of the very derivation that produced the inequality (2). We believe Star centers should be selected with a metric that tries to maximize the average intra-cluster similarity, i.e. metric that takes into consideration the weight of the edges at any given vertex rather than just its degree. The derivation (2) can therefore be used to estimate the average intra-cluster similarity. For a cluster of n vertices and center v, the average intra-cluster similarity is:

$$\frac{\sum_{(v_i, v_j) \in v.adj \, x \, v.adj} \cos(\gamma_{i,j})}{n^2} \geq \frac{\left(\sum_{v_i \in v.adj} \cos(\alpha_i)\right)^2 + \frac{\sigma}{\sigma+1}\left(\sum_{v_i \in v.adj} \sin(\alpha_i)\right)^2}{n^2}$$

(3)

where $\gamma_{i,j}$ is the angle between vertices v_i and v_j, α_i is the angle between v and vertex v_i, and where $v.adj$ is the set of vertices adjacent to v in G_σ (i.e. the vertices in the cluster). This is computed on the pruned graph, i.e. after edges with weights lower that σ has been removed from the graph. For each vertex v in G_σ, we let:

$$lb(v) = \frac{\left(\sum_{v_i \in v.adj} \cos(\alpha_i)\right)^2 + \frac{\sigma}{\sigma+1}\left(\sum_{v_i \in v.adj} \sin(\alpha_i)\right)^2}{n^2}$$

(4)

We call the metrics $lb(v)$, the lower bound. This is the theoretical lower bound on the actual average intra-cluster similarity when v is Star center and $v.adj$ are its satellites. We introduce several similarity metrics that tries to maximize this lower bound of intra-cluster similarity with the hope of improving the actual intra-cluster similarity.

Among the metrics that we introduce are (a) Markov Stationary Distributions that uses the idea of random walk to find important vertices

in the graph that are potentially good candidates for star centers, (b) Lower Bound that chooses vertices which maximize the value of lower bound derived in (4) as star centers, (c) Average that chooses vertices which maximize the function $ave(v)$ as star centers (where $ave(v) = \sum_{vi \in v.adj} \cos(\alpha_i) / degree(v)$; and α_i is the angle between v and vertex v_i), and (d) Sum that chooses vertices which maximize the function $sum(v)$ as star centers (where $sum(v) = \sum_{vi \in v.adj} \cos(\alpha_i)$; where α_i is the angle between v and vertex v_i)

Note that our function $ave(v)$ is the square-root of the first term in the lower bound $lb(v)$ metric. Thus we expect $ave(v)$ will be a good approximation for $lb(v)$. Coincidentally, $ave(v)$ which aims to maximize the average similarity between a Star center and its satellites is related to the idea used by K-means algorithm whereby, at each iteration, the algorithm tries to maximize the average similarity between centroids and their vertices.

Incorporating these metrics in Star algorithms, we sort vertices by sum and average and pick un-marked vertex with highest sum and average to be the new Star center, respectively. We incorporate the lower bound, average and sum metrics in the original Star algorithms by using $lb(v)$, $sum(v)$ and $ave(v)$ in the place of $degree(v)$. We empirically studied the performance of our variants of Star clustering for the task of document clustering.

Our empirical results (Wijaya & Bressan, 2007) confirm our hypothesis: selecting star centers based on degree performs almost as poorly as a random selection. One needs to use a metrics that maximizes intra-cluster similarity such as the lower bound metrics. While it indeed yields the best results, it is expensive to compute. The average metrics is a fast and good approximation of the lower bound metrics. For the offline version of the algorithm, it yields up to 4.53% improvement of F_1 (harmonic mean of precision and recall) with a 19.1% improvement on precision and 1.77% on recall over the original Star clustering algorithm. For the online (dynamic) version, it yields an outstanding 20.81% improvement of F_1 with a

20.87% improvement on precision and 20.67% on recall over the original Star clustering algorithm.

MST-SIM: PROPOSED VARIANTS OF MST CLUSTERING

Our proposed variants of MST clustering algorithms, called MST-Sim, builds clusters while executing Kruskal's algorithm or Borůvka's algorithm for finding minimum spanning tree (MST) in the graph. They leverage the properties that the minimum spanning sub-trees created during the execution of Kruskal's and Borůvka's algorithms exhibit good inter-cluster sparseness and intra-cluster similarities; as the way these sub-trees are created aims to maximize the minimum spacing between sub-trees and minimize the maximum spacing within sub-tree (spacing being the inverse of weights of edges that reflect similarity between two vertices).

During the execution of either Kruskal's or Borůvka's algorithms, MST-Sim decides whether or not to merge two sub-trees into one sub-tree based on metrics measuring inter- and intra- similarity between the two sub-trees. To do so, when MST-Sim encounters an edge connecting two vertices from different sub-trees, using a similarity metric Z, it first calculates the inter-cluster similarity (based on the weights of edges between the sub-trees) and intra-cluster similarity (based on the weights of edges within the sub-tree). MST-Sim then merges the two sub-trees only if their inter-cluster similarity is bigger than either one of their intra-cluster similarities times an inflation parameter c which is a fine tuning parameter: lower values favor recall while higher values favor precision as fewer clusters are merged. We study several similarity metrics: Eta-, Beta-, and Diameter-index proposed in (Rodrigue, 2009). The clusters are the resulting final sub-trees.

MST-Sim is different in several aspects from the existing MST clustering algorithms. Firstly, it does not require any input information such as desired number of clusters or threshold to be provided before clustering. At most they use an inflation parameter that gives a fine tuning capability for effectiveness. Secondly, it finds clusters while constructing the MST rather than a posteriori – hence it is more easily adaptable to an online (or dynamic) application than the original MST clustering algorithm that requires the MST to be built first before determining edges to prune to create clusters. Thirdly, MST-Sim considers both inter-cluster sparseness – edges in-between clusters and intra-cluster density – edges within clusters when constructing clusters. We empirically studied the performance of our variants of Star clustering for the task of document clustering. We use document collections from Reuters-21578, TIPSTER–AP and our original collection: Google (Wijaya & Bressan, 2007). Our empirical result shows that on average over all document collections in our empirical study, MST-Sim (using Kruskal algorithm for finding MST and Diameter-index for similarity metric) achieves 11.0% increase in F_1 value over the best F_1 values achieved by Zahn's and 61.8% increase in F_1 value over the F_1 values achieved by single-link clustering with optimum number of clusters given. In comparison with other state-of-the-art clustering algorithms, on average over all collections in our empirical study, MST-Sim (using Kruskal algorithm and Diameter-index for similarity metric) achieves 37.1% improvement in F_1 over Star clustering (with average similarity of documents in the given collection used as threshold), 0.93% improvement in F_1 over Markov Clustering (with the optimum inflation parameter used), 21.1% improvement in F_1 over K-medoids (with the optimum number of clusters given).

Ricochet: A Family of Unconstrained Graph Clustering Algorithms (Wijaya & Bressan, 2009)

Unlike Star clustering algorithm that is parameterized by the edge threshold and MST clustering that is parameterized by the inflation parameter, our proposed clustering algorithm Ricochet is unconstrained. Ricochet algorithms alternate two phases: the choosing of vertices to be the centroids of clusters and the assignment of vertices to existing clusters. The motivation underlying Ricochet is that: (1) Star clustering algorithm provides a metric of selecting Star centers that are potentially good cluster centroids for maximizing intra-cluster similarity, (2) K-means provides an excellent vertices assignment and reassignment, and a convergence criterion that increases intra-cluster similarity at each iteration, (3) MST algorithm provides a means to select edges to merge clusters that potentially maximizes intra-cluster similarity. By using Star clustering for selecting Star centers, we find potential cluster centroids without having to supply the number of clusters. By using K-means re-assignment of vertices, we update and improve the quality of these clusters and reach a termination condition without having to determine any threshold. By using MST algorithm, we select edges to merge clusters to maximize the clusters' intra-cluster similarities. Hence, similar to our proposed variant of Star algorithm (Wijaya & Bressan, 2007), Ricochet chooses centroids in descending order of the value of the metric combining degree with the weight of adjacent edges. Similar to K-means, Ricochet assigns and reassigns vertices; and the iterative assignment of vertices is stopped once these conditions are met: (1) no vertex is left unassigned and (2) no vertex is candidate for re-assignment. Similar to MST algorithm, for each centroid, Ricochet selects the unprocessed edge with minimum spacing (maximum similarity weight) adjacent on the centroid. Ricochet algorithm has been devised by spinning the metaphor of ripples created by the throwing of stones in a pond. Clusters' centroids are stones and rippling is the iterative assignment of objects to clusters.

The Ricochet family is twofold. In the first Ricochet sub-family, centroids are chosen one after the other. In the second Ricochet sub-family,

centroids are chosen at the same time. We call the former algorithms Sequential Rippling, and the latter Concurrent Rippling. The algorithms in the Sequential Rippling, because of the way they select centroids and assign or re-assign vertices, are intrinsically hard clustering algorithms, i.e. they produce disjoint clusters. The algorithms in the Concurrent Rippling are soft clustering algorithms, i.e. they produce possibly overlapping clusters.

Sequential Rippling

The algorithms in the Sequential Rippling can be perceived as somewhat straightforward extensions to the K-means clustering.

The first algorithm of the subfamily is called Sequential Rippling (or SR in figure 1). In this algorithm, *vertices* are ordered in descending order of the average weight of their adjacent edges (later referred to as the weight of a vertex). The vertex with the highest weight is chosen to be the first centroid and a cluster is formed by assigning all other vertices to the cluster of this first centroid. Subsequently, new centroids are chosen one by one from the ordered list of vertices. When a new centroid is added, vertices are re-assigned to a new cluster if they are closer to the new centroid than they were to the centroid of their current cluster (if no vertex is closer to the new centroid, no new cluster is created). If clusters are reduced to singletons during re-assignment, they are assigned to the nearest non-singleton cluster. The algorithm stops when all vertices have been considered.

The second algorithm of the subfamily is called Balanced Sequential Rippling (BSR in figure 2). The difference between BSR and SR is in its choice of subsequent centroid. In order to balance the distribution of centroids in the graph, BSR chooses a next centroid that is both a reasonable centroid for a new cluster (i.e. has large value of weight) as well as sufficiently far from the previous centroids. Subsequent centroid is chosen to maximize the ratio of its weight to the sum of its similarity to the centroids of already existing

Figure 1. Sequential rippling algorithm

```
Given a Graph G = (V, E). V contains vertices, N = |V|. Each vertex has a weight
which is the average similarity between the vertex and its adjacent vertices. E
contains edges in G (self-loops removed) with similarity as weights.

Algorithm: SR ( )
Sort V in order of vertices' weights
Take the heaviest vertex v from V
listCentroid.add (v)
Reassign all other vertices to v's cluster
While (V is not empty)
      Take the next heaviest vertex v from V
      Reassign vertices which are more similar to v than to other centroid
      If there are re-assignments
            listCentroid.add (v)
            Reassign singleton clusters to its nearest centroid
For all i ε listCentroid return i and its associated cluster
```

Figure 2. Balanced sequential rippling algorithm

```
Algorithm: BSR ( )
Sort V in order of vertices' weights
Take the heaviest vertex v from V
listCentroid.add (v)
Reassign all other vertices to v's cluster
Reassignment = true
While (Reassignment and V is not empty)
      Reassignment = false
      Take a vertex v ∉listCentroid from V whose ratio of its weight to
       the sum of its similarity  to existing centroids is the maximum
      Reassign vertices which are more similar to v than to other centroid
      If there are re-assignments
            Reassignment = true
            listCentroid.add (v)
            Reassign singleton clusters to its nearest centroid
For all i ε listCentroid return i and its associated cluster
```

clusters. This is a compromise between weight and similarity. We use here the simplest possible formula to achieve such compromise. It could clearly be refined and fine-tuned. As in SR, when a new centroid is added, vertices are re-assigned to a new cluster if they are closer to the new centroid than they were to the centroid of their current cluster. The algorithm terminates when there is no re-assignment of vertices.

Concurrent Rippling

Unlike sequential rippling which chooses centroids one after another, concurrent rippling treats all vertices as centroids of their own singleton clusters initially. Then, each centroid concurrently 'ripples its influence' using its adjacent edges to other vertices. As the rippling progresses, some centroids can lose their centroid status (i.e. become non-centroid) as the cluster of smaller weight centroid is 'engulfed' by the cluster of bigger weight centroid.

The first algorithm of the sub-family is called Concurrent Rippling (CR in figure 3). In this algorithm, for each vertex, the adjacent edges are ordered in descending order of weights. Iteratively, all edges whose weights are heavier or equal than the minimum of the next (unprocessed) heaviest edges of all vertices are processed concurrently. Two cases are possible: (1) if the edge connects a centroid to a non-centroid, the non-centroid is added to the cluster of the centroid (notice that at this point the non-centroid belongs to at least two clusters), (2) if the edge connects two centroids, the cluster of one centroid is assigned to the cluster of the other centroid (i.e. it is 'engulfed' by the other centroid), if and only if its weight is smaller than that of the other centroid. The two clusters are merged and the smaller weight centroid becomes a non-centroid. The algorithm terminates when the centroids no longer change.

The second algorithm of the sub-family is called Ordered Concurrent Rippling (OCR in Figure 4). In this algorithm, the constant speed of rippling is abandoned to be approximated by a simple ordering of adjacent edges according to their weights to the vertex. The method allows to process only the best 'ripple' (i.e. heaviest adjacent edge) for each vertex each time. We empirically studied the performance of our variants of Star clustering for the task of document clustering (Wijaya & Bressan, 2009).

In comparison with constrained algorithms, BSR and OCR are found to be the most effective among Ricochet family of algorithms. BSR achieves higher precision than K-medoids supplied with the correct number of clusters, Star and our best Star variant: Star-ave in (Wijaya & Bressan, 2007) on all our document collections (Wijaya & Bressan, 2009). We believe BSR achieves higher precision because at each step it tries to maximize the average similarity between vertices and their centroids through reassignment of vertices. Choices of centroids that are of heavy weights and as far away from each other as possible may also have positive effects on the purity of clusters produced.

OCR achieves a balance between high precision and recall, and obtains higher or comparable F1-value than K-medoids, Star and Star-Ave on all our document collections. In terms of F1 value, OCR is 8.7% better than K-medoids, 23.5% better than Star, and 7.9% better than Star-Ave.

In comparison with unconstrained algorithm, although Markov Clustering at its best inflation setting is slightly more effective than Ricochet algorithms (9% more effective than OCR), OCR, is not only respectably effective but also significantly more efficient (70.8% more efficient) than Markov Clustering. Furthermore OCR does not require the setting of any fine tuning parameters like the inflation parameter of Markov Clustering that, when set incorrectly, can have adverse effect on its performance (OCR is in average, 334% more effective than Markov Clustering at its worst inflation setting). More recently, an empirical study is conducted to compare the accuracy and scalability of various graph clustering algorithms for the task of duplicate detection in large databases (Hassanzadeh, Chiang, Lee, & Miller, 2009). The source relation is represented as a graph where each vertex represents a record in the base relation and each edge connects two nodes only if their similarity score is above a specified threshold. The task of partitioning the relation is equivalent to clustering the vertices in the graph. The clusters produced by clustering algorithms are groups of potential duplicates in the database. Among the

Figure 3. Concurrent rippling algorithm

```
For each vertex v, v.neighbor is the list of v's adjacent vertices sorted by their similarity to v
from highest to lowest. If v is a centroid (v.centroid == 1); v.cluster contains the list of
vertices ≠ v assigned to v

Algorithm: CR ( )
1. Sort E in order of the edge weights
2. CentroidChange = true
3. index = 0
4. While (CentroidChange && index < N-1 && E is not empty)
     5. CentroidChange = false
     6. For each vertex v, take its edge e_vw connecting v to its next
        closest neighbor w; i.e. w = v.neighbor [index]
     7. Store these edges in S
     8. Find the lowest edge weight in S, say low, and empty S
     9. Take all edges from E whose weight >= low
     10. Store these edges in S
     11. PropagateRipple (S)
     12. index ++
13. For all i ε V, if i is a centroid, return i and i.cluster


Sub Procedure: PropagateRipple (list S)
/* This sub procedure is to propagate ripples for all the centroids. If the ripple of one centroid
touches another, the heavier weight centroid will engulf the lighter centroid and its cluster. If
the ripple of a centroid touches a non-centroid, the non-centroid is assigned to the centroid.
A non-centroid can be assigned to more than one centroid, allowing overlapping between
clusters, a generally desirable feature */
While (S is not empty)
     Take the next heaviest edge, say e_vw, from S
     If v ∉ x.cluster for all x ε V
             If w is a centroid, compare v's weight to w's weight
             If (w.weight > v.weight)
                 add v and v.cluster into w.cluster
                 Empty v.cluster
                 If v is a centroid
                     v.centroid = 0
                     CentroidChange = true
             Else
                 add w and w.cluster into v.cluster
                 Empty w.cluster
                 w.centroid = 0
                 CentroidChange = true
             Else if w is not a centroid
                 v.cluster.add (w)
                 If v is not a centroid
                     v.centroid = 1
                     CentroidChange = true
```

clustering algorithms investigated are Star cluster-ing, Markov clustering and Ricochet. SR and BSR are found to be the least sensitive to the threshold value. Ricochet algorithms are also found to be relatively more robust on datasets with different amounts of errors; however they are sensitive to the distribution of duplicates in the data. Ricochet algorithms produce high quality clustering when used with uniformly distributed duplicates but

Figure 4. Ordered concurrent rippling algorithm

```
For each vertex v, v.neighbor is the list of v's adjacent vertices sorted by their
similarity to v from highest to lowest. If v is a centroid (i.e. v.centroid == 1);
v.cluster contains the list of vertices ≠ v assigned to v

Algorithm: OCR ( )
public CentroidChange = true
index = 0
While (CentroidChange && index < N-1)
    CentroidChange = false
    For each vertex v, take its edge e_vw connecting v to its next closest
    neighbor w; i.e. w = v.neighbor [index]
    Store these edges in S
    PropagateRipple (S)
    index ++
For all i ε V, if i is a centroid, return i and i.cluster
```

failed in other distributions mainly due to the inability of Ricochet in finding singleton clusters.

FUTURE RESEARCH DIRECTIONS

For the domain of graph clustering algorithms, further improvements in the algorithms and applications to other domains (such as duplicate detection) can be explored in the future.

In terms of the pre-processing time for graph clustering algorithms, for example, one crucial weakness of graph-based clustering algorithms is that they need to compute pair wise similarities between vertices in the graph before clustering. In future, methods such as indexing, stream processing, bootstrapping can be explored to reduce the number of pair wise similarities that the algorithm need to pre-compute. It will also be interesting if randomized graph algorithms such as the one in (Karger, Klein, & Tarjan, 1995) can be explored to do clustering. Interesting relationship between matrix factorizations and clustering can also be explored (Ding & He, 2004 and Ding, He, and Simon, 2005). Further, the cut and cycle property

of graphs maybe further exploited to do clustering. The cut property maybe related to inter-cluster density while the cycle property maybe related to intra-cluster sparseness. Another interesting idea is in using the notion of heavy or light edges in randomized MST algorithm to remove "unnecessary" edges from the graph thus thresholding the graph before conducting any clustering on the graph.

CONCLUSION

In this chapter we have presented an overview of graph algorithms for clustering vertices in a weighted graph. We present existing graph clustering algorithms: Star clustering, MST clustering, and Markov clustering algorithms, and our proposed variants of Star Clustering, MST clustering and Ricochet. All the algorithms presented are discussed in the light of an extensive comparative empirical performance evaluation.

Our novel variants of Star clustering algorithm explore different techniques, including random walk algorithm, to choose centroids (Star centers). Our variants of Star clustering are more effective than, and as efficient as, the original Star clustering algorithms.

Based on our study of minimum spanning tree algorithm, we propose a novel family of clustering algorithms: MST-Sim that uses minimum spanning tree algorithm and adds to it intra- and inter-cluster similarity metrics. MST-Sim algorithms are generally very fast and efficient in comparison with other state of the art graph clustering algorithms.

Based on our study of Star clustering, minimum spanning tree and K-means, we propose an unconstrained family of graph-based clustering algorithms named Ricochet that does not require any parameter to be defined a priori. While the fact that Ricochet is unconstrained is already an advantage, Ricochet algorithms are competitive to other state of the art clustering algorithms. One of them, OCR, yields a very respectable effectiveness while being efficient

REFERENCES

Aslam, J., Pelekhov, K., & Rus, D. (2004). The Star Clustering Algorithm. *Journal of Graph Algorithms and Applications, 8*(1), 95–129.

Boruvka, O. (1926). O jistém problému minimálním (About a certain minimal problem). *Práce Mor. Prírodoved. Spol., v Brne III*(3), 37–58.

Brin, S., & Page, L. (1998). The anatomy of a large-scale hypertextual Web search engine. *Computer Networks and ISDN Systems, 30*(1-7), 107–117.

Croft, W. B. (1977). Clustering large files of documents using the single-link method. *Journal of the American Society for Information Science American Society for Information Science*, 189–195.

Ding, C., & He, X. (2004). *K-means clustering via principal component analysis*. In *Proceedings of the 21ˢᵗ International Conference on Machine learning*, Banff, Alberta, Canada.

Ding, C., He, X., & Simon, H. D. (2005). *On the equivalence of nonnegative matrix factorization and spectral clustering*. In *Proceedings SIAM International Conference Data Mining*, Newport Beach, CA.

Gondran, M., Minoux, M., & Vajda, S. (1984). *Graphs and algorithms*. New York, NY: John Wiley and Sons.

Grygorash, O., Zhou, Y., & Jorgensen, Z. (2006). *Minimum spanning tree based clustering algorithms*. Paper presented at the 18th IEEE International Conference on Tools with Artificial Intelligence, Washington, DC.

Hassanzadeh, O., Chiang, F., Lee, H. C., & Miller, R. J. (2009). *Framework for evaluating clustering algorithms in duplicate detection*. Paper presented at the 35ᵗʰ International Conference on Very Large Data Bases, Lyon, France.

He, Y., & Chen, L. (2005). A threshold criterion, auto-detection and its use in MST-based clustering. *Intelligent Data Analysis, 9*(3), 253–271.

Jain, A. K., Murty, M. N., & Flynn, P. J. (1999). Data clustering: A review. *ACM Computing Surveys, 31*(3). doi:10.1145/331499.331504

Karger, D. R., Klein, P. N., & Tarjan, R. E. (1995). A randomized linear-time algorithm to find minimum spanning trees. *Journal of the ACM, 42*(2), 321–328. doi:10.1145/201019.201022

Kruskal, J. B. (1956). On the shortest spanning subtree and the traveling salesman problem. *Proceedings of the American Mathematical Society, 7*, 48–50. doi:10.1090/S0002-9939-1956-0078686-7

Nieland, H. (2000). Fast graph clustering algorithm by flow simulation. *Research and Development*. (ERCIM News 42)

Rodrigue, J. (2009) Graph theory: Measures and indices. *The geography of transport systems.* Retrieved June, 2010, from: http://people. hofstra. edu/geotrans/eng/ch1en/meth1en/ch1m3en.html.

Skiena, S. S. (1998). *The algorithm design manual.* New York, NY: Telos/Springer-Verlag.

Van Dongen, S. M. (2000). *Graph clustering by flow simulation.* Universiteit Utrecht, Netherlands: Tekst. – Proefschrift.

Voorhees, E. (1985). *The cluster hypothesis revisited.* In Proceedings of the 8th SIGIR, Montreal, Canada.

Wijaya, D., & Bressan, S. (2007). *Journey to the centre of the star: Various ways of finding star centers in star clustering.* 18th International Conference on Database and Expert Systems Applications (DEXA), Regensburg, Germany.

Wijaya, D., & Bressan, S. (2009). *Ricochet: A family of unconstrained algorithms for graph clustering.* 14th International Conference on Database Systems for Advanced Applications, Brisbane, Australia.

Zahn, C. T. (1971). Graph theoretical methods for detecting and describing gestalt clusters. *IEEE Transactions on Computers, C-20*(1). doi:10.1109/T-C.1971.223083

KEY TERMS AND DEFINITIONS

Clustering: The assignment of a set of observations into subsets (called clusters) so that observations in the same cluster are similar in some sense.

Markov Clustering: A fast and scalable unsupervised cluster algorithm for networks (also known as graphs) based on simulation of (stochastic) flow in graphs.

Minimum Spanning Tree Clustering: Clustering that is based on Minimum Spanning Tree algorithm. Given a connected, undirected graph, a spanning tree of that graph is a subgraph which is a tree and connects all the vertices together. A minimum spanning tree (MST) is then a spanning tree with weight less than or equal to the weight of every other spanning tree.

Star Clustering: Clustering that is based on covering graphs by dense subgraphs that are star-shaped.

Weighted Graph: A weighted graph associates a label (weight) with every edge in the graph.

Chapter 13
Large Scale Graph Mining with MapReduce:
Counting Triangles in Large Real Networks

Charalampos E. Tsourakakis
Carnegie Mellon University, USA

ABSTRACT

In recent years, a considerable amount of research has focused on the study of graph structures arising from technological, biological and sociological systems. Graphs are the tool of choice in modeling such systems since they are typically described as sets of pairwise interactions. Important examples of such datasets are the Internet, the Web, social networks, and large-scale information networks which reach the planetary scale, e.g., Facebook and LinkedIn. The necessity to process large datasets, including graphs, has led to a major shift towards distributed computing and parallel applications, especially in the recent years. MapReduce was developed by Google, one of the largest users of multiple processor computing in the world, for facilitating the development of scalable and fault tolerant applications. MapReduce has become the de facto standard for processing large scale datasets both in industry and academia.

In this Chapter, we present state of the art work on large scale graph mining using MapReduce. We survey research work on an important graph mining problem, counting the number of triangles in large-real world networks. We present the most important applications related to the count of triangles and two families of algorithms, a spectral and a combinatorial one, which solve the problem efficiently.

INTRODUCTION

The total digital output is expected to exceed 1.2 ZetaBytes in 2010 (Blake, 2010). The New York Stock Exchange generates about one terabyte of new trade data per day and Facebook hosts approxi-
mately 10 billion photos, taking up one PetaByte of storage (White, 2009). It has become apparent that as the amount of data generated increases at this unprecedented rate, scalability of algorithms is crucial. In recent years, MapReduce (Dean et al., 2008) and Hadoop (Hadoop Wiki, 2010), its

DOI: 10.4018/978-1-61350-053-8.ch013

open source implementation, have become the de facto standard for analyzing large datasets. Despite its limitations, the MapReduce framework stands out for making the programmer's life who uses MapReduce to develop applications easy. Specifically, from the programmer's perspective, MapReduce is just a library imported at the beginning of the program, like any other common library. MapReduce takes care of the parallelization and all its details including distributing the data over the cluster and fault tolerance. In the next Section we provide more details on MapReduce and Hadoop. According to (Hadoop Users, 2010) over 70 major companies over the world use Hadoop. Furthermore, innovative commercial ideas like Amazon's Elastic Compute Cloud (EC2) where users can upload large data sets and rent processor time in a large Hadoop cluster have proved successful. Besides companies, MapReduce and Hadoop have become also the de facto standard for research. Several universities including Carnegie Mellon University, Cornell and Berkeley are using Hadoop clusters for research purposes. Projects include text processing, analysis of large astronomical datasets and graph mining. Currently, (Pegasus CMU, 2010) provides an open source Hadoop-based library for performing important graph mining operations.

In this Chapter, we survey state-of-the-art work related to triangle counting using MapReduce. The interested reader is urged to study the original publications (Tsourakakis, 2008), (Tsourakakis et al., 2009a), (Tsourakakis et al., 2009b), (Tsourakakis et al., 2009c), (Tsourakakis, 2010), (Tsourakakis et al., 2011) which we survey in this Chapter for the full details of the algorithms. The outline of this Chapter is as follows: in Section 2 we provide a brief description of MapReduce and Hadoop, an open source package which includes a freely available implementation of MapReduce. In Section 3 we present work related to the triangle counting problem, in Section 4 the implementation details and in Section 5 future research directions. Finally,

in Section 6 we conclude. For the interested reader, we provide at the end of the Chapter additional reading material.

BACKGROUND

MapReduce

While the PRAM model (Jaja, 1992) and the bulk-synchronous parallel model (BSP) (Valiant, 1990) are powerful models, MapReduce has largely "taken over" both industry and academia (Hadoop Users, 2010). In few words, this success is due to two reasons: first, MapReduce is a simple and powerful programming model which makes the programmer's life easy. Secondly, MapReduce is publicly available via its open source version Hadoop. MapReduce was introduced in (Dean et al, 2008) by Google, one of the largest users of multiple processor computing in the world, for facilitating the development of scalable and fault tolerant applications. In the MapReduce paradigm, a parallel computation is defined on a set of values and consists of a series of *map*, *shuffle* and *reduce* steps. Let $(x_1,.., x_n)$ be the set of values, *m* denote the mapping function which takes a value x and returns a pair of a key k and a value *u* and *r* the reduce function.

1. In the map step a mapping function *m* is applied to a value x_i and a pair (k_i,u_i) of a key k_i and a value u_i is generated.
2. The shuffle step starts upon having mapped all values x_i for i=1 to n to pairs. In this step, a set of lists is produced using the key-value pairs generated from the map step with an important feature. Each list is characterized by the key k and has the form L_k = {k: $u_1,..,u_{j(k)}$} if and only if there exists a pair (k,u_i) for i=1 to j.
3. Finally in the reduce step, the reduce function *r* is applied to the lists generated from

the shuffle step to produce the set of values $(w_1, w_2, \ldots)$.

To illustrate the aforementioned abstract concepts consider the problem of counting how many times each word in a given document appears. The set of values is the "bag-of-words" appearing in the document. For example, if the document is the sentence "The dog runs in the forest", then $\{x_1, x_2, x_3, x_4, x_5, x_6\} = \{the, dog, runs, in, the, forest\}$. One convenient choice for the MapReduce functions is the following and results in the following steps:

- The map function m will map a value x to a pair of a key and a value. A convenient choice for m is something close to the identity map. Specifically, we choose m(x) $=(x,\$)$, where we assume that the dollar sign $\$$ a especially reserved symbol.
- The shuffle step for our small example will produce the following set of lists: (the:$\$,\$$), (dog:$\$$) (runs:$\$$), (in:$\$$), (runs:$\$$), (forest:$\$$)
- The reduce function r will process each list defined by each different word appearing in the document by counting the number of dollar signs $\$$. This number will also be the count of times that specific word appears in the text.

Hadoop -as already mentioned- implements MapReduce and was originally created by Doug Cutting. Even if Hadoop is well known for MapReduce it is actually a collection of subprojects that are closely related to distributed computing. For example HDFS (Hadoop filesystem) is a distributed filesystem that provides high throughput access to application data and HBase is a scalable, distributed database that supports structured data storage for large tables (column-oriented database). Another subproject is Pig, which is a high-level data-flow language and execution framework for parallel computation (Gates, 2009). Pig runs on HDFS and MapReduce. For more details and other subprojects, the interested reader can visit the website that hosts the Hadoop project (Hadoop Wiki 2010).

The MapReduce (*MRC*) Complexity Class

Karloff, Suri and Vassilvitskii in (Karloff et al. 2010) in their fundamental paper towards understanding which problems can be solved efficiently in MapReduce present a formal computation model for MapReduce and compare it to the popular PRAM model. There are three main aspects of the MapReduce complexity class (*MRC*) are the following:

- Memory: the input to any mapper and any reducer should be sublinear in the size of the data.
- Machines: the total number of machines should also be sublinear in the data size.
- Time: both map and reduce functions run in time polynomial with respect to the original input size.

Clearly, the requirements are well grounded. For example, if the memory requirement did not hold, then we could use a single reducer to solve the problem. However, this is against the parallel programming paradigm in which we are interested in. Furthermore, imagine requiring a superlinear number of machines, for example for n^2 machines where n is the size of the Web graph. This is unrealistic and this is why we require a sublinear number of machines. Similarly, the third requirement is in accordance to Complexity theory where a polynomial time algorithm implies an efficient solution. The algorithm we present in Section 4 is in accordance with this model of computation. For the details of the *MRC* complexity class, the interested reader is encouraged to study the (Karloff et al. 2010) paper.

TRIANGLE COUNTING

Motivation

The number of triangles is a significant and computationally expensive graph statistic in complex network analysis, in random graph models and in various important applications. Specifically, in complex network analysis (Newman, 2003) a frequently used statistic is the transitivity of the graph which is defined as the ratio of the triangles by the number of triples in the graph times 3 (Newman et al., 2002). Other metrics which involve triangle counting are the clustering coefficients of the vertices and the clustering coefficient of the graph (Schank et al, 2004), (Watts et al., 1998). Two popular statistical models for real-world networks are the exponential random graph model (ERGM) (Frank, 1991), (Wasserman et al., 1996) and its predecessor, the Markov graph (Frank et al., 1986). The count of triangles is the most common statistic used in the likelihood functions defined by the aforementioned models which is computationally expensive. Furthermore, triangles play a significant role in social network analysis since friends of friends tend to become friends themselves (Wasserman et al., 1994) Therefore, many studies on the evolution of networks e.g., (Leskovec et al., 2008) focus on triads. Triangles also play an important role in motif detection in protein interaction networks (Lotem et al., 2004). Interestingly, triangles have found several real-world applications. Specifically, triangles are used for spam detection (Beccheti et al., 2008), for uncovering the thematic structure of the Web (Eckmann et al., 2002) and for link recommendation (Tsourakakis et al., 2011). Given the large size of numerous graphs -according to (Becchetti et al., 2008) the total number of nodes indexable by search engines is in the order of 10^{10} and the expected number of hyperlinks per web page between 20 and 30-, the computational cost of triangle counting and the fact that for the aforementioned applications, the exact count of triangles is not crucial, high quality and fast approximation algorithms are necessary.

It is worth mentioning that triangles play an important role in theoretical computer science. Specifically, the problem of detecting whether a graph is triangle-free (Alon et al., 2006) arises in numerous combinatorial problems such as the minimum cycle detection problem (Itai et al., 1977), the approximate minimum vertex cover in planar graphs (Bar-Yehuda et al., 1982 and recognition of median graphs (Imrich et al., 1999). Recently, it was shown that detecting a triangle is equivalent to boolean matrix multiplication under the notion of subcubic reductions (Williams et al., 2010) contrary to common belief (Spinrad, 2003).

In the following we present two families of algorithms for counting triangles in large networks. The first family is based on the special spectral properties of real-world networks (Tsourakakis, 2008), (Tsourakakis, 2010), (Tsourakakis et al., 2009a), (Tsourakakis et al., 2011) whereas the second is a randomized, combinatorial algorithm which works on graphs with at least O(npolylog(n)) triangles (Tsourakakis et al., 2009b), (Tsourakakis et al., 2009c).

EIGENTRIANGLE: SPECTRAL COUNTING OF TRIANGLES

Theorems

The following theorem connects the number of triangles in which node i participates with the eigenvalues and eigenvectors of the adjacency matrix.

Theorem 1 (EigenTriangleLocal)

Let G be an undirected, simple graph and A is adjacency matrix representation.

The number of triangles Δ_i that node i participates in satisfies the following equation:

$$\Delta_i = \frac{\sum_j u_{ij}^2 \lambda_j^3}{2}$$

where u_{ij} is the i-th entry of the j-th eigenvector and λ_j is the j-th eigenvalue of the adjacency matrix.

The following lemma holds and the proof of Theorem 1, see (Tsourakakis, 2008).

Lemma 1 (EigenTriangle)

The total number of triangles $\Delta(G)$ in the graph is given by the sum of the cubes of the eigenvalues of the adjacency matrix divided by six, i.e.,:

$$\Delta(G) = \frac{\sum_j \lambda_j^3}{6}$$

The importance of Theorem 1 and of Lemma 1 lies in the fact that they provide us with an alternative way to compute the total number of triangles and the number of triangles in the graph. Specifically, we can count the total number of triangles and the number of triangles each node participates in using the eigenvalues and eigenvectors of the adjacency matrix representation of the graph. However, the above theorems do not justify why an algorithm which relies on the above Theorem and Lemma for counting triangles should be efficient. In other words, it is not immediately apparent why such an alternative computation should be more effective than a naive enumeration of triples in the graph since the full eigendecomposition of the adjacency matrix runs also in $O(n^3)$ time. In the following, we propose the EIGENTRIANGLE algorithms and then we explain why they are effective for counting triangles in real-world networks.

Algorithms

Figure 1 and Figure 2 show the two spectral based algorithms for counting triangles in large real world networks, the EigenTriangle and the

EigenTriangleLocal algorithm respectively. The former is based on Lemma 1 whereas the latter on Theorem 1 respectively. Both algorithms take as input the n x n adjacency matrix A and a tolerance parameter *tol*, where n is the number of nodes in the graph G. The EigenTriangle algorithm keeps computing eigenvalues until the contribution of the cube of the current eigenvalue is considered to be significantly smaller than the sum of the cubes of the previously computed eigenvalues. The tolerance parameter determines when the algorithm will stop looping, i.e., when we consider that the currently computed eigenvalue contributes little to the total number of triangles. The idea behind them is that due to the special spectral properties of real-world networks few iterations suffice to output a good approximation. We elaborate more on this fact in the next subsection. Specifically, EigenTriangle starts with computing the first eigenvalue λ_1. It then computes the second eigenvalue λ_2 and checks using the condition in the *repeat* loop if λ_2 contributes significantly or not to the current estimate of triangles the algorithm keeps iterating and keeps computing eigenvalues until the stopping criterion is satisfied. Then, it outputs the estimate of the total number of triangles $\Delta'(G)$ using the computed eigenvalues and Lemma 1. EigenTriangleLocal additionally stores the eigenvectors corresponding to the top eigenvalues in order to make an estimate of Δ_i using Theorem 1. The *repeat* loop as in EigenTriangle computes eigenvalue-eigenvector pairs until the stopping criterion is met and the *for* loop computes the estimates Δ'_I of Δ_i, for i=1..n.

Both algorithms use the subroutine *Lanczos-Method* (Demmel, 1997) as a black box. Observe that in order to simplify the presentation, depending on the number of output arguments, Lanczos returns either the eigenvalues only or the eigenvalues and the corresponding eigenvectors as well. The required time is practically the same in both cases to compute a low-rank eigendecomposition of the adjacency matrix. Lanczos method is a well studied projection based method for solving the

Figure 1. The EigenTriangle algorithm

Algorithm 1 The EIGENTRIANGLE algorithm

Require: Adjacency matrix A $(n \times n)$
Require: Tolerance *tol*
Output: $\Delta'(G)$ global triangle estimation
$\quad \lambda_1 \leftarrow LanczosMethod(A, 1)$
$\quad \Lambda \leftarrow [\lambda_1]$
$\quad i \leftarrow 1$ {initialize i, Λ}
$\quad$**repeat**
$\quad\quad i \leftarrow i + 1$
$\quad\quad \lambda_i \leftarrow LanczosMethod(A, i)$
$\quad\quad \Lambda \leftarrow [\Lambda \ \lambda_i]$
$\quad$**until** $0 \leq \dfrac{|\lambda_i^3|}{\sum_{j=1}^{i} \lambda_j^3} \leq tol$
$\quad \Delta'(G) \leftarrow \frac{1}{6} \sum_{j=1}^{i} \lambda_j^3$
$\quad$**return** $\Delta'(G)$

Figure 2. The EigenTriangleLocal algorithm

Algorithm 2 The EIGENTRIANGLELOCAL algorithm

Require: Adjacency matrix A $(n \times n)$
Require: Tolerance *tol*
Output: $\Delta'(G)$ per node triangle estimation
$\quad \langle \lambda_1, \boldsymbol{u_1} \rangle \leftarrow LanczosMethod(A, 1)$
$\quad \Lambda \leftarrow [\lambda_1]$
$\quad \mathbf{U} \leftarrow [\boldsymbol{u_1}]$
$\quad i \leftarrow 1$
$\quad$ {initialize $i, \Lambda, \mathbf{U}$}
$\quad$**repeat**
$\quad\quad i \leftarrow i + 1$
$\quad\quad \langle \lambda_i, \boldsymbol{u_i} \rangle \leftarrow LanczosMethod(A, i)$
$\quad\quad \Lambda \leftarrow [\Lambda \ \lambda_i]$
$\quad\quad \mathbf{U} \leftarrow [\mathbf{U} \ \boldsymbol{u_i}]$
$\quad$**until** $0 \leq \dfrac{|\lambda_i^3|}{\sum_{j=1}^{i} \lambda_j^3} \leq tol$
$\quad$**for** $j = 1$ to n **do**
$\quad\quad \Delta'_j = \dfrac{\sum_{k=1}^{i} u_{jk}^2 \lambda_k^3}{2}$
$\quad$**end for**
$\quad \Delta'(G) \leftarrow [\Delta'_1, .., \Delta'_n]$
$\quad$**return** $\Delta'(G)$

---

symmetric eigenvalue problem using Krylov subspaces. It is based on simple matrix-vector multiplications. Furthermore, high quality software implementing Lanczos method is publicly available (ARPACK, Parallel ARPACK, MATLAB etc.). It is worth noting how easy it is to implement our algorithm in a programming language that offers routines for eigenvalue computation. For example, assuming that a k-rank approximation of the adjacency matrix gives good results, the piece of MATLAB code described in Table 1 will output an accurate estimate of the number of triangles. This function takes two input arguments, A and k which are the adjacency matrix representation of the graph and the desired rank of the low rank approximation respectively.

Analysis of EigenTriangle Algorithms

As we mentioned previously, EigenTriangle and EigenTriangleLocal perform efficiently on real world networks. But how do we define the term "real world network"? It is hard to define this term rigorously in mathematical terms since real world networks are diverse, exhibiting contradictory properties. For example a real network which represents the electrical system of a country is a planar graph, a characteristic which does not appear in large social networks for example. Typically by the term real world network one means networks which exhibit some special properties, such as small-worldness, scale-freeness and self-similarity characteristics. A common characteristic of large scale real world networks is the skewed degree distribution. This is an important feature for our work since it affects the spectrum distribution of the network (Mihail et al., 2002). For our work, the special spectral properties are crucial.

Figure 3 shows the spectrum of a real world network, a small network with approximately 1,2K nodes and 17K edges. It is representative of the typical spectrum of a real-world network. The Figure plots the value of the eigenvalue versus its rank. For example, the largest (with respect to the absolute value) eigenvalue is 74.08, the second largest is 59.94 and the third largest is -29.36. Also observe that the rest eigenvalues are significantly smaller than the top three eigenvalues and furthermore almost symmetrically distributed around 0. These two features of the spectrum are crucial for the EigenTriangle and the EigenTriangleLocal algorithms. Specifically, the following features allow EigenTriangle and EigenTriangleLocal to estimate efficiently the count of triangles in large real world networks:

1. The absolute values of the few top eigenvalues are skewed, typically following a power law. Taking their cubes amplifies the difference in magnitude with respect to the cubes of the rest of the eigenvalues.
2. The signs of the eigenvalues tend to alternate for the bulk of the eigenvalues and thus their cubes almost cancel out.

In other words, the contribution of the bulk of the eigenvalues is negligible compared to the contribution of the few top eigenvalues to the

Table 1. Matlab Implementation of EigenTriangleLocal. The input is the adjaceny matrix A and the rank k of the approximation, the output is a vector x containing the triangle estimate per node.

```
function x = EigenTriangleLocal(A,k)
n = size(A,1);
x = zeros(n,1);
opts.isreal=1; opts.issym=1;
[u l] = eigs(A,k,'LM',opts);
l = diag(l)';
for j=1:n
    x(j) = sum(l.^3.*u(j,:).^2)/2
end
```

Figure 3. Spectrum plot for a real world network (Political Blogs, 17K edges, 1.2K nodes), representing the spectrum of several real world networks. The figure plots the eigenvalue versus its rank. Observe that few top eigenvalues are well detached from the bulk which is almost symmetrically distributed around 0.

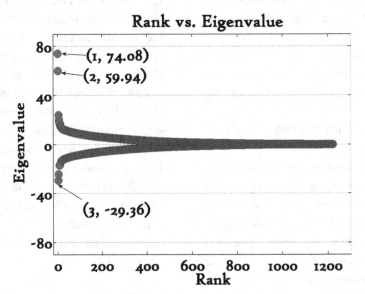

total number of triangles. For example in the Political Blogs network whose spectrum is shown in Figure 3, three eigenvalues suffice to obtain a high accuracy estimate of the count of triangles. These simple facts allow us to discard the largest part of the spectrum. Therefore we can keep just a handful of eigenvalues and approximate fast and well the number of triangles. Experimentally 1 to 25 eigenvalues, see (Tsourakakis, 2008), lead to a satisfactory approximation. The time complexity of our proposed algorithms is O(cm), where m is the number of edges and c is the total number of matrix vector multiplications executed by Lanczos method. Typically as explained in (Tsourakakis, 2010) c is small, i.e., at most O(logn). This means that the computation of a handful of the top eigenvalues results in a small number of iterations c and therefore the performance of our methods is fast.

Performance

An extensive experimental evaluation has been conducted in order to evaluate the performance of the EigenTriangle and the EigenTriangleLocal

algorithms in practice. Since the knowledge for the spectrum of real world networks is limited, such an evaluation was necessary. The interested reader can find this evaluation in (Tsourakakis, 2008) and in (Avron, 2010). Here we show just one of the figures of (Tsourakakis, 2008). Figure 4 shows the performance of EigenTriangleLocal on three large real world networks. ASN stands for an anonymous social network with approximately 400,000 nodes and 2,2 million edges, Reuters for an information network with 13,000 nodes and 17,000 edges, and PolBlogs for the Political Blogs network which as mentioned before has 1,200 nodes and 17,000 edges. Figure 4 plots the quality of the approximation, quantified by the Pearson's correlation coefficient, versus the rank of the approximation. As we observe, with just one eigenvalue for the Political Blogs, the Reuters and the ASN networks we obtain approximately 94%, 97% and 99% accuracy, With three eigenvalues, this accuracy reaches the optimal value 1 for all three networks. It is worth mentioning that the fact of obtaining a better approximation with a single eigenvalue as the size of the network increases is

Figure 4. EigenTriangleLocal algorithm's performance on three real world networks, an anonymous social network (ASN), Reuters network and the Political Blogs network. The figure plots Pearson's correlation coefficient ρ versus the approximation rank k. Notice that with three eigenvalues for all three networks, the accuracy is almost optimal.

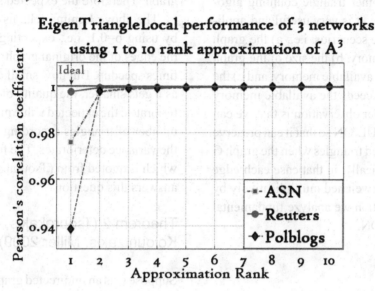

not random. Typically, as the size of the network increases, so do the top eigenvalues, see (Mihail et al., 2002). This implies that with fewer eigenvalues we obtain better approximation in large networks, assuming of course the special spectral properties. Another more subtle detail which is related with Lanczos method, is that the larger the spectral gaps between the top eigenvalues, the less iterations are needed for convergence. Since this is not the focus of the Chapter, we omit the details here. The interested reader is urged to read (Demmel, 1997) for an introduction in numerical linear algebra and (Tsourakakis, 2010) for the details with respect to triangle counting and the Lanczos method.

DOULION: Counting Triangles with a Coin

Algorithm

In this section we present a simple and effective randomized algorithm for counting triangles in real

world network. The algorithm is called DOULION and was introduced in (Tsourakakis et al., 2009b). The algorithm takes as input an unweighted graph G, a sparsification parameter p and outputs the estimate of the number of triangles. The steps of the algorithm are the following:

1. For each edge toss a biased coin with success probability p of keeping the edge.
2. Count the number of triangles in the sparsified graph and output as the estimate the count multiplied by $1/p^3$.

Before we go into the details of the analysis of the algorithm let's consider few simple aspects of it. The DOULION algorithm in step 2 counts the number of triangles in the sparsified graph. Any triangle counting algorithm can be used for this task. For example, in practice one can use the Node Iterator (for each node count the number of edges among its neighbors), the Edge Iterator (for each edge count the number of common neighbors of its endpoints) or their variations, see (Schank et al. 2004). This makes DOULION a triangle preserving sparsifying algorithm and therefore DOULION is a "friend" rather than a competitor of the other triangle counting algorithms. Furthermore, it is very useful and applicable in all possible scenarios, i.e., a) the graph fits in the main memory, b) the size of the graph exceeds slightly the available memory, and c) the size of the graph exceeds the available memory significantly. Another observation is that we can slightly modify DOULION so that it can preserve the count of weighted triangles when the graph G is weighted. Specifically, in that case each edge which survives is reweighed multiplicatively by $1/p$. In the next section we analyze fundamental aspects of DOULION.

Analysis

The following Lemma states that the expected number of triangles that DOULION outputs is the true number of triangles.

Lemma 2

Let T be the estimate of DOULION and t the true number of triangles in G. Then $E[T]=t$.

Lemma 3 answers the basic question: what is the expected speedup of DOULION algorithm. Of course the answer depends on the complexity of the triangle counting algorithm that will be used in the second step. For a practical choice, such as the Node Iterator the speedup is quadratic. Specifically:

Lemma 3

The expected speedup of using DOULION with the Node Iterator algorithm in its second step is $1/p^2$.

Proof

If R is the running time after the removal of edges, then $R=\Sigma_i D^2(v_i)$ where D(v) is the degree of vertex v after coin-tossing. Therefore, the expected running time is given by

$$E[R]=p^2 \Sigma_i d^2(v_i)$$

where d(v) is the degree of vertex v in the original graph. Therefore the expected speedup is $1/p^2$.

The above Lemma tells us that for example by using p=0.1, i.e., expecting to keep 10% of the edges of the original graph, will result in 100 times speedup. But how small can p be? Clearly, as p gets smaller, the quality of the estimator deteriorates: the expected value may still be the true number of triangles according to Lemma 2, but the variance deteriorates. The following theorem which is quoted from (Tsourakakis et al., 2009c) answers this question.

Theorem 2 (Tsourakakis, Kolountzakis, Miller 2009)

Suppose G is an undirected graph with n vertices, m edges and t triangles. Let also Δ denote the size of the largest collection of triangles with a common edge. Let G' be the random graph that arises from G if we keep every edge with probability p and write T for the number of triangles of G'. Suppose that $\gamma>0$ is a constant and the following conditions hold for $n \geq n_0$ sufficiently large:

$$\frac{pt}{\Delta} \geq \log^{6+\gamma} n, \ \ if \ p^2\Delta \geq 1 \ (1)$$

$$p^3t \geq \log^{6+\gamma} n, \ \ if \ p^2\Delta < 1 \ (2)$$

Then for any constants K, $\varepsilon >0$ and all large enough n (depending on ε, K, n_0) the following concentration inequality holds:

$$PR[|\ T - E[T]\ |\geq \varepsilon E[T]] \leq n^{-K}$$

The proof of the theorem is based on state of the art results for concentration of measure inequalities for multivariate polynomials. For the proof of this theorem, the interested reader should read

(Tsourakakis et al., 2009c). The performance of the algorithm is excellent as is shown in (Tsourakakis et al., 2009b), (Tsourakakis et al., 2009c).

IMPLEMENTATION DETAILS

In this section we provide the implementation details for counting triangles in the MapReduce framework. Specifically we will illustrate how the node iterator algorithm is implemented. Before we give the details, note that the main limitation that we have to tackle with is the fact that the whole input cannot fit onto a single machine. This suggests that nodes which have large degree O(n) require $O(n^2)$ pairs to be checked which is infeasible due to the space constraints. Therefore a simple implementation where each reducer receives all the key-value pairs with the key being the node id can fail. Furthermore, observe that such a scenario is very likely to happen in real-world networks where there exist few nodes with huge degree. The key idea which is implemented in (Hofman et al. 2010) is to filter the input, i.e., sparsify it in order to reduce its size to $O(n^{1-\varepsilon})$, i.e., sublinear. The key idea is the following: we distinguish two types of triangles. The first type consists of triangles which have at least one participating vertex of low degree, i.e., $d(v) \leq \sqrt{n}$. The second type of triangle consists of triangles where all participating vertices have large degree $d(v) \geq \sqrt{n}$. Then we first count triangles of the first type since we can "pivot" on the low degree vertex and avoid the linear complexity. After counting the triangles of the first type, we remove all the low degree vertices. The remaining graph is sparse and it cannot have many high degree nodes. So again we can use the same idea to count the remaining triangles.

Assume the input consists of tuples of the form <u,d(u),v,d(v)> for every edge (u,v), where d(u),d(v) are the degrees of vertices u and v

respectively. It is worth pointing out that if the input consists of tuples <u,v> where (u,v) is an edge then one can apply the method in (Karloff et al.), Section 6.1.1 for k=0, and bring the input in the form we require here. In the first Map phase the algorithm distinguishes the edges that have at least one vertex of low degree from the edges whose endpoints are both of large degree. This is achieved by using an extra bit which is set to 1 in the latter case. After the shuffle stage, each reducer receives a vertex u and its neighborhood N(u). Depending on whether the special bit is 0 or 1 the reduce phase outputs all neighbors of u or just its high degree neighbors correspondingly. Map 2 performs load balancing before redirecting the length two paths to the reducer. Reduce 2 phase guarantees that each triangle is exactly once for each node. To compute the total number of triangles that each node participates one can use again (Karloff et al. 2010) Section 6.1.1 to compute the first frequency moments.

The algorithm description follows in detail:

Map 1

```
Input:   <u,d(u),v,d(v)>
Output:  if d(u)≤n^{1/2-ε} emit <u;v>
         if d(v)≤n1^{1/2-ε} emit <v;u>
         otherwise emit <u';v>
```

Observe that each key is a vertex id, which can be primed or unprimed. The prime can be represented as an extra bit which denotes the type of the key-vertex. Specifically if vertex u is of high degree, then its type is 1, otherwise it is type 0.

Reduce 1

```
Input: <u; N(u)> where N(u)={v_1,...,v_k}
is the neighborhood of vertex u
         <u';N'(u)> where N'(u) is the
         set of neighbors of u with
         high degree
```

```
Output: pivot(<u;N(u)>):= {<v_i,v_j;u>}
where v_i,v_j ∈ N(u)
        pivot(<u';N(u)>):= {<v_i,v_j;u>}
where v_i,v_j ∈ N'(u)
```

Now, in the second phase, the input to the mapper will be the output of the reduce 1 phase and the original edge file. In the following we assume that the dollar sign \$ is a unique special character.

Map 2

```
For every input key-value pair
<v_i,v_j;u> emit <v_i,v_j,r; u> where r=u
mod n^ε
For every input key-value pair
<v_i,v_j;u> emit <v'_i,v'_j; u'>
For every <u,d(u),v,d(v);> 
if d(u)≤n^{1/2-ε} or d(v)≤n^{1/2-ε} emit
<vi,_vj,_1;$>,.., <vi,_vj,_nε;$>
For every <u,d(u),v,d(v);> if
d(u)>n^{1/2-ε} and d(v) >n1/2-ε emit
<v'i,v'_j;$>
```

Reduce 2

```
If <vi,_vj,_r; u1,..,uk> emit ∅
If <v'i,_v'j; u'1,..,u'k> emit ∅
If <vi,_vj,_r;u1,..,uk,_s> then for each
uk output <vi;_1/tk>,<vj;_1/tk>,<uk;_1/
tk> where tk is the number of nodes
in triangle (vi,_vj,_uk) which have type
0 (low degree nodes)
If <v'i,_v'j;_u'1,..,u'k,_s> then output
<vi;_k/3>,<vj;_k/3>,<u1;_1/3>,..,<uk;_1/3>
```

As Hofman, Suri and Vassilvitskii show the above algorithm satisfies the requirements we have set for any efficient algorithm in the MapReduce framework and also computes correctly the number of triangles per node. Specifically the size of the output of Map 1 is 2m, the input to any reducer in the Reduce 1 phase is at most $O(n^{1-\varepsilon})$, the size of the output of Map 2 is $O(n^{2^{(1-\varepsilon)}})$ and the input to any reducer in Reduce 2 has length at most $O(n^{1-\varepsilon})$. It is worth mentioning that if there are no low degree vertices in the graph then one can first apply DOULION and then the Hofman et al. method.

FUTURE RESEARCH DIRECTIONS

In the following, we propose several research directions with respect to the triangle counting problem and more general research directions with respect to large scale graph mining using distributed computing:

1. Spectrum of real-world networks: as we saw in Section 3, the efficiency of the EigenTriangle algorithm and its extensions relies on special spectral properties. These properties as outlined empirically appear in many real-world social networks, i.e., networks with skewed degree distributions. However, there is not enough knowledge to justify these properties fully theoretically. Most of the existing knowledge is on the distribution of the top eigenvalues of the adjacency matrix of the Laplacian spectrum.

2. Extensive experimental study of randomized linear algebra algorithms for triangle counting: (Tsourakakis, 2010) provided a new direction for triangle counting via randomized Singular Value Decomposition (SVD) algorithms. Therein, Tsourakakis used the algorithm proposed in (Drineas et al., 1999). Since then several faster algorithms have appeared. An experimental work which compares the performance of existing randomized SVD algorithms with respect to triangle counting is missing currently.

3. Concentration of measure for the DOULION algorithm: (Tsourakakis et al. 2009c) proved using state of the art results on concentration for multivariate polynomials that more than $O(n\log^7(n))$ triangles in a graph with n

nodes suffices for DOULION to obtain a concentrated estimate. We conjecture that $O(n\log(n))$ triangles suffice.

4. Creating a library for most common graph mining algorithms: despite existing attempts to create such a library (Kang et al., 2009), there exists a lot of space for new research.

CONCLUSION

We surveyed state of the art work on the triangle counting problem for large real world networks using MapReduce. MapReduce has become the *de facto* standard for distributed computing in both academia and industry. Even if there exist several other powerful models for distributed computing, MapReduce due to its simplicity offers the programmer the ability to use MapReduce as a simple library that is imported at the beginning of the program, like any other library. However, implementing several graph algorithms becomes non-trivial. For example (Kang et al, 2010) implemented a non-trivial algorithm for estimating the diameter of the largest graph ever analyzed since existing algorithms did not scale. Attempts to create a library with primitives commonly used (Kang, 2009) have already been done but are at a preliminary stage and there is definitely a lot of space for research. In this Chapter we focused on an important graph mining problem, counting the number of triangles in a graph. We presented two families of algorithms, a spectral and a combinatorial/randomized one. Both families perform excellently on large scale networks. The combinatorial algorithm though is preferable since it comes with strong guarantees for its performance, despite the fact that the spectral based algorithm empirically works excellently as well. Finally, we presented new research directions with respect to triangle counting, graph mining and distributed computing using MapReduce.

REFERENCES

Alon, N., Kaufman, T., Krivelevich, M., & Ron, D. (2006). Testing triangle-freeness in general graphs. In *Proceedings of the 17th Annual ACM-SIAM Symposium on Discrete Algorithms (SODA '06)* (pp. 279-288). New York, NY, USA: Association for Computing Machinery

Avron, H. (2010*) Counting Triangles in Large Graphs using randomized trace estimation*. In Proceedings of the 2nd Workshop on Large Scale Data Mining, Theory and Applications (LDMTA '10).

Bar-Yehuda, R., & Even, S. (1982). On approximating a vertex cover for planar graphs. In *Proceedings of the 14th Annual Association for Computing Machinery Symposium on Theory of Computing* (STOC '82) (pp. 303-309). New York, NY, USA: ACM.

Becchetti, L., Boldi, P., Castillo, C., & Gionis, A. (2008). Efficient semi-streaming algorithms for local triangle counting in massive graphs. In *Proceeding of the 14th ACM SIGKDD International Conference on Knowledge Discovery and Data Mining* (KDD '08) (pp. 16-24). New York, NY, USA: Association for Computing Machinery.

Blake, H. (2010, May 04). *Digital universe to smash 'zettabyte' barrier for first time*, The Telegraph. Retrieved from http://www.telegraph.co.uk/.

Chierichetti, F., Kumar, R., & Tomkins, A. (2010). Max-Cover in MapReduce. In *Proceedings of the 19th International Conference on World Wide Web* (pp. 231-240). New York, NY, USA: ACM.

Dean, J., & Ghemawat, S. (2008). Mapreduce: Simplified data processing on large clusters . *Communications of the ACM, 51*(1), 107–113. doi:10.1145/1327452.1327492

Demmel, J. W. (1997). *Applied numerical linear algebra*. Philadelphia, PA: SIAM.

Drineas, P., Frieze, A., Kannan, R., Vempala, S., & Vinay, V. (1999). Clustering in Large Graphs and Matrices. In *Proceedings of the 10ᵗʰ Annual ACM-SIAM Symposium on Discrete Algorithms (SODA '99)* (pp. 291-299). New York, NY: ACM.

Eckmann, J.-P., & Moses, E. (2002). Curvature of co-links uncovers hidden thematic layers in the World Wide Web. *Proceedings of the National Academy of Sciences of the United States of America*, *99*(9), 5825–5829. doi:10.1073/pnas.032093399

Frank, O. (1991). Statistical analysis of change in networks. *Statistica Neerlandica*, *45*(3), 283–293. doi:10.1111/j.1467-9574.1991.tb01310.x

Frank, O., & Strauss, D. (1986). Markov graphs *. Journal of the American Statistical Association*, *8*(395), 832–842. doi:10.2307/2289017

Gates, A., Natkovich, O., Chopra, S., Kamath, P., Narayanamurthy, S., & Olston, C. …Srivastava, S. (2009). Building a high-level dataflow system on top of map-reduce: The pig experience. Proc. *VLDB Endow. 2*(2), 1414-1425.

Hadoop Users. (2010), from http://wiki.apache.org/hadoop/PoweredBy

Hadoop Wiki. (2010), from http://hadoop.apache.org/

Imrich, W., Klavzar, S., & Mulder, M. (1999). Median graphs and triangle-free graphs . *SIAM Journal on Discrete Mathematics*, *12*(1), 111–118. doi:10.1137/S0895480197323494

Itai, A., & Rodeh, M. (1977). Finding a minimum circuit in a graph. In *Proceedings of the 9ᵗʰ Annual ACM Symposium on Theory of Computing (STOC '77)* (pp. 1-10). New York, NY, USA: ACM.

JaJa. J. (1992). *An introduction to parallel algorithms*. Redwood City, CA, USA: Addison Wesley Longman Publishing Co., Inc.

Kang, U., Tsourakakis, C., Appel, A., Leskovec, J., & Faloutsos, C. (2010a). *Hadi: Mining radii of large graphs*. ACM Transactions on Knowledge Discovery from Data.

Kang, U., Tsourakakis, C., Appel, A., Leskovec, J., & Faloutsos, C. (2010b). *Radius plots for mining TeraByte scale graphs: Algorithms, patterns, and observations*. SIAM International Conference on Data Mining.

Kang, U., Tsourakakis, C., & Faloutsos, C. (2009). *Pegasus: A peta-scale graph mining system-implementation and observations*. Paper presented at the IEEE International Conference on Data Mining.

Karloff, H., Suri, S., & Vassilvitskii, S. (2010). A model of computation for MapReduce. In *Proceedings of the 21ˢᵗ Annual ACM-SIAM Symposium on Discrete Algorithms (SODA '10)*. Philadelphia, PA: Society for Industrial and Applied Mathematics.

Leskovec, J., Backstrom, L., Kumar, R., & Tomkins, A. (2008). Microscopic evolution of social networks. In *Proceeding of the 14th ACM SIGKDD International Conference on Knowledge Discovery and Data Mining* (pp. 462-470). New York, NY, USA: ACM.

Lotem, E., Sattath, S., Kashtan, N., Itzkovitz, S., Milo, R., & Pinter, R. …Margalit, H. (2004). Network motifs in integrated cellular networks of transcription-regulation and protein-protein interaction. In *Proceedings of National Academy of Sciences*, USA, (*101(*16), 5934-5939).

Mihail, M., & Papadimitriou, C. (2002). On the Eigenvalue Power Law: Randomization and approximation techniques. In *Proceedings of the 6th International Workshop on Randomization and Approximation Techniques*, Cambridge, MA, USA *(RANDOM '02)* (pp. 254-262). London, UK: Springer-Verlag.

Newman, M., Watts, D., & Strogatz, S. (2002). Random graph models of social networks. *Proceedings of the National Academy of Sciences of the United States of America, 99*(1), 2566–2572. doi:10.1073/pnas.012582999

Newman, M. E. J. (2003). The structure and function of complex networks. *SIAM Review, 45*, 167–256. doi:10.1137/S003614450342480

Pegasus project. CMU (2010), from http://www.cs.cmu.edu/~pegasus

Schank, T., & Wagner, D. (2004). Approximating clustering-coefficient and transitivity. *Journal of Graph Algorithms and Applications, 9*(2), 265–275.

Spinrad, J. (2003). *Efficient graph representations. Fields Institute Monographs*. American Mathematical Society.

Tsourakakis, C. (2008). Fast counting of triangles in large real networks without counting: Algorithms and laws. *ICDM . IEEE Computer Society, 2008*, 608–617.

Tsourakakis, C. (in press). Counting triangles in real-world networks using projections. *Knowledge and Information Systems*.

Tsourakakis, C., Drineas, P., Michelakis, E., Koutis, I., & Faloutsos, C. (2009a). *Spectral counting of triangles in power-law networks via element-wise Sparsification*. Advances in Social Networks Analysis and Mining (ASONAM '09) (pp. 66-71).

Tsourakakis, C., Drineas, P., Michelakis, E., Koutis, I., & Faloutsos, C. (in press). Spectral counting of triangles via element-wise sparsifcation and triangle-based link recommendation. In *Journal of Social Network Analysis and Mining, 2011*.

Tsourakakis, C., Kang, U., Miller, G., & Faloutsos, C. (2009b). DOULION: Counting triangles in massive graphs with a coin. In *Proceedings of the 15th ACM SIGKDD International Conference on Knowledge Discovery and Data Mining(KDD '09)*, Paris, France (pp. 837-846). New York, NY, USA: ACM.

Tsourakakis, C., Kolountzakis, M., & Miller, G. L. (2009c). *Approximate triangle counting*, CoRR, *abs/0904.3761*.

Valiant, L. (1990). A bridging model for parallel computation. *Communications of the ACM, 33*(8), 103–111. doi:10.1145/79173.79181

Vassilevska, V., & Williams, R., (Preprint 2010). *Triangle detection versus matrix multiplication: A study of truly subcubic reducibility.*

Wasserman, S., & Faust, K. (1994). *Social network analysis: Methods and applications*. Cambridge, UK: Cambridge University Press.

Wasserman, S., & Pattison, P. (1996). Logit models and logistic regressions for social networks: I. An introduction to Markov graphs and "p." . *Psychometrika, 61*(3), 401–425. doi:10.1007/BF02294547

Watts, D., & Strogatz, S. (1998). Collective dynamics of 'small-world' networks . *Nature, 393*(6684), 440–442. doi:10.1038/30918

White, T. (2009). *Hadoop: The definitive guide* (1st ed.). CA, USA: O'Reilly Media.

ADDITIONAL READING

Hadoop Related Papers. (2010). Retrieved from http://atbrox.com/2009/10/01/mapreduce-and-hadoop-academic-papers/

KEY TERMS AND DEFINITIONS

Concentration of Measure: is a principle that is applied in measure theory, probability and combinatorics, and has consequences for other fields such as Banach space theory. Informally, it states that Lipschitz functions that depend on many parameters are almost constant.

Eigenvalue: The eigenvectors of a square matrix are the non-zero vectors which, after being multiplied by the matrix, remain proportional to the original vector.

Graph: An abstract representation of a set of objects where some pairs of the objects are connected by links.

MapReduce: A patented software framework introduced by Google to support distributed computing on large data sets on clusters of computers.

Randomized Algorithm: An algorithm which employs a degree of randomness as part of its logic.

Spectral Graph Theory: The study of properties of a graph in relationship to the characteristic polynomial, eigenvalues, and eigenvectors of its adjacency matrix or Laplacian matrix.

Triangle: A cycle of length three in a graph G.

Chapter 14
Graph Representation and Anonymization in Large Survey Rating Data

Xiaoxun Sun
Australian Council for Educational Research, Australia

Min Li
University of Southern Queensland, Australia

ABSTRACT

We study the challenges of protecting privacy of individuals in the large public survey rating data in this chapter. Recent study shows that personal information in supposedly anonymous movie rating records is de-identified. The survey rating data usually contains both ratings of sensitive and non-sensitive issues. The ratings of sensitive issues involve personal privacy. Even though the survey participants do not reveal any of their ratings, their survey records are potentially identifiable by using information from other public sources. None of the existing anonymisation principles can effectively prevent such breaches in large survey rating data sets. We tackle the problem by defining a principle called (k, ε)-anonymity model to protect privacy. Intuitively, the principle requires that, for each transaction t in the given survey rating data T, at least $(k - 1)$ other transactions in T must have ratings similar to t, where the similarity is controlled by ε. The (k, ε)-anonymity model is formulated by its graphical representation and a specific graph-anonymisation problem is studied by adopting graph modification with graph theory. Various cases are analyzed and methods are developed to make the updated graph meet (k, ε) requirements. The methods are applied to two real-life data sets to demonstrate their efficiency and practical utility.

DOI: 10.4018/978-1-61350-053-8.ch014

INTRODUCTION

The problem of privacy-preserving data publishing has received a lot of attention in recent years. Privacy preservation on relational data has been studied extensively. A major type of privacy attack on relational data includes re-identifying individuals by joining a published data set containing sensitive information with the external data sets modeling background knowledge of attackers (Sweeney et al. 2002, Machanavajjhala et al. 2006). Most of the existing work is formulated in contexts of several organizations, such as hospitals, publishing detailed data (also called microdata) about individuals (e.g. medical records) for research or statistical purposes.

Privacy risks of publishing microdata are well-known (Kifer et al. 2006, Wang et al. 2006, Zhang et al. 2008). Famous attacks include de-anonymisation of the Massachusetts hospital discharge database by joining it with a public voter database and privacy breaches caused by AOL search data (Sweeney et al. 2002, Machanavajjhala et al. 2006). Even if identifiers such as names and social security numbers have been removed, the adversary can use linking (Sweeney et al. 2002), homogeneity and background attacks (Machanavajjhala et al. 2006) to re-identify individual data records or sensitive information of individuals. To overcome the re-identification attacks, the mechanism of k-anonymity was proposed (Sweeney et al. 2002). Specifically, a data set is said to be k-anonymous if, on the quasi-identifier (QID) attributes (the maximal set of join attributes to re-identify individual records), each record is identical with at least $(k-1)$ other records. The larger the value of k, the better the privacy protection is. Although k-anonymity has been well adopted, Machanavajjhala et al. 2006 showed that a k-anonymous data set may still have some subtle but severe privacy problems due to the lack of diversity in sensitive attributes. Particularly, a large body of research contributes to trans-forming a data set to meet a privacy principle (k-anonymity (Samarati 2001), l-diversity (Machanavajjhala et al. 2006), (α, k)-anonymity (Wong et al. 2006), t-closeness (Li et al. 2007)) using techniques such as generalization, suppression (removal), permutation and swapping of certain data values while minimizing certain cost metrics (Wang et al. 2004, Bayardo et al. 2005, Fung et al. 2005, LeFevre et al. 2005, He et al. 2009).

Recently, a new privacy concern has emerged in privacy preservation research: how to protect the privacy of individuals in published large survey rating data. For example, movie rating data, supposedly to be anonymized, is de-identified by linking un-anonymized data from another source. On October 2, 2006, Netflix, the world's largest online DVD rental service, announced a \$1-million Netflix Prize for improving their movie recommendation service. To aid contestants, Netflix publicly released a data set containing 100,480,507 movie ratings, created by 480,189 Netflix subscribers between December 1999 and December 2005. Narayanan and Shmatikov have shown that an attacker only needs a little bit information of an individual to identify the anonymized movie rating transaction of the individual in the data set. They re-identified Netflix movie ratings using the Inter-net Movie Database (IMDb) as a source of auxiliary information and successfully identified the Netflix records of known users, uncovering their political preferences and other potentially sensitive information. In this chapter, we will refer to two types of data as "survey rating data" and "relational data".

MOTIVATION

The structure of large survey rating data is different from relational data, since it does not have fixed personal identifiable attributes. The lack of a clear set of personal identifiable attributes makes the anonymisation challenging (Ghinita et al. 2008, Xu et al. 2008, Zhou et al. 2008). In addition, survey rating data contains many attributes, each of which corresponds to the response to a survey question, but not all participants need to rate all issues (or answer all questions), which means a lot of cells in a data set are empty. For instance, Figure 1(a) is a published survey rating data set containing ratings of survey participants on both sensitive and non-sensitive issues. The higher the rating is, the more preferred the participant is towards the issue. "null" means the participant did not rate the issue. Figure 1(b) contains comments on non-sensitive issues of some survey participants, which might be obtained from public information sources such as personal weblogs or social network.

However, individuals in the anonymous survey rating data set are potentially identifiable based on their public comments from other sources. By matching the ratings of non-sensitive issues with publicly available preferences, an adversary can identify a small number of candidate groups that contain the record of the victim. It is unfortunate if there is only one record in the candidate group. For example, Alice is at risk of being identified in Figure 1(a), since t1 is unique and could be

linked to Alice's comments in Figure 1(b). This example motivates the first challenge:

• *How to preserve individual's privacy through identity protection in a large survey rating data set?*

Though several models and algorithms have been proposed to preserve privacy in relational data, most of the existing studies can deal with relational data only (Machanavajjhala et al. 2006, Li et al. 2007, Wong et al. 2006). Divide-and-conquer methods are applied to anonymize relational data sets due to the fact that tuples in a relational data set are separable during anonymisation. In other words, anonymizing a group of tuples does not affect other tuples in the data set. However, anonymizing a survey rating data set is much more difficult since changing one record may cause a domino effect on the neighborhoods of other records, as well as affecting the properties of the whole data set (details in Section 5.3). Hence, previous methods can not be applied directly to survey rating data and it is much more challenging to anonymize large survey rating data than

Figure 1. (a) A published survey rating data set containing ratings of survey participants on both sensitive and non-sensitive isues. (b) Public comments on some non-sensitive issues of some participants of the survey. By matching the ratings on non-sensitive issues with public available preferences, t_1 is linked to Alice, and her sensitive rating is revealed.

	non-sensitive			sensitive
ID	issue 1	issue 2	issue 3	issue 4
t_1	6	1	*null*	6
t_2	1	6	*null*	1
t_3	2	5	*null*	1
t_4	1	*null*	5	1
t_5	2	*null*	6	5

(a)

	non-sensitive issues		
name	issue 1	issue 2	issue 3
Alice	excellent	so bad	-
Bob	awful	top	-
Jack	bad	-	good

(b)

for relational data. Therefore, the second arising challenge is:

- *How to anonymize a large survey rating data while maintaining the least amount of distortion?*

CONTRIBUTIONS

Faced with these challenges, in this chapter we study privacy preserving techniques for large survey rating data sets, and propose a new model and methods to preserve privacy in published large survey rating data sets.

This chapter presents a systematic study towards the identity protection in large survey rating data sets. Firstly, we propose a privacy principle called (k, ε)-anonymity, which demands that for each transaction in a given survey rating data set, there are at least other $(k-1)$ similar transactions, where similarity is measured by ε. (k, ε)-anonymity guarantees that no individual is identifiable with confidence up to a function of ε with probability greater than $1/k$. Both k and ε define the degree of identity protection from different perspectives. The parameter ε specifies, for each transaction t, the length of ε-proximate neighborhood, whereas $1/k$ limits the probability that an adversary realizes t falling in that ε-proximate neighborhood.

Secondly, we formulate the (k, ε)-anonymity model using a graphical representation, design a metric to quantify graph modification operations and formally define the graph-anonymisation problem that, given a graphical representation G, asking for the k-decomposable graph stemmed from G with the minimum number of graph modification operations. Given a survey rating data set T and ε, we prove that if the graphical representation G of T is k-decomposable, then T is (k, ε)-anonymous. This interpretation of anonymity prevents the re-identification of individuals by adversaries with a priori knowledge of the degree of certain nodes. Then, we make a thorough analysis of the modification strategies and prove the correctness and completeness of the proposed modification strategies. Finally, we apply the approaches to real-world rating data sets and demonstrate that the utility of the anonymous rating as well as the statistical properties are well preserved, and our methods are efficient.

The rest of the chapter is organized as follows. Section 3 surveys related work. Section 4 discusses fundamental concepts and proposes the novel (k, ε)-anonymity principle for identity protection in a large survey rating data set. Section 5 introduces the graphical representation of (k, ε)-anonymity models and develops the anonymisation method for large survey rating data sets. Section 6 includes the results of experimental evaluations on two real-life data sets. Finally, Section 7 concludes the chapter with directions for future work.

RELATED WORK

Privacy preserving data publishing has received considerable attention in recent years, especially in the context of relational data (Aggarwal 2005, Li et al. 2007, Samarati 2001, Machanavajjhala et al. 2006). All these works assume a given set of attributes QID on which an individual is identified, and anonymize data records on the QID. Aggarwal 2005 presents a study on the relation- ship between the dimensionality of QID and information loss, and concludes that, as the dimensionality of QID increases, information loss increases quickly. Large survey rating data sets present a worst case scenario for existing anonymisation ap- proaches because of the high dimensionality of QID and sparseness of the data sets. To our best knowledge, all existing solutions in the context of k-anonymity (Sweeney 2002, Samarati 2001), l-diversity (Machanavajjhala et al. 2006) and t-closeness (Li et al. 2007) assume a relational table, which typically has a low dimensional QID. Survey rating data sets, on the other hand, are characterized by sparseness and high dimensionality, which makes the current state-of-art principles incapable handling the anonymisation of large survey rating data sets.

There are few previous works considering the privacy of large rating data. In collaboration with MovieLens recommendation service, Frankowski et al. correlated public mentions of movies in the MovieLens discussion forum with the users' movie rating histories in the internal Netflix data set. Recent study reveals a new type of attack on anonymized MovieLens data. The supposedly anonymized movie rating data is re-identified by linking non-anonymized data from other sources. Our recent work [33] discusses how to determine whether or not the survey rating data satisfy the specified privacy requirements, but we do not investigate the anonymization of survey rating data. To our best knowledge, no anonymisation models and methods exist for preserving privacy for large survey rating data sets.

Privacy-preservation of transactional data has been acknowledged as an important problem in the data mining literature (Atzori et al. 2005, Atzori et al. 2008, Ginita et al. 2008, Liu et al .2008, Zhou et al. 2008, Sun et al. 2010). The privacy threats caused by publishing data mining results such as frequent item sets and association rules is addressed in (Atzori et al. 2008). The work in (Atzori et al. 2005, Verykios et al. 2004) focus on publishing anonymous patterns, where the patterns are mined from the original data, and the resulting set of rules is sanitized to present privacy breaches. In contrast, our work addresses the privacy threats caused by publishing a large survey rating data. Recent work (Ginita et al. 2008, Liu et al .2008, Zhou et al. 2008) targets anonymisation of transaction data. Our work aims to prevent individual identity disclosure in a large survey rating data set.

Graph approaches have been applied in solving anonymization problems (Liu et al .2008, Zhou et al. 2008). Liu and Terzi (Liu et al .2008) study a specific graph-anonymization problem. A graph is called k-degree anonymous if for every node

v, there exists at least k − 1 other nodes in the graph with the same degree as v. This definition of anonymity prevents the re-identification of individuals by adversaries with a priori knowledge of the degree of certain nodes. The anonymization problem we consider in this chapter is partially related to it but different. We not only study how to modify the graph to make it k-decomposable, but also analyze how to anonymize the underlying data set, which is beyond the study of (Liu et al .2008). Pei and Zhou in (Zhou et al. 2008) consider yet another definition of graph anonymity - a graph is k-anonymous if for every node there exist at least k−1 other nodes that share isomorphic neighborhoods; in this case the neighborhood of a node is defined by its immediate neighbors and the connections between them. This definition of anonymity in graphs is different from ours. In a sense it is a stricter one. Given the difference in the definition, the corresponding algorithmic problems arising in (Zhou et al. 2008) are also different from the problems we consider in this chapter

(K, E)-ANONYMITY

In this section, we formally define the (k, ε)-anonymity model for protecting privacy in a large survey rating data set.

We assume that survey rating data publishes people's ratings on a range of issues. Some issues are sensitive, such as income level and sexuality frequency, while some are non-sensitive, such as the opinion of a book, a movie or a kind of food. Each survey participant is cautious about his/her privacy and does not reveal his/her ratings. However, an attacker can use auxiliary information to identify an individual's sensitive ratings in supposedly anonymous survey rating data. The auxiliary information of an attacker includes: (i) knowledge that a victim is in the survey rating data and; (ii) preferences of the victims on some non-sensitive issues. For instance, an attacker may find a victim's preference (not exact rating scores) by personal familiarity or by reading the victim's comments on some issues from personal weblogs or social networks. We assume that attackers know preferences of non-sensitive issues of a victim but do not know exact ratings and want to find out the victim's ratings on some sensitive issues. Our objective is to design an effective model to protect privacy of people's sensitive ratings in published survey rating data.

Given a survey rating data set T, each transaction contains a set of numbers indicating the ratings on some issues. Let $(o_1, o_2, ..., o_p, s_1, s_2 ..., s_q)$ be a transaction $o_i \epsilon \{1:r, null\}$, i-1,2,...,p and $s_j \in \{1:r, null\}$, j=1,2,...,q, where r is the maximum rating and null indicates that a survey participant did not rate. $o1 ... op$ stand for non-sensitive ratings and $s1 ..., sq$ denote sensitive ratings. Each transaction belongs to a survey participant. Let $T_A = \{o_{A_1}, o_{A_2}, \cdots, o_{A_p}, s_{A_1}, s_{A_2}, \cdots, s_{A_q}\}$ be the ratings for a survey participant A and $T_B = \{o_{B_1}, o_{B_2}, \cdots, o_{B_p}, s_{B_1}, s_{B_2}, \cdots, s_{B_q}\}$ be the ratings for a participant B. We define the dissimilarity between two non-sensitive rating scores as follows.

$$Dis(o_{A_i}, o_{B_i}) = \begin{cases} |o_{A_i} - o_{B_i}| & \text{if } o_{A_i}, o_{B_i} \in \{1:r\} \\ 0 & \text{if } o_{A_i} = o_{B_i} = null \\ r & \text{otherwise} \end{cases} \quad (1)$$

Definition 1 (ε-proximate). Given a small positive number ε, if for $1 \leq i \leq p$, $Dis(o_{A_i}, o_{B_i}) \leq \varepsilon$, then transactions T_A and T_B are ε-proximate.

If two transactions are ε-proximate, the dissimilarity between their non-sensitive ratings is bound by ε. In Figure 1(a), if ε = 1, ratings 5 and 6 may have no difference in interpretation, so t_4 and t_5 are 1-proximate based on their non-sensitive rating.

Definition 2 ((k, ε)-anonymity). A survey rating data set is (k, ε)-anonymous if every transaction

in the survey rating data set has at least (k − 1) ε-proximate neighbors.

The idea behind (k, ε)-anonymity is to make each transaction in a survey rating data set similar with at least other (k − 1) transactions in order to avoid linking to individual's sensitive ratings. (k, ε)-anonymity can well protect identity privacy, since it guarantees that no individual is identifiable with confidence up to a function of ε with probability greater than 1/k. Both parameters k and ε are intuitive and operable in real-world applications. By varying the values of k or ε, we strengthen the protection from different perspectives. Specifically, the parameter ε captures the protection proximate neighborhood of each survey participant in that raising ε enlarges the protection range of each sensitive value. The purpose of elevating k is to lower an adversary's chance of beating that protection.

Given a survey rating data set T and the values of k, ε, the objective of (k, ε)-anonymisation is to modify T to make it satisfy the k, ε requirements. Generally speaking, if T has already met this privacy requirement, we can publish it without any modifications; otherwise, we need develop modification techniques for satisfying the (k, ε) requirements. Next, we discuss this problem.

SURVEY RATING DATA ANONYMIZATION

In this section, we describe our modification strategies through the graphical representation of the (k, ε)-anonymity model. Firstly, we introduce some preliminaries and quantify the distortion caused by anonymization. Secondly, we present the (k, ε)-anonymity model with graphs. Finally, we describe the modification strategies in detail.

Given a survey rating data set T, we define a binary flag matrix F (T) to record if there is a rating or not for each non-sensitive issue (column). $F(T)_{ij} = 1$ if the ith participant rates the jth issue

Figure 2. Sample survey rating data (I)

ID	non-sensitive			sensitive
	issue 1	issue 2	issue 3	issue 4
t_1	3	6	null	6
t_2	2	5	null	1
t_3	4	7	null	4
t_4	5	6	null	1
t_5	1	null	5	1
t_6	2	null	6	5

and F $(T)_{ij} = 0$ otherwise. For instance, the flag matrix associated with the rating data of Figure 2 is

$$F = \begin{pmatrix} 1 & 1 & 0 \\ 1 & 1 & 0 \\ 1 & 1 & 0 \\ 1 & 1 & 0 \\ 1 & 0 & 1 \\ 1 & 0 & 1 \end{pmatrix} \quad (2)$$

in which each row corresponds to survey participants and each column corresponds to non-sensitive issues. In order to measure the distance between two vectors in the flag matrix, we borrow the concept of Hamming distance .

Definition 3 (Hamming Distance). Hamming distance between two vectors in the flag matrix of equal length is the number of positions for which the corresponding symbols are different. We denote the Hamming distance between two vectors v_1 and v_2 as H (v_1, v_2).

In other words, Hamming distance measures the minimum number of substitutions required to change one vector into the other, or the number of errors that trans- formed one vector into the other. For example, if $v_1 = (1, 1, 0)$ and $v_2 = (1, 0, 1)$, then H $(v_1, v_2) = 2$. If the Hamming distance between two vectors is zero, then these two vectors are identical. In order to categorize identical vectors in the flag matrix, we introduce the concept of Hamming group.

Definition 4 (Hamming Group). Hamming group is the set of vectors in which the Hamming distance between any two vectors of the flag matrix is zero. The maximal Hamming group is a Hamming group that is not a subset of any other Hamming group.

For example, there are two maximal Hamming groups in the flag matrix (2) made up of vectors $\{(1, 1, 0), (1, 1, 0), (1, 1, 0), (1, 1, 0)\}$ and $\{(1, 0, 1), (1, 0, 1)\}$ and they correspond to groups $\{t_1, t_2, t_3, t_4\}$ and $\{t_5, t_6\}$ of T.

DISTORTION METRICS

Definition 5 (Tuple distortion). Let $t = (t_1, ... t_m)$ be a tuple and $t' = (t_1', ... t_m')$ be an anonymized tuple of t. Then the distortion of this anonymization is defined as:

$$\text{Distortion\_additon}(t, t') = \sum_{i=1}^{m} |t_i - t_i'|$$

Definition 6 (Total distortion). Let $t = (t_1, ..., t_m)$ be a tuple and $t' = (t_1', ... t_m')$ be an anonymized tuple of t. Then the total distortion of this anonymization is defined as:

$$\text{Distortion}(T, T') = \sum_{i=1}^{n} \text{Distortion\_addition}(t_i, t_i')$$

GRAPHICAL REPRESENTATION

Given a survey rating data set T $= =(t_1, ..., t_n)$, its graphical representation is the graph G = (V, E), where V is a set of nodes, and each node in V corresponds to a record t_i ($i=1,...,n$) in T, and E is the set of edges, where two nodes are connected by an edge if and only if the distance between two records is bounded by ε with respect to the non-sensitive ratings (Equation (1)).

Two nodes t_i and t_j are called connected if G contains a path from t_i to t_j $(1 \leq i, j \leq n)$. The graph G is called connected if every pair of distinct nodes in the graph can be connected through some paths. A connected component is a maximal connected subgraph of G. Each node belongs to exactly one connected component, as does each edge. The degree of the node t_i is the number of edges incident to t_i $(1 \leq i \leq n)$.

Theorem 1. Given the survey rating data set T with its graphical representation G, T is (k, ε)-anonymous if and only if the degree of each node of G is at least $(k - 1)$.

Proof. "⇐": Without loss of generality, we assume that G is a connected graph. If for every node v in G, the degree of v is greater than $(k - 1)$, which means there are at least $(k - 1)$ other nodes connecting with v, then according to the construction of the graph, two nodes have an edge connection if and only if their distance is bounded by ε. Therefore, T satisfies (k, ε)-anonymity property.

"⇒": If T is (k, ε)-anonymous, then according to the definition of (k, ε)-anonymity, each record in T is ε-proximate with at least $(k - 1)$ other records, and then in the graphical representation G of T, the degree of each node should be at least $(k - 1)$.

With the equivalent condition proven in Theorem 1, we see that in order to make T (k, ε)-anonymous, we need to modify its graphical representation G to ensure that each node in G has degree of at least $(k - 1)$. Next, we introduce the general graph anonymization problem. The input to the problem is a simple graph $G = (V, E)$ and an integer k. The requirement is to use a set of graph-modification operations on G in order to construct a graph $G' = (V', E')$ with the degree of each node in G' is at least $k - 1$. The graph modification operation considered in this chapter is edge addition (adding edge is by modifying values of transactions represented as nodes). We require that the output graph be over the same set of nodes as the original graph, that is, $V' = V$. Given T and ε, we denote the graphical representation of T as G and D(G) the distortion function of anonymiz-

ing G. In order to meet k and ε requirements, we modify G to G', and the underlying data set T is changed into T'. We capture the distortion between T and T' as the distortion of anonymizing G to G', i.e., D(G) = Distortion(T, T').

Problem 1. Given a graph $G = (V, E)$ and an integer k, find a graph $G' = (V, E')$ with $E' \cap E = E$ by modifying values of some tuples so that the degree of each node of the corresponding graph is at least $(k - 1)$ such that the distortion D(G) is minimized.

Even though we can present the equivalent connection between the problem of anonymizing survey rating data and Problem 1, it is not easy to solve the Problem 1. The main difficulty as we will illustrate next is the domino effects. If the degree of a node is less than $(k - 1)$, we need to add some edges to make its degree $(k - 1)$.

However, this simple operation could cause the domino effects to other nodes. The domino effect is a chain reaction that occurs when a small change causes a similar change nearby, which then will cause another similar change, and so on. In the graphical representation of the survey rating data set, if we add an edge to two nodes that are originally not connected, then the distance between these two nodes should be bounded by ε. Since the distance between these two nodes are changed, it is mostly likely that the distance between these two nodes and other nodes are affected as well. If this happens, it is hard to regulate the modification either on the graphical representation or on the survey rating data set. Take Figure 4 as an example. Since node b is connected with nodes a, c, e, g, if we are going to change the degree of b, all the nodes are subject to this change, and the whole structure of the graph would be different. To avoid this domino effect, we further reduce the anonymization problem to ensure that the change of one node's degree has no effects on other nodes. In this chapter, we adopt the concept of k-clique for the reduction.

G is a clique if every pair of distinct nodes is connected by an edge. The k-clique is a clique

322

with at least k nodes. The maximal k-clique is a k-clique that is not a subset of any other k-clique. We say the connected component G = (V, E) is k-decomposable if G can be decomposed into several k-cliques. The graph is k-decomposable if all its connected components are k-decomposable.

Proposition 1. If a graph G = (V, E) is k_1-decomposable, then it is also k_2-decomposable, for every $k_2 \leq k_1$.

For instance, the graphical representation of the survey rating data in Figure 2 with ε = 2 is shown in Figure 2(a). In Figure 2(a), there are two connected components, G_1 and G_2, where G_2 is the 2-clique. G_{134} is a maximal 3-clique in G_1 (shown in Figure 2(b)). G is 2-decomposable, since both G_1 and G_2 are 2-decomposable. Two

Figure 3. Sample survey rating data (II)

	non-sensitive			sensitive
ID	issue 1	issue 2	issue 3	issue 4
t_1	3	6	null	6
t_2	2	5	null	1
t_3	4	7	null	4
t_4	5	6	null	1
t_5	1	null	5	1
t_6	2	null	6	5
t_7	6	null	6	3
t_8	5	null	5	2

Figure 4. An example of domino effects

possible 2-decompositions of G_1, G_{11} and G_{12} are shown in Figure 3.

Note that if G is k-decomposable, then the degree of each node is at least (k − 1). However, on the other hand, if the degree of every node in G is at least (k − 1), G is not necessarily k-decomposable. A counterexample is shown in Figure 7. For each node of G, the degree is at least 3, but G is not 4-decomposable. Although k-decomposability of G is a stronger condition than requiring the degree of the nodes in G to be at least (k − 1), it can avoid the domino effect through edge addition operations. From Theorem 1, we have the following corollary.

Corollary 1. Given the survey rating data set T with its graphical representation G, if G is k-decomposable, then T is (k, ε)-anonymous.

For instance, the survey rating data shown in Figure 2 is (2, 2)-anonymous since its graphical representation (Figure 2(a)) is 2-decomposable.

Problem 2. Given a graph G = (V, E) and an integer k, modify values of some tuples to make the corresponding graph G' = (V, E') k-decomposable with E' ∩ E = E such that the distortion D(G) is minimized.

Note that Problem 2 always has feasible solutions. In the worst case, all edges not present in each connected component of the input graph can be added. In this way, the graph becomes the union of cliques and all nodes in each connected component have the same degree; thus, any pri-

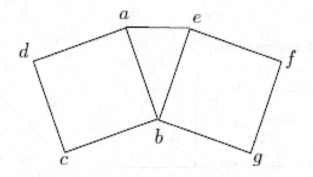

vacy requirement is satisfied (due to Proposition 1). Because of Corollary 1, Problem 1 always has a feasible solution as well.

If a given survey rating data set T satisfies the anonymity requirement, we can publish the data directly. On the other hand, if T is not (k, ε)-anonymous, we need to do some modifications in order to make it anonymous. Due to the hardness of computing Problem 1, in this chapter, we investigate the solutions of Problem 2. We provide the heuristic methods to compute (k, ε)-anonymous solution, which starts from each connected component. More specifically, we consider three scenarios that may happen during the computation. Firstly, if each connected component is already k-decomposable, then we do nothing since it has satisfied the privacy requirements. Secondly, if some connected components are k-decomposable while others are not. We reinvestigate their Hamming groups to see whether two different connected components belonging to

the same Hamming group can be merged together. Third, if none of the above situations happen, we consider borrowing nodes from connected components that belonging to different Hamming groups. In Section 5.4, we discuss the possible graphical modification operations, and in Section 5.5, we apply the graphical modifications to the survey rating data sets by the metrics defined in Section 5.2.

GRAPH MODIFICATION

Given the survey rating data set T with its graphical representation G, the number of connected components in G can be determined by the flag matrix of T. If two trans- actions are in different Hamming groups in the flag matrix, there must be no edge between these two nodes in G. For instance, the flag matrix of Figure 5 is shown in Equation (2), obviously there are two connected

Figure 5. Graphical representation example

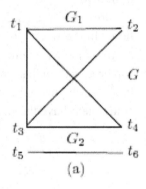 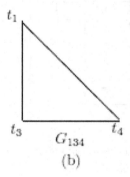

Figure 6. Two possible 2-decompose of G₁

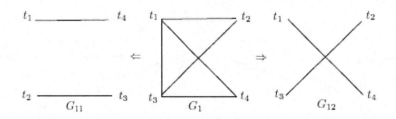

components in G (shown in Figure 5). However, the converse is not true, since it may happen that two transactions are in the same Hamming group in the flag matrix, but their distance is greater than the given ε. For instance, although there are still two groups in the flag matrix of Figure 6, there would be three connected components in its graphical representation (see Figure 5(a)).

The number of Hamming groups decided by the flag matrix is not sufficient to determine the number of connected components of G, but it is enough to determine the minimum number of connected graphs of G. The graph anonymisation process starts from the connected component of the graphical representation. We test the (k, ε) requirements for each connected component of G, and have the following three cases:

- Case 1: (Trivial case) If all the connected components of G are k-decomposable, then we publish the survey rating data without any changes.
- Case 2: (Merging case) There exists at least one connected component containing at least two nodes that is not k-decomposable. If some of the connected components do not satisfy the requirement, it may happen that some of them belong to the same Hamming group in the flag matrix. For example, with k = 3 and ε = 2, the two connected components G_2 and G_3 do not satisfy this requirement, but they belong to the

same Hamming group in the flag matrix of Figure 9 whose graphical representation is shown in Figure 8(a). In this situation, we merge them first, and then do modifications in order to make them meet the requirement. Figure 8(b) illustrates how the merging process and modification works.

At the initial stage, there are three connected components G_1, G_2 and G_3. If the privacy requirement is k = 3 and ε = 2, we verify this requirement for each component, and it turns out that none of the components satisfy the requirement. We further know that records t_5, t_6, t_7, t_8 are in the same Hamming group of the flag matrix of Figure 9, so we merge them into one connected components G_{23} by adding four edges among them. To make G_1 meet the requirement, it is enough to add one edge between t_2 and t_4. The added edges are shown in bold Figure 8(b). After the merging and modification process, Figure 8(b) is 4-decomposable, and according to Corollary 1, the survey rating data set shown in Figure 9 satisfies the privacy requirement. Now, we could make the graph k-decomposable by edge addition operations.

- Case 3: (Borrowing case) There exists at least one connected component that is not k-decomposable and in the case that we could not make G k-decomposable through merging and modification process, we need to borrow some nodes from other connected components without affecting other connected components. In order to pro- duce no effect to other groups, we find the maximal k-clique.

Take Figure 8 (graphical representation in Figure 8(a)) as an example with k = 3, ε = 2. We need to borrow at least one point from G_1 for G_2 in order to satisfy the given k. In order not to affect the structure of G_1, we find the maximal 3-clique G_{134} of G_1, and the left point t_2 is the one we borrow from G_1. Then, we add edges between t_2, t_5

Figure 7. A counter example

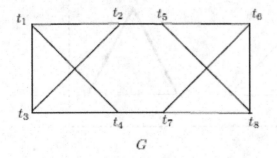

and t_2, t_6 to make it 3-decomposable. The process is shown in Figure 9

- Case 3.1: If the k-clique is unique in the connected graph, then we borrow the point from the left ones. However, there might not be a unique k-clique. For example, either t_1, t_2, t_3 or t_1, t_3, t_4 form a 3-clique of G_1. In either case, the left point is t_4 or t_2. In order to determine which one we should choose, we need to define the objective of our problem and measure the information loss. We discuss appropriate metrics in the next section. Generally speaking, our objective is to find a solution with minimum distortion.
- Case 3.2: It might happen that there is no k-clique in some connected components. For example, the graphical representation

of some sample data is shown in Figure 10 with the privacy requirement k = 3, ε = 2. In Figure 10(a), there are two connected components G_1 and G_2. With the requirement of k = 3, there is no 3- clique in G_1.. Instead, we find a 2-clique. Generally, if there is no k-clique, we find a $(k - 1)$-clique, and since 2-clique always exists, this recursive process will end.

If we find the 2-cliques, the next question is how to combine them into a 3-clique. In the example above, there are three possible 2-cliques consisting of $\{t_1, t_2\}$, $\{t_1, t_3\}$ and $\{t_3, t_4\}$. If we choose $\{t_1, t_2\}$ and $\{t_1, t_3\}$ to merge together, there will be information loss in adding the edge between t2 and t3 (Figure 10(b)). If we choose $\{t_1, t_3\}$ and $\{t_3, t_4\}$ to merge together, there will be information loss in adding the edge between t_1 and t_4 (Figure

Figure 8. Merging and modification process for subcase 2. 1

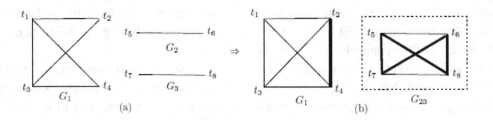

Figure 9. Borrowing nodes from other connected graph

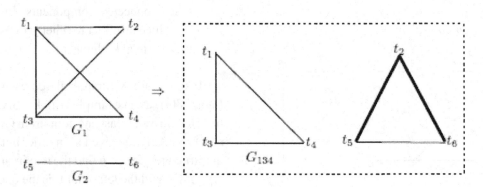

10(c)). The decision of choosing which kind of operation is depended on the distortion incurred by the edge addition operation. Distortion metrics are introduced in previous section.

EXPERIMENTS

In this section, we experimentally evaluate the effectiveness and efficiency of the proposed survey rating data publication method. Our objectives are three-fold. Firstly, we verify that publishing the survey rating data satisfying (k, ε)-anonymity via our proposed approaches is fast and scalable. Secondly, we show that the anonymous survey rating data sets produced permit accurate data analysis. Finally, we perform the statistical analysis on both original and anonymized data sets.

DATA SETS

Our experimentation uses two real-world databases, MovieLens and Netflix. The MovieLens data set was made available by the GroupLens Research Project at the University of Minnesota. The data set contains 100,000 ratings (5-star scale), 943 users and 1682 movies. Each user has rated at least 20 movies. The Netflix data set was released by Netflix for competition. This movie rating data set contains over 100,480,507 ratings from 480,189 randomly-chosen Netflix customers over 17,000 movie titles. The Netflic data were collected between October, 1998 and December, 2005 and reflected the distribution of all ratings received during this period. The ratings are on a scale from 1 to 5 stars. In both data sets, a user is considered as a survey participant while a movie is regarded as an issue to respond. Many entries are empty since each participant only rated a small number of movies. We consider all the movies as non-sensitive attributes, and add one sensitive issue "income level" to each data set, in which the ratings scales from 1 to 5. We randomly generate a rating from 1 to 5 and assign it to each record. The correspondence of the income level and income interval is shown in Table Figure 11, where the classification of income interval is referred as the Australia Tax Rates 2008-2009.

EFFICIENCY

Data used for Figure 12(a) is generated by resampling the Movielens and Netflix data sets while varying the percentage of data from 15% to 100%. For both data sets, we evaluated the running time for the (k, ε)-anonymity model with the default set- ting k = 20, ε = 1. For both testing data sets, the execution time for (k, ε)-anonymity

Figure 10. Combining two 2-cliques

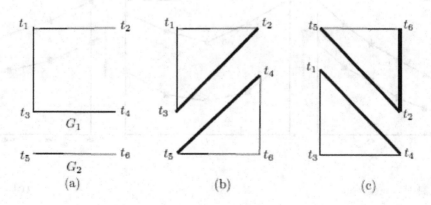

327

Figure 11. Correspondence of income level and income interval

income level (1-5)	income interval
1	$0-$6,000
2	$6,001-$35,000
3	$35,001-$80,000
4	$80,001-$180,000
5	>$180,001

is increased by enlarging the percentage of both data sets. This is because as the per- centage of data increases, the computation cost increases too. The result is expected since the overhead is increased with the more dimensions.

Next, we evaluated the effect of the parameters k, ε on the cost of computing. The data sets used for this experiment are the whole MovieLens and Netflix databases and we evaluate by varying the value of ε and k. With k = 20, Figure 12(b) shows the computational cost as a function of ε, in determining (k, ε)-anonymity for both data sets. Interestingly, in both data sets, as ε increases, the cost initially becomes lower but then increases monotonically. This phenomenon is due to a pair of contradicting factors that push up and down

the running time, respectively. At the initial stage, when ε is small, fewer edges are contained in the graphical representation of the data set, and therefore, more computation efforts are put into edge addition and data modification operations. This explains the initial descent of overall cost. However, as ε grows, there are more possible (k, ε)-anonymous solutions and searching for the one with least distortion requires a larger overhead, and this causes the eventual cost increase. Setting ε = 2, Figure 12(c) displays the results of execution time by varying k from 20 to 60 for both data sets. The cost drops as k grows. This is expected because fewer search efforts for possible (k, ε)-anonymous solutions are needed for a greater k, allowing our algorithm to terminate earlier.

DATA UTILITY

Having verified the efficiency of our technique, we proceed to test its effectiveness. We measure data utility as the error in answering average rating queries ion the anonymized survey rating data it produces by running 100 random queries of the rating of a movie.

Figure 12. Running time on MovieLens and Netfliz data sets vs. (a) Data percentage varies; (b) ε varies; (c) k varies

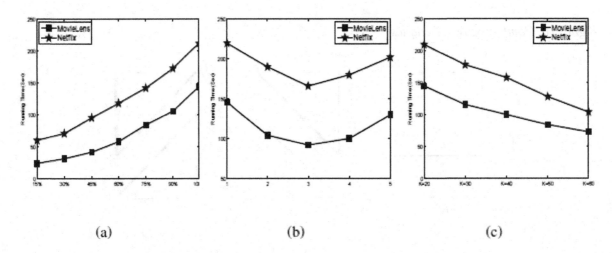

(a)　　　　　　　(b)　　　　　　　(c)

We first study the influence of ε (i.e., the length of a proximate neighborhood) on data utility. Towards this, we set k to 10. With $(10, \varepsilon)$-anonymity, Figure 13(a) plots the average error on both data sets as a function of ε. (k, ε)-anonymity produces useful anonymized data with average error below 15%. The anonymisation strategies incur higher error as ε increases. This is expected, since a larger ε demands stricter privacy preservation, which reduces data utility. Next, we examined the utility of (k, ε)-anonymous solutions with different k when $\varepsilon = 2$. Figure 13(b) presents the average error of 100 random queries of the average rating as a function of k. The error grows with k because a larger k demands tighter anonymity control. Nevertheless, even for the greatest k, the data still preserves fairly good utility by our

technique, incurring an error of no more than 20% for Movielens and 25% for Netflix. Figure 13(c) plots the query accuracy by changing the parameter pair (k, ε). We vary the k from 20 to 40 with ε changing from 1 to 2. From the graph we can see, when ε (k) is fixed, the accuracy is increasing with k (ε), which is consistent with the results obtained from Figures 13(a) and (b).

Since our objective is to anonymize large survey rating data, we adopt another criterion to evaluate data utility called membership changing ratio. This proportion of data points changing cluster memberships from clusters on the original data set to clusters on the anonymized data set when a clustering algorithm (e.g., k-means algorithm) runs on both data sets. We first anonymize the original dataset by our anonymisation method,

Figure 13. Performance comparison on MovieLens and Netflix data sets: (a) Query accuracy vs. ε; (b) Query accuracy vs. k; (c) Query accuracy vs. (k,ε); (d) Clusters changes vs. k.

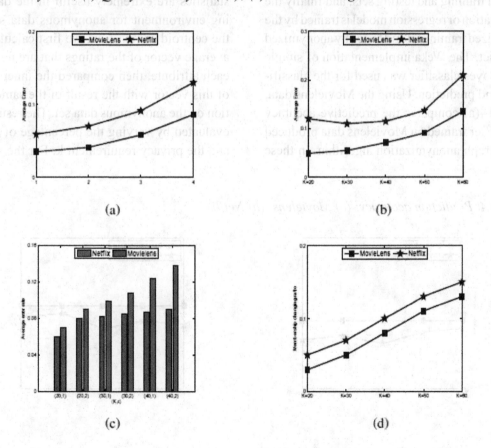

(a)

(b)

(c)

(d)

and then we run a k-means algorithm over both the original and anonymous data sets, keeping the same initial seeds and identical k. We use the proportion of data points changing cluster memberships as another measure of utility. Generally, the lower the membership changing ratio is, the higher the data utility is preserved. Figure 13(d) plots clustering membership changing ratio versus k. The membership changing ratio increases with increasing k. When k = 60, the membership changing ratio is less than 15% for both data sets. This shows that our data modification approach preserves the grouping quality of anonymized data very well.

Figures 14(a) and (b) evaluate the classification and prediction accuracy of the graph anonymization algorithm. Our evaluation methodology is that we first divide data into training and testing sets, and we apply the graph anonymization algorithm to the training and testing sets to obtain the anonymized training and testing sets, and finally the classification or regression model is trained by the anonymized training set and tested by anonymized testing set. The Weka implementation of simple Naive Bayes classifier was used for the classification and prediction. Using the Movielens data, Figure 14(a) compares the predictive accuracy of classifier trained on Movielens data produced by the graph anonymization algorithm. In these

experiments, we generated 50 independent training and testing sets, each containing 2000 records, and we fixed $\varepsilon = 1$. The results are averaged across these 50 trials. For comparison, we also include the accuracies of classifier trained on the (not anonymized) original data. From the graph, we can see that the average prediction accuracy is around 75%, very close to the original accuracy, which preserves better utility for data mining purposes. In Figure 14(b), similar results are obtained by using the Netflix rating data.

STATISTICAL PROPERTIES

We further performed the statistical analysis on the original and anonymous data sets. In this series of evaluations, we compare some key statistical properties, centroid and standard deviation with the original and anonymized data, since these statistics are extremely useful in the data mining environment for anonymous data sets. For the centroid comparison, we first calculated the average vector of the ratings that are not null of each attribute, then compared the inner product of this vector with the result of the same operation on the anonymous data set. The results were evaluated by varying the percentage of the data and the privacy requirement k. For the standard

Figure 14. Prediction accuracy: (a) Movielens; (b) Netflix

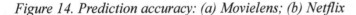

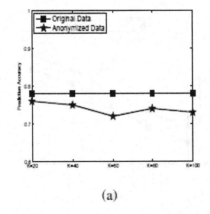

(a)

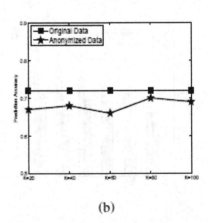

(b)

deviation, we computed the average standard deviation among all the attributes for the original and anonymous data sets. The experiments were conducted by varying ε.

We first compared the centroid before and after anonymisation while varying the percentage of the data set. We set k = 20, ε = 2 and let the percentage of the data vary from 20% to 100%. The result is shown in Figure 15(a). We can see that al- though the centroid between original and anonymous data sets are different, they do not differ much which makes the data useful for the data mining purposes, and the results suggest that our modification strategies preserve the centroid of the data. We then fixed the data set with ε = 2 and varied the privacy requirement k from 5 to 35. The result is shown in Figure 15(b). No matters what kind of operations is used, the centroids before and after the operation are similar to each other. Figure 15(c) compares average standard deviations before and after data anonymisation. The average standard deviation remains constant for the original data, since parameter ε has no effect on it. For the anonymous data set, the standard deviation is bounded by some specific value for a given ε. Similar results were obtained on Netflix data sets as well.

CONCLUSION AND FUTURE WORK

In this chapter, we alleviate a privacy threat to a large survey rating data set with an anonymisation principle called (k,ε)-anonymity. We apply a graphical representation to formulate the problem and provide a comprehensive analysis of the graphical modification strategies. Extensive experiments confirm that our technique produces anonymized data sets that are highly useful and preserve key statistical properties.

This work also initiates several directions for future investigations on our research agenda. Firstly, the (k, ε)-anonymity model introduced in the chapter is targeted at identify protection in a large survey rating data set, it is also important to address the issue of how to prevent attribute disclosures. The privacy principle similar to l-diversity might be considered. Secondly, in this chapter, we consider only edge addition operations for graph modification, and it is interesting to investigate the case when the privacy requirement is achieved by deleting some transactions from the survey rating data. Finally, it is also interesting to employ dimensionality reduction techniques for more effective anonymisation.

Figure 15. Statistical properties analysis (Movielens Dataset): (a) centroid vs. data percentage; (b) centroid vs. k; (c) standard deviation vs. ε

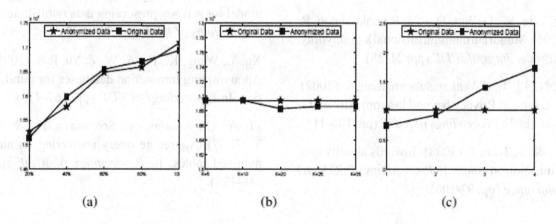

(a)   (b)   (c)

REFERENCES

Aggarwal, C. C. (2005). On k-Anonymity and the curse of dimensionality. In *Proceedings of VLDB* (pp. 901-909).

Atzori, M., Bonchi, F., Giannotti, F., & Pedreschi, D. (2005). Blocking anonymity threats raised by frequent itemset mining. In *Proceedings of ICDM* (pp. 561-564).

Atzori, M., Bonchi, F., Giannotti, F., & Pedreschi, D. (2008). Anonymity preserving pattern discovery. In *Proceedings of VLDB J.* (pp. 703-727).

Fung, B. C. M., Wang, K., & Yu, P. S. (2005). Top-down specialization for information and privacy preservation. In *Proceedings of ICDE* (pp. 205-216).

He, Y., & Naughton, J. F. (2009). Anonymization of set-valued data via top-down, local generalization. In *Proceedings of PVLDB* (pp. 934-945).

Jr, R. J. B., & Agrawal, R. (2005). Data privacy through optimal k-anonymization. In *Proceedings of ICDE* (pp. 217-228).

Kifer, D., & Gehrke, J. (2006). Injecting utility into anonymized datasets. In *Proceedings of SIGMOD Conference* (pp. 217-228).

LeFevre, K., DeWitt, D. J., & Ramakrishnan, R. (2005). Incognito: Efficient full-domain k-anonymity. In *Proceedings of SIGMOD Conference* (pp. 49-60).

LeFevre, K., DeWitt, D. J., & Ramakrishnan, R. (2006). Mondrian multidimensional k-anonymity. In *Proceedings of ICDE* (pp. 21-28).

Li, N., Li, T., & Venkatasubramanian, S. (2007). T-closeness: Privacy beyond k-anonymity and l-diversity. In *Proceedings of ICDE* (pp. 106-115).

Liu, K., & Terzi, E. (2008). Towards identity anonymization on graphs. In *Proceedings of SIGMOD Conference* (pp. 93-106).

Machanavajjhala, A., Kifer, D., Gehrke, J., & Venkitasubramaniam, M. (2007). L-diversity: Privacy beyond k-anonymity. In *Proceedings of TKDD* (pp. 120-140).

Samarati, P. (2001). Protecting respondents' identities in microdata release. In *Proceedings of IEEE Trans. Knowl. Data Eng.* (pp. 1010-1027).

Sun, X., Wang, H., & Li, J. (2010). Satisfying privacy requirements: One step before anonymization. In *14th Pacific-Asia Conference on Knowledge Discovery and Data Mining (PAKDD '10)* (pp. 181-188).

Sweeney, L. (2002). K-anonymity: A model for protecting privacy . In *Proceedings of International Journal of Uncertainty* (pp. 557–570). Fuzziness and Knowledge-Based Systems.

Verykios, V. S., Elmagarmid, A. K., Bertino, E., Saygin, Y., & Dasseni, E. (2004). Association Rule Hiding. In *Proceedings of IEEE Trans. Knowl. Data Eng.* (pp. 434-447).

Wang, K., & Fung, B. C. M. (2006). Anonymizing sequential releases. In *Proceedings of KDD* (pp. 414-423).

Wang, K., Yu, P. S., & Chakraborty, S. (2004). Bottom-up generalization: A data mining solution to privacy protection. In *Proceedings of ICDM* (pp. 249-256).

Wong, R. C., Li, J., Fu, A. W., & Wang, K. (2006). (Alpha, k)-anonymity: An enhanced k-anonymity model for privacy preserving data publishing. In *Proceedings of KDD* (pp. 754-759).

Xu, Y., Wang, K., Fu, A. W., & Yu, P. S. (2008). Anonymizing transaction databases for publication. In *Proceedings of KDD* (pp. 767-775).

Zhang, Q., Koudas, N., Srivastava, D., & Yu, T. (2007). Aggregate query answering on anonymized tables. In *Proceedings of ICDE* (pp. 116-125).

Zhou, B., & Pei, J. (2008). Preserving privacy in social networks against neighborhood attacks. In *Proceedings of ICDE* (pp. 506-515).

ADDITIONAL READING

Aggarwal, G., Panigrahy, R., Feder, T., Thomas, D., Kenthapadi, K., Khuller, S., & Zhu, A. (2010). Achieving anonymity via clustering. In *Proceedings of ACM Transactions on Algorithms* (21-58).

Agrawal, R., & Srikant, R. (2000). Privacy-preserving data mining. In *Proceedings of SIGMOD Conference* (439-450).

Campan, A., & Truta, T. M. (2008). Data and structural k-anonymity in social networks. In *Proceedings of PinKDD* (33-54).

Dinur, I., & Nissim, K. (2003). Revealing information while preserving privacy. In *Proceedings of PODS* (202-210).

Fung, B. C. M., Wang, K., & Yu, P. S. (2007). Anonymizing classification data for privacy preservation. In *Proceedings of IEEE Trans. Knowl. Data Eng* (711-725).

LeFevre, K., DeWitt, D. J., & Ramakrishnan, R. (2006). Mondrian multidimensional k-anonymity. In *Proceedings of ICDE* (114-120).

Meyerson, A., & Williams, R. (2004). On the complexity of optimal k-anonymity. In *Proceedings of PODS* (223-228).

Samarati, P., & Sweeney, L. (1998). Generalizing data to provide anonymity when disclosing information (abstract). In *Proceedings of PODS*.

Sun, X., Wang, H., & Li, J. (2008). L-diversity based dynamic update for large time-evolving microdata. In *Proceedings of Australasian Conference on Artificial Intelligence* (pp. 461-469).

Sun, X., Wang, H., Li, J., & Truta, T. M. (2008). Enhanced p-sensitive k-anonymity models for privacy preserving data publishing. In *Proceedings of Transactions on Data Privacy* (pp. 53-66).

Terrovitis, M., Mamoulis, N., & Kalnis, P. (2008). Privacy-preserving anonymization of set-valued data. In *Proceedings of PVLDB* (pp. 115-125).

Wang, H., & Lakshmanan, L. V. S. (2006). Probabilistic privacy analysis of published views. In *Proceedings of WPES (pp. 81-84).*

KEY TERMS AND DEFINITIONS

Anonymity: Anonymity typically refers to the state of an individual's personal identity.

Hamming Distance: Between two strings of equal length is the number of positions at which the corresponding symbols are different.

Clique: An inclusive group of people who share interests, views, purposes, patterns of behavior, or ethnicity.

Complete Graph: A simple graph in which every pair of distinct vertices is connected by a unique edge.

Centroid: In geometry, the centroid, geometric center, or barycenter of a plane figure or two-dimensional shape X is the intersection of all straight lines that divide X into two parts of equal moment about the line.

Mean: The expected value of a random variable, which is also called the population mean.

Standard Deviation: It shows how much variation or "dispersion" there is from the "average" (mean, or expected/budgeted value).

Section 3
Graph Database Applications in Various Domains

Chapter 15
Querying RDF Data

Faisal Alkhateeb
Yarmouk University, Jordan

Jérôme Euzenat
INRIA & LIG, France

ABSTRACT

This chapter provides an introduction to the RDF language as well as surveys the languages that can be used for querying RDF graphs. Then it reviews some of the languages that can be used for querying RDF and provides a comparison between these query languages.

INTRODUCTION

The Resource Description Framework (RDF) (Manola & Miller, 2004) is the W3C recommended data model for the representation of information about resources on the Web. Nowadays, more resources are annotated via RDF due to its simple data model, formal semantics, and a sound and complete inference mechanism. A query language that provides a range of querying paradigms is therefore needed.

The SPARQL query language (Prud'hommeaux & Seaborne, 2008) is a W3C recommendation developed in order to query an RDF knowledge base. The heart of a SPARQL query, the graph pattern, is an RDF graph (and more precisely an RDF graph with variables). The maps that

are used to compute answers to a graph pattern query in an RDF knowledge base are exploited by (Perez, Arenas, & Gutierrez, 2006) to define answers to the more complex, more expressive SPARQL queries (using, for example, disjunctions or functional constraints).

This chapter provides an introduction to RDF as well as surveys the languages that can be used for querying RDF graphs. In particular, it introduces the RDF language: its syntax and its semantics. Then it reviews some of the well known graph query languages used for querying structured or semi-structured data bases, presents some of RDF query languages, and details the SPARQL query language. It then presents some extensions of the SPARQL query language. Finally, it provides a comparison between these query languages.

DOI: 10.4018/978-1-61350-053-8.ch015

The RDF Language

The Resource description Framework (RDF) is a W3C standard language dedicated to the annotation of resources within the Semantic Web (Manola & Miller, 2004). The atomic constructs of RDF are statements, which are triples (subject, predicate, object) consisting of the resource (the subject) being described, a property (the predicate), and a property value (the object).

For example, the assertion of the following RDF triples {<book1 rdf:type publication>, <book1 title "Ontology Matching">, <book1 author "Jérôme Euzenat">, <book1 publisher "Springer">} means that "Jérôme Euzenat" is an author of a book titled "Ontology Matching" whose publisher is "Springer".

A collection of RDF statements (RDF triples) can be intuitively understood as a directed labeled graph: resources are nodes and statements are arcs (from the subject node to the object node) connecting the nodes. The language is provided with a model-theoretic semantics [Hayes, 2004], that defines the notion of consequence (or entailment) between two RDF graphs, i.e., when an RDF graph is entailed by another one. Answers to an RDF query (the knowledge base and the query are RDF graphs) can be computed using a particular map (a mapping from terms of the query to terms of the knowledge base preserving constants), a graph homomorphism [Gutierrez, Hurtado &Mendelzon, 2004; Baget, 2005].

RDFS (RDF Schema) [Brickley & Guha, 2004] is an extension of RDF designed to describe relationships between resources and/or resources using a set of reserved words called the RDFS vocabulary. In the above example, the reserved word rdf:type can be used to relate instances to classes, e.g., book1 is of type publication.

This section is devoted to the presentation of Simple RDF without RDF/RDFS vocabulary (Brickley & Guha, 2004). We first recall its abstract syntax [Carroll & Klyne, 2004] and its semantics

(Hayes, 2004). Then we compare the RDF data model with database models and focus on those that are based upon the graph structure.

RDF Syntax

RDF can be expressed in a variety of formats including RDF/XML [Beckett, 2004], Turtle (Beckett, 2006), etc. We use here its abstract syntax (triple format), which is sufficient for our purpose. To define the syntax of RDF, we need to introduce the terminology over which RDF graphs are constructed.

RDF TERMINOLOGY

The RDF terminology T is the union of three pairwise disjoint infinite sets of terms [Hayes, 2004]: the set U of URIrefs, the set L of literals (itself partitioned into two sets, the set Lp of plain literals and the set Lt of typed literals), and the set B of variables. The set $V = U \cup L$ of names is called the vocabulary. From now on, we use different notations for the elements of these sets: a variable will be prefixed by ? (like ?b1), a literal will be between quotation marks (like "27"), and the rest will be urirefs (like foaf:Person — foaf: is a namespace prefix used for representing personal information—ex:friend or simply friend).

RDF Graphs as Triples

RDF graphs are usually constructed over the set of urirefs, blanks, and literals [Carroll & Klyne, 2004]. "Blanks" are vocabulary specific to RDF and SPARQL currently considers them as constant values without giving them their existential semantics [Hayes, 2004]. For the sake of simplicity, we do not use blanks in the definition of RDF syntax.

Definition (RDF graph). An RDF triple is an element of $V \times V \times V$. An RDF graph is a finite set of RDF triples.

Example 1. The following set of triples represents an RDF graph:

```
{
< ex:person1 foaf:name "Faisal" >,
< ex:person1 ex:daughter ex:person2 >,
< ex:person2 foaf:friend ex:person3 >,
< ex:person3 foaf:knows ex:person1 >,
< ex:person3 foaf:name "Sara" >
}
```

Intuitively, this graph means that there exists an entity named (foaf:name) "Faisal" that has a daughter (ex:daughter) that has a friend relation with another entity, whose name is "Sara", and who knows (foaf:knows) the entity named "Faisal".

Graph Representation of RDF Triples

If G is an RDF graph, we use T(G), U(G), L(G), B(G), V(G) to denote the set of terms, urirefs, literals, variables or names that appear in at least one triple of G. In a triple <s, p, o>, s is called the subject, p the predicate and o the object. It is possible to associate to a set of triples G a labeled directed multi-graph, such that the set of nodes is the set of terms appearing as a subject or object at least in a triple. By drawing these graphs, the nodes resulting from literals are represented by rectangles while the others are represented by rectangles with rounded corners. In what follows, we do not distinguish the two views of RDF syntax

(as sets of triples or labeled directed graphs). We will then speak interchangeably about its nodes, its arcs, or the triples it is made of. For example, the RDF triples given in Example 1 can be represented graphically as shown in Figure 1.

Simple RDF Semantics

Several semantics for RDF graphs have been introduced in (Hayes, 2004). In this section, we present only the simple semantics without RDF/RDFS vocabulary (Brickley & Guha, 2004). The definitions of interpretations, models, and entailment correspond to the simple interpretations, simple models, and simple entailments of (Hayes, 2004). It should be noticed that RDF and RDFS consequence (or entailment) can be polynomially reduced to simple entailment via RDF or RDFS rules (Baget, 2003, ter Horst, 2005).

Interpretations

An interpretation describes possible way(s) the world might be in order to comply the truth-value of any ground RDF graph. It does this by specifying for each URIref, what is its denotation. In addition, if it is used to indicate a property, what values that property has for each thing in the universe. Interpretations that assign particular meanings to some names in a given vocabulary will be named from that vocabulary, e.g. RDFS interpretations (Brickley & Guha, 2004). An interpretation with

Figure 1. An RDF graph

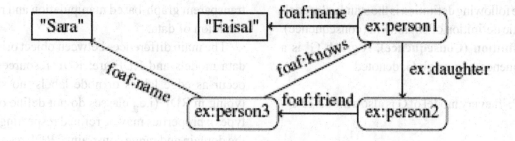

no particular extra conditions on a vocabulary (including the RDF vocabulary itself) will be simply called an interpretation.

Definition (Interpretation of a vocabulary). An interpretation of V is a tuple I = <IR, IP, IEXT, i> where:

- IR is a set of resources that contains $V \cap L$;
- IP is a set of properties;
- IEXT: IP $\to 2^{IR \times IR}$ associates to each property a set of pairs of resources called the extension of the property;
- the interpretation function i: V $\to$ IR associates to each name in V a resource of IR, if $v \in L$, then $i(v) = v$.

Models

By providing RDF with formal semantics, [Hayes, 2004] expresses the conditions under which an RDF graph truly describes a particular world (i.e., an interpretation is a model for the graph).

Intuitively, a ground triple (i.e., a triple without variables) <s, p, o> in an RDF graph will be true under the interpretation I if p is interpreted as a property, s and o are interpreted as a pair of resources, and the pair of resources belongs to the extension of that property.

An interpretation I is a model of an RDF graph G if all triples are true under I.

Definition (Model of an RDF graph). Let V be a vocabulary, and G be an RDF graph such that every name appearing in G is also in V (V(G) $\subseteq$ V). An interpretation I = I =<IR, IP, IEXT, i> of V is a model of G iff for each triple <s, p, o> of G, $i(p) \in$ IP and $< i$ (s), i (o)$> \in$ IEXT (i (p)).

The following definition is the standard model-theoretic definition of entailment (consequence).

Definition (Consequence). A graph G' is a consequence of a graph G, denoted

G |= G', iff every model of G is also a model of G'.

RDF vs. Database Models

In order to compare RDF query languages with those of database, we first need to identify the differences in the underlying data models. In this section, we provide a brief presentation of the RDF data model with some of the database models, and stress on those that are based on a graph model (see (Angles & Gutiérrez, 2008)) for a survey of database models and (Kerschberg, Klug & Tsichritzis, 1976) for a taxonomy of data models).

Relational Models

The relational data model is introduced in (Codd, 1970) to separate the physical and logical levels. It is a simple model based on the notions of sets and relations with a defined algebra and logic. SQL is its standard query and manipulation language.

The main differences between the relational model and RDF are that the data have a predefined structure with simple record-type, and the schema is fixed and difficult to extend. The same differences between RDF and the object data models also apply to the relational data model (see the following subsection).

Object Data Models

Object data models are based on the object-oriented programming paradigms (Kim, 1990), representing data as a collection of objects interacting among them by methods. Among object oriented data models are: O2 (Lécluse, Richard & Vélez) based on a graph structure, and Good (Gyssens, Paredaens & Gucht, 1990) that has a transparent graph-based manipulation and representation of data.

The main differences between object oriented data models and RDF are: RDF resources can occur as edge labels or node labels; no strong typing in RDF (i.e., classes do not define object types); properties may be refined respecting only the domain and range constraints; RDF resources can be typed of different classes, which are not necessarily pairwise related by specialization, i.e., the instances of a class may have associated quite different properties such that there is no other class on which the union of these properties is defined.

Semi-Structured Data Models

Semi-structured data models are oriented to model semi-structured data (Buneman, 1997, Abiteboul, 1997). They deal with data whose structure is irregular, implicit, and partial, and with schema contained in the data.

One of these models is OEM (Object Exchange Model) (Papakonstantinou, Garcia-Molina & Widom, 1995). It aims to express data in a standard way to solve the information exchange problem. This model is based on objects that have unique identifiers, and property value that can be simple types or references to objects. However, labels in the OEM model cannot occur in both nodes (objects) and edges (properties), and OEM is schemaless while RDF may be coupled with RDFS. Moreover, nodes in RDF can be also blanks.

Another data model is the XML data model (Bray, Paoli, Sperberg-McQueen, Maler, & Yergeau, 2006). RDF has substantial differences with the XML data model (Bray, Paoli, Sperberg-McQueen, Maler, & Yergeau, 2006). XML has an ordered-tree like structure against the graph structure of RDF. Also, information about data in XML is part of the data while RDF expresses explicitly information about data using relation between entities. In addition, we cannot distinguish in RDF between entity (or node) labels and relation labels, and RDF resources may have irregular structures due to multiple classification.

Graph Data Models

The Functional Data Model (Shipman, 1981) is one of the models considering an implicit structure of graphs for the data, aiming to provide a "conceptually natural" database interface. A different approach is the Logical Data Model proposed in (Kuper & Vardi, 1993), where an explicit graph model is considered for representing data. In this model, there are three types of nodes (namely basic, composition and collection nodes), all of which can be modeled in RDF. Among the models that have explicit graph data model are: G-Base (Kunii, 1987) representing complex structures of knowledge; Gram (Amann & Scholl, 1992) representing hypertext data; GraphDB [Gting, 1994] modeling graphs in object oriented databases; and Gras (Kiesel, Schurr & Westfechtel, 1996). They have no direct applicability of a graph model to RDF since RDF resources can occur as edge or node labels. Solving this problem requires an intermediate model to be defined, e.g. bipartite graphs (Hayes & Gutierrez, 1996).

QUERY LANGUAGES FOR THE SEMANTIC WEB

A query language can be understood as a mechanism for searching, manipulating and/or inferencing data from valid instances of the data model.

This section surveys the languages that can be used for querying RDF graphs. In particular, it reviews some of the well-know graph query languages used for querying structured or semi-structured data bases. Then it presents some of RDF query languages as well as details the SPARQL query language. After that, some extensions of SPARQL are introduced. Finally, a comparison between some of the existing query languages is provided.

Graph Query Languages

Query languages for structured graph data base models can be used for querying RDF viewing RDF data as a graph that may contain transitive or repetitive patterns of relations. Among them, G [Cruz, Mendelzon & Wood, 1987] and its extension G+ [Cruz, Mendelzon & Wood, 1988] are two languages for querying structured databases. A simple G+ query has two elements, a query graph that specifies the pattern to be matched and a summary graph that defines graphically how the answers are to be structured and then presented to the user.

Example 2. Given a graph that represents relations between people, the G+ query of Figure 2 finds pairs of people who share a common ancestor. The left hand side of the bold arrow is the pattern to be matched in the knowledge base while the right hand side is the summary graph. Graphlog — a visual query language which has been proven equivalent to linear Datalog [Consens & Mendelzon, 1990] — extends G+ by combining it with the Datalog notation. It has been designed for querying hypertext. A Graphlog query is only a graph pattern containing a distinguished edge

or arc (i.e., it is a restructuring edge, which corresponds to the summary graph in G+).

Example 3. Figure 3 shows a Graphlog query: dashed lines represent edge labels with the positive closure, a crossed dashed line represents a negated label (e.g. !descendant+ between ?person2 and ?person3), person is a unary predicate, and finally a bold line represents a distinguished edge that must be labeled with a positive label. The effects of this query is to find all instances of the pattern that occur in the database, i.e., finding descendant of ?person1 which are not descendant of ?person2. Then, for each of them, define a virtual link represented by the distinguished edge.

These query languages (namely G, G+ and Graphlog) support graphical queries that are limited to finding simple paths (cycle-free paths). The main problem with finding only simple paths, is that there are situations in which answers to

Figure 2. A G+ query to find common ancestor

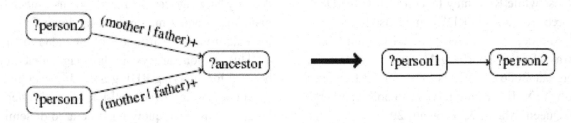

Figure 3. A Graphlog query

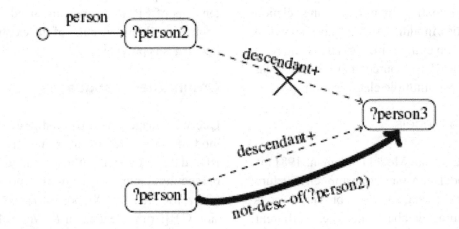

such queries are all non simple, e.g. if the only paths matching a regular expression pattern have cycles (see the example of non-simple paths in (Anyanwu, Maduko, & Sheth, 2007). In addition, the complexity of finding simple paths is NP-complete even without variables in regular expressions (Wood, 1988).

Moreover, these languages do not provide complex functionalities, for example, for filtering, ordering, projection, union of graph patterns; optional graph patterns and other useful features (see SPARQL features and examples below).

(Semi)-Structured Query Languages

Lorel (Abiteboul, Quass, McHugh, Widom, & Wiener, 1997) is an OEM-based language for querying semi-structured documents. It uses regular expression patterns for traversing object hierarchy paths, restricted to simple path semantics (or acyclic paths). UnQL (uneman, Davidson, Hillebrand, & Suciu, 1996) is a language closely related to Lorel for querying semi-structured data. It is based on a data model similar to OEM (Buneman, Davidson & Suciu, 1995). A particular aspect of the language is that it allows some form of restructuring even for cyclic structures. A traverse construct allows one to transform a database graph while traversing it, e.g. by replacing all labels A by the label A0. This powerful operation combines tree rewriting techniques with some control obtained by a guided traversal of the graph. For instance, one could specify that the replacement occurs only if a particular edge, say B, is encountered on the way from the root. STRUQL (Fernandez, Florescu, Levy & Suciu, 1997), a query language for web-site management, incorporates regular expressions and has precisely the same expressive power as stratified linear Datalog.. WebSQL (Mendelzon, Mihaila, & Milo, 1997), incorporates regular expressions for querying distributed collection of documents connected by hypertext links. It has a cost based query evaluation mechanism, i.e., it evaluates how much of the network must be visited to answer a particular query.

A Logic that incorporates a kind of constrained regular expressions has been proposed for XPath (Genevès, Layaïda & Schmitt, 2007). However, XPath operates on trees (not on graphs), and only defines monadic queries (Clark & DeRose, 1999). Several works attempt to adapt PDL-like or μ-calculus based on monadic queries for querying graphs, for example (Alechina, Demri, & de Rijke, 2003).

RDF Query Languages

Several query languages have been proposed for RDF (Haase, Broekstra, Eberhart & Volz, 2004). Most of them use a query model based on relational algebra (Codd, 1970), where RDF graphs are viewed as a collection of triples and the queries are triple-based formulas expressed over a single relation. In spite of the benefits gained from the existing relational database systems such as indexing mechanisms, underlying storage of triples as relations (Harris & Shadbolt, 2005), query optimization techniques, and others; relational queries cannot express recursive relations and even the most simple form, the transitive closure of a relation (Aho & Ullman, 1979), directly inherited from the graph nature of RDF triples.

There are many real-world applications, inside and outside the domain of the semantic web, requiring data representation that are inherently recursive. For that reason, there are several attempts to extend relational algebra to express complex query modeling. Outside the domain of the semantic web, we mention (Agrawal, 1988) extends the relational algebra to represent transitive closure and (Jagadish, 1989) represents query hierarchies. In the domain of RDF, some query languages such as RQL (Karvounarakis, Alexaki, Christophides, Plexousakis, and Scholl, 2002) attempts to combine the relational algebra with some special class hierarchies. It supports a form of transitive expressions over RDFS transitive properties (i.e., subPropertyOf and subClassOf) for navigating through class and property hierarchies. Versa (Olson & Ogbuji, 2002), RxPath (Souzis, 2004), PRDF (Alkhateeb, Baget, & Euzenat, 2005; Alkhateeb, 2007) and (Matono, Amagasa, Yoshikawa & Uemura, 2005) are all path-based query languages for RDF that are well suited for graph traversal but do not support SQL-like functionalities. WILBUR (Lassila, 2002) is a toolkit that incorporates path expressions for navigation in RDF graphs. The authors of (Zhang & Yoshikawa, 2008) discuss the usage of a Concise Bounded Description (CBD) of an RDF graph, which is defined as a subgraph consisting of those statements which together constitute a focused body of knowledge about a given resource (or a node) in a given RDF graph. It also defines a Dynamic version (DCBD) of CBD as well as proposes a query language for RDF called DCBDQuery, which mainly addresses the problem of finding meaningful (shortest) paths with respect to DCBD.

SQL-like query languages for RDF include SeRQL (Broekstra, 2003), RDQL (Seaborne, 2004) and its current successor – a W3C recommendation – SPARQL (Prud'hommeaux & Seaborne, 2008). Since it is defined by the W3C's Data Access Working Group (DAWG) and becomes the most popular query language for RDF, we chose to build our work on SPARQL and avoid reinventing another query language for RDF. So, SPARQL will be presented below in more details than the other languages.

THE SPARQL QUERY LANGUAGE

SPARQL query answering is characterized by defining maps from query patterns to the RDF knowledge base (Perez, Arenas, & Gutierrez, 2006).

SPARQL Syntax

The heart of SPARQL queries is graph patterns. Informally, a graph pattern can be one of the following (cf. (Prud'hommeaux & Seaborne, 2008) for more details):

- A triple pattern: a triple pattern corresponds to an RDF triple with variables;
- A basic graph pattern: a set of triple patterns (or an RDF graph with variables) is called a basic graph patterns;
- A union of graph patterns: we use the keyword UNION in SPARQL to represent alternatives;
- An optional graph pattern: SPARQL allows optional results to be returned determined by the keyword OPTIONAL;
- A constraint: constraints in SPARQL are boolean-valued expressions that limit the number of answers to be returned. They can be defined using the keyword FILTER. As atomic FILTER expressions, SPARQL allows unary predicates like BOUND; binary (in)equality predicates (= and ! =); comparison operators like <; data type conversion and string functions which will be omitted here. Complex FILTER expressions can be built using !, || and &&;
- A group graph pattern: is a graph pattern grouped inside { and }, and determines the scope of SPARQL constructs like FILTER and variable nodes;

Definition (Triple pattern). A triple pattern is an element of $T \times T \times T$.

Definition (SPARQL graph pattern). A SPARQL graph pattern is defined inductively in the following way:

- Every triple pattern is a basic SPARQL graph pattern;

- If P1, P2 are SPARQL graph patterns and C is a SPARQL constraint, then {P1}, {P1 AND P2}, {P1 UNION P2}, {P1 OPTIONAL P2}, and {P1 FILTER C} are SPARQL graph patterns.

Example 4. The following graph pattern:

```
{ ?person foaf:knows "Faisal" . }
```

is a basic graph pattern that can be used in a query for finding persons who know Faisal.

```
{
{ ?person ex:liveIn ex:France . }
UNION
{ ?person ex:hasNationality ex:French
. }
}
```

is a union of two basic graph patterns that searches the persons who either live in France or have a French nationality.

The following graph pattern

```
{ ?person foaf:knows "Faisal" .
OPTIONAL
{ ?person foaf:mbox ?mbox . }
}
```

contains an optional basic graph pattern searching the mail boxes, if they exist, of persons who know Faisal.

```
{
?person ex:liveIn ex:France .
?person ex:hasAge ?age .
FILTER (?age < 40) .
}
```

the constraint in this graph pattern limits the answers to the persons who live in France whose ages are less than 40.

```
{ { ?person foaf:knows "Faisal" . }
{
?person ex:liveIn ex:France .
?person ex:hasAge ?age .
FILTER (?age < 40) .
}
}
```

SPARQL query: A SELECT SPARQL query is expressed using a form resembling the SQL SELECT query: SELECT B FROM u WHERE P where u is the URL of an RDF graph G, P is a SPARQL graph pattern and B is a tuple of variables appearing in P. Intuitively, an answer to a SPARQL query is an instantiation π of the variables of B by the terms of the RDF graph G such that π is a restriction of a proof that P is a consequence of G.

SPARQL provides several result forms other than SELECT that can be used for formatting the query results. For example, CONSTRUCT that can be used for building an RDF graph from each answer, ASK that returns TRUE if there is an answer to a given query and FALSE otherwise, and DESCRIBE that can be used for describing a resource RDF graph. The following example queries give an insight of these query forms.

Example 5. The following ASK query:

```
ASK
WHERE { ?person foaf:name "Faisal" .
        ?person ex:hasChild ?child .
      }
```

returns TRUE if a person named Faisal has at least one child, FALSE otherwise.

The following CONSTRUCT query:

```
CONSTRUCT { ?son1 ex:brother ?son2 .}
WHERE { ?person foaf:names "Faisal" .
      ?son1 ex:sonOf ?person .
      ?son2 ex:sonOf ?person .
      FILTER (?son1 != ?son2) .
    }
```

The following query:

```
DESCRIBE <example.org/person1>
```

Returns a description of the resource identified by the given URIref, i.e., returns the set of triples involving this URIref.

SPARQL uses post-filtering clauses which allow, for example, to order (ORDER BY clause), or to limit (LIMIT and/or OFFSET clauses) the answers of a query. The reader is referred to the SPARQL specification (Prud'hommeaux & Seaborne, 2008) for more details or to (Perez, Arenas, & Gutierrez, 2006) for formal semantics of SPARQL queries.

Example 6. The following SPARQL query:

```
SELECT ?name
WHERE {
        ?person ex:liveIn ex:France .
        ?person foaf:name ?name .
        }
ORDER BY ?name
LIMIT 10
OFFSET 5
```

Formal Semantics: Answers to SPARQL Queries

SPARQL query constructs are defined through algebraic operations on assignments from a set of variables to terms, i.e., that preserves names, called maps.

Definition (Map). Let $V1 \subseteq T$, and $V2 \subseteq T$ be two sets of terms. A map from $V1$ to $V2$ is a mapping $\mu: V1 \rightarrow V2$ such that $\forall x \in (V1 \cap V)$, $\mu(x) = x$.

Operations on maps: If μ is a map, then the domain of μ, denoted by $\text{dom}(\mu)$, is the subset of T on which μ is defined. If P is a graph pattern, then $\mu(P)$ is the graph pattern obtained by the substitution of $\mu(b)$ to each variable $b \in B(P)$. Two maps $\mu1$ and $\mu2$ are compatible when $\forall x \in \text{dom}(\mu1) \cap \text{dom}(\mu2)$, $\mu1(x) = \mu2(x)$. Otherwise,

they are said incompatible and this is denoted by $\mu1 \perp \mu2$. If $\mu1$ and $\mu2$ are two compatible maps, then we denote by $\mu = \mu1 \oplus \mu2: T1 \cup T2 \rightarrow T$ the map defined by: $\forall x \in T1; \mu(x) = \mu1(x)$ and $\forall x \in T2; \mu(x) = \mu2(x)$. The join and difference of two sets of maps $\Omega1$ and $\Omega2$ are defined as follows [Perez, Arenas, & Gutierrez, 2006]:

(join) $\Omega1 \bowtie \Omega2 = \{\mu1 \oplus \mu2 \mid \mu1 \in \Omega1, \mu2 \in \Omega2$ are compatible$\}$;

(difference) $\Omega1 \setminus \Omega2 = \{\mu1 \in \Omega1 \mid \forall \mu2 \in \Omega2, \mu1$ and $\mu2$ are not compatible$\}$.

Definition (Answer to a SPARQL graph pattern). Let G be an RDF graph and P be a SPARQL graph pattern. The set $S(P,G)$ of answers of P in G is defined inductively in the following way:

1. If P is a triple pattern, $S(P,G) = \{\mu \mid \mu(P) \in G\}$;
2. If $P = (P1 \text{ AND } P2)$, $S(P,G) = S(P1,G) \bowtie S(P2,G)$;
3. If $P = (P1 \text{ UNION } P2)$, $S(P,G) = S(P1,G) \cup S(P2,G)$;
4. If $P = (P1 \text{ OPTIONAL } P2)$, $S(P,G) = (S(P1,G) \bowtie S(P2,G)) \cup (S(P1,G) \setminus S(P2,G))$;
5. If $P = (P1 \text{ FILTER } C)$, $S(P,G) = \{\mu \in S(P1,G) \mid \mu(C) = T\}$.

The semantics of SPARQL FILTER expressions is defined as follows: given a map μ and a SPARQL constraint C, we say that μ satisfies C (denoted by $\mu(C) = T$), if:

- C is $\text{BOUND}(x)$ with $x \in \text{dom}(\mu)$;
- C is $(x = c)$ with $x \in \text{dom}(\mu)$ and $\mu(x) = c$;
- C is $(x = y)$ with $x; y \in \text{dom}(\mu)$ and $\mu(x) = \mu(y)$;
- C is $(x != c)$ with $x \in \text{dom}(\mu)$ and $\mu(x) != c$;
- C is $(x != y)$ with $x; y \in \text{dom}(\mu)$ and $\mu(x) != \mu(y)$;
- C is $(x < c)$ with $x \in \text{dom}(\mu)$ and $\mu(x) < c$;

- C is $(x < y)$ with x; $y \in dom(\mu)$ and $\mu(x) < \mu(y)$;
- C is !C1 with $\mu(C1) = \perp$ (μ does not satisfy C1);
- C is $(C1\|C2)$ with $\mu(C1) = T$ or $\mu(C2) = T$;
- $C = (C1\&\&C2)$ with $\mu(C1) = T$ and $\mu(C2) = T$.

Let Q =SELECT B FROM u WHERE P be a SPARQL query, G be the RDF graph identified by the URL u, and Ω is the set of maps of P in G. Then the answers of the query Q are the instantiation of elements of Ω to B. That is, for each map μ of Ω, the answer of Q associated to μ is $\{(x; y) \mid x \in B$ and $y = \mu(x)$ if $\mu(x)$ is defined, null otherwise}.

Example 7. Consider the following SPARQL query Q:

```
SELECT ?name ?mbox
FROM <http://example.org/index1.ttl>
WHERE {
    ?b1 foaf:name "Faisal" .
    ?b1 ex:daughter ?b2 .
    ?b2 ex:friend ?b3 .
    ?b3 foaf:knows ?b1 .
```

```
    ?b3 foaf:name ?name .
    OPTIONAL {
        ?b2 foaf:mbox ?mbox .
    }
}
```

WORK ON SPARQL

(Cyganiak, 2005) presents a relational model of SPARQL, in which relational algebra operators (join, left outer join, projection, selection, etc.) are used to model SPARQL SELECT clauses. The authors propose a translation system between SPARQL and SQL to make a correspondence between SPARQL queries and relational algebra queries over a single relation. (Harris & Shadbolt, 2005) presents an implementation of SPARQL queries in a relational database engine, in which relational algebra operators similar to (Cyganiak, 2005) are used. The definition of mapping for SPARQL from a logical point of view has been addressed in (de Bruijn, Franconi & Tessaris, 2005). A preliminary formalization of the semantics of SPARQL as well as a definition to an answer set to a basic graph

Figure 4. An RDF graph

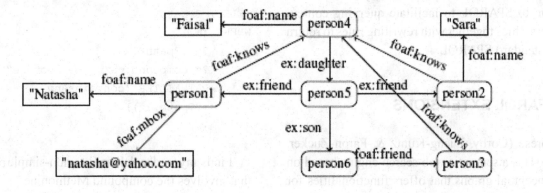

Table 1.

?name	?mbox
Sara	Null
Natasha	natasha@yahoo.com

pattern query using partial functions have been provided in (Franconi & Tessaris, 2005). The authors use high level operators (Join, Optional, etc.) from sets of mappings to sets of mappings, but currently they do not have formal definitions for them, stating only their types. (Polleres, 2007) provides translations from SPARQL to Datalog with negation as failure, some useful extensions of SPARQL, like set difference and nested queries, are proposed. Finally, (Perez, Arenas, & Gutierrez, 2006) presents the semantics of SPARQL using traditional algebra, and gives complexity bounds for evaluating SPARQL queries. The graph pattern facility are used to capture the core semantics and complexities of the language, and discussed their benefits.

An implementation of the SPARQL query language in Corese search engine is found in (Corby, Dieng-Kuntz & Faron-Zucker, 2004, Corby & Faron-Zucker, 2007a). In particular, it describes a graph homomorphism based algorithm for answers SPARQL queries that integrates SPARQL constraints during the search process (i.e., while matching the query against RDF graphs). (Corby & Faron-Zucker, 2007) presents a design pattern to handle contextual metadata hierarchically organized and modeled within RDF. (Corby & Faron-Zucker, 2007) proposes a syntactic extension to SPARQL to facilitate querying context hierarchies together with rewriting rules to return to standard SPARQL.

SPARQL EXTENSIONS

Corese (Corby, Dieng-Kuntz & Faron-Zucker, 2004) is a semantic web search engine based on conceptual graphs that offers functionalities for querying RDF graphs. At the time of writing, it supports only fixed path length queries and no other path expressions such as variable-length paths or constraints on internal nodes, though this seems to be planned.

Two extensions of SPARQL have been defined: SPARQLeR and SPARQ2L. SPARQLeR (Kochut & Janik, 2007) extends SPARQL by allowing query graph patterns involving path variables. Each path variable is used to capture simple (i.e., acyclic) paths in RDF graphs, and is matched against any arbitrary composition of RDF triples between the two given nodes. This extension offers good functionalities like testing the length of paths and testing if a given node is in the found paths.

Example 8. The following SPARQLeR query:

```
SELECT %path
WHERE {
        <r> %path <s> .
        FILTER (length(%path) < 10).
            }
```

SPARQ2L (Anyanwu, Maduko, & Sheth, 2007) also allows using path variables in graph patterns and offers features like constraints in nodes and edges, i.e., testing the presence or absence of nodes and/or edges; constraints in paths, e.g. simple or non-simple paths, presence of a pattern in a path.

Example 9. The following SPARQ2L query:

```
SELECT ??path
WHERE {
      ?x ??path ?x .
      ?z compound:name "Methionine" .
      PATHFILTER (containsAny
      (??path,?z)).
      }
```

Finds any feedback loop (i.e., non-simple path) that involves the compound Methionine.

(Alkhateeb, Baget, & Euzenat, 2009) presents an extension of the SPARQL query language called PSPARQL. PSPARQL adds regular expressions to SPARQL and fully preserves SPARQL. CP-SPARQL is further an extension of PSPARQL that allows expressing constraints in the edges and/or nodes of the traversed paths (i.e., paths encoded by regular expressions) (Alkhateeb, Baget, & Euzenat, 2008). In addition, (Alkhateeb, 2008) shows that (C)PSPARQL can be used to answer SPARQL queries over RDF graphs considering RDFS semantics.

Example 10. The following PSPARQL query:

```
SELECT ?City1 ?City2
WHERE {
?City1 (train | plane)+ ?City2 .
?City1 cityIn France .
?City2 cityIn Italy .
  }
```

Another extension of SPARQL, called nSPAR-QL, to a restricted fragment of RDFS is proposed in (Arenas, Gutierrez, & Pérez, 2008). This extension allows using nested regular expressions, i.e., regular expressions extended with branching axis borrowed from XPath.

Other extensions to SPARQL include: SPARQL-DL (Sirin & Parsia, 2007) that extends SPARQL to support Description Logic semantic queries, SPARQL++ (Polleres, Scharffe & Schindlauer, 2007) extending SPARQL with external functions and aggregates which serves as a basis for declaratively describing ontology mappings, and iSPARQL (Kiefer, Bernstein, Lee, Klein & Stocker, 2007) extends SPARQL to allow for similarity joins which employ several different similarity measures.

COMPARISON BETWEEN DIFFERENT QUERY LANGUAGES

This section provides a comparison between different query languages based on (Haase, Broekstra, Eberhart & Volz, 2004, Angles & Gutiérrez, 1995). The authors of (Haase, Broekstra, Eberhart & Volz, 2004) compare several RDF query languages using 14 distinct tests (or features). Among them were Path expression, Optional path and Recur-

sion tests. The interpretation of these three tests is given respectively as follows: using graph patterns, optional graph patterns, and recursive expressions. To remove ambiguity with the interpretation of path or regular expressions, we rename the three tests to be: Graph pattern, Optional pattern, and Recursion (or Regular expression).

From (Angles & Gutiérrez, 1995), we include the following features: Adjacent nodes, Adjacent edges, Fixed-length path, Degree of a node, Distance between nodes, and Diameter. We also add the following features: Regular expression variable, Constraints, Path variable, Constrained regular expression, Inverse path, and Non-simple path. We mean by "Regular expression variable" that the use of variables in the predicates or regular expressions of graph patterns. The query languages are restricted to this feature when they allow the use of variables only in the atomic predicates. A simple path is a path whose nodes are all distinct. There were 8 query languages in the original comparison (Haase, Broekstra, Eberhart & Volz, 2004) from which we choose RQL, RDQL, SeRQL, and Versa which seem to represent the most expressive languages for supporting the two types of querying paradigms (i.e., path-based and relational-based models); we include G+, GraphLog, STRUQL, LOREL from (Angles & Gutiérrez, 1995); and we add SPARQL, Corese, SPARQ2L, SPARQLeR and (C)PSPARQL.

Figure 5 Summarizes the main differences between the current SPARQL extensions and other query languages. In Figure 5, columns represent query languages and rows represent features or queries. Moreover, we use - to denote that the feature has no support in the query language, ° to denote that there exists a partial (restricted) support, and finally • to denote the full support of the feature.

As it is appearing in the table, (C)PSPARQL and SPARQ2L are the two languages that support most of the features. However, SPARQ2L supports only simple-paths and its semantics does not work with non-simple paths.

Figure 5. Comparison of RDF query languages and graph query languages: white circle for partial (restricted) support, a dash for no support, and full circle for full support

	SPARQL	Corese	SPARQ2L	SPARQLeR	(P/CP)SPARQL	G+	GraphLog	STRUQL	RDQL	SeRQL	Versa	RQL	LOREL
Graph pattern	•	•	•	•	•/•	•	•	•	•	•	•	•	•
Optional pattern	•	•	•	•	•/•	-	-	-	-	•	•	○	-
Union	•	•	•	•	•/•	-	-	-	-	•	•	•	•
Constraints	•	•	•	•	•/•	-	-	-	•	•	•	•	•
Difference	•	•	•	•	•/•	-	-	-	•	•	○	•	-
Quantification	-	-	-	-	-/-	-	-	-	•	-	•	•	•
Aggregation	-	○	-	-	○/○	-	-	-	-	-	•	•	•
Reification	•	•	•	•	•/•	-	-	-	○	•	○	○	-
Collections and Containers	○	○	○	○	○/○	-	-	-	○	○	○	•	-
Namespace	•	•	•	•	•/•	-	-	-	○	•	-	•	-
Language	•	•	•	•	•/•	-	-	-	-	•	-	-	-
Lexical space	•	•	•	•	•/•	-	-	-	•	•	•	•	-
Value space	•	•	•	•	•/•	○	○	○	○	•	-	•	•
Entailment	-	•	-	○	•/•	-	-	-	○	•	-	•	•
Recursion (Regular expression)	-	-	•	•	•/•	•	•	•	-	-	•	○	•
Regular expression variable	-	-	-	-	•/•	•	•	•	-	-	○	○	•
Constrained regular expression	-	-	○	○	-/•	-	-	-	-	-	-	-	-
Fixed-length path	-	•	○	○	•/•	•	•	•	○	○	-	•	•
Path variable	-	•	•	•	•/•	-	-	-	-	-	-	-	•
Inverse Path	-	-	-	•	-/•	•	•	-	-	-	-	-	-
Non-simple path	-	-	•	-	•/•	-	-	-	-	-	-	-	-
Adjacent nodes	•	•	•	•	•/•	•	•	•	○	○	○	○	•
Adjacent edges	•	•	•	•	•/•	•	•	•	○	-	○	○	○
Degree of a node	-	-	-	-	-/-	•	•	•	-	-	-	○	-
Distance between nodes	-	-	-	-	-/-	•	•	•	-	-	-	-	-
Diameter	-	-	-	-	-/-	•	•	•	-	-	-	-	-

CONCLUSION

Nowadays, more resources are annotated via RDF due to its simple data model, formal semantics, and a sound and complete inference mechanism. RDF itself can be used as a query language for an RDF knowledge base. Nonetheless, the use of RDF as a query language is still limited for answering queries. In particular, answering those that contain complex relations requires complex constructs. It is impossible, for example, to answer the query "find the names and addresses, if they exist, of persons who either work on query languages or ontology matching" using an RDF graph patterns.

Therefore the need for added expressivity in queries has led to define several query languages on top of graph patterns that are basically RDF with variables. This chapter gave an overview of some languages that have been designed or can be used for querying RDF graphs, and discussed the main differences between them in terms of expressiveness and limitations.

As shown in this chapter through the use of examples, SPARQL allows for asking sophisticated queries. But many types of queries remain inexpressible. The development of the SPARQL recommendation has not prevented many extensions to be proposed, which are presented and compared in this chapter and may be integrated in a SPARQL recommendation update.

REFERENCES

Abiteboul, S. (1997). Querying semi-structured data. In *Proceeding of the 6th International Conference on Database Theory (ICDT) (*1186 of LNCS, pp 1-18). Springer-Verlag.

Abiteboul, S., Quass, D., McHugh, J., Widom, J., & Wiener, J. (1997). The Lorel query language for semistructured data. *Journal on Digital Libraries, 1*(1), 68–88.

Agrawal, R. (1988). Alpha: An extension of relational algebra to express a class of recursive queries. *IEEE Transactions on Software Engineering, 14*(7), 879–885. doi:10.1109/32.42731

Aho, A., & Ullman, J. (1979). Universality of data retrieval languages. In *Proceedings of the 6th ACM SIGACT-SIGPLAN Symposium on Principles of Programming Languages (POPL 1979),* New York, NY, USA (110–119). ACM.

Alechina, N., Demri, S., & de Rijke, M. (2003). A modal perspective on path constraints. *Journal of Logic and Computation, 13*, 1–18. doi:10.1093/logcom/13.6.939

Alkhateeb, F. (2007). Une extension de RDF avec des expressions régulières. In *Actes de 8e Rencontres Nationales des Jeunes Chercheurs en Inteligence Artificielle (RJCIA)* (pp. 1–14).

Alkhateeb, F. (2008). Querying RDF(S) with regular expressions. *Thèse d'informatique, Université Joseph Fourier*, Grenoble (FR), 2008.

Alkhateeb, F., Baget, J., & Euzenat, J. (2005). Complex path queries for RDF graphs. In *Poster Proceedings of the 4th International Semantic Web Conference (ISWC'05),* Galway (IE).

Alkhateeb, F., Baget, J., & Euzenat, J. (2008). Constrained regular expressions in SPARQL. In *Proceedings of the 2008 International Conference on Semantic Web and Web Services (SWWS'08)* (91–99).

Alkhateeb, F., Baget, J., & Euzenat, J. (2009). Extending SPARQL with regular expression patterns (for querying RDF). *Journal of Web Semantics, 7*(2), 57–73. doi:10.1016/j.websem.2009.02.002

Amann, B., & Scholl, M. (1992). Gram: A graph data model and query language. In *Proceedings of European Conference on Hypertext (ECHT) (*201–211).

Angles, R., & Gutiérrez, C. (1995). Querying RDF data from a graph database perspective. In *Proceedings of the European Semantic Web Conference (ESWC),* (pp. 346–360).

Angles, R., & Gutiérrez, C. (2008). Survey of graph database models. *ACM Computing Surveys, 40*(1), 1–39. doi:10.1145/1322432.1322433

Anyanwu, K., Maduko, A., & Sheth, A. (2007). SPARQ2L: Towards support for subgraph extraction queries in RDF databases. In *Proceedings of the 16th International Conference on World Wide Web (WWW'07)* (pp. 797–806).

Arenas, M., Gutierrez, C., & Pérez, J. (2008). An extension of SPARQL for RDFS. In *Post Proceedings of Joint SWDB and ODBIS Workshop on Semantic Web, Ontologies, Databases (SWDB-ODBIS'07)*, Vienna, Austria (LNCS, vol. 5005, pp. 1–2).

Baget, J. (2003). Homomorphismes d'hypergraphes pour la subsomption en RDF. In *Proceedings of the 3e Journées Nationales sur les Modèles de Raisonnement (JNMR)*, Paris, France (pp. 1–24).

Baget, J. (2005). RDF entailment as a graph homomorphism. In *Proceedings of the 4th International Semantic Web Conference (ISWC'05)*, Galway (IE) (pp. 82–96).

Beckett, D. (2004). RDF/XML syntax specification (revised). *W3C recommendation*, February 2004.

Beckett, D. (2006). *Turtle - terse RDF triple language. Technical report.* Bristol, UK: Hewlett-Packard.

Bray, T., Paoli, J., Sperberg-McQueen, C., Maler, E., & Yergeau, F. (2006). Extensible markup language (XML) 1.0. *Recommendation, W3C, August 2006*. Retrieved from http://www.w3.org/TR/REC-xml/.

Brickley, D., & Guha, R. (2004). RDF vocabulary description language 1.0: RDF schema. *W3C recommendation, 2004*. Retrieved from http://www.w3.org/TR/2004/REC-rdf-schema-20040210/.

Broekstra, J. (2003). SeRQL: Sesame RDF query language. In *SWAP Delivrable 3.2*. Method Design.

Buneman, P. (1997). Semistructured data. In *Tutorial in Proceedings of the 16th ACM Symposium on Principles of Database Systems* (pp. 117–121).

Buneman, P., Davidson, S., Hillebrand, G., & Suciu, D. (1996). A query language and optimization techniques for unstructured data. In *Proceedings of the ACM SIGMOD International Conference on the Management of Data* (pp. 505–516).

Buneman, P., Davidson, S., & Suciu, D. (1995). Programming constructs for unstructured data. In *Proceedings of the 1995 International Workshop on Database Programming Languages* (p. 12).

Carroll, J., & Klyne, G. (2004). *RDF concepts and abstract syntax. W3C recommendation, W3C*, February 2004.

Clark, J., & DeRose, S. (1999). XML path language (XPath). *W3C Recommendation*, 1999. Retrieved from http://www.w3.org/TR/xpath.

Codd, E. (1970). A relational model of data for large shared data banks. *Communications of the ACM, 13*(6), 377–387. doi:10.1145/362384.362685

Consens, M., & Mendelzon, A. (1990). Graphlog: A visual formalism for real life recursion. In *Proceedings of the 9th ACM SIGACT-SIGMOD-SIGART Symposium on Principles of Database Systems* (pp. 404–416).

Corby, O., Dieng-Kuntz, R., & Faron-Zucker, C. (2004). Querying the Semantic Web with Corese search engine. In *Proceedings of the 16th European Conference on Artificial Intelligence (ECAI'2004), sub-conference (PAIS'2004)*, Valencia, Spain (pp. 705–709).

Corby, O., & Faron-Zucker, C. (2007). RDF/SPARQL design pattern for contextual metadata. In *Proceedings of the IEEE/WIC/ACM International Conference on Web Intelligence (WI'07)*, Washington, DC, USA (pp. 470–473).

Corby, O., & Faron-Zucker, C. (2007a). Implementation of SPARQL query language based on graph homomorphism. In *Proceedings of the 15th International Conference on Conceptual Structure (ICCS'07)*, Sheffield, UK (pp. 472–475).

Cruz, I., Mendelzon, A., & Wood, P. (1987). A graphical query language supporting recursion. In *Proceedings of the 1987 ACM SIGMOD International Conference on Management of Data*, New York, NY, USA (pp. 323–330).

Cruz, I., Mendelzon, A., & Wood, P. (1987). G+: Recursive queries without recursion. In *Proceedings of 2ⁿᵈ International Conference on Expert Database Systems* (pp. 355–368).

Cyganiak, R. (2005). A relational algebra for SPARQL. *Technical Report HPL-2005-170, HP Labs, 2005*. Retrieved on http:// www. hpl. hp. Com / techreports/ 2005/ HPL-2005-170.html.

De Bruijn, J., Franconi, E., & Tessaris, S. (2005). Logical reconstruction of normative RDF. In *International Workshop on OWL: Experiences and Directions (OWLED 2005)*, Galway, Ireland.

Fernandez, M., Florescu, D., Levy, A., & Suciu, D. (1997). A query language for a Web-Site management system. *SIGMOD Record, 26*(3), 4–11. doi:10.1145/262762.262763

Franconi, E., & Tessaris, S. (2005). The semantics of SPARQL. *W3C working draft, November 2005*. Retrieved from http://www.inf.unibz.it/krdb/w3c/sparql/.

Genevès, P., Layaïda, N., & Schmitt, A. (2007). Efficient static analysis of XML paths and types. In *Proceedings of PLDI'07* (pp. 342–351).

Gting, R. (1994). GraphDB: Modeling and querying graphs in databases. In *Proceedings of 20th International Conference on Very Large Databases* (pp. 297–308).

Gutierrez, C., Hurtado, C., & Mendelzon, A. (2004). Foundations of Semantic Web databases. In *ACM Symposium on Principles of Database Systems (PODS)*, (pp. 95–106).

Gyssens, M., Paredaens, J., & Gucht, D. (1990). A graph-oriented object model for database end-user interfaces. *SIGMOD Record, 19*(2), 24–33. doi:10.1145/93605.93616

Haase, P., Broekstra, J., Eberhart, A., & Volz, R. (2004). A comparison of RDF query languages. In *Proceedings 3rd International Semantic Web Conference*, Hiroshima, Japan (pp. 502–517).

Harris, S., & Shadbolt, N. (2005). SPARQL query processing with conventional relational database systems. In *Web Information Systems Engineering (WISE'05 Workshops)* (235–244).

Hayes, J., & Gutierrez, C. (1996). Bipartite graphs as intermediate model for RDF. In *Proceedings of the 3th International Semantic Web Conference (ISWC)*, (pp. 47U"–61).

Hayes, P. (2004). *RDF semantics. W3C Recommendation*, February 2004.

Jagadish, H. (1989). Incorporating hierarchy in a relational model of data. In *Proceedings of the 1989 ACM SIGMOD International Conference on Management of Data*, Portland, Oregon (pp. 78-87. ACM Press. Karvounarakis, G., Alexaki, S., Christophides, V., Plexousakis, D., & Scholl, M. (2002). RQL: A declarative query language for RDF. In *Proceedings of the 11th International Conference on the World Wide Web (WWW2002)*.

Kerschberg, L., Klug, A., & Tsichritzis, D. (1976). A taxonomy of data models. In *Proceedings of Systems for Large Data Bases* (pp. 43–64). North Holland & IFIP.

Kiefer, C., Bernstein, A., Lee, H., Klein, M., & Stocker, M. (2007). Semantic process retrieval with iSPARQL. In *Proceedings of the 4th European Semantic Web Conference (ESWC '07)*. Springer, 2007.

Kiesel, N., Schurr, A., & Westfechtel, B. (1996). A graph oriented software engineering database system. In *IPSEN Book* (pp. 397–425). GRAS.

Kim, W. (1990). Object-oriented databases: Definition and research directions. *IEEE Transactions on Knowledge and Data Engineering, 2*(3), 327–341. doi:10.1109/69.60796

Kochut, K., & Janik, M. (2007). SPARQLeR: Extended SPARQL for semantic association discovery. In *Proceedings of 4th European Semantic Web Conference (ESWC'07)* (pp. 145–159).

Kunii, H. (1987). DBMS with graph data model for knowledge handling. In *Proceedings of the 1987 Fall Joint Computer Conference on Exploring technology: today and tomorrow*, Los Alamitos, CA, USA (pp. 138–142). IEEE Computer Society Press.

Kuper, G., & Vardi, M. (1993). The logical data model. *ACM Transactions on Database Systems, 18*(3), 379–413. doi:10.1145/155271.155274

Lassila, O. (2002). Taking the RDF model theory out for a spin. In *Proceedings of the 1st International Semantic Web Conference on The Semantic Web (ISWC 2002)*, London, UK (pp. 307–317). Springer-Verlag.

Lécluse, C., Richard, P., & Vélez, F. (2002). An object oriented data model. *SIGMOD Record, 17*(3), 424–433. doi:10.1145/971701.50253

Manola, F., & Miller, E. (2004). RDF primer. *W3C recommendation*, 2004. Retrieved from http://www.w3.org/TR/REC-rdf-syntax/.

Matono, A., Amagasa, T., Yoshikawa, M., & Uemura, S. (2005). A path-based relational RDF database. In *Proceedings of the 16th Australasian database conference (ADC'05)*, Darlinghurst, Australia (pp. 95–103). Australian Computer Society, Inc.

Mendelzon, A., Mihaila, G., & Milo, T. (1997). Querying the world wide web. *Int. J. on Digital Libraries, 1*(1), 54–67. Retrieved from citeseer.ist.psu.edu/mendelzon97querying.html.

Olson, M., & Ogbuji, U. (2002). *Versa: Path-based RDF query language*, 2002. http://copia.ogbuji.net/files/Versa.html.

Papakonstantinou, Y., Garcia-Molina, H., & Widom, J. (1995). Object exchange across heterogeneous information sources. In P. S. Yu & A. L. P. Chen (Eds.), *Proceedings of 11th Conference on Data Engineering*, Taipei, Taiwan (pp. 251–260). IEEE Computer Society.

Perez, J., Arenas, M., & Gutierrez, C. (2006). Semantics and complexity of SPARQL. In *Proceedings of the 5th International Semantic Web Conference*, Athens, Georgia (pps. 30–43).

Polleres, A. (2007). From SPARQL to rules (and back). In *Proceedings of the 16th World Wide Web Conference (WWW)* (pp. 787–796).

Polleres, A., Scharffe, F., & Schindlauer, R. (2007). SPARQL++ for mapping between RDF vocabularies. In *Proceedings of OTM Conferences* (pp. 878–896).

Prud'hommeaux, E., & Seaborne, A. (2008). *SPARQL query language for RDF. W3C Recommendation*, January 2008.

Seaborne, A. (2004). RDQL - *A query language for RDF. Member submission, W3C*, 2004.

Shipman, D. (1981). The functional data model and the data languages DAPLEX. [TODS]. *ACM Transactions on Database Systems, 6*(1), 140–173. doi:10.1145/319540.319561

Sirin, E., & Parsia, B. (2007). SPARQL-DL: SPARQL query for OWL-DL. In *Proceedings of the 3rd OWL Experiences and Directions Workshop (OWLED 2007)*.

Souzis, A. (2004). RxPath specification proposal. Retrieved from http://rx4rdf.liminalzone.org/RxPathSpec.

Ter Horst, H. (2005). Completeness, decidability and complexity of entailment for RDF schema and a semantic extension involving the OWL vocabulary. *Journal of Web Semantics, 3*(2), 79–115. doi:10.1016/j.websem.2005.06.001

Wood, P. (1988). *Queries on Graphs. PhD thesis, Department of Computer Science*, University of Toronto, 1988.

Zhang, X., & Yoshikawa, M. (2008). "DCBD-Query: Query language for RDF using dynamic concise bounded description". In *Proceedings of the Data Engineering Workshop (DEWS2008)*, 2008.

Chapter 16
On the Efficiency of Querying and Storing RDF Documents

Maria-Esther Vidal
Universidad Simón Bolívar, Venezuela

Amadís Martínez
Universidad Simón Bolívar & Universidad de Carabobo, Venezuela

Edna Ruckhaus
Universidad Simón Bolívar, Venezuela

Tomas Lampo
University of Maryland, USA

Javier Sierra
Universidad Simón Bolívar, Venezuela

ABSTRACT

In the context of the Semantic Web, different approaches have been defined to represent RDF documents, and the selected representation affects storage and time complexity of the RDF data recovery and query processing tasks. This chapter addresses the problem of efficiently querying and storing RDF documents, and presents an alternative representation of RDF data, Bhyper, which is based on hypergraphs. Additionally, access and optimization techniques to efficiently execute queries with low cost, are defined on top of this hypergraph based representation. The chapter's authors have empirically studied the performance of the Bhyper based techniques, and their experimental results show that the proposed hypergraph based formalization reduces the RDF data access time as well as the space needed to store the Bhyper structures, while the query execution time of state-the-of-art RDF engines can be sped up by up to two orders of magnitude.

DOI: 10.4018/978-1-61350-053-8.ch016

INTRODUCTION

Emerging infrastructures such as the Semantic Web, the Semantic Grid, Service Oriented architectures and the Cloud of Linked Data support on-line access to a wealth of ontologies, data sources and Web services. Ontologies play an important role in these infrastructures, and provide the basis for the definition of concepts and relationships that make the recovery and integration of Web data and resources possible. Particularly, in the context of the Cloud of Linked Data, a large number of diverse datasets have become available, and an exponential growth has occurred during the last years. In October 2007, datasets consisted of over 2 billion RDF triples, which were interlinked by over 2 million RDF links. By May 2009 this had grown to 4.2 billion RDF triples interlinked by around 142 million RDF links. At the time this chapter was written, there were 13,112,409,691 triples in the Cloud of Linked Data; datasets can be on medical publications, airport data, drugs, diseases, and clinical trials, among others.

Furthermore, the number of available Web services has rapidly increased during the last few years. For example, the molecular biology databases collection currently includes 1,078 databases (Galperin, 2008) which is 110 more than the previous year (Galperin, 2007). Tools and services as well as the number of instances published by these resources follow a similar progression (Benson, 2007). In addition, thanks to this wealth, users rely more on various digital tasks such as data retrieval from public data sources or from the Cloud of Linked Data, as well as data analysis with Web tools or services organized in complex workflows. Thus, Web architectures need to be tailored for the provision of efficient storage structures and the processing of large number of resources and instances, in order to scale up to user requests.

In the context of the Semantic Web, several query engines have been developed to access RDF documents efficiently (e.g., AllegroGraph; Harth

et al., 2007; Ianni et al., 2009; JENA; JENATDB; Neumann & Weikum, 2008; Wielemaker, 2005). The majority of these approaches have developed techniques to generate evaluation plans, and execution engines where these plans can be executed in a way that the processing time is reduced (e.g., AllegroGraph; Neumann & Weikum, 2008; Lampo et al., 2009; Vidal et al., 2010). Additionally, some of these approaches have implemented structures to efficiently store and access RDF data. Tuple Database or TDB (JENATDB) is a persistent graph storage layer for Jena. TDB works with the Jena SPARQL query engine (ARQ) to support SPARQL together with a number of extensions (e.g., property functions, aggregates, arbitrary length property paths).

YARS2 (Yet Another RDF Store, Version 2) (Harth et al., 2007) is a repository for queries against an indexed federation of RDF documents; three types of in-memory indices are used to scan keywords, perform atomic operations on RDF documents, and speed up combinations of patterns or values. RDF-3X (Neumann & Weikum, 2008) focuses on an index system, and its optimization techniques were developed to explore the space of plans that benefit from these index structures. Hexastore (Weiss et al., 2008) is a main memory indexing technique that uses the triple nature of RDF as an asset. RDF data is also indexed in six possible ways, one for each possible triple pattern permutation. Finally, secondary-memory index-based representations for large RDF datasets are presented in (e.g., Fletcher & Beck, 2009; McGlothlin & Khan, 2009; Weiss & Bernstein, 2009).

All these approaches may reduce the execution time of RDF queries; however, for some queries, the solution identified can be far from optimal. For instance, as we will show in this chapter, some queries can be reordered and grouped into small-sized star-shaped groups, and the execution time can be orders of magnitude less than the execution time of the original query. However, because these approaches are not tailored to identify this type of plans or to use their storage structure properties to exploit the benefits of these plans, the performance of these state-of-the-art RDF engines can be poor for this type of queries.

In this chapter, we address the problems of storing RDF documents and processing SPARQL queries, and describe an integrated engine that implements star-shaped based optimization and evaluation techniques (Lampo et al., 2009); we also have implemented the star-shaped operators in several of the above-mentioned state-of-the-art RDF engines. In all cases, we have observed that our proposed techniques are able to speed up query execution time by at least one order of magnitude. Initial results of these techniques have been already presented in (Martinez & Vidal, 2007; Lampo et al., 2009; Vidal et al., 2010).

The chapter is comprised of seven additional sections. Section 2 presents the definition of some of the concepts required to understand our approach and a motivating example; it also summarizes the existing state-of-the-art approaches to store and index RDF documents; additionally, existing optimization and evaluation techniques for SPARQL queries are presented in conjunction with an analysis of the advantages and limitations of each approach. Section 3 describes our index-based approach, named Bhyper. Then, we propose query optimization techniques that exploit the properties of Bhyper index structures, and are able to identify query execution plans where the number of intermediate results and evaluation time are minimized. Finally, we present an execution engine that offers a set of physical operators to efficiently evaluate query plans against the Bhyper structures. In Section 4, the quality and performance of the proposed techniques are empirically evaluated against state-of-the-art solutions. We report on the efficiency and effectiveness of Bhyper structures. Future directions of this research are described in Section 5, and the conclusions of our work are pointed out in Section 6. Finally, additional readings that may be of interest are presented in Section 7, and key terms and definitions are given in Section 8.

BACKGROUND

In this section we present the concepts required to understand the problems treated in this chapter. Then, we describe state-of-the-art approaches to store and index RDF documents, and existing optimization and evaluation techniques for SPARQL queries; for each approach, we outline its advantages and limitations.

Preliminaries

We developed the OneQL system which is based on a typical database management architecture as the one presented in Figure 1. This architecture is comprised of a Query Planner, an Execution engine, and an Ontology catalog (Ruckhaus et al., 2007).

Ontologies are modeled as a deductive database (DOB) which is composed of an extensional and an intensional database. The extensional database (EDB) is comprised of meta-level predicates that represent the information explicitly modeled by the ontology; for each ontology language built-in vocabulary term, there is a meta-level predicate (e.g., *subClassOf*). The intensional database (IDB) corresponds to the deductive rules that express the semantics of the vocabulary terms (e.g., the transitive properties of the *subClassOf* term). In the case of RDF documents, OneQL only maintains extensional predicates in the EDB.

Ontologies and statistics are stored in the Ontology catalog; statistics include for each RDF predicate, cardinality of different subjects and objects, as well as the number of different predicates. These statistics are used by the hybrid cost model to estimate the cost of a given query plan. A hypergraph-based structure named Bhyper is used to index RDF triples and to speed up the tasks of query processing.

Queries are described in SPARQL and posted to the system through a SPARQL-based API. Each query is translated into OneQL internal structures that keep information about the query joins and

Figure 1. The OneQL System Architecture

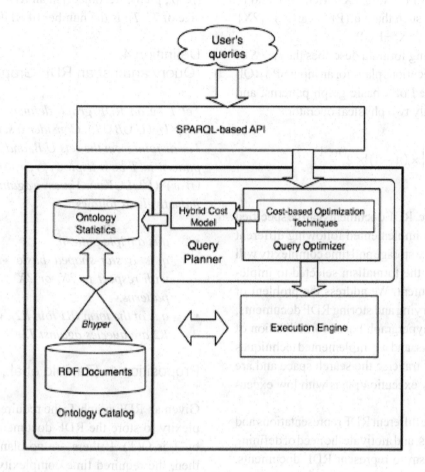

instantiations. This internal representation is then passed to the optimizer, which uses statistics stored in the catalog to identify an efficient query execution plan. Finally, the plan is given to the execution engine, which evaluates it against data stored in the catalog.

An execution plan is a reordering and grouping of the basic graph patterns in the input SPARQL query; physical operators are also assigned for each join. We consider two physical operators: *njoin* and *gjoin*. The former implements a classic index nested loop join; it scans the triples of the first pattern and loops on the second pattern for matching triples. The latter independently evaluates each *join* argument and then matches their results. Also, execution plans can be of any shape, and in this work we are particularly interested in

generating plans comprised of small-sized star-shaped groups (Vidal et al., 2010). Formally, we define a SPARQL triple pattern and a star-shaped basic graph pattern as follows:

Definition 1. (SPARQL Triple Pattern)

A Triple Pattern (or a basic graph pattern, respectively) is an RDF triple (or a set of RDF triples, resp.) where variables may occur in the subject, predicate or object position.

Definition 2.
(?X*−BGP (Vidal et al., 2010))

Each triple pattern {?X p o} or {s p?X} such that s ≠?X, p ≠?X, and o ≠?X is a Star-shaped basic graph pattern w.r.t. ?X, or ?X*−BGP. If P and P' are ?X*-BGPs such that var(P) ∩ var(P')={?X} then P∪ P' is an ?X*−BGP.

The following formula describes the size *S* of the space of executions plans for an input SPARQL query comprised of *n* basic graph patterns, and considering only two physical operators:

$$S = \binom{2(n-1)}{n-1} \times (n-1)! \times 2^{(n-1)}$$

Furthermore, RDF documents can be specified and eventually implemented following different formalisms. The storage and time complexity will be affected by the formalism selected to implement the document. We address the problem of efficiently querying and storing RDF documents; we defined a hypergraph based formalization of RDF documents, and we implemented techniques that efficiently traverse the search space and are able to identify execution plans with low execution cost.

We describe different RDF representations and their limitations, and motivate the need of defining a new formalism to represent RDF documents. First, an RDF document can be represented as a graph, where each node is a resource and each arc represents a property. Formally, an RDF graph is defined as follows (Gutiérrez et al., 2004): Suppose there is an infinite set *U* (URI references), an infinite set $B = \{b_j : j \in N\}$ (blank nodes), and an infinite set *L* (RDF literals). A triple $(s,p,o) \in (U \cup B) \times U \times (U \cup B \cup L)$ is called an RDF triple where, *s* represents a subject, *p* a predicate, and *o* an object.

Definition 3. (RDF Graph)

An RDF graph T is a set of RDF triples: T = {(s,p,o) ∈ (U ∪ B)×U×(U ∪ B∪ L)

The universe of an RDF graph *T*, *univ(T)*, is the set of elements of $U \cup B \cup L$ that occur in the triples of *T*. *sub(T)* (resp., *pred(T)*, *obj(T)*) is the set of all elements in *univ(T)* that occur as a subject

(resp., predicate, object) in an RDF graph *T*. The size of *T*, |*T*|, is the number of RDF triples in *T*.

Definition 4.
(Query against an RDF Graph)

Let T be an RDF graph defined on the set (U ∪B)×U×(U ∪B ∪ L). Consider a set of variables Var disjoint from the sets U,B, and L. Let a triple pattern in T be a triple $(v_1, v_2, v_3) \in (U \cup Var) \times (U \cup Var) \times (U \cup L \cup Var)$. A query q against T is defined inductively as follows:

- *q is a triple pattern.*
- *q is a star-shaped basic graph pattern with respect to ?X, or ?X*-BGP on triple patterns.*
- *q is of the form (R1 join R2), where R1 and R2 are queries against T.*[1]

Proposition 1. (Zaniolo et al., 1997)

Given an RDF graph T, the required space complexity to store the RDF document represented by T is O(T). If there are no blank nodes in T then, the required time complexity to answer a query Q against an RDF document represented by T is O(|T|^m) where m is the number of triple patterns in Q.

RDF graphs have been represented as: labeled directed graphs (Gutiérrez et al., 2004; Klyne & Carroll, 2004), undirected hypergraphs (Hayes, 2004), bipartite graphs (Hayes, 2004; Hayes & Gutiérrez, 2004), and directed hypergraphs (Martinez & Vidal, 2007).

In the labeled directed graph model, given an RDF graph *T*, the set of nodes *W* is comprised of elements in *sub(T)∪obj(T)*, and the set of arcs *E* is composed of elements in *pred(T)*. Thus, each RDF triple $(s,p,o) \in T$ is represented by a labeled arc, $s \xrightarrow{p} o$. The number of nodes and arcs for directed labeled graphs representing RDF graphs is $|W| \leq 2|T|$ and $|E|=|T|$. Thus, given an RDF graph T, the space complexity of the problem of storing an RDF document represented by T using this model is $O(|T|)$.

The representation of RDF documents as labeled directed graphs has two main drawbacks. First, a resource may simultaneously appear as a predicate, a subject and/or an object in the same RDF graph. This situation can be modeled by allowing multiple occurrences of the same resource in the resulting labeled directed graph, as arc or node labels. However, this assumption compromises one of the most important properties of graph theory: the intersection between the node and arc labels must be empty. Second, a predicate may relate to other predicates in an RDF graph. This situation can be modeled by extending the notion of arc, allowing connections between arcs. However, the resulting structure is not a graph in the strict mathematical sense, because the set of arcs must be a subset of the Cartesian product of the set of nodes. Since these two simple situations violate some graph constraints, it is not possible to use concepts and search algorithms of graph theory to manipulate RDF graphs. Thus, while the labeled directed graph model is the most widely used representation, it cannot be considered a formal model for RDF (Dau, 2006a).

In the undirected hypergraph model, given an RDF graph T, each RDF triple $t=(s,p,o)T$ is a hyperarc and each element of t (subject s, predicate p, and object o) is a node. The number of nodes and hyperarcs for undirected hypergraphs representing RDF graphs is $|W|=|univ(T)|$ and $|E|=|T|$. Thus, given an RDF graph T, the required space complexity to store the RDF document represented by T using this model is $O(\max(|univ(T)|, |T|))$. However, this representation does not respect the concept of direction in RDF graphs, which is necessary to accomplish the tasks of query answering and semantic reasoning. Additionally, it may not be easy to graphically visualize large RDF graphs.

In the bipartite graph model, given an RDF graph T, there are two types of nodes in W: state-

ment nodes S_t (one for each RDF triple $(s,p,o) \in T$) and value nodes Va; (one for each element $w \in univ(T)$). Arcs in E relate statement and value nodes as follows: each $t \in S_t$ has three out-coming arcs that point to the corresponding node for the subject, predicate, or object of the RDF triple represented by the statement node t. The number of nodes and arcs of bipartite graphs representing RDF graphs is $|S_t|=|T|$, $|VAL|=|Univ(T)|$, and $|E|=3|T|$. Thus, given an RDF graph T, the required space complexity to store the RDF document represented by T using this model is $O(\max(|univ(T)|, |T|))$. While bipartite graphs satisfy the requirement of a formal graph representation for RDF, issues such as query answering have not been addressed yet.

To overcome the above-mentioned drawbacks, we propose a hypergraph representation of RDF documents, and optimization and evaluation techniques to exploit the properties of this representation.

Related Work

In the context of the Semantic Web, several query engines have been developed to access RDF documents efficiently (e.g., AllegroGraph; Harth et al., 2007; Ianni et al., 2009; JENA; JENATDB; Neumann & Weikum, 2008; Wielemaker, 2005). Jena (JENA; Wilkinson et al., 2003) provides a programmatic environment for SPARQL, and it includes the ARQ query engine and indices, which provide an efficient access to large datasets. Tuple Database or TDB (JENATDB) is a persistent graph storage layer for Jena. TDB works with the Jena SPARQL query engine (ARQ) to support SPARQL together with a number of extensions (e.g., property functions, aggregates, arbitrary length property paths). Sesame (Wielemaker, 2005) is an open source Java framework for storage and querying RDF data. It supports SPARQL and SeRQL queries, which are translated to Prolog.

YARS2 (Harth et al., 2007) is a federated repository for queries against indexed RDF documents. YARS2 supports three types of indices that enable keyword lookups, perform atomic lookup operations on RDF documents, and speed up combinations of patterns or values. Indices are implemented by using an in-memory sparse index data structure that refers to on-disk block entries which contain the indexed entry; six combinations of triple patterns are indexed. A general query processor on top of a distributed Index Manager was implemented, and SPARQL queries are supported.

RDF-3X (Neumann & Weikum, 2008) focuses on an index system, and its optimization techniques were developed to explore the space of plans that benefit from these index structures. The RDF-3X query optimizer implements a dynamic programming-based algorithm for plan enumeration, which imposes restrictions on the size of queries that can be optimized and evaluated. AllegroGraph (AllegroGraph) uses a native object store for on-disk binary tree-based storage of RDF triples. AllegroGraph also maintains six indices to manage all the possible permutations of subject (s), predicate (p) and object (o). The standard indexing strategy is to build indices whenever there are more than a certain number of triples. The query optimizer is based on *join* ordering for the generation of execution plans; no bushy plans are generated.

Hexastore (Weiss et al., 2008) is a main memory indexing technique that exploits the role of the arguments of an RDF triple. Six indices were designed so that each one could efficiently retrieve a different access pattern; thus, each possible ordering and combination of the subject, property and object is materialized in different indices. A dictionary to encode URI's and literal values and a mapping function that relates the resource values to the identifiers are maintained. Although the index schema proposed by Hexastore is able to speed up typical query operators, the prime drawback of Hexastore lies in storage space usage. It may require a five-fold increase in storage space compared to a triple table; also, the same resource can appear in multiple indices depending of the

role played by the resource in the stored triple. A secondary-memory-based solution for Hexastore has been presented in (Weiss & Bernstein, 2009); this solution scales up to larger datasets, however, this persistent version still suffers of the main disadvantages of the main-memory version.

Furthermore, two additional secondary-memory index-based representations and evaluation techniques are presented in (Fletcher & Beck, 2009; McGlothlin & Khan, 2009). Fletcher et al. (Fletcher & Beck, 2009) propose indexing the universe of RDF resource identifiers, regardless of the role played by the resource; although they are able to reduce the storage costs of RDF documents, since the proposed *join* implementations are not closed, the properties of the index-based structures can only be exploited in *join*s on basic graph patterns.

In contrast, MacGlothlin et al. (McGlothlin, 2010) propose an index-based representation for RDF documents that materializes the results for subject-subject *join*s, object-object *join*s and subject-object *join*s. This approach has been implemented on top of MonetDB (Idreos et al., 2009) and it can exploit the MonetDB cache management system. MonetDB and C-store (Stonebraker et al., 2005) are column oriented relational database management systems able to achieve high performance on complex queries. These column oriented databases are partitioned into one or more indexed groups according to the column values, and *join* indices are built on top of group indices to speed up query processing time. Although these structures can speed up the performance of *join*s, this solution may not scale up to very large strongly connected RDF graphs or complex SPARQL queries.

Abadi et al. (Abadi et al., 2007, 2009) and Sidirourgos et al. (Sidirourgos et al., 2008) propose different RDF store schemas to implement an RDF management system on top of a relational database system. They empirically show that a physical implementation of vertically partitioned

RDF tables, may outperform the traditional physical schema of RDF tables.

Recently, Atre et al. (Atre et al., 2010) proposed the BitMat approach, which is supported on a fully inverted index structure that implements a compressed bit-matrix structure of the RDF data. An RDF engine has been developed on top of this bit-based structure, which exploits its properties and avoids the storage of intermediate results generated during query evaluation. Although BitMat does not use cache techniques, it has been shown that thanks to the BitMat structures, its performance is competitive with existing RDF engines that provide an efficient cache management. Similarly to some of the existing state-of-the-art RDF systems, the optimization and evaluation techniques are not tailored to the storage data structures; thus, optimizers may not be able to identify optimal plans, or the execution engine may not exploit all the properties of the physical structures.

Finally, Nguyen et al. (Nguyen et al., 2010) propose a hybrid structure named B+Hash that combines the benefits of the B+tree and the Hash Map structures; this combination supports range queries in logarithmic time as well as key-based queries in constant-time. Additionally, HypergraphDB is a database for storing hypergraphs. It is built on top of Berkeley DB where large size hypergraphs can be managed. Both B+Hash trees and HypergraphDB[2] provide the basis to implement Bhyper; in the future we plan to develop Bhyper on top of these two platforms and compare their performance with the Bhyper implementations reported in this chapter.

RDF BASED STORAGE AND QUERY EVALUATION

In this section we present our proposed approach. First, we motivate the problem of efficiently evaluating SPARQL queries in large datasets. Then, we describe our index-based approach named Bhyper.

Next, we present query optimization techniques that exploit the properties of Bhyper index structures, and are able to identify query execution plans where the number of intermediate results and evaluation time are minimized. Finally, we describe an execution engine that offers a set of physical operators to efficiently evaluate the query plans against the Bhyper structures.

Motivating Example

Consider the dataset that publishes the US Congress bills voting process[3]. Suppose the following instances are available: $D_1 = \{(:id0, type, Term), (:id0, forOffice, AZ), (AZ, type, Office), (Office, subClassOf, Organization), (Country, subClassOf, Organization), (forOffice, range, Organization), (forOffice, domain, Term)\}$, where the resource *forOffice* occurs as a predicate and a subject. This situation can be modeled by allowing multiple occurrences of the same resource in the resulting labeled directed graph, as arcs or nodes labels (Figure 2). However, the intersection between the node and arc labels is not empty and this structure cannot be formally considered a graph.

Second, a predicate may be related to other predicates in an RDF document. For example, in the RDF document $D_2 = \{(Rush, sponsor, HR45), (:id1, supported, SJ37), (sponsor, subPropertyOf, supported)\}$ the predicate *subPropertyOf* connects the predicates sponsor and supported. This situation can be modeled extending the notion of arc, allowing a connection between arcs (Figure 3). However, the set of arcs is not a subset of the Cartesian product of the set of nodes and again this structure cannot be formally considered a graph. In both cases, the definition of a graph is not completely respected. Thus, while the labeled directed graph model is the most widely used representation, it cannot be considered a formal model for RDF (Dau, 2006b). Our proposed hypergraph-based model, named Bhyper, overcomes these limitations.

Figure 2. RDF Graph Representation-Multiple occurrences of the same resource

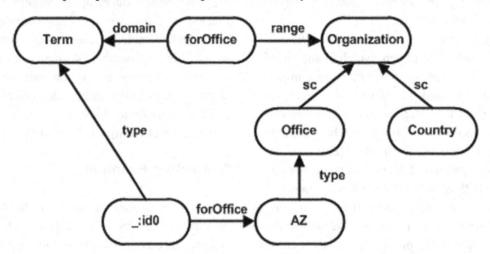

Given an RDF document *D*, each node corresponds to an element $w \in univ(D)$. Thus, the information is only stored in the nodes, and the hyperarcs only preserve the role of each node and the concept of direction of RDF graphs. An advantage of this representation is that each resource (subject, property, or value) is stored only once, and the space required to store an RDF document is reduced if a resource appears multiple times in the document. In this way, the space complexity of our approach is lower than the complexity of the graph-based RDF representation. Besides, concepts, techniques, and algorithms of hyper-graph theory can be used to manipulate RDF documents more efficiently. Additionally, Bhyper is implemented on top of Tokyo Cabinet[4], taking advantage of all the provided physical structures and operators.

Furthermore, to motivate the need of developing evaluation and optimization techniques that exploit the shape of execution plans and the Bhyper structures, consider the following query against the dataset of the US Congress bills voting process: *Select all the bills and their title where "Nay" was the winner, and at least one voter voted for the same option as the voter L000174.*

Figure 3. RDF Graph Representation-Extending Arc Definition

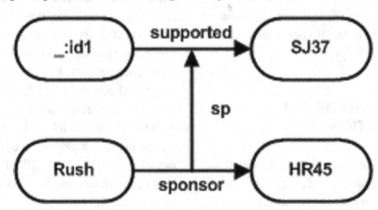

```
PREFIX vote: <tag:govshare.
info,2005:rdf/vote/>
PREFIX dc: <http://purl.org/dc/
elements/1.1/>
PREFIX people: <http://www.rdfabout.
com/rdf/usgov/congress/people/>
SELECT ?E ?T FROM <http://example.
org/votes>
WHERE {?E vote:winner 'Nay' .
    ?E dc:title ?T . ?E
    vote:hasBallot ?I .
    ?I vote:option ?X .?J vote:
    option ?X .
    E vote:hasBallot ?J .
    ?J vote:voter 'people:
    L000174'}
```

To evaluate this query, in addition to deciding the physical operators that need to be used, reorderings and groupings of the query triple patterns have to be generated. For example, if the former left linear plan is run in RDF-3X, its evaluation time is 8,466.0 secs.

On the other hand, consider the following plan where the triple patterns are grouped and reordered according to small-sized star-shaped groups, and the operator *gjoin* is used to evaluate the *join* operator between groups. This plan can be executed in 122.0 secs in GRDF-3X[5], i.e., one order of magnitude cheaper than the left linear plan.

```
PREFIX vote: <tag:govshare.
info,2005:rdf/vote/>
PREFIX dc: <http://purl.org/dc/
elements/1.1/>
PREFIX people: <http://www.rdfabout.
com/rdf/usgov/congress/people/>
SELECT ?E ?T FROM <http://example.
org/votes>
WHERE {
    {?E vote:winner 'Nay' . ?E
    vote:hasBallot ?J .
    ?E dc:title ?T . ?E vote:
    hasBallot ?I} gjoin
```

```
{?J vote:voter 'people:
L000174'.
?J vote:option ?X .?I vote:
option ?X }}
```

The majority of state-of-the-art optimization techniques are only able to generate left linear plans whose cost can be far from optimal. In contrast, our proposed techniques can identify plans whose cost is close to the optimal if the list of triple patterns of the query can be decomposed into small-sized star-shaped groups.

Bhyper: A Hypergraph-Based Representation for RDF Documents

In RDF documents, a resource can play the role of a subject, predicate or value in a large number of triples. A data structure that exploits this property can positively impact on the amount of RDF document storage space as well as on the query evaluation time. We propose the Bhyper directed hypergraph-based data structure to represent RDF documents. In Bhyper, RDF triples are implemented as nodes, while hyperarcs correspond to sets of triples, from which roles played by a resource can be extracted; six complementary index structures, inspired on the Hexastore indexing approach, are used to provide direct access to the nodes and the hyperarcs. These indices exhaustively link the RDF-triples and all their combinations (pairs and single values).

Basically, a directed hypergraph is defined by a set of nodes and a set of hyperarcs, each one of them maps a set of source nodes (named tail of the hyperarc) to a set of target nodes (named head of the hyperarc). Directed hypergraphs have been successfully used as a tool to represent concepts and structures in different areas: formal languages, relational databases, production and manufacturing systems, public transportation systems, topic maps, among others (e.g., Auillans et al., 2002; Gallo et al., 2003; Gallo & Scutella, 1999). An RDF directed hypergraph is defined as follows:

Definition 5. (RDF Hypergraph)

Let D be an RDF document. We define a Bhyper RDF representation of D, as a tuple H(D)=(W,E,ρ), such that:

- $W=\{w:w \in D\}$ *is the set of nodes.*
- $E=\{e_i:1\le i{\le}|D|\}$ *is the set of hyperarcs, each hyperarc is a set of triples. For each resource $r \in$ univ(D) there is a hyperarc.*
- $\rho : univ(D) \times E \rightarrow \{'s','p','o'\}$ *is the role function of resources with respect to hyperarcs. Let $t \in D$ be an RDF triple, $e \in E$ a hyperarc, and $r \in$ univ(D) a resource. Then the following must hold:*
  - $(\rho(r,e) = 's') \Leftrightarrow (t \in e) \land (r \in subject(\{t\}))$
  - $(\rho(r,e) = 'p') \Leftrightarrow (t \in e) \land (r \in predicate(\{t\}))$
  - $(\rho(r,e) = 'o') \Leftrightarrow (t \in e) \land (r \in object(\{t\}))$

Given a document D we construct a Bhyper RDF for D as follows: initially for each triple t in D a hyperarc is created. However, if there are two triples t_1 and t_2 such that there is an element a that appears in both triples as subject, property

or object, we merge the corresponding hyperarcs. Merges are performed until all the triples that share the same subject, property or object are in the same hyperarc. Inside a hyperarc, triples that share the same subject are grouped together; similarly, the triples that share the same property and the same object. Thus, all the triples where a particular element appears, are stored in the same hyperarc; thus there will be as many hyperarcs as resources in an RDF document. Note that a triple may appear in several hyperarcs.

Figures 4 and 5 show the RDF directed hypergraphs representing RDF documents D_1 and D_2, respectively. In Bhyper, given an RDF document D, each node corresponds to triple $w \in D$, and the resources in *univ(D)* are encoded. Thus, resources that appear in a triple, are represented by their corresponding identifiers in the hyperarcs. An advantage of this representation is that each resource (subject, property, or value) is stored only once, and the space required to store an RDF document is reduced if a resource appears several times in the document. In this way, the space complexity

Figure 4. Hypergraph Representation Document D_1

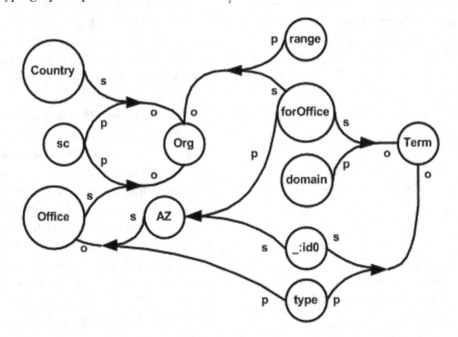

of our approach is lower than the complexity of the graph-based RDF representation.

Bhyper has been implemented in main and secondary-memory. First, we provided a naive main-memory implementation in Prolog in the OneQL system previously described; then, we also implemented a main-memory solution in C++; finally, we exploited the benefits of the Tokyo Cabinet library to provide a more complete and scalable secondary-memory approach.

OneQL Bhyper Implementation

Given a hypergraph $H(D)=(W,E,\rho)$, the OneQL Prolog implementation of Bhyper is based on the following predicates:

- *resources(ID,r)*: for each resource $r \in univ(D)$.
- *subject(sID,LPO)* iff $\rho(sID,e) = 's'$ and $LPO=\{(pID,oID)|(sID,pID,oID) \in e\}$. The predicate *subject* associates a resource identifier *sID* with the list of pairs *(pID,oID)* where it appears as a subject.

- *object(oID,LSP)* iff $\rho(oID,e) = 'o'$ and $LSP=\{(pID,oID)|(sID,pID,oID) \in e\}$. The predicate *object* maps an object value *oID* with the list of pairs *(sID,pID)* where it appears as an object.
- *property(pID,LSO)* iff $\rho(pID,e) = 'p'$ and $LSO=\{(sID,oID)|(sID,pID,oID) \in e\}$. The predicate *property* maps a resource identifier property value *pID* with the list of pairs *(sID,oID)* where it appears as a property. Prolog predicates *subject*, *object* and *property* are indexed on the first argument. Given a resource $r \in univ(D)$ with identifier *id(r)* such that *subject(id(r),LPO)*, *object(id(r),LSP)* and *property (id(r),LSO)*, the hyperarc associated with *r* is comprised of LPO_r, LSP_r and LSO_r.

Bhyper Main-Memory Implementation

In the second in-memory implementation we also adopted the approach of replacing all terms in the document vocabulary by unique identifiers (*ids*) using a mapping dictionary. Thus, we define

Figure 5. Hypergraph Representation Document D₂

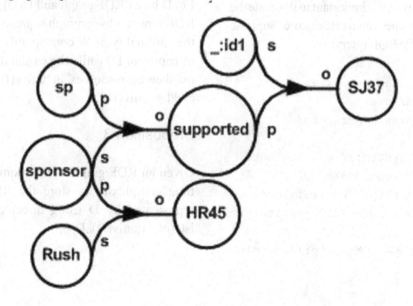

two index dictionaries: the *resourceToID* and the *idToResource*. The former maps terms to their *ids*, and the latter maps *ids* to their terms. Based on this encoding, each RDF triple *t = (s, p, o)* is also represented as *r=(id(s),id(p),id(o))*. Thus, given a hypergraph *H(D)=(W,E,ρ)*, we have defined the following main-memory structures:

- *resourceToID: univ(D)→idSet* and *idToResoure: idSet→univ(D)* where *idSet* is a set of identifiers for the resources in *D*.
- A hash function *Hyperarcs(id(r))* $= \langle (subject, LS), (property, LP), (object, LO) \rangle$, where for each $r \in univ(D)$, there exists $e \in E$, such that $LS \cup LP \cup LO = e$.
- A hash function *subject(sID)=LPO* iff $\rho(sID, e) = {}'s{}'$ and $LPO=\{(pID,oID)|(sID,pID,oID) \in e\}$.
- A hash function *property(pID)=LSO* iff $\rho(pID, e) = {}'p{}'$ and $LSO=\{(sID,oID)|(sID,pID,oID) \in e\}..$
- A hash function *object(oID)=LSP* iff $\rho(oID, e) = {}'o{}'$ and $LSP=\{(sID,pID)|(sID,pID,oID) \in e\}..$

The hash functions resemble the access patterns provided by Hexastore (Weiss et al., 2008); each one of them materializes an access pattern over the hyperarcs. However, it is important to illustrate the advantages of Bhyper versus Hexastore. Suppose the following SPARQL query:

```
PREFIX vote: <tag:govshare.
info,2005:rdf/vote/>
PREFIX dc: <http://purl.org/dc/
elements/1.1/>
PREFIX people:<http://www.rdfabout.
com/rdf/usgov/congress/people/>
PREFIX votes:<http://www.rdfabout.
com/rdf/usgov/congress/108/senate/
votes/>
SELECT ?A ?B ?C FROM <http://example.
org/votes>
```

```
WHERE {
?A vote:voter <http://www.rdfabout.
com/rdf/usgov/congress/people/
L000174>.
?A vote:option ?B . ?A vote:hasBallot
?C }
```

To execute the former query using Hexastore, first, the instantiations of ?A should be recovered by using the index PO; then, for each retrieved value of ?A, the index SP should be accessed to retrieve the instantiations of ?B, and the index PO to retrieve the instantiations of ?C. In contrast, by using Bhyper, once the instantiations of ?A are found, the corresponding hyperarcs will be accessed to recover the instantiations of ?B and ?C. Thus, in addition to consuming less space, Bhyper execution time is also reduced. In Bhyper, the hyperarcs structure will be accessed a number of times equal to the number of instantiations of ?A plus one; in Hexastore, the PO index will be accessed once, and the SP index accesses will be twice the number of instantiations of ?A.

This main-memory Bhyper implementation has the following space and time complexity:

Proposition 2

Let D be an RDF graph and H(D)=(W,E,ρ)be an RDF directed hypergraph representing D. Then, the cardinality of W corresponds to the number of triples in D, while the cardinality of E is the number of resources in unive(D), i.e.,|W|=|D| and|E|=|univ(D)|.

Proposition 3

Given an RDF graph D, the required space and time complexity to store the RDF document represented by D using directed hypergraphs isO(max(|univ(D)|,D|))..

Bhyper Secondary-Memory Implementation

Finally, the Bhyper secondary-memory approach maintains the mapping dictionaries and the set of hyperarcs in indexed file structures. Mapping dictionaries, their indices, and the set of nodes and hyperarcs are implemented as hash-files, and B+-tree structures implement the hash functions induced by the ρ function. Thus, given a hypergraph $H(D)=(W,E,\rho)$, we have defined the following main-memory structures:

- **DICTIONARY** is a hash file with an entry for each resource in *univ(D)* and its corresponding identifier.
- **NODES** is a hash file with an entry for each $w \in W$.
- **HYPERARCS** is a hash file with an entry in *univ(D)*, i.e., entries in **HYPERARCS** are the identifiers of the resources in D and the range corresponds to the set of hyperarcs in the hypergraph $H(D)=(W,E,\rho)$. Thus, **HYPERARCS**$(id(r))= \langle (subject, LS), (property, LP), (object, LO) \rangle$ where for each $r \in univ(D)$, there exists $e \in E$, such that $LS \cup LP \cup LO = e$.
- **subject**: a B+-tree defined on the access key (sID) in a way that an entry in a leaf of subject is a pair (sID, LPO) iff $\rho(sID, e) = 's'$ and $LPO = \{(pID, oID) | (sID, pID, oID) \in e\}..$
- **property**: a B+-tree defined on the access key (pID) in a way that an entry in a leaf of property is a pair (pID, LSO) iff $\rho(pID, e) = 'p'$ and $LSO = \{(sID, oID) | (sID, pID, oID) \in e\}.$
- **object**: a B+-tree defined on the access key (oID) in a way that an entry in a leaf of object is a pair (oID, LSP) iff $\rho(oID, e) = 'o'$ and $LSP = \{(sID, pID) | (sID, pID, oID) \in .$

Hash based implementations of HYPERARCS and NODES support a direct access to the data and provide a constant-time solution to key based queries. On the other hand, indices property, subject, and object provide a logarithmic solution to range queries.

The following example illustrates the Bhyper approach in secondary-memory. Consider the following RDF document:

```
_:id0 <type> <Term>
_:id0 <forOffice> <AZ>
<AZ> <type> <Office>
<Office> <subClassOf> <Organization>
<Country> <subClassOf> <Organization>
<forOffice> <range> <Organization>
<forOffice> <domain> <Term>
<Rush> <sponsor> "HR45"
_:id1 <supported> "SJ37"
<sponsor> <subPropertyOf> <supported>
```

Figure 6 shows the hyperarcs for the resources: *forOffice, _:id0, AZ* and *Office*; note that all the triples where a given resource participates, are stored in the same hyperarc, and two hyperarcs intersect if they share at least one triple. Figure 7 presents the Bhyper secondary-memory structures and indices that are created. The structures **DICTIONARY** and **HYPERARCS** store the resources and hyperarcs, respectively. For each resource, there exists a hyperarc, and the role played by it in each triple of the hyperarc, is explicitly represented; thus, the resource is not repeated multiple times. Hash-based structures index these two structures, and three B+-trees index the table **HYPERARCS**.

Optimizing and Evaluating SPARQL queries

We have implemented query optimization and execution techniques to support the evaluation of SPARQL queries and to exploit the properties of the Bhyper structures.

Figure 6. Hyperarcs for RDF Triples

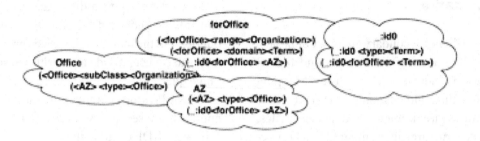

The proposed optimization techniques are based on a cost model that estimates the execution time or intermediate RDF triples generated during query evaluation; they are able to produce query plans of any shape. The execution engine is supported by physical operators that efficiently execute bushy plans.

The Query Optimizer (Lampo et al., 2009) is built on top of the following two sub-components (Ruckhaus et al., 2006, 2007, 2008; Vidal et al.,

2010): (a) a hybrid cost model that estimates the cardinality and evaluation cost of execution plans, (b) optimization strategies to identify bushy plans.

Execution Query Engine

The query execution engine implements different strategies (operators) used to retrieve and combine intermediate generated RDF triples. We have defined different operators and make use of

Figure 7. Bhyper Secondary-Memory Structures and Indices

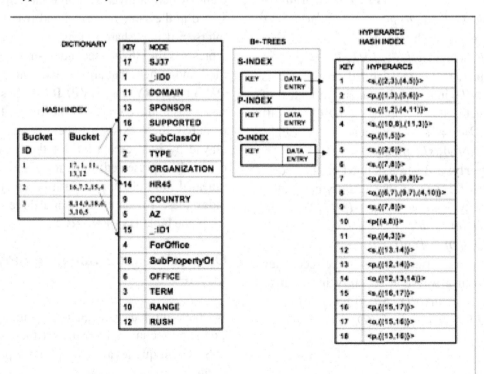

the recovery techniques provided by the Bhyper-based structures:

Star-Shaped Groups (*starScan*): the main idea of this operator is to evaluate the first pattern in the star-shaped group and identify the bindings/instantiations of the shared variable. These instantiations are used to retrieve the corresponding hyperarc from where all the instantiations of the rest of the triple patterns will be recovered. Figure 8 illustrates the behavior of the *starScan* operator. Note that for each instantiation of the first triple of the group, the corresponding hyperarc is recovered to retrieve the instantiations of the rest of the triples in the group. The *starScan* operator requires one access to the RDF data to recover the instantiations of the first triple, and for each of the recovered instantiations, one access to the hyperarcs. Thus, if the first triple is very selective, the *starScan* can be very efficient. If we assume that a resource appears in a number of triples that require *t* pages and *#Instantiations* is the number of valid instantiations of the *join* variable in the group then, the time complexity of the *starScan* is:

$$Cost_{starScan} = (1+t) + \#Ins\tan tiations \times (1+t)$$

Index Nested-Loop Join (*njoin*): For each matching triple in the first pattern, we retrieve the matching triples in the second pattern, i.e., the *join* arguments[6] are instantiated in the second pattern through the sideways passing of variable bindings. Similarly to the starScan operator, Bhyper hyperarcs are used to access the instantiations of the inner patterns of the *join* operator, i.e., instantiations of the rest of the joined patterns are recovered from the hyperarcs. The time complexity of R1 *njoin* R2 is:

$$Cost_{njoin}(R1,R2) = Cost(R1) + \#Ins\tan tiations \times (1+t)$$

The first term of the formula represents the cost of evaluating the outer argument of the *join*

operator. The second term counts the cost of retrieving the hyperarc bucket of each particular instantiation and the t pages where the triples of the hyperarc are stored.

Group Join (*gjoin*): The main idea of this operator is to partition the patterns that appear in the 'WHERE' clause of a query into groups that are comprised of triple patterns whose evaluation is small-sized. Given two groups *R1* and *R2*, each of them is independently evaluated, and the results are combined into a hash table to identify the compatible mappings. If answers of *R1* and *R2* are small-sized, no disk access will be required to identify the compatible mappings, and the cost will be reduced to the cost of executing R1 and R2. The time complexity of *R1 gjoin R2* is:

$$Cost_{gjoin}(R1,R2) = Cost(R1) + Cost(R2) + 2 \times (Card(R1) + Card(R2))$$

We have implemented these three operators on top of all the Bhyper versions that we have developed; additionally, we implemented the *njoin* and *gjoin* on top of other state-of-the-art RDF engines like Jena and RDF-3X (Vidal et al., 2010). The physical implementations of *njoin* and *gjoin* in Bhyper main-memory are closed, i.e., the result of evaluating these operators over two hypergraphs is also a hypergraph indexed by all the indices that we previously defined. This property allows us to implement an efficient RDF query engine, as we will show in the experimental results.

Star-Shaped Group Optimization Techniques

The implemented query optimization techniques able to identify query execution plans where the execution cost is minimized. This optimization problem is a combinatorial problem formally defined as follows.

Figure 8. starScan for the group {?X1 <forOffice><AZ>. ?X1 <type> ?Y. ?X1 <supported> ?Z}

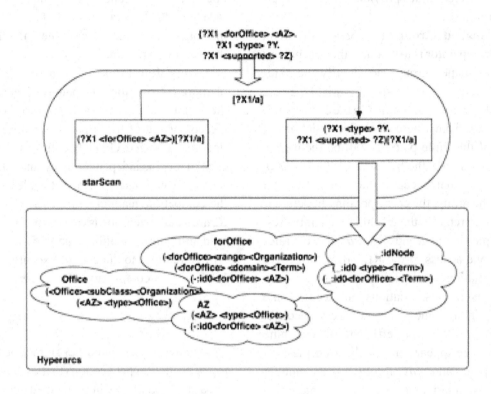

Definition 6. (Query Optimization Problem)

Given an RDF document D and an SPARQL query Q. The Query Optimization Problem is represented by a tuple (H(D),S,cost), where:

- $H(D)=(W,E,\rho)$ is the Bhyper RDF representation of D,
- $S=\{p: p$ is an execution plan for Q$\}$,
- cost: $S\rightarrow R$, where cost(p) maps the plan p to the estimate of the number of intermediate triples generated during the execution of p.

And, the **Query Optimization Problem** corresponds to identifying an execution plan *p* for *Q*, such that, the *cost(p)* is minimized.

To solve this combinatorial problem, dynamic-based or randomized algorithms are applied to identify a good ordering or grouping of the input SPARQL query patterns. On one hand, the dynamic-programming algorithm works on iterations, and during each iteration the best intermediate sub-plans are chosen based on the cost and the cardinality that were estimated by the hybrid cost model. In the last iteration of the algorithm, final plans are constructed and the best plan is selected in terms of the estimated cost. This optimal ordering corresponds to the plan among the set of generated plans that minimizes the estimate of the number of intermediate triples. The dynamic-programming algorithm is used in queries where the number of triple patterns is not large.

On the other hand, the randomized algorithm performs random walks over the search space of bushy execution plans. The query optimizer implements a *Simulated Annealing* algorithm.

Random walks are performed in stages, where each stage consists of an initial *plan generation step* followed by one or more *plan transformation steps*. An equilibrium condition or a number of iterations determines the number of transformation steps. At the beginning of each stage, a query execution plan is randomly created in the plan generation step. Then, successive *plan transformations* are applied to the query execution plan during the plan transformation steps, in order to obtain new plans.

The probability of transforming a current plan *p* into a new plan *p'* is specified by an acceptance probability function $P(p, p', T)$, that depends on a global time-varying parameter *T* called the temperature, which reflects the number of stages to be executed.

The function P may be non-zero when $\cos t(p') > \cos t(p)$, meaning that the optimizer can produce a new plan even when it is worse than the current one, i.e., it has a higher cost. This feature prevents the optimizer from becoming stuck in a local minimum. Temperature *T* is decreased during each stage and the optimizer concludes when *T*=0. Transformations applied to the plan during the random walks correspond to the SPARQL axioms of the physical operators implemented by the query and reasoning engine (Vidal et al., 2010). The Simulated Annealing-based optimizer scales up to queries of any shape and number of triple patterns, and is able to produce execution plans of any shape comprised of small-sized star-shaped groups.

A Hybrid Cost Model

To estimate the cost of a plan *p*, we defined a hybrid cost model, where evaluation cost is measured in terms of the number of intermediate RDF triples generated during the execution of *p*, and the cardinality corresponds to the number of valid answers of *p*. This model is described as follows:

- To estimate the cardinality and cost of star-shaped groups of a SPARQL query

against an RDF document, we applied the *Adaptive Sampling* Technique (Lipton & Naughton, 1990). This method executes samples of each star-shaped group where its variables are instantiated to constants. Then, the method estimates the cost and cardinality of a star-shaped group as the average of the cardinality and cost of the executed instantiations of this group. The instantiations are randomly sampled without replacement from a set of values taken from the RDF document or population. The number of samples or sampling stop conditions are defined to ensure that the estimates are within a predetermined accuracy and confidence level.

- To estimate the cardinality and cost of a plan comprised of several star-shaped groups, we use a cost model à la System R (Selingerl et al., 1979). Similarly to System R, we store for each RDF predicate *pr*, the number of different subjects *s* and objects *o*, such that the triple *(s, pr, o)* belongs to the RDF document. Formulas for computing the cost and cardinality are similar to the different physical *join* formulas in relational queries and also ensure that the estimates are within a predetermined accuracy and confidence level.

The objective of our hybrid cost model is to estimate cost and cardinality of the execution of a query plan *p*, *cost(p)* and *card(p)*, respectively, so that with a high confidence (at least α) the relative error of the estimates is greater than some given constant ε, i.e.,

$$\Pr\left(\left|\frac{realCost(p) - \cos t(p)}{realCost(p)}\right| \geq \varepsilon\right) = \alpha$$

Formally, our hybrid cost model is defined as follows:

Definition 7. (Cost Model)

Let p and H(D)=(W,E,ρ) be an execution plan and a Bhyper RDF representation of an RDF document D, respectively. The cost and cardinality of p are defined inductively by the followings rules:

- *p is a star-shaped basic graph pattern w.r.t. ?X, ?X*−BGP then,*

$$\cos t(p) = \left(\sum\nolimits_{a \in M} realCost(p_a)\right) \times \frac{|M|}{N}$$

and $card(p) = \left(\sum_{a \in M} realCard(p_a)\right) \times \frac{|M|}{N}$,

where:

- *N is the number of different valid instantiations of the variable ?X of p in H(D),*
- *M is the set of valid instantiations of the variable ?X of p sampled from H(D),*
- *p_a is an instantiation of p where the variable ?X is bound to a,*
- *the sum $s = \left(\sum\nolimits_{a \in M} realCost(p_a)\right) \times \frac{|M|}{N}$*

  (resp., $s = \left(\sum_{a \in M} realCard(p_a)\right) \times \frac{|M|}{N}$) and

  |M| satisfies $\left(s \geq k_1 \times b \times \left(\frac{1}{\varepsilon} + 1\right) \times \frac{1}{\varepsilon}\right)$ and

  $\left(|M| \geq k_2 \times h^2\right)^7$, where:

  - *ε is the relative error of the estimate,*
  - *b corresponds to an upper bound of the cost/cardinality of the evaluation of any instantiation of p,*
  - *$h=100 \times \varepsilon$*
  - *k_1 is a constant and considers the case when the cost/cardinality variance of all the instantiations of p is normally distributed,*
  - *k_2 is constant and represents the situation when the cost/cardinality variance of all the instantiations of p is not normally distributed.*
- *if p=(R1 gjoin R2) then, cost(p)=cost(R1) +cost(R2)+card(R1)+card(R2)*

- *if p=(R1 njoin R2) then, $\cos t(p) = \cos t(R1) + card(R1) \times \cos t(R2')$, where $\cos t(R2')$ corresponds to the cost of evaluating the plan R2 where the join variables between R1 and R2, are bound by the results produced by R1,*
- *card((R1gjoinR2))=card((R1njoinR2)) =card(R1)×card(R2)×selectivityFactor (R1,R2) where:*

If Y is the set of join variables between R1 and R2, and max(?Y) is the maximum number of different values of variable ?Y $\in$ Y then,

$$selectivityFactor(R1, R2) = \frac{1}{\prod\limits_{?Y \in Y} \max(?Y)}$$

Consider the following star-shaped group: *P={?A1 vote:voter people:L000174. ?A1 vote:option ?O1 . ?E1 vote:hasBallot ?A1}.* Let *PP* be the population from which *M* instantiations are sampled; *PP* corresponds to all the valid instantiations of the triple pattern *?A1 vote:voter people:L000174* in the dataset of the US Congress vote results. Suppose *N* is the number of different instantiations of *?A1* in *PP*, and *realCost* returns the real execution cost of a plan. Then, the *cost* of *P* is computed as follows:

cost(P)=

$\left(\sum\nolimits_{a \in M} realCost(a \ vote{:}option \ ?O1.?E1 \ vote{:}hasBallot \ a)\right) \times \frac{|M|}{N}$

EXPERIMENTAL STUDY

We conducted an experimental study to empirically analyze the effectiveness of the index-based approach and the optimization and evaluation techniques. We report on the load and index time and compare the performance of the Bypher-based query engine with respect to the following RDF engines: RDF-3X version 0.3, AllegroGraph RDFStore version 3.0.1, Jena version 2.5.7, Jena with TDB version 0.7.3 and an implementation of Hexastore available at http://github.com/kasei/hexastore. Additionally, we report on the execution time of bushy plans identified by our proposed query optimizer; also, we show the cache usage during query execution time.

Datasets and Query Benchmarks

We used four different datasets: the Lehigh University Benchmark (LUBM) (Guo et al., 2004), wikipedia[8], the real-world dataset on US Congress vote results of 2004, and the real-world ontology YAGO[9]. We generated the LUBM datasets for 1, 5, 10, 20 and 50 universities. The size of each dataset is described in Table 1. We considered four sets of queries. Benchmark one is a set of nine queries which are described in Table 2 in terms of the number of patterns in the WHERE clause and the answer size; all the queries have at least one pattern whose object is instantiated with a constant. Benchmark two is a set of 20 queries, which have between one and seven *gjoin(s)* among small-sized groups of patterns and have more than 12 triple patterns. Benchmark three has 10 queries which are comprised of between 17 and 25 basic patterns; for all these queries the answer is empty, except q6 that produces 551 triples. Finally, benchmark four is comprised of the first

eight queries of the LUBM benchmark. The first three benchmarks are published in http:www.ldc.usb.ve/~mvidal/OneQL/datasets.

Evaluation Metrics

We report on runtime performance, which corresponds to the user time produced by the time command of the Unix operation system. The experiments on dataset one were evaluated on a Solaris machine with a Sparcv9 1281 MHz processor and 16GB RAM; experiments on the dataset YAGO and RDF-3X were executed on a Linux Ubuntu machine with an Intel Pentium Core2 Duo 3.0 GHz and 8GB RAM. Experiments were run in both cold and warm caches. To run cold cache, we cleared the cache before running each query by performing the command sh -c "sync ; echo 3 > /proc/sys/vm/drop caches". To run on warm cache, we executed the same query five times by dropping the cache just before running the first iteration of the query. The machines were dedicated to exclusively run these experiments.

Query Engine Implementations

The star-shaped group randomized query optimizer implements a Simulated Annealing algorithm that was run for twenty iterations and an initial temperature of 700. OneQL was implemented in SWI-Prolog (Multi-threaded, 64 bits, Version

Table 1. Dataset Cardinality

Dataset	Number of triples	Size
LUBM *Univ(1,0)*	103,074	17.27 MB
LUBM *Univ(5,0)*	645,649	108.28 MB
LUBM *Univ(10, 0)*	1,316,322	220.79 MB
LUBM *Univ(20, 0)*	2,781,322	468.68 MB
LUBM *Univ(50, 0)*	6,888,642	1.16 GB
US Congress votes 2004	67,392	3.61 MB
YAGO	44,000,000	4.0 GB
wikipedia	47,000,000	6.9 GB

Table 2. Benchmark One Query Set

Query	#Patterns	Answer Size
q1	4	3
q2	3	14,033
q3	7	3,908
q4	4	14,868
q5	4	10,503
q6	4	47
q7	3	6,600
q8	3	963
q9	7	13,177

5.6.54); RDF-3X 0.3.4 is implemented in gcc/g++ v4.3.3. We have extended RDF-3X 0.3.4 to respect query execution plans produced by the OneQL query optimizer; *gjoin* is implemented as the RDF-3X *Hash Join*, while *njoins* between star-shaped groups correspond to RDF-3X *Merge Joins*; we call this version GRDF-3X.

Finally, the Bhyper prototypes were developed using the C++ programming language and compiled with g++ 4.4.3. The main-memory approach was developed using the Standard Template Library (STL), while the secondary-memory

prototype exploited the benefits of the database library Tokyo 1.4.45 Cabinet[10]. Hash-files were used to store and index mapping dictionaries and to store node and hyperarc sets; B+-trees were used to index hyperarc sets.

Effectiveness of the Bhyper-Based Representation in OneQL

Figure 9 compares the evaluation cost of queries of benchmark two in log. scale, when the Bhyper structures in OneQL, are used to index the RDF data, and when the Bhyper structures are not used to index the RDF data. The results indicate that the indices improve the performance of the physical operators in OneQL, while the evaluation time is reduced by up to two orders of magnitude in queries comprised of a large number of *gjoins* between groups of instantiated triples.

Effectiveness of the Optimization and Evaluation Techniques of Bhyper in OneQL

We studied the benefits of the optimization and evaluation techniques implemented by OneQL by

Figure 9. Performance of the OneQL Bhyper-based index representation

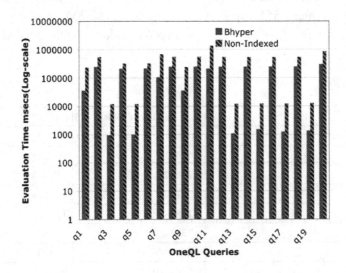

empirically analyzing the quality of the OneQL optimized plans compared to the plans optimized by the RDF-3X query optimizer. Queries of benchmark one were generated by OneQL and RDF-3X; then, both types of plans were run in OneQL with and without Bhyper indices. Each plan optimized by RDF-3X was run using the *gjoin* and *njoin* operators to evaluate the groups in the bushy plans. Figure 10 reports the evaluation time (log. scale) of these query combinations. We can observe that the Bhyper-based representation is able to speed up the evaluation time of all the versions of the queries comprised of instantiated triples. Second, the evaluation time of the OneQL and RDF-3X optimized plans are competitive, except for queries *q1* and *q6*, where OneQL was able to identify plans where all the triples are instantiated, and the most selective ones are evaluated first. These results indicate that the OneQL optimization and evaluation techniques may be used in conjunction with the state-of-the-art techniques to provide more efficient query engines. This encouraged us to develop our own physical operators in existing RDF engines such as RDF-3X.

Efficiency of Bhyper in Main-Memory

We compared the load and index time of Bhyper with respect to Jena. We report on the average execution time, and the amount of main-memory required to store Bhyper structures.

Figure 11 reports on the time (seconds and log. scale) required to load and index all triples of each dataset while Figure 12 reports on the amount of main-memory required for the structures to store all triples on a dataset (MB and log. scale). Bhyper in-memory was faster than Jena, loading and indexing the LUBM datasets. In our experiments, Bhyper consumed in average 16.92% of the time needed for Jena, Similarly, Bhyper consumed less main-memory, requiring in average just 57.25% of the memory consumed by Jena. The observed savings are achieved thanks to the representation of the hyperarcs where each resource is associated with all the triples where it plays the role of subject, property or object. In contrast, Jena represents all the triples in a way that the same resource is repeated in all of the triples where it appears.

Figure 10. Performance of the OneQL optimization and evaluation techniques

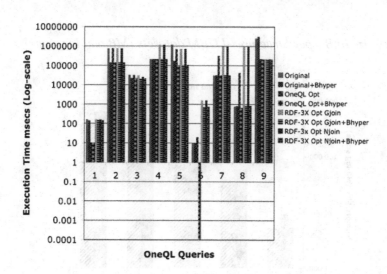

Figure 11. Load and index time of Bhyper Structures-LUBM datasets (secs. and log scale)

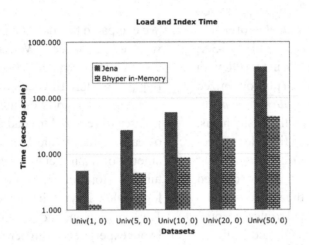

Effectiveness of the Optimization and Evaluation Techniques of Bhyper in Main-Memory

We studied the effects on the query execution time of our optimization and evaluation techniques when Bhyper index based structures are kept in main-memory. We executed all the queries of benchmark four against the LUBM datasets for 1, 5, 10, 20, and 50 universities. Figure 13 reports on the average query evaluation time over each

LUBM dataset (seconds and log. scale). In the five datasets, Bhyper in main-memory overcomes Jena. We must highlight that, in contrast to Jena, the queries that were ran on Bhyper were not optimized. Thus, time improvements were just produced by the Bypher data structures and the indices on the original RDF documents and on the intermediate results produced by the execution engine.

Figure 12. Memory size of Bhyper Structures-LUBM datasets (MB and log scale)

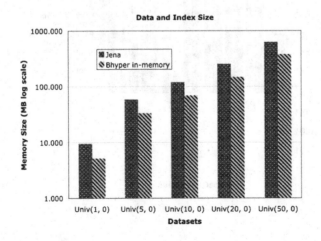

Figure 13. Average query execution time-benchmark four (secs. and log. scale)

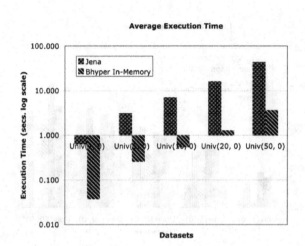

Efficiency and Effectiveness of Bhyper in Secondary-Memory

We also studied the effects on the query execution time of our optimization and execution techniques when Bhyper index-based structures are kept in secondary-memory. We evaluated Bhyper performance in the LUBM datasets for 1, 5, 10, 20, and 50 universities, YAGO and wikipedia. We executed all the queries of benchmark four against the LUBM datasets for 1, 5, 10, and 50 universities and queries of benchmark three against YAGO. We considered RDF-3X, AllegroGraph, Jena TDB, and two versions of Hexastore: one that implements native persistent storage structures and the other that is built on top of Tokyo Cabinet. In all the experiments we could observe that Bhyper outperformed the majority of existing RDF engines, showing a competitive behavior with RDF-3X in all of the experiments.

First, we loaded the wikipedia dataset in Bhyper, RDF-3X, AllegroGraph, and Jena TDB. We could observe that Bhyper only required 447.86 secs., representing approximately 1/4 of the load and index time consumed by RDF-3X, which had the best results among AllegroGraph, Jena, and Jena TDB. In addition, Bhyper consumed 1.12 GB to store all triples out of the 6.9 GB required

to store the flat file, and 1/2 of the memory space used by RDF-3X. Then, we loaded LUBM datasets for 1, 5, 10, 20 and 50 universities in Bhyper, RDF-3X, AllegroGraph, Jena TDB, and the two versions of Hexastore. Figure 14 reports on the time (seconds and log. scale) required to load and index all triples of each dataset. We could observe that the version of Hexastore built on top of Tokyo Cabinet that is available at http://github.com/kasei/hexastore, was not able to load the LUBM dataset for 50 universities; also, because data is compressed into Tokyo Cabinet internal structures the time consumed in all the datasets, was higher. In contrast, Bhyper was faster than the other RDF engines, loading and indexing the LUBM datasets for 1, 5, 10, and 20 universities. In some cases, Bhyper just consumed 2/3 of the time needed for RDF-3X, which was the fastest among AllegroGraph, Jena TDB, and Hexastore Tokyo Cabinet.

Figure 15 reports on the amount of memory required for the structures to store all triples of a dataset (MB and log. scale). Although data is not compressed in Bhyper, it consumed less memory than AllegroGraph, Jena TDB, and the two versions of Hexastore. However, RDF-3X makes use of LZ77 compression in conjunction with byte-wise Gamma encoding for all the IDs and gap

Figure 14. Load and index time of Bhyper Structures-LUBM datasets (secs. and log scale)

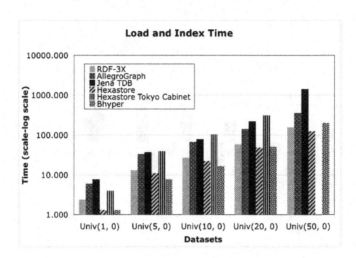

Figure 15. Memory size of Bhyper Structures-LUBM datasets (MB and log scale)

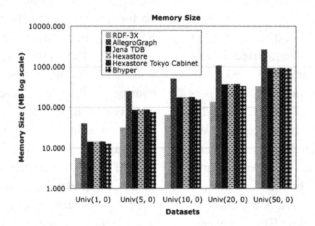

compression (Neumann & Weikum, 2009); thus, although RDF-3X respects a graph based representation of RDF documents, it is still able to consume less memory than Bhyper.

Figure 16 reports on the average query evaluation time over each LUBM dataset (seconds and log. scale). We compare the behavior of RDF-3X, Hexastore and Bhyper in both cold and warm caches. In the five datasets, Bhyper in secondary-memory overcomes AllegroGraph, Jena TDB, and Hexastore. We must highlight that, in contrast to RDF-3X, AllegroGraph and JenaTDB, the

queries that ran on Bhyper were not optimized. Thus, time improvements were just produced by Bypher data structures and indices on the original RDF documents, and on the intermediate results produced by the execution engine.

In case of Jena TDB, we turned off the optimizer and we could observe that queries against the dataset with 50 universities timed out after 14 hours; the Bypher engine overcame the Jena TDB engine in at least one order of magnitude for the rest of the datasets. Although Jena TDB is implemented in Java and Bhyper is implemented in

Figure 16. Average query execution time-benchmark four (secs. and log. scale)

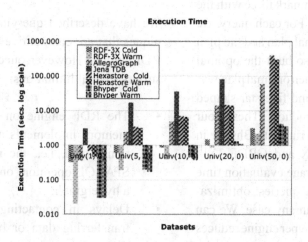

Table 3. Efficiency of Bhyper in Secondary-Memory (Size in MB and Time in seconds)

Bhyper Structure	Size (MB)	Load and Index Time (secs.)
nodes	766.40	250.00
hyperarcs	1,100.00	250.00
node-index	740.10	139.40
s-index	596.40	337.54
p-index	424.00	84.91
o-index	651.00	633.11

C++, this difference between the evaluation costs may suggest that Bhyper structures in conjunction with the physical implementations of *starScan*, *njoin* and *gjoin*, speed up the evaluation time of RDF queries even when optimization techniques are not performed.

We also studied the efficiency and effectiveness of the secondary-memory implementation of Bhyper on large datasets, and we loaded and indexed the YAGO dataset in Bhyper secondary-memory structures and in RDF-3X. The rest of the engines could not load YAGO. Table 3 shows the amount of memory required to store each of Bhyper secondary-memory structures and the time consumed when these structures were created. We could observe that the same value can appear as the object in many different triples; thus, the time to

create the o-index was the highest and represents 28% of total load and index time.

Additionally, the size of the Bhyper structures represents 300% of the size of the RDF-3X compressed file and 163.4% of the size of YAGO in N-triples format; the time to load and index Bhyper structures is 273.4% of the time required by RDF-3X. These results may be understood as disadvantages of Bhyper. However, it is important to highlight that Bhyper stores different types of secondary-memory indices for three access patterns, while RDF-3X implements sophisticated compress algorithms to store the data in flat files. These access patterns allow Bhyper to outperform RDF-3X in large queries.

Finally, we studied the effects of the OneQL optimization techniques in the secondary-memory version of Bhyper; we compare the Bypher evaluation time of queries of benchmark three with the time consumed by RDF-3X. For each query, we computed the RDF-3X optimal plan and the plan produced by OneQL. We also built the optimal plan of each query by hand; each optimal plan was comprised of between two and five star-shaped groups free of Cartesian products. These four versions of the queries were run with Bhyper in secondary-memory, RDF-3X and GRDF-3X[11]. Figure 17 reports on the average evaluation time (seconds-log. scale) of these queries; optimization time is not considered in any case. We can observe that in average the Bhyper engine reduces the RDF-3X evaluation time by up to one order of magnitude. Also, the plans produced by RDF-3X and OneQL and the optimal plan produced by hand, reduce in average the execution time in the Bhyper engine more than in RDF-3X. Finally, we observe that GRDF-3X outperforms Bhyper and RDF-3X; this is because GRDF-3X is able to use statistics to determine when sub-plans produce empty results, and avoids processing the rest of the query. In the future we plan to incorporate our current Bhyper engine with a cost-based optimizer and catalog to overcome these limitations.

FUTURE RESEARCH DIRECTIONS

We have described querying and storing techniques that are competitive with state-of-the-art RDF engines. However, our current approach still suffers several limitations:

- The RDF engine on Bhyper secondary-memory implements a non closed execution model, i.e., the result of evaluating SPARQL operators on hypergraphs is not a hypergraph.
- Delays in contacting external datasets, transferring data or bursty arrivals from data sources are not hidden.
- Non-uniform distributions of the values in the RDF documents, as well as correlations between the values, are not considered in the cost models.

To overcome these disadvantages, we plan to define physical implementations of *njoin* and *gjoin* that produce intermediate Bhyper structures; this feature will speed up the execution engine on Bhyper secondary-memory version. Additionally, to hide the effects of Web source delays, we are

Figure 17. Query Execution Time Bhyper versus RDF-3X-Benchmark Three (secs. and log. scale)

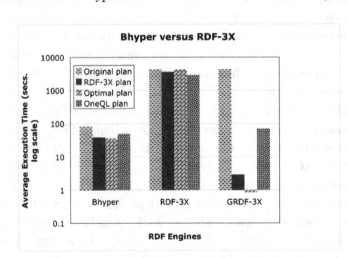

defining an adaptive version of our execution engine, where operators are able to incrementally produce results as the data becomes available; thus, we plan to extend the *Symmetric hash join* (Deshpande et al., 2007) to process RDF data depending on availability. Also, the engine itself can detect when data sources get blocked and modify the execution plan on-the-fly. These new features will provide the basis to efficiently evaluate data on the Cloud of Linked Data. We also will enhance the OneQL cost model with Bayesian inference capabilities to consider correlations between the different patterns that can appear in an RDF query.

CONCLUSION

This chapter has defined Bhyper, a hypergraph based representation for RDF documents that reduces the space and time complexity of the tasks of storing and querying RDF documents. Then, the OneQL system was described with the aim to illustrate the performance of Bhyper structures when SPARQL queries are evaluated. The chapter also addressed the challenges of scaling up to large RDF documents and complex SPARQL queries. The chapter's authors reported on the performance of optimization and evaluation techniques for SPARQL queries, and the time spent loading and indexing Bhyper structures; the described functionalities support an efficient evaluation of RDF queries against single datasets. To provide a more complete solution able to efficiently scale to linked datasets as the ones in the Cloud of Linked Data, the proposed techniques have to be extended mainly to hide source delays, to efficiently store and index intermediate results, and to relax the uniformity and independence assumptions on which the OneQL cost model is based.

REFERENCES

Abadi, D. J., Marcus, A., Madden, S., & Hollenbach, K. (2009). SW-Store: A vertically partitioned DBMS for Semantic Web data management. *The VLDB Journal*, *18*(2), 385–406. doi:10.1007/s00778-008-0125-y

Abadi, D. J., Marcus, A., Madden, S., & Hollenbach, K. J. (2007). Scalable Semantic Web data management using vertical partitioning. *In Proceedings of VLDB* (pp. 411–422).

AllegroGraph. (2009). *AllegroGraph*. Retrieved from http:// www. franz. com/ agraph/ allegrograph/.

Atre, M., Chaoji, V., Zaki, M. J., & Hendler, J. A. (2010). Matrix "bit" loaded: A scalable lightweight join query processor for RDF data. In *Proceedings of the WWW* (pp. 41–50).

Auillans, P., de Mendez, P. O., Rosenstiehl, P., & Vatant, B. (2002). A formal model for topic maps. In *Proceedings of the 3rd International Semantic Web Conference (ISWC 2004)*.

Basca, C., & Bernstein, A. (2010). Avalanche: Putting the spirit of the Web back into Semantic Web querying. In *Proceedings of the 6th International Workshop on Scalable Semantic Web Knowledge Base Systems at ISWC*.

Benson, G. (2007). Editorial. *Nucleic Acids Research, 35(Web-Server-Issue)*, 1.

Chen, C.-M., & Roussopoulos, N. (1994). Adaptive selectivity estimation using query feedback. In *Proceedings of SIGMOD Conference* (pp. 161–172).

Da Costa, P. C. G., Ladeira, M., Carvalho, R. N., Laskey, K. B., Santos, L. L., & Matsumoto, S. (2008a). A first-order Bayesian tool for probabilistic ontologies. In *Proceedings of FLAIRS Conference* (pp. 631–636).

Da Costa, P. C. G., Laskey, K. B., & Laskey, K. J. (2008b). Pr-owl: A Bayesian ontology language for the Semantic Web. In *Proceedings of URSW (LNCS Vol.)* (pp. 88–107).

Dau, F. (2006a). RDF as graph-based, diagrammatic logic. In *Proceedings of the 16th ISMIS, Italy* (vol. 4203 of LNCS) (pp. 332–337).

Dau, F. (2006b). RDF as graph-based, diagrammatic logic. In *Proceedings of the 16th International Symposium on Methodologies for Intelligent Systems (ISMIS 2006)*.

Davison, D. L., & Graefe, G. (1995). Dynamic resource brokering for multi-user query execution. In *Proceedings of SIGMOD Conference* (pp. 281–292).

Deshpande, A., Ives, Z. G., & Raman, V. (2007). Adaptive query processing. *Foundations and Trends in Databases*, *1*(1), 1–140. doi:10.1561/1900000001

Fletcher, G., & Beck, P. (2009). Scalable indexing of RDF graph for efficient join processing. In *Proceedings of CIKM09*.

Gallo, G., Longo, G., Pallottino, S., & Nguyen, S. V. (2003). Directed hypergraphs and applications. *In discrete applied mathematics*.

Gallo, G., & Scutella, M. G. (1999). Directed hypergraphs as a modelling paradigm. *In Tech. Rep. TR-99-02, Universita di Pisa*, Italy.

Galperin, M. (2007). The molecular biology database collection: 2007 update. *Nucleic Acids Research*, *35*(Database issue). Retrieved from http://view.ncbi.nlm.nih.gov/pubmed/17148484. doi:10.1093/nar/gkl1008

Galperin, M. (2008). The molecular biology database collection: 2008 update. *Nucleic Acids Research*, *36*(Database issue), D2–D4. Retrieved from http://dx.doi.org/10.1093/nar/gkm1037. doi:10.1093/nar/gkm1037

Getoor, L. (2006). An introduction to probabilistic graphical models for relational data. *IEEE Data Eng. Bull.*, *29*(1), 32–39.

Goldsmith, J., & Laskey, K. B. (2010). Introduction to the special issue on Bayesian model views. *International Journal of Approximate Reasoning*, *51*(2), 165–166. doi:10.1016/j.ijar.2009.08.001

Gunter Ladwig, T. T. (2010). Linked data query processing strategies. In *Procddings of the International Semantic Web Conference (ISWC)*.

Guo, Y., Pan, Z., & Heflin, J. (2004). An evaluation of knowledge base systems for large OWL datasets. In *Proceedings of the 3rd ISWC, Japan* (pp. 274–288).

Gutiérrez, C., Hurtado, C. A., & Mendelzon, A. O. (2004). Foundations of Semantic Web databases. In *Proceedings of the 23rd SIGMOD/PODS, France* (pp. 95–106).

Harth, A., Hose, K., Karnstedt, M., Polleres, A., Sattler, K.-U., & Umbrich, J. (2010). Data summaries for on-demand queries over linked data. *In Proceedings of WWW*.

Harth, A., Umbrich, J., Hogan, A., & Decker, S. (2007). YARS2: A federated repository for querying graph structured data from the Web. *In Proceedings of ISWC/ASWC* (pp. 211–224).

Hartig, O., Bizer, C., & Freytag, J. C. (2009). Executing SPARQL queries over the Web of linked data. In *Proceedings of the International Semantic Web Conference (ISWC)* (pp. 293–309).

Hartig, O., Sequeda, J., Taylor, J., & Sinclair, P. (2010). How to consume linked data on the Web: Tutorial description. In *Proceedings of WWW* (pp. 1347–1348).

Hayes, J. (2004). A graph model for RDF. *Master's thesis, Technische Universitt Darmstadt,* Department of Computer Science, Darmstadt, Germany.

Hayes, J., & Gutiérrez, C. (2004). Bipartite graphs as intermediate model for *RDF.* In *Proceedings of the International Semantic Web Conference ISWC, vol. 3298 of LNCS,* Japan (pp. 47–61).

Ianni, G., Krennwallner, T., Martello, A., & Polleres, A. (2009). A rule system for querying persistent RDFS data. *In Proceedings of the 6th European Semantic Web Conference (ESWC2009).* Heraklion, Greece: Springer. Demo Paper.

Idreos, S., Kersten, M. L., & Manegold, S. (2009). Self-organizing tuple reconstruction in column-stores. In *Proceedings of SIGMOD* (pp. 297–308).

JENA. (2009). The JenaOntology Api. Retrieved from http:// jena. sourceforge. net/ ontology/ index.html.

JENATDB. (2009). Jena TDB. Retrieved from http://jena.hpl.hp.com/wiki/TDB.

Kaoudi, Z., Kyzirakos, K., & Koubarakis, M. (2010). Sparql query optimization on top of DHTs. In *Proceedings of the International Semantic Web Conference (ISWC).*

Klyne, G., & Carroll, J. J. (2004). Resource description framework (RDF): Concepts and abstract syntax. *Tech. Rep. Recommendation, W3C.*

Lampo, T., Ruckhaus, E., Sierra, J., Vidal, M.-E., & Martinez, A. (2009). OneQL: An ontology-based architecture to efficiently query resources on the Semantic Web. *In The 5th International Workshop on Scalable Semantic Web Knowledge Base Systems at ISWC.*

Li, Y., & Heflin, J. (2010). Using reformulation trees to optimize queries over distributed heterogeneous sources. In *Proceddings of the International Semantic Web Conference (ISWC).*

Lipton, R., & Naughton, J. (1990). Query size estimation by adaptive sampling (extended *abstract).* In *Proceedings of SIGMOD*

Martinez, A., & Vidal, M.-E. (2007). A directed hypergraph model for RDF. In *Proceedings of KWEPSY.*

McGlothlin, J. (2010). RDFVector: An efficient and scalable schema for Semantic Web knowledge bases. In *Proceedings of the PhD Symposium ESWC.*

McGlothlin, J., & Khan, L. (2009). RDFJoin: A scalable of data model for persistence and efficient querying of RDF dataasets. *In Proceedings of VLDB.*

Mihaylov, S. R., Jacob, M., Ives, Z. G., & Guha, S. (2010). Dynamic join optimization in multi-hop wireless sensor networks. *PVLDB, 3*(1), 1279–1290.

Neumann, T., & Weikum, G. (2008). RDF-3X: A RISC-style engine for RDF. *PVLDB, 1*(1), 647–659.

Neumann, T., & Weikum, G. (2009). Scalable join processing on very large RDF graphs. In *Proceedings of SIGMOD* (pp. 627–640).

Nguyen, M. K., Basca, C., & Bernstein, A. (2010). B+Hash tress: Optimizing query execution times for on-disk Semantic Web data structures. In *The 6th International Workshop on Scalable Semantic Web Knowledge Base Systems at ISWC.*

raefe, G. (1995). The cascades framework for query optimization. *IEEE Data Eng. Bull., 18*(3), 19–29.

raefe, G. (2000). Dynamic query evaluation plans: Some course corrections? *IEEE Data Eng. Bull., 23*(2), 3–6.

Ruckhaus, E., Ruiz, E., & Vidal, M. (2006). Query evaluation and optimization in the Semantic Web. In *Proceedings ALPSWS2006: 2nd International Workshop on Applications of Logic Programming to the Semantic Web and Semantic Web Services.*

Ruckhaus, E., Ruiz, E., & Vidal, M. (2007). OnEQL: An ontology efficient query language engine for the Semantic Web. In *Proceedings ALPSWS.*

Ruckhaus, E., Ruiz, E., & Vidal, M. (2008). *Query evaluation and optimization in the Semantic Web.* TPLP.

Selingerl, P., Astrahan, M., Chamberlin, D., Lorie, R., & Price, T. (1979). Access path selection in a relational database management system. In *Proceedings of SIGMOD.*

Sen, P., Deshpande, A., & Getoor, L. (2008). Exploiting shared correlations in probabilistic databases. *PVLDB, 1*(1), 809–820.

Sidirourgos, L., Goncalves, R., Kersten, M. L., Nes, N., & Manegold, S. (2008). Column-store support for RDF data management: Not all swans are white. *PVLDB, 1*(2), 1553–1563.

Stonebraker, M., Abadi, D. J., Batkin, A., Chen, X., Cherniack, M., & Ferreira, M. …Zdonik, S. B. (2005). C-store: A column-oriented *DBMS.* In *Proceedings of VLDB (pp. 553–564).*

Tran, T., Zhang, L., & Studer, R. (2010). Summary models for routing keywords to linked data sources. In *Proceedings of the International Semantic Web Conference (ISWC).*

Udrea, O., Subrahmanian, V. S., & Majkic, Z. (2006). Probabilistic RDF. *In Proceedings of IRI* (pp. 172–177).

Urhan, T., & Franklin, M. J. (2000). Xjoin: A reactively-scheduled pipelined join operator. *IEEE Data Eng. Bull., 23*(2), 27–33.

Urhan, T., & Franklin, M. J. (2001). Dynamic pipeline scheduling for improving interactive query performance. In *Proceedings of VLDB* (pp. 501–510).

Urhan, T., Franklin, M. J., & Amsaleg, L. (1998). Cost based query scrambling for initial delays. In *Proceedings of SIGMOD* (pp. 130–141).

Vidal, M.-E., Ruckhaus, E., Lampo, T., Martinez, A., Sierra, J., & Polleres, A. (2010). Efficiently joining group patterns in SPARQL queries. In *Proceedings of the 7th Extended Semantic Web Conference (ESWC2010).*

Weiss, C., & Bernstein, A. (2009). On-disk storage techniques for SemanticWeb data- Are b-trees always the optimal solution? In *The 5th International Workshop on Scalable Semantic Web Knowledge Base Systems at ISWC.*

Weiss, C., Karras, P., & Bernstein, A. (2008). Hexastore: Sextuple indexing for Semantic Web data management. *PVLDB, 1*(1), 1008–1019.

Wielemaker, J. (2005). An optimised Semantic Web query language implementation in prolog. In *Proceedings of ICLP* (pp. 128–142).

Wilkinson, K., Sayers, C., Kuno, H., Reynolds, D., & Database, J. (2003). Efficient RDF storage and retrieval in Jena2. In. *Proceedings of EXPLOITING HYPERLINKS, 349,* 35–43.

Zaniolo, C., Ceri, S., Faloutsos, C., Snodgrass, R. T., Subrahmanian, V., & Zicari, R. (1997). *Advanced database systems.* San Francisco, CA, USA: Morgan Kaufmann.

ADDITIONAL READING

Probabilistic-based Ontologies and Cost Models: (e.g., da Costa et al., 2008b,a; Getoor, 2006; Goldsmith & Laskey, 2010; Sen et al., 2008; Udrea et al., 2006).

Adaptive Query Processing: (e.g., Chen & Roussopoulos, 1994; Davison & Graefe, 1995; Deshpande et al., 2007; Graefe, 1995, 2000; Mihaylov et al., 2010; Urhan et al., 1998; Urhan & Franklin, 2000, 2001).

Query Execution of Web and Linked Data: (e.g., Basca & Bernstein, 2010; Harth et al., 2010; Hartig et al., 2009, 2010; Li & Heflin, 2010; Kaoudi et al., 2010; Gunter Ladwig, 2010; Tran et al., 2010).

KEY TERMS AND DEFINITIONS

Cost Model: Statistic tool to estimate the cost or quality of evaluating a query.

Execution Engine: DBMS component that provides a set of physical operators to execute queries against a data source.

Hypergraph: A pair (V, E), where V is a set of vertices, and E is a set of hyperarcs between the vertices. Each hyperedge is a set of vertices: $E \subseteq \{\{u, v, \ldots\} \subseteq 2^V\}$.

Indices: Structures able to provide a direct access to a particular piece of data.

Linked Data: A paradigm to link resources published on the Web.

Query Execution Plan: Structure that represents the order, steps and physical operators that must be followed to evaluate a particular query.

Query Optimization Techniques: Set of strategies to identify a query execution plan for a query such as the evaluation cost is minimized.

Resource Description Framework (RDF): A recommendation from the W3C to describe the semantics of the data on the Web.

SPARQL: A recommendation from the W3C to specify queries against RDF documents.

ENDNOTES

[1] In this work we do not consider UNION or OPTIONAL.

[2] http://www.kobrix.com/hgdb.jsp

[3] http://www.govtrack.us/data/rdf/

[4] 1978th.net/tokyocabinet/

[5] GRDF-3X is an extension of RDF-3X that offers the *gjoin* operator and evaluates bushy plans.

[6] The join arguments are the common variables in the two predicates that represent the patterns.

[7] The first sub-condition imposes an upper bound on the sum of the cost/card of *p*. The second sub-condition establishes a sanity bound and controls the termination of the sampling process when *b* is high and an oversampling can arise.

[8] http://labs.systemone.net/wikipedia3

[9] Ontology available for download at http://www.mpi-inf.mpg.de/yago-naga/yago/

[10] 1978th.net/tokyocabinet/

[11] GRDF-3X is the extension of RDF-3X where we implemented our own physical operators.

Chapter 17
Graph Applications in Chemoinformatics and Structural Bioinformatics

Eleanor Joyce Gardiner
University of Sheffield, UK

ABSTRACT

The focus of this chapter will be the uses of graph theory in chemoinformatics and in structural bio-informatics. There is a long history of chemical graph theory dating back to the 1860's and Kekule's structural theory. It is natural to regard the atoms of a molecule as nodes and the bonds as edges (2D representations) of a labeled graph (a molecular graph). This chapter will concentrate on the algorithms developed to exploit the computer representation of such graphs and their extensions in both two and three dimensions (where an edge represents the distance in 3D space between a pair of atoms), together with the algorithms developed to exploit them. The algorithms will generally be summarized rather than detailed. The methods were later extended to larger macromolecules (such as proteins); these will be covered in less detail.

INTRODUCTION

Chemistry space is exceedingly large. Recent estimates put the number of potentially 'drug-like' molecules at anything between 10^{12} and 10^{180} (Gorse, 2006). The overwhelming majority of

these molecules never has been, and never will be, synthesized but methods are nevertheless required to determine which of these potential compounds should be made. Some large pharmaceutical/agrochemical companies maintain corporate databases of millions of molecules. The discovery of New Chemical Entities (NCEs) which may become drugs depends on the successful mining

DOI: 10.4018/978-1-61350-053-8.ch017

of the information stored in these databases. Such information may be explicit (e.g. the molecules may be annotated with chemical reaction or activity data) or may be implicit in the structure of a molecule. For many years isomorphism algorithms have formed the basis of structural comparison between pairs of molecules in these databases, designed to extract this implicit information. The main purpose of this chapter is to introduce the concept of chemoinformatics to practitioners from the field of graph theory and to demonstrate the widespread application of graph-theoretic techniques to the solving of chemoinformatics problems. However, many graph-theoretic algorithms from chemoinformatics have subsequently been adapted for the structural comparison of macromolecules in the field known as structural bioinformatics. A secondary aim of the chapter is to provide a brief overview of these applications.

The layout of the chapter will now be described. In the Background section some definitions of chemoinformatics are given and the topic is placed within the context of the drug discovery process. Structural bioinformatics is also defined and the necessary graph theoretic notation is introduced. The two main sections deal with the use of algorithms from graph theory in chemoinformatics and structural bioinformatics respectively. In the Chemoinformatics section the reader is introduced to the concept of a molecule as a molecular graph; this concept informs the rest of the section. Then the use of algorithms for graph labeling in order to register molecules is discussed, followed by the use of graph invariants as part of a molecular description. The use of subgraph isomorphism algorithms for molecular substructure searching is considered and the importance of the Ullmann algorithm is emphasized. Next the important concept of molecular similarity is considered along with the reformulation of this problem as a maximum clique problem. Two key clique-detection algorithms in chemoinformatics, Bron-Kerbosch and RASCAL, are considered in more detail. These algorithms are then shown to

be important in protein-ligand docking, pharmacophore elucidation and molecular clustering. Reduced graphs for molecular representation and searching are then introduced and example graph reductions are considered. In the Structural Bioinformatics section the necessary elements of protein structure are first presented. Many methods from chemoinformatics have been adapted for use in structural bioinformatics: some of these are described here, in particular uses of the Ullmann algorithm for substructural searching and the Bron-Kerbosch algorithm for similarity searching and protein-protein docking. The final sections are the Future Directions section, where the need for graph-theoreticians to present algorithms in a way which is accessible to chemoinformaticians is discussed, and the Conclusions section where the chapter is summarized.

BACKGROUND

The first question to be answered is "What is chemoinformatics?" Chemoinformatics (also known as cheminformatics) is an interface science (N. Brown, 2009) which includes expertise from chemistry, biology, physics, mathematics and computer science. No definitive definition of the term "chemoinformatics" has ever been given but, as chemoinformaticians, we know what we mean when we say it. The term chemoinformatics was first used by Frank Brown:

The use of information technology and management has become a critical part of the drug discovery process. Chemoinformatics is the mixing of those information resources to transform data into information and information into knowledge for the intended purpose of making better decisions faster in the area of drug lead identification and optimization. (F. K. Brown, 1998).

Other definitions from leading practitioners in the field include:

Chemoinformatics is the application of informatics methods to solve chemical problems. (Gasteiger, 2006).

...the computer manipulation of two- or three-dimensional chemical structures and excludes textual information. This distinguishes the term from chemical information, largely a discipline of librarians and does not include the development of computational methods. Willett, 2002 cited in (Russo, 2002).

So generally speaking, by the term chemoinformatics we mean the use of computers to design and manipulate small molecular structures. NB Small molecules are frequently called *ligands* in the chemoinformatics literature, particularly in the context of their binding to a target protein.

The main fields of application for chemoinformatics are the pharmaceutical and agrochemical industries. It takes many years and hundreds of millions of dollars to bring a drug to market (Di-Masi, Hansen, & Grabowski, 2003).The process goes through several stages, starting with the identification of a protein target whose eventual interaction with a drug molecule will alter the progression of a disease. Many molecules are screened against the target, in a High Throughput Screen (HTS) to determine whether or not they are active (i.e. modify the action of the protein); such active molecules are termed *hits*. A subset of the hits (with suitable physio-chemical properties) will be pursued as *leads*. These leads will be *optimized* and eventually some candidate drugs may enter pre-clinical and then clinical trials. The rate of attrition is very high; at all stages molecules fail for numerous reasons (difficulties with yield, synthesizability, toxicology and regulatory problems to name but a few). Chemoinformatics is involved at all stages of the drug discovery process, but in particular the earlier stages. For example, when some hits have been identified in HTS, then a database of molecular structures may be searched to locate similar molecules; this is termed *ligand-based virtual screening*.

We also need to define what is meant by structural bioinformatics. The central dogma of molecular biology is that DNA sequence determines protein structure which determines protein function. Bioinformatics is the application of computational techniques to understand and organize the information now available from the sequenced genomes of many organisms (Luscombe, Greenbaum, & Gerstein, 2001) and there are very many applications of graph theory in bioinformatics (De Jong, 2002) which are outside the scope of this review.

The completion of the Human Genome Project (Lander & al., 2001; Venter & al., 2001) means that the sequence of the estimated 20000-25000 genes present in human DNA is known. However it is not the sequence but rather the 3D structure of the proteins coded for by these genes which determines their function and in most cases this remains unknown. Whilst similar sequences usually lead to proteins with similar 3D structure, it is also true that proteins with very different sequence can have similar 3D folds which may mean that they have similar functions. In 2003 the Protein Structure Initiative (http://www.nigms.nih.gov/psi/) was launched with the aim of determining the structure of as large a representative subset of the human proteome as possible. Their method was to organize known protein sequences into families and then select family representatives as targets. The 3D structures of these targets were to be solved by means of techniques such as X-ray crystallography or NMR spectroscopy. (NB *solving a structure* means determining the 3D atomic coordinates). These structures would then serve as the basis for determining the structure of other family members by, for example, homology modeling. Solved structures are deposited in the Protein Data Bank (PDB) (Bernstein et al., 1977) - to date more than 9000 of the 67000 structures in the PDB have been deposited under this initiative. Although many of these structures are of unknown function, knowledge of the structure can be crucial in assigning function to a protein. Such an assignment is typically derived either from a generalized assignment based on a similarity of fold to other proteins (e.g. (Hwang, Chung, Kim, Han, & Cho, 1999)) or even from the chance observation of similar ligand binding (e.g. (Zarembinski et al., 1998)).

Structural bioinformatics focuses on the representation, storage, retrieval, analysis, and display of structural information at the atomic and sub-cellular spatial scales. (Gu & Bourne, 2009)

When mining the literature of an unfamiliar field, it is often difficult to know where to begin. The most important journal in the field of chemoinformatics is the *Journal of Chemical Information and Modeling* which was first known as the *Journal of Chemical Documentation*, subsequently renamed the *Journal of Chemical Information and Computer Science* and gained its current name in 2007. Other specialist journals in the field include the *Journal of Computer-Aided Molecular Design*, the *Journal of Molecular Graphics and Modelling* (formerly the *Journal of Molecular Graphics*) and *Molecular Informatics* (formerly *QSAR*). Other important journals which often contain chemoinformatics methodological articles include the *Journal of Medicinal Chemistry*, the *Journal of the American Chemical Society* (*JACS*) and *Drug Discovery Today*. The most important source of articles for structural bioinformatics is probably *Proteins: Structure, Function and Genetics* which is often abbreviated to *Proteins* and was formerly known as *Proteins: Structure, Function and Bioinformatics*. The journal *Bioinformatics*, although originally specializing in sequence-based bioinformatics, now contains many articles on structural methods and has also recently started to include chemoinformatics articles. NB these lists are not exhaustive and reflect the journal-reading habits of the author.

Now we introduce the notation necessary for the remainder of the chapter.

NOTATION

An undirected *graph*, G = (V,E) is composed of a set V of *vertices* and a set E of *edges* where E $\subseteq$ {(u,v): u,v $\in$ V}. A graph G'=(V',E') is a *subgraph* of G if V' $\subseteq$ V and E' $\subseteq$ {(u,v): u,v $\in$ V' and (u,v) $\in$ E}. (Informally, E' $\subseteq$ E.) Two vertices *u* and *v* are *adjacent* if (u,v) $\in$ E; an edge e = (u,v) connects *u* and *v*. The edge (u,v) may be referred to simply as *uv*. The subgraph G' is *induced* if u,v $\in$ V' and uv $\in$ E => uv $\in$ E'. The *degree* of a vertex *v* is the number of vertices to which *v* is adjacent (Golumbic, 1980). A graph is *complete* if every vertex is adjacent to every other vertex. A *clique* is a maximal complete subgraph, i.e., a complete subgraph which is not properly contained in any other. An *isomorphism* between two graphs G = (V,E) and G' = (V',E') is a one-to-one mapping ¢: G → G' such that if *uv* $\in$ E then ¢(u)¢(v) $\in$ E'. Thus isomorphism preserves adjacency. If the graph is labeled, then isomorphism must also preserve the labeling (Read and Corneil, 1977). Clearly |V| = |V'|. A *subgraph isomorphism* is a mapping from a graph G to a subgraph H of G', such that G is isomorphic to H. A *common subgraph* of two graphs, G_1 and G_2, consists of a subgraph H_1 of G_1 and subgraph H_2 of G_2 such that H_1 is isomorphic to H_2.

USE OF ALGORITHMS FROM GRAPH THEORY IN CHEMOINFORMATICS

Molecular Graphs

Chemists naturally think in terms of structure diagrams of molecules (Figure 1). Such diagrams are clearly also labeled undirected graphs whose vertices are atoms (labeled with atomic type) and

Figure 1. A molecule as a (hydrogen-suppressed) graph. a) Structure diagram, unlabeled atoms are carbons. b) Molecular graph, atoms are replaced by labeled nodes where no label is the (implicit) label carbon. Bonds become labeled edges, 1 indicates a single bond, 2 indicates a double bond.

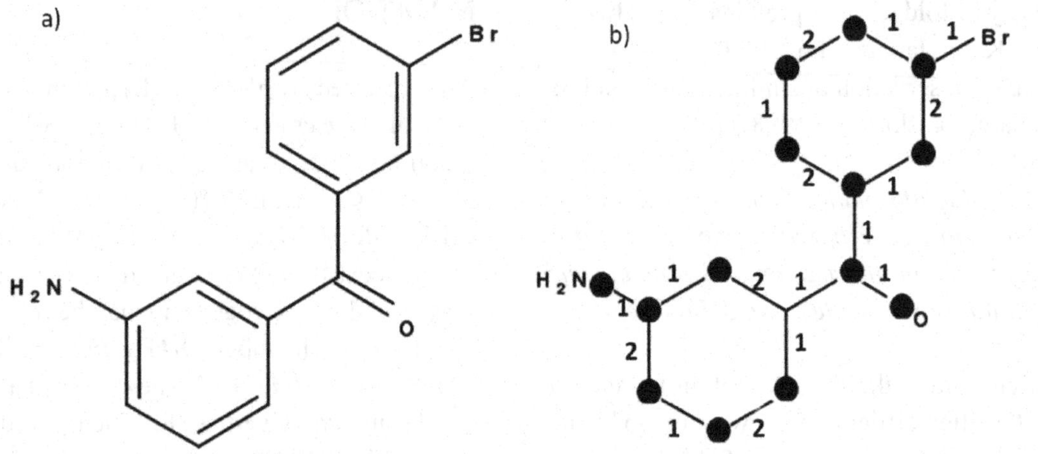

whose edges are bonds (labeled with the bond type, single, double or triple). It is common to ignore hydrogen atoms when constructing the molecular graph – such a representation is called hydrogen-suppressed. However it is important to remember that the structure diagram is a simplified abstraction of a flexible three-dimensional entity.

As a *molecular graph*, a chemical structure may be represented by its adjacency lists which in this context are called a connection table (CT). For a 2D chemical structure, the CT contains, for each non-hydrogen atom, a list of each non-hydrogen atom to which it is attached together with the bond type which forms the connection. A CT as just described is *redundant* due to the symmetric nature of the table; if the information is only stored once the CT is *non-redundant*. NB the rules of chemistry mean that the existence of, and attachment to, hydrogen atoms can be inferred from the 2D CT. A 2D description of a molecule is often referred to as being *topological* (A.R. Leach & Gillet, 2007). Common file formats include the MDL mol and SDF formats and the Sybyl mol2 format developed by Tripos. All these are text files, generally with separate sections for

atoms, bonds and other information (such as atom coordinates), separated by specific delimiters. An example of a molecule and its representation as a mol2 file are given in Figure 2.

Another well-studied molecular graph is the 2D (topological) distance matrix, often denoted D. Here the vertices are again atoms whilst the edges are bond distances (see Figure 4b).

For a 3D molecular graph one needs to determine the atomic coordinates. This has been done experimentally for a large number of molecules using techniques such as x-ray crystallography. For example, the Cambridge Structural Database (Allen, 2002) contains the structures of more than 525,000 experimentally determined organic compounds. However most molecules have no experimental structure available. Their structures must be generated using sets of rules based on standard bond lengths, bond angles and torsion angle preferences and the minimization of any unfavourable interactions. Two commonly used programs are CONCORD (Rusinko, Skell, Balducci, & Pearlman, 1986) and OMEGA (Hawkins, Skillman, Warren, Ellingson, & Stahl). Unfortunately most molecules are flexible – the different

Figure 2. mol2 file format a) Simple molecule. b) Mol2 representation: in this representation the carbon bonded to 3 hydrogens (atoms 6, 7, 8) is atom 1, the central carbon is atom 2, the oxygen double-bonded to atom 2 is atom 3, the nitrogen is atom 4, the other oxygen is atom 5.

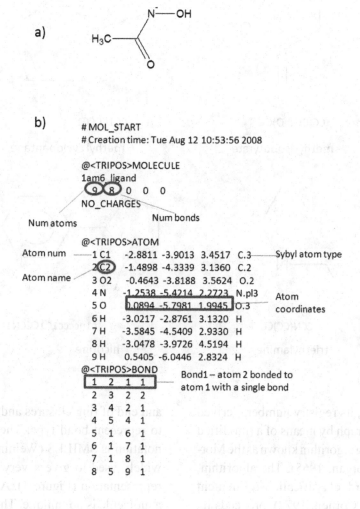

shapes which a molecule can adopt are known as its *conformers*. It is therefore a gross simplification to consider merely a single low-energy molecular conformation, but it is a simplification which is frequently made and which can work well in practice. Once a 3D structure has been obtained, the edges in the 3D molecular graph represent the inter-atomic distances. Both the distance matrix and the 3D molecular graph are complete.

There are many public and commercial repositories of 2D and 3D structural chemistry data.

Reviews are given by (Jonsdottir, Jorgensen, & Brunak, 2005; Southan, Varkonyi, & Muresan, 2007; Villar & Hansen, 2009).

Graph-Labeling

A CT, as described above, provides an unambiguous representation of a molecule but it is not unique. The need for a unique and unambiguous labeling for chemical graphs arose from the desire to register compounds. The Chemical Abstracts Service (CAS) gives each compound a unique

Figure 3. Examples SMILES strings. Brackets represent branches, pairs of integers represent ring closures, lowercase letter sequences represent aromatic (alternating single/double) bonds.

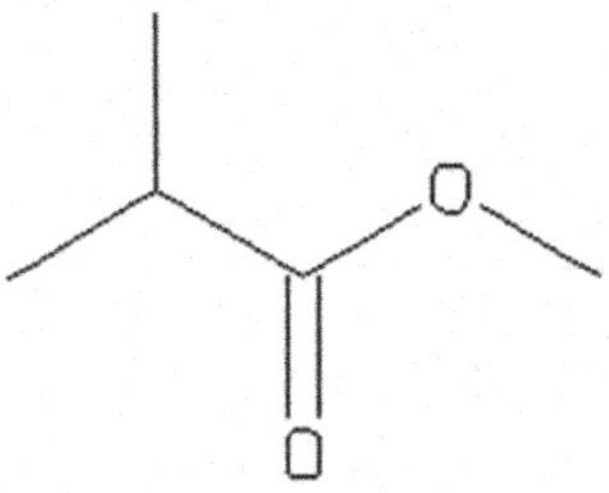

CC(C)C(=O)OC

methyl isobutyrate

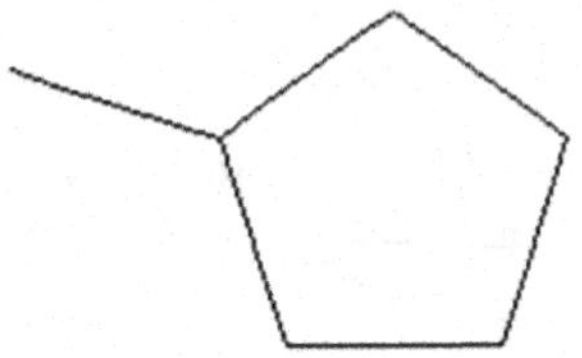

CC1CCCC1

methyl cyclopentane

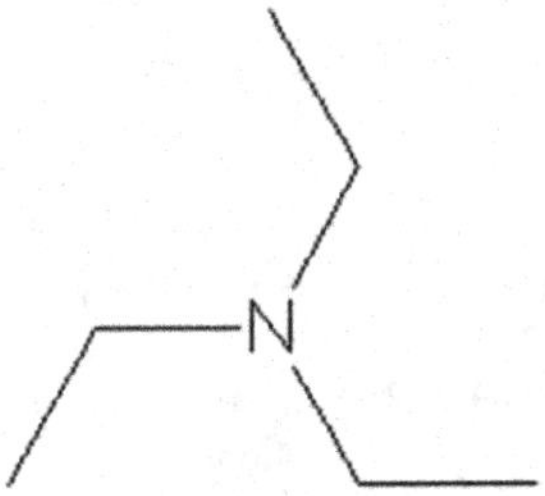

CCN(CC)CC

triethylamine

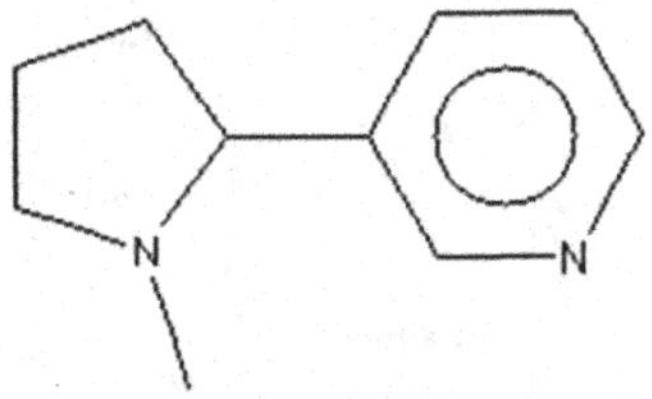

c1ncccc1C1CCCN1C

nicotine

alphanumeric label, its registry number, derived from its chemical graph by means of a (modified version of a) labeling algorithm known as the Morgan Algorithm (Morgan, 1965). The algorithm, which is a standard classification-refinement algorithm (Read & Corneil, 1977), proceeds by generating a set of labelings and then choosing the lexicographically lowest as the unique label. The nature of chemical graphs (each vertex has connectivity at most 4, there are a limited number of atom types which are the vertex labels) plus the intelligent heuristics used in the algorithm means that the number of labelings which have to be generated before the lowest can be chosen is not too large to be prohibitive.

Molecular graphs can also be represented by strings of atom symbols, with parentheses used to represent branches, integers used for the start

and end of ring closures and other symbols used to represent bond type. The most popular such notation is SMILES (Weininger, 1988) which is widely used to give a very compact molecular representation (Figure 3). A SMILES string for a molecule is not unique. The use of the Morgan algorithm however allows the SMILES generation to proceed in a standard order producing a *canonical* SMILES string.

Graph Invariants

Graphs may be classified by any one of a huge number of so-called *graph invariants*. A graph invariant is a number calculated for a graph from its structure, its value is independent of how the graph is drawn or labeled (Rucker, Rucker, & Meringer, 2002). Graphs which are isomorphic

Figure 4. Formation of a correspondence graph. a) Two molecules. b) Generate complete graphs where the edge between two atoms is labeled with the shortest path between them. c) Generate the vertices, all ordered pairs of atoms, one from each graph, where the atoms (labels) are of the same type. So, for example, C1 can match C1' and C2'. N3 can match N3' and O, S do not match. Join two vertices if the 'distance' (= edge label) in the first graph is same as the distance in the second graph. So C1 – N3 has label 2, so does C1' and N3', therefore they are joined. It is immediately apparent that any common subgraph is induced. d) The MCS.

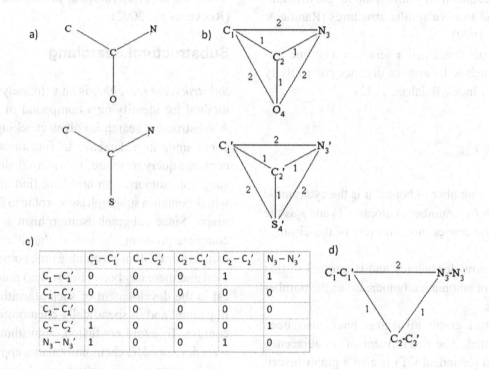

will have the same graph invariants although the converse is, of course, false, i.e. graph invariants are degenerate. Chemists have long been interested in graph invariants, many of which capture some essential property of the molecule whose graph is under consideration. Graph invariants calculated simply from the CT or 2D distance matrix are often called *Topological Indices (TIs)*. TIs are a kind of *molecular descriptor*, a numerical value which characterizes the property of a molecule (A.R. Leach & Gillet, 2007) and as such a set of TIs may be calculated for all the molecules in a database, as is done using the MOLCONN-Z computer program (Molconn-Z). The most obvious graph invariants are the number of edges and the number of vertices. There is also much interest discovering more discriminating graph invariants, with a balance needed between ease of calculation and discrimination.

The first graph invariant to become established was a TI, the Wiener Index, W (Wiener, 1947).

$$W = \frac{1}{2} \sum_{i,j} D_{ij}$$

where D_{ij} is the shortest path between two non-hydrogen atoms, i and j. Wiener showed that W was linearly correlated with the boiling point of a series of alkanes. This is a simple example of a Quantitative Structure Activity Relationship (QSAR), which is an important field in chemoinformatics (Kier & Hall, 1986). However the Wiener index shows a fairly high degree of degeneracy.

Randic and co-workers developed many path-based TIs. The distribution of path lengths for a molecule can be characteristic of a molecule, so that molecules with similar path length distributions tend to have similar structures (Randic & Wilkins, 1979).

Balaban developed a series of TIs: one important such is the average distance connectivity index or J index(Balaban, 1982).

$$J = \frac{q}{\mu + 1} \sum_{edge, si, j} \left(s_i s_j \right)^{-1/2}$$

where q = number of bonds, μ is the cyclomatic number = (q – number of atoms + 1) and s_i is the sum of the entries in the ith row of the distance matrix.

J has low degeneracy and is unusual in that it does not automatically increase as the number of atoms.

Spectral graph invariants have also been investigated. The determinant of an adjacency matrix (a redundant CT) is also a graph invariant, as is its characteristic polynomial and thus so are its eigenvalues (its spectrum). These spectral invariants are slower to calculate than the simple topological indices but might be expected to be more discriminating since they contain more information. However the smallest cospectral (having the same spectrum) simple graphs have only 6 vertices (Balaban & Harary, 1971), degeneracy beginning at the same size molecule as that of Balaban's far simpler J index.

Since 2D molecualr graphs are relatively simple, with all vertices having degree at most four, it may seem likely that there is a graph invariant which can uniquely characterize such graphs. However to date, despite vast amounts of effort having been expended in the search, no such invariants have been found. However, for some applications well-discriminating indices, or combinations thereof, do suffice. For example Rucker et al demonstrate that for some classes of saturated hydrocarbons their program NISMG is able to find all distinct subgraphs with fewer than ten vertices using a combination of Balaban's J index and the eigenvalues of the distance matrix (Rucker et al., 2002).

Substructural Searching

Substructural searching is an extremely popular method for identifying a compound of interest. A substructure search involves checking all the compounds in a database to find those which contain a query structure. This is equivalent to the subgraph isomorphism problem: find all graphs which contain a subgraph isomorphic to the query graph. Since subgraph isomorphism is an NP-complete problem, the use of algorithms which can perform within acceptable time constraints is vital and there has been (and still is) much interest in the development of such algorithms both in general and in specifically chemoinformatics context. To avoid confusion, algorithms which were developed for chemoinformatics applications will be referred to as substructural search algorithms whilst those developed in a more general context and adapted for substructure search will be referred to as subgraph isomorphism algorithms. Although published nearly 20 years ago a review of substructure searching algorithms by Barnard (Barnard, 1993) still provides an excellent overview of work in the field – indeed there have been few recent advances in this area.

Many substructural searching algorithms employ a depth-first search strategy. In depth-first search all nodes are initially marked as unvisited. A node k is chosen as the root node, marked as visited, and then all unvisited nodes connected to k are (recursively) visited. Alternatively, in breadth-first search all nodes connected to k are visited, followed by all nodes two edges distant from k etc (Decker, Lenz, & Borgelt, 2007; Sedgewick,

1998). The first substructural searching algorithm was that of (Ray & Kirsch, 1957) but this was a very inefficient depth-first back-tracking algorithm. Back-tracking algorithms assign an initial mapping to from a single atom of the query structure to an atom of the database compound (the target) of the same atom type. The algorithm then proceeds iteratively to match neighbors of the query atom to neighbors of the target atom, then neighbors of query neighbors to neighbors of target neighbors, etc. If at some point no match can be found, the algorithm backtracks to the previous successfully matched atom and attempts an alternative match. If at some point all query atoms are successfully matched then the query structure has been found within the target structure.

Other techniques, usually used in conjunction with back-tracking, include vertex-partitioning and relaxation. Vertex-partitioning is based initially on atom typing in the two structures being matched. If, for example, the query contains an oxygen bonded to two carbons, then it can only be matched to an oxygen with the same connections in the target structure, and so a partition can be constructed containing all oxygen atoms of the target which fulfill this criterion. Relaxation is then used to refine the partitions, usually by iteratively considering more distant neighbors. Substructure algorithms which use these techniques include (Figueras, 1972; Sussenguth, 1965; Vonscholley, 1984).

Chemoinformatics as a discipline is particularly concerned with the development of efficient algorithms and, as a corollary, with the comparison of published algorithms to determine which, if any, is the most efficient on the specific data domain to which it is to be applied. Such a comparison of substructure and subgraph isomorphism algorithms by Brint and Willett led to the widespread adoption of the Ullmann algorithm (Ullmann, 1976) as the algorithm of choice for substructural searching (Brint & Willett, 1987b).

The Ullmann subgraph isomorphism algorithm is a combination of back-tracking and refinement

(Barnard, 1993) and operates on the adjacency matrices of the query, **Q**, and the target **T**. If the query substructure contains q atoms and the target molecule contains t atoms, a new $q \times t$ matrix, the matching matrix, **M** is constructed. The initial entries of M indicate possible correspondences between atoms of Q and T (indicated by a value of 1) and definite non-correspondences (if, for example the atom types are different, indicated by a value of 0). Successive refinement steps attempt to replace 1's by 0's so that each row of M contains a single 1 and each column contains no more than one 1. For each instance of the query within the target the matching matrix **M** must satisfy $\mathbf{M(MT)}^{\mathrm{T}} = \mathbf{Q}$. In this case **M** will define a mapping from **Q** to **T** where atom i of **Q** maps to atom j of **T**.

Although the Ullmann algorithm is very efficient, it remains relatively time-consuming for use in databases containing hundreds of thousands of compounds. The standard method of substructure search is therefore first to screen the database and eliminate all those compounds which cannot possibly contain the query substructure. Modern efficient fragment-based screening systems mean that more than 99% of the potential candidates can be omitted from the more rigorous substructure search procedure.

More recent developments include the feature-based similarity search of Yan and co-workers (Yan, Zhu, Yu, & Han, 2006) which uses filtering and pre-indexed structural patterns (Yan, Yu, & Han, 2004) to avoid time-consuming structural comparisons. Graph-matching is regarded as an edit operation and so the similarity between a pair of graphs is the percentage of retained edges when the first graph has been transformed into the second.

Similarity Searching in 2D and 3D Using Maximum Clique Algorithms

An extremely important principle in chemoinformatics is the similar-property principle which states that molecules that are structurally similar are likely to exhibit similar activity (M. A. Johnson & Maggiora, 1990). Thus if one has an active molecule of interest (the query) and a database of chemical structures, the database can be ranked in order of similarity to the query with the highest ranked molecules (the *nearest neighbors*) being most likely to be similarly active. A disadvantage of substructure searching is that it is a binary solution to the problem of identifying molecules of interest. The database is partitioned into two sets of molecules, those which contain a query substructure and those which do not. There is no control over the size of the output. Similarity searching overcomes this disadvantage – one can select the top n% most similar molecules in decreasing order of similarity (P. Willett, Barnard, & Downs, 1998).

In order to conduct a similarity search one needs a method of determining the similarity between a pair of molecules. Whilst the purpose of this review is to describe the use of graph theory in chemoinformatics, it would be highly misleading to assume that graph-theoretic methods are the most commonly used methods for searching chemical databases. Indeed other molecular representations and searching methods have proved highly efficient and effective. The most common method of representing a molecule is by a means of a binary *fingerprint*, with bits set on (off) to represent the presence (absence) of particular topological substructures or fragments (Peter Willett, 2006). The similarity between a pair of molecules can then be determined simply by comparing their bitstrings. The most commonly-used similarity coefficient is the Tanimoto coefficient, in which the similarity between a pair of molecules, A and B, represented by binary bitstrings, is

$$Similarity_{AB} = \frac{c}{a + b - c}$$

where a, b are the number of bits set on in A, B and c is the number of bits set on in both A and B (A.R. Leach & Gillet, 2007).

However fragment-based approaches may retrieve only molecules which are very similar to the query molecule. Recently there has been much interest in the ability to find molecules with a different "scaffold" (i.e. central ring system) to that of the query molecule – this process is known as *scaffold-hopping* and is highly desirable for a number of reasons. The chief of these is the ability to circumvent patents held by competitors. An intuitively appealing measure of the similarity between two molecules is the "largest" substructure which the two molecules have in common, which, in graph-theoretic terms, is a *Maximum Common Subgraph* (MCS). There are two definitions of MCS which can be considered, the Maximum Common Induced Subgraph (MCIS) and the Maximum Common Edge Subgraph (MCES). A *vertex-induced subgraph* is a set of vertices and all the edges which connect them. An *edge-induced subgraph* is a set of edges and all the vertices which are at their end points. The MCIS is the largest vertex-induced common subgraph and the MCES is the largest edge-induced common subgraph. The MCES is also known as the Maximum Overlapping Set (MOS) (Raymond, Gardiner, & Willett, 2002a).

It is well-known that the problem of determining the MCS between two graphs is equivalent to finding the maximum cliques of a different graph (Barrow and Burstall, 1976). This equivalence is very frequently used in chemoinformatics. So, given two graphs, G_1 and G_2, it is possible to form a third graph, called a *correspondence graph* C (also known as a *compatibility graph*, an *association graph*, a *modular product graph*), such that the cliques of the correspondence graph correspond to the MCIS's between the two graphs. The vertices of C are the set of ordered pairs of vertices of G_1 and G_2 where the atom types are the same. Then a pair of vertices of C, (I, X) and (J,Y), are adjacent if the interatomic distance I → J is the same as that of X → Y (to within some user defined tolerance). In the case of 2D molecular graphs, the "distance" between two vertices is the number of bonds between the atoms, which, in graph-theoretic terms, is the shortest path between them. A maximum clique of the correspondence graph then provides a mapping between the vertices of an MCIS of the two molecules. The formation of a correspondence graph from two simple molecules is illustrated in Figure 4.

In the case of the MCES, we first form the line graphs of the molecular graphs (Figure 5). In a line graph L(G) the vertices of L are the edges of G and an edge is formed in L(G) between two vertices if they have an endpoint in common. A correspondence graph is then generated, as before, but this time from the line graphs, not from the molecular graphs. Then the cliques of the correspondence graph map back to the common subgraphs of the line graphs, which correspond to the MCES of the original graphs, as long as a ΔY graph interchange has not occurred (see Figure 6) (Whitney, 1932).

The graph similarity between two molecules is frequently measured using a variation of the Tanimoto coefficient for graph comparison:

$$Similarity_{AB} = \frac{|G_{AB}|}{|G_A| + |G_B| - |G_{AB}|}$$

where $|G_{AB}|$ is the number of vertices in the MCS, $|G_A|$ is the number of vertices in G_A and $|G_B|$ is the number of vertices in G_B.

Whilst quantifying the similarity between two molecules, the MCS also provides an overlay. An algorithm such as (Kabsch, 1976) can be used to generate an alignment from the matching atoms identified in the MCS.

Clique-Detection Algorithms in Similarity Searching

Determining all the cliques in a graph is well-known to be an NP-complete problem and so efficient algorithms are particularly important. In 2D there are few examples of the successful use of MCS similarity measures. One example is that developed by Hagadone which made significant use of heuristics to determine an upper bound on the size of the MCS before applying an approximate MCS procedure to the surviving pairs of molecules (Hagadone, 1992).

Figure 5. Forming the line graph. a) Molecule; b) its line graph

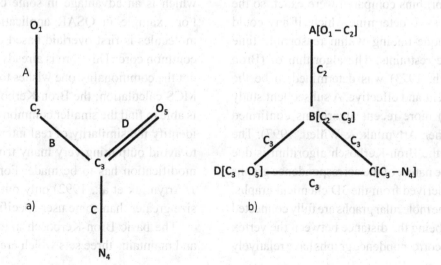

Figure 6. Delta Y interchange: a) two non-isomorphic graphs, K3 and K1,3; b) the line graphs are isomorphic

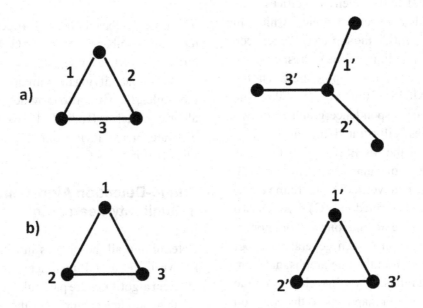

However in 3D, MCS algorithms have found a wider application. (Crandell & Smith, 1983) first developed an algorithm to overlay two molecules in order to determine their MCS. (Brint & Willett, 1987a) conducted comparisons of clique-detection algorithms for determining the MCIS between pairs of small molecules in 3D. All the algorithms compared were exact, so the intention was to determine which, if any could perform clique-finding within reasonable time and storage restraints. The algorithm of (Bron & Kerbosch, 1973) was determined to be the most efficient and effective. A subsequent study with (then) more recent algorithms confirmed this (Gardiner, Artymiuk, & Willett, 1997). The success of the Bron-Kerbosch algorithm is due to the sparse nature of the correspondence graphs which are derived from the 3D chemical graphs. Although the molecular graphs are fully connected (the edges being the distance between the vertex atoms), the correspondence graphs have relatively low edge density (usually less than 10% of the possible edges are formed). Most clique-detection algorithms are designed to perform well on graphs of high edge density, which is not a requirement for comparing small molecules.

The Bron-Kerbosch algorithm finds all the cliques of a graph, not just the maximum cliques, which is an advantage in some circumstances. For example in QSAR applications, a set of molecules is first overlaid based on some large common core. This core is already known and is not the commonality one wishes to find using an MCS calculation; the Bron-Kerbosch algorithm is able to find the smaller common cliques which identify the similarity of real interest. However, to avoid outputting very many trivial cliques, a modification has to be made. For example, (P. J. Artymiuk et al., 1992) only output cliques of size greater than some user-specified parameter.

The basic Bron-Kerbosch algorithm creates and maintains three sets which are:

1. *compsub*. This is the set of vertices which currently form a complete subgraph. Thus every vertex of *compsub* is connected to every other vertex. The cardinality of *compsub* corresponds to the current depth of the search tree.
2. *candidates*. This is the set of vertices which are currently available to extend the present configuration of *compsub*. Thus these vertices are also connected to every vertex of *compsub*.
3. *not*. This is the set of vertices which has already been used to extend the present *compsub* and thus these vertices are also connected to every vertex of *compsub*. These vertices are explicitly excluded from being *candidates*.

This set-triple is maintained for every depth, d, of the search tree; (i.e. at every level d there exist sets $compsub_d$, $candidates_d$ and not_d).

An "extension operator" is applied to $compsub_d$, $candidates_d$ and not_d. This generates all extensions (additions of just one vertex) of $compsub_d$ which it can make from the set $candidates_d$ and still exclude all members of not_d. The extension operator is recursive and for each of the new sets (now at level $d+1$) the extension process is repeated.

Clearly, for $compsub_d$ to be a clique, $candidates_d$ must be empty. However, by the definition of the sets, if not_d is non-empty then $compsub_d$ has already been contained in a larger complete subgraph and so cannot now be a clique. Thus $compsub_d$ is a clique if and only if $candidates_d$ and not_d are both empty.

The basic algorithm is given in 5 steps. These are:

1. Choose a candidate vertex from $candidates_d$.
2. Add the candidate to $compsub_d$ to give $compsub_{d+1}$.
3. Create new sets $candidates_{d+1}$ and not_{d+1} by removing all points (from both sets) not connected to the chosen candidate.
4. Call the extension operator to operate on $compsub_{d+1}$, $candidates_{d+1}$ and not_{d+1}.
5. Upon return, remove chosen candidate from $compsub_{d+1}$, $candidates_d$ and add to not_d.

The algorithm as described will find all cliques, but is just a backtracking search tree and so is very inefficient. The heart of the algorithm is the choice of candidate to extend compsub. Consider the set *not*. For a clique to be found, *not* must be empty. The only time points are removed from *not* is at step 3 of the algorithm where all points not connected to the chosen candidate vertex are removed. Thus, if there exists a vertex x in not_d which is connected to every vertex of $candidates_d$ then x can never be removed from not_d or subsequent *not*s. This is therefore a bound condition for the algorithm. A well-chosen candidate is one for which the bound is reached soonest. (In this way, ultimately unsuccessful paths can be eliminated higher up the tree).

Bron and Kerbosch accomplish this by keeping track (at each level d) of the vertex p_d, of not_d which is disconnected to the smallest number of vertices of $candidates_d$ (and therefore connected to the most) and always choosing a candidate which is not connected to p_d. The operation of the algorithm on a simple graph is illustrated in Figure 7.

The Bron-Kerbosch algorithm was adopted in various similarity-searching systems, for example the DISCO program (Martin et al., 1993) although it was not fast enough for searching in databases of hundreds of thousands of molecules (P. Willett, 2005) especially in 2D where the density of the correspondence graphs is high.

More recently the RASCAL (RApid Similarity CAcuLation) has been developed (Raymond et al., 2002a; Raymond, Gardiner, & Willett, 2002b; Raymond & Willett, 2002a, 2002b) and this has

Figure 7. Operation of the Bron-Kerbosch Algorithm. d is the depth of the recursion. For details of the sets see the text.

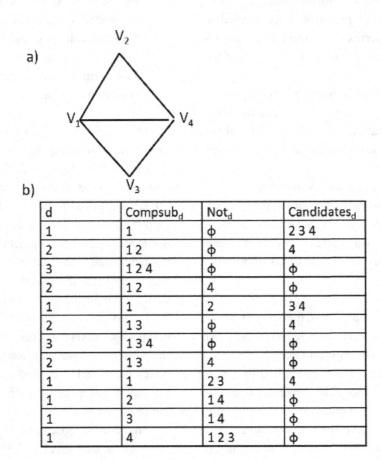

d	Compsub$_d$	Not$_d$	Candidates$_d$
1	1	φ	2 3 4
2	1 2	φ	4
3	1 2 4	φ	φ
2	1 2	4	φ
1	1	2	3 4
2	1 3	φ	4
3	1 3 4	φ	φ
2	1 3	4	φ
1	1	2 3	4
1	2	1 4	φ
1	3	1 4	φ
1	4	1 2 3	φ

revived interest in the use of MCS calculations in very large databases. RASCAL is an MCES algorithm and uses an alternative measure of similarity developed from that of Johnson (M. Johnson, 1985) and given by

$$sim(G_A, G_B) = \frac{(|V(G_{AB})| + |E(G_{AB})|)^2}{(|V(G_A)| + |E(G_A)|)(|V(G_B)| + |E(G_B)|)}$$

where G_{AB} is the MCES of G_A and G_B.

The RASCAL algorithm comprises two main parts with the first part being an upper bound procedure used to screen out molecules which cannot be similar enough to the target. RASCAL uses a user-defined *Minimum Similarity Index* (MSI): a

value of 0.7 was found to discriminate between molecules whose structural similarity was sufficiently "chemically sensible" and the remainder (Raymond et al., 2002b). Only if the molecules are sufficiently similar are they subjected to the clique-detection procedure which is more computationally demanding. The upper bound procedure itself is in two tiers, sim^{cost1} and sim-^{cost2}, the upper bound being tightened by a second computation, sim^{cost2}, for those molecules which survive the first cut. The upper-bound procedures are both *cost-based*, meaning that the similarities they approximate are a measure of the number of edit operations required to transform one graph into another. The upper-bound procedures have the property, for any two graphs G_A and G_B, that $\text{sim}^{\text{cost1}}(G_A, G_B) \geq \text{sim}^{\text{cost2}}(G_A, G_B) \geq \text{sim}(G_A, G_B)$.

The first tier similarity, $\text{sim}^{\text{cost1}}$, is based on sorted degree sequences and can be performed in $O(n)$ time (where n is the number of atom types present in the molecules). The second tier similarity, $\text{sim}^{\text{cost2}}$, is based on a linear assignment procedure and can be performed in $O(n^3)$ time (where n is again the number of atom types present in the molecules).

The clique-detection procedure in RASCAL is a branch and bound procedure which contains a number of novel pruning, node selection, lower-bounding and upper-bounding heuristics which are applicable to general MCS problems; these are too complex to be described here and are detailed in (Raymond et al., 2002b). RASCAL uses the line graph/ correspondence graph formulation of the MCES problem described above. An advantage of this formulation is that, in a chemical context, the MCES is the common structure with the largest number of bonds rather than the most atoms (which is the MCIS). In the context of overlaying chemical structures, maximising the number of bonds in the overlay makes more sense. RASCAL was shown in tests to be able to compute similarities between thousands of pairs of molecules per second on a desktop PC.

Pharmacophore Elucidation

An important concept in chemoinformatics is that of the *pharmacophore* which describes the three-dimensional arrangement of chemical features required for a ligand to bind to a protein target. The pharmacophore can be considered as the largest common denominator shared by a set of active molecules (A. R. Leach, Gillet, Lewis, & Taylor). Thus in the absence of knowledge about a protein target, significant information can be deduced from the pharmacophore defined by a set of ligands which bind to it. Since most molecules are flexible, pharmacophore elucidation is a very difficult problem involving the search of con-

former space to find matching subsets of feature points from the different molecules. Identifying the correct solution can also be extremely difficult. One of the difficulties is that, even if the correct set of pharmacophoric features are overlaid, if the molecules are not in their binding conformations, the deduced pharmacophore will be incorrect. Since their common MCS provides an intuitive alignment of a set of ligands, MCS (equivalently clique-detection) methods have been widely used for pharmacophore elucidation.

Usually, in pharmacophore applications, each ligand is pre-processed to determine its potential pharmacophore points. As an example, a cyclin-dependent kinase inhibitor is shown in Figure 8, with its hydrogen bond donor, hydrogen bond acceptor and hydrophobic features annotated.

Several groups use graph-theoretic methods as part of a wider pharmacophore elucidation program. (Cheeseright, Mackey, Rose, & Vinter, 2006) use clique-detection to overlay the extrema (called field points) of their XED force-field to generate a pairwise alignment of two molecules. Four types of field points can be calculated: positive, negative; hydrophobic and van der Waals, depending on the potential used. The alignments are optimised using a simplex algorithm. PharmID described by (Feng, Sanil, & Young, 2006) uses a Gibbs sampler to find sets of conformations, one from each ligand, that have a high probability of containing common configurations. This set is then subjected to clique detection to find common configurations. (Gardiner, Cosgrove, Taylor, & Gillet, 2009) use a multi-objective genetic algorithm which searches ligand conformational space on the fly rather than by using pre-generated conformers. However its performance was much improved when the initial population of potential pharmacophores was generated using a conformer library. The Bron-Kerbosch algorithm was used to overlay subsets of conformers and the cliques generated were used as the basis for the initial population.

Figure 8. cdk2 inhibitor with its potential pharmacophore points highlighted. D1-D2 are hydrogen bond donors, A1-A2 are hydrogen bond acceptors and H1-H3 are hydrophobic centres.

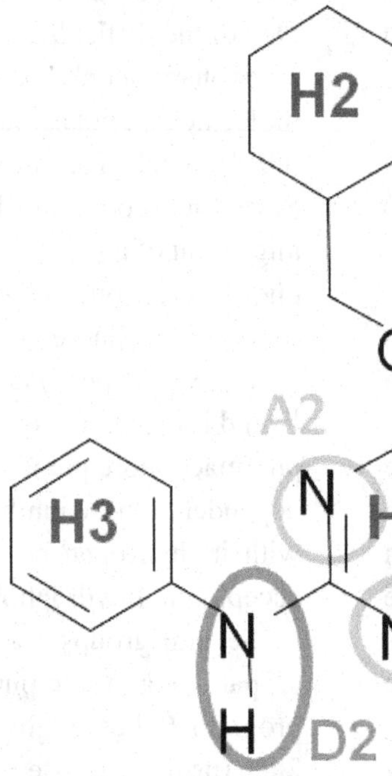

An entirely clique-based approach is described by (Podolyan & Karypis, 2009) in a method they call *frequent clique detection*. The method exploits the fact that although a molecule may have many different conformers, a pair of conformers will share a large degree of structural similarity. Each conformer is described as a graph (a conformer graph) whose vertices are pharmacophore points. The inter-point distances are binned and the edges are labeled with both their own bin and the closest neighboring bin. Points which are relatively distant are not connected by edges. The conformer graphs are also vertex-labeled using a canonical graph labeling based on the minimum adjacency matrix (Kuramochi & Karypis, 2007) for improved efficiency. Then a potential common pharmacophore (a clique) is a set of labeled points plus edges which is embedded in at least one conformer of each of the molecules. A big advantage of the method is that the number of molecules for which

this is true (termed the *support* of the clique) can be relaxed, meaning that the algorithm is able to find partial pharmacophores, something many pharmacophore programs are unable to do. The embedded cliques are found using one of two algorithms developed by the authors, termed the *Multiple Conformer Miner* and the *Unified Conformer Miner* algorithms.

Once a pharmacophore has been elucidated, it can be used in a database similarity search. Again this can be done using an MCS calculation, as in for example the CLIP program (Rhodes, Willett, Calvet, Dunbar, & Humblet, 2003).

Clique-Detection Algorithms in Protein-Ligand Docking

The aim of protein-ligand docking is ".. to predict the 3D structure (or structures) formed when one or more molecules form an intermolecular complex" (A.R. Leach & Gillet, 2007). Docking was initially a very time-consuming process, focused on the detailed analysis of only a few complexes. Recent advances in computer power means that now large numbers of ligands can be docked into the binding site of a protein target to identify those which might bind, a process known as structure-based virtual screening. Docking is a two stage process. Since there are very many ways in which a ligand can be fitted into the binding site of a protein, a large number of putative 3D structures is generated (often called a pose) and each of these must be scored. Here the focus is on graph-based docking algorithms rather than scoring functions.

Docking algorithms are based on the idea of some sort of 'complementarity' between the two interacting molecules. This idea was expressed by Pauling and Delbruck (1940) '...to achieve maximum stability, the two molecules must have complementary surfaces, like die and coin, and also a complementary distribution of active groups.'

Docking methods are usually classified as being either shape-based or energy-based (Hart & Read, 1992). Shape-based methods essentially try to find maximal regions of surface complementarity between the two molecules. Energy-based methods seek to minimise the interaction energy of the docked complex. Most graph-based methods are shape-based.

The obvious approach (initially adopted by (Kuntz, Blaney, Oatley, Langridge, & Ferrin, 1982) in their highly influential DOCK algorithm) is to identify the two surfaces as the two domains of a bipartite graph and to look for maximum matchings between the two. Although intuitively attractive, this approach is very demanding computationally. Subsequently their bi-partite method was replaced by the Bron-Kerbosch clique detection algorithm (Ewing & Kuntz, 1997). An alternative, correspondence graph approach is taken by (Kuhl, Crippen, & Friesen, 1984). This representation of the two molecules by a single graph means that clique detection can be used. Kuhl et al. use the

Bron and Kerbosch algorithm. Clique detection is also used in the FLOG program (Miller, Kearsley, Underwood, & Sheridan, 1994). In an alternative approach, the Ullmann algorithm is used by (Kasinos, Lilley, Subbarao, & Haneef, 1992).

Clustering

Chemical databases are routinely clustered, for several different purposes. One is the selection of a diverse but representative set of compounds. This is based on an application of the similar property principle. If structurally similar molecules exhibit similar activity then the selection of a set of structurally diverse compounds should maximize the coverage of the activities represented in the database (A.R. Leach & Gillet, 2007). One method for achieving this is to cluster the database and then pick a molecule to represent each cluster.

For clustering purposes one needs a set of objects to be clustered, a method for quantifying the similarity between pairs of objects and an algorithm which processes the similarities in order to decide which objects belong in the same cluster. The most widely used similarity measure for chemical clustering is the fingerprint/Tanimoto coefficient combination described above whilst the two most popular clustering algorithms are the Jarvis-Patrick (Jarvis & Patrick, 1973) and Wards (Ward, 1963). Until the development of the RASCAL algorithm, clustering using a graph-based similarity measure was impractical for large databases. (Raymond, Blankley, & Willett, 2003) showed that RASCAL-derived MCS similarities could be used with both Ward's and the Jarvis-Patrick method. They also used a new clustering algorithm, CAST, originally developed for clustering gene expression data (Ben-Dor, Shamir, & Yakhini, 1999) which is based on an approximate clique-detection algorithm. A further algorithm comparison by (Stahl, Mauser, Tsui, & Taylor, 2005) demonstrated that, of the six algorithms tested, RASCAL was the most efficient and effective algorithm for clustering– interestingly the

Bron-Kerbosch algorithm was included in this comparison. Subsequently the RASCAL algorithm was also used in refining clusters generated by a different method (Stahl & Mauser, 2005).

Reduced Graphs

Reduced graphs (RGs) provide summary representations of molecules. Groups of atoms are reduced to single vertices with the connectivity between the vertices reflecting the connectivity of atoms in the original chemical graph. Many different criteria can be used to generate the RG vertices, depending on the application (Gillet et al., 1987). Figure 9 shows several different types of graph reduction. RGs were originally developed at Sheffield University for searching in patents (Gillet, Downs, Holliday, Lynch, & Dethlefsen, 1991) (Lynch & Holliday, 1996) and are extensively used in commercial software such as MARPAT (Ebe, Sanderson, & Wilson, 1991) for this purpose. A drug patent is designed to cover a whole class of compounds. This can achieved by using a generic (or Markush) structure, consisting of a core structure and so-called R-groups which are used to represent lists of possible substituents. In most cases, the substituents can be classified as either ring or non-ring series, meaning that the Markush structure can be represented by a reduced graph

with ring/non-ring vertex types, a very simple example of which is shown in Figure 10.

RGs can also be used for similarity searching. When applied to similarity searching, the graph reduction process focuses on features of molecules that are likely to be important for interaction with a receptor, such as ring systems, charged groups and groups having hydrogen bonding ability. In this context reduced graphs are sometimes referred to as topological pharmacophores – the aim is to find sets of molecules with common functionalities without the need for the consideration of conformational flexibility. Various levels of specificity may be chosen. For example, rings may be split into sub-types, such as aromatic and aliphatic. Features are usually classified by their ability to accept or donate hydrogen bonds. Atoms having no functional classification may be grouped into non-feature vertices (sometimes called linkers). Such definitions usually result in about 12 vertex types (depending on the level of specificity). Ring systems are identified using ring perception algorithms such as that of Figueras (Figueras, 1996). Figure 11 shows two molecules with the same reduced graph.

In similarity searching applications RGs have often been represented as fingerprints (Barker, Gardiner, Gillet, Kitts, & Morris, 2003; Gillet, Willett, & Bradshaw, 2003) and their similarity

Figure 9. Different types of graph reduction

(a)

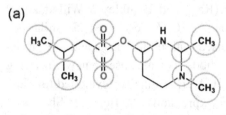

Cyclic/Acyclic Reduction

(b)

(c) **Homeomorphic Reduction**

Carbon/Heteroatom Reduction

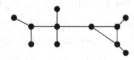

(d)

● Ring Node
● Non-ring node

● Heteroatom Node
● Carbon Node

Figure 10. A Markush structure and a corresponding reduced graph

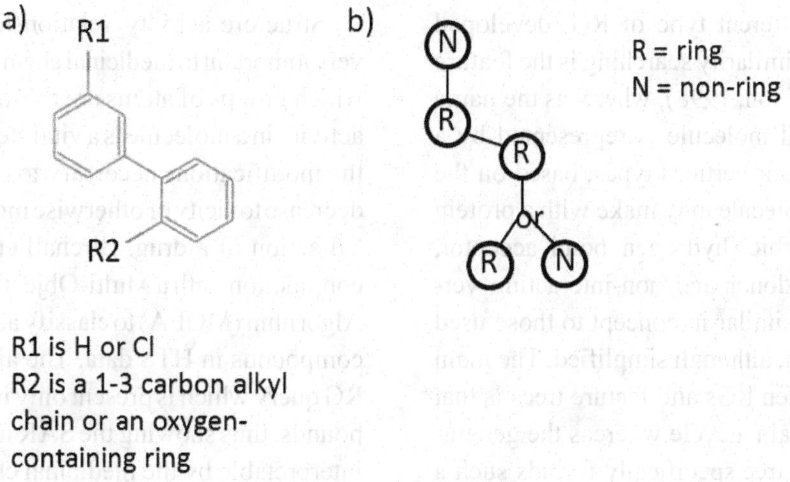

a)

R1

R2

R1 is H or Cl
R2 is a 1-3 carbon alkyl
chain or an oxygen-
containing ring

b)

R = ring
N = non-ring

has also been measured using an "edit-distance" (Harper, Bravi, Pickett, Hussain, & Green, 2004). All these studies showed that RGs were of comparable effectiveness to conventional 2D fingerprints when used for similarity searching and, additionally, tended to retrieve different subsets of the active compounds. The relatively small size of RGs means that the use of MCS algorithms for similarity searching is feasible and several groups have used RGs for just such a purpose (Takahashi, Sukekawa, & Sasaki, 1992). Since a single RG

vertex type, for example a hydrogen-bond donor, may represent many different groups of atoms, it was hypothesized that similarity searching using RGs might produce scaffold hops. Barker et al implemented both the RASCAL and Bron-Kerbosch algorithms in a comparison with searching using a traditional fingerprint method. They showed that RGs could indeed successfully be used for scaffold-hopping (Barker et al., 2006). Stiefl at al showed a similar ability to scaffold

Figure 11. Two molecules with the same reduced graph. The light grey RG vertex is an aromatic ring; the black vertex is an acid.

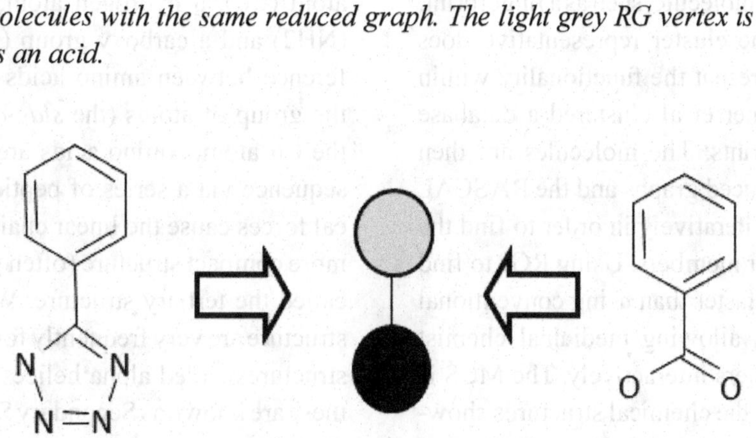

hop using their version of RGs (Stiefl, Watson, Baumann, & Zaliani, 2006).

A slightly different type of RG, developed specifically for similarity searching is the feature tree (Rarey & Dixon, 1998), where, as the name suggests, a small molecule is represented by a tree. There are four vertices types, based on the interactions a molecule may make with a protein target: hydrophobic, hydrogen bond acceptor, hydrogen bond donor and non-interacting vertices. These are similar in concept to those used in RG generation, although simplified. The main difference between RGs and feature trees is that an RG may contain a cycle whereas the generation of a feature tree specifically forbids such a construct. The advantage of feature trees is that trees are simple and there are fast algorithms for their comparison. Rarey and Dixon developed two such algorithms, termed match-search and split-search.

RGs have been used to cluster high throughput screening data (Harper et al., 2004). Each molecule is represented by several motifs, which include its reduced graph, with molecules sharing common motifs being placed in the same cluster. RGs have also recently been used for cluster representation. Chemical databases can be very large and one of the aims of clustering is to use a representative of the cluster to represent the molecules within the cluster. However clustering using an abstract representation of a molecule, such as a fingerprint, may mean that the cluster representative does not obviously represent the functionality within the cluster. Gardiner et al clustered a database using 2D fingerprints. The molecules are then represented as reduced graphs and the RASCAL algorithm applied iteratively in order to find the MCS of the cluster members. Using RGs to find the MCS is much faster than using conventional molecular graphs, allowing medicinal chemist to browse the clusters interactively. The MCS is mapped back onto the chemical structures showing the common functional features which may

be responsible for the cluster activity. (Gardiner, Gillet, Willett, & Cosgrove, 2007).

Structure-activity relationships (SARs) are very important to medicinal chemists. Determining which groups of atoms are responsible for which activity in a molecule is a vital step in determining the modifications necessary to enhance potency, decrease toxicity or otherwise modify the biological action of a drug. Birchall et al used RGs in conjunction with a Multi-Objective Evolutionary Algorithm (MOEA) to classify active and inactive compounds in HTS data. The aim is to evolve a RG query which is present only in the active compounds, thus showing the SAR in a form which is interpretable by the medicinal chemist (Birchall, Gillet, Harper, & Pickett, 2008a, 2008b).

USE OF ALGORITHMS FROM GRAPH THEORY IN STRUCTURAL BIOINFORMATICS

Before considering some applications of graph theory in structural bioinformatics, it is necessary to briefly consider some aspects of protein structure. Proteins are composed of a linear sequence of amino acids (often also called residues) of which twenty occur naturally. All amino acids are composed of the same 9-atom core, called the *main-chain* atoms, comprising a central carbon atom (Cα), a hydrogen atom, an amino group (NH2) and a carboxy group (COOH). The difference between amino acids is determined by the group of atoms (the *side-chain*) attached to the Cα atom. Amino acids are joined along the sequence via a series of peptide bonds. Chemical forces cause the linear chain to fold up into a more compact structure (often globular) which is called the tertiary structure. Within this tertiary structure are very frequently found two main substructures called alpha helices and beta strands; these are known as Secondary Structure Elements (SSEs) and are often joined by short flexible links of amino acids known as linker regions. Beta strands often also associate to form a section of the protein called a beta sheet. Simple sections of protein containing two alpha helices and two beta strands are shown in Figure 12 whilst Figure 13 shows the complete tertiary structure of the 126-residue protein kinase C interacting protein (PDB code 1av5) which has six alpha helices and ten beta strands in two sheets. The helix/strand representation is a huge simplification of the 126 residues which contain 1749 atoms, but this turns out to be extremely useful.

As discussed in the Background section, a protein's structure determines its function. Thus the discovery of structural resemblance between proteins is a very important method of assigning function to a protein whose function is unknown. It may be obvious, but perhaps is worth stating at this point, that determining some measure of structural similarity between a pair of proteins provides a means of aligning them, based on their

common structural elements, and, conversely, any meaningful alignment will provide a set of some common structural elements.

There has been a substantial crossover of graph-theoretic methods from chemoinformatics to structural bioinformatics and vice versa. At Sheffield University many collaborations between the chemoinformatics and structural biology groups have resulted in important algorithmic developments in methods for determining structural resemblances between proteins. One of the first resulted from using the simplified SSE protein representation described above. Both alpha helices and beta strands are approximately linear structures, and can thus be described as vectors (see Figure 12 c and f). A protein SSE graph can then be constructed whose vertices are labeled SSEs (i.e. labeled either H or S) and where the edge between a pair of vertices is labeled with a set of distances and torsion angles between the

Figure 12. Different representations of alpha helices and beta strands. a) space-filling representation of a portion of a protein containing two alpha helices joined by a linker region; b) when just the backbone atoms are shown the helical structure is much more apparent; c) the vector representation of the approximately linear helices. d) space-filling representation of a portion of a protein containing two beta strands joined by a linker region; b) when just the backbone atoms are shown the linear strand structure is much more apparent; c) the vector representation of the approximately linear strands.

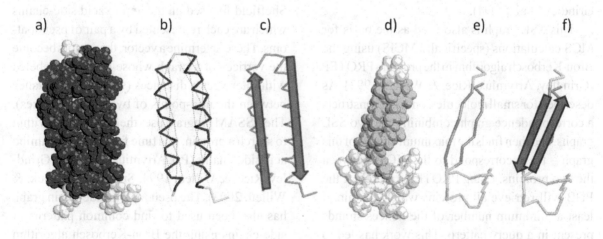

a) b) c) d) e) f)

Figure 13. Alpha helices and betas strands of protein kinase C interacting protein

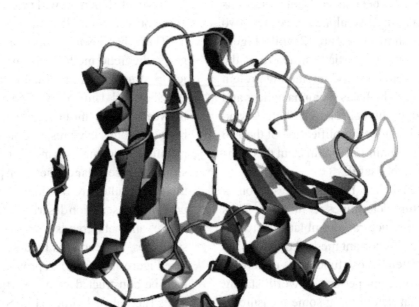

two SSEs. The program POSSUM then uses the Ullmann subgraph isomorphism algorithm to search for proteins containing a specific query pattern of SSEs (Mitchell, Artymiuk, Rice, & Willett, 1990), in a similar manner to that described above for substructural searching in small molecule databases. This type of search is very useful for annotating protein structures (P. J. Artymiuk, Grindley et al., 1994).

This SSE graph is also used as the basis for MCS calculations (specifically MCIS) using the Bron-Kerbosch algorithm in the program PROTEP (Grindley, Artymiuk, Rice, & Willett, 1993). As described for small molecules, one first constructs a correspondence graph combining the two SSE graphs, and then finds the maximum cliques of this graph – these correspond to the MCSs between the two proteins. Using PROTEP a search of the PDB will retrieve all proteins which contain at least a minimum number of the helices/strands present in a query pattern. This work has led to important discoveries of previously unknown

structural resemblances (P.J. Artymiuk, Poirrette, Rice, & Willett, 1997). More recently these ideas have been closely followed in the SSM program (Krissinel & Henrick, 2004) where a modified Ullmann algorithm (instead of Bron-Kerbosch) is used in the MCS-finding step.

A more complex protein representation is to use the residues as vertices of a graph. Work at Sheffield focused on the amino acid side-chains which are each represented by a pair of pseudoatoms. These determine a vector; the vectors become the vertices of a graph whose edges are labeled with inter-vector distances (such as the distance between the mid-points of two vector vertices). The ASSAM program uses the Ullmann algorithm to search a protein, this time for patterns of amino acid side-chains (P. J. Artymiuk, Poirrette, Grindley, Rice, & Willett, 1994; Spriggs, Artymiuk, & Willett, 2003). The pseudoatom side-chain graph has also been used to find common patterns of side-chains using the Bron-Kerbosch algorithm in a similar manner to PROTEP (P. J. Artymiuk,

Grindley, Kumar, Rice, & Willett, 1993). The graphs are larger (more vertices) and denser than the SSE graphs and so, in a novel approach, the correspondence graphs can first be pre-screened with a different clique-detection algorithm (Carraghan & Pardalos, 1990) to give an upper bound on the size of the maximum clique (which is the size of the MCS). Only those proteins which pass this screening step are subject to the full Bron-Kerbosch algorithm (Gardiner et al., 1997).

The most widely used program for 3D protein alignment is DALI (Holm & Sander, 1993, 1995, 1998). This is based on a graph with vertices at the Cα positions of the residues. Two protein graphs are then represented by distance matrices and these matrices are aligned using a Monte Carlo procedure.

There are many other protein structural databases besides the PDB. Each gives a different view of protein structure and most have programs developed specifically to perform some kind of structure comparison within their data. For example, the eF-site database contains the molecular electrostatic potential, calculated on the protein surface. (Kinoshita & Nakamura, 2003) form graphs whose vertices are sets of local maxima/minima in the surface curvature and edges labeled with the inter-vertex distance. They use the Bron-Kerbosch clique-detection algorithm to compare protein surfaces and assign function based on surface similarity. They were able to assign nucleotide binding function to a protein based on surface similarity to proteins of a different fold.

Another very important problem in structural bioinformatics is that of predicting the structure of the complex formed between two or more proteins, an area of research known as *protein-protein docking*. This problem is fundamental to all aspects of biological function since proteins must recognise their protein-partners, antibodies their antigens, etc. Equally importantly, molecules must be able to discriminate between molecules to which they should bind and all the others. The problem of whether two proteins interact can be solved experimentally by biochemists and molecular biologists and the mode of interaction can, in favourable cases, be elucidated experimentally by structure techniques such as crystallography. However the problem of crystallizing a protein-protein complex is much more difficult than that of crystallizing a single protein and in many cases, although structures of both components of a complex are known, the complex itself is not, and therefore theoretical techniques must be employed.

Protein-protein docking is inherently more difficult than protein-ligand docking since the 'ligand' to be docked is itself a protein and so the size of the interface between the interacting molecules is much larger. Some graph-theoretic protein-ligand docking methods have been used in protein-protein docking, viz DOCK (Ewing & Kuntz, 1997) but although the concepts are similar many of the techniques used for protein-ligand docking do not transfer to protein-protein docking. (Gardiner, Willett, & Artymiuk, 2000) developed the first graph-theoretic method specifically for protein-protein docking, which uses clique-detection in a docking graph. The protein surfaces are first pre-processed to assign vectors at the positions of potential hydrogen bond donors and acceptors on the proteins' surfaces and then a docking graph is formed (see Figure 14), defined such that the maximum cliques of this graph correspond to maximum sets of matching hydrogen bond donor/acceptor pairs. The Bron-Kerbosch algorithm is used to find the maximum cliques. A limitation of the approach is the very many possible cliques which need to be scored in order to find the actual docking conformation.

Other types of macromolecules have also been represented as graphs with the aim of database searching. For example, (Bruno, Kemp, Artymiuk, & Willett, 1997) represented complex carbohydrate structures as labeled directed graphs and used the Ullmann algorithm to identify query patterns in the Complex Carbohydrate Structure

Figure 14. Constructing the docking graph. Two proteins are involved. The hashed areas represent protein interiors. H1,H2,h1 and h2 are hydrogen atoms; E1, e1, e2 are hydrogen bond acceptors. D1, D2, d1, d2 are pseudo donor atoms and A1,a1,a2 are pseudo acceptor atoms. The ordered pairs (H1 ,e1),(H1,e2),(H2,e1),(H2,e2),(E1,h1) and (E1,h2) are the vertices of the docking graph. X and y are outer distances whilst x and Y are inner distances. Vertices (H1,e1), (E1,h2) will be joined if the inner distance Y matches with the outer distance y and the outer distance X matches with the inner distance x, to within a user-defined tolerance.

Protein 1

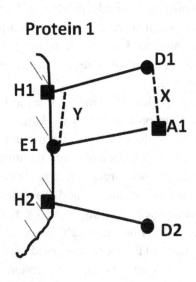

Protein 2

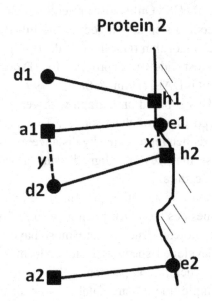

Database (Doubet, Bock, Smith, Darvill, & Albersheim, 1989).

FUTURE RESEARCH DIRECTIONS

The focus of this chapter has been on the use of graph-theoretic algorithms in chemoinformatics and structural bioinformatics. However, a quick glance at the chapter would certainly give the impression that a review of applications of the Bron-Kerbosch clique-detection algorithm had been attempted. Although this no doubt reflects the interests of the author, it is certainly true that the Bron-Kerbosch algorithm is extremely widely used. One might venture to suggest that one reason for this is the simplicity of the algorithm and a second is the clarity with which the original paper was

written. In addition, the paper contains ALGOL-like pseudo code which this author (and probably many others) had simply to translate into C code and then run. For chemoinformaticians without a background in graph theory, these factors are very influential. Several algorithm comparisons also demonstrated the superiority of this algorithm for computing cliques in small molecules (Brint & Willett, 1987a; Gardiner et al., 1997). Such comparisons are highly influential, but can only investigate a very few of the available relevant algorithms published each year.

In contrast, the more recent RASCAL algorithm, developed to include (if desired) heuristics to speed the searching of small molecules, is very complex. RASCAL is demonstrably superior to the Bron-Kerbosch algorithm in terms of speed and is being adopted by the chemoinformatics community (Stahl et al., 2005), although its speed of take-up is hampered by the complexity of the algorithm. Most chemoinformaticians are not graph theoreticians or computer scientists and so naturally gravitate towards algorithms which are simpler to understand. This has at least three implications for graph theory specialists. Firstly, if their algorithms are to find a wider application, they should be written clearly, preferably with step-by-step examples. Secondly there are probably very many published algorithms, which are suitable for use in chemoinformatics applications, but which non-specialists have little chance of understanding and implementing. Thirdly, it has been repeatedly demonstrated that graphs derived from molecular structures bear little resemblance to the typical graphs generated for the benchmark comparison of graph theory algorithms (Gardiner et al., 1997; D. S. Johnson & Trick, 1996). Graph theory specialists – here is an opportunity for you (Pardalos & Rebennack). Develop new algorithms or implement old ones, in collaboration with chemoinformaticians. Benchmark them on realistic test data and then publish the results in a journal which chemoinformaticians read, such as the Journal of Chemical Information and Modeling.

CONCLUSION

This chapter has provided an overview of the use of graph-theoretic algorithms in chemoinformatics and structural bioinformatics. Several important concepts in chemoinformatics have been introduced, the most important of which is probably the similar-property principle. The natural correspondence between graphs and 2D molecular structure diagrams has been illustrated. The widespread use of graph-theoretic algorithms in molecule registration, substructure search and both 2D and particularly 3D similarity searching has been demonstrated. A major theme has been the widespread use of MCS algorithms, since the maximum common substructure between

two molecules gives a natural measure of their similarity. The key concept of re-casting an MCS problem as a clique-detection problem has been discussed together with the widespread use of the Bron-Kerbosch and RASCAL clique-detection algorithms and also of the Ullmann subgraph isomorphism algorithm. The crossover between algorithm in chemoinformatics and structural bioinformatics has also been considered.

In this chapter I have aimed to give an overview of several areas of chemoinformatics and structural bioinformatics, rather than a narrower focus on specific applications or case studies. However, I have no doubt that many useful application areas have been omitted, some unwittingly and others, such as graph kernel methods, reluctantly due to lack of space – articles introducing some of the latter may be found in the additional readings section. In conclusion, despite the inevitable omissions, I hope that this chapter provides a useful introduction to the way that chemoinformaticians use algorithms from graph theory. Many problems in chemoinformatics have been solved by the use of subgraph isomorphism and especially clique-detection algorithms. The challenge now lies in casting other chemoinformatics problems as problems in graph theory and then finding algorithms to solve them.

REFERENCES

Allen, F. H. (2002). The Cambridge structural database: A quarter of a million crystal structures and rising. *Acta Crystallographica. Section B, Structural Science*, *58*, 380–388. doi:10.1107/S0108768102003890

Artymiuk, P. J., Bath, P. A., Grindley, H. M., Pepperrell, C. A., Poirrette, A. R., & Rice, D. W. (1992). Similarity searching in databases of 3-dimensional molecules and macromolecules. *Journal of Chemical Information and Computer Sciences*, *32*(6), 617–630. doi:10.1021/ci00010a007

Artymiuk, P. J., Grindley, H. M., Kumar, K., Rice, D. W., & Willett, P. (1993). 3-dimensional structural resemblance between the ribonuclease-h and connection domains of hiv reverse-transcriptase and the atpase fold revealed using graph-theoretical techniques. *FEBS Letters, 324*(1), 15–21. doi:10.1016/0014-5793(93)81523-3

Artymiuk, P. J., Grindley, H. M., Poirrette, A. R., Rice, D. W., Ujah, E. C., & Willett, P. (1994). Identification of beta-sheet motifs, of psi-loops, and of patterns of amino-acid-residues in 3-dimensional protein structures using a subgraph-isomorphism algorithm. *Journal of Chemical Information and Computer Sciences, 34*(1), 54–62. doi:10.1021/ci00017a007

Artymiuk, P. J., Poirrette, A. R., Grindley, H. M., Rice, D. W., & Willett, P. (1994). A graph-theoretic approach to the identification of 3-dimensional patterns of amino-acid side-chains in protein structures. *Journal of Molecular Biology, 243*(2), 327–344. doi:10.1006/jmbi.1994.1657

Artymiuk, P. J., Poirrette, A. R., Rice, D. W., & Willett, P. (1997). A polymerase 1 palm in adenylyl cyclase? *Nature, 388*, 33–34. doi:10.1038/40310

Balaban, A. T. (1982). Highly discriminating distance-based topological index. *Chemical Physics Letters, 89*(5), 399–404. doi:10.1016/0009-2614(82)80009-2

Balaban, A. T., & Harary, F. (1971). Characteristic polynomial does not uniquely determine topology of a molecule. *Journal of Chemical Documentation, 11*(4), 258. doi:10.1021/c160043a020

Barker, E. J., Buttar, D., Cosgrove, D. A., Gardiner, E. J., Kitts, P., & Willett, P. (2006). Scaffold hopping using clique detection applied to reduced graphs. *Journal of Chemical Information and Modeling, 46*(2), 503–511. doi:10.1021/ci050347r

Barker, E. J., Gardiner, E. J., Gillet, V. J., Kitts, P., & Morris, J. (2003). Further development of reduced graphs for identifying bioactive compounds. *Journal of Chemical Information and Computer Sciences, 43*(2), 346–356. doi:10.1021/ci0255937

Barnard, J. M. (1993). Substructure searching methods - old and new. *Journal of Chemical Information and Computer Sciences, 33*(4), 532–538. doi:10.1021/ci00014a001

Ben-Dor, A., Shamir, R., & Yakhini, Z. (1999). Clustering gene expression patterns. *Journal of Computational Biology, 6*(3-4), 281–297. doi:10.1089/106652799318274

Bernstein, F. C., Koetzle, T. F., Williams, G. J. B., Meyer, E. F., Brice, M. D., & Rodgers, J. R. (1977). Protein data bank - computer-based archival file for macromolecular structures. *Journal of Molecular Biology, 112*(3), 535–542. doi:10.1016/S0022-2836(77)80200-3

Birchall, K., Gillet, V. J., Harper, G., & Pickett, S. D. (2008a). Evolving interpretable structure - Activity relationship models. 2. Using multiobjective optimization to derive multiple models. *Journal of Chemical Information and Modeling, 48*(8), 1558–1570. doi:10.1021/ci800051h

Birchall, K., Gillet, V. J., Harper, G., & Pickett, S. D. (2008b). Evolving interpretable structure - Activity relationships. 1. Reduced graph queries. *Journal of Chemical Information and Modeling, 48*(8), 1543–1557. doi:10.1021/ci8000502

Brint, A. T., & Willett, P. (1987a). Algorithms for the identification of 3-dimensional maximal common substructures. *Journal of Chemical Information and Computer Sciences, 27*(4), 152–158. doi:10.1021/ci00056a002

Brint, A. T., & Willett, P. (1987b). Pharmacophoric pattern-matching in files of 3d chemical structures - Comparison of geometric searching algorithms. *Journal of Molecular Graphics, 5*(1), 49–56. doi:10.1016/0263-7855(87)80045-0

Bron, C., & Kerbosch, J. (1973). Finding all cliques of an undirected graph. *Communications of the ACM, 16*(9), 575–577. doi:10.1145/362342.362367

Brown, F. K. (1998). Chemoinformatics: What is it and how does it impact drug discovery? *Annual Reports in Medicinal Chemistry, 33*, 375–384. doi:10.1016/S0065-7743(08)61100-8

Brown, N. (2009). Chemoinformatics-An introduction for computer scientists. *ACM Computing Surveys, 41*(2), 38. doi:10.1145/1459352.1459353

Bruno, I. J., Kemp, N. M., Artymiuk, P. J., & Willett, P. (1997). Representing and searching of carbohydrate structures using graph-theoretic techniques. *Carbohydrate Research, 304*, 61–67. doi:10.1016/S0008-6215(97)00196-1

Carraghan, R., & Pardalos, P. M. (1990). An exact algorithm for the maximum clique problem. *Operations Research Letters, 9*(6), 375–382. doi:10.1016/0167-6377(90)90057-C

Cheeseright, T., Mackey, M., Rose, S., & Vinter, A. (2006). Molecular field extrema as descriptors of biological activity: Definition and validation. *Journal of Chemical Information and Modeling, 46*(2), 665–676. doi:10.1021/ci050357s

Crandell, C. W., & Smith, D. H. (1983). Applications of artificial intelligence for chemical interference. 44. Computer-assisted examination of compounds for common 3-dimensional substructures. *Journal of Chemical Information and Computer Sciences, 23*(4), 186–197. doi:10.1021/ci00040a009

De Jong, H. (2002). Modeling and simulation of genetic regulatory systems: A literature review. *Journal of Computational Biology, 9*(1), 67–103. doi:10.1089/10665270252833208

Decker, R., Lenz, H. J., & Borgelt, C. (2007). Canonical forms for frequent graph mining. In *Advances in Data Analysis* (pp. 337–349). Berlin, Heidelberg: Springer. doi:10.1007/978-3-540-70981-7

DiMasi, J. A., Hansen, R. W., & Grabowski, H. G. (2003). The price of innovation: New estimates of drug development costs. *Journal of Health Economics, 22*(2), 151–185. doi:10.1016/S0167-6296(02)00126-1

Doubet, S., Bock, K., Smith, D. H., Darvill, A., & Albersheim, P. (1989). The complex carbohydrate structure database. *Trends in Biochemical Sciences, 14*, 475–477. doi:10.1016/0968-0004(89)90175-8

Ebe, T., Sanderson, K. A., & Wilson, P. S. (1991). The chemical abstracts service generic chemical (Markush) structure storage and retrieval capability. 2. The MARPAT file. *Journal of Chemical Information and Computer Sciences, 31*(1), 31–36. doi:10.1021/ci00001a004

Ewing, T. J. A., & Kuntz, I. D. (1997). Critical evaluation of search algorithms for automated molecular docking and database screening. *Journal of Computational Chemistry, 18*(9), 1175–1189. doi:10.1002/(SICI)1096-987X(19970715)18:9<1175::AID-JCC6>3.0.CO;2-O

Feng, J., Sanil, A., & Young, S. S. (2006). PharmID: Pharmacophore identification using Gibbs sampling. *Journal of Chemical Information and Modeling, 46*(3), 1352–1359. doi:10.1021/ci050427v

Figueras, J. (1972). Substructure search by set reduction. *Journal of Chemical Documentation, 12*(4), 237–244. doi:10.1021/c160047a010

Figueras, J. (1996). Ring perception using breadth-first search. *Journal of Chemical Information and Computer Sciences, 36*(5), 986–991. doi:10.1021/ci960013p

Gardiner, E. J., Artymiuk, P. J., & Willett, P. (1997). Clique-detection algorithms for matching 3-dimensional molecular structures. *Journal of Molecular Graphics & Modelling, 15*(4), 245–253. doi:10.1016/S1093-3263(97)00089-2

Gardiner, E. J., Cosgrove, D. A., Taylor, R., & Gillet, V. J. (2009). Multiobjective optimization of Pharmacophore hypotheses: Bias toward low-energy conformations. *Journal of Chemical Information and Modeling, 49*(12), 2761–2773. doi:10.1021/ci9002816

Gardiner, E. J., Gillet, V. J., Willett, P., & Cosgrove, D. A. (2007). Representing clusters using a maximum common edge substructure algorithm applied to reduced graphs and molecular graphs. *Journal of Chemical Information and Modeling, 47*(2), 354–366. doi:10.1021/ci600444g

Gardiner, E. J., Willett, P., & Artymiuk, P. J. (2000). Graph-theoretic techniques for macromolecular docking. *Journal of Chemical Information and Computer Sciences, 40*(2), 273–279. doi:10.1021/ci990262o

Gasteiger, J. (2006). The central role of chemoinformatics. *Chemometrics and Intelligent Laboratory Systems, 82*(1-2), 200–209. doi:10.1016/j.chemolab.2005.06.022

Gillet, V. J., Downs, G. M., Holliday, J. D., Lynch, M. F., & Dethlefsen, W. (1991). Computer-storage and retrieval of generic chemical structures in patents. 13. Reduced graph generation. *Journal of Chemical Information and Computer Sciences, 31*(2), 260–270. doi:10.1021/ci00002a011

Gillet, V. J., Downs, G. M., Ling, A., Lynch, M. F., Venkataram, P., & Wood, J. V. (1987). Computer-storage and retrieval of generic chemical structures in patents. 8. Reduced chemical graphs and their applications in generic chemical-structure retrieval. *Journal of Chemical Information and Computer Sciences, 27*(3), 126–137. doi:10.1021/ci00055a007

Gillet, V. J., Willett, P., & Bradshaw, J. (2003). Similarity searching using reduced graphs. *Journal of Chemical Information and Computer Sciences, 43*(2), 338–345. doi:10.1021/ci025592e

Gorse, A.-D. (2006). Diversity in medicinal chemistry space. *Current Topics in Medicinal Chemistry, 6*, 3–18. doi:10.2174/156802606775193310

Grindley, H. M., Artymiuk, P. J., Rice, D. W., & Willett, P. (1993). Identification of tertiary structure resemblance in proteins using a maximal common subgraph isomorphism algorithm. *Journal of Molecular Biology, 229*(3), 707–721. doi:10.1006/jmbi.1993.1074

Gu, J., & Bourne, P. E. (2009). *Structural bioinformatics* (2nd ed.). NJ, USA: Wiley-Blackwell.

Hagadone, T. R. (1992). Molecular substructure similarity searching - Efficient retrieval in 2-dimensional structure databases. *Journal of Chemical Information and Computer Sciences, 32*(5), 515–521. doi:10.1021/ci00009a019

Harper, G., Bravi, G. S., Pickett, S. D., Hussain, J., & Green, D. V. S. (2004). The reduced graph descriptor in virtual screening and data-driven clustering of high-throughput screening data. *Journal of Chemical Information and Computer Sciences, 44*(6), 2145–2156. doi:10.1021/ci049860f

Hart, T. N., & Read, R. J. (1992). A multiple-start Monte-Carlo docking method. *Proteins-Structure Function and Genetics, 13*(3), 206–222. doi:10.1002/prot.340130304

Hawkins, P. C. D., Skillman, A. G., Warren, G. L., Ellingson, B. A., & Stahl, M. T. (2010). Conformer generation with OMEGA: Algorithm and validation using high quality structures from the protein databank and Cambridge structural database. *Journal of Chemical Information and Modeling, 50*(4), 572–584. doi:10.1021/ci100031x

Holm, L., & Sander, C. (1993). Protein-structure comparison by alignment of distance matrices. *Journal of Molecular Biology*, *233*(1), 123–138. doi:10.1006/jmbi.1993.1489

Holm, L., & Sander, C. (1995). DALI - A network tool for protein-structure comparison. *Trends in Biochemical Sciences*, *20*(11), 478–480. doi:10.1016/S0968-0004(00)89105-7

Holm, L., & Sander, C. (1998). Touring protein fold space with Dali/FSSP. *Nucleic Acids Research*, *26*(1), 316–319. doi:10.1093/nar/26.1.316

Hwang, K. Y., Chung, J. H., Kim, S. H., Han, Y. S., & Cho, Y. J. (1999). Structure-based identification of a novel NTPase from *Methanococcus Jannaschii*. *Nature Structural Biology*, *6*, 691–696. doi:10.1038/10745

Jarvis, R. A., & Patrick, E. A. (1973). Clustering using a similarity measure based on shared near neighbors. *IEEE Transactions on Computers*, *C-22*(11), 1025–1034. doi:10.1109/T-C.1973.223640

Johnson, D. S., & Trick, M. A. (1996). *Cliques, Colorings and Satifiability: 2nd DIMACS Implementation Challenge*. Bellcore and the American Mathematical Society.

Johnson, M. (1985). Relating metrics, lines and variables defined on graphs to problems in medicinal chemistry. In Alavi, Y., Chartrand, G., Lesniak, L., Lick, D., & Wall, C. (Eds.), *Graph theory and its applications to algorithms and computer science* (pp. 457–470). New York: Wiley.

Johnson, M. A., & Maggiora, G. M. (1990). *Concepts and applications of molecular similarity*. New York: Wiley Inter-Science.

Jonsdottir, S. O., Jorgensen, F. S., & Brunak, S. (2005). Prediction methods and databases within chemoinformatics: Emphasis on drugs and drug candidates. *Bioinformatics (Oxford, England)*, *21*(10), 2145–2160. doi:10.1093/bioinformatics/bti314

Kabsch, W. (1976). Solution for best rotation to relate 2 sets of vectors. *Acta Crystallographica Section A*, *32*(SEP1), 922–923.

Kasinos, N., Lilley, G. A., Subbarao, N., & Haneef, I. (1992). A robust and efficient automated docking algorithm for molecular recognition. *Protein Engineering*, *5*(1), 69–75. doi:10.1093/protein/5.1.69

Kier, L. B., & Hall, L. H. (1986). *Molecular connectivity in structure-activity analysis*. Chichester, UK: John Wiley and Sons.

Kinoshita, K., & Nakamura, H. (2003). Identification of protein biochemical functions by similarity search using the molecular surface database eF-site. *Protein Science*, *12*(8), 1589–1595. doi:10.1110/ps.0368703

Krissinel, E., & Henrick, K. (2004). Secondary-structure matching (SSM), a new tool for fast protein structure alignment in 3 dimensions. *Acta Crystallographica. Section D, Biological Crystallography*, *60*, 2256–2268. doi:10.1107/S0907444904026460

Kuhl, F. S., Crippen, G. M., & Friesen, D. K. (1984). A combinatorial algorithm for calculating ligand-binding. *Journal of Computational Chemistry*, *5*(1), 24–34. doi:10.1002/jcc.540050105

Kuntz, I. D., Blaney, J. M., Oatley, S. J., Langridge, R., & Ferrin, T. E. (1982). A geometric approach to macromolecule-ligand interactions. *Journal of Molecular Biology*, *161*(2), 269–288. doi:10.1016/0022-2836(82)90153-X

Kuramochi, M., & Karypis, G. (2007). Discovering frequent geometric subgraphs. *Information Systems, 32*(8), 1101–1120. doi:10.1016/j.is.2005.05.005

Lander, E. S., Linton, L., Birren, B., Nusbaum, C., Zody, M., & Baldwin, J. (2001). Initial sequencing and analysis of the human genome. *Nature, 409,* 860–921. doi:10.1038/35057062

Leach, A. R., & Gillet, V. J. (2007). *An introduction to chemoinformatics* (2nd ed.). Dordrecht, Netherlands: Springer. doi:10.1007/978-1-4020-6291-9

Leach, A. R., Gillet, V. J., Lewis, R. A., & Taylor, R. (2010). 3-dimensional Pharmacophore methods in drug discovery. *Journal of Medicinal Chemistry, 53*(2), 539–558. doi:10.1021/jm900817u

Luscombe, N. M., Greenbaum, D., & Gerstein, M. (2001). What is bioinformatics? A proposed definition and overview of the field. *Methods of Information in Medicine, 40*(4), 346–358.

Lynch, M. F., & Holliday, J. D. (1996). The Sheffield generic structures project - A retrospective review. *Journal of Chemical Information and Computer Sciences, 36*(5), 930–936. doi:10.1021/ci9501731

Martin, Y. C., Bures, M. G., Danaher, E. A., Delazzer, J., Lico, I., & Pavlik, P. A. (1993). A fast new approach to Pharmacophore mapping and its application to dopaminergic and benzodiazepine agonists. *Journal of Computer-Aided Molecular Design, 7*(1), 83–102. doi:10.1007/BF00141577

Miller, M. D., Kearsley, S. K., Underwood, D. J., & Sheridan, R. P. (1994). FLOG - A system to select quasi-flexible ligands complementary to a receptor of known 3-dimensional structure. *Journal of Computer-Aided Molecular Design, 8*(2), 153–174. doi:10.1007/BF00119865

Mitchell, E. M., Artymiuk, P. J., Rice, D. W., & Willett, P. (1990). Use of techniques derived from graph theory to compare secondary structure motifs in proteins. *Journal of Molecular Biology, 212,* 151–166. doi:10.1016/0022-2836(90)90312-A

Molconn-Z. Retrieved December 15, 2010, from http:////www.edusoft-lc.com/molconn

Morgan, H. L. (1965). Generation of a unique machine description for chemical structures-A technique developed at Chemical Abstracts Service. *Journal of Chemical Documentation, 5*(2), 107. doi:10.1021/c160017a018

Pardalos, P. M., & Rebennack, S. (2010). Computational Challenges with Cliques, Quasi-cliques and Clique Partitions in Graphs. In Festa, P. (Ed.), *Experimental Algorithms, Proceedings* (*Vol. 6049,* pp. 13–22). Berlin, Germany: Springer-Verlag Berlin. doi:10.1007/978-3-642-13193-6_2

Podolyan, Y., & Karypis, G. (2009). Common Pharmacophore identification using frequent clique detection algorithm. *Journal of Chemical Information and Modeling, 49*(1), 13–21. doi:10.1021/ci8002478

Randic, M., & Wilkins, C. L. (1979). Graph-based fragment searches in polycyclic structures. *Journal of Chemical Information and Computer Sciences, 19*(1), 23–31. doi:10.1021/ci60017a008

Rarey, M., & Dixon, J. S. (1998). Feature trees: A new molecular similarity measure based on tree matching. *Journal of Computer-Aided Molecular Design, 12*(5), 471–490. doi:10.1023/A:1008068904628

Ray, L. C., & Kirsch, R. A. (1957). Finding chemical records by digital computers. *Science, 126*(3278), 814–819. doi:10.1126/science.126.3278.814

Raymond, J. W., Blankley, C. J., & Willett, P. (2003). Comparison of chemical clustering methods using graph- and fingerprint-based similarity measures. *Journal of Molecular Graphics & Modelling, 21*(5), 421–433. doi:10.1016/S1093-3263(02)00188-2

Raymond, J. W., Gardiner, E. J., & Willett, P. (2002a). Heuristics for similarity searching of chemical graphs using a maximum common edge subgraph algorithm. *Journal of Chemical Information and Computer Sciences, 42*(2), 305–316. doi:10.1021/ci010381f

Raymond, J. W., Gardiner, E. J., & Willett, P. (2002b). RASCAL: Calculation of graph similarity using maximum common edge subgraphs. *The Computer Journal, 45*(6), 631–644. doi:10.1093/comjnl/45.6.631

Raymond, J. W., & Willett, P. (2002a). Effectiveness of graph-based and fingerprint-based similarity measures for virtual screening of 2D chemical structure databases. *Journal of Computer-Aided Molecular Design, 16*(1), 59–71. doi:10.1023/A:1016387816342

Raymond, J. W., & Willett, P. (2002b). Maximum common subgraph isomorphism algorithms for the matching of chemical structures. *Journal of Computer-Aided Molecular Design, 16*(7), 521–533. doi:10.1023/A:1021271615909

Read, R. C., & Corneil, D. G. (1977). The graph isomorphism disease. *Journal of Graph Theory, 1*, 339–363. doi:10.1002/jgt.3190010410

Rhodes, N., Willett, P., Calvet, A., Dunbar, J. B., & Humblet, C. (2003). CLIP: Similarity searching of 3D databases using clique detection. *Journal of Chemical Information and Computer Sciences, 43*(2), 443–448. doi:10.1021/ci025605o

Rucker, C., Rucker, G., & Meringer, M. (2002). Exploring the limits of graph invariant- and spectrum-based discrimination of (sub)structures. *Journal of Chemical Information and Computer Sciences, 42*(3), 640–650. doi:10.1021/ci010121y

Rusinko, A., Skell, J. M., Balducci, R., & Pearlman, R. S. (1986). Concord - Rapid generation of high-quality approximate 3-dimensional molecular coordinates. [-COMP.]. *Abstracts of Papers of the American Chemical Society, 192*, 12.

Russo, E. (2002). Chemistry plans a structural overhaul. *Nature, 419*(6903), 4–7. doi:10.1038/nj6903-04a

Southan, C., Varkonyi, P., & Muresan, S. (2007). Complementarity between public and commercial databases: New opportunities in medicinal chemistry informatics. *Current Topics in Medicinal Chemistry, 7*(15), 1502–1508. doi:10.2174/156802607782194761

Spriggs, R. V., Artymiuk, P. J., & Willett, P. (2003). Searching for patterns of amino acids in 3D protein structures. *Journal of Chemical Information and Computer Sciences, 43*(2), 412–421. doi:10.1021/ci0255984

Stahl, M., & Mauser, H. (2005). Database clustering with a combination of fingerprint and maximum common substructure methods. *Journal of Chemical Information and Modeling, 45*(3), 542–548. doi:10.1021/ci050011h

Stahl, M., Mauser, H., Tsui, M., & Taylor, N. R. (2005). A robust clustering method for chemical structures. *Journal of Medicinal Chemistry, 48*(13), 4358–4366. doi:10.1021/jm040213p

Stiefl, N., Watson, T. A., Baumann, K., & Zaliani, A. (2006). ErG: 2D Pharmacophore descriptions for scaffold hopping. *Journal of Chemical Information and Modeling, 46*(1), 208–220. doi:10.1021/ci050457y

Sussenguth, E. H. (1965). A graph-theoretic algorithm for matching chemical structures. *Journal of Chemical Documentation*, 5(1), 36. doi:10.1021/c160016a007

Takahashi, Y., Sukekawa, M., & Sasaki, S. (1992). Automatic identification of molecular similarity using reduced-graph representation of chemical-structure. *Journal of Chemical Information and Computer Sciences*, 32(6), 639–643. doi:10.1021/ci00010a009

Ullmann, J. R. (1976). Algorithm for subgraph isomorphism. *Journal of the ACM*, 23(1), 31–42. doi:10.1145/321921.321925

Venter, J. C., Adams, M., Myers, E., Li, P., Mural, R., & Sutton, G. (2001). The sequence of the human genome. *Science*, 291, 1304–1351. doi:10.1126/science.1058040

Villar, H. O., & Hansen, M. R. (2009). Mining and visualizing the chemical content of large databases. *Current Opinion in Drug Discovery & Development*, 12(3), 367–375.

Vonscholley, A. (1984). A relaxation algorithm for generic chemical-structure screening. *Journal of Chemical Information and Computer Sciences*, 24(4), 235–241. doi:10.1021/ci00044a009

Ward, J. H. (1963). Hierarchical grouping to optimize an objective function. *Journal of the American Statistical Association*, 58(301), 236. doi:10.2307/2282967

Weininger, D. (1988). SMILES, a chemical language and information-system. 1. Introduction to methodology and encoding. *Journal of Chemical Information and Computer Sciences*, 28(1), 31–36. doi:10.1021/ci00057a005

Whitney, H. (1932). Congruent graphs and the connectivity of graphs. *American Journal of Mathematics*, 54, 150–168. doi:10.2307/2371086

Wiener, H. (1947). Structural determination of paraffin boiling points. *Journal of the American Chemical Society*, 69(1), 17–20. doi:10.1021/ja01193a005

Willett, P. (2005). Searching techniques for databases of 2- and 3-dimensional chemical structures. *Journal of Medicinal Chemistry*, 48(13), 4183–4199. doi:10.1021/jm0582165

Willett, P. (2006). Similarity-based virtual screening using 2D fingerprints. *Drug Discovery Today*, 11(23-24), 1046–1053. doi:10.1016/j.drudis.2006.10.005

Willett, P., Barnard, J. M., & Downs, G. M. (1998). Chemical similarity searching. *Journal of Chemical Information and Computer Sciences*, 38(6), 983–996. doi:10.1021/ci9800211

Yan, X. F., Yu, P. S., & Han, J. (2004). *Graph indexing: A frequent structure-based approach.* Paper presented at the SIGMOD'04 (International Conference on Management of Data), Paris.

Yan, X. F., Zhu, F. D., Yu, P. S., & Han, J. W. (2006). Feature-based similarity search in graph structures. *ACM Transactions on Database Systems*, 31(4), 1418–1453. doi:10.1145/1189769.1189777

Zarembinski, T. I., Hung, L. W., Mueller-Dieck-mann, H. J., Kim, K. K., Yokota, H., & Kim, R. ... Kim, S. H. (1998). Structure-based assignment of the biochemical function of a hypothetical protein: A test case of structural genomics. In *Proceedings of the National Academy of Sciences of the United States of America*, 95, 15189-15193.

ADDITIONAL READING

Artymiuk, P. J., Spriggs, R. V., & Willett, P. (2005). Graph theoretic methods for the analysis of structural relationships in biological macromolecules. *Journal of the American Society for Information Science and Technology*, 56(5), 518–528. doi:10.1002/asi.20140

Bajorath, J. (2004). *Chemoinformatics: Concepts, methods and tools for drug discovery*. Totowa, N.J.: Humana Press.

Balaban, A. T. (1995). Chemical graphs - looking back and glimpsing ahead. *Journal of Chemical Information and Computer Sciences, 35*, 339–350. doi:10.1021/ci00025a001

Barnard, J. M. (1993). Substructure searching methods - old and new. *Journal of Chemical Information and Computer Sciences, 33*(4), 532–538. doi:10.1021/ci00014a001

Brown, N. (2009). Chemoinformatics-an introduction for computer scientists. *ACM Computing Surveys, 41*(2), 38. doi:10.1145/1459352.1459353

Butenko, S., & Wilhelm, W. E. (2006). Clique-detection models in computational biochemistry and genomics. *European Journal of Operational Research, 173*(1), 1–17. doi:10.1016/j.ejor.2005.05.026

Faulon, J.-L., & Bender, A. (2010). *Handbook of chemoinformatics algorithms*. Routledge.

Grindrod, P., & Kibble, M. (2004). Review of uses of network and graph theory concepts within proteomics. *Expert Review of Proteomics, 1*(2), 229–238. doi:10.1586/14789450.1.2.229

Gu, J., & Bourne, P. E. (2009). *Structural bioinformatics* (2nd ed.). Wiley-Blackwell.

Halperin, I., Ma, B. Y., Wolfson, H., & Nussinov, R. (2002). Principles of docking: An overview of search algorithms and a guide to scoring functions. *Proteins-Structure Function and Genetics, 47*(4), 409–443. doi:10.1002/prot.10115

Hashimoto, K., Goto, S., Kawano, S., Aoki-Kinoshita, K. F., Ueda, N., & Hamajima, M. (2006). KEGG as a glycome informatics resource. *Glycobiology, 16*(5), 63R–70R. doi:10.1093/glycob/cwj010

Jones, S., & Thornton, J. M. (2004). Searching for functional sites in protein structures. *Current Opinion in Chemical Biology, 8*(1), 3–7. doi:10.1016/j.cbpa.2003.11.001

King, R. B., & Rouvray, D. H. (1987). *Graph theory and topology in chemistry*. Oxford: Elsevier.

Koehle, P. (2006). Protein structure classification. In Lipkowitz, K. B., Cundari, T. R., & Gillet, V. J. (Eds.), *Reviews in computational chemistry*. Hoboken, New Jersey: Wiley. doi:10.1002/0471780367.ch1

Leach, A. R., & Gillet, V. J. (2007). *An introduction to chemoinformatics* (2nd ed.). Dordrecht: Springer. doi:10.1007/978-1-4020-6291-9

Leach, A. R., Gillet, V. J., Lewis, R. A., & Taylor, R. (2010). Three-dimensional pharmacophore methods in drug discovery. *Journal of Medicinal Chemistry, 53*(2), 539–558. doi:10.1021/jm900817u

Lozano, M. A., & Escolano, F. (2006). Protein classification by matching and clustering surface graphs. *Pattern Recognition, 39*(4), 539–551. doi:10.1016/j.patcog.2005.10.008

Mahe, P., & Vert, J. P. (2009). Graph kernels based on tree patterns for molecules. *Machine Learning, 75*(1), 3–35. doi:10.1007/s10994-008-5086-2

Martin, Y. C., & Willett, P. (1998). *Designing bioactive molecules. Three-dimensional techniques and applications*. Washington, D.C.: American Chemical Society.

Rupp, M., & Schneider, G. (2010). Graph kernels for molecular similarity. *Molecular Informatics, 29*(4), 266–273.

Schietgat, L., Ramon, J., Bruynooghe, M., & Blockeel, H. (2008). An efficiently computable graph-based metric for the classification of small molecules. *Discovery Science Proceedings, 5255*, 197–209.

Smith, G. R., & Sternberg, M. J. E. (2002). Prediction of protein-protein interactions by docking methods. *Current Opinion in Structural Biology, 12*(1), 28–35. doi:10.1016/S0959-440X(02)00285-3

Trinajstic, I. (1983). *Chemical Graph Theory.* Chichester: Ellis Horwood.

Willett, P. (2005). Searching techniques for databases of two- and three-dimensional chemical structures. *Journal of Medicinal Chemistry, 48*(13), 4183–4199. doi:10.1021/jm0582165

Willett, P. (2008). From chemical documentation to chemoinformatics: 50 years of chemical information science. *Journal of Information Science, 34*(4), 477–499. doi:10.1177/0165551507084631

Willett, P., Barnard, J. M., & Downs, G. M. (1998). Chemical similarity searching. *Journal of Chemical Information and Computer Sciences, 38*(6), 983–996. doi:10.1021/ci9800211

KEY TERMS AND DEFINITIONS

Docking: Predicting the 3D structure of a complex formed between two molecules.

Protein-Ligand Docking: Docking a small molecule and a protein.

Protein-Protein Docking: Predicting the 3D structure of a protein-protein complex.

Pharmacophore: The 3D arrangement of chemical features required for a ligand to bind to a protein target.

Pharmacophore Elucidation: The determination of the pharmacophore common to two or more ligands.

Structural Bioinformatics: The representation and manipulation of structural information regarding macromolecules such as proteins, DNA and carbohydrates.

Chapter 18
Business Process Graphs:
Similarity Search and Matching

Remco Dijkman
Eindhoven University of Technology, The Netherlands

Marlon Dumas
University of Tartu, Estonia

Luciano García-Bañuelos
University of Tartu, Estonia

ABSTRACT

Organizations create collections of hundreds or even thousands of business process models to describe their operations. This chapter explains how graphs can be used as underlying formalism to develop techniques for managing such collections. To this end it defines the business process graph formalism. On this formalism it defines techniques for determining similarity of business process graphs. Such techniques can be used to quickly search through a collection of business process graphs to find the graph that is most relevant to a given query. These techniques can be used by tool builders that develop tools for managing large collections of business process models. The aim of the chapter is to provide an overview of the research area of using graphs to do similarity search and matching of business processes.

INTRODUCTION

Nowadays, most organizations describe their operations in terms of business processes models. As a consequence they have large repositories of business process models. For example, the Reference Model for Dutch Local Government (Documentair Structuurplan, n.d.) contains around 600 business process models and the SAP Reference

Model (Curran & Keller, 1999) contains a similar number of business process models.

As the size of these repositories increases, automated techniques for managing them become important. This includes techniques for searching through a repository of business process models in order to retrieve models that are similar to a given one. We call this form of search *similarity search*. Similarity search can be used for various purposes. For example, when two organizations merge, their business analysts need to understand

DOI: 10.4018/978-1-61350-053-8.ch018

the similarity and overlap between the business processes that were previously ran separately, in order to establish the opportunities for operational consolidation. If both organizations have their operations described in terms of business process models, a search through their collections for business process models that are similar would reveal such opportunities. As another example, an organization that maintains a large collection of business process models may want to inspect that collection on a regular basis in order to identify pairs of groups of models with high similarity. High similarity between models may indicate that anti-patterns such as overlap exist in the collection, which should be removed by means of refactoring.

This chapter explains how graph theory can be used as a basis for similarity search. To this end it presents the concept of business process graph and subsequently defines several techniques for graph-based business process similarity search. The chapter aims to present a comprehensive overview of work that we have undertaken in this area (Dijkman, Dumas & García-Bañuelos, 2009; Dijkman, Dumas, García-Bañuelos & Käärik, 2009; Dijkman, van Dongen, Dumas, Käärik & Mendling, 2010; van Dongen, Dijkman & Mendling, 2008).

The remainder of this chapter is structured as follows. First, we explain the general concept of business process similarity, including the work that others have done in this area. Second, we present the concept of business process graph and define the various techniques for measuring business process similarity. Third, we present future research direction on the topic of graph-based business process similarity and finally we present conclusions.

BACKGROUND

A business process is a collection of related tasks that can be performed to achieve a certain goal. A business process model represents the tasks in a

business process as well as their relations. Typically, the model is enriched with nodes that affect the order in which tasks can be performed. These are called *control-nodes or gateways*. Figure 1 shows six examples of business process models in the Business Process Modeling Notation (BPMN). Rounded rectangles represent tasks. Circles represent events that occur during a process. An empty circle represents an event that signals the start of the process. Consequently, in the first process, at the start of the process the task 'buy goods' is performed. A bulls-eye represents an event that signals the completion of the process. Diamonds represent gateways. A diamond marked with an 'X' is called an exclusive gateway and it represents a decision point at which the process can continue along exactly one out of a number of alternative paths. An exclusive gateway can also be used to merge multiple alternative paths. Similarly a diamond marked with an 'O' (called an inclusive gateway) represents a point at which one or more alternative paths can be chosen or merged while a diamond marked with a '+' (called a parallel gateway) represents a point where multiple outgoing parallel threads are started, or a point where multiple incoming threads must be synchronized before the execution of the process can continue.

In this Chapter, we will review several approaches to defining business process similarity metrics. For uniformity, we define a business process similarity metric as a function that, given two business process models, returns a value between 0 and 1 (inclusive) that indicates the similarity between these business process models. The similarity metric should correspond to human judgment, such that models that are perceived to be more similar have a higher similarity value.

A business process similarity metric can be used as a query tool in order to perform similarity search queries. A similarity search query returns those models from a collection that have a sufficiently high similarity value when compared to a given model. In that case the models from the collection are called document models and the input

Figure 1. A query model and five document models

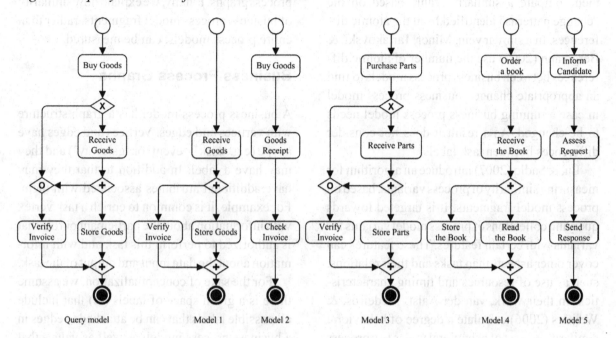

model is called the query model. Figure 1 shows an example. The figure shows a collection of five document models and a query model. Given the query model a query tool could return document models 1, 2 and 3 (ranked in some way). However, the exact models that would be returned of course depend on the similarity metric that is used and the threshold value that decides which similarity values are considered to be 'sufficiently' high to return the document model.

The topic of business process similarity has received some attention recently. Dijkman, Dumas, García-Bañuelos & Käärik (2009) provide an overview of the area. They distinguish several options for computing business process similarity. In particular, they distinguish business process similarity that is computed based on:

1. The text in the labels of the business process only;
2. The structural properties of the business process; and
3. The behavioral semantics of the business process.

Within this framework, we can identify several initiatives. Nejati, Sabetzadeh, Chechik, Easterbrook, & Zave (2007) propose a similarity metric for computing the similarity of statecharts. Although their technique uses a different formalism than business process models, many of its elements can also be used to determine similarity of business process models. To determine similarity of statecharts, they use text in the labels of models, as well as an approximation of bi-similarity (a measure of behavioral equivalence). In addition to that, they use the hierarchical structure of a statechart, which is usually composed of sub-statecharts, as a structural property to determine similarity. Wombacher (2006) also introduces a technique for determining similarity of statecharts.

Li, Reichert, & Wombacher (2007) propose a structural approach to determine the similarity between business process models. Their approach first determines 'atomic' differences between business process models (inserting, deleting or substituting nodes or edges) and subsequently groups these differences using so-called "change patterns" that they defined in earlier work. They then compute a similarity value based on the "change patterns" identified from the atomic differences. In a similar vein, Minor, Tartakovski, & Bergmann (2007) use the number of atomic differences between business process models to find an appropriate changed business process model in case a running business process model needs to be changed. As a result it does not consider differences between task labels.

Lu, & Sadiq (2007) introduce an algorithm for measuring similarity of process variants, based on process model fragments. It is targeted towards querying collections of process model variants for variants with certain features. These features can cover other aspects than tasks and their relations, such as use of resources and timing characteristics. In their work, van der Aalst, Medeiros, & Weijters (2006) calculate a degree of behavioral similarity of a set of behavioral traces to a process model. This technique can be used indirectly to determine the similarity of two process models, by first generating representative sets of traces for both process models and subsequently computing the similarity of each of the sets of traces to the other process model. Finally, Ehrig, Koschmider, & Oberweis (2007) match task labels based, among other options on synonyms.

SIMILARITY SEARCH AND MATCHING

In this chapter we use graph theory as the basis for defining business process similarity metrics. We do that by interpreting business process models as graphs.

Below, we introduce these similarity metrics in four parts. First, we introduce the concept of business process graph and four techniques for measuring similarity of business process graphs. Next, we define similarity metrics between pairs of nodes. These similarity metrics are then used to define similarity metrics on entire business

process graphs. Finally, we explain how similarity of business process model fragments, rather than entire process models, can be measured.

Business Process Graphs

A business process model has a graph structure with vertices and edges. Vertices and edges have a type (e.g. 'task', 'event' or 'gateway') and they may have a label. In addition to that they may have additional attributes associated with them. For example, it is common to enrich a task vertex with information about the participant or role that is authorized to perform this task and with information about the data input and output of the task.

For the sake of conceptualization, we assume there is a given space of labels (Ω) that include all possible labels that can be attached to edges in a business process model, as well as values that can be taken by node attributes in the process model. We assume that edges may have labels, even though it is unusual for business process models to have labeled edges. One exception is in the case of edges that emanate from a decision gateway. Such edges are generally labeled with Boolean conditional expressions. On this basis, we define a Business Process Graph (BPG) as an attributed graph.

Definition 1 (Business Process Graph). Let T be a set of types and Ω be a set of text labels. A Business Process Graph is a tuple (N, E, τ, λ, α), in which:

- N is a finite set of nodes;
- E: N × N is a finite set of edges;
- τ: (N ∪ E) → T associates nodes and edges with their allowed attribute names;
- λ: (N ∪ E) → Ω associates nodes and edges with labels; and
- α: (N ∪ E) → (T → Ω) associates nodes and edges with attributes, where an attribute always is a combination of an attribute name and a label.

In a BPG certain types of nodes can be ignored by removing them from the set of nodes and replacing paths of ignored nodes by direct edges. For example, Figure 2 shows the BPGs for the business process models from Figure 1. In these BPGs only vertices that have the type 'task' are considered, other vertices are ignored (especially: gateways). The purpose of removing nodes is to make the graph smaller and therewith make computation of various forms of similarity faster. Clearly, removing nodes means that comparison (for similarity or matching) of BPGs with respect to those nodes is no longer possible. This is not necessarily a problem, because comparison is done on an abstraction of the BPGs, removing nodes simply increases the level of abstraction. In case this abstraction is not acceptable, the nodes should not be removed.

Similarity and Matching of Business Process Graph Nodes

In many applications of graphs, equivalent nodes can be assumed to have equivalent labels. For example, when representing a DNA structure as a graph (e.g. to find a DNA match in a database) each node is labeled with one of four labels 'A', 'T', 'C' or 'G' and a node should only be matched to another node if it has the same label. However, in business process graphs that assumption does not hold, because different process modelers may have used a different label to represent the same task. For example, one process modeler may have

used the label 'check application' to represent the task of checking whether the information on a loan application is correct, while another process modeler may have used the label 'verify information on loan application' to represent the same task. Therefore, to determine similarity of business process graphs, first similarity of their nodes must be determined.

A number of techniques exist for computing node similarity. These techniques vary with respect to the attributes that they use to determine node similarity and the additional information that they use to determine similarity. In this chapter we explain three representative techniques that illustrate the various options for including attributes and additional information from a dictionary. Other techniques are described by Dijkman, Dumas, García-Bañuelos and Käärik (2009) and by Weidlich, Dijkman and Mendling (2010).

Syntactic Label Similarity

The simplest technique is based on syntactic similarity of node labels. Syntactic similarity can be computed by measuring the number of atomic string operations needed to transform one label into the other. This is known as the 'string edit distance' (Levenshtein, 1966). Atomic string operations include inserting a character, deleting a character and substituting one character for another. The string edit distance yields a number between 0 and the length of the longest string, because in the worst case the longest label can be

Figure 2. A query BPG and five document BPGs

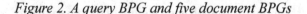

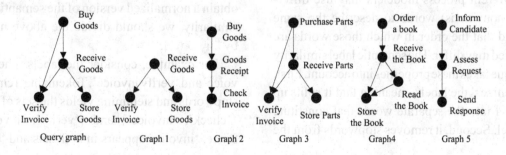

transformed into the other label by deleting the number of characters that the longest label has more than the shortest label and then substituting the remaining characters for the characters from of the shortest label (e.g. to transform 'abcd' into 'ef' we can delete characters 'cd' and substitute 'ab' for 'ef'). However, a similarity score should be in between 0 and 1. Therefore, we define a similarity metrics based on the string edit distance as follows.

Definition 2 (Syntactic label similarity): Let $l_1, l_2 \in \Omega$ be two labels, let $|l|$ represent the number of characters in a label $l \in \Omega$ and let $ed(l_1, l_2)$ represent the string edit distance between l_1 and l_2. Then the syntactic label similarity of l_1 and l_2, denoted $syn(l_1, l_2)$, is:

$$syn(l_1, l_2) = \frac{ed(l_1, l_2)}{\max(|\, l_1 \,|, |\, l_2 \,|)}$$

For example, the syntactic label similarity of the labels 'customer inquiry' and 'customer inquiring' is 3/18, because the string edit distance is 3 (delete 'n' and 'g' from 'customer inquiring', then substitute 'i' for 'y') and the length of the maximum string is 18.

To improve the quality of the syntactic label similarity special characters can be removed from the label and all characters can be transformed into lowercase characters.

Semantic Label Similarity

The syntactic label similarity technique is an easy to use, but it is rather naïve. It disregards that different process modelers may use different (synonymous) words to describe the same task and that the order in which those words are presented may differ. The semantic label similarity technique takes these properties into account. First, it 'tokenizes' the labels, meaning that it splits up the label into the separate words that constitute the label. Second, it removes stopwords from the tokenized labels. Stopwords are words that occur so frequently in a language that their presence or absence does not provide much information; in our case evidence that the two labels are similar. Examples of stopwords are 'an' and 'about'. Third, the technique returns words to their stem form, such that different forms of the same word can be compared (e.g.: 'doing' and 'done' are returned to the same stem form 'do'). Finally, the technique determines the similarity of the two labels as the fraction of words that the two labels have in common and the fraction of words in one label for which there is a synonymous word in the other label. Consequently, semantic label similarity can be defined as follows.

Definition 2 (Semantic label similarity): Let $l_1, l_2 \in \Omega$ be two labels, let $\mathbf{W}$ be the set of all possible words, let $\mathbf{SW}$ be the set of all stop words, let $tk: \Omega \rightarrow \wp\, \mathbf{W}$ be a function that tokenizes a label into a set of words and $stem: \mathbf{W} \rightarrow \mathbf{W}$ be a function that returns the stem form for a word. Furthermore, let $synonym: \mathbf{W} \times \mathbf{W}$ be a predicate that is true for synonymic words. Then, the semantic similarity of l_1 and l_2, denoted $sem(l_1, l_2)$, is:

$$sem(l_1, l_2) = |\, w_1 \cap w_2 \,| + \theta_* |\{t_1 \mid t_1 \in w_1 - w_2, \exists t_2 \in w_2 - w_1, synonym(t_1, t_2)\}|$$

$$+ \theta_* |\{t_2 \mid t_2 \in w_2 - w_1, \exists t_1 \in w_1 - w_2, synonym(t_2, t_1)\}|$$

where $w_i = \{stem(w) \mid w \in tk(l_i) - \mathbf{SW}\}$

In this function, θ is a number between 0 and 1 that can be assigned as desired to capture the relative importance of an exact match of words (which has a weight of one) versus a match of synonyms (which has a weight of θ). If we wish to obtain a normalized version of the semantic label similarity, we should divide the above number by $|\, w_1 \cup w_2 \,|$.

For example, consider the labels 'check invoice' and 'verify invoice'. Tokenizing, removing stopwords and stemming yields the sets of words {'check', 'invoice'} and {'verify', 'invoice'}. Since, 'invoice' appears in both sets and 'check' and 'verify' are synonyms, the semantic label similarity of the two labels is $1 + \theta \cdot 2$. If we take $\theta = 0.7$, the semantic label similarity is 2.4. The normalized value of the similarity is then $2.4/3 = 0.8$.

Now let us consider the labels 'goods receipt' and 'receive goods'. After stemming, we obtain the sets {'good', 'receipt'} and {'receive', 'good'}. Again, we have that 'good' appears in both sets, and 'receipt' and 'receive' are synonyms, so the semantic label similarity is again $1 + \theta \cdot 2$.

To improve the quality of the semantic label similarity technique, not only words that are a synonym can be considered, but also words that are a synonym of a synonym, etc. Also, metrics can be used that can determine the semantic similarity of two words, based on their relation in a dictionary. Budanitsky and Hirst (2006) compared a number of such metrics. Alternatively, domain specific ontologies can be used to determine the semantic relation of words.

Virtual Document Similarity

Attribute values of a node can easily be included into the set of words that is used to determine the semantic similarity. However, the drawback of using this approach is that the number of occurrences of words is then ignored, while this is important information that can be exploited. In particular, it is common to include task descriptions or work instructions as attributes of a task. These are pieces of text that describe the task or that tell the person who should execute the task what to do. If, for example, the word 'check' appears often in the description of a task, this provides a strong hint as to what the nature of the task is.

The virtual document approach that we propose is inspired by the work of Qi, Hu and Cheng (2006). It is based on the observation that for any structured collection of information a document can be constructed. This document consists of the terms and the frequencies of these terms in the documents. Information on terms and term frequencies is sufficient to use common search engine techniques to determine the similarity of the documents (Raghavan, & Wong, 1986; Salton, & McGill, 1983).

As a simple example, consider a task with label 'check application' that uses the data object 'client application' and has as task description 'check the client application'. This task has as its virtual document: 'check' (2 occurrences), 'application' (2 occurrences), 'client' (2 occurrences), 'the' (1 occurrences).

Similarity of Business Process Graphs

Having abstracted business process models as graphs, we can use graph matching as a basis for defining similarity measures. Specifically, we can define measures of similarity between pairs of process models based on the notion of graph-edit distance (Messmer 1995; Bunke & Shearer 1997). The graph-edit distance between two graphs is the minimum number of operations (e.g. insertions, deletions, substitutions) needed in order to transform one graph into the other. Different notions of graph-edit distance can be defined depending on the choice of operations, and the cost associated to each operation. In general, the following types of operations are considered when defining graph-edit distances:

- Node substitution: a node from one graph is substituted for a node from the other graph.
- Node insertion/deletion: a node is inserted into or deleted from a graph.
- Edge substitution: an edge from one graph is substituted for an edge from the other graph. Edge substitutions are not relevant in the context of BPGs because edges in BPGs do not have labels.

- Edge insertion/deletion: an edge is inserted into or deleted from a graph.

Let us consider for example the process graphs in Figure 2. In order to transform the query graph into Graph 1 we need to delete node "Buy Goods", which means that we also have to delete the two edges of which "Buy Goods" is the source. Meanwhile, in order to transform the query graph into Graph 2, we need to delete node "Store Goods" (and its incoming edge), substitute node "Receive Goods" with "Goods Receipt", substitute node "Verify Invoice" with "Check Invoice" and finally delete the edge between "Buy Goods" and "Check Invoice". Another solution would be to substitute "Verify Invoice" with "Store Goods" and then to delete "Check Invoice" instead of deleting "Store Goods". Intuitively, the former option is preferable, because "Verify Invoice" has more similarity with "Check Invoice" than with "Store Goods" – a conclusion we can reach using either semantic or syntactic similarity. Next, in order to transform query graph into Graph 4, we need to substitute "Buy Goods" with "Order a book", "Receive Goods" with "Receive the Book", "Store Goods" with "Store the Book", delete node "Verify Invoice" and its incoming edge and finally add node "Read the Book" and its incoming edge. Instead of deleting "Verify Invoice" and adding "Read the Book", we could substitute "Verify Invoice" with "Read the Book", but this would be counter-intuitive because these two activities have nothing in common.

From these examples, we can see that we sometimes have to choose between one node substitution and another, or between node substitution and node addition/deletion. In the context of graph-edit distance, this choice is made by means of a *cost function*, that is, a function that given an operation returns a real number. For example, we can adopt a cost function that assigns a cost function like the following one:

- The cost of a node substitution is equal to the similarity between the nodes being compared (using syntactic or semantic similarity or a combination thereof).
- The cost of insertions and deletions of nodes and edges is a constant value (e.g. a cost of 0.25 for edge insertion/deletion and a cost of 0.5 for node insertion and node deletion).

Other cost functions could be adopted, but it is important to keep in mind that:

- Insertions and deletions of nodes (or edges) should be given the same cost in order to make the distance symmetric. Indeed, a node deletion operation when going from G1 to G2 becomes a node insertion operation in the other direction, and thus these two operations should be assigned the same cost.
- If the node similarity between two nodes N1 and N2 is zero, meaning that they have nothing in common, the cost of substituting N1 with N2 (and their associated edges) should be the same as the cost of deleting node N1 and then inserting back node N2 with the same edges as before. Conversely, the cost of substituting node N1 with N2 when the similarity between N1 and N2 is zero, should be zero because this is equivalent to leaving the graph intact.

One can easily check that the above cost function satisfies these properties.

We also observe from the above examples that a transformation from a BPG to another can be conceptually represented by means of: (i) a mapping of the nodes of one graph to the nodes of the other graph; and (ii) a set of edges to be inserted/deleted.

Intuitively, the mapping tells us which nodes are substituted. All nodes that do not appear in the mapping are nodes that need to be deleted or nodes that need to be inserted.

We also note that the set of edges to be inserted/deleted can be derived from the source and the target graphs and the mapping. Indeed, a node deletion implies that we have to delete the edges that are incident to this node in the source graph, while a node insertion means that we have to add all edges that are incident to this node in the target graph.

Thus we retain that a transformation between two BPGs can be represented by a partial mapping from the nodes in the source BPG to the nodes in the target BPG. This mapping has to be injective, meaning that one node in the target BPG can only be a substitute for at most one node in the source BPG.

Given the above observations, the graph-edit distance between two graphs (in particular two BPGs) is defined as follows:

Definition 3 (Graph Edit Distance): *Let $B_1 = (N_1, E_1, \tau_1, \lambda_1, \alpha_1)$ and $B_2 = (N_2, E_2, \tau_2, \lambda_2, \alpha_2)$ be two BPGs and let Sim be one of the similarity metrics between node labels as defined above (syntactic of semantic label similarity or a combination thereof). Finally, let $M: N_1 \rightarrow N_2$ be a partial injective mapping.*

Let $n \in N_1 \cup N_2$ be a node. n is substituted if and only if $n \in dom(M)$ or $n \in cod(M)$. sb is the set of all substituted nodes. n is inserted or deleted if and only if it is not substituted. sn is the set of all inserted and deleted nodes.

Let $(n, m) \in E_1$ be an edge. (n,m) is inserted in or deleted from B_1 if and only if there do not exist mappings $(n,n') \in M$ and $(m,m') \in M$ and edge $(n', m') \in E_2$. Edges that are inserted in or deleted from B_2 are defined similarly. se is the set of all inserted or deleted edges.

Finally, let cn be the cost assigned to node deletion/insertion and ce be the cost assigned to edge deletion/insertion.

The distance induced by the mapping is defined as:

$$cn \cdot |sn| + ce \cdot |se| + 2 \cdot \sum_{(n,m) \in M} 1 - Sim(n,m)$$

The graph edit distance is the minimal possible distance induced by a mapping between B_1 and B_2.

For example, let us consider again Figure 2 and compare the query graph with Graph 2. Let us consider the mapping that relates "Receive Goods" with "Goods Receipt" and "Verify Invoice" with "Check Invoice". This mapping implies that we need to delete node "Store Goods" and its incoming edge, and the edge between "Buy Goods" and "Check Invoice". Recall that the semantic similarity between "Receive Goods" with "Goods Receipt" is 0.8 (with $\theta = 0.7$), and the same applies to "Goods Receipt" and "Verify Invoice". We have that $|sn| = 1$, $|se| = 2$ and there are two node substitutions with node similarity of 0.8, and thus 1-Sim(n1, n2) is 0.2. Let us now set *cn* to 0.5 and *ce* to 0.25. The graph-edit distance induced by this mapping is: 0.5 + 2*0.25 + 2*0.2 = 1.4. If we explored the other possible mappings, we would find that they induce larger graph-edit distances. In particular, if we take the mapping that relates "Receive Goods" with "Goods Receipt" and "Verify Invoice" with "Store Goods", we would obtain a similarity higher than 1.2 because the similarity between "Verify Invoice" and "Store Goods" is zero, thus the corresponding term 1-Sim(n1, n2) is 1, and additionally there is a node deletion and an edge deletion.

There is one small inconvenience with the above definition: the distance is an absolute value. In the context of comparing BPGs, we would like to be able to report a similarity as a relative score (from 0 to 1), such that a similarity close to one means that the models are very similar, and a similarity close to 0 means that the models are completely different. In other words, we would like to define a normalized similarity.

Accordingly, we define the graph edit distance similarity as one minus the average of the fraction of inserted or deleted nodes, the fraction of inserted of deleted edges and the average distance of substituted nodes.

Definition 4 (Graph Edit Distance Similarity): *Let $B_1 = (N_1, E_1, \tau_1, \lambda_1, \alpha_1)$ and $B_2 = (N_2, E_2, \tau_2, \lambda_2, \alpha_2)$ be two BPGs and let Sim be one of the similarity metrics between node labels defined above.*

Furthermore, let M: $N_1 \rightarrow N_2$ be the partial injective mapping that induces the graph-edit distance between the two processes and let sn and se be defined as in Definition 3. We define the graph edit distance similarity *as:*

simged(B_1,B_2)=avg(snv,sev,svb)

Where:

$$snv = \frac{|sn|}{|N_1| + |N_2|}$$

$$sev = \frac{|se|}{|E_1| + |E_2|}$$

$$sbv = \frac{2 \cdot \sum_{(n,m)\in M} 1 - Sim(n,m)}{|N_1| + |N_2| - |sn|}$$

Variations of this similarity measure can be obtained by replacing the arithmetic average with a weighted average of the fractions of skipped nodes, substituted nodes and skipped edges (like in the definition of graph-edit distance where we used costs). In this case, the user must choose the appropriate weights.

Conceptually, a graph-edit distance algorithm must try possible combinations of transformations (i.e. mappings) between the two input graphs, and return the one with the minimal total cost. It has been shown that computing the graph-edit distance is an NP-complete problem (Messmer 1995). This is not only a theoretical limitation but a practical one. We have experimentally observed that for real-life process models with more than 20 nodes, exhaustive graph matching algorithms

for computing lead to combinatorial explosion. Therefore, heuristics are needed that strike a tradeoff between computational complexity and precision.

A known family of methods to compute the graph edit distance is based on the A* search algorithm (Messmer 1995). The idea is to construct possible mappings incrementally. The algorithm starts by picking one node in the first graph, and pairing it with each node in the second graph. This leads to a set of |G2| mappings of size 1, where |G2| is the size of the second BPG. The algorithm will then iterate to create larger mappings, until it finds a complete mapping. In other words, the algorithm iterates until no more pairs can be added to the current mapping. In each iteration, the algorithm takes the best partial mapping so far, picks a new node n1 in G1 that it not yet in this current mapping, pairs it with each node in n2 in G2 that is not yet in the current mapping, and produces a new mapping for each such pair *(n1, n2)*. This way, the algorithm produces mappings of larger size, by always extending the best mapping so far.

In one of its variants, the algorithm backtracks if the current (best) mapping has a cost above a maximum acceptable threshold. When a solution is found, the cost of the solution is taken as the new maximum threshold, and the search can continue with a tighter threshold.

A major issue with these A*-like method is the large number of partial mappings that must be maintained during the search $- O(m^n)$ in the worst case, where *m* and *n* are the numbers nodes in the graphs (Messmer 1995). Our experiments have shown that this is problematic for process models with over 20 nodes (Dijkman, Dumas & García-Bañuelos, 2009). Accordingly, we proposed to address this issue by forbidding pairs of nodes to be added to a mapping if their labels are too different from one another -- but this hinders the optimality of the obtained solution. Other experiments (Grigori, Corrales & Bouzeghoub 2008) show that the technique can be scaled to around

50 nodes but on highly structured BPGs (e.g. business processes written using the structured subset of the BPEL language).

In (Dijkman, Dumas & García-Bañuelos, 2009) we proposed three other heuristics for calculating the similarity of business process models based on graph matching. These heuristics are also based on the idea of constructing partial mappings of increasing size by looking at pairs of nodes that have not yet been mapped and adding them to the currently maintained set of mapping(s). One of these algorithms follows the principles of "greedy" heuristics. We start with an empty mapping, and add the pair of nodes *(n1, n2)* that least increases the graph edit distance. Then among the nodes that have not yet been included in the mapping, we pick again the one that least increases the graph edit distance, and so on until no more pairs of nodes can be added to the current mapping. This greedy heuristic algorithm is highly scalable.

In (Dijkman, Dumas & García-Bañuelos, 2009) we reported experimental results in the context of similarity search of business process models. The problem of similarity search is the following: given a model (the *query model*), and a collection of models, find the models in the collection that most resemble the *query* model. We compared an A*-like heuristics and the three other heuristics (including the greedy one) in terms of their ability to appropriately rank the models in a collection of 100 models with respect to 10 query models. For each query model, the ranking given by each heuristics and for each query was compared with a manual ranking. The results suggest that the greedy algorithm, while more scalable, has a mean average precision within 5-10% of that of the A*-like heuristics.

In the above discussion, we have only considered elementary graph-edit operations (deletion, insertion and substitution), meaning that only 1-to-1 node mappings are constructed. In (Grigori, Corrales & Bouzeghoub 2008), the set of graph-edit operations is extended with node splitting and node merging, i.e. N-to-M mappings

are constructed. In (Dumas, García-Bañuelos and Käärik 2009), we observed that the number of partial mappings grows combinatorially when node splitting and merging operations are integrated and proposed an alternative two-step approach. First, the basic A-star algorithm is used to obtain a 1-to-1 mapping. In the second step, all deleted/inserted nodes are combined with adjacent nodes and we check if this improves the mapping. Combining a deleted node with a matched one is similar to node merging, while combining an inserted node with a matched one is similar to node splitting. In this way, the N-to-M mapping can be computed while maintaining the memory requirements of the 1-to-1 mapping approach. Weidlich, Dijkman and Mendling (2010) further extended this idea by considering not only adjacent nodes, but also groups of nodes around a given one based on four types of groups: sequences, splits, joins and distance-bounded groups (i.e. all activities within a given distance of a given node). This leads to a broader exploration of the set of possible 1-to-N mappings.

We evaluated the performance of the graph edit distance metric for computing similarity between business process graphs, using different settings and different techniques for computing the similarity of nodes (Dijkman, van Dongen, Dumas, Käärik & Mendling, 2010). The evaluation was performed on two test sets, one in which the search query models were taken from the collection of models that was searched and one in which search query models were taken from another collection. The main goal of the evaluation was to compare the performance of the different metrics to a text-based search engine. The results showed that for both test sets the graph edit distance based metrics outperformed the text-based search engine. For the first test set the text-based search engine had a first-10 precision of 0.70, while the graph-edit distance based metric had a first-10 precision of 0.78. For the second test set the performance was 0.55 and 0.65, respectively. Interestingly, the results did not differ much depending on whether syntactic or semantic node similarity was used. We attribute this to the fact that in for the first test set, similar nodes had very similar labels, such that the syntactic similarity measure lead to sufficiently good results, while in the second test set, similar nodes had such different labels that even semantic similarity did not improve the results much.

Similarity of Business Process Graph Fragments

In addition to checking similarity between business process models as a whole, we can check similarity between smaller fragments of a business process model. Such similarity checks can, among other things, be used to find overlap between business process models. In general good design practice requires that (large) overlap should be avoided, because it complicates updates of business process models. In case an update must be performed on a part of a business process model that appears in multiple process models, the update must be performed on each of those business process models. If an update is performed on one fragment, but not on another, overlapping, fragment, then a collection of business process models becomes inconsistent. In addition similarity checks between business process fragments can be used to determine similarity of a business process model fragment to a (anti-)pattern, thus finding position to apply a pattern or improve a process.

The problem with determining similarity between business process model fragments is that it has exponential complexity; each business process has 2^N possible fragments where N is the number of nodes in the business process, because a fragment can or cannot contain a node. Therefore, a heuristic must be used to select the business process fragments for which to determine similarity.

We use a parsing technique that is called the Refined Process Structure Tree (RPST) (Vanhatalo, Völzer, & Koehler, 2009). Figure 3 shows an example of such decompositions for the query

model and models 1 and 2 from Figure 1. A fragment is a connected subgraph, such that control enters the fragment via a single *entry node* and leaves the fragment via a single *exit node*. The RPST defines a unique decomposition, i.e., a hierarchy of fragments, that can be computed in linear time (Vanhatalo, Völzer, & Koehler, 2009). Consequently, it does not suffer from exponential complexity.

The Refined Process Structure Tree can be defined as follows. Let G be a business process graph with a unique source and a unique sink, such that every node is on a path from the source to the sink. Let F be a connected subgraph of G. A node of F is an *interior* node of F if it is connected only to nodes in F, otherwise it is a *boundary node* of F. A boundary node u of F is an *entry* of F if no incoming edge of u belongs to F or if all outgoing edges of u belong to F. A boundary node v of F in an *exit* of F if no outgoing edge of v belongs to F or if all incoming edges of v belong to F. F is a *fragment* if it has exactly two boundary nodes, one entry and one exit. A fragment is *trivial* if it only contains a single edge. Note that every singleton edge forms a trivial fragment.

We say that two fragments are *nested* if one is a subgraph of the other, they are *disjoint* if their sets of edges are disjoint. If they are neither nested nor disjoint, we say that they *overlap*. A fragment is said to be *canonical* if it does not overlap with any other fragment. The RPST of G is the set of canonical fragments of G. It follows that any two canonical fragments are either nested or disjoint and hence they form a hierarchy. This hierarchy can be shown as a tree, where the parent of a canonical fragment F is the smallest canonical fragment that contains F. In particular, the RPST is capable of discovering sequences, parallel paths (that are formed by a related split and a join node), trivial fragments and rigid fragments that represents all fragments that are not a sequence, parallel path or trivial fragment. Figure 4 shows a tree representation of the RPST for the Query model RPST from Figure 3.

Figure 3. The Refined Process Structure Trees of three business process models

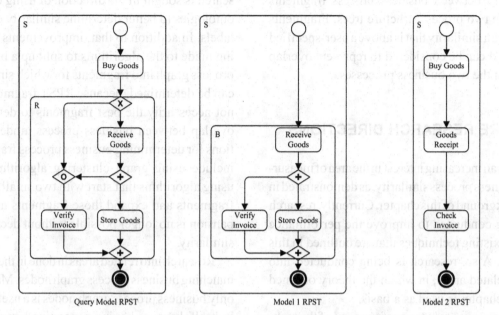

The RPST thus divides a business process graph into a collection of fragments. Subsequently, we can check a pair of business process graphs for pairs of fragments that are overlapping (i.e. that have a sufficiently high similarity, using one of the metrics from the previous section).

Figure 5 summarizes the complete procedure of determining similarity between business process fragments. Given two business process models, the first step is to create the respective process structure trees. This step separates the business process models into collections of canonical fragments. The second step is to determine the

Figure 4. A Tree Representation of a Refined Process Structure Tree

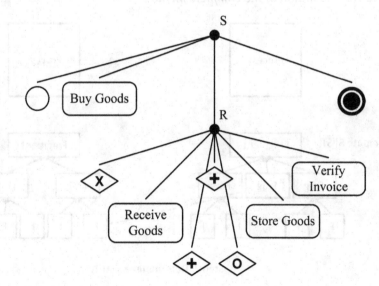

similarity between business process fragments from the two process structure trees. Fragments that have a similarity that is above a user-specified threshold can be considered to represent overlap between the two business processes.

FUTURE RESEARCH DIRECTIONS

There is an increasing interest in the area of measuring business process similarity, as demonstrated in the background of this chapter. Currently, research is being conducted to improve the performance of the existing techniques that are outlined in this chapter. Also, research is being conducted into more related areas, in which the theory outlined in this chapter is used as a basis.

Improvements in the performance of the techniques in this chapter are sought both in terms of improving the computational performance and in terms of improving the quality (e.g. accuracy) of the results of business process similarity search. In terms of computational performance, algorithms are being developed to quickly compute similarity. The work by Dijkman, Dumas, & García-Bañuelos (2009) is a first effort in this direction. Improvement of the quality of business process similarity

search is sought in the direction of using domain ontologies to better determine similarity of node labels. In addition to that, improvements are being made to the algorithms to split up a business process graph into fragments for which similarity can be determined, because RPST fragments are not necessarily the best fragments to determine overlap between business process models. Options for determining business process fragments include using graph clustering algorithms and using algorithms that start with two small similar fragments and expand those fragments until expansion is no longer possible without decreasing similarity.

Research into related areas in done in the area of matching business process graph nodes. Matching only business process graph nodes is a useful goal in itself, because having a mapping between the nodes of two business process graphs is often a prerequisite for other forms of analysis of business process models (e.g.: analyzing conformance of one business process model to another, or analyzing equivalence of business process models). An important area of future work for business process graph node matching is finding matches between groups of nodes, because often business process graphs are not modeled at the same level

Figure 5. A graphical representation of the complete method

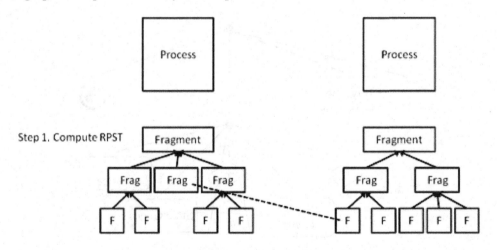

of granularity, leading to a single node in one business process graph that corresponds to multiple nodes in another business process graph, or even multiple nodes in one business process graph that correspond to multiple nodes in the other. The architecture developed by Weidlich, Dijkman, & Mendling, (2010) is a first step into the direction of developing matches between groups of nodes.

Another related research area is the area of business process query languages and algorithms for executing queries expressed in such languages (e.g. BPMN-Q (Awad, Polyvyanyy & Weske, 2008)). A business process query can be used to specify a search for business process models in a collection that have certain properties. Such properties may be defined on the basis of temporal logic – see for example (Awad, Decker & Weske 2008) – or in terms of languages inspired by SQL or to the Object Constraint Language (OCL). In principle, graph theory could be used to define mechanisms to perform business process model searches based on their graph structure. These mechanisms could enable searches that return approximate matches to the search query, rather than only exact matches.

Research is also ongoing in the area of computing the collection of fragments of a graph. In particular research is ongoing into creating a more refined classification of fragments (<TODO: add reference>). Currently fragments can be classified as a sequence, parallel paths, trivial or rigid, where every fragment that is not a sequence a set of parallel paths or a trivial fragment. A further classification of rigid fragments is being developed.

The research in this chapter is focused on business process similarity, but strongly related research is done in the area of (web) service similarity and matching. Research in this area uses similar techniques, such as determining fragments of a service behavior description (Eshuis & Grefen, 2007), similarity search (Grigori, Corrales, Bouzeghoub, & Gater, 2010) and matching (Nezhad, Xu, & Benatallah, 2010).

CONCLUSION

This chapter explained how graph theory can be used to measure the similarity of business process models, by interpreting a business process model as a special type of graph. Subsequently, graph edit distance can be used to determine the similarity of business process graphs. In addition to that the Refined Process Structure Tree can be used to partition a graph into smaller fragments and determine graph similarity of the fragments.

There is a wide range of applications of these techniques. The most obvious use of the graph similarity techniques is to use them for searching a collection of business process models for business process models that are most similar to a given business process model (similarity search). In addition to that, the techniques can be used to determine overlap between business process models in a collection, which then can be reduced, thus improving the quality of that collection.

In future work specific extensions of the techniques are envisioned, with the goal of improving the computational performance of the techniques and the quality of the results that they return. In addition to that the techniques can be combined with other techniques to support matching of business process tasks and to support business process query languages.

REFERENCES

Awad, A., Decker, G., & Weske, M. (2008). Efficient compliance checking using BPMN-Q and temporal logic. In *Proceedings of the 6th International Conference on Business Process Management (BPM)*, Ulm, Germany (pp. 326-341). Berlin, Heidelberg, Germany: Springer.

Awad, A., Polyvyanyy, A., & Weske, M. (2008). Semantic querying of business process models. In *Proceedings of the 12th International EDOC Conference (EDOC)*, Munich, Germany (pp. 85-94).

Budanitsky, A., & Hirst, G. (2006). Evaluating WordNet-based measures of lexical semantic relatedness. *Computational Linguistics, 32*(1), 13–47. doi:10.1162/coli.2006.32.1.13

Bunke, H., & Shearer, K. (1998). A graph distance metric based on the maximal common subgraph. *Pattern Recognition Letters, 19,* 255–259. doi:10.1016/S0167-8655(97)00179-7

Curran, T. A., & Keller, G. (1999). *SAP R/3 Business Blueprint - Business Engineering mit den R/3-Referenzprozessen.* Bonn, Germany: Addison-Wesley.

Dijkman, R.M., Dongen, B.F. van, Dumas, M., Käärik, R., & Mendling, J. (2010). Similarity of business process models: Metrics and evaluation. Accepted for publication in: *Information Systems.*

Dijkman, R. M., Dumas, M., & García-Bañuelos, L. (2009). Graph matching algorithms for business process model similarity search. In, *Proceedings of the 7th International Conference on Business Process Management* (pp. 48-63). Berlin, Germany: Springer.

Dijkman, R. M., Dumas, M., García-Bañuelos, L., & Käärik, R. (2009). Aligning business process models. In, *Proceedings of the 13th IEEE EDOC Conference* (pp. 45-53).

Documentair Structuurplan. (n.d.). Retrieved May 10, 2010 from: http://www.model-dsp.nl.

Ehrig, M., Koschmider, A., & Oberweis, A. (2007). Measuring similarity between semantic business process models. In, *Proceedings of the 4th Asia-Pacific Conference on Conceptual Modeling* (pp. 71–80). Darlinghurst, Australia: Australian Computer Society.

Eshuis, R., & Grefen, P. (2007). Structural matching of BPEL processes. In *Proceedings of the 5th European Conference on Web Services* (pp. 171-180). Halle (Saale), Germany. Washington, DC, USA: IEEE Computer Society.

Grigori, D., Corrales, J. C., & Bouzeghoub, M. (2008). Behavioral matchmaking for service retrieval: Application to conversation protocols. *Information Systems, 33*(7-8), 681–698. doi:10.1016/j.is.2008.02.004

Grigori, D., Corrales, J. C., Bouzeghoub, M., & Gater, A. (2010). Ranking BPEL processes for service discovery. *IEEE Transactions on Services Computing, 3,* 178–192.

Levenshtein, I. (1966). Binary code capable of correcting deletions, insertions and reversals. *Cybernetics and Control Theory, 10*(8), 707–710.

Li, C., Reichert, M., & Wombacher, A. (2007). *On measuring process model similarity based on high-level change operations.* (Report No. TR-CTIT-07-89). Enschede, The Netherlands: Centre for Telematics and Information Technology.

Lu, R., & Sadiq, S. (2007). On the discovery of preferred work practice through business process variants. In *Conceptual Modeling - ER 2007* (pp. 165–180). Berlin, Germany: Springer. doi:10.1007/978-3-540-75563-0_13

Madhusudan, T., Zhao, L., & Marshall, B. (2004). A case-based reasoning framework for workflow model management. *Data & Knowledge Engineering, 50*(1), 87–115. doi:10.1016/j.datak.2004.01.005

Messmer, B. (1995). *Efficient graph matching algorithms for preprocessed model graphs.* PhD thesis, University of Bern, Switzerland.

Minor, M., Tartakovski, A., & Bergmann, R. (2007). Representation and structure-based similarity assessment for agile workflows. In *Proceedings of the 7th International Conference on Case-Based Reasoning* (pp. 224–238). Berlin, Germany: Springer.

Nejati, S., Sabetzadeh, M., Chechik, M., Easterbrook, S., & Zave, P. (2007). Matching and merging of statecharts specifications. In *29th International Conference on Software Engineering* (pp. 54–63).

Nezhad, H. R. M., Xu, G. Y., & Benatallah, B. (2010). Protocol-aware matching of Web service interfaces for adapter development. In *Proceedings of WWW* (pp. 731-740).

Qu, Y., Hu, W., & Cheng, G. (2006). Constructing virtual documents for ontology matching. In *Proceedings of WWW, 2006*, 23–31.

Raghavan, V. V., & Wong, S. K. M. (1986). A critical analysis of vector space model for information retrieval. *JASIS, 37*(5), 279–287.

Salton, G., & McGill, M. H. (1983). *Introduction to modern information retrieval*. New York, NY: McGraw-Hill.

van der Aalst, W., Medeiros, A., & Weijters, A. (2006). Process equivalence: Comparing two process models based on observed behavior. In *Proceedings of BPM 2006*, (pp. 129–144). Berlin, Germany: Springer.

van Dongen, B. F., Dijkman, R. M., & Mendling, J. (2008). Measuring similarity between business process models. In, *Proceedings of the 20th International Conference on Advanced Information Systems Engineering* (pp. 450-464). Berlin, Germany: Springer.

Vanhatalo, J., Völzer, H., & Koehler, J. (2009). The refined process structure tree. *Data & Knowledge Engineering, 68*(9), 793–818. doi:10.1016/j.datak.2009.02.015

Weidlich, M., Dijkman, R. M., & Mendling, J. (2010). The ICoP framework: Identification of correspondences between process models. In *Proceedings of the 22th International Conference on Advanced Information Systems Engineering* (pp. 483-498). Berlin, Germany: Spinger.

Wombacher, A. (2006). Evaluation of technical measures for workflow similarity based on a pilot study. In *Proceedings of the 14th International Conference on Cooperative Information Systems* (pp. 255–272). Berlin, Germany: Springer.

KEY TERMS AND DEFINITIONS

Business Process: A collection of related tasks that must be performed to achieve a certain goal.

Business Process Repository: A tool that facilitates management of a collection of business processes.

Business Process Graph: An abstraction of a business process model in the form of a graph.

Similarity Search: Searching a collection of documents for those documents that are similar to a given query document.

Edit Distance: The number of operations necessary to transform one object into another.

Matching: Determining which elements from one document are similar to which elements from another document.

Refined Process Structure Tree: A tree-based representation of a business process, in which the business process is broken down into smaller fragments, each of which has a single entry point and a single exit point.

Chapter 19
A Graph–Based Approach for Semantic Process Model Discovery

Ahmed Gater
Universite de Versailles Saint-Quentin en Yvelines, France

Daniela Grigori
Universite de Versailles Saint-Quentin en Yvelines, France

Mokrane Bouzeghoub
Universite de Versailles Saint-Quentin en Yvelines, France

ABSTRACT

One of the key tasks in the service oriented architecture that Semantic Web services aim to automate is the discovery of services that can fulfill the applications or user needs. OWL-S is one of the proposals for describing semantic metadata about Web services, which is based on the OWL ontology language. Majority of current approaches for matching OWL-S processes take into account only the inputs/outputs service profile. This chapter argues that, in many situations the service matchmaking should take into account also the process model. We present matching techniques that operate on OWL-S process models and allow retrieving in a given repository, the processes most similar to the query. To do so, the chapter proposes to reduce the problem of process matching to a graph matching problem and to adapt existing algorithms for this purpose. It proposes a similarity measure used to rank the discovered services. This measure captures differences in process structure and semantic differences between input/outputs used in the processes.

INTRODUCTION

Semantic web services envision a greater access to services on the web and a more automatic support to their management by providing the ability to describe their semantics in a formal and machine-processable manner. One of the key tasks in the service oriented architecture that semantic web services aim to automate is the discovery of services that can fulfill user needs.

DOI: 10.4018/978-1-61350-053-8.ch019

Majority of approaches for semantic web services discovery are based on formal descriptions of both service advertisements (published by providers in a registry) and queries, i.e., the service that a user is looking for.

These descriptions are written in the same description language (for example, OWL-S (Martin et al, 2004)) and defined in an underlying decidable description logic based ontology language, such as OWL-DL, and OWL-Lite. This way, description logic reasoning can be used to automatically determine services that semantically match a given service request based on the terminological concept subsumption relations computed in the underlying ontology. Examples of such logic-based approaches to semantic service matchmaking are the OWL-S UDDI matchmaker (Kawamura et al. 2003) and WSMO discovery approach (Keller et al. 2005).

OWL-S is one of the proposals for describing semantic metadata about web services that is based on the OWL ontology language. OWL-S covers three main parts: the service profile for advertising and discovering of services; the process model, which gives a detailed description of a service's actions and behavior; and the grounding, which provides details on how to cooperate with a service.

Current approaches for discovering semantic services take into account only the service profile, by exploiting the relations between inputs and outputs concepts in the ontology (Klusch et al. 2006). As we will see in next section, discovering services using only their inputs/outputs is not sufficient for some applications. For instance, when searching services for integrating in a given application, the process model specifying how to interact with the provider service has to be taken into account in the discovery process. Other application example is the scientific workflow discovery, where scientists look in a workflow repository for existing workflows that could support their research. Recent works (Goderis et al. 2006, Goderis et al. 2009) showed that scientists

require tools for service discovery based on their underlying process model.

These applications show that the discovery based on the profile has to be complemented by integrating the process model. In our view, service discovery can be reformulated as a three-phase process (see Figure 1):

- Phase 1: profile-based selection which uses classical information retrieval techniques to select the first bunch of services based on keywords and vectorial model matching, possibly improved by some ontological knowledge;
- Phase 2: structure-based selection which exploits behavioral properties given in the business process specification, usually leading to graph or automata matching;
- Phase 3: service ranking of the results provided by the previous phase, based on constraints satisfaction and quality features.

This chapter is concerned by phase 2. We present matching techniques that operate on OWL-S process models and allow retrieving in a given repository, the processes most similar to the query. As process models are usually represented as graphs, the problem of process matching can be reduced to a graph matching problem. In this chapter we show how existing graph matching algorithms can be adapted and extended for this purpose. We propose a graph-based similarity measure that will be used to rank the discovered services. This measure captures differences in process structure and semantic differences between inputs/outputs used in the process. In this chapter we present our matching approach as a step in the process of service discovery, but it can be used in several applications (merging processes, delta analysis, auto completion mechanism for modeling processes, ...) requiring the matching semantic process models.

Figure 1. Service discovery steps

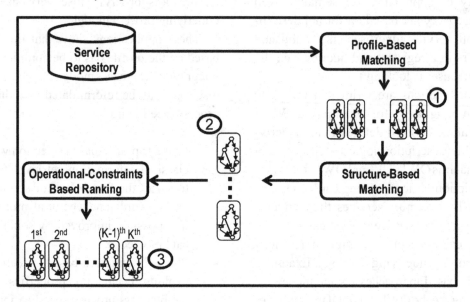

In Section 2, we present two motivating scenarios where process model matchmaking is necessary. Section 3 presents existing approaches for service retrieval and shows their drawbacks for the presented scenarios. In Section 4, we give an overview on the OWL-S ontology, by focusing on the process models. In Section 5, we show how the process model matchmaking is reduced to a graph matching problem. Section 6 shows how the graph matching algorithm can be used for OWL-S process model matchmaking. The matchmaking algorithm is illustrated through an example in Section 7. Finally, Section 8 presents some open problems and conclusions.

MOTIVATING SCENARIO

With the increasing importance of processes in current information systems and service oriented architecture, we are witnessing the emergence of a growing need for tools allowing matching processes. Examples of such applications are numerous: web service integration, retrieving scientific workflow, delta analysis, version management, compatibility and replaceability, analysis of business protocols, behavior based service discovery...

Due to space limitations, we limit ourselves to the presentation of two scenarios: web service integration, retrieving scientific workflow.

Web Services Integration

Consider a company that uses a service to order office suppliers. Suppose that the company wants to replace its current partner or to find a new retailer (say WalMart or Target). Many existing services are programmed to exchange data according to a specified protocol. The allowed message exchange sequences are called process model and can be expressed for example using BPEL abstract processes (Andrews et al. 2007) or OWL-S (for process models consisting of semantically annotated web services). Thus the company will search for a service having a process model that is compatible with service's process model. Among retailer services, the most compatible one has to be found. If the service is not fully compatible, the company will adapt it or will develop an adaptor in order to interact with the retrieved service. In both situations, the

Figure 2. Granularity level differences

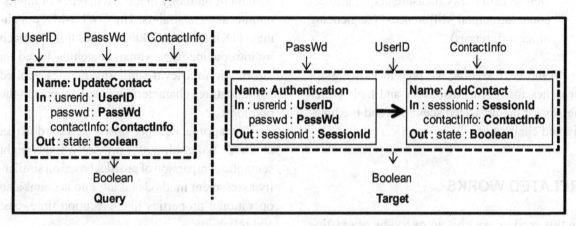

differences between the process models have to be automatically identified. In the former case, finding the most similar service allows to minimize the development cost. In the latter case, identifying automatically the differences between protocols is the first stage in the process of semi-automatically adapters development (Benatallah et al., 2005). An approach for mediating two OWL-S process models (provider and requester) was proposed in (Vaculn et al. 2007). But, complementary to this approach, a method is needed to retrieve within a repository of OWL-S services, those having the process models that are the most similar to the user query.

Retrieving Scientific Workflows

Collaboratories emerge on the web, allowing scientists to share and re-use the scientific workflows describing their experiments. As an example, myExperiment (www.myexperiement.org) is one of the current public workflow repositories containing hundreds of distinct scientific workflows, contributed by hundreds of users. While current retrieval facilities in workflow repositories are mostly limited to browsing and keywords based searches, recent works (Goderis et al. 2006, 7) elicited requirements for workflow discovery through an experiment with scientists and developers form the myGrid workflow environment.

The experiments showed: (i) the willingness of users to share and reuse workflows, (ii) the limits of current retrieval facilities and (iii) that process based discovery is a required feature. As some of these repositories use ontologies to describe and discover services (see (Wroe et al. 2003) as an example in a bioinformatics domain), they require methods and tools to retrieve semantic based process models based on the underlying process description.

To achieve efficient process model matchmaking techniques, for these applications, we must tackle three issues:

- Identify similar activities in the two graphs by using all sources of evidence: their names, inputs and outputs.

- Detect granularity differences between the two graphs: the same functionality can be implemented by a developer as an activity, while another developer could decompose it in several activities. Figure 2 shows an example of such granularity differences. The query process specifies user update contact functionality as a single activity (UpdateContact), while the target one implements it as a sequence of two sub-activities (Authentication followed by AddContact).

• Define a similarity measure taking into account structural differences (sequencing order differences)

In the next section, we present existing approaches for service discovery and their weaknesses for the presented scenarios and the highlighted challenges.

RELATED WORKS

In this section, we give an overview of existing approaches for service retrieval and show their limits for the presented scenarios.

Currently, Web services discovery in registers like UDDI or ebXML are based on a search by keywords or tables of correspondence of couples (key-value). Within the framework of the semantic Web, description logics were proposed for a richer and precise formal description of services. Since semantic models provide a shared agreement on the meaning of terms regardless the underlying format (syntax and structure), annotating requirements and capabilities of Web services with these models introduces an additional level of abstraction that can improve significantly the relevance of web service discovery engines. Specifically, these models allow the definition of ontologies (for example OWL-S) which are used as a basis for semantic matching between a declarative description of the required service and descriptions of the offered services (Paolucci et al. 2002, Bernstein et al. 2002, Benatallah et al. 2003).

In Paolucci et al. 2002, Benatallah et al. 2003, a published service is matched against a required service when the inputs and outputs of the required service match the inputs and outputs of the published service. Two inputs/outputs, which are concepts in a given domain ontology, match if they have the same type or one is a generalization of the other.

In (Kawamura et al. 2003), several filters are defined for service retrieval: the namespace, the domain of ontology that is used, types of inputs/outputs and constraints. The OWLS-MX matchmaker (Klusch et al. 2006) extends this approach by introducing approximate matching based on information retrieval similarity metrics applied to the features characterizing the concepts in the ontology.

The approaches presented in (Cardoso et al. 2003, Wu et al. 2005) provide a lightweight semantic comparison of profiles based on similarity assessment methods taking into account also operational properties like execution time, cost and reliability.

Recently, the World Wide Web Consortium (W3C) produced a standard set of Semantic Annotations for WSDL (SAWSDL) (Farrell et al. 2007), aiming at disambiguating the semantic of Web services description during discovery. For a survey on approaches for semantic matchmaking of web service interfaces, see (Bellur et al. 2008).

Authors in (Bansal et al. 2003) argue that the matchmaking based only on service profile (inputs and outputs of the service) is not sufficient as some outputs data may be produced only under certain internal conditions.

Service discovery based on keywords or on the service profile, even if enriched by semantic annotations, is still insufficient for many applications such as those presented in the previous section. Therefore, recent approaches (Nejati et al. 2007, Ehrig et al. 2007, Wombacher et al. 2004, Minor et al. 2007, Dijkman et al. 2009, Dongen et al. 2008])take into account the process model to enhance the service discovery engines accuracy.

In (Nejati et al. 2007), authors propose process model similarity metric for processes captured as hierarchical statecharts, where each state represents an atomic activity. The similarity between two activities is evaluated on the basis of their labels and on their behavioral semantics. The algorithm iteratively computes a similarity degree for every pair of activities by aggregating the similarity degrees between their neighbors (successor of a state). The algorithm iterates until either the similarity degrees between all state pairs stabilize, or a maximum number of iterations is reached.

In (Ehrig et al. 2007), authors propose a similarity measure for semantic process models specified using Petri nets. The proposed similarity is an aggregation of syntactic, linguistic and structural similarities of Petri net elements. Authors use Levenhstein distance (Gater et al. 2010) to evaluate the syntactic similarity of element label, while the linguistic similarity relies on WordNet dictionary to determine element synonyms. The structural similarity of two elements is defined as the weighted average of the similarities of all elements which may influence it.

In (Dijkman et al. 2009), authors reduce the process model (specified as rooted graphs) matchmaking problem into a graph matchmaking problem. They propose a structural similarity based on the notion of graph-edit distance (Messmer 1995). The graph-edit distance is based on the minimum cost of edit operations (node/edge insertion and substitution) that are necessary to transform one graph to another. Moreover, authors define syntactic and lexical metrics to compute the similarity between the vocabularies of different models.

Another structure-based metric is proposed in (Minor et al. 2007) to evaluate the distance between two process models captured as rooted graphs. The distance is viewed as being the number of activities and control flow constraints that are not shared by the two process models. The distance between two process models P_1 and P_2 is expressed by the following formula: $\delta(P_1, P_2) = |A_1| + |E_1| + |A_2| + |E_1|$; where A_1 (resp. A_2) are nodes within P_1 (resp. P_2) but not within P_2 (resp P_1), and E_1 (resp. P_2) are edges within P_1 (resp. P_2) but not within P_2 (resp. P_1).

In (Wombacher et al. 2004), authors give a formal semantics to the matchmaking of process model specified using finite state machines (FSM). In this approach, the process model matchmaking problem is formulated as FSM intersection, where two FSMs match if they share a non-empty set of common execution paths.

In (Dongen et al. 2008), it is proposed a technique for matching process models based on causal footprints. A causal footprint is defined as a tuple $P = (N, L_{lb}, L_{la})$, where N is a finite set of activities, $L_{lb} \subseteq (P(N) \times N)$ is a set of look-back links, and $L_{la} \subseteq (P(N) \times N)$ is a set of look-ahead links. Each look-ahead link $(a, B) \in L_{la}$ means that the execution of a is followed at least by the execution of an element $b \in B$. Each look-back link in $(A, b) \in L_{lb}$ means that the execution of b is preceded at least by the execution of an element $a \in A$. Process models are represented as vectors, and their similarity is considered as the cosine of the angle between their respective vectors. The dimensions composing the vectors are activities, look-ahead links and look-back links belonging to at least one of the two causal footprints.

Other area of related works (Vaculn et al. 2007, Beeri et al. 2008, Awad et al. 2008) concerns process query languages allowing to retrieve in a repository process models satisfying structural constraints. In (Vaculn et al. 2007), a query language for services is defined, which allows to find services by specifying conditions on the activities composing them, the exceptions treated, the flow of the data between the activities.

BP-QL (Beeri et al. 2008) is a graph-based language for querying BPEL processes which allows to navigate along the path-dimension inside a single process graph and to zoom across process graphs of the used services.

BPMN-Q (Awad et al. 2008) is another query language for processes expressed using Business Process Modeling Notation (BPMN). In order to deal with heterogeneity of activity names, semantic expansion of BPMN-Q queries is realized by constructing new queries using similar activities to the ones employed in the query and returning results that match either the original query or any of its derivatives.

These query languages are based on an exact matching between the query pattern and the target process model. They not allow to retrieve patterns similar to the query, i.e. if a graph containing the query pattern does not exist, but a graph containing a similar one exist, it will not be returned to the user.

Complementary to the work presented here, are recent works that try to uncover the particular similarity metrics people use for establishing workflow similarity. Authors in (Bernstein et al. 2005) look for the best semantic similarity measures to rank business processes from the MIT Process Handbook, based on process ontology. The work presented in (*) seeks to elicit the similarity metrics used by workflow researchers when comparing the control flow of workflows described by Finite State Machines (FSMs). Both works show that a general similarity measure reflecting human similarity assessments can hardly be found, the first one suggesting personalizing the similarity measures according to the user's similarity assessment style.

To summarize, the need to take into account the service process model in the retrieval process was underlined by several authors and some very recent proposals exist (Nejati et al. 2007, Wombacher et al. 2004).

However, most of these approaches do not consider all activity attributes that can make the calculation of distance between process activities more efficient. In this sense, we defined a similarity measure between process activities that takes into account all sources of evidence: inputs, outputs and name.

Moreover, granularity differences may exist between two processes: the same functionality can be implemented by a developer as an activity, while other developer could decompose it in several activities. While majority of existing approaches considers only simple matches (1-1 activity correspondences), we introduce in this chapter a technique that allows identifying complex matches (1-Many activity correspondences) between activities based on their inputs/outputs semantics and control flow dependencies.

An approximate matching technique addressing these issues is defined in (*) for service retrieval

based on BPEL process model. This technique is extended in (*) for semantic annotated process models (OWL-S process model). Hereafter, we present in details these techniques.

OVERVIEW OF OWL-S ONTOLOGY

OWL-S (*) is an ontology for web services description that enables greater access to web services by offering a set of markup language constructs for describing the properties and capabilities of Web services in an unambiguous, computer-interpretable form. OWL-S ontology covers three main parts: service profile, service grounding and, the service process model.

The profile gives mechanisms for specifying service functionality, provider information, and non-functional properties. Service functionality describes the function the service offers in terms of required inputs to produce the expected outputs. Furthermore, it describes the preconditions under which the service operates, and the effects resulting from the execution of the service. The provider information consists of the contact information about the entity offering the service; it may include geographic locations of the company offering the service, the operator responsible of marketing or running. The non-functional properties allow describing an unbounded list of service parameters that can contain service category, quality rating, geographic availability, time response, etc.

The grounding of a service specifies the details of how to access the service in terms of protocol and message formats, serialization, transport, and addressing. Concrete messages are specified explicitly in the grounding part. OWL-S adopts Web Services Description Language (WSDL) for concrete message specification. The process model gives a detailed description of a service's actions and behavior. It captures the temporal and logical dependencies (control flow) of process model activities. The elementary unit of the process model is an atomic process, which represents one indivisible operation that the client can perform by sending a particular message (possibly complex) to the service and receiving a corresponding response message (possibly complex). Atomic processes are specified by means of their inputs, outputs, preconditions, and effects (IOPEs). Types of inputs and outputs are defined as concepts in some domain ontology or as simple XSD data-types.

Atomic processes can be combined into composite processes by using the following control constructs: Sequences, Any-Order, Choice, If-Then-Else, Split, Split-Join, Repeat-Until and Repeat-While.

Sequence describes a list processes to be executed in the order they appear. *Split* specifies a bag of processes to be executed concurrently. *Split* completes as soon as all of its sub processes have been scheduled for execution. *Split-Join* specifies the concurrent execution of its branches and completes when all of these branches have completed. *Any-Order* specifies a set of processes that have to be executed in some unspecified sequence but not concurrently. Processes of an *Any-Order* construct cannot overlap. *Choice* specifies a set of unconditional branches, where any of them may be chosen for execution. The *If-Then-Else* control construct describes a conditional branching. If the condition holds, the branch associated to Then is executed, otherwise, the Else branch is executed. A *Repeat-While- condition*, executes the process if the condition is true and loops, and exits if the condition is false. *Repeat-Until* executes the process, tests for the condition, exits if it is true, and otherwise loops.

Figure 3 sketches an example of OWL-S process model specification (*BankCodes*) taken from the bank domain. The *BankCodes* process model allows retrieving, through the bank name its local and international identifiers. The specification is divided in two parts. The first one specifies the process model (*CompositeProcess* XML element of the specification depicted in Figure 3), and the second one defines the atomic processes composing the composite one (*AtomicProcess* XML

element of the specification shown in Figure 3). Figure 4 shows the ontologies used to annotate *BankCodes* atomic processes inputs and outputs.

A GRAPH-BASED APPROACH FOR PROCESS MODEL SIMILARITY EVALUATION

In this section we show how the process model matchmaking is reduced to a graph matchmaking problem. By transforming query and target OWL-S process models to graphs, the process model matchmaking turns into a graph matching problem which is formulated as a search for graph or sub-graph isomorphism. To develop matching techniques allowing the delivery of inexact matches and the evaluation of the semantic distance between target models and user query, we adapt error-correcting sub-graph isomorphism (ECSI) detection algorithm(*) that integrates the concept of error correction into the matching process by using graph edit operations. The principle behind ECSI algorithm is to apply edit operations over the target graph until there exists a sub-graph isomorphism to the query graph. Each edit operation is assigned a cost function depending on the application. The goal is then to find the sequence of edit operations leading to an isomorphism that minimizes the graph-edit distance.

Background and Basic Definitions

Our choice to represent the process models using graphs is motivated by the following reasons. First, the procedure to transform process models to graphs is simple (nodes represent service operations and edges represent constraints between them). Secondly, graphs are a general and powerful data structure for the representation of objects that have been successfully applied in different applications for evaluating objects similarities. In the following we give the definitions of error correcting graph matching as given by (*). A

Figure 3. OWL-S process model specification example

```
<process:CompositeProcess rdf:ID=« BankCodes">
  <process:Choice>
    <process:sequence>
      <atomic process:GetBranchNumber>
      <atomic process: GetNationalCode >
    </process:sequence>
    <process:sequence>
      <atomic process:GetNationalCode>
      <atomic process: GetBankCounter>
    </process:sequence>
  </process:Choice>
</process:CompositeProcess>
....
<process:AtomicProcess rdf:ID=" GetNationalCode ">
  <process:hasInput>
    <process:input >&Bank;#BankName</process:input>
  </process:Input>
  <process:hasOutput>
    <process:Output >&Bank;#ABI</process:Output>
  </process:hasOutput>
</process:AtomicProcess>
<process:AtomicProcess rdf:ID=" GetBranchNumber ">
  <process:hasInput> ......
```

directed graph is a set of labeled nodes that are related by directed edges. Its formal description is given by the Definition 1.

Definition 1. Directed labeled graph. Let L_V and L_E be the sets of node labels and edges labels respectively, a directed labeled graph is a tuple G = (V,E,α,β), in which:

- V is the set of vertices,
- E $\subset$ V$\times$V is the set of edges,
- α: V $\rightarrow$ L_V is the vertex labeling function

Figure 4. Ontologies used in the example of Figure 3

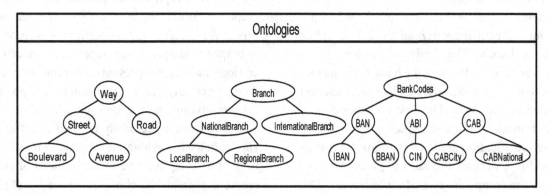

- β: E → L$_E$ is the edge labeling function.

Given a graph G and a sequence of edit operations $\Delta = (\delta_1, \delta_2,..., \delta_k)$, the edited graph $\Delta(G) = \delta_k(...\delta_2(\delta_1(G)))...)$ is obtained by applying successively the operations of Δ over the graph G.

Given a graph G, a graph edit operation δ on G is any of the following: substituting the label α (v) of vertex v by l, substituting the label β(e) of edge e by l', deleting the vertex v from G, deleting the edge e from G, inserting an edge between two existing vertices, decomposing a vertex v into two vertices v_1, v_2 joining two vertices v_1, v_2 into a vertex v.

Definition 2. Edited graph. Given a graph and a sequence of edit operations $\Delta = (\delta_1, \delta_2,..., \delta_k)$, the edited graph $\Delta(G)$ is $\Delta(G) = \delta_k(...\delta_2(\delta_1(G)))...)$.

Definition 3. Ec-sub-graph isomorphism. Given two graphs G and G', an error correcting (ec) sub-graph isomorphism f from G to G' is a 2-tuple $f = (\Delta, f_\Delta)$ where Δ is a sequence of edit operations and f_Δ is a sub-graph isomorphism from $\Delta(G)$ to G'.

For each edit operation δ, a certain cost is assigned C(δ). The cost of an ec-sub-graph isomorphism $f = (\Delta, f_\Delta)$ is the cost of the edit operations Δ, i.e., $C(\Delta) = \sum_{i=1}^{k} C(\delta_i)$.

The sub-graph edit distance is then defined to be the minimum cost taken over all sequences of edit operations that are necessary to obtain a sub-graph isomorphism.

From OWL-S Process Model to a Semantic Process Graph

An OWL-S process model is transformed into an attributed graph, called semantic process graph. A semantic process graph, whose formal description is given by Definition 4, consists of a set of activity and connector nodes connected via edges labeled with optional guards. A semantic process graph has one *START* node marking the beginning

of the process and can have multiple *END* nodes representing the termination of the process.

OWL-S atomic processes are represented by activity nodes that are described by their names, a set of inputs and a set of outputs. The formal description of an activity node is given by the Definition 5.

Connector nodes capture the execution logic of the process model and represent split and join rules of types *XOR* or *AND*. *AND-Split* connector triggers all of its outgoing concurrent branches which are synchronized by a corresponding *AND-Join* connector. The *XOR-Split* represents a choice between one of several alternative branches which are merged by the corresponding *XOR-Join*. Outgoing branches of a *XOR-Split* may be labeled by the branching conditions. A connector node has two attributes: connector type (CT) (*AND-Split*, *AND-Join*, *XOR- Split*, *XOR-Join*) and connector source (CS) that records the control structure captured by the node. Its formal description is given in Definition 6.

Definition 4. Semantic Process Graph is a tuple SPG = (A,C,E,P,O,AD,CDτ,λ,φ), where:

- A is the set of activity nodes,
- C is the set of connector nodes,
- $E \subseteq ((A \cup C) \times (A \cup C))$ is the set of edges,
- P is the set of branching conditions,
- O is the set of ontological concepts,
- AD is the set of activity descriptor,
- CD is the set of connector descriptor,
- τ: A → AD is a function that maps activity node to an activity description,
- λ: C → CD is a function that maps a connector node to its type,
- φ : E → P ∪ {true} is a function that maps each edge to its branching condition or true (edge without condition).

Definition 5. Activity Descriptor is a tuple AD = (Name,OA, In,Out, θ), where:

- Name is the name of activity,
- $O_A \subseteq O$ is the set of ontological concepts,
- In is the set of input attributes,
- Out is the set of output attributes,
- $\theta : (In \cup Out) \rightarrow O$ is the function that maps input/output attributes to ontological concepts

Definition 6. Connector Descriptor is a tuple CD = (Type, ConnectorSource), where:

- Type $\in$ { AND-Split, AND-Join, XOR-Split, XOR-Join }
- ConnectorSource $\in$ {If-Then-Else, Choice, Any-Order, Repeat, Split, Split-Join, Repeat-Until, Repeat-While}

To transform an OWL-S process model to a semantic process graph, we propose an algorithm similar to the flattering strategy algorithm presented in (*). The general idea is to map structured activities to their respective process graph fragments. The algorithm traverses the nested structure of OWL-S control flow in a top-down manner and applies recursively a transformation routine specific to each type of structured activity. A *sequence* is transformed by connecting all nested sub-processes with edges; each sub-process is then transformed recursively to its process graph fragment. For a *While* control structure a loop is created between an *XOR-Join* and an *XOR-Split*, the edge is labeled with the loop condition. The graph representation of an *If-Then-Else* consists of a block of alternative branches, labeled with

Figure 5. Correspondences between OWL-S control flow structures and graph fragments

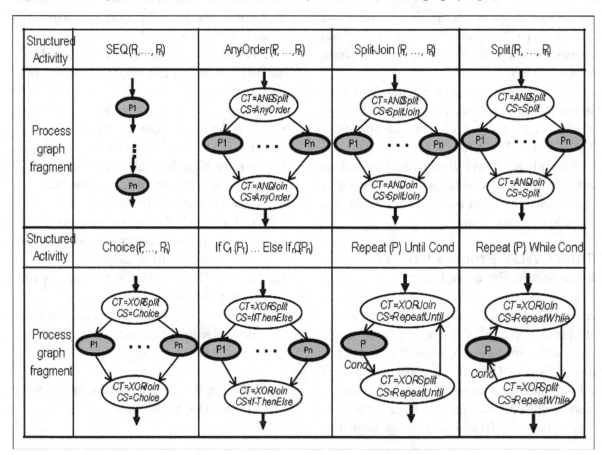

the branching conditions, between an *XOR-Split* and an *XOR-Join*. The alternative branches of a *Choice* start from a *XOR-Split* and merge in a *XOR-Join*. A *Flow* is transformed into a block of parallel branches triggered by an *AND-Split* and synchronized with an *AND-Join*. An *Any-Order* structure is transformed to a block of parallel branches starting with an *AND-Split* and synchronized with an *AND-Join*. Figure 5 resumes the correspondences between OWL-S control flow structures and process graph fragments.

Figure 6 shows the transformation of the OWL-S process model specification given in Figure 3.

We observe that the same behavior can be specified, in OWL-S, using different syntactical structures. We defined five syntactic equivalence rules allowing transforming equivalent syntactical structures to the same graph fragments. These rules are the followings:

- Choice $(P_1,$ Choice$(P_2,P_3))$ ↔ Choice (Choice $(P_1,P_2),$ $P_3)$ ↔ Choice$(P_1,P_2,$ $P_3)$
- Split-Join $(P_1,$ Split-Join$(P_2,P_3))$↔ Split-Join(Split-Join$(P_1,P_2),$ $P_3)$ ↔ Split-Join (P_1,P_2,P_3)
- Split $(P_1,$ Split $(P_2,P_3))$ ↔ Split (Split$(P_1,$ $P_2,)$ $P_3)$ ↔ Split (P_1,P_2,P_3)
- Any-Order$(P_1,$Any-Order$(P_2,P_3))$ ↔ Any-Order (Any-Order$(P_1,P_2),P_3)$ ↔ Any-Order(P_1,P_2,P_3)
- If Cond$_1$ (If Cond$_2$ (P_1) Else (P_2)) Else P_3 ↔ If ((Cond$_1$ and Cond$_2$) (P_1)) Else ((If (Cond$_1$ and !Cond$_2$) (P_2)) Else (If (!Cond$_1$) (P_3)))

OWL-S Graph Matchmaking

In this section we illustrate the use of the error-correcting graph matching algorithm for OWL-S process models matchmaking. We first give an overview of the matchmaking process and

Figure 6. Transformation of the OWL-S process of Figure 2 to its SPG

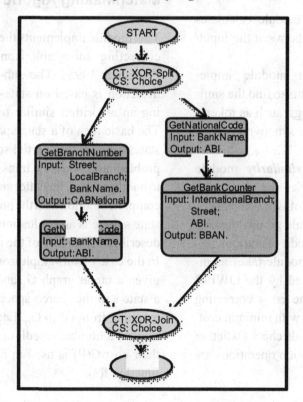

Figure 7. OWL-S Process Model Matchmaking

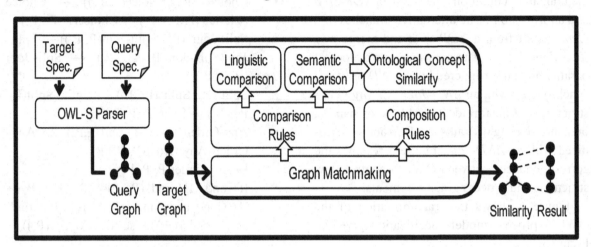

then we discuss each step in detail. Our OWL-S matchmaking approach, illustrated in Figure 7 is composed of the following steps. First, the OWL-S process models to be compared are transformed to graphs. Next, the similarity between the two graphs is evaluated by a similarity analyzer that is composed of the following modules (Figure 7):

- *Semantic comparison* module calculates the semantic similarity between the input/output concepts.
- *Linguistic comparison* module implements different algorithms to find the similarity between two strings, such as tokenization, NGram, Check synonym, Check abbreviation.
- *Ontological concepts similarity* module contains different metrics for measuring the degree of similarity of two concepts.
- *Comparison rules* module groups the cost functions for the graph edit operations.
- *Graph matchmaking* module takes as inputs the graphs produced by the OWL-S parser and finds out the error correcting sub-graph isomorphism with minimal cost.
- *Composition rules* module checks whether composition/decomposition operations are

necessary and add their cost to the total distance.

In the next subsections, we present in details the functionalities of these modules.

Semantic Process Graph Matchmaking Algorithm

This module implements the algorithm for error-correcting sub-graph isomorphism detection (Messmer 1995). The sub-graph isomorphism detection is based on state-space searching using an algorithm similar to A* (Bunke 2000). The basic idea of a state-space search is to have states representing partial solutions of the given problem and to define transitions from one state to another. Thus, the latter state represents a more complete solution than the previous state. For each state s there is an evaluation function f(s) which describes the quality of the represented solution. In the case of sub-graph isomorphism detection, given a target graph G_T and a query graph G_Q, a state s in the search space represents a partial mapping from G_T to G_Q. Each partial mapping P implies a number of edit operations ($\delta_1..\delta_i$) and their cost C(P) is used to define the evaluation function f(s).

Algorithm 1. Error-correcting sub-graph isomorphism detection

```
1. INPUTS T(A_T, C_T, E_T, O), Q(A_Q, C_Q, E_Q, O)
2. OUTPUTS Similarity
3. Initialize OPEN: Match the first activity node a ∈ A_T against each activity node b ∈ A_Q ∪{$}
       IF feasible(v1;w) THEN
               3.1 Create a mapping P = {(a,b)}
               3.2 Calculate the cost of this mapping C(P) and Add it to OPEN.
4. IF No Satisfactory Matcher for a try CompositionNodes
5. IF OPEN is empty THEN Exit.
6. Select P from OPEN such that C(P) is minimal and remove it from OPEN
7. IF P represents a complete mapping from T to Q THEN
               7.1 Output P; Set acceptable threshold = C(P); Goto 3.
8. Let P be the current mapping that maps k nodes from A_T .
9. Extending P to P' by mapping a_{k+1} ((k + 1)^{th} activity node of A_T
FOR each activity node b ∈ A_Q ∪{$} that is not yet mapped to a corresponding node ∈ A_T
IF feasible(a_{k+1},b) THEN
               9.1 P' = P ∪ {(a_{k+1},b)}.
               9.2 Calculate the cost of this mapping C(P').
               9.3 IF C(P')<= Accept threshold THEN OPEN = OPEN ∪ {P'}
10. IF No Satisfactory Matcher for a_{k+1} try CompositionNodes
11. Goto 3.
```

In other words, the algorithm starts by mapping the first activity node of G_T with all the activity nodes of $G_Q \cup \{\$\}$ (symbol $\$$ is used to denote deleting activity nodes in the target graph G_T) with respect to the pruning function *feasible* (line 1 of Algorithm 1) and chooses the best mapping (with minimal cost) (Algorithm 1, line 6). This represents a partial mapping that will be extended by adding one activity node at a time (line 9). The process terminates when either a state representing an optimal ec-subgraph isomorphism from G_T to G_Q has been reached or all states in the search space have edit costs that exceed a given acceptance threshold.

The cost of the mapping C (P') (line 9.2) represents the cost of extending the current mapping P with the next activity node in G_T. Extending the mapping by matching an activity $b \in A_Q$ that is not yet mapped to an activity node a in the target graph (that does not belong to the current mapping) implies an activity node edit operation and an edge/connector edit operations: First, the attributes of a must be substituted by attributes of b, and secondly, for each mapping $(a',b') \in P$ it must be ensured that any link (two activity nodes can be connected either by an edge or via

a connector node) between b' and b in the G_Q can be mapped to a link between a and a' in G_T by means of edge and connector edit operations. Since connector nodes express control flow constraints, they are compared in a manner similar to edges. Thus, when matching two graphs, we are not interested in finding all the correspondences between similar connector nodes, but comparing how mapped activity nodes are connected.

Pruning the State-Space Search

The major problem with such an exhaustive algorithm is its complexity evaluated to $O(M^2N^2)$ in the best case (when the distance between the target and the query graphs is minimal) and $O(M^N N)$ in the worst case (when the two graphs are completely disparate). "M" and "N" are respectively the total number of nodes in the query and target graphs. Experiments shows that this algorithm can be used, with a low cost, for matching process graphs having less than 30 activities (*). Thus, to deal with larger process sizes, we should define effective criterion allowing reducing the search-space while guaranteeing finding satisfactory matchers.

Figure 8. Example of edit connector

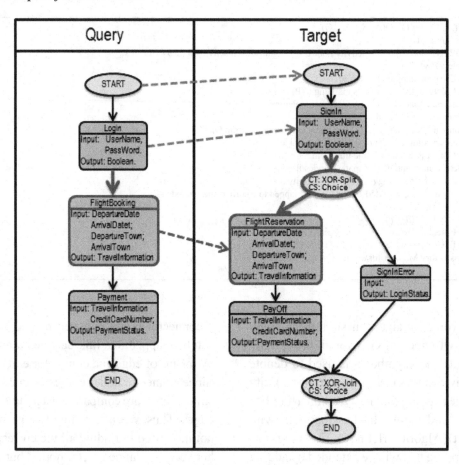

The first criterion relates to the maximum cost that a mapping must never exceed. Thus, the mappings having a cost exceeding an *acceptable threshold* are dropped. When a complete mapping is found, its cost becomes the new acceptable threshold.

The second criterion concerns the maximum cost that a new pair of matches must never exceed. Clearly, it is not interesting to extend a mapping by adding a new pair of activity nodes that don't match at all. In the example shown by Figure 8, matching the query activity *"Login"* against the target one *"PayOff"* is completely senseless.

Suppose that a state, representing a partial mapping P between the query and the target graphs, is extended by matching a couple of activity nodes (a,b) ($a \in A_T$ and $b \in A_Q$). This extension is not a promising one when the distance between a and b exceeds a given threshold *MatchThreshold(MDThreshold,SSThreshold)*.

This threshold specifies the minimum similarity (*SSThreshold*) between two activity nodes and the minimal matching degree (*MDThreshold*) that inputs/outputs of a and b should respect to be added to P. However, deleting an activity is still permitted. Accordingly, the new matches that don't meet this pruning condition are discarded. *feasible* function (Algorithm 2) implements this pruning rule.

Our experiments (*) show that by setting the *MatchThreshold* to *(PlugIn, 0.5)*, and acceptable threshold to 10, our matchmaking algorithm can be used, with acceptable execution time, for process graphs having less than 40 activity nodes.

Algorithm 2. Function feasible

```
1. INPUTS: a,b, MatchThreshold (MatchingDegree, DistanceNode)
2. OUTPUT: BOOL
3. Threshold: Struct
4. RETURN
      (w=$ (/*deleting a node is always feasible*/)
      or
      (AtomicProcessMatch(a,b).DegreeMatch >= NodeThreshold.DegreeMatch and
      AtomicProcessMatch(a,b).DistanceNode <= NodeThreshold.DistanceNode))
```

Algorithm 3. LinguisticSimilarity

```
1. INPUTS Token₁, Token₂
2. OUTPUTS Similarity
3. IF (Ngram(Token₁, Token₂)=1)
      Return 1 ;
4. ELSE IF (Synonyms(Token₁, Token₂)=1)
      Return 1;
5. ELSE IF (Abbreviation(Token₁, Token₂)=1)
      Return 1
      ELSE
Return {Ngram(Token₁,Token₂) + Synonyms(Token₁,Token₂) }/2
```

SIMILARITY METRICS

One of the major issues in our technique is the ability to determine the degree of resemblance of two activities. To estimate this similarity, we combine multiple sources of evidence: name, inputs and outputs. We make usage of linguistic similarity for computing activity names similarity, since they are human-assigned, and ontological similarity for evaluating the similarity of inputs/outputs similarity, since they are taken within a domain ontology.

Linguistic Similarity

Activity names are human-assigned and are often formed by a combination of words and can contain abbreviations. Therefore, their similarity is computed using linguistic and textual similarity techniques. To obtain a linguistic distance between two names, we use existing algorithms: N-Gram, Check synonym, Check abbreviation and tokenization.

The tokenization algorithm tokenizes the name into its component words, removes stopwords, stems the words to their linguistic roots and then N-Gram, Check synonym and Check abbreviation algorithms are applied on each pair of tokens.

The *N-Gram* algorithm estimates the similarity according to a number of common q-grams between words (*). The *Check abbreviation* algorithm uses a custom abbreviation dictionary to check whether a token is an abbreviation of another.

The *Check synonym* algorithm uses a linguistic dictionary to compute the similarity between tokens. We used in our implementation the free *WordNet::Similarity API* (*). This *API* provides six similarity metrics implemented over the *WordNet* dictionary. These measures take as input two words, and return a value representing their similarity degree according to their relationships in the dictionary.

Algorithm 3 shows details of the routine that computes the similarity of two tokens. If two tokens are the same (*Ngram* function returns similarity value equal to 1), the *LinguisticSimilar-*

ity routine returns 1. Otherwise, the *Linguistic-Similarity* routine checks the synonymy (*Synonyms* function of algorithm 3) of the tokens and return 1 if they are synonym. If the tokens are not synonym, the algorithm checks whether one token is an abbreviation of another and returns 1 if it's the case. Finally, if the three functions values are between 0 and 1, the similarity of the tokens is the average of them.

There are other possible ways to measure name similarity: Levenshtein edit distance algorithm, techniques borrowed from the information retrieval area like TF-IDF or a combination of techniques can be considered. However, defining a clever function for syntactic similarity is outside the scope of this chapter, since the focus of our work is on behavior similarity.

Ontological Similarity

Inputs and outputs are concepts taken from a domain ontology and therefore the similarity between two concepts c_q (input of the query) and c_t (input of the target) is defined on the basis of their semantic relationship in the ontology. We can distinguish three cases. The first case (Exact), which is trivial, c_q and c_t are the same concept and then their similarity is 1. The second case is when c_q is a specialization of c_t (Plug-In); then the similarity is 1, since this guarantees that target activity will be executable with the provided input (c_q). The third case includes the cases when c_q is a generalization of c_t (Subsume) and the case when c_q and c_t have a common ancestor (Fail). In these cases, we use ontological concept similarity metric.

The similarity between two concepts is assessed using a pair of parameters, matching degree (MD) and semantic similarity (SS). The matching degree (MD) records the logical matching between two concepts. The MDs are ordered according to their levels of restriction: *EXACT > PLUG-IN > SUBSUMES > FAIL*. SS is a real number ranging between 0 and 1 and reflects the degree of resemblance between two concepts.

Algorithm 4 describes the routine for computing concepts similarity.

Many metric similarities between ontological concepts have been proposed in past research. These measures can be divided into three main approaches (*):

- Feature-theoretical approach: the similarity between two concepts is related to both common and different characteristics. The more characteristic they share, the more they are similar.

- Edge-based approach: the similarity between two concepts is related to the path length between them. The shorter the path from one concept to another, the more similar they are. The links connecting two nodes are weighted to overcome the limitation imposed by the uniform distance.

- Information theoretic models: the similarity between two concepts is defined as the information content of the lowest common ancestors of them. The information content of a concept c is defined as the negative log likelihood of the probability of encountering an instance of the concept. The intuition behind the use of negative likelihood is that the more probable a concept is of appearing, the less information it conveys.

Depending on the expressiveness of the used ontology, a metric can been preferred to another. These different metrics can be implemented in the *Ontological concepts similarity metrics* module. In our implementation, we use a well known path-based metric to compute the distance between two concepts c_q (query concept) and c_t (target concept):

OntologySim(c_q, c_t) = 1 - (*), where lca(c_q, c_t) is the least common ancestor of c_q and c_t and $\omega(c)$ is the weight of the concept c in the ontology.

Function *ConceptSimilarity* is the basic block to calculate the similarity between two sets of concepts that is processed by *MatchSet* function. *MatchSet* calculates the best matching between two sets (D_q, D_t) of concepts that maximizes the total of semantic similarities (SS). The formula of *MatchSet* is given in Equation 1.

MatchSet function returns also the set *MD-Set* of mapped pairs (I,J). This brings us to the definition of semantic comparison between two sets of concepts. The semantic similarity and the matching degree between two sets of concepts are, respectively, the average of semantic similarities and the minimum of matching degrees of all the concept-matched pairs within *MDSet*.

$$ConceptSimilarity(D_r, D_s).SS = \frac{MatchSet(D_r, D_s).SS}{min(|D_r|, |D_s|)}$$

$$ConceptSimilarity(D_r, D_s).MD = \min_{(I,J) \in MDset} (ConceptSimilarity(I,J).MD$$

COMPARISON RULES

The Comparison rules module contains all the application-dependent functions allowing calculating the cost of graph edit operations. These functions are used by the graph matching module for calculating the distance between two graphs. In the following, we explain the cost functions

Equation 1.

$$MatchSet(D_r, D_s).SS =$$
$$[Max(MatchSet.SS(D_r - I, D_s - I) + CS(I, I).SS \text{ if } D_r \neq \varnothing, D_s \neq \varnothing, I \in D_r, J \in D_s]$$

Algorithm 4. Function ConceptSimilarity

```
1. INPUTS: c_q, c_t
2. OUTPUT:Sim: Struct(SS,MD)
3. IF (c_q = c_t) THEN
    Sim.SS = 1 ; Sim.MD = Exact
4. ELSE IF c_t > c_q THEN
    Sim.SS = 1 ; Sim.MD = Plug-In
5. ELSE IF c_q > c_t THEN
    Sim.SS = OntologySim(c_q, c_t) ; Sim.MD = Subsumes
6. ELSE
    Sim.SS = OntologySim(c_q, c_t) ; Sim.MD = Fail
Return Sim
```

used for OWL-S process model matchmaking. The cost for inserting, deleting edges and vertices can be set to a constant. The cost for editing vertices (activity and connector nodes) is presented below.

Matching Activity Nodes

The distance between two activity nodes is computed by the function *Activity Node Distance Evaluation* (see algorithm 5), and is computed on the basis of inputs, outputs and name similarities. Activity names similarities are computed by the module *Linguistic Comparison*, while inputs and outputs sets similarities are computed using *ConceptSetSimilarity* module. Finally, the distance between the two activities (*DistanceNode*) is the difference between 1 and the weighted average of inputs/outputs semantic similarity and names similarity. Weights ω_{io} and ω_{name} indicate the contribution of semantic similarity of Input/Output and name similarity respectively ($0 < \omega_{io} < 1$ and $0 < \omega_{name} < 1$). The function returns also the matching degree of the two Input/Output sets which is defined as the minimum of the two matching degrees of inputs and outputs.

Algorithm 5. Function Activity Node Distance Evaluation

```
1. INPUTS: A (Name_A, Input_A, Output_A), B(Name_B, Input_B, Output_B)
2. OUTPUT: MatchingDegree ; ActivityDistance
3. LOCAL InSimilarity, OutSimilarity: Struct(MD,SS)
4. Calculate Name Similarity NameSimilarity = LinguisticSimilarity(Name_A, Name_B)
5. IF (NameSimilarity=0) return (Fail,1).
6. Calculate Input/Output Similarity
5.1 InSimilarity = ConceptSetSimilarity(Input_A, Input_B)
    5.2 OutSimilarity = ConceptSetSimilarity(Output_B, Output_A)
    5.3 IOSimilarity = (InSimilarity.SS + OutSimilarity.SS) /2
    5.4 DegreeMatch = min (InSimilarity.MD, OutSimilarity.MD)
6. Calculate Distance Node
ActivityDistance = 1 – (ω_io * IOSimilarity + ω_name *NameSimilarity) / (ω_io + ω_name)
    7. RETURN (DegreeMatch, ActivityDistance).
```

Matching Connector Nodes

As mentioned above, the connector nodes define the execution logic of the process models. Thus, we are not interested in finding all the correspondences between similar connector nodes, but comparing how mapped activities are linked (by edge or via a connector node). Suppose that the current mapping p is extended by matching a against b ($a \in A_T$ and $b \in G_Q$). Thus, for each mapping $(a',b') \in P (a' \in A_T$ and $b' \in G_Q)$ such that there is a link ($link_1$) between a and a' in graph G_T and there is a link ($link_2$) between b and b' in graph G_Q, it checks whether an edit operation is needed or not. $link_i$ can be either an edge or a connector node. Figure 8 shows an example of editing connector node. The current mapping *{(Start,Start),(Login, SignIn)}* is extended by matching *FlightBooking* (of the query) against *FlightReservation* (in the target). In the query graph, *Login* is linked to *FlightBooking* via an edge, while in the target graph *SignIn* is linked to *FlightReservation* via a connector node (of type Xor-Split). Thus, this mapping induces an editing link whose cost is the cost of deleting an edge and adding a connector. Figure 9 shows all cases that may be encountered when computing the cost of editing links (edge and connectors). Constants *PA* (parallel to any-order), *BD* (branch deletion), *LI* (loop insertion), *AP* (any-order to parallel), *BI* (branch insertion), *CD* (condition deletion), *CI* (condition insertion),

LD (loop deletion), C_{ed} (edge deletion), C_{ci} (connector insertion), C_{cd} (connector deletion) C_{ei} (edge insertion). Since there is no consensus on the definition of similar behavior (*), this table allows the user to express his own perception of behavioral equivalences/differences by specifying its own edit operation costs.

GRANULARITY LEVEL COMPARISON

As shown by the example of Figure 2, the models to be compared may have different granularity levels for achieving the same functionality. The classical edit operations take into account only 1-1 matches between activity nodes of the two graphs. Using the example of the Figure 2, a matching algorithm based only on the classical edit operations would match the query activity *UpdateContact* with one of the two target activities *Authentication* and *AddContact* and delete the other.

To solve this kind of mismatches, we need edit operations that allow discovering both simple matches (1-1) and complex matches (1-many or many-1). A complex match specifies that a combination of activities (connected sub-graph) in one process model corresponds to a combination of activities in the other.

Given a process graph *G*, these edit operations are the followings:

Figure 9. Node editing cost table

Link(a',a) \ Link(a,b)		And-Split/Join		XOR-Split/Join		XOR-Join/Split	Edge	No link
		Split/Split-Join	Any	If-then-else	Choice	While/Repeat		
And-Split/Join	Split/Split-Join	0	PA	BD	BD	LI	$C_{cd}+C_{ei}$	C_{cd}
	Any	AP	0	BI	BD	LI	$C_{cd}+C_{ei}$	C_{cd}
XOR-Split/Join	If-then-else	BI	BI	0	CD	LI	$C_{cd}+C_{ei}$	C_{cd}
	Choice	BI	BI	CI	0	LI	$C_{cd}+C_{ei}$	C_{cd}
XOR-Join/Split	While/Repeat	LD	LD	LD	LD	0	$C_{cd}+C_{ei}$	C_{cd}
Edge		$C_{ed}+C_{ci}$	$C_{ed}+C_{ci}$	$C_{ed}+C_{ci}$	$C_{ed}+C_{ci}$	$C_{ed}+C_{ci}$	0	C_{ed}
No link		C_{ic}	C_{ic}	C_{ic}	C_{ic}	C_{ic}	C_{ei}	0

- Decomposing an activity node a into a set of activity nodes $\{a_1 \dots a_n\}$.
- Composing a set of activity nodes $\{a_1 \dots a_n\}$ into a single activity node a.

Suppose that no satisfactory matcher is found for a target activity a: $\forall b_i \in T'$, *ActivityDistance(a,b_i) > threshold* (T' is the set of nodes that are not yet mapped in the current mapping), we then try to compose activities from T' to a find satisfactory matcher for a.

The composition is done iteratively until the termination conditions of the composition are no longer met.

Thus, at each iteration, the activities of T' are composed 2-2 and only compositions respecting composition conditions (enumerated bellow) are treated and considered as potential matchers of a. Each composition is then considered as an atomic activity and added to T'. T' is ordered according to the distance between its elements and this activity (a). This procedure is reiterated until composition conditions are no more satisfied. At the end of this procedure, the activity node a (for which we look for satisfactory matcher) is then matched against the last composition result.

Given two nodes b_1(Name$_1$, Input$_1$,Output$_1$) and b_2(Name$_2$, Input$_2$,Output$_2$) that are in T', the composition is permitted when:

- **Condition 1**: b_1 and b_2 are composable iff they are in parallel (AND(b_1,b_2)), in conditional/unconditional (XOR(b_1,b_2)) or in sequence (SEQ(b_1,b_2)).
- **Condition 2**: b_1 and b_2 share at least one input or one output with a:
  ○ (Input$_1$ ∩ Input$_a$) ∪ (Output$_1$ ∩ Output$_a$) ≠ φ
  ○ (Input$_2$ ∩ Input$_a$) ∪ (Output$_2$ ∩ Output$_a$) ≠ φ
- **Condition 3**: the cost of the composition of the (I + 1)th iteration is less than the cost of the Ith one. The cost of the first iteration is the activity distance between activity node a and the first activity node in T'. b_1 may be

Figure 10. Matchmaking example

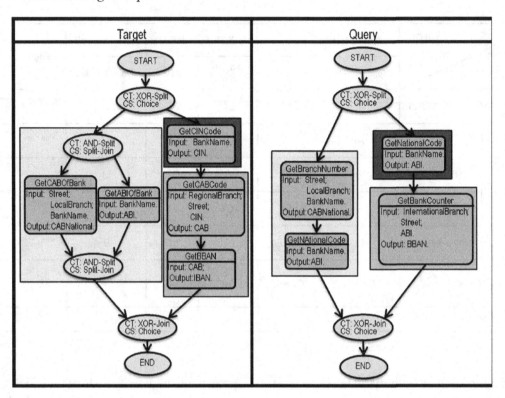

an activity node originally belonging to *T'* or the result of the previous compositions.

The composition of two activity nodes $b_1(Name_1, Input_1, Output_1)$ and $b_2(Name_2, Input_2, Output_2)$ leads to an activity node $b_{12}(Name_{12}, Input_{12}, Output_{12})$ defined as follows:

- $Name_{12} = concat(Name_1, Name_2)$
- $Input_{12} = Input_1 \cup Input_2 - (Output_1 \cap Input_2)$
- $Output_{12} = Output_1 \cup Output_2 - (Output_1 \cap Input_2)$

The composition routine is given by the algorithm 6. When several synchronized activities of the query graph correspond to one activity in the target graph, a decomposition of this node is necessary. Therefore, the same approach can be followed to define the decomposition algorithm.

Matching Example

The Figure 10 shows two process models (Query and Target) taken from the Bank domain. The Query process model is that of the Figure 6. The example highlights the challenging aspects that are handled by our algorithm to provide an effective technique for process model similarity evaluation.

The first one is related to the mismatches between metadata (name, inputs and outputs) describing atomic processes. The rules we defined to compare atomic processes allow mapping atomic processes even if they are described differently. For instance, target atomic process *GetCINCode* is matched against query atomic process *GetNationalCode*. Whatever their names are not exactly the same and the output of the second process subsumes the output of the first, the two activities match approximately.

Algorithm 6. Function Composition

```
INPUTS: a,P,T',OPEN
While T' is not empty
{
FOR each couple of activities b₁ and b₂ ∈ T'
{
IF (Condition 3(b₁,b₂) is false)
    1.1 Remove b₁ and b₂ from T'.
    1.2 IF (Distance(a, b₁) < Threshold) Add P ∪ {(a,b₁)} to OPEN.
    1.3 IF (Distance(a, b₂) < Threshold) Add P ∪ {(a,b₂)} to OPEN.

ELSE IF (Condition 1(b₁,b₂) and Condition 2(b₁,b₂)
    2.1 Remove b₁ and b₂ from T'.
    2.2 Add the composition result of b₁ and b₂ to T'.
}
}
```

The second one is related to the granularity level differences between the two process models, where the atomic process *GetBankCounter* in the query is matched against the sequence of *GetCABCode* and *GetBBAN* activities in the target. The rules of compositions that are based on inputs/outputs semantic allow detecting with accuracy granularity differences.

The third aspect concerns behavior differences and equivalences. For instance, *GetBranchNumber* and *GetNationalCode* activities of the query are in sequence, while their corresponding activities in the target are in parallel. The algorithm detects and matches equivalent behaviors even if they are specified using different control constructs and it is able to consider user behavioral equivalences/differences perception(through the table of connector node edit operation costs).

CONCLUSION

In this chapter, we described a graph-based approach for semantic process retrieval. The approach was illustrated using OWL-S, but can be adapted to other semantic process models. Two motivating scenarios were presented showing the need to develop process matching techniques. In order to allow an approximate matching, a graph error correcting matching algorithm was adapted and extended. The matchmaking algorithm returns a similarity score and a matching degree (reflecting the terminological concept subsumption relationship between inputs/outputs of atomic processes); it outputs also the edit operations needed to transform one process into the other. These graph edit operations could be useful for applications that require the development of adapters to solve differences between process models describing business protocols of two web services to be integrated.

An interesting future extension consists in learning matchmaking parameters starting from user preferences and rankings in order to provide personalizable similarity measures.

While the approach presented in this chapter allows the matchmaking of two process models, optimization techniques (indexing, filtering) have to be proposed for the case when one process model has to be compared with a set of models. Recent developments in graph indexing could be adapted for this purpose.

REFERENCES

Andrews, T., Curbera, F., Dholakia, H., Goland, Y., Klein, J., & Leymann, F. ...Weerawarana, S. (d. u.). *Business Process Execution Language for Web Services Version 1.1*. Retrieved from http://www.ibm.com/developerworks/library/specification/ws-bpel/

Awad, A., Polyvyanyy, A., & Weske, M. (2008). *Semantic querying of business process models* (pp. 85–94). EDOC.

Bansal, S., & Vidal, J. M. (2003). Matchmaking of Web services based on the DAML-S service model. In *Proc. of Int. Joint Conference on Autonomous Agents and Multiagent Systems* (926–927).

Beeri, C., Eyal, A., Kamenkovich, S., & Milo, T. (2008). Querying business processes with bp-ql. *Information Systems, 33*(6), 477–507. doi:10.1016/j.is.2008.02.005

Benatallah, B., Casati, F., Grigori, D., Motahari Nezhad, H. R., & Toumani, F. (2005). *Developing adapters for Web services integration*. In Proc. of CAISE.

Benatallah, B., Hacid, M., Rey, C., & Toumani, F. (2003). *Semantic reasoning for Web services discovery*. In Proc. of WWW Workshop on E-Services and the Semantic Web.

Bernstein, A., Kaufmann, E., Brki, C., & Klein, M. (2005). How similar is it? Towards personalized similarity measures in ontologies. In 7 Internationale Tagung Wirtschaftsinformatik.

Bernstein, A., & Klein, M. (2002). *Towards high-precision service retrieval*. In Proc. of Int. Semantic Web Conference (ISWC).

Bunke, H. (2000). Recent developments in graph matching. In *Proc. of 15th Int. Conf. on Pattern Recognition* (117 – 124).

Cardoso, J., & Sheth, A. (2003). Semantic e-workflow composition. *Journal of Intelligent Information Systems, 21*, 191–225. doi:10.1023/A:1025542915514

Dijkman, R. M., Dumas, M., & García-Bañuelos, L. (2009). *Graph matching algorithms for business process model similarity search* (pp. 48–63). BPM.

Dongen, B.V., Dijkman, R., & Mendling, J. (2008). *Measuring similarity between business process models*. In advanced Information Systems Engineering, CAiSE.

Ehrig, M., Koschmider, A., & Oberweis, A. (2007). Measuring similarity between semantic business process models. In J. F. Roddick, & A. Hinze (Eds.), *APCCM Vol. 67 of CRPIT.*, Australian Computer Society (71–80).

Farrell, J., & Lausen, H. (2007). Semantic annotations for WSDL and XML schema. Technical report, W3C candidate recommendation.

Gater, A., Grigori, D., & Bouzeghoub, M. (2010). *OWL-S process model matchmaking*. In IEEE International Conference on Web Services, Miami, Florida, USA.

Goderis, A., Li, P., & Goble, C. (2006). Workflow discovery: The problem, a case study from e-science and a graph-based solution. In *International Conference on Web Services (ICWS '06)* (312–319).

Goderis, A., Roure, D. D., Goble, C., Bhagat, J., Cruickshank, D., & Fisher, P. …Tanoh, F. (2009). *Discovering scientific workflows: The my experiment benchmarks*. In Technical Report UNSPECIFIED, School of Electronics and Computer Science, University of Southampton.

Grigori, D., Corrales, J., & Bouzeghoub, M. (2008). Behavioral matchmaking for service retrieval: Application to conversation protocols. In *Information Systems. Advances in Data and ServiceIntegration, 33*(7-8), 681-698.

Grigori, D., Corrales, J. C., & Bouzeghoub, M. (2008). Behavioral matchmaking for service retrieval: Application to conversation protocols. *Information Systems, 33*, 681–698. doi:10.1016/j.is.2008.02.004

Kawamura, T., De Blasio, J., Hasegawa, T., Paolucci, M., & Sycara, K. (2003). A preliminary report of a public experiment of a semantic service matchmaker combined with a UDDI business registry. In *Proc. of 1st International Conference on Service Oriented Computing (ICSOC)*.

Keller, U., Lara, R., Lausen, H., Polleres, A., & Fensel, D. (2005). *Automatic location of services* (pp. 1–16). ESWC.

Klusch, M., Fries, B., & Sycara, K. (2006). *Automated Sematic Web discovery with owls-mx*. In Proceedings of the 5th International Joint Conference on Autonomous Agents and Multiagent Systems.

Martin, D., Burstein, M., Hobbs, J., Lassila, O., McDermott, D., & McIlraith, S. ...Sycara, K. (2004). *OWLS: Semantic markup language for Web Services*. In: W3C Member Submission, Retrieved from http://www.w3.org/Submission/OWL-S. (2004)

Messmer, B. (1995). *Graph matching algorithms and applications*. PhD thesis, University of Bern.

Minor, M., Tartakovski, A., & Bergmann, R. (2007). *Representation and structure-based similarity assessment for agile workflows*. In Proceedings of the 7th International Conference on Case-Based Reasoning.

Nejati, S., Sabetzadeh, M., Chechik, M., Easterbrook, S., & Zave, P. (2007). *Matching and merging of state charts specifications*. In Proceedings of the 29th International Conference on Software Engineering.

Paolucci, M., Kawamura, T., Payne, T. R., & Sycara, K. (2002). *Semantic matching of Web services capabilities*. In Proc. of 1st International Semantic Web Conference (ISWC).

Pedersen, T., Patwardhan, S., & Michelizzi, J. (2004). *(d. u.). WordNet: Similarity - Measuring the relatedness of concepts* (pp. 1024–1025). AAAI.

Song, L., & Ma, J. H.L.L.L., & Zhang, D. (2007). *Fuzzy semantic similarity between ontological concepts*. In Advances and Innovations in Systems, Computing Sciences and Software Engineering.

Vaculn, R., & Sycara, K. (2007). *Towards automatic mediation of owl-s process models*. In IEEE International Conference on Web Services, ICWS 2007.

Wombacher, A. (2006). *Evaluation of technical measures for workflow similarity based on a pilot study*. In CoopIS, Montpellier, France.

Wombacher, A., Mahleko, B., Fankhauser, P., & Neuhold, E. (2004). *Matchmaking for business processes based on choreographies*. In Proc. of IEEE International Conference on E-technology, E-commerce and E-service.

Wroe, C., Stevens, R., Goble, C., Roberts, A., & Greenwood, M. (2003). A suite of daml+oil ontologies to describe bioinformatics Web services and data. *In Intl. J. of Cooperative Information Systems* (197224).

Wu, J., & Wu, Z. (2005). *Similarity-based Web service matching*. In Proc. of IEEE International Conference on Services Computing.

KEY TERMS AND DEFINITIONS

Process Discovery: Designates techniques allowing retrieving in a given repository, the process most similar to the query.

Process Matching: Provides a mapping between two process models and a similarity metric evaluating how they are similar.

Process Model: Captures the temporal and logical dependencies (control flow) of a bag of business activity.

Semantic Process Graph: An abstract representation of OWL-S process models. It can be used to capture several process model descriptions.

Semantic Web Services: Aim to provide mechanisms to represent the requirements and capabilities of Web services in an unambiguous and machine interpretable form.

Similarity Metric: Evaluates the degree of resemblance of two objects.

Web Service: A decoupled software component allowing communication between heterogeneous applications.

Chapter 20
Shortest Path in Transportation Network and Weighted Subdivisions

Radwa Elshawi
National ICT Australia (NICTA) - University of Sydney, Australia

Joachim Gudmundsson
National ICT Australia (NICTA) - University of Sydney, Australia

ABSTRACT

The shortest path problem asks for a path between two given points such that the sum of its edges is minimized. The problem has a rich history and has been studied extensively since the 1950's in many areas of computer science, among them network optimization, graph theory and computational geometry.

In this chapter we consider two versions of the problem; the shortest path in a transportation network and the shortest path in a weighted subdivision, sometimes called a terrain.

INTRODUCTION

The Shortest Path Problem (SPP) is one of the most studied optimization problem and come in numerous different flavors. The earliest reference to problems of this form is by Euler in the 1700's. His "Königsberg bridge" question is often considered the starting point of this class

of problems. Finding a shortest path in a given graph is probably the most well-known variant.

The most popular algorithm to compute the shortest path from any source node to all other nodes of the graph was given by Dijkstra (1959). Early implementations of Dijkstra's algorithm required $O(v^2)$ time, or $O(e \log v)$ where v denotes the number of vertices and e denotes the number of edges in the graph. Using Fibonacci heaps, Fredman and Tarjan (1987) gave an $O(e + v \log v)$ time implementation, and argued that this is optimal

DOI: 10.4018/978-1-61350-053-8.ch020

in a comparison-based model of computation. Recently there has again been a flurry of results focusing on shortest path computation and distance oracles in graphs, see Thorup (1999), Thorup (2004), Thorup and Zwick (2005), Gudmundsson et al. (2008) and Pătraşcu and Roddity (2010).

In this chapter we discuss two variants of the shortest path problem. These include shortest paths in transportation networks and shortest paths in weighted regions.

Transportation networks are an integral part of our infrastructure. They can be modeled as a set of nodes and a set of edges on which transportation activities can be carried out. For example nodes may represent cities, street crossings, train or bus stations, and edges in a transportation network may represent streets, roads, air routes or railway tracks. A transportation network is usually embedded in an underlying metric, thus outside the network a traveler can move at unit speed in any direction. This model was introduced by Aurenhammer and Klein (2000) and it assumes that one can enter and exit the network at any point of the graph (including any point on a road). The induced distance is called the transportation distance.

The second problem we consider is the SPP in a weighted subdivision, also known as a terrain (Mitchell and Papadimitriou, 1991). The plane is divided into n triangular regions; each of which has an associated positive weight. This can be used to model different geographical features of regions, such as deserts, forests, grasslands and lakes, in which the travelling costs are different. The *cost* of a path p is defined to be the weighted length of p. The aim is to find a shortest path through the triangulation taking the path cost into consideration.

We will also consider the query version. That is, can we preprocess the data into a data structure that allows us to answer shortest path queries efficiently? To speed up the query time many researchers consider approximate versions, that is, instead of reporting the exact shortest path, an approximate shortest path is reported. Designing an approximate shortest path query processing data

structure raises many crucial questions such as: How to construct these data structures efficiently? How good is the approximation quality? What are the tradeoffs between some important parameters such as pre-processing time, storage, query time, and approximation quality?

The aim of this chapter is to present the most common techniques used for solving the shortest path problems in a transportation network and in a weighted subdivision. It is impossible to cover all the literature for both problems in a short chapter so we have chosen to discuss the most well-known approaches.

The chapter is divided into two main parts. In the first part, we briefly review the most relevant theoretical results for the SPP in a transportation network. The second part is devoted to SPP in a weighted subdivision.

Shortest Paths in a Transportation Network

A transportation network consists of nodes and roads; nodes are endpoints of roads or intersections and roads are segments (edges) along which one can move. Also, edges may be assigned weights such as the expected travel times, distances or speeds. Throughout the chapter we will assume that there are no crossings between roads but roads can share endpoints. This structure can generally be represented as a planar straight-line graph $G=(V, E)$ with speed $v(e)$ on each road $e \in E$, where V is the set of nodes and E is the set of roads. Outside the network G, one moves at unit speed in any direction. The model assumes that one can enter and exit G at any point of the graph (including any point on a road).

In the presence of a transportation network, the distance between two points is defined to be the shortest elapsed time among all possible paths joining the two points. We call such an induced distance a *transportation distance*. In the literature (Aichholzer et al., 2004) it is also known as, the *time distance* or the *city metric* (in the L_1 metric).

Figure 1. Enter the highway at q_{li}

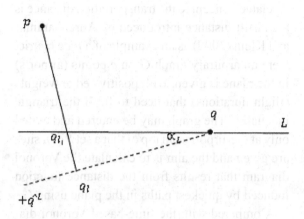

Voronoi Based Techniques

Closest point problems have received great attention in computational geometry. Given a set S of n sites in the plane, the *Voronoi diagram* of S is a partition of the plane into regions, one for each site, such that the region of site p contains all the points of the plane that are closer to p than to any other site in S. For more information see the survey by Aurenhammer and Klein (2000).

In the following we show how variants of the Voronoi diagram can be used to compute a quickest path in a transportation network. We will discuss the Time-based Voronoi diagram, followed by the Airlift Voronoi diagram and, finally, we consider the concept of a needle which was used by Bae and Chwa (2004) to develop an $O(nm^2+m^3+nm \log n)$ time algorithm to compute the Voronoi diagram for a transportation network in the Euclidean plane, where n is the number of given sites and m is the complexity of the given transportation network.

Time-Based Voronoi Diagram Techniques

In this section we consider the Voronoi diagram of a set of n points induced by the transportation

metric, which we call a *time-based Voronoi diagram*. The model wa and $-\hat{q}^L$, originated from q^L of slopes $+\tan \alpha_L$ and $-\tan \alpha_L$ respectively, where $\sin \alpha_L = \dfrac{v0}{v'} + \hat{q}^L$ is called the plus-hat of q^L, and $-\hat{q}^L$ is called the minus-hat of q^L. Figure 1 shows the case when q lies on L, in which case $q^L=q$. The transportation distance between p and q is defined to be the minimum of $d(p,q)$, $d(p,q_l)$, and $d(p,q_r)$, where $q_l \in +\hat{q}^L$ and $d(p,q_l)$, is $\min_{x \in +\hat{q}^L} \{d(q,x)\}$, and $q_r \in -\hat{q}^L$, and $d(p,q_r)$ is $\min_{x \in -\hat{q}^L} \{d(q,x)\}$.

In Figure 2, it is shown that the time taken by the path from p to q_r is equal to the time taken by the three-segment path from p to q_{ri}, then following the highway from q_{ri} to q_{ro} and finally, from q_{ro} to q. We refer to the three-segment path as a *highway* path.

Next consider the case when q and p lies on opposite sides of L. Then the transportation distance between p and q is considered to be the minimum of $d(p,q_l)$ and $d(p,q_r)$, where $q_l \in +\hat{q}$ and $d(p,q_l)=\min_{x \in +\hat{q}} \{d(q,x)\}$,, and $q_r \in -\hat{q}$ and $d(p,q_r)=\min_{x \in -\hat{q}} \{d(q,x)\}$. Let $+\hat{q}$ and $-\hat{q}$ be the half-lines originating from q with slopes $\tan \alpha L$ and $-\tan \alpha L_r$ respectively and let $+\hat{p}$ and $-\hat{p}$ be the half-lines originating from p with slopes $\tan \alpha L_a$ nd $-\tan \alpha L_r$ respectively.

The time-based Vonoroi diagram of a set S of sites in the presence of a highway L (such that L positioned horizontally) is reduced to the following. The time-based Voronoi diagram in the half-plane above L will be the ordinary Voronoi diagram defined by the set of sites p that lie above L, their associated hats, $+\hat{p}^L$, $-\hat{p}^L$, and by the sets of sites q that lie below L and their associated hats $+\hat{q}$ and $-\hat{q}$. The time-based Voronoi diagram in the half-plane below L is defined similarly. If q and p are on the same side, the transportation distance between q to p must be one of the Eu-

Figure 2. The time-distance of three-segment path equals the time-distance from p to $-\hat{q}^L$

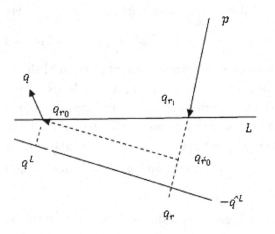

clidean distances from q to $p, +\hat{p}^L, -\hat{p}^L$. Otherwise, the time distance between q to p must be one of the Euclidean distances from q to $p, +\hat{p}, -\hat{p}$.

Lee et al. (2004) extended the results in Abellanas et al. (2003) by considering multiple highways as follows:

- All highways are straight lines, denoted L_1, ..., L_k.
- Travellers can enter the highways at any point and travel in both directions. The travelling speed allowed on highway L_i is v_i for all i.
- Outside the highways travellers can move freely in the plane, and the travelling speed in any direction is v_0.

Lee et al. (2004) show that the Voronoi diagram in the two-highway model of a set of n points can also be computed in $O(n \log n)$ time. They extend their method and present an $O(k^3 \log k + k^2 n \log n)$ time algorithm for the multiple-highway model, provided that the highways pairwise satisfy the so-called good angle condition (see Lee et al. (2004) for details) .

Airlift Voronoi Diagrams

A related concept to the transportation distance is the airlift distance introduced by Aurenhammar and Klein (2000) as an example of a *nice* metric. Here an arbitrary graph G on c points (airports) in the plane is given, with positive edge weights (flight durations) that need to fulfil the triangle inequality. The graph may be entered and exited only at the airports. On top of that a set S of n sites are given and the aim is to calculate the Voronoi diagram that results from the distance function induced by quickest paths in the plane using G.

Compared with the time-based Voronoi diagram this is a considerably simpler diagram. In fact, denying access to the transportation network C except at designated points yields an instance of the airlift Voronoi diagram, where the weight of a segment of C is its length divided by the network speed v. Note that such weights do obey the triangle inequality. Aurenhammar and Klein (2000) show that the airlift Voronoi diagram can be constructed for any L_p metric, $p \geq 1$, in time $O(n \log n + c^2)$ by using a reduction to an L_p Voronoi diagram for $n+c$ circles in this metric.

Voronoi Diagrams for Needles

The concept of needles, a generalized Voronoi site, was introduced by Bae and Chwa (2004). They used this concept to develop an $O(nm^2 + m^3 + nm \log n)$ time algorithm that computes the Voronoi diagram for a transportation network in the Euclidean plane, where n is the number of given sites and m is the complexity of the given transportation network. Note that a resulting diagram of their algorithm is in fact a refined diagram of the real Voronoi diagram so that it consists of shortest-paths information in each cell and it can also serve as a shortest path map structure.

The transportation metric has some special properties that make computing the Voronoi diagrams under it a difficult task, for example the bisector between two sites might be cyclic.

In order to solve this problem, one has to analyse the plane with a transportation network carefully. First, consider the basic case when the network consists of only a single road. For this case Abellanas et al. (2003) showed how to find a shortest path. From their results, it is easy to extract the following properties:

1. Every segment along a shortest path is a straight line.
2. To reach a destination as quickly as possible, in accessing a road e, the entering or exiting angle with the road e should be $\pi / 2 \pm \alpha$, where $\sin \alpha = \dfrac{1}{v(e)}$. If this is impossible then access the road e through the node of e closest to the source (Bae and Chwa (2004)).

From the above properties, one can find the t-neighborhood of a point p in the plane under the transportation metric with G, defined as $\{x \mid d_G(x, p) \leq t\}$, for any $t \geq 0$. We shall denote it by $N_G(p, t)$. Figure 3 shows four cases for the boundary of $N_G(p, t)$. In the case when G is a single road network, $N_G(p, t)$ can be seen as a union of one large disk centred at p and two needle shaped regions along the road, such that each needle is a union of a set of disks whose radii are linearly decreasing along the road. The idea by Bae and Chwa (2004) is to consider each needle-shaped region produced from p as an independent Voronoi site under the Euclidean metric.

They defined a needle as a generalized Voronoi site under a transportable distance d. A needle p under d can be represented by a 4-tuple $(p_1(p), p_2(p), t_1(p), t_2(p))$ with $t_2(p) \geq t_1(p) \geq 0$, where $p_1(p), p_2(p)$ are two endpoints and $t_1(p), t_2(p)$ are additive weights of the two endpoints. In addition, a needle under d is d-straight in the sense that it can be viewed as a set of weighted points on the d-straight path from $p_2(p)$ to $p_1(p)$. . Let $s(p)$ be the set of points on the d-straight path from $p_2(p)$ to $p_1(p)$, and $v(p)$ be the speed of p, defined by $d(p_2(p), p_1(p)) / (t_2(p) - t_1(p))$.

From any point x to a needle p, the distance is measured as $d(x, p) = \min_{y \in s(p)} \{d(x, y) + w_p(y)\}$, where $w_p(y)$ is the weight assigned to y on p, given as $w_p(y) = t_1(p) + d(y, p_1(p)) / v(p),$, for all $y \in s(p)$.

For the Euclidean case, the Voronoi diagram for pairwise non-piercing needles has been shown to be an abstract Voronoi diagram. In addition, two needles are called non-piercing if the bisector between them contains at most one connected component.

As stated in the beginning of this section the resulting diagram of this algorithm consists of shortest-paths information in each cell and it can also serve as a shortest path map structure. For more details, we refer to Bae and Chwa (2004).

A Different Approach

El Shawi et al. (2010) used a slightly different approach and showed that given two points s and t in the Euclidean plane, the quickest path between s and t using a transportation network can be computed in $O(n^2 \log n)$ time using $O(n^2)$ space. Their approach also works in the case when the edges of the network are directed. Note that their approach does not depend on Voronoi diagrams, instead they used the following properties:

Consider an optimal path P and let $C_p = \langle c_1, c_2, ..., c_k \rangle$ be the sequence of roads that are encountered and followed in order along P. Each road $c_i = (u_i, v_i)$ has assigned a weight $\alpha_i \in (0,1]$.

Note that a road can be encountered, and followed, several times by a path. For each road $c_i \in C_p$ let s_i and t_i be the first and last point on c_i

Figure 3. Illustrations of t-neighborhoods when G has a single road

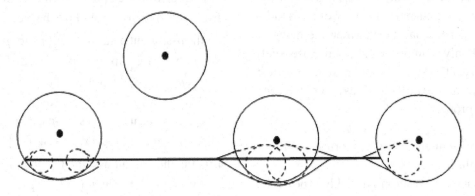

encountered for each occasion by P. Without loss of generality, we assume that t_{i+1} lies below s_i when studying two consecutive roads in C_p. We have:

1. For any two consecutive roads c_i and c_{i+1} in C_p the subpath of P between t_i and s_{i+1} is the straight line segment (t_i, s_{i+1}).
2. If t_i lies in the interior of c_i or s_{i+1} lies in the interior of c_{i+1} then $\varphi_{i+1}=arccos(\alpha_{i+1})$, where φ_{i+1} denote the angle $\angle(t_i, s_{i+1}, u_{i+1})$, as illustrated in Figure 4.
3. There exists an optimal path P' of total cost $wt(P)$ with $C_p'= C_p$ that fulfils properties 1 and 2 such that for any two consecutive roads c_i and c_{i+1} in C_p' the straight-line segment (t_i, s_{i+1}) of P' must have an endpoint at an endpoint of c_i or c_{i+1}, respectively.

In addition, El Shawi et al. (2010) show how the transportation network can be preprocessed in $O(n^2 log\ n)$ time into a data structure of size $O(n^2)$ such that $(1+\varepsilon)$-approximate fastest path queries between any two points in the plane can be answered in $O(1/\varepsilon^4 log\ n)$ time.

Shortest Path in a Weighted Subdivision

The SPP in an undirected transportation network can be regarded as a special and degenerate case of the shortest path problem in a weighted subdi-

vision. In this section we study the 2D *weighted subdivision optimal path problem* (Mitchell and Papadimitriou, 1991). The plane is partitioned into n triangular regions; each of which has an associated positive weight that reflects the speed of movement in that region. This can be used to model different geographical features, such as deserts, forests, grasslands and lakes, in which the travelling costs are different. Given a weighted triangulation T of the plane, a source point s and a destination point t in the plane, find a path with minimum cost within T from s to t. The cost of an edge is the length of the edge times the weight of the underlying region. The unit cost of traversing a region is uniform within the region but it may vary between regions. Figure 5 shows an example of an optimal path in the plane among four triangular weighted regions. In this figure we assume that the darker the region, the greater weight it has.

There are several variations of the weighted subdivision problem, for example where the weights are either 0 or 1 (Gewali et al., 1988). Solutions of the exact version of the problem seem to be infeasible, because computing the exact distances requires a solution of high degree algebraic equations (Aleksandrov et al., 2010). In the following we focus on studying $(1+\varepsilon)$-*approximation algorithms.*

The section is organized as follows. First we list some basic characteristics of the SPP in a

Figure 4. Illustrating property 2

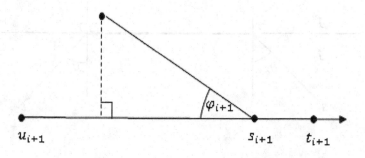

weighted subdivision. Then we highlight some of the existing algorithmic results for the problem.

Characteristics of Shortest Path on Weighted Subdivision

A shortest path through a weighted subdivision has several interesting characteristics. In this section it is assumed that the weights of the triangular regions and boundary edges are greater than 0. In addition, it is assumed that the weight of an edge is the minimum weight of all faces that share this edge. In the following we list the main characteristics of an optimal path (shortest path) through the weighted subdivision (Bemmelen et al., 1993).

1. An optimal path through a convex region does not bend.
2. When an optimal path enters a new region, it obeys Snells Law of Refraction: $a_f sin(\theta) = a_{f'}$ $sin(\theta')$, where θ and θ' are the angles of entry and exit and a_f and $a_{f'}$ are the weights of regions f and f'.
3. Let e be a boundary edge between the two regions f and f'. The edge that connects regions f and f' along an optimal path has a fixed orientation θ_c, (called the critical angel) with the edge e where $\theta_c = \arcsin(a/ a_f)$, as shown in Figure 6. When this path travels from a region with high weight to a region with small weight, it goes along the edge e. If the path moves back into the same

Figure 5. Optimal path in a weighted subdivision

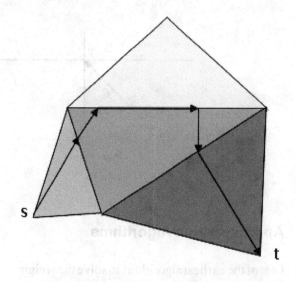

face after travelling along the edge, then the path is critically reflected (see Figure 7). In the case when the path does not move back into f then the path follows e, enters f' with an angle of θ_c.

4. The shortest path between two points interior to a face is not necessarily the line connecting them, the path might exit and enter the face again later.

Next we review the most well-known algorithms for the optimal path through weighted subdivisions.

Figure 6. The path from s to t critically reflected from edge e

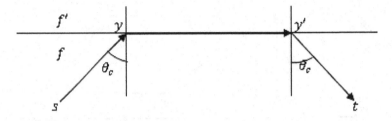

Figure 7. The path from s to t critically uses edge e

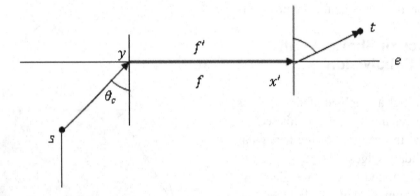

Approximation Algorithms

One of the earliest algorithms to solve the weighted region problem was presented by Mitchell and Papadimitriou (1991). Their algorithm constructs a (restricted) "shortest path map" with respect to a given source point is presented. The output is a partitioning of each edge of the subdivision into intervals of ε-optimality, allowing an ε-optimal path to be traced from the source to any query point along any edge. The algorithm computes the geodesic weighted shortest path in

$$O\left(n^8 \log\left(\frac{nNW}{\varepsilon w}\right)\right)$$ time using the "continuous

Dijkstra method", where $W(w)$ is the maximum (minimum) weight of a face. A wavelet descents from the source vertex, and a structure is built that allows to find the shortest path from the source vertex to any other vertex. The main problem with this algorithm is whenever the source vertex changes, the algorithm needs to be run again.

Many of the approximation algorithms are based on what is called *discrete vector approaches*. In this type of approach, the geometric continuous problem is transformed into a discrete combinatorial problem (graph problem). In most of the cases, this graph is built by placing points, called Steiner points, on the boundary of the triangles. For every triangular region a subgraph is built using the Steiner points and original vertices of the region. The cost of an edge of the subgraph corresponds to its Euclidean length multiplied by the corresponding weight of the face that contains the edge. Then, all the subgraphs are combined into one. On the resulting graph, denoted G, one can compute a shortest path, which can be proven to be an approximate shortest path in the original setting. In the following we mention some discretization techniques that have been used in solving the shortest path on weighted subdivisions.

Mata and Mitchell (1997) presented $O\left(n^3 \dfrac{N^2 W}{\varepsilon w}\right)$ time (1+ε)-approximation algorithm, using edge subdivision where ε>0 is any user-specified degree of precision. The algorithm discretizes the original continuous space by evenly placing m points along each boundary edge. The algorithm is then based on constructing a relatively sparse graph, a "pathnet", that links selected pairs of subdivision vertices (and "critical points of entry") with locally optimal paths. The pathnet can be searched for paths that are provably close to optimal, as one varies the parameter that controls the sparsity of the pathnet. Lanthier et al. (1997) presented a similar scheme where the Steiner points are placed at uniform distance from each other along every edge. The cost of an approximate path is $\left(1 + W|L|\right)$ times the cost of the optimal path, where L denote the longest edge length of the triangulation T and W denote the largest weight of any face of T. The time complexity of their algorithm is $O(n^5)$ which was improved to $O\left(\dfrac{n^3}{\varepsilon} + n^3 \log n\right)$ in the same paper by computing the shortest path in an ε–spanner of G instead of the whole graph.

Aleksandrov et al. (1998) placed Steiner points in a non uniform fashion; more precisely, in a logarithmically progressive way. The placement can be seen in Figure 8, where the density of the Steiner points increases when the distance to a vertex decreases. This results in an (1+ε) approximation with a time complexity of $O\left(N^2 \log\left(\dfrac{NW}{w\varepsilon}\right) \dfrac{n}{\varepsilon^2} \log\left(\dfrac{nN}{\varepsilon}\right)\right)$, where N is the largest integer coordinate of any vertex and $W(w)$ is the maximum (minimum) weight of a face.

This result was improved in several follow-up papers (Aleksandrov et al., 2000 and Aleksandrov et al., 2005). Instead of placing Steiner points on

Figure 8. The placement of Steiner points

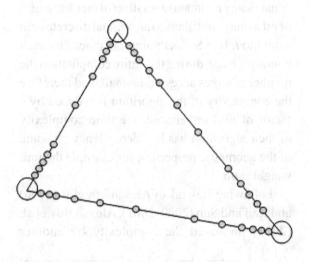

edges of the polyhedral surface, Steiner points are placed on bisectors of the angles of each triangle region and edges are defined between them. This results in a sparser graph and the time complexity is improved to $O(N^2 \log\left(\dfrac{NW}{w}\right) \dfrac{n}{\sqrt{\varepsilon}} \log \dfrac{n}{\varepsilon} \log \dfrac{1}{\varepsilon})$. Aleksandrov et al. (2005) achieve this improved time complexity as follows: Instead of placing a number of Steiner points nearby the regions' vertices they defined a small polygonal region around each vertex such that no Steiner points are added in this area. This area is called the vertex vicinity. The Steiner points are placed on bisectors and edges are defined instead of placing Steiner points on edges of the polyhedral surface. Although the ε-spanner causes an additional term of error, the approximate optimal path computed remains $O(\varepsilon)$-good.

Instead of applying Dijkstra's algorithm to the resulting graph G, Sun and Reif (2006), give an approximation algorithm that uses a discrete search algorithm called BUSHWHACK. The algorithm can compute optimal discrete paths on both uniform and logarithmic discretizations more efficiently than the ones in Lanthier et al. (1997) and Alexandrov et al. (2000, 2005). For each Steiner point v, the BUSHWHACK algorithm dynamically maintains a small set of incident edges of v that may contribute to an optimal discrete path from s to t. If m Steiner points are placed on each boundary edge, during the entire computation the number of edges accessed is small, and therefore the complexity of the algorithm is reduced by a factor of m. Furthermore, the time complexity of their algorithm has less dependency on some of the geometric properties, for example the unit weight ratio.

Following the work by Alexandrov et al. (2000) and Reif and Sun (2000, 2001), Alexandrov et al. (2003) improved the complexity by another $O\left(\dfrac{1}{\sqrt{\varepsilon}}\right)$ factor. They achieve it by using a novel discretization method that places Steiner points on bisectors of triangular regions instead of on boundary edges. While still guaranteeing the same ε error bound. They then apply a discrete algorithm similar to BUSHWHACK to compute an optimal discrete path in such a discretization.

Query Version

In this section we present a query structure that returns approximate shortest paths on a polyhedral surface presented by Aleksandrov et al. (2010). The approximation algorithm takes an approximation parameter $\varepsilon \in (0,1)$ and a query time parameter q as an input, and then builds a data structure that answers an ε-approximate distance query in $O(q)$ time.

This algorithm combines three different techniques: (1) Efficient solution of the approximate single source shortest path (SSSP) tree problem on weighted surfaces, (2) local Voronoi diagrams and (3) weighted Surface Partitioning. In the following we briefly discuss these techniques, and then we show how they are combined.

The problem of approximating the SSSP tree has been studied extensively; see Aleksandrov et

al. (1998, 2003, 2005). The problem is as follows: given a source vertex on a weighted polyhedral surface of size n and an approximation parameter $\varepsilon \in (0,1)$, one can compute ε-approximate distances from the source vertex to all other vertices of the surface. For the approximate SSSP tree problem, the solution is based on discretizing the "continuous" SSSP tree problem to a SSSP tree problem in a graph $G_\varepsilon = (V_\varepsilon, E_\varepsilon)$, called an approximation graph. The nodes of the graph G_ε are the vertices of the weighted triangulated surface P and a set of additional points, called Steiner points, inserted along the bisectors of the faces of P, similar the technique in Aleksandrov et al. (2005). The edges of G_ε connect nodes in neighbouring faces and have cost equal to the cost of the shortest "local" paths between their endpoints. Then, the algorithm from Aleksandrov et al. (2005) is used to solve the SSSP tree problem in G_ε.

The second main technique used is the Local Voronoi Diagrams (LVD). Each pair of adjacent faces determines a LVD. The LVD data structures are combined with a SSSP tree in the graph G_ε in order to provide a solution to the approximate Single Source Query (SSQ) problem.

The last technique used in the combined approach is the partitioning techniques. These techniques have been successfully used for shortest path problems in both graphs and geometric environments, see Arikati el al. (1996), and Chen and Xu (2000). Aleksandrov et al. (2010) developed a partitioning technique to solve the approximate All Pairs Query (APQ) problem. In the following we briefly explain the partitioning technique used.

First, compute a special set of faces S, called a separator, whose removal from P partitions the surface into disjoint, connected regions $R_1,...,R_k$. The APQ data structure consists of a collection of SSQ data structures constructed with respect to this partitioning, one for each region R_i. To find a "good" partitioning of P, the dual graph P^* of P

is considered and the partitioning problem for P is formulated as a graph separator problem for P^*.

Open Problems?

One direction for future research is trying to use structural information about shortest paths to reduce the number of Steiner points. One direction for further research in the shortest path queries in transportation network is to accelerate the preprocessing using parallel processing, or to execute multiple queries in parallel. Finally, study the SPP in a weighted subdivision in higher-dimensional spaces is a natural question.

REFERENCES

Abellanas, M., Hurtado, F., Sacristan, V., Icking, C., Ma, L., Klein, R., & Palop, B. (2003). Voronoi Diagram for services neighboring a highway. *Information Processing Letters, 86*, 283–288. doi:10.1016/S0020-0190(02)00505-7

Aichholzer, O., Aurenhammer, F., & Palop, B. (2004). Quickest paths, straight skeletons, and the city Voronoi diagram. *Discrete & Computational Geometry, 31*(1), 17–35. doi:10.1007/s00454-003-2947-0

Aleksandrov, L., Djidjev, H., Guo, H., Maheshwari, A., Nussbaum, D., & Sack, J.-R. (2010). Algorithms for approximate shortest path queries on weighted polyhedral surfaces. *Discrete & Computational Geometry, 44*(4), 762–801. doi:10.1007/s00454-009-9204-0

Aleksandrov, L., Lanthier, M., Maheshwari, A., & Sack, J.-R. (1998). An epsilon-approximation algorithm for weighted shortest paths on polyhedral surfaces. In *Proceedings of the 6th Scandinavian Workshop on Algorithm Theory. Lecture Notes in Computer Science 1432*.

Aleksandrov, L., Lanthier, M., Maheshwari, A., & Sack, J.-R. (2003). An improved approximation algorithm for computing geometric shortest paths. In *Proceedings of the 14th International Symposium on Fundamentals of Computation Theory. Lecture Notes in Computer Science 2751*.

Aleksandrov, L., Maheshwari, A., & Sack, J.-R. (2000). Approximation algorithms for geometric shortest path problems. In *Proceedings of the 32nd Annual ACM Symposium on Theory of Computing*, 286-295.

Aleksandrov, L., Maheshwari, A., & Sack, J.-R. (2005). Determining approximate shortest paths on weighted polyhedral surfaces. *Journal of the ACM, 52*(1), 25–53. doi:10.1145/1044731.1044733

Arikati, S., Chen, D., Chew, L., Das, G., Smid, M., & Zaroliagis, C. (1996). Planar spanners and approximate shortest path queries among obstacles in the plane. In *Proceedings of the 4th European Symposium on Algorithms. Lecture Notes in Computer Science 1136*.

Aurenhammer, F., & Klein, R. (2000). Voronoi Diagrams. *Handbook on computational geometry*.

Bae, S., & Chwa, K. (2004). Voronoi diagrams with a transportation network on the Euclidean Plane. In *Proceedings of the 15th International Symposium on Algorithms and Computation*.

Bemmelen, J., Quak, W., Hekken, M., & Oosterom, P. (1993). Vector vs. Rasterbased algorithms for cross country movement planning. *Proceedings Auto-Carto, 11*, 304–317.

Daescu, O., Mitchell, J., Ntafos, S., Palmer, J., & Yap, C.-K. (2005). K-Link shortest paths in weighted subdivisions. *9th International Workshop of Algorithms and Data Structures*, 325-337.

Dijkstra, E. (1959). A note on two problems in connection with graphs. *Numerische Mathematik, 1*, 269–271. doi:10.1007/BF01386390

El Shawi, R., Gudmundsson, J., & Levcopoulos, C. (2010). Quickest path queries on transportation network. *CoRR, abs/1012.0634.*

Frederickson, G. (1987). Fast algorithms for shortest paths in planar graphs. *SIAM Journal on Computing, 16,* 1004–1022. doi:10.1137/0216064

Fredman, M., & Tarjan, R. (1987). Fibonacci heaps and their uses in improved network optimization algorithms. *Journal of the ACM, 34*(3), 596–615. doi:10.1145/28869.28874

Gewali, L., Meng, A., Mitchell, J., & Ntafos, S. (1988). Path planning in 0/1/infinity weighted regions with applications. In *Proceedings of the 4th Annual Symposium on Computational Geometry,* 266-278.

Gudmundsson, J., Levopoulos, C., Narasimhan, G., & Smid, M. (2008). Approximate distance oracles for geometric spanners. *ACM Transactions on Algorithms, 4*(1).

Lanthier, M., Maheshwari, A., & Sack, J.-R. (1997). Approximating shortest paths on weighted polyhedral surfaces. In *Proceedings of the 13th Symposium on Computational Geometry, 30*(4), 527-562. *Journal version in Algorithmica, 30*(4): 527-562, 2001.

Lee, D., Liao, C.-S., & Wang, W.-B. (2004). Time-based Voronoi diagram. In *Proceedings of the 1st International Symposium on Voronoi Diagrams in Science and Engineering,* 229-243.

Mata, S., & Mitchell, J. (1997). A new algorithm for computing shortest paths in weighted planar subdivisions. In *Proceedings of the 13th Annual Symposium on Computational Geometry,* 264-273.

Mitchell, J., Mount, D., & Papadimitriou, C. (1987). The discrete geodesic problem. *SIAM Journal on Computing, 16*(4), 647–668. doi:10.1137/0216045

Mitchell, J., & Papadimitriou, C. (1991). The weighted region problem: Finding shortest paths through a weighted planar subdivision. *Journal of the ACM, 38*(1), 18–73. doi:10.1145/102782.102784

Pătraşcu, M., & Roditty, L. (2010). Distance oracles beyond the Thorup-Zwick bound. In *Proceedings of the 51st IEEE Symposium on Foundations of Computer.*

Reif, J. H., & Sun, Z. (2000). An efficient approximation algorithm for weighted region shortest path problem. In *Proceedings of the 4th Workshop on Algorithmic Foundations of Robotics (WAFR2000)* (pp. 191–203).

Sun, Z., & Reif, J. (2003). Adaptive and compact discretization for weighted region optimal path finding. In *Proceedings of Foundations of Computation Theory,* 258-270.

Sun, Z., & Reif, J. (2006). On finding approximate optimal paths in weighted regions. *Journal of Algorithms, 58,* 1–32. doi:10.1016/j.jalgor.2004.07.004

Thorup, M. (1999). Undirected single source shortest paths with positive integer weights in linear time. *Journal of the ACM, 46*(3), 362–394. doi:10.1145/316542.316548

Thorup, M. (2004). Integer priority queues with decrease key in constant time and the single source shortest paths problem. *Journal of Computer and System Sciences, 69*(3), 330–353. doi:10.1016/j.jcss.2004.04.003

Thorup, M., & Zwick, U. (2005). Approximate distance oracles. *Journal of the ACM, 52*(1), 1–24. doi:10.1145/1044731.1044732

About the Contributors

Sherif Sakr is a Research Scientist in the Managing Complexity Group at National ICT Australia (NICTA), ATP lab, Sydney, Australia. He is also a Conjoint Lecturer in The School of Computer Science and Engineering (CSE) at University of New South Wales (UNSW) and an Adjunct Lecturer with the Department of Computing in the Division of Information and Communication Sciences at Macquarie University . In 2011, he held a visiting research scientist position at Microsoft Research Laboratories, Redmond, USA. Dr. Sakr received his PhD degree in Computer Science from Konstanz University, Germany in 2007. He received his BSc and MSc degree in Computer Science from the Information Systems department at the Faculty of Computers and Information in Cairo University, Egypt, in 2000 and 2003 respectively. His research interest is data and information management in general, particularly in areas of indexing techniques, query processing and optimization techniques, graph data management, social networks, data management in cloud computing.

Eric Pardede is a lecturer in the Department of Computer Science and Computer Engineering at La Trobe University, Melbourne, Australia. From the same university, he received his Doctor of Philosophy and Master of Information Technology in 2006 and 2002 respectively. He has research interests in data modelling, data quality, data security and data privacy in XML and Web Databases as well as data repository for social networks.

***

Faisal Alkhateeb is an assistant professor inthe department of computer science at Yarmouk University. He holds a B.Sc. (Yarmouk University, 1999), M.Sc. (Yarmouk University, 2003), M.Sc. (Grenoble 1, 2004), and Ph.D. (Grenoble 1, 2008). He is interested in knowledge-based systems, knowledge representation and reasoning, constraint satisfaction and optimization problems. More on http://faculty.yu.edu.jo/faisal/.

Ghazi Al-Naymat is an Assistant Professor at University of Tabuk. He previously held a Research Fellow at the School of Computer Science and Engineering at The University of New South Wales, Australia. He received his PhD degree in May 2009 from the school of Information Technologies at The University of Sydney, Australia. Dr. Al-Naymat research focuses on developing novel data mining techniques for different applications and datasets such as: graph, spatial, spatio-temporal, and time series databases. He has published a number of papers in excellent international journals and conferences.

Ana Paula Appel received the B.Sc. degree in computer science from Federal University of São Carlos, Brazil in 2001 and the M.Sc. and Ph.D. degrees in computer science from the University of São Paulo, Brazil, in 2003 and 2010, respectively. She was a visit scholar at CMU in 2008 working with Professor Faloutsos. She is currently also a professor with the Engineering and Computer Science Department of the Federal University of Espirito Santo at São Mateus, Brazil and a Post-Doc at Federal University of São Carlos, Brazil. Her research interests include graph mining, data mining and databases. She is a member of SBC.

Norbert Martinez Bazan. Software Engineer and Master in Computer Architecture, Networks and Systems (Universitat Politècnica de Catalunya). With more than 25 years as a software architect and director of multidisciplinary software development teams, he has designed and coordinated many commercial software projects for Windows and Linux, such as Win-Logo (Idealogic, 1989), a programming language for teaching, and Synera (Synera Systems, 1997), a database management system based on columns with embedded data mining. He is currently the manager of the technology transfer group of DAMA-UPC, where he has designed DEX (2007), a highly efficient graph database management system for very large networks. His research work has resulted in several patents and publications in scientific journals and conferences in the areas of graph databases, computational psychometrics and complex systems.

Mokrane Bouzeghoub is a full professor in Computer Science at the University of Versailles SQY (since 1992). Before, he was Associate Professor at University P.& M. Curie (ParisVI). Prof. Bouzeghoub is currently leading a research group on Advanced Modeling of Adaptive Information Systems. His research topics mainly concern data integration, data warehousing, data quality, context-aware applications, query personalization, web services discovery. During 15 years he was a collaborator of different INRIA Teams (Sabre, Rodin, Caravel) where he participated to various research projects on object databases, active databases and data warehousing. Prof. Bouzeghoub published several papers in different journals and conferences and co-authored six books on database systems, object technology and design methodogies. He was also editor of several LNCS Proceedings of various international conferences and guest editor of Journal special issues such as Information Systems and Data & Knowledge Engineering. Prof. Bouzeghoub participated as a program committee member of many international conferences (including VLDB, EDBT, ER/Conceptual Modeling, CoopIS, CAiSE, DOLAP, DaWak, ...).

Stéphane Bressan is Associate Professor in the Computer Science department of the School of Computing (SoC) at the National University of Singapore (NUS). He is also adjunct Associate Professor at Malaysia University of Science and Technology (MUST). He received his Ph.D. in Computer Science in 1992 from the Laboratoire D'informatique Fondamentale of the University of Lille. In 1990, Stéphane joined the European Computer-industry Research Centre (ECRC) of Bull, ICL, and Siemens in Munich (Germany). From 1996 to 1998, he was research associate at the Sloan School of Management of the Massachusetts Institute of Technology (MIT). Stéphane's research interest is the integration and management of information from heterogeneous, distributed and autonomous information sources. In his current projects he investigates the integration and privacy preservation of information in Web2.0 applications, and the integration and management of business process definitions.

Jiefeng Cheng received his bachelor and master degrees in computer science and engineering at the Northeastern University, China, in 2000 and 2003, and obtained his PhD from The Chinese University of Hong Kong in 2007, respectively. Dr Cheng is currently a PostDoc Fellow in the Department of Computer Science, The University of Hong Kong. He has been working on graph reachability queries, graph distance query processing, and graph pattern matching. His PhD thesis is entitled ¡°Query Processing for Graph-Structured Data¡±.

Remco Dijkman is an assistant professor in Information Systems at Eindhoven University of Technology. Previously, he worked as a postdoctoral researcher and as a research assistant towards a Ph.D. in the area of Architecture of Distributed Systems at the University of Twente. Before that he combined work as a research assistant towards a Ph.D. and consultancy work in positions at the Open University of the Netherlands and Ordina. He has been a visitor of the Business Process Management group at Queensland University of Technology. Remco holds a M.Sc. degree, cum laude, in Computer Science from the University of Twente and a Ph.D. degree in Computer Science from the same university.

David Dominguez-Sal is currently working as a postdoc researcher in DAMA-UPC. He obtained his computer engineering degree at the Facultat d'Informatica de Barcelona in 2004 and his PhD in Computer Architecture from Universitat Polit\`{e}cnica de Catalunya in 2010. His main research interests are question answering, distributed systems and graph data management.

Marlon Dumas is Professor of Software Engineering at University of Tartu, Estonia. He is also Strategic Area Leader at the Software Technology and Applications Competence Centre (STACC). From 2000 to 2007, he held various academic appointments at Queensland University of Technology in Brisbane, Australia. He has also been visiting professor at University of Grenoble (France), Visiting Professor at University of Nancy (France) and Visiting Scholar at University of Macau. His current research interests are in he areas of business process management and service-oriented computing.

Radwa El Shawi is a PhD student at Sydney University and National ICT Australia (NICTA). She received his M.Sc. in Computer Science from Arab Academy for Science and Technology, Egypt, where she was a research and teaching assistant. Her research interests are in the areas of computational geometry, approximation algorithms, data structure and Date mining.

Jérôme Euzenat is senior research scientist at INRIA (Montbonnot, France). He holds a PhD (1990) and a habilitation (1999) in computer science, both from Joseph-Fourier university of Grenoble. Before joining INRIA he has worked for Cognitech, Bull and Ilog. He has contributed to reasoning maintenance systems, object-based knowledge representation, symbolic temporal granularity, collaborative knowledge base construction, multimedia document adaptation and semantic web technologies. His all time interests are tied to the relationships holding between various representations of the same situation. Dr Euzenat has set up and leads the INRIA Exmo team devoted to "Computer-mediated communication of structured knowledge".

Christos Faloutsos is a Professor at Carnegie Mellon University. He has received the Presidential Young Investigator Award by the National Science Foundation (1989), the Research Contributions Award in ICDM 2006, the Innovation Award in KDD 2010, fifteen ``best paper'' awards, and four teaching awards. He has served as a member of the executive committee of SIGKDD; he has published over 200 refereed articles, 11 book chapters and one monograph. He holds five patents and he has given over 30 tutorials and over 10 invited distinguished lectures. His research interests include data mining for graphs and streams, fractals, database performance, and indexing for multimedia and bio-informatics data.

Alfredo Ferro received the BS degree in mathematics from Catania University, Italy, in 1973 and the Ph.D. in Computer Science from New York University in 1981 (Jay Krakauer Award for the best dissertation in the field of sciences at NYU). He is currently professor of computer science at Catania University and has been director of graduate studies in computer science for several years. Since 1989 he has been the director of the International School for Computer Science Researchers (Lipari School http://lipari.cs.unict.it). He is the co-director of the International School on Computational Biology and BioInformatics (http://lipari.cs.unict.it/bio-info/). His research interests include bioinformatics, algorithms for large data sets management, data mining, computational logic and networking.

Hong Gao received the BS degree in computer science from the Heilongjiang University, China, the MS degree in computer science from the Harbin Engineering University, China, and the PhD degree in computer science from the Harbin Institute of Technology, China. She is currently a professor in the Department of Computer Science and Technology at the Harbin Institute of Technology, China. Her research interests include graph data management, sensor networks, and massive data management.

Luciano García-Bañuelos received his PhD in Computer Science from the Grenoble Institute of Technology in 2003 for his contribution to the development and evaluation of the PERSEUS open-source middleware platform. After completing his PhD, he moved to University of Tlaxcala (Mexico) where he participated in several research projects related to transactional information systems and transactional business processes. In 2009, he joined University of Tartu as a senior researcher. His current research interests are in the areas of business process modeling and social network analysis.

Eleanor Gardiner is a researcher in the Chemoinformatics group of the Information School at the University of Sheffield. She has a Masters degree in pure mathematics and a PhD in computational bioinformatics. Her interests centre on the application of mathematical techniques to problems in chemo- and bioinformatics, specialising in graph-theoretical algorithms and evolutionary algorithms. Graph theoretic work includes the comparison of clique-detection algorithms, the use of clique-detection for protein-protein docking and pharmacophore elucidation, the development of reduced graphs for scaffold-hopping and contributions to the development of the RASCAL algorithm. She has also developed a genetic algorithm for protein-protein docking and a multi-objective genetic algorithm for pharmacophore elucidation.

Ahmed Gater received his engineering degree from Institut National d'Informatique (Algeria) and Master form the University of Versailles SQY in Computer Science in 2007 and 2008 respectively. At present, he is a Ph.D. student within Advanced Modeling of Adaptive Information Systems team of the University of Versailles SQY, France. His research interests include web service discovery, business process management and modeling.

Rosalba Giugno is an Assistant Professor at the department Mathematics and Computer Science at the University of Catania, Italy. She received the BS degree in computer science from Catania University in 1998 and the PhD degree in computer science from Catania University in 2003. She has been visiting researcher at Cornell University, Maryland University and New York University. She is co-director of Lipari School on BioInformatics and Computational Biology (Lipari School http://lipari.cs.unict.it). Her research interests include Data Mining on structured data and algorithms for Bioinformatics.

Daniela Grigori is an associate professor at the University of Versailles (since 2002). She received her degree in Computer Engineering from Technical University of Iasy (Romania) and PhD degree in computer science from University Nancy I (in 2001). Previously she worked several years at Romanian Research Institute for Informatics on developing information retrieval methods and tools. Her current research interests include web services, process management systems, business process intelligence. She has a number of papers in international conferences and journals and has served as organizer and program committee member in many conferences. She is co-author of a book on process management systems.

Joachim Gudmundsson is a Principal Researcher at National ICT Australia (NICTA) and is also an honorary associate at University of Sydney. He received his PhD degree in 2000 in the area of Computational Geometry from Lund University, Sweden. Prior to joining NICTA Joachim was STINT postdoctoral Researcher at Utrecht University and an NWO veni postdoctoral researcher at the Technical University of Eindhoven, the Netherlands. His research interests are in the areas of computational geometry, approximation algorithms, discrete geometry and trajectory analysis. He is in the editorial board of International Journal of Computational Geometry and a managing editor of Journal of Computational Geometry.

Jun (Luke) Huan has been an assistant professor in the Electrical Engineering and Computer Science department at the University of Kansas since 2006. He is an affiliated member of the Information and Telecommunication Technology Center (ITTC), Bioinformatics Center, Bioengineering Program, and the Center for Biostatistics and Advanced Informatics—all KU research organizations. Dr. Huan received his Ph.D. in Computer Science from the University of North Carolina at Chapel Hill in 2006. Before joining KU, he worked at the Argonne National Laboratory (with Ross Overbeek) and the GlaxoSmithKline plc. (with Nicolas Guex). Dr. Huan was a recipient of the NSF Faculty Early Career Development (CAREER) Award in 2009. He serves on the program committees of leading international conferences including ACM SIGKDD, IEEE ICDE, ACM CIKM, IEEE ICDM.

Tomas Lampo (tlampo@umd.edu) is a Computer Engineer from the Universidad Simón Bolívar, Caracas, Venezuela. He graduated as the second best student in Computer Science, and was awarded the "Best Student of 2008 Award". He has been working as a researcher since 2008 and has published 4 papers since. While he was studying at the Universidad Simón Bolívar, he joined the Databases Group, where he did research on the Semantic Web and worked on the optimization and extension of existing engines to speed up query processing time. He was also part of the Artificial Intelligence Group and used to take part in Robotics Contests for Students. In 2007, his team won the first place on Venezuela's Third IEEE Robotics Contest, and then won the second place on Latin America's Sixth IEEE Robotics Contest for students, held in Mexico. After his graduation, he specialized in writing iPhone applications and has sent more than 10 applications to Apple's App Store. He is currently a PhD student in Computer Science at the University of Maryland in the United States and works at the MIND lab, where he is in charge of the mobile apps for the University.

Jianzhong Li is a professor in the Department of Computer Science and Technology at the Harbin Institute of Technology, China. In the past, he worked as a visiting scholar at the University of California at Berkeley, as a staff scientist in the Information Research Group at the Lawrence Berkeley National Laboratory, and as a visiting professor at the University of Minnesota. His research interests include data management systems, data mining, data warehousing, sensor networks, and bioinformatics. He has published extensively and been involved in the program committees of all major database conferences, including SIGMOD, VLDB, and ICDE. He has also served on the boards for varied journals, including the IEEE Transactions on Knowledge and Data Engineering. He is a member of the IEEE.

Min Li received her B.Sc. degree in Department of Mathematics, Hebei Normal University and her M.Sc. degree in Department of Mathematics, Ocean University of China in 2006. She is a Ph.D. student in the Department of Mathematics & Computing at University of Southern Queensland. She is a student member of IEEE, and her research interests lie at the intersection of databases, data mining, security and privacy.

Amadís Martínez (aamartin@uc.edu.ve) is currently an Associate Professor at the Computer Science Department of the Faculty of Sciences and Technology of the University of Carabobo, Valencia, Venezuela. He obtained his Computer Engineer degree and M.S. degree in Computer Science from the Universidad Simón Bolívar, Caracas, Venezuela, where he is currently a student of the Ph.D. program in Computer Science. He has advised over 12 master and undergraduate students. Professor Martínez has over 15 publications in international and national conferences and journals. Also, he has been reviewer in several national conferences and journals. Professor Martínez is a Member of the National Committee of the ACM Collegiate Programmin Contest, where he has participated in the Program, Organizing and Judge Committees in several national and international contests.

Victor Muntés-Mulero is an associate professor at the Universitat Politècnica de Catalunya. He obtained his PhD in 2007. His work is focused on efficiently managing large amounts of data. In recent years, he has been working in massive graph management performance aspects. He is also the co-founder of Sparsity S.L., a company that commercializes DEX, a graph database management system. He is also interested in performance of relational DBMS and data privacy and anonymization.

Peter Neubauer, Neo Technology. Peter has been deeply involved in programming for 10 years and is co-founder of a number of Open Source projects like Neo4j, Tinkerpop, OPS4J and Qi4j. In the last years, Peter has been involved in establishing the concept of Graph Databases as a concept and Neo4j a high performance implementation a Graph Database it in particular.

Josep Lluis Larriba Pey is associate professor with the Computer Architecture Department at Universitat Politècnica de Catalunya and director of the DAMA-UPC research group www.dama.upc.edu. He has been coordinating different research and technology development projects with different companies and administrations, in projects related to high performance data management for large data sets and, in particular, for data integration and graph management.

Alfredo Pulvirenti is an Assistant Professor at the department Mathematics and Computer Science at the University of Catania. He received the BS degree in computer science from Catania University, Italy, in 1999 and the PhD degree in computer science from Catania University in 2003. He has been visiting researcher at New York University. He is co-director of Lipari School on BioInformatics and Computational Biology (Lipari School http://lipari.cs.unict.it). His research interests include Data Mining and machine learning, and algorithms for Bioinformatics (sequences and structures).

Marko A. Rodriguez focuses his time and energy on various topics in the emerging graph database space. His primary interests are in the development of graph traversal languages, algebras, and engines.

Edna Ruckhaus (ruckhaus@ldc.usb.ve, http://www.ldc.usb.ve/~ruckhaus) is a Full Professor of the Computer Science department at the Universidad Simón Bolívar, Caracas, Venezuela since 1998. Visiting scholar of the research group Mindswap (Maryland Information and Network Dynamic Lab Semantic Web Agents Project), 2004-2005. Over 20 publications in international and national conferences and journals. She has been reviewer and has participated in the Program Committee of several International Conferences. Member of the Organizing Committee of the Workshop on Applications of Logic Programming to the Semantic Web and Semantic Web Services (ALPSWS'2007) co-located with the International Conference on Logic Programming, and co-Chair of the Organizing Committee of the ESWC 2011 Workshop on Resource Discovery (RED 2011).

Hiroto Saigo received the PhD degree in Informatics from Kyoto University in 2006. From 2003 to 2004, he studied as a visiting student at University of California at Irvine, US. He has held postdoctoral researcher positions at Max Planck Institute of Biological Cybernetics, Germany from 2006 to 2008 and at Max Planck Institute of Informatics, Germany from 2008 to 2010. Since 2010 he is working as an associate professor in the Department of Bioscience and Bioinformatics at Kyushu Institute of Technology, Japan. His research focus is on machine learning and its applications to biological data. He has served as a program committee for bioinformatics / machine learning conferences and as a reviewer for journals. He has received a best paper award at MLG2006 and an incentive award in DMSS2007.

Dennis Shasha is a professor of computer science at the Courant Institute of New York University where he works with biologists on pattern discovery for microarrays, combinatorial design, network inference, and protein docking; with physicists, musicians, and financial people on algorithms for time series; on database applications in untrusted environments; and on tree and graph matching. Because he likes to type, he has written six books of puzzles about a mathematical detective, a biography about great computer scientists, and technical books about database tuning, biological pattern recognition, time series, and statistics. He has co-authored over sixty journal papers, seventy conference papers, and fifteen patents. He has written the puzzle column for various publications including Scientific American and Dr. Dobb's Journal.

Javier Sierra(jsierra@ldc.usb.ve) is a Computer Engineer from the Universidad Simón Bolívar, Caracas, Venezuela. He graduated as the fifth best student in Computer Science, and was awarded a cum-laude mention. He has been working as a researcher since 2007 and has published 6 papers since. While he was studying at the Universidad Simón Bolívar, he joined the Databases Group, where he did research on the Semantic Web and worked on a query optimization engine for SPARQL queries based on cost heuristics. He was also part of the Artificial Intelligence Group and used to take part in Robotics Contests for Students. In 2007, his team won the first place on Venezuela's Third IEEE Robotics Contest, and then won the second place on Latin America's Sixth IEEE Robotics Contest for students, held in Mexico. In 2009 Javier received the "Eureka Innovation Award" for his undergrad thesis work. After obtaining his degree he opened his own consulting firm developing Web Management Systems for multinational clients.

Srinath Srinivasa is an Associate Professor at the International Institute for Information Technology, Bangalore (IIIT-B). His research interests include multi-agent systems and analysis of co-occurrence patterns in different data-sets. Srinath holds a PhD in information systems from the Berlin-Brandenburg Graduate School for Distributed Information Systems, Germany and an MS from IIT-Madras. He has also worked in Wipro Infotech at Bangalore as an R&D Engineer. Currently, he heads the Open Systems Lab at IIIT-B and serves on the technical and organizational committees for various international conferences. He has served and continues to serve as a technical reviewer for many journals like IEEE TKDE and the VLDB Journal. He is a member of CSI (Computer Society of India), IEEE and ACM and has been active in the COMAD series of conferences by the Computer Society of India. He has joined the IEEE CS Executive Committee for the Bangalore Chapter from June 2010.

Xiaoxun Sun received his B.Sc and M.Sc. degree in Department of Mathematics, Ocean University of China in 2006. He is currently a Ph.D. candidate in the Department of Mathematics & Computing at University of Southern Queensland. His research interests include access control, data privacy and security, data mining, and applied cryptography.

Caetano Traina Jr. received the B.Sc. degree in electrical engineering, the M.Sc. and Ph.D. degrees in computer science from the University of São Paulo, Brazil, in 1978, 1982 and 1987, respectively. He is currently a full professor with the Computer Science Department of the University of São Paulo at São Carlos, Brazil. His research interests include access methods for complex data, data mining, similarity searching and multimedia databases. He is a member of IEEE, ACM, SIGMOD, SIAM and SBC.

Charalampos E. Tsourakakis is a graduate student at the Department of Mathematical Sciences at Carnegie Mellon university working under the supervision of Prof. Alan Frieze. He graduated from the National Technical University of Athens (Dipl. Ingenieur, ECE) and from the Machine Learning Department at CMU (MSc,SCS). Research wise, he is interested in certain aspects of probability theory, graph theory and linear algebra: probability on graphs, randomized algorithms, spectral graph theory and machine learning.

Koji Tsuda is Senior Research Scientist at AIST Computational Biology Research Center. He is also affiliated with ERATO Minato Project, Japan Science and Technology Agency (JST). After completing his Dr.Eng. in Kyoto University in 1998, he joined former Electrotechnical Laboratory (ETL), Tsukuba, Japan, as Research Scientist. When ETL is reorganized as AIST in 2001, he joined newly established Computational Biology Research Center, Tokyo, Japan. In 2000-2001, he worked at GMD FIRST (current Fraunhofer FIRST) in Berlin, Germany, as Visiting Scientist. In 2003-2004 and 2006-2008, he worked at Max Planck Institute for Biological Cybernetics, Tuebingen, Germany, first as Research Scientist and later as Project Leader. He has published more than 70 papers in refereed conferences and journals, and served as an area chair and a program committee member in leading machine learning conferences such as NIPS and ICML. IPSJ Nagao Award (2009).

Maria-Esther Vidal (mvidal@ldc.usb.ve, http://www.ldc.usb.ve/~mvidal) is a Full Professor of the Computer Science department at the Universidad Simón Bolívar, Caracas, Venezuela. She has been Research Associate and Visiting Researcher at the Institute of Advanced Computer Studies of the University of Maryland, and Visiting Professor at Universidad Politecnica de Catalunya and University of Laguna Spain. Has participated in several international projects supported by NFS (USA), AECI (Spain) and CNRS (France). She has advised five PhD students and more than 45 master and undergraduate students. Professor Vidal has published more than 50 papers in International Conferences and Journals of the Database and The Semantic Web areas. She has been reviewer and has participated in the Program Committee of several International Journals and Conferences. Co-chair of iiWAS Internationa Workshop on REsource Discovery (RED'2010), co-Chair of the Organizing Committee of the ESWC 2011 Workshop on Resource Discovery (RED 2011), and accompanying professor of On the Move Academy (OTMa).

Hongzhi Wang received his BS, MS and PhD in Computer Science from Harbin Institute of Technology, Harbin, China, in 2001, 2003 and 2008, respectively. He is currently an Associate Professor of the Department of Computer Science and Engineering at Harbin Institute of Technology. His research interests include XML data management, data quality and information integration. He is the author of more than 70 research papers published at national and international journals and conference proceedings. He has been involved in the program committees of many international conferences. He has also served as reviewers for varied journals He has been awarded Microsoft Fellow, IBM PHD Fellowship and Chinese Excellent Database Engineer.

Xiaohong Wang received her master degree in Computer Science from University of Kansas. Before studying in KU, she worked in Southerwest Jiaotong University, Chengdu, P. R.China, where she received her Bachelor and Master degrees in Electrical Engineering in 1999 and 2002, respectively. Her research interest is to effectively obtain knowledge from data by applying computational and mathematical principles. The research areas cover bioinformatics, machine learning and power system.

Fang Wei is an assistant professor at the University of Freiburg, Germany. She obtained her PhD from the University of Freiburg. Her current research interests are graph algorithms, graph databases, Semantic Web and distributed data management.

Derry Tanti Wijaya is a Ph.D. student in Language Technologies Institute (LTI), School of Computer Science, Carnegie Mellon University (CMU). She received her Bachelor and Master degree in Computer Science from National University of Singapore in 2004 and 2008 respectively. From 2004 to 2006, she was a lecturer at Business Information Technology department in Institute of Technical Education (ITE) Singapore. In 2008 she did an internship in Google Zurich, Switzerland. In 2009-2010 she was a graduate research assistant at Artificial Intelligence Laboratory in University of Geneva, Switzerland. She is currently involved in project Read the Web at CMU. Her research interests are information extraction, semantic processing and opinion mining of documents in the web.

Jeffrey Xu Yu received his B.E., M.E. and Ph.D. in computer science, from the University of Tsukuba, Japan, in 1985, 1987 and 1990, respectively. Dr. Yu held teaching positions in the Institute of Information Sciences and Electronics, University of Tsukuba, Japan, and the Department of Computer Science, The Australian National University. Currently, he is a Professor in the Department of Systems Engineering and Engineering Management, the Chinese University of Hong Kong. Dr. Yu served as an associate editor of IEEE Transactions on Knowledge and Data Engineering, and is serving as a VLDB Journal editorial board member, and an ACM SIGMOD Information Director. His current main research interest includes graph database, graph mining, keyword search in relational databases, XML database, and Web-technology. He has published over 190 papers including papers published in reputed journals and major international conferences.

Index

Symbols

2D weighted subdivision optimal path problem 468
2-hop code 115
2-hop cover 123-124, 132, 135, 217

A

adjacency lists 3-7, 18, 390
adjacency matrix 2-3, 7, 10, 18-19, 21, 64, 76, 94,
 240-241, 245, 247-248, 287, 302-303, 305,
 310, 314, 394, 402
adjacent query 172
adjacent relationship 144, 158, 172
algorithm design 216, 298-299
All Pairs Query (APQ) 472
ancestor table 150, 152
approximation algorithms 13, 26, 224, 302, 470,
 473
atomicity, consistency, isolation and durability 50
Attributed Relational Graph (ARG) 56, 67, 106

B

balanced graph bisection 11
Basic Graph Pattern (BGP) 14-16, 88, 342-343,
 357-358, 372
basis graph 58-60
BerkeleyDB 18, 20
bidimensional boolean matrix 4
Bi-HGJoin 130, 143, 152-154, 164
bijective mapping 145, 173
bindingDB data sets 191, 202
bioinformatics 49, 53, 66, 87-88, 95, 105-110,
 176-177, 179, 198, 209-210, 212, 214-215,
 386-389, 406-407, 409-411, 414-416, 419-420,
 441, 461
biomolecular motif counting 97
biorthogonal wavelet 181
bi-partite 51, 403

bitmatrix 15
boolean junction 2
boolean values 2
Boost Graph Library (BGL) 17-19
Breadth First Search (BFS) 7-8, 10, 13, 27-28, 214-
 217, 227-228, 231-232, 234-236
Breadth First Search Layout (BFSL) 7-8
B+Tree 20, 361
BUSHWHACK algorithm (BUSHWHACK) 471-
 472
business process graph 421-422, 424-425, 432-435,
 437
business process repository 437

C

CBi-query 146, 154, 158
CBi-subquery 152, 156
chemical database 176, 199, 201
chemoinformatics 176-177, 199-200, 209, 260, 262,
 386-389, 394-396, 401, 407, 410-411, 413-416,
 419-420
clique detection 99, 386, 401-403, 412, 416-417
cloud computing 299
cluster coefficient 242-243, 245-246, 253-254
clustering 23, 67, 81, 108, 257, 280, 285-292, 294-
 298, 302, 312, 329-330, 333, 387, 403, 406,
 412, 414-415, 417, 419, 434
color coding 97-99, 105
COMPLEX NETWORK 241, 244-245, 253-254,
 258, 302
computer science 29, 44, 67, 105-106, 170, 211,
 237, 281, 287, 302, 353, 382, 387, 389, 415,
 460, 463, 473
concentration of measure 308, 310, 314
Connection Table (CT) 390-391, 393-394, 447, 454
Controlled Decomposition Model (CDM) 49
C-Store 16, 28, 360, 384